All in One®

Social Science

CBSE Class 9

Focused Theory ▪ Practice Exercises ▪ Sample Papers

Recommended by Teachers
Trusted by Toppers

All in One®

Social Science

CBSE Class 9

Focused Theory ▪ Practice Exercises ▪ Sample Papers

Author
Kriti Arora

arihant
SUCCESS AND NOTHING LESS

arihant
SUCCESS AND NOTHING LESS

ARIHANT PRAKASHAN
(School Division Series)

卐 *ADMINISTRATIVE & PRODUCTION OFFICES*
Regd. Office
'Ramchhaya' 4577/15, Agarwal Road, Darya Ganj, New Delhi -110002
Tele: 011- 47630600, 43518550; Fax: 011- 23280316
卐 *Head Office*
Kalindi, TP Nagar, Meerut (UP) - 250002, Tel: 0121-7156203, 7156204

卐 *SALES & SUPPORT OFFICES*
Agra, Ahmedabad, Bengaluru, Bareilly, Chennai, Delhi, Guwahati, Hyderabad, Jaipur, Jhansi, Kolkata, Lucknow, Nagpur & Pune.

PO No : TXT-XX-XXXXXXX-X-XX

Published By Arihant Publications (India) Ltd.

For further information about the books published by Arihant, log on to www.arihantbooks.com or e-mail at info@arihantbooks.com
Follow us on

卐 *PRICE* ₹515.00

PRODUCTION TEAM

Publishing Managers
Mahendra Singh Rawat & Keshav Mohan

Cover Designer
Salman Shaikh

Inner Designer
Ankit Tyagi

Project Head
Shivam Gupta

Page Layouting
Sundar Bisht

Proof Reader
Sundip Giri

Index *cum* Study Planner

One Book- Endless Features

to Help you Succeed

Chapter Intro

A quick information about the coverage of the chapter to explain students about what they are going to study.

CHAPTER 1

The French Revolution

The French revolution is a landmark in the history of Europe and the world. It ended the monarchial system in France. The slogan of French Revolution i.e. *liberty, freedom* and *equality* became important ideas of the new era.

1.1 French Society During the Late 18th Century

In 1774, **Louis XVI** of Bourbon family became the king of France. He was married to the Austrian Princess Marie Antoinette. When Louis XVI became the king, he got an empty treasury. Long years of war and maintenance of the court of the Palace of Versailles were the main reasons of it.

Louis XVI helped thirteen American colonies to gain their independence from Britain. As a result of this, more than 1 billion livres[1] were added to the debt which had already risen to more than 2 billion livres. The lenders who gave the credit began to charge an interest of 10 per cent on loans.

To meet the expenses like maintaining the army, the court, running government offices and universities etc, the state was forced to increase the taxes.

However this measure was not sufficient as French society was divided into three estates in 18th century and only members of the third estate paid taxes.

The society of estates was part of the feudal[2] system of the middle ages. The society and institution of France before 1789 was considered as old regime[3].

The three estates of France at that time were

First Estate (the Clergy)

It comprised of the group of persons, who have special functions in the Church. They owned vast land and wealth.

They enjoyed certain privileges by birth, like exemption from paying taxes to the state.

The Church levied a tax, called *'Tithe'* from the peasants, which comprised of one-tenth of the agricultural produce.

Try These

A set of Questions given after topic end, helps students to remain connected with topic while studying. They can instantly assess themselves for their understanding.

Complete Theory

Each chapter has Complete, Easy to Understand and Simplified theory covering latest syllabus and rationalized NCERT Textbook.

Try These

1. How many American colonies got independence by the help of Louis XVI?
2. How much debt was increased because of the war in France?
3. It was a direct tax of the third estate given to the state in the French society. Name this tax.
4. Who formed the 'National Assembly' in France in 1789?
5. In the Constitution of 1791, the powers were divided among whom?

Mind Map

A quick revision visual tool for the complete chapter.

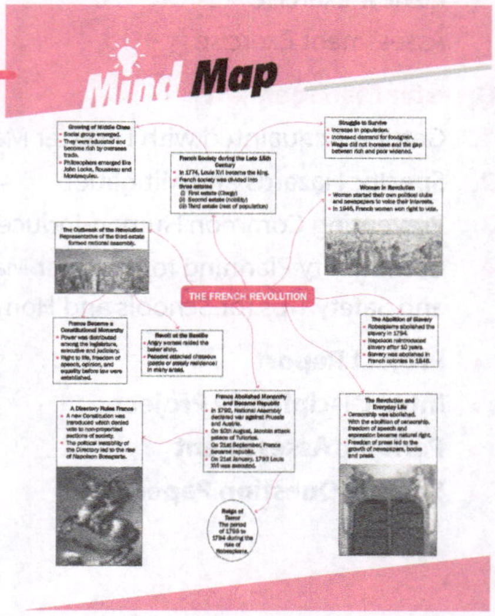

NCERT Folder

Complete explanations of all the questions of NCERT Exercises.

NCERT FOLDER | Covering Intext Questions and Exercises of NCERT

INTEXT QUESTIONS

Q.1 Identify the symbols which stand for liberty, equality and fraternity.

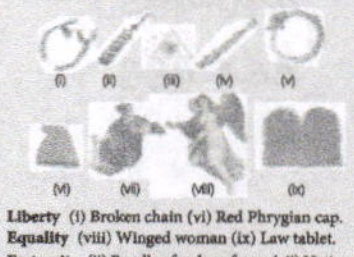

Ans. Liberty (i) Broken chain (vi) Red Phrygian cap.
Equality (viii) Winged woman (ix) Law tablet.
Fraternity (ii) Bundle of rods or fasces (vii) National colours of France, *viz*, Blue-White-Red.

Q.2 Explain the meaning of the painting of the Declaration of Rights of Man and Citizen by reading only the symbols.

The Declaration of the Rights of Man and Citizen, painted by the artist Le Barbier in 1790. The figure on the right represents France. The figure on the left symbolises the law.

One Book- Endless Features

to Help you Succeed

Review Exercise

Chapter exercise having all types of questions; MCQs, Assertion-Reason, Matching, Case based, VSA, SA, LA.

REVIEW EXERCISE

Including Competency Based Questions

Multiple Choice Questions (MCQs)

1. When did Louis XVI become the king of France?
(a) In 1770 (b) In 1772
(c) In 1774 (d) In 1787

2. The 18th century witnessed the emergence of which new social group in France, viz
(a) Middle class (b) Nobility
(c) Working class (d) None of these

3. The book 'The Spirit of the Laws' was written by
(a) John Locke (b) Montesquieu
(c) Rousseau (d) None of these

4. An extreme situation in which the basic means of livelihood are endangered is known as
(a) subsistence crisis (b) struggle to survive
(c) economic crisis (d) None of these

5. When did Louis XVI call an assembly of the Estates General to pass proposals for new taxes?
(a) On 5th May, 1789 (b) On 4th April, 1789
(c) On 5th May 1788 (d) On 3rd February 1788

6. Who is the composer of the National Anthem Marseillaise?
(a) Roget de L'Isle (b) Mirabeau
(c) Abbé Sieyès (d) None of these

7. Who wrote the 'Declaration of the Rights to Woman and Citizen'?
(a) Olympe de Gouges (b) Mirabeau
(c) Abeé Sieyès (d) None of these

8. When did French women march to Versailles and brought the king Louis XVI back with them to Paris?
(a) 5th October, 1789 (b) 10th October, 1789
(c) 10th November, 1791 (d) 10th June, 1790

9. When was slavery finally abolished in the French colonies?
(a) In 1842 (b) In 1845
(c) In 1848 (d) In 1850

10. When did Napoleon Bonaparte crown himself as Emperor of France?
(a) In 1798 (b) In 1800 (c) In 1804 (d) In 1802

Sample Question Papers

There are 5 Sample Question Papers at the end. All these Sample Questions Papers are exactly prepared on the latest syllabus & pattern of examination.

Sample Question Paper 1 (Solved)
Social Science

Time : 3 hrs M.M. : 80

General Instructions

1 Question paper comprises Six Sections – A, B, C, D, E and F. There are 37 questions in the question paper. All questions are compulsory.
2 Section A – From Question 1 to 20 are MCQs of 1 mark each.
3 Section B – Question no. 21 to 24 are Very Short Answer Type Questions, carrying 2 marks each. Answer to each question should not exceed 40 words.
4 Section C – Contains Questions 25 to 29 are Short Answer Type Questions, carrying 3 marks each. Answer to each question should not exceed 60 words
5 Section D – Question no. 30 to 33 are long answer type questions, carrying 5 marks each. Answer to each question should not exceed 120 words.
6 Section E – Questions no from 34 to 36 are case based questions with three sub questions and are of 4 marks each.
7 Section F – Question no. 37 is map based, carrying 5 marks with two parts, 37a from History (2 marks) and 37b from Geography (3 marks).

Section A (1 × 20 = 20)

1. Renu lives in Rajasthan, she wanted to visit Dudhwa national park with her family. Dudhwa National park located in which region? (1)
(a) Uttar Pradesh (b) Andhra Pradesh
(c) Madhya Pradesh (d) Gujarat

2. Complete the following table with correct information regarding India. (1)

India (Size)	Area of India	Total Geographical area of the World	Total length of Indian Coastline
	3.28 million sq km	A-?	7516.6 km

(a) 3.2% (b) 2%
(c) 2.4% (d) 3%

3. Match the following. (1)

List I	List II
A. Rajasthan	1. Tropic of Cancer passes through it
B. Andhra Pradesh	2. Located on West coast
C. Kerala	3. Located in East coast
D. Mizoram	4. North of the Tropic of Cancer

Codes

	A	B	C	D
(a)	4	3	2	1
(b)	1	2	3	4
(c)	4	1	2	3
(d)	3	4	1	2

4. Consider the following statements about the Kaveri Basin and select the correct option. (1)
I. Kaveri river originates in the Brahmagiri range of the Western Ghats.
II. If flows into the Bay of Bengal, South of the Cuddalore in Tamil Nadu.
III. The length of the river is about 760 km.
Codes
(a) Only I (b) Only II (c) Both I and III (d) All of these

5. Identify the season with the help of following information. (1)
- The season begins from mid-November and stays till February.
- In Northern parts of India, December and January are the coldest months.
- The temperature decreases from South to North.
- Days are warm and nights are cold during this season.

Options
(a) The cold weather season (b) The hot weather season
(c) Raining season (d) Summer season

Assessment Exercise

Complete Test of chapter in Exam format.

ASSESSMENT EXERCISE

Multiple Choice Questions (MCQs)

1. The Bastille fortress was hated by all because it
(a) stood for the despotic power of the king.
(b) imprisoned common men.
(c) was located in a secluded place.
(d) provided no facilitiy for living.

2. The French Government increased the taxes to meet the needs of
(a) maintaining army (b) maintaining the court
(c) running government offices (d) All of these

3. Who was the famous leader of Jacobin club?
(a) Robespierre (b) Napoleon
(c) Desmoulins (d) Roget de L'Isle

4. The period from .... to .... is referred to as the 'Reign of Terror'.
(a) 1789, 1791 (b) 1793, 1794
(c) 1789, 1790 (d) 1792, 1793

Latest Course *Structure*

History (India and Contemporary World-I)			**Suggestive no. of periods = 60**	**20 inclusive of map pointing**
Section	**Chapter No.**	**Chapter Name**	**No. of Periods**	**Marks Allocated**
I Events and Process	I	The French Revolution	15	18 + 2 map pointing
	II	Socialism in Europe and the Russian Revolution	15	
	III	Nazism and the Rise of Hitler	15	
II Livelihoods, Economies and Societies	IV	Forest Society and Colonialism		
		Interdisciplinary project as part of multiple assessments (Internally assessed for 5 marks)	5	–
	V	Pastoralists in the Modern World (To be assessed as part of Periodic Assessment only)	10	–

Geography (Contemporary India-I)		**Suggestive no. of periods = 55**	**20 inclusive of map pointing**
Chapter No	**Chapter Name**	**No. of Periods**	**Marks Allocated**
1	India - Size and Location	17	17 + 3 map pointing*
2	Physical Features of India	-	
3	Drainage	10	
4	Climate	12	
5	Natural Vegetation and Wildlife (Only map pointing to be evaluated in the annual examination)	3	
	Interdisciplinary project as part of multiple assessments (Internally assessed for 5 Marks)	5	–
6	Population	8	*Marks as mentioned above

Political Science (Democratic Politics-I)		Suggestive no of periods = 50	20 Marks
Chapter No.	Chapter Name	No. of Periods	Marks Allocated
1	What is Democracy? Why Democracy?	10	20
2	Constitutional Design	10	
3	Electoral Politics	8	
4	Working of Institutions	12	
5	Democratic Rights	10	

	Economics	Suggestive no. of periods = 50	20 Marks
Chapter No.	Name of the Chapter	No. of Periods	Marks Allocated
1	The Story of Village Palampur (To be assessed as part of Periodic Assessment only)	10	
2	People as Resource	10	20
3	Poverty as a Challenge	15	
4	Food Security in India	15	

List of Map Items

S. No.	Subject	Name of the Chapter	List of Areas to be Map Pointed
I	History	French Revolution	Outline political map of France Locate/label/identify; • Bordeaux, Nantes, Paris, Marseille
		Socialism in Europe	Outline political map of world locate/label/identify major countries of World War (central powers- Germany, Austria-Hungary, Turkey (Ottoman Empire) Allied Powers-France, England, Russia, USA
		Nazism and the Rise of Hitler	Outline political map of the World. Locate/label/identify major countries of Second World War: Axis Powers - Germany, Italy, Japan Allied Powers - UK, France, Former USSR, USA
II	Geography	India: Size & Location	• India-States with Capitals • Tropic of Cancer, Standard Meridian (Location and Labelling) • Neighbouring countries
		India Physical Features	Mountain Ranges : The Karakoram, The Zasker, The Shivalik, The Aravali, The Vindhya, The Satpura, Western and Eastern Ghats • Mountain Peaks – K2, Kanchanjunga, Anaimudi • Plateau - Deccan Plateau, Chota Nagpur Plateau, Malwa Plateau • Coastal Plains - Konkan, Malabar, Coromandel & Northern Circar (Location and Labelling)
		Drainage System	Rivers: (Identification only) • The Himalayan River Systems-The Indus, The Ganges, and The Sutlej • The Peninsular Rivers-The Narmada, The Tapi, The Kaveri, The Krishna, The Godavari, The Mahanadi • Lakes- Wular, Pulicat, Sambhar, Chilika
		Climate	• Annual rainfall in India, Monsoon wind directions
		Population	• Population density of all states • The state having highest and lowest density of population

The French Revolution

CHAPTER 1

The French Revolution is a landmark event in the history of Europe and the world. It ended the monarchial system in France. The slogan of French Revolution i.e. 'Liberty, Freedom and Equality' became important ideas of the new era.

1.1 French Society During the Late 18th Century

In 1774, **Louis XVI** of Bourbon family became the king of France. He was married to the Austrian Princess Marie Antoinette. When Louis XVI became the king, he got an empty treasury. Long years of war and maintenance of the court of the Palace of Versailles were the main reasons of it.

Louis XVI helped thirteen American colonies to gain their independence from Britain. As a result of this, more than 1 billion livres[1] were added to the debt which had already risen to more than 2 billion livres. The lenders who gave the credit began to charge an interest of 10 per cent on loans.

To meet the expenses like maintaining the army, the court, running government offices and universities, etc the state was forced to increase the taxes.

However, this measure was not sufficient as French society was divided into three estates in 18th century and only members of the third estate paid taxes.

The society of estates was part of the feudal[2] system of the middle ages. The society and institution of France before 1789 was considered as old regime[3].

The three estates of France at that time were

First Estate (the Clergy)

It comprised of the group of persons, who have special functions in the Church. They owned vast land and wealth. They enjoyed certain privileges by birth, like exemption from paying taxes to the state.

The Church levied a tax, called ***'Tithe'*** from the peasants, which comprised of one-tenth of the agricultural produce.

Second Estate (the Nobility)

It comprised of rich, aristocrat people of the state. They also enjoyed the privilege of exemption from paying taxes to the state.

They enjoyed feudal privileges, i.e. feudal dues, which they collected from the peasants.

Third Estate

It comprised of the rest of the population i.e., businessmen, merchants, court officials, lawyers, peasants, artisans, landless labour, servants, etc.

They had no privilege as they had to pay direct taxes called Taille[4] to the state as well as a number of indirect taxes levied on articles of everyday consumption, like salt, tobacco, etc.

Peasants made up about 90 per cent of the population of France. Only a small number of them owned the land they cultivated. 60 per cent of the land was owned by nobles, the Church and other richer members of the third estate.

Peasants were forced to work in the house of nobles and their lands, to serve in the army or to participate in building roads.

1 Livres These refer to units of currency in France at that time, which was discontinued in 1794.
2 Feudal It was a social system that existed during the middle ages in Europe. In this system, people were given land and protection by a nobleman and had to work and fight for him in return.
3 Old Regime This term is usually used to describe the society and institution of France before 1789.
4 Taille It was a tax to be paid directly to the state.

The Struggle to Survive

During 1715-1789, the population of France increased rapidly which led to rapid increase in demand for food grains.

Insufficient production increased the price of bread. However, the wages of the workers did not match the rise in prices. So, the gap between the poor and the rich widened.

Situation became worse when bad weather conditions reduced the harvest. This condition created **subsistence crisis**[5].

A Growing Middle Class

In the past, peasants and workers had revolted against high taxes and food shortages. However, they lacked the resources and plans to bring about big changes in the social and economic order. This responsibility was taken on by the more prosperous and educated groups within the third estate.

In the 18th century, a new social group emerged who were known as the **middle class**. They had become rich by expansion of overseas trade and manufacturing goods like woolen and silk textiles.

In addition to merchants and manufacturers, there were lawyers and administrative officials, who were educated. They believed that no group of society should be privileged by birth. Rather, a person's social position must depend on his merit.

The news that Louis XVI planned to impose more taxes to meet the expenses of the state, generated anger and protest against the system of privileges among the people.

Philosophers like John Locke, Jean Jacques Rousseau and Montesquieu spread the ideas of freedom, equal laws and opportunities for all.

The ideas of philosophers were as follows

(i) **John Locke** in his **Two Treatises of Government** criticised the doctrine of divine and absolute right of the monarch (king).

(ii) **Rousseau** in his book **The Social Contract** proposed the form of the government based on social contract between people and their representatives.

(iii) **Montesquieu** in his book **The Spirit of the Laws**, proposed the concept of separation of powers between the Legislature, the Executive and the Judiciary. This model of government was accepted by the USA, after the thirteen colonies declared their independence from Britain.

The American Constitution and its guarantee of individual rights was an important example for political thinkers in France.

The ideas of these philosophers were spread among the people through the books and newspapers. These were often read aloud in groups to help people who could not read or write.

1.2 The Outbreak of the Revolution

In France, the monarch did not have the power to impose taxes on his own. He had to call a meeting of the **Estates General**, a political body. All three estates sent their representatives to this body to pass proposals for new taxes.

Only the King could decide when to call a meeting. The last meeting was in 1614.

On 5th May, 1789, Louis XVI called for an assembly of the Estates General to pass the proposals for new taxes.

The first and second estates sent 300 representatives each, who were seated in rows facing each other on two sides.

The 600 members of the third estate had to stand at the back. The third estate was represented by richer and educated members. Peasants, artisans and women were not allowed in the assembly. Their problems and demands were written in 40,000 letters brought by the representatives.

Voting in the Estate General in the past had been conducted according to the principle that each estate had one vote.

The members of the third estate demanded that voting should be conducted by taking assembly as a whole where each member should have one vote. However, the king rejected this proposal and members of the third estate walked out of assembly in protest.

National Assembly of Third Estate

On 20th June, 1789, the representatives of the third estate assembled in the hall of an indoor tennis court in Versailles.

They declared themselves a National Assembly. They also declared to draft a new Constitution for France that would limit the powers of the monarch.

The representatives of the third estate were led by **Mirabeau** and **Abbé Sieyès**. Mirabeau was born in a noble family, but discarded his feudal privileges. Abbe Sieyes was originally a priest. He wrote an influential pamphlet called 'What is the third Estate?'

5 **Subsistence Crisis** It refers to an extreme situation where the basic means of livelihood are endangered.

Revolt at the Bastille

In France, due to severe winter, harvest was severely affected, which led to the increase in price of bread.

The bakers exploited this situation and stored supplies. After spending hours in long queues at the bakery, crowds of angry women raided the shops. At the same time, the King ordered troops to move into Paris.

On 14th July, 1789, an agitated (worried) crowd destroyed the Bastille. **The Bastille was hated by all French people as it symbolised the dominating power of the king.**

In the countryside, rumours spread from village to village that the lords of the manor[6] had hired the gang of robbers to destroy the ripe crops. After hearing this rumour, peasants attacked chateaux[7] in many areas of France.

The peasants looted stored grain and burnt documents containing records of manorial dues. Due to all these, a large number of nobles moved to neighbouring countries.

As a result of the revolt, Louis XVI finally granted recognition to the National Assembly and accepted the principle, that his powers would be checked by a Constitution.

On 4th August, 1789, the Assembly passed a law of abolishing the feudal system of obligations and taxes.

The members of clergy were also forced to give up their privileges. Tithes[8] were abolished and lands owned by the Church were seized by authority. This gave the government assets worth 2 billion livres.

France Became a Constitutional Monarchy

The National Assembly completed the draft of the Constitution in 1791. Its main objective was to limit the powers of the monarch.

Now, the powers were separated and assigned to different institutions like the Legislature, Executive and Judiciary. This change of powers made France a constitutional monarchy.

The new Constitution granted the power to make laws in the National Assembly. The assembly was indirectly elected *i.e.* active citizens voted for a group of electors, who in turn chose the assembly members. The main features of the changed system were

- Men who were above 25 years of age and who paid taxes equal to atleast 3 days of a labourer's wage, were given the status of **active citizens**, i.e. they had right to vote. The remaining men and all women were classed as **passive citizens.**
- To qualify as an elector and then as a member of the assembly, a man had to belong to the highest group of taxpayers.
- The Constitution began with a Declaration of the Rights of Man and Citizen. Rights such as the right to life, freedom of speech, freedom of opinion and equality before law were established as 'natural and inalienable' rights. These rights belonged to everyone by birth and could not be taken away. It was the duty of the state to protect these rights.

Try These

1. **How many American colonies got independence by the help of Louis XVI?**
2. **How much debt was increased because of the war in France?**
3. **It was a direct tax of the third estate given to the state in the French society. Name this tax.**
4. **Who formed the 'National Assembly' in France in 1789?**
5. **In the Constitution of 1791, the powers were divided among whom?**

1.3 France Abolished Monarchy and became a Republic

Rulers of France's neighbouring countries were worried by the developments in France. They made plans to send troops to put down the events taking place since 1789.

In April 1792, the National Assembly declared war against Prussia and Austria. Thousands of volunteers came from the provinces to join the army. They saw it as a fight of the people against Kings and nobles in Europe.

The patriotic song sung by volunteers was the *Marseillaise* which was composed by the poet **Roget de L'Isle**. It was sung for the first time by volunteers from Marseilles as they marched into Paris. It later became the **National Anthem of France.**

The revolutionary wars caused losses and economic problems for the people. While men fought, women had to work and take care of families. Many believed the revolution should go further, as the 1791 Constitution gave political rights only to the rich.

Political clubs became important for people to discuss government policies and plan actions. The most successful was the **Jacobin Club**, named after the former St. Jacob convent in Paris. Women, who were active, also formed their own clubs.

---

6 Manor It refers to an estate consisting of the Lord's lands and his mansion.
7 Chateaux It is a castle or stately residence belonging to a king or a nobleman.
8 Tithes These taxes were levied by the Church, comprising one-tenth of the agricultural produce.

The Jacobin Club

Members of the Jacobin club belonged mainly to the less prosperous sections of society. They included shopkeepers, artisans, cooks, shoe-makers, watch-makers, printers, servants and daily-wage workers. Their leader was **Maximilian Robespierre**.

They dressed differently by wearing long striped trousers similar to those worn by dock workers. It was a way of declaring the end of the power held by the nobles who wore knee breeches.

They came to be known as '*sans-culottes*' meaning 'people without knee breeches'. Sans-culottes men wore a red cap that symbolised liberty. However, women were not allowed to do this.

The Convention : Newly Elected Assembly

On 10th August, 1792, the Jacobins attacked the Palace of the Tuileries with large number of Parisians who were angered by the short supplies and high price of food.

They killed the King's guards and held the King himself as hostage for several hours. Later, the assembly voted to imprison the royal family.

Elections were held and now all men above 21 years of age were allowed to vote regardless of their wealth.

The **newly elected assembly** was called the **Convention**. It abolished monarchy on 21st September, 1792, and France was declared a **Republic**. A republic is a form of government where the people elect the government and also the head of the government.

Louis XVI was sentenced to death by a court on the charge of treason[9]. On 21st January, 1793, Louis XVI was executed publicly at the Place de la Concorde. After some time, the Queen Marie Antoinette was also sentenced to death.

The Reign of Terror

The period from 1793 to 1794 is referred to as the 'Reign of Terror' in France. This was due to the policy of severe control and punishment followed by Robespierre.

During this period following events took place

- Many people were arrested and tried by a revolutionary tribunal (court). These included all those people who were considered enemies (like ex-nobles, clergy and members of other political parties) of republic by Robespierre. If the court found them guilty, they were guillotined[10].
- Laws were made to set a limit on wages and prices.
- Peasants were forced to transport their grain to the cities and sell it at the prices fixed by the government.
- The use of expensive white flour was forbidden. Meats and breads were rationed.
- People were forced to eat the *pain d'egalite* (equality bread), a loaf made of whole wheat.
- Instead of Monsieur (Sir) and Madame (Madam), all French men and women were called as **Citoyen** and **Citoyenne** (citizen).
- Churches were shut down and their buildings were converted into barracks or offices.
- Robespierre was so determined to follow his plans that even his supporters demanded moderation. He was finally convicted by a court and guillotined in July, 1794.

A Directory Rules France

After the fall of the Jacobins, the wealthier middle classes seized power. A new Constitution was introduced which denied the vote to non-propertied sections of society.

It provided for two elected Legislative Councils. These councils appointed a Directory, an Executive made up of five members.

This was done to prevent concentration of power in a one-man hand, as under the Jacobins.

Sometimes, the Directors clashed with the Legislative Councils and the councils often dismissed these Directors.

This political instability paved the way for the rise of **Napoleon Bonaparte**, a military dictator. Inspite of all these changes, the ideals of freedom, equality and fraternity remained inspiring ideals that motivated political movements for France and the rest of the Europe.

1.4 Women in Revolution

Women played a very significant role in the French Revolution. They hoped their involvement would pressure the government to make their lives better. Most of the women belonging to the third estate worked for a living.

9 Treason It means betrayal of one's country or government.

10 Guillotine It is a device for beheading a person by means of a heavy blade that is dropped between two posts serving as guides. It was widely used during the French Revolution.

They worked as seamstresses[11] or laundresses, sold flowers, fruits and vegetables in the market, employed as domestic servants in rich family, etc.

Most of the women did not have access to education or job training. Only the daughters of nobles and wealthier members of the third estate could study at a convent.

Besides caring for their families, the French women had to cook, fetch water, stand in queues for bread, look after the children, etc. Their wages were always lower than the men.

Women in France were disappointed with the Constitution of 1791. It reduced them to passive citizens who had no political rights.

They demanded political rights, viz. Right to Vote, to be elected to the assembly and to hold political office. To express their own views and demands, women started their own political clubs and newspapers.

There were about sixty clubs of women in French cities of which, **The Society of Revolutionary and Republican Women was the most famous.**

In the early years, laws were passed to improve the lives of women. The changes brought about by these laws were

- Women gained access to education with the introduction of state schools and a system of compulsory education for girls.
- Women could no longer be forced into marriages by their fathers and they could marry according to their will.
- Marriage was now a contract which could be registered under civil law.
- Divorce was made legal. Both men and women could apply for it.
- Women could train for jobs, become artists or run small business.

French Women Got Right to Vote

During the Reign of Terror, the government ordered for the closure of women's clubs and banned their political activities. Many prominent women were arrested and executed.

Women's struggle for voting and equal political rights was carried on through an international suffrage movement during the late 19th and early 20th century. Finally in 1946, French women won the Right to Vote.

11 Seamstresses It refers to a woman who earns her living by sewing.

Olympe de Gouges (1748-1793)

Olympe de Gouges (1748-1793) was one of the most important politically active women in revolutionary France. She protested against the Constitution and the Declaration of Rights of Man and Citizen. This was because they excluded women from basic rights that each human being deserved.

In 1791, she wrote a **Declaration of the Rights of Woman and Citizen**, in which she addressed the Queen and the members of the National Assembly.

In 1793, Olympe de Gouges criticised the Jacobin government for forcibly closing down women's clubs. She was tried by the National Convention, which charged her with treason. Soon after, she was executed.

1.5 The Abolition of Slavery

The greatest social reform made by the Jacobin government was to abolish slavery in French colonies. The French colonies in the Caribbean like **Martinique, Guadeloupe** and **San Domingo** were important suppliers of tobacco, indigo, sugar, coffee, etc.

The French needed workers for plantations in its colonies but the Europeans did not want to work in distant, unknown lands.

Thus, a three way trade in slaves started between Europe, Africa and America in the 17th century. This was known as **triangular slave trade**.

French merchants travelled from the ports of Bordeaux or Nantes to the African coast, where they bought slaves from local chieftains. These port cities owed their economic prosperity to the flourishing slave trade. The slaves were branded, chained and tightly packed into ships for the three-month voyage across the Atlantic to the Caribbean, where they were sold to plantation owners. The exploitation of slave labor helped meet the growing demand in European markets for sugar, coffee, and indigo.

Throughout the 18th century, there was little criticism of slavery in France. The National Assembly had long debates about whether the rights of man should be given to all French people, including those in the colonies. However, they did not make any laws, fearing opposition from businessmen who made money from the slave trade.

After long debates, the National Convention passed a law in 1794 which declared slavery illegal and freed all slaves in France's overseas colonies.

After ten years, Napoleon reintroduced slavery.

Plantation owners believed their freedom included the right to enslave African **Negroes**[12] for their economic interests. Slavery was ended in French colonies in 1848.

1.6 The Revolution and Everyday Life

After 1789, many changes took place in the lives of women, men and children in France. The revolutionary governments made laws to turn the ideas of liberty and equality into everyday actions.

One important law that came into effect in 1789 was the **abolition of censorship**. According to censorship, all written material and cultural activities could be performed or published only after they had been approved by the censors of the king.

With the abolition of censorship and the Declaration of the Rights of Man and Citizen, freedom of speech and expression became a natural right of man.

This led to the growth of newspapers, pamphlets, books and printed pictures. Freedom of the press meant that opposing opinions could be expressed.

Each side tried to convince the other through print. Plays, songs, and celebrations attracted large crowds. This was a way for people to understand ideas like liberty and justice, which political philosophers wrote about in texts that only a few educated people could read.

Conclusion

In 1804, Napoleon Bonaparte, crowned himself Emperor of France. He conquered neighbouring European countries, dispossessed dynasties and created kingdoms where he placed members of his family.

He saw himself as a moderniser of Europe. He introduced many laws such as the protection of private property and a uniform system of weights and measures provided by the decimal system.

Initially, many people saw Napoleon as a liberator who would bring freedom for the people. But soon his army came to be viewed everywhere as an invading force.

Finally, Napoleon was defeated at the **Waterloo** in 1815. Even after his defeat, ideas of Napoleon on liberty and modern laws continued to impact other parts of Europe.

The ideas of liberty and democratic rights were the most important legacy of the French Revolution which spread all over Europe. This led to abolition of feudal systems and freedom of colonised nations.

KNOWLEDGE PLUS **Tipu Sultan and Raja Rammohan Roy** are some of the Indians who were inspired by the ideas of the French Revolution.

Try These

1. **Who composed the song 'Marseillaise'?**
2. **Who were known as 'Sans-culottes?**
3. **When was the monarchy abolished by the convention?**
4. **In which year Napoleon was defeated at waterloo?**
5. **Name the Indians who were inspired by the ideas of the French Revolution.**

TIME LINE

Covering Major Events with their Time Periods in Chronological Order

Year	Important Event
1774	Louis XVI ascended throne of France.
5th May, 1789	The king called an assembly of the Estates General to pass proposals for new taxes.
20th June, 1789	Third estate representatives assembled and took the Tennis Court Oath. They formed a National Assembly.
14th July, 1789	Storming of the Bastille; French Revolution started.
4th August, 1789	National Assembly passed a decree to abolish the feudal system of obligations and taxes.
5th Oct, 1789	Women marched to Versailles and brought back King Louis XVI with them to Paris.
1791	National Assembly completed draft of new Constitution; Revolutionary woman Olympe de Gouges writes 'Declaration of the Rights of Woman and Citizen'.
April, 1792	National Assembly voted to declare war against Prussia and Austria.
21st Sep, 1792	Monarchy abolished and France declared a republic.
21st Jan, 1793	Louis XVI executed.
1793 -1794	All slaves in French overseas possessions freed, but decision overturned by Napoleon ten years later.
Sep 1793-July 1794	'Reign of Terror'.
July 1794	Robespierre arrested and executed.
1804	Napoleon Bonaparte crowned himself Emperor of France.
1815	Napoleon finally defeated at Waterloo.
1848	Slavery finally abolished in French colonies.
1946	Women in France won the right to vote.

12 **Negroes** It is a term used for the indigenous people of Africa living South of the Sahara. It is a derogatory term not in common use any longer.

Mind Map

Growing of Middle Class
- Social group emerged.
- They were educated and become rich by overseas trade.
- Philosophers like John Locke, Rousseau and Montesquieu emerged.

French Society during the Late 18th Century
- In 1774, Louis XVI became the king.
French society was divided into three estates
(i) first estate (elergy)
(ii) Second estate (nobility)
(iii) Third estate (rest of population)

Struggle to Survive
- Increase in population.
- Increased demand for foodgrain.
Wages did not increase cause the gap between rich and poor.

Women in Revolution
- Women started their own political clubs and newspapers to voice their interests.
- In 1946, French women won right to vote.

The Outbreak of the Revolution
Representative of the third Estate formed national assembly.

THE FRENCH REVOLUTION

The Abolition of Slavery
- The National Convention abolished the slavery in 1794.
- Napoleon reintroduced slavery after 10 years.
- Slavery was abolished in French colonies in 1848.

France became a Constitutional Monarchy
- Power was distributed among the legislature, executive and judiciary.
- Right to life, freedom of speech, opinion, and equality before law were established.

Revolt at the Bastille
- Angry women raided the baker shop.
- Peasant attack chateaux (castle or stately residence) in many areas.

The Revolution and Every day Life
- Censorship was abolished. With the abolition of censorship, freedom of speech and expression became natural right.
- Freedom of press led to the growth of newspapers, books and press.

A Directory Rules France
- A new constitution was introduced which denied vote to non-properties sections of society.
- The political instability of the Directory led to the rise of Napoleon Bonaparte.

France Abolished Monarchy and Became Republic
- In 1792, National Assembly declared war against Prussia and Austria.
- On 10th August, Jacobin attack palace of Tuileries,
- On 21st september, France became republic.
- On 21st January, 1793 Louis XVI was executed.

Reign of Terror
The period of 1793 to 1794 during the rule of Robespierre

NCERT FOLDER

Covering Intext Questions and Exercises of NCERT

INTEXT QUESTIONS

Q.1 Identify the symbols which stand for liberty, equality and fraternity.

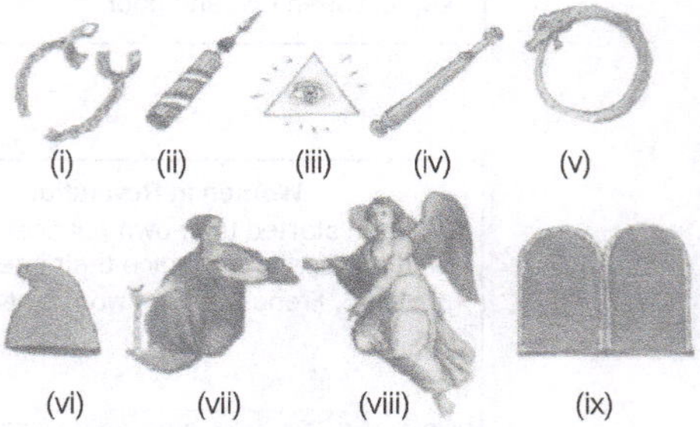

Ans. Liberty (i) Broken chain (vi) Red Phrygian cap.
Equality (viii) Winged woman (ix) Law tablet.
Fraternity (ii) Bundle of rods or fasces (vii) National colours of France, *viz*, Blue-White-Red.

Q.2 Explain the meaning of the painting of the Declaration of Rights of Man and Citizen by reading only the symbols.

The Declaration of the Rights of Man and Citizen, painted by the artist Le Barbier in 1790. The figure on the right represents France. The figure on the left symbolises the law.

Ans. The figure on the left symbolises the right to liberty, property, equality, etc enshrined in the new Constitution of France. The figure on the right symbolises the law. The law tablet signifies equality before the law for all.

Q.3 Compare the political rights which the Constitution of 1791 gave to the citizens with Articles 1 and 6 of the Declaration (Source C). Are the two documents consistent? Do the two documents convey the same idea?

Source C

The Declaration of Rights of Man and Citizen

1. Men are born and remain free and equal in rights.
2. The aim of every political association is the preservation of the natural and inalienable rights of man; these are liberty, property, security and resistance to oppression.
3. The source of all sovereignty resides in the nation; no group or individual may exercise authority that does not come from the people.
4. Liberty consists of the power to do whatever is not injurious to others.
5. The law has the right to forbid only actions that are injurious to society.
6. Law is the expression of the general will. All citizens have the right to participate in its formation, personally or through their representatives. All citizens are equal before it.
7. No man may be accused, arrested or detained, except in cases determined by the law.

11. Every citizen may speak, write and print freely; he must take responsibility for the abuse of such liberty in cases determined by the law.

13. For the maintenance of the public force and for the expenses of administration a common tax is indispensable; it must be assessed equally on all citizens in proportion to their means.

17. Since property is a sacred and inviolable right, no one may be deprived of it, unless a legally established public necessity requires it. In that case a just compensation must be given in advance.

Ans. The two documents are consistent and convey the same idea that human beings are born equal and all citizens are equal before the law.

Q.4 Which groups of French society would have gained from the Constitution of 1791? Which groups would have had reason to be dissatisfied? What developments does Marat (Source B) anticipate in the future?

Source B

The revolutionary journalist Jean-Paul Marat commented in his newspaper *L'Ami du peuple* (The friend of the people) on the Constitution drafted by the National Assembly:

'The task of representing the people has been given to the rich...... the lot of the poor and oppressed will never be improved by peaceful means alone. Here we have absolute proof of how wealth influences the law.

Yet laws will last only as long as the people agree to obey them. And when they have managed to cast off the yoke of the aristocrats, they will do the same to the other owners of wealth'

Source An extract from the newspaper *L'Ami du peuple*.

Ans. Only some members of the third estate, who were rich and propertied, would have gained from this Constitution.

Members of the first and second estates would have been dissatisfied as their privileges were abolished and they had to pay taxes.

Marat anticipated another revolution in which the poor would rebel against the rich persons of the third estate and overthrow them, just like they had done to the noblemen and clergy.

Q.5 Imagine the impact of the events in France on neighbouring countries such as Prussia, Austria-Hungary or Spain, all of which were absolute monarchies. How would the kings, traders, peasants, nobles or members of the clergy here have reacted to the news of what was happening in France?

Ans. The reaction of the kings, traders, peasants, nobles, clergy and other privileged sections of these countries was that they would become fearful about what has happened in France can happen in their country also. The peasants would welcome the developments in France and sympathise with the peasants and underprivileged sections of that country.

Q.6 Source D

What is liberty? Two conflicting views:

The revolutionary journalist Camille Desmoulines wrote the following in 1793. He was executed shortly after, during the Reign of Terror.

'Some people believe that Liberty is like a child, which needs to go through a phase of being disciplined before it attains maturity. Quite the opposite. Liberty is Happiness, Reason, Equality Justice, it is the Declaration of Rights... You would like to finish off all your enemies by guillotining them.

Has anyone heard of something more senseless? Would it be possible to bring a single person to the scaffold without making ten more enemies among his relations and friends? On 7th February, 1794, Robespierre made a speech at the Convention, which was then carried by the newspaper *Le Moniteur Universal*. Here is an extract from it.

'To establish and consolidate democracy, to achieve the peaceful rule of constitutional laws, we must first finish the war of liberty against tyranny... . We must annihilate the enemies of the republic at home and abroad, or else we shall perish. In time of Revolution, a democratic government may rely on terror. Terror is nothing but justice, swift, severe and inflexible; ... and is used to meet the most urgent needs of the fatherland. To curb the enemies of Liberty through terror is the right of the founder of the Republic'.

Ans. Robespierre felt that use of terror by a democratic government was justified, as it preserved the ideals of the revolution. However, Desmoulins saw liberty as freedom to do anything which was based on principles of equality, reason and justice without being injurious to others.

Robespierre saying, 'the war of liberty against tyranny' meant that they should kill the enemies of the republic both in France and outside France.

Desmoulins perceived liberty as laid down in the Declaration of Rights, i.e. it was happiness, reason, equality and justice.

The constitutional laws on the rights of individuals laid down the rights of liberty, equality, property, security and resistance to oppression.

Q.7 Compare the views of Desmoulins and Robespierre (Source D). How does each one understand the use of state force? What does Robespierre mean by 'the war of liberty against tyranny'?

How does Desmoulins perceive liberty? Refer once more to Source C. What did the constitutional laws on the rights of individuals lay down? Discuss your views on the subject in class.

Describe the persons represented in figure below their actions, their postures, the objects they are carrying. Look carefully to see whether all of them come from the same social group.

What symbols has the artist included in the image? What do they stand for? Do the actions of the women reflect traditional ideas of how women were expected to behave in public? What do you think: does the artist sympathise with the women's activities or is he critical of them? Discuss your views in the class.

- Parisian women on their way to Versailles

This print is one of the many pictorial representations of the events of 5th October, 1789, when women marched to Versailles and brought the king back with them to Paris.

Ans. Desmoulins and Robespierre had different views on state force during the French Revolution. Robespierre believed in using force to protect the revolution and secure liberty, seeing it as a 'war of liberty against tyranny,' where violence was justified to eliminate oppression and safeguard freedom. Desmoulins, on the other hand, was more cautious, emphasizing the need for liberty but criticizing excessive violence.

The constitutional laws, like the Declaration of Rights of Man and Citizen, emphasized equality, liberty, property and security. They asserted that sovereignty belongs to the nation and individual's should be protected. However, they also allowed for restrictions on liberty in cases harmful to society and emphasised the importance of the law.

The persons represent in the figure are all women and belong to the same social group, i.e. the underprivileged. The symbols that are included in the image are the agricultural implements, the clothes, symbol of justice, woman on the horse and the drum.

The agricultural implements in their hands confirm that they are peasants. The clothes also show their poverty. The symbol of justice held by one woman depicts that they are striving for it.

The woman on the horse symbolises power and strength. The drum symbolises that they are proclaiming their march to all concerned.

The actions of the women do not reflect the traditional ideas of how women should publicly behave. The artist definitely sympathises with the activities of the women.

EXERCISE

Q.1 Describe the circumstances leading to the outbreak of revolutionary protest in France.

Ans. The outbreak of revolutionary protest in France was a culmination of social, political, economic and intellectual factors. These were

- **Social Causes or Social Conditions** French society was divided into three estates. The first estate and the second estate belonged to the privileged section who were exempt from payment of state taxes. The third estate consisted of the lower and middle classes. The third estate was represented by its more prosperous and educated members but they were who bore the burden of the taxes. They did not have any political rights and social status.
- **Political Causes** Louis XVI, the King of France, was an autocratic, inefficient ruler who led a luxurious life with his queen. People of France became tired of this rotten system of administration and wanted a change.
- **Economic Causes** The treasury of the king was empty on account of long wars, involvement in the American War of Independence, luxurious living of the king and faulty system of taxation. The state also had to a great debt.
- **Influence of the Philosophers and Writers** There were many French Philosophers and thinkers like Montesquieu, Roussean, Voltaire, Mirabeau who exposed the evils prevailing in the system. Their ideas were discussed intensively in salons and coffee-houses and spread among people through books and newspapers. They inspired people with the idea of liberty, equality and fraternity.
  There was a wide gap between rich and poor people in the society. Increasing price of staple food caused a wide spread anger among masses.
- **Immediate Cause** Forced by financial bankruptcy, Louis XVI was compelled to call an assembly of the Estates General to pass proposals for new taxes in 1789. This time, voting method was not accepted by the third estate. They demanded that each member should have one vote. This controversy led to agitation among the people which became the immediate cause of the French Revolution.

Q.2 Which groups of French society benefitted from the revolution? Which groups were forced to relinquish power? Which sections of society would have been disappointed with the outcome of the revolution?

Ans. All the groups which formed the third estate were benefited from the revolution. These groups included workers, businessmen, merchants, court officials, lawyers, teachers, doctors etc. Previously, these people had to pay state taxes and they did not enjoy equal status. But after the revolution they began to be treated equally with the upper sections of the society.

The classes which formed the privileged sections of society like the nobility and clergy were forced to relinquish (give up) their executive powers and privileges.

The privileged classes, would have been disappointed with the outcome of the revolution because their privileges were taken away from them.

Q.3 Describe the legacy of the French Revolution for the people of the world during the 19th and 20th centuries.

Ans. The legacy of the French Revolution for the people of world during 19th and 20th centuries can be discussed in the following ways

- The idea of liberty expressed in the Declaration of the Rights of Man and Citizen laid the foundation of a new social order. The ideals of freedom and liberty formed the basis of national sovereignty.
- The idea of equality led to the end of a society based on privileges. 'All individuals have the same rights' became the new slogan for world politics.
- The idea of fraternity promotes the ideals of love, unity and cooperation among different sections of society.
- Another great legacy of the French Revolution was the idea of nationalism. The French Revolution promoted the concept of 'nationalist' which inspired the people of Poland, Germany and Italy to establish nation- states in their countries.

- These ideas played a great role in reshaping the boundaries of Europe and South America. In India, Tipu Sultan and Raja Ram Mohan Roy got deeply influenced by the ideas of revolution. Even today, people get inspiration by the great ideals of the French Revolution.

Q.4 Draw up a list of democratic rights we enjoy today whose origins could be traced to the French Revolution.

Ans. Some of the democratic rights which we enjoy today whose origins could be traced to the French Revolution are given in the Indian Constitution. They are

- **Right to Equality** The Right to Equality has its origin in the French Revolution. In the Indian Constitution, Right to Equality means equality before law, prohibition of discrimination and equality of opportunity in matters of employment.
- **Right to Liberty or Freedom** The origin of this right can also be traced to the French Revolution. In the Preamble to the Indian Constitution, Right to Liberty or Freedom means 'freedom of thought, expression, belief, faith and worship'.
- **Encouraging the Spirit of Fraternity** The French Revolution introduced the growth of the spirit of fraternity and social welfare. In the Indian Constitution, the concept of 'fraternity' abolishes untouchability and local or provincial anti-social feelings.
- **Inspiring the Spirit of Democracy** The French Revolution inspired the spirit of democracy which ensured many rights, *viz.*, right against exploitation, right to life, right to vote, etc which we are enjoying today.

Q.5 Would you agree with the view that the message of universal rights was beset with contradictions? Explain.

Ans. Yes, I agree that the message of universal rights was beset with contradictions. Many ideals in the "Declaration of Rights of Man and Citizen" were not clear in their meanings. For example,

- "The law has the right to forbid only actions injurious to society" did not mention about criminal offences against individuals.
- The declaration stated that "law is the expression of the general will. All citizens have the right to participate in its formation. All citizens are equal before it." Although, France became a Constitutional Monarchy, millions of citizens (men under the age of 25 and women) were still not allowed to vote at all.
- Women were still regarded as passive citizens. They did not have any political rights, such as right to vote and hold political offices like men. Thus, their position contradicts the concept 'men are born and remain free and equal in rights.'
- French colonies and slavery still continued till the 19th century. All these were in striking contrast to the ideals that the revolution supported.

Q.6 How would you explain the rise of Napoleon Bonaparte.

Ans. The rise of Napoleon Bonaparte was the result of following reasons

- **Poltitical Instability** The rise of Napoleon Bonaparte was an indirect result of the French Revolution. After the revolution, there was a struggle for power going on in France.
- **New Constitution** After the fall of the Jacobin government, a new Constitution was introduced. It provided for two elected legislative councils and a Directory which was made of five members. The Directory often clashed with the legislative councils, who then sought to dismiss them. Napoleon took advantage of this instability and become a military dictator.
- **Napoleon became the Emperor** In 1804, Napoleon Bonaparte crowned himself Emperor of France. Many people saw him as a liberator, who would bring freedom for the people. But his rise to power did not last for a long time. In 1815, at Waterloo, he was finally defeated.

REVIEW EXERCISE

Including Competency Based Questions

Part I

Multiple Choice Questions (MCQs)

1. When did Louis XVI become the king of France?

(a) In 1770 (b) In 1772
(c) In 1774 (d) In 1787

2. The 18th century witnessed the emergence of which new social group in France, viz

(a) Middle class (b) Nobility
(c) Working class (d) None of these

3. The book 'The Spirit of the Laws' was written by

(a) John Locke (b) Montesquieu
(c) Rousseau (d) None of these

4. An extreme situation in which the basic means of livelihood are endangered is known as

(a) subsistence crisis
(b) struggle to survive
(c) economic crisis
(d) None of the above

5. When did Louis XVI call an assembly of the Estates General to pass proposals for new taxes?

(a) On 5th May, 1789 (b) On 4th April, 1789
(c) On 5th May, 1788 (d) On 3rd February, 1788

6. Who is the composer of the National Anthem Marseillaise?

(a) Roget de L'Isle (b) Mirabeau
(c) Abbé Sieyès (d) None of these

7. Who wrote the 'Declaration of the Rights to Woman and Citizen'?

(a) Olympe de Gouges (b) Mirabeau
(c) Abeé Sieyès (d) None of these

8. When did French women march to Versailles and brought the king Louis XVI back with them to Paris?

(a) 5th October, 1789 (b) 10th October, 1789
(c) 10th November, 1791 (d) 10th June, 1790

9. When was slavery finally abolished in the French colonies?

(a) In 1842 (b) In 1845
(c) In 1848 (d) In 1850

10. When did Napoleon Bonaparte crown himself as Emperor of France?

(a) In 1798 (b) In 1800
(c) In 1804 (d) In 1802

11. Consider the following statements and select the correct one.

(a) First estate in France demanded that each member of an estate would have one vote.
(b) Second estate in France demanded that each member of an estate would have one vote.
(c) Third estate in France demanded that each member of an estate would have one vote.
(d) Both second and third estate in France demanded that each member of an estate would have one vote.

12. Consider the following statements and select the correct one.

(a) Tax to be paid directly to the state in French society is known as Tithe.
(b) Tax to be paid directly to the state in French Society is known as Taille.
(c) Tax to be paid directly to the state in French society is known as Livre.
(d) Tax to be paid directly to the state in French society is known as Directory.

13. Which of the following statements defines convent?

(a) Building belonging to a community devoted to a religious life.
(b) Building belonging to a community devoted to a social life.
(c) Building belonging to a community devoted to a political life.
(d) Building belonging to a community devoted to a economic life.

14. Which of the following statements defines chateaux?

(a) Castle belongs to a king.
(b) Stately residence belongs to a nobleman.
(c) Castle belongs to the Army Chief.
(d) Both (a) and (b)

15. Which of the following is incorrect about Marseillaise?

(a) The Marseillaise is the National Anthem of France.
(b) The Marseillaise is a patriotic song.
(c) This song is composed by Poet Roget de L'Isle.
(d) The song was first sung by the Jacobins.

16. In the 18th century, the middle class emerged, earning wealth through overseas trade and textile manufacturing. This group, along with professionals like lawyers and officials, believed in merit-based social positions rather than birth privilege.

Which philosophers influenced the belief in social mobility based on merit during the emergence of the middle class in the 18th century? Competency Based

(a) Aristotle and Plato
(b) John Locke and Jean Jacques Rousseau
(c) Thomas Hobbes and Immanuel Kant
(d) John Locke and Montesquieu

17. Which French colonies played a crucial role in the supply of commodities like tobacco, indigo, sugar and coffee?

(a) South-East Asia (b) North America
(c) Caribbean (d) South America

18. Arrange in sequence.

I. France became a republic
II. Louis XVI became the King of France
III. A Constitution is framed to limit the powers of the king
IV. Napolean became Emperor of France

Codes

(a) II, III, I, IV (b) II, I, III, IV
(c) I, II, IV, III (d) IV, I, II, III

19. Identify the person with the help of given information. Competency Based

- He becomes emperor of France in 1804.
- He saw himself as a moderniser of Europe.
- Many people saw him as a liberator who would bring freedom for the people.
- He was defeated in the Battle of Waterloo in 1815.

Options

(a) Napoleon Bonaparte (b) Louis XVI
(c) Vladimir Lenin (d) Tsar Nicholas II

20. Identify the reason, how Louis XVI of France helped the American colonies. Choose from the following statements.

I. By giving them less trade tax
II. By giving them the army support
III. To gain their independence from the Germany.
IV. To gain their independence from the common enemy, British.

Options

(a) Statements I and II are appropriate.
(b) Statements I, II and III are appropriate.
(c) All the statements are appropriate.
(d) Only statement IV is appropriate

21. Consider the statements given below and choose the correct answer. Competency Based

Statement I The population of France rose from about 40 million in 1715 to 30 million in 1789.

Statement II The term Old Regime is usually used to describe the society and institutions of France before 1789.

Options

(a) Statement I is correct and statement II is incorrect
(b) Statement I is incorrect and statement II is correct
(c) Both statements I and II are incorrect
(d) Both statements I and II are correct

Answers

1. (c)	**2.** (a)	**3.** (b)	**4.** (a)	**5.** (a)
6. (a)	**7.** (a)	**8.** (a)	**9.** (c)	**10.** (c)
11. (c)	**12.** (b)	**13.** (a)	**14.** (d)	**15.** (d)
16. (b)	**17.** (c)	**18.** (a)	**19.** (a)	**20.** (d)
21. (b)				

Match the Following

1.

List I	List II
A. French Colonies	1. Bordeaux, Nantes
B. Port Cities related to Slave trade	2. Extravagant court
C. Palace of Versailles	3. Martinique, San Domingo

Codes

	A	B	C		A	B	C
(a)	1	2	3	(b)	3	1	2
(c)	2	1	3	(d)	3	2	1

2.

List I	List II
A. The Broken Chains	1 Symbol of royal power
B. The Bundle of Rods	2 Act of becoming free
C. Sceptre	3 Strength lies in unity

Codes

	A	B	C		A	B	C
(a)	1	2	3	(b)	3	2	1
(c)	2	3	1	(d)	2	1	3

3.

List I	List II
A. Unit of Currency	1 Tax levied by the Church
B. Tithe	2 Livre
C. Taille	3 Tax directly to be paid to the state

Codes

	A	B	C		A	B	C
(a)	2	1	3	(b)	1	2	3
(c)	2	3	1	(d)	3	1	2

Ans. 1. (b) 2. (c) 3. (a)

Assertion-Reason

1. Assertion (A) Finally in 1946, the women in France won the right to vote.

Reason (R) Women's struggle for equal political rights continued for more than two hundred years after the French Revolution.

Codes

(a) Both A and R are true and R is the correct explanation of A
(b) Both A and R are true, but R is not the correct explanation of A
(c) A is true, but R is false
(d) A is false, but R is true

2. Assertion (A) Louis XVI faced significant financial challenges upon ascending the throne in 1774, leading to economic struggles in France.

Reason (R) French society was divided into Five estates, and only members of the fifth estate paid taxes.

Codes

(a) Both A and R are true and R is the correct explanation of A
(b) Both A and R are true, but R is not the correct explanation of A
(c) A is true, but R is false
(d) A is false, but R is true

3. Assertion (A) The combination of population growth, food shortages, and stagnant wages exacerbated the gap between the rich and poor in pre-revolutionary France, contributing to a climate of unrest.

Reason (R) In addition to merchants and manufacturers, the third estate included professions such as lawyers or administrative officials.

Codes

(a) Both A and R are true and R is the correct explanation of A
(b) Both A and R are true, but R is not the correct explanation of A
(c) A is true, but R is false
(d) A is false, but R is true

4. **Assertion** (A) In many ways, the French Revolution was a very significant event in the history of the world.

Reason (R) The French Revolution not only inspired French citizens to take action, but also inspired many philosophers and leaders across the globe.

Codes

(a) Both A and R are true and R is the correct explanation of A
(b) Both A and R are true, but R is not the correct explanation of A
(c) A is true, but R is false
(d) A is false, but R is true

5. **Assertion** (A) After his accession, Louis XVI found an empty treasury.

Reason (R) Long years of war had drained the financial resources of France.

Codes

(a) Both A and R are true and R is the correct explanation of A
(b) Both A and R are true, but R is not the correct explanation of A
(c) A is true, but R is false
(d) A is false, but R is true

Ans. 1. (a) Both A and R are true and R is the correct explanation of A

2. (c) A is true, but R is false

3. (b) Both A and R are true, but R is not the correct explanation of A

4. (a) Both A and R are true and R is the correct explanation of A

5. (a) Both A and R are true and R is the correct explanation of A

Picture Based Questions

1. What did the artist want to depict in this picture?

(a) The poor men brought everything for his lord.
(b) The nobleman bought the grains from the peasant in a low rate.
(c) The nobleman was the spider and the peasant was the fly.
(d) Both (a) and (c)

2. The special features about this painting is/are

(a) It is one of the rare paintings by a woman artist.
(b) The painting is a female allegory of liberty.
(c) It symbolises the new Constitution of France.
(d) Both (a) and (b)

3. What is the significance of this picture?

(a) It describes the emancipation of slaves
(b) It suggests the condition of slave trade
(c) It depicts the uncivilised African slaves
(d) All of the above

4. What is the name of this couple in the picture ?

(a) Sans-culottes couple
(b) Jacobin couple
(c) Noble couple
(d) Revolutionary couple

Ans. 1. (d) Both (a) and (c)

2. (d) Both (a) and (b)

3. (a) It describes the emancipation of slaves

4. (a) Sans-culottes couple

Case Based Question

1. Read the source given below and answer the questions that follow.

Louis XVI had to increase taxes for reasons you have learnt in the previous section. In France of the Old Regime the monarch did not have the power to impose taxes according to his will alone. Rather, he had to call a meeting of the Estates General which would then pass his proposals for new taxes. The Estates General was a political body to which the three estates sent their representatives. However, the monarch alone could decide when to call a meeting of this body. The last time it was done in 1614. On 5 May, 1789, Louis XVI called together an assembly of the Estates General to pass proposals for new taxes. A resplendent hall in Versailles was prepared to host the delegates. The first and second estates sent 300 representatives each, who were seated in rows facing each other on two sides, while the 600 members of the third estate had to stand at the back.

(i) What voting system did the Third Estate propose in the Estates General?

(a) Each estate has one vote

(b) Each representative has one vote, regardless of estate

(c) Two-thirds majority vote

(d) Voting based on social standing

(ii) Who was the noble leader who advocated for social reforms and supported the Third Estate?

(a) Lafayette (b) Marie Antoinette

(c) Mirabeau (d) Sieyès

(iii) Where did the representatives of the Third Estate declare themselves a National Assembly?

(a) At the Palace of Versailles

(b) In a Parisian theater

(c) In the Hall of Mirrors

(d) In an indoor tennis court

(iv) How were the grievances and demands of the common people communicated to the assembly?

(a) Through written petitions and letters

(b) Through social media

(c) Through speeches delivered by representatives

(d) Through public protests and demonstrations

Ans. (i) (b) Each representative has one vote, regardless of estate

(ii) (c) Mirabeau

(iii) (d) In an indoor tennis court

(iv) (a) Through written petitions and letters

Part II

Very Short Answer Type Questions

1. When did the French Revolution begin?

Ans. The French Revolution began on 14th July, 1789 with the storming of the Bastille prison just outside Paris.

2. Louis XVI belonged to which dynasty?

Ans. Louis XVI belonged to the Bourbon dynasty.

3. Which family was ruling in France when the French Revolution took place?

Ans. The Bourbon family was ruling in France when the French Revolution took place.

4. Name the classes which formed the privileged estates.

Ans. The clergy and the nobility constituted the privileged estates.

5. Which estate of French society paid all taxes?

Ans. The third estate paid all the taxes in French society.

6. What was the name of the direct tax collected by the state from the peasants in 18th century France?

Ans. The name of the direct tax was *taille* collected by the state from the peasants in 18th century France.

7. Name the authors of the following books.

(i) The Social Contract

(ii) Two Treatises of Government

Ans. (i) The Social Contract was written by Jean Jacques Rousseau.

(ii) Two Treatises of Government was written by John Locke.

8. Which section of French society was forced to give up their powers after the French Revolution?

Ans. The first and second estates were forced to give up their power after the French Revolution.

9. When and where was Napoleon Bonaparte finally defeated?

Ans. Napoleon was finally defeated at the Battle of Waterloo in 1815.

10. Which Indian individuals responded to the ideas coming from revolutionary France?

Ans. Tipu Sultan and Raja Rammohan Roy are two examples of Indian individuals who responded to the ideas coming from revolutionary France.

11. 'The end of the Reign of Terror came on 28th July, 1794, when Maximilien Robespierre, the most prominent member of the Committee of Public Safety, and his closest colleagues were executed. Robespierre's fellow revolutionaries and previous collaborators turned on him amid indications that he was planning to attack them.................'

Source (edited) : The Washington Post **Competency Based**

(i) **What role did peasants play in the economic policies of Robespierre's government?**

(ii) **When and how did Robespierre meet his end?**

Ans. (i) The peasants played a key role in the economic policies of Robespierre's government during the French Revolution. They were compelled to transport their grain to the cities and sell it at prices fixed by the government.

(ii) Robespierre met his end in July, 1794 because of his cruel policies. He issued laws placing a maximum ceiling on wages and prices, forced peasants to transport and sell their grain to the cities at the fixed price. His reign was known as 'reign of terror'. Even his supporter demanded moderation of the policies. Finally, he was convicted by a court and guillotined.

12. Councils then appointed a Directory, an executive made up of five members. This was meant as a safeguard against the concentration of power in a one-man executive as under the Jacobins. However, the Directors often clashed with the legislative councils, who then sought to dismiss them.

Why did the legislative councils often clash with the Directors? **Competency Based**

Ans. The legislative councils often clashed with the Directors due to power struggles and disagreements over governance. The Directors, as the executive branch, and the legislative councils, which were responsible for making laws, had different visions and interests.

13. The colonies in the Caribbean - Martinique, Guadeloupe and San Domingo- were important suppliers of commodities such as tobacco, indigo, sugar and coffee. But the reluctance of Europeans to go and work in distant and unfamiliar lands meant a shortage of labour on the plantations. So, this was met by a triangular slave trade between Europe, Africa and the Americas.

What was the most revolutionary social reform of the Jacobin regime? **Competency Based**

Ans. One of the most revolutionary social reforms of the Jacobin regime was the abolition of slavery in the French colonies, particularly in the Caribbean colonies such as Martinique, Guadeloupe, and San Domingo. All these were the important suppliers of commodities like tobacco, indigo, sugar and coffee.

14. From the very beginning women were active participants in the events which brought about so many important changes in French society. They hoped that their involvement would pressurise the revolutionary government to introduce measures to improve their lives. Most women of the third estate had to work for a living.

What were the typical occupations of most women in the third estate during that time? **Competency Based**

Ans. During that time, most women in the third estate were engaged in occupations such as seamstresses, laundresses, selling flowers, fruits, and vegetables at the market, or working as domestic servants in the houses of prosperous individuals.

15. The people of Paris rose up against years of mistreatment under the monarchy, and the storming of the Bastille stands as a monumental victory against tyranny. On the first anniversary of this triumph, representatives from across France gathered in Paris for a joyous event called Fête de la Fédération (Festival of the Federation) ....'

Source (edited): Livemint

What was the primary reason for the riots in Paris? **Competency Based**

Ans. The primary reason for the riots in Paris was the high price of bread. Most people, both in Paris and the countryside, were protesting against the rising cost of this essential need. The protests against economic hardships laid the groundwork for broader societal and political changes during the French Revolution.

Short Answer Type Questions

1. Describe the events of 14th July, 1789.

or **Describe the incident which took place in the morning of 14th July, 1789 in France.**

Ans. The following events took place in the morning of 14th July, 1789 in France

- In the morning of 14th July, 1789 the King ordered his troops to move into Paris. There was a rumour that he ordered his army to open fire upon the citizens.
- Some 7000 men and women gathered in front of the town hall and decided to form a people's militia.
- Agitated crowd broke into a number of government building in search of arms.
- A group of several hundred people stormed the fortress prison, the Bastille, where they hoped to find hoarded ammunition.
- The crowd destroyed the Bastille, the commander of the Bastille was killed and the seven prisoners released.

2. Which three causes led to the 'subsistence crisis' in France during the Old Regime?

or **What is 'subsistence crisis'? Explain any three factors responsible for the same.**

Ans. 'Subsistence crisis' can be defined as an extreme situation where the basic means of livelihood are endangered. During the Old Regime, France faced the 'subsistence crisis' because

- The population of France had increased from 23 million in 1715 to 28 million in 1789 which led to a rapid increase in the demand for foodgrains. But the production of grains could not keep pace with this demand.
- Most workers got fixed wages which did not keep pace with the rising prices of objects of daily use. So the gap between the poor and rich increased.
- Things became worse when drought or hail reduced the harvest, causing shortages.

3. Describe the divisions in French society before the French Revolution.

Ans. The French society was divided into three estates as follows

- **First Estate** It comprised of the clergy which was a group of persons which had special functions in the church. They were exempted from paying taxes to the state.
- **Second Estate** This estate comprised of nobility which were the aristocrats and landlords. They were considered above law and exempted from paying taxes.
- **Third Estate** This comprised the big businessmen, merchants, peasants, artisans, city workers and the middle class people like teachers, doctors, lawyers, writers, landless labour, servants etc. All such people had no political rights.

They had to pay many kinds of taxes like tithes (to church by peasants) and a direct tax, i.e. taille and also a number of indirect taxes were given by all member of third estate.

4. Give reasons as to why was the National Assembly formed by the people of the third estate.

Ans. The National Assembly was formed by the people of the Third Estate due to following reasons

- Louis XVI called together an assembly of the Estates General on 5th May, 1789 to pass proposals for new taxes.
- The first and second estates sent 300 representatives each, while third estate sent 600 members.
- Louis XVI wanted to continue with old voting system in which each estate had one vote. But members of third estate wanted a new voting system, where each member have one vote.
- The King rejected their proposal and on 20th June, 1789 third estate declared themselves as National Assembly.

5. What was the contribution of Mirabeau and Sieyes to the formation of the National Assembly?

Ans. The contribution of Mirabeau and Sieyes to the formation of National Assembly were

- Mirabeau and Sieyes led the movement of representatives of the third state who declared themselves a National Assembly. They demanded that voting in the Estate General to be conducted by the assembly as a whole in which each member would have one vote. However, the demand was rejected by the king.
- During the formation of National Assembly, Mirabeau brought out a journal and through his writings and powerful speeches, he tried to inspire the representatives.
- Sieyes wrote an important pamphlet 'What is the Third Estate' to further inspire the representatives of National Assembly.

6. Explain the immediate causes of the outbreak of the revolt in France in 1789.

Ans. Many causes contributed to the outbreak of the revolt of France in 1789. The following are the immediate causes

- Louis XVI called a meeting of Estate General to increase taxes. The representatives from first and second estate were seated in rows facing each other on two sides, while the members of the third estate had to stand at the back. This disrespect of the third estate was the first cause which create a feeling of disrespect which further led to revolution.
- Another cause was that some representatives of the third estate such as some peasants, artisans and women were denied entry to the assembly.
- The last cause was that the demand of the third state of one vote for each member was rejected by the king in this assembly.

7. How did peasants protest against the feudal lords or nobles of France?

Ans. Peasants protested against the feudal lords or nobles of France in the following ways

- These was rumour that the landlords hired criminals to destroy the ripe crops of the peasants. Being afraid of the situation, peasants in several districts seized hoes and pitch forks (a farm tool) and attacked chateaux (castles belonging to king or nobleman).
- The peasants looted the hoarded grain.
- They even burnt the documents containing records of manorial dues.

8. How did France become a constitutional monarchy?

Ans. France became a constitutional monarchy in the following ways

- The first step was the drafting of the Constitution by the National Assembly in 1791. Its main objective was to limit the powers of the monarch.
- The next step was that the powers, instead of being concentrated in the hands of the monarch, were separated and divided between the Legislature, the Executive and the Judiciary by the Constitution.

- Finally, the Constitution of 1791 vested the power to make laws in the National Assembly which was indirectly elected.

9. Explain any three features of the Constitution of France drafted in 1791.

Ans. Three features of the Constitution of France drafted in 1791 were

- The Constitution reduced the king's powers by distributing them between three institutions called the Legislature, Executive and Judiciary.
- The Constitution gave the power of making of laws to the National Assembly, which was indirectly elected by a group of electors who, in turn, were elected by the registered voters.
- According to Constitution, only men above 25 years and paying a certain minimum amount of tax were allowed to vote. The remaining men and women remained passive citizens.

10. Who were the Jacobins? Write about them in three points.

Ans. The Jacobins was one of the most successful clubs, which got its name from the former convent of St Jacob in Paris.

The Jacobins are described in the following ways

- The Jacobins club became an important rallying point for people who wished to discuss government policies and plan their own forms of action.
- The members of the Jacobin club belonged mainly to the less prosperous section of society which included small shopkeepers, artisans like shoe-makers, pastry cooks, watch-makers, printers, servants, daily-wage workers etc.
- The member of Jacobins club wore striped trousers known as 'Sans-culottes' which meant 'those without knee breeches' and red cap that symbolised liberty.

11. What was the condition of women in France before the revolution?

Ans. The condition of the women in France before the revolution was as follows

- All women were classified as passive citizens. They did not have voting powers.
- They worked as seamstresses or laundresses, sold flowers, fruits and vegetables or worked as domestic servants.
- Their wages were lower than those of men.
- They looked after their children, did the cooking, fetched water and queued up for bread.
- Most women did not have access to education or job training. Only daughters of wealthy parents could study at a convent, after which they were married off.

12. Differentiate between active and passive citizens of France. **Competency Based**

Ans. Following were the differences between active and passive citizens of France

Active Citizens	Passive Citizens
Only men above 25 years of age, who paid taxes equal of at least 3 days of a labourer's wage were given the status of active citizens.	The remaining men as well as women were called passive citizens.
They were entitled to vote.	They were not entitled to vote.

13. What do you understand by the term 'Reign of Terror'? Discuss.

Ans. The period from September 1793 to July 1794 was referred to as the 'Reign of Terror'. During this period, Robespierre, who ruled France at that time, followed a policy of severe control and punishment and terrorised people with his harsh measures.

All those whom he regarded as 'enemies' of the republic e.g. nobles, clergy or members of his or other political parties, were arrested and tried by a revolutionary tribunal. If they were found guilty, they were guillotined. More than 15000 persons were guillotined during this period.

The 'Reign of Terror' became intolerable and people resented Robespierre and his followers. Finally, Robespierre was convicted and guillotined in July 1794 and the 'Reign of Terror' ended with his death.

14. Read the statements given below regarding French Revolution. **Competency Based**

Statement I (S1) Rulers of other neighbouring countries too were worried by the developments in France.

Statement II (S2) The revolutionary wars brought losses and economic difficulties to the people.

Explain how these statements are reflecting in French Revolution.

Ans. **Statement I** reflects the impact of the French revolution on neighbouring countries. The rulers of neighbouring countries were worried by the developments in France. In France the people were fighting for their rights and inequality that prevailed in the society.

1789 revolt at Bastile forced the King Louis XVI to accept the National Assembly and abolish federal system of obligations and taxes.

Statement II reflects the consequences of the revolutionary wars on the people. During the period of revolution, the prices of the foodgrains increased. During the reigen of terror, many people lost their life. There was no economic development in the country. Utimately, it brought significant losses and economic difficulties.

Long Answer Type Questions

1. What were the causes for the empty treasury of France under Louis XVI? Assess any three causes.

or **State any five causes for the empty treasury of France under Louis XVI.**

Ans. The causes for the empty treasury of France under Louis XVI were

- **Long Years of wars** The seven years war (1756-63) and the Revolutionary War in America had drained the financial resources of France. Under Louis XVI, France helped the thirteen American colonies to gain their independence from Britain.
- **Debt Trap** The war added more than a billion livres to a debt that had already risen to more than 2 billion livres, Lenders who had given the state credit, began to charge 10% interest on the existing loans.
- **Extravagant Court** The extravagant court of France required huge amount of money for its maintenance.
- **Unfair Taxation System** Taxes were levied only on third estate and exempted first and second estates who were rich.
- **Increasing Expenditure** As the lender increased rate of interest, the French government was obliged to spend an increasing percentage of its budget on interest payment alone.

  To meet the regular expenses, like the cost of maintaining the army, the court, running government offices and universities, the state was forced to increase the taxes on the third estate.

2. The French Revolution popularised many symbols. Each symbol depicted some basic values. Mention the symbols and related values.

Ans. The symbols and their related values are stated in the points below

- **The Broken Chain** Chains were used to fetter slaves. A broken chain symbolised freedom from slavery.
- **The Bundle of Rods or Fasces** One rod can be easily broken, but not an entire bundle. It symbolises that strength lies in unity.
- **The Eye within a Triangle Radiating Light** The all seeing eye stands for knowledge. The rays of the Sun will drive away the clouds of ignorance. It depicts that knowledge removes ignorance.
- **Sceptre** It was a symbol of royal power. It depicted the power of autocracy.
- **Snake Biting its Tail to form a Ring** This type of ring has neither beginning nor end. It is a symbol of eternity.
- **Red Phrygian Cap** It was worn by a slave upon becoming free. It symbolises freedom from bondage or slavery.
- **Blue-White-Red** These were the national colours of France. The use of these colours depicted nationalism.
- **The Winged Woman** Personification of the law. It symbolised the power of law.
- **The Law Tablet** The law is the same for all and all are equal before it. It symbolised equality and justice.

3. What was the contribution of the French philosophers in the outbreak of the Revolution of 1789 in France?

or **What is the role of philosophers in the French Revolution?**

Ans. The revolutionary ideas of philosophers encouraged people to fight for their rights. These philosophers and their ideas were

- **Voltaire** He believed that man's destiny was in his own hands.
- **John Locke** He criticised the divine and absolute rights of the monarch in his book 'Two Treatises of Government'.
- **Rousseau** He put forward the idea of formation of a government based on a social contract between people and their representatives. Men had the right to change their government if they were not satisfied with it.
- **Montesquieu** He believed that all powers should not be concentrated in one person's hand. They should be divided between the Legislative, the Executive and the Judiciary.
- The ideas of these philosophers were discussed by common people in salons and coffee-houses and inspired them to fight for their rights.

4. What landmark decisions were taken by the National Assembly led by the third estate on the 4th August, 1789? What were its result?

or **"The National Assembly led by the third estate took some landmark decisions on 4th August, 1789 which brought landmark changes in French society." Justify the statement.**

Ans. On 20th June, 1789, the representatives of the third estate declared themselves as a National Assembly. They drafted a Constitution for France, which brought some land mark changes in French society on 4th August, 1789. These were

- They discarded the power of absolute monarchy.
- On 4th August, 1789, the Assembly passed a decree abolishing the feudal system of obligations and taxes.
- Members of the clergy were forced to give up their privileges.
- Tithe, a tax levied by the Church, comprising one-tenth of the agricultural produce, was abolished and lands owned by the Church were also confiscated.

The results of these decisions were

- As a direct consequence of these measures taken by the government, the government acquired assets worth at least 2 billion livres.
- France became a Constitutional monarchy. Powers were now separated and assigned to three different institutions i.e. the Legislative, the Executive and the Judiciary.
- The Constitution began with a Declaration of the Rights of Man and Citizen which established right to life, freedom of speech, freedom of opinion and equality before law as 'natural and inalienable' rights. It was the duty of the state to protect these rights.

5. What changes were seen in the regime of Robespierre's government?

Ans. The following changes were seen in the regime of Robespierre's government

- Robespierre's government issued laws placing a maximum ceiling on wages and prices. Meat and bread were rationed.
- Peasants were forced to transport their grain to the cities and sell it at fixed prices by the government.
- The use of expensive white flour was forbidden and all citizens were forced to eat the equality bread, *i.e.* a loaf made of whole wheat.
- Instead of the traditional Monsieur (Sir) and Madame (Madam), all French men and women were called as Citoyen and Citoyenne (citizen).
- Churches were also shut down and their buildings were converted into barracks or offices.

6. Name one of the most important politically active women in revolutionary France. What do you know about her?

Ans. Olympe de Gouges was one of the most important politically active women in revolutionary France.

She was a playwright and political activist whose feminist writings reached a large audience. She was an outspoken advocate for improving the conditions of slaves in France.

She wrote a 'Declaration of the Rights of Woman and Citizen' and demanded that French women should be given the same rights as French men. In 1793, she criticised the Jacobin government for forcibly closing down women's clubs. She was executed by guillotine during the 'Reign of Terror' for attacking Robespierre.

She is best known today as an early feminist who challenged the practice of male authority and the notion of male-female inequality.

7. How was slavery abolished in France? Explain.

Ans. Slavery was abolished in France in the following ways

- The abolition of slavery in the French colonies was first took up by the Jacobin regime in their social reforms.
- Secondly, the National Assembly held long debates and discussion for abolishing slavery. However, it did not pass any laws for abolition of slavery as it was fearing opposition from businessmen whose income depended on the slave trade.
- The third attempt to abolition of slavery was taken up by the convention in 1794 which legislated to free all slaves in the French overseas. However, it was a short term measure as after ten years slavery was reintroduced by Napoleon.
- Finally, slavery was abolished in French colonies in 1848 when plantation owners understood their freedom as including the right to enslave African Negroes in pursuit of their economic interests.

8. What changes did people witness in everyday life after the revolution of 1789 in France?

Ans. The people of France observed following changes after the revolution of 1789

- The revolutionary ideas of liberty and equality changed the clothes people wore, the language they spoke and the books they read.
- Censorship was abolished, flooding the country with newspapers, pamphlets, books and printed pictures.
- Freedom of the press implied that opposing views of events could be expressed. Each side tried to convince the other through the print medium.
- Act flourished in the form of plays, songs and festive processions attracted large crowds of people, as the largely uneducated population was able to identify with the new ideas.
- Slavery was abolished.

9. Olympe de Gouges in 1791 started a protest in France. She protested against the Constitution and the Declaration of Rights of Man and Citizen as they excluded women from basic rights that each human being was entitled to. The protest gained popularity in France. And then revolutionary government decided to pass a law for women's Rights. Explain how this law improved the lives of women and how it contributed to societal development?

Competency Based

Ans. This law improved lives of women by granting different rights like

(i) Women gained access to education with the introduction of state schools and a system of compulsory education for girls.

(ii) Women could no longer be forced into marriages and legalisation of divorce promised women's freedom.

(iii) Laws allowing women to train for jobs and enter various profession expanded economic opportunities for them.

These laws expanded access to education and workforce participation of women which enriched labour market and cultural landscape that led to the development of society.

10. Read the information about French Revolution and answer the question that follows.

On 5th May, 1789, Louis XVI called together an assembly of the Estates General to pass proposals for new taxes. A resplendent hall in Versailles was prepared to host the delegates. The first and second estates sent 300 representatives each, who were seated in rows facing each other on two sides, while the 600 members of the third estate had to stand at the back. The third estate was represented by its more prosperous and educated members. Peasants, artisans and women were denied entry to the assembly. However, their grievances and demands were listed in some 40,000 letters which the representatives had brought with them.

How did the Estates General function as a political body in France during the Old Regime, and who were the representatives sent by the three estates to participate in this assembly? **Competency Based**

Ans. During the Old Regime in France, the Estates General functioned as a political body responsible for advising the monarch on important matters, particularly financial issues such as taxation. The Estates General comprised representatives from each of the three estates, and their role was to discuss and pass proposals, including those related to new taxes.

The representatives sent by the three estates to participate in the assembly of the Estates General were

- Representatives of the first estate included high-ranking members of the clergy, such as bishops and abbot.
- The second estate was represented by members of the nobility, which encompassed aristocrats, landowners, and military officers.
- The third estate was represented by individuals from various backgrounds, including professionals, merchants, peasants, and laborers.

Case Based Questions

1. Read the source given below and answer the questions that follow.

The period from 1793 to 1794 is referred to as the Reign of Terror. Robespierre followed a policy of severe control and punishment. All those whom he saw as being 'enemies' of the republic-ex-nobles and cleargy, members of other political parties, even members of his own party who did not agree with his methods-were arrested, imprisoned and then tried by a revolutionary tribunal. If the court found them 'guilty' they were guillioned. The guillotine is a device consisting of two poles and a blade with which a person is beheaded. It was named after Dr Guillotin who invented it.

Robespierre's government issued laws placing a maximum ceiling on wages and prices. Meat and bread were rationed. Peasants were forced to transport their grain to the cities and sell it at prices fixed by the government.

The use of more expensive white flour was forbidden; all citizens were required to eat the pain degalite (equality bread), a loaf made of wholewheat. Equality was also sought to be practised through forms of speech and address. Instead of the traditional Monsieur (Sir) and Madame (Madam) all French men and women were hence forth Citoyen and Citoyenne (Citizen). Churches were shut down and their buildings converted into barracks or offices.

Robespierre pursued his policies so relentlessly that even his supporters began to demand moderation. Finally, he was convicted by a court in July 1794, arrested and on the next day sent to the guillotine.

(i) Enemies of the French Republic was tried by a revolutionary tribunal. Justify.

(ii) Laws of Robespierre's government were very repressive. Explain it by giving an example.

(iii) The ideas of equality was applied in French society. Justify the claim by giving an example.

Ans. (i) During the Reign of Terror, Robespierre followed a policy of severe control and punishment. According to this policy ex-nobles, clergy, member of other parties, even members of his own party who disagreed with his method were considered as enemies of the french republic and were tried and imprisoned by a revolutionary tribunal.

(ii) Laws of Robespierre's government were very repressive and applicable to all of the republic. Peasants of France were forced to transport their grain to the cities and sell it only at the prices fixed by the government, otherwise they would be punished.

(iii) One of the most important ideas of French Revolution, equality was applied by the Jacobins in French society. During that period, all Frenchmen and women were known as citoyen and citoyenne (citizen) instead of traditional Monsieur (Sir) and Madame (Madam) for aristocrat people.

2. Read the sources given below and answer the questions that follow.

Source A End of Special Privileges in France

Faced with the power of his revolting subject, Louis XVI finally accorded recognition to the Nation Assembly and accepted the principle that his powers would from now on be checked by a Constitution. On the night of 4th August, 1789, the Assembly passed a decree abolishing the feudal system of obligations and taxes. Members of the clergy too were forced to give up their privileges. Tithes were abolished and lands owned by the church were confiscated. As a result, the government acquired assets worth at least 2 billion livres.

(i) The powers of revolting subjects forced Louis XVI to curtail his own power. Justify the statement.

Source B France Becomes a Constitutional Monarchy

The National Assembly completed the draft of the Constitution in 1791. Its main objective was to limit the powers of the monarch. These powers instead of being concentrated in the hands of one person, were now separated and assigned to different institutions-the Legislature, Executive and Judiciary. This made France a constitutional monarchy.

(ii) The National Assembly advocated for the separation of powers instead of monopoly of power. Explain.

Source C Laws of the National Assembly

The Constitution of 1971 vested the power to make laws in the National Assembly, which was indirectly elected. That is, citizens voted for a group of electors, who in turn chose the Assembly. Not all citizens, however, had the right to vote. Only men above 25 years of age who paid taxes equal to atleast 3 days of a labourer's wage were given the status of active citizens, that is, they were entitled to vote.

The remaining men and all women were classed as passive citizens. To qualify as an elector and then as a member of the Assembly, a man had to belong to the highest bracket of taxpayers.

(iii) Is it true that political rights are only enjoyed by the active citizens of France? Give reasons.

Ans. (i) It is correct as when Louis XVI was faced with the power of his revolting subjects, he admitted the existence of the National Assembly of the third estate. He was forced to recognise the Constitution of the National Assembly which curtailed the powers of the monarch.

(ii) As the main aim of the National Assembly was to limit the powers of the monarch, it suggested the separation of powers between different organs like Legislative, Executive and Judiciary.

(iii) It is true that political rights are only enjoyed by the active citizens of France. According to the Constitution of the National Assembly, only men above 25 years of age who paid taxes equal to at least 3 days of a labourer's wage were regarded as active citizens. They were only given the right to vote. They were the people who gave the highest amount of tax and enjoyed the political rights to vote.

Map Based Question

1. Three items A, B and C are shown in the given outline map of France. Identify these items with the help of the following information and write their correct names on the lines marked on the map.

(a) Ports of France related to the slave trade.
(b) Capital of France.
(c) A place from where volunteers sang National Anthem of France.

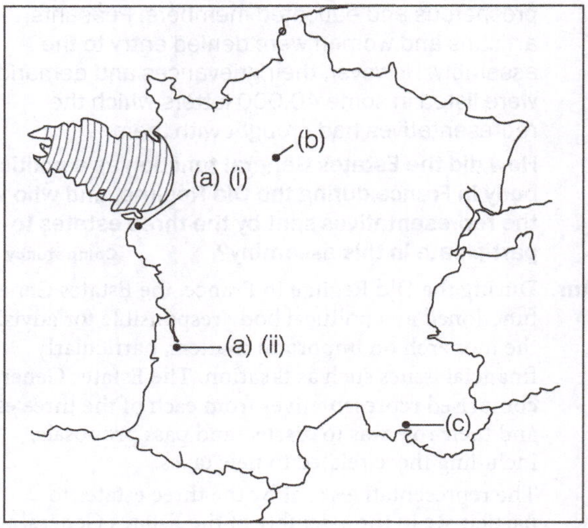

Ans.

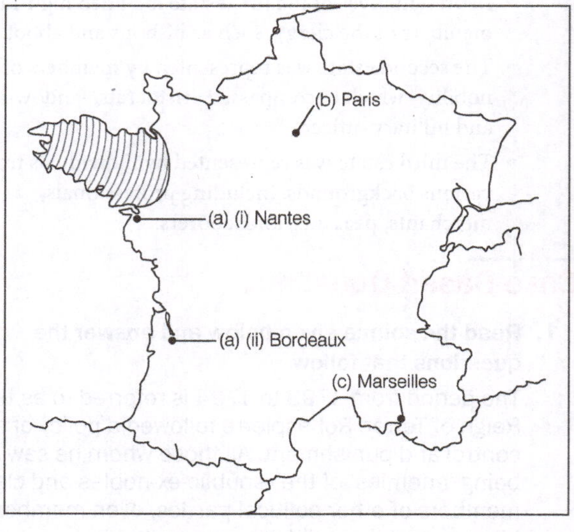

ASSESSMENT EXERCISE

Multiple Choice Questions (MCQs)

1. The Bastille fortress was hated by all because it
(a) stood for the despotic power of the king.
(b) imprisoned common men.
(c) was located in a secluded place.
(d) provided no facility for living.

2. The French Government increased the taxes to meet the needs of
(a) maintaining army (b) maintaining the court
(c) running government offices (d) All of these

3. Who was the famous leader of Jacobin club?
(a) Robespierre (b) Napoleon
(c) Desmoulins (d) Roget de L'Isle

4. The period from .... to .... is referred to as the 'Reign of Terror'.
(a) 1789, 1791 (b) 1793, 1794
(c) 1789, 1790 (d) 1792, 1793

5. Match the following.

List I		List II
A.	Louis XVI became the King of France	1. 1789
B.	Third Estate forms National Assembly	2. 1792-93
C.	Robespierre is guillotined	3. 1774
D.	France became a Republic	4. 1794

Codes

	A	B	C	D
(a)	1	3	2	4
(b)	3	1	4	2
(c)	4	1	3	2
(d)	2	3	4	1

Subjective Questions (VSA, SA & LA)

1. Name the group of people which did not belong to the Jacobin club.

2. What was the reason for the Bastille being hated by all in France?

3. What laws were introduced by the revolutionary government to improve the lives of women in France?

4. Explain how the new political system of Constitutional monarchy in France worked.

5. How can you say that Louis XVI was a despotic ruler?

6. How was French society organised? What privileges did certain sections of the society enjoy?

7. What changes were seen after the rise of population of France in 1789?

CHAPTER 2

Socialism in Europe and the Russian Revolution

In the 19th century, new political ideas, especially socialism, began to emerge as a response to the hardships caused by industrialisation and inequality. Socialism aimed to improve the lives of workers and promote equality. The Russian Revolution of 1917 was a key event where socialism transformed society, influencing the world in the 20th century.

2.1 The Age of Social Change

The French Revolution opened up the possibility of creating a new social structure. Before the 18th century, society was broadly divided into estates and orders. It was the aristocracy and church who controlled economic and social power.

In India, Raja Rammohan Roy and Derozio pointed out the significance of the French Revolution and many others discussed the ideas of post-revolutionary Europe.

After the French Revolution, new ideas about 'individual right's and 'societal changes' began to be discussed in Europe and Asia.

There were groups who wanted to change society according to their thoughts and visions. Liberals, Radicals and Conservatives were the three main groups that emerged during this period.

Liberals

- They suggested to change the society and supported the idea based on 'Tolerance of all Religions'.
- They opposed the uncontrolled powers of dynastic rulers.
- They wanted to safeguard the rights of individuals against governments.
- They supported a representative, elected parliamentary government and an independent judiciary.
- Liberals were not democrats as they did not favour Universal Adult Franchise (Right to Vote). They favoured voting rights only for men with property and not for women.

Radicals

- They supported the Government based on majority of country's population.
- They opposed the privileges given to great landowners and wealthy factory owners.
- Many of them also supported women's suffragette movements[1].
- They supported private property but disliked concentration of property in the hand of few.

Conservatives

- They opposed the views of Radicals and Liberals.
- Earlier, they opposed the idea of change but by the 19th century, they accepted some changes.
- They asserted that past must be respected.
- They wanted change but at a slow pace.

Industrial Society and Social Change

During the Industrial Revolution, many changes came in the society and economy. Some of them were

- New cities, new industrial regions and new railway lines were developed.
- Men, women and children worked in factories.
- Working hours were often long and wages were poor.
- Unemployment was common due to low demand for industrial goods.
- Housing and sanitation were problems since towns were growing rapidly.

Liberals and Radicals searched for solutions to these issues. Many of the factory owners were Liberals and Radicals. Both Liberals and Radicals felt that worker's efforts must be encouraged. They also held that its benefits would be achieved if the workforce in the economy is healthy and citizens were educated.

They believed in hardwork, effort and enterprise, instead of privileges by birth.

1 **Suffragette Movements** These refer to movements for giving women the right to vote.

Many working women and men who wanted changes in the world rallied around liberal and radical groups in the early 19th century.

Some Nationalists, Liberals and Radicals wanted revolutions to put an end to the kind of governments established in Europe in 1815. They worked to overthrow existing monarchs in **France, Italy, Germany** and **Russia.**

Nationalists emphasised on revolutions that would create 'nations' where all citizens would have equal rights.

After 1815, **Giuseppe Mazzini,** an Italian nationalist conspired with others to achieve this in Italy.

The Coming of Socialism to Europe

By the mid of 19th century in Europe, socialism was a well-known body of ideas that attracted widespread attention. Socialists were against the idea of **private property** but had differing ideas on how a society without property could operate.

Some of the visions of socialists are as follows

- **Robert Owen** (1771-1858) He believed in setting up of a cooperative community called New Harmony in Indiana (USA).
- **Louis Blanc** (1813-1882) He was a French socialist who wanted the government to encourage cooperatives and replace capitalist enterprises. These cooperatives were associations of people who produced goods together and divided the profits according to the work done by members.
- **Karl Marx** (1818-1883) He believed that the industrial society was capitalist. Capitalists owned the capital invested in factories and the profit of capitalists was produced by workers.

  The conditions of workers could not improve till the profit was accumulated by private capitalists. He believed that to remove capitalism, workers had to construct a radically socialist society in which all property would be socially controlled. This would be a communist society.
- **Friedrich Engels** (1820-1895) He suggested that workers have to remove capitalism and the rule of private property.

Support for Socialism

The spread of socialist ideas through Europe by the 1870s led to the formation of an international body i.e. the **Second International.** The association of workers in England and Germany began to be formed.

They were formed due to the following reasons

- To improve the working and living conditions of workers.
- They set up funds to help member workers in difficult times.
- To demand reduction of working hours and the right to vote.
- In Germany, these associations worked closely with the **Social Democratic Party** (SDP) and helped it win parliamentary seats.

By 1905, socialists and trade unionist formed a **Labour Party** in **Britain** and a **Socialist Party** in **France.** However, till 1914, the socialists were not able to form a government in Europe. Socialists were represented by strong figures in Parliamentary politics, but governments continued to be run by conservatives, liberals and radicals.

Try These

1. **Identify the group who accepted slow changes by the 19th century?**
2. **Which group opposed the uncontrolled powers of dynastic rulers and supported representative parliamentary government?**
3. **Who believed in setting up a cooperative community called New Harmony in Indiana, USA?**
4. **Who proposed that the government encourage cooperatives to replace capitalist enterprises?**

2.2 The Russian Revolution

The decline of monarchy in February 1917, and the events of October are generally known as Russian Revolution. Socialists took over the government in Russia through the October Revolution of 1917.

The Russian Empire in 1914

In 1914, **Tsar**[2] **Nicholas II** ruled Russia and its empire. The Russian Empire included territory around Moscow, present day Finland, Latvia, Lithuania, Estonia, parts of Poland, Ukraine and Belarus.

The empire stretched to the Pacific and comprised today's Central Asian states, as well as Georgia, Armenia and Azerbaijan. The majority religion was Russian Orthodox Christianity along with Catholics, Protestants, Muslims and Buddhists.

2 **Tsar** It referred to the title of the Emperor of Russia.

Economy and Society

At the beginning of the 20th century, about 85 per cent of the Russian empire's population earned their living from agriculture. The percentage of agriculturalists in Russia was higher than most European countries. For instance, in France and Germany, the proportion was between 40% and 50%.

Russia was a major exporter of grain in the Empire and cultivators produced for the market as well as for their own needs.

Industries were very few in number. Prominent industrial areas were **St Petersburg** and **Moscow**. Craftsmen did most of the production, but large factories also worked alongside small workshops. Many factories were set up in the 1890's, when Russian rail network was extended and foreign investment in industries also increased. As a result, coal production was doubled while Iron and Steel output increased four times.

Most of the industries were privately owned. Large factories were supervised under the Government to ensure minimum wages and limited hours of work.

Factory rules were broken in craft units and small workshops as the working hours exceeded to 15 hours, compared with 10 or 12 hours in factories.

Workers were a divided social group. Some stayed connected to their villages, while others settled in cities permanently.

Workers were also divided on the basis of 'skill' as a social group. For example, metal workers were considered as aristocrats because they were more trained and skilled.

Women made up about 31 per cent of the factory labour force by 1914, but they were paid less than man. Despite divisions, workers were united when they disagreed with employers about dismissals or work conditions. Strikes were common in textile industry during 1896 and 1897 and in metal industry during 1902.

Peasants in the Countryside

In the countryside, peasants were another social group who cultivated land owned by nobility, crown and orthodox church. They were divided on religious basis but united against the nobles.

Nobles got their power and position through their services to the Tsar, not through local popularity.

In France, during French Revolution in Brittany, peasants respected nobles and fought for them.

However, in Russia, peasants wanted the land of the nobles to be given to them. They refused to pay rent and even murdered landlords. In 1902, such events occurred on a large scale in South Russia, but later in 1905 such incidents spread all over Russia.

Russian peasants were different from other European peasants. They accumulated their land together periodically and later divided it on the basis of needs of individual families. Peasant community was called **'commune'** (mir).

Socialism in Russia

All political parties were illegal in Russia before 1914. The **Russian Social Democratic Workers Party** was founded in 1898 by socialists who respected Marx's ideas. Due to government policies, the party operated as an illegal organisation. It started its own newspaper, mobilised workers and organised strikes.

Some Russian socialists felt that the Russian peasant custom of dividing land periodically made them natural socialists. Therefore, peasants rather than workers would be the main force of the revolution.

Socialists in the countryside formed the **Socialist Revolutionary Party** in 1900. This party struggled for peasant's rights and demanded that land belonging to nobles would be transferred to peasants.

Social Democrats disagreed with socialists revolutionaries about peasants. **Lenin** felt that peasants were not one united group due to financial differences. Due to these differences, they could not be a part of socialist movement. The Social Democratic Party was later divided into two wings, the **Bolsheviks**[3] and the **Mensheviks**[4].

Vladimir Lenin who led the Bolshevik group thought that in a repressive society like Tsarist Russia, the party should be disciplined and should control the number and quality of its members. On the other hand, Mensheviks wanted party to be opened to all (as in Germany).

3 **Bolsheviks** It refers to the majority group of the Russian Social Democratic Workers Party led by Lenin based on the ideology of Karl Marx and Friedrich Engels.

4 **Mensheviks** It refers to the minority group of Russian Social Democratic Workers Party formed in 1898. They favoured a parliamentary model of government like that of Britain and France.

The 1905 Revolution

In the beginning of 20th century, Russia was still an **autocracy**[5] and the Tsar was not responsible to the Parliament.

During the revolution of 1905, Liberals wanted to end this state of affairs. They joined hands with social democrats and socialist revolutionaries worked with peasants and workers to demand a **Constitution**.

They were supported in the Russian empire by nationalists (e.g. in Poland) and in Muslim-dominated areas by **jadidists**[6], who wanted modernised Islam to lead their societies.

Some of the reasons responsible for the 1905 revolution were

- In 1904, prices of essential goods rose so quickly that **Real wages**[7] of the workers declined by 20 per cent.
- Four members of the Putilov Iron works were dismissed that called for the industrial action.

Many workers in St Petersburg went on strike demanding a reduction in the working day to eight hours, an increase in wages and improvement in working conditions.

The procession of workers led by **Father Gapon** reached the Winter Palace. However, they were attacked by police and the **Cossacks**[8]. In this incident, many workers were killed and wounded.

This came to be known as **Bloody Sunday** and started a series of events that came to be known as 1905 revolution. These events were

- Trend of strikes spread all over the country.
- Universities closed down when students complained about the lack of civil liberties.
- Doctors, lawyers, engineers and other middle-class workers established the Union of Unions and demanded a Constituent Assembly.
- A large number of trade unions and factory committees consisted of factory workers also existed for short time.
- Severe restrictions were placed on political activity.

Under the widespread revolution, the Tsar allowed the creation of an **Elected Consultative Parliament** or **Duma**[9]. He dismissed the **first Duma** within 75 days and re-elected the **second Duma** within 3 months.

He did not want any questioning of his authority or any reduction in his power. He changed the **voting laws** and made the **third Duma** with conservative politicians. Liberals and revolutionaries were kept out.

The First World War and the Russian Empire

In 1914, the First World War started between two European alliances that were **Germany, Austria** and **Turkey** (the central powers) and **France, Britain** and **Russia**, (Later **Italy** and **Romania**).

The First World War was fought outside Europe as well as in Europe.

Initially, the war was popular in Russia and the people rallied around Tsar Nicholas II. As the war continued, the Tsar refused to consult the main parties in the Duma and there was loss of support for Tsar.

Anti German feeling got stronger, e.g. **St. Peterberg** which was a German name renamed as **Petrograd**. The Tsarina Alexandra's German origin and her advisor Rasputin (a German monk) made the autocracy unpopular.

The armies in First World War fought from two direction i.e. Eastern and Western.There was a difference between **Eastern army** and **Western army** of the First World War.

The Western army fought from trenches stretched along Eastern France, whereas the Eastern army fought battle by leaving large casualties.

Russia suffered shocking defeats along with heavy casualties in the war. Russian armies lost badly in **Germany** and **Austria** between 1914 and 1916.

The effects of this war were

- The Russian army destroyed crops and buildings to prevent the enemy from being able to live off the land. It led to over 3 million refugees in Russia.
- The war also affected the industry. Russia's own industries were few in number and the country was cut off from other suppliers of industrial goods by German control of the Baltic sea.
- By 1916, railway lines began to break down.
- Able-bodies men were called up to the war. This led to shortage of labour and shut down of small workshops.

---

5 **Autocracy** It is a system of government which is ruled by one person who has complete power.
6 **Jadidists** Muslim reformers within the Russian empire.
7 **Real wages** Reflects the quantities of goods which the wages will actually buy.
8 **Cossacks** A group of predominantly East slavic people who were members of democratic, semi-military communities in Ukraine and Southern Russia.
9 **Duma** The Russian Parliament or Legislature. Its members were elected and charged with the responsibility of making laws.

- Large supplies of grain were sent to feed the army. This leads to scarcity of bread and flour for the people in cities. By the winter of 1916, riots at breadshops were common.

Try These

1 **What percentage of the Russian Empire's population earned their living from agriculture at the beginning of the 20th century?**

2 **Which event in 1905 sparked a series of events known as the 1905 Revolution?**

3 **Name the main religion in the Russian Empire during the early 20th century.**

4 **What was the name of the elected consultative Parliament allowed by the Tsar during the 1905 Revolution?**

2.3 The February Revolution in Petrograd

In winter 1917, Petrograd faced hard times. Workers lived on the right bank of River Neva, while the left bank had fashionable areas and the winter palace.

Food shortages hit workers hard during the freezing winter. Parliament opposed the Tsar's plan to dissolve the Duma.

On 22nd February, a lockout took place at a factory. This led to protests and strikes against the factory joined by women. This day came to be known as **International Women's Day**.

Demonstrating workers crossed from the factory quarters to the centre of the capital, **Nevskii Prospekt**. At this stage, no political party was actively ogranising the movement.

Curfew was imposed by the government and to restrict the demonstrators, **cavalry** and **police** was called out. On 25th February, the government suspended the Duma. Politicians spoke out against this measure.

On 26th February, demonstrators returned on the streets whereas on 27th February, the police headquarters were attacked and damaged.

Workers demonstrated on the streets, raising slogans about bread, wages, better hours and democracy. The government tried to control the situation through cavalry but it refused to fire on demonstrators.

An officer was shot at the barracks of a regiment. Three other regiments revolted and voted to join the striking workers. The cavalry soldiers joined the workers and jointly formed a **Soviet** or **Council** in the same building where the Duma met. This was the **Petrograd Soviet**.

On 28th February, a delegation went to see the Tsar. Tsar resigned the throne on the advice of the military commanders on 2nd March, 1917.

Soviet leaders and Duma leaders formed a **provisional government** to run the country. A Constituent Assembly was elected on the basis of **universal adult suffrage** in Russia. The February Revolution in Petrograd brought down the monarchy in February 1917.

After February

Army officials, landowners and industrialists played an important role in the Provisional Government. But, the liberals as well as socialists among them worked towards an elected government. Restrictions on public meetings and associations were removed.

The Bolshevik leader Vladimir Lenin returned to Russia from his exile in **April 1917**. He wanted the soviets to take over power. Lenin gave his 'April Theses' in which he made three demands

(i) The war should be brought to an end.
(ii) The land must be transferred to the peasants.
(iii) The banks should be nationalised.

Lenin wanted the Bolshevik Party to be renamed as **Communist Party** to indicate its new radical aims.

The Worker's Movement spread throughout the summer. In industrial areas, factory committees were formed which began questioning the way industrialists operated their factories.

Soldier's committees were also formed in the army. In June, about 500 soviets sent representatives to an All Russian Congress of Soviets. The power of provisional government was reduced and the Bolshevik influence increased.

The Provisional Government decided to take strong steps against the discontent of the workers. It resisted attempts by workers to run factories and began arresting leaders.

Popular demonstrations under the Bolsheviks in July, 1917 were strictly repressed.

In the countryside, peasants and their socialist revolutionary leaders demanded for a **redistribution of land** for which land committees were formed.

Peasants were encouraged by the socialist revolutionaries and seized land between July and September 1917.

The Revolution of October 1917

As the conflict grew between the Provisional Government and Bolsheviks, Lenin feared that the Provisional Government would set up a dictatorship. In September, he began discussions for an uprising against the government.

On 16th October, 1917, Lenin persuaded the Petrograd Soviet and the Bolshevik Party to agree to a socialist seizure of power. To organise the seizure, **Military Revolutionary** Committee was appointed by the Soviet under **Leon Trotskii**.

As the uprising began on 24th October, 1917, Prime Minister **Kerenskii** left the city to summon troops in fear. In the evening, loyal military men of government captured the building of two Bolshevik newspapers. Pro-government troops were sent to capture telephone and telegraphy offices' and protect the winter palace.

In response, the Military Revolutionary Committee ordered its supporters to capture government offices and arrest ministers. Later the ship **Aurora** protected the winter palace. Other vessels sailed down the River Neva and took over different military points.

The revolution ended with all Russian Congress of Soviets in Petrograd approving the Bolshevik action. There was heavy fighting especially in Moscow but by December, the Bolsheviks controlled the Moscow-Petrograd area.

2.4 Changes After October

- The Bolsheviks nationalised the banks and industries in November 1917.
- The Bolsheviks declared land as a social property and allowed peasants to capture land of nobles.
- The Bolsheviks banned old titles of aristocracy and big houses were partitioned according to the family needs.
- New uniforms were designed for the army and officials and the Soviet hat *(budeonovka)* was also designed.
- The **Bolshevik Party** was renamed as the **Russian Communist Party** (Bolshevik).
- The Bolsheviks were totally opposed to **private property**.
- In November 1917, the Bolsheviks conducted the elections to the Constituent Assembly, but they failed to gain majority support.
- In January 1918, the Assembly rejected Bolshevik measures and Lenin dismissed the Assembly. He believed that All Russian Congress of Soviets was more democratic than an assembly elected in uncertain conditions.
- In March 1918, the Bolsheviks entered into a treaty with Germany at Brest Litovsk. The Bolsheviks became the only party to participate in the elections to All Russian Congress of Soviets which was the parliament of the country and they won.
- **Russia** became a **one-party state** and trade unions were kept under party control. Those who criticised Bolsheviks were punished by secret police (Cheka and later OGPU and NKVD).
- Many young writers and artists opposed the party because it stood for socialism and change. This led to experiments in the field of arts and architecture after October 1917.
- After October 1917, many Bolshevik followers became disillusioned by the way the party functioned.

The Civil War

The decision of redistribution of land by Bolsheviks caused breakup of army. Soldiers, who were mostly peasants, wished to go home for the redistribution and deserted.

Non-Bolshevik socialist, liberals and supporters of autocracy condemned the Bolshevik uprising. Their leaders moved to South Russia and organised troops to fight the Bolshevik.

The pro-Tsarists (the 'whites') and the Socialist Revolutionaries (the 'greens') fought a Civil War with Bolshevik (the 'reds') troops during 1918 and 1919.

The pro-Tsarists and socialists were supported by French, American, British and Japanese troops. These forces were worried at the growth of socialism in Russia. Supporters of private property among 'whites' took harsh steps with peasants who had seized land. This made them unpopular.

By January 1920, the Bolsheviks controlled most of the former Russian Empire. They succeeded due to cooperation with non-Russian nationalists and Muslim Jadidists.

In Khiva in Central Asia, Bolshevik colonists brutally killed local nationalists in the name of defending socialism. In this situation, many were confused about what the Bolshevik government wanted.

In 1922, most non-Russian nationalist were given **political autonomy**[10] in the USSR (which was the state created from the Russian Empire in **December 1922**) by the Bolsheviks. However, the Bolshevik Government discouraged **nomadism**[11] and this led to partial success to win over the different nationalities of this region.

10 **Political Autonomy** The right to govern themselves.

11 **Nomadism** Lifestyle of those who do not live in one place, but move from area to area to earn their living.

Making a Socialist Society

During the civil war, the Bolsheviks kept industries and banks nationalised. They permitted peasants to cultivate the captured land to show collective work.

Centralised planning was introduced with the introduction of five year plans. The government fixed all prices to promote industrial growth during the first two 'plans' (1927-32 and 1933-38).

Centralised planning led to economic growth. New factory cities came into being. Industrial production increased between 1929 and 1933 by 100 per cent in the field of oil, coal and steel.

Rapid construction led to poor working conditions for workers. In **Magnitogorsk**, a steel plant was constructed in three years. Workers did not have even basic facilities of toilet, health care, etc.

Measures taken to improve status of workers were

- An extended **schooling system** developed and arrangement were made for factory workers and peasants to enter universities.
- **Creches** (day boarding) were established in factories for the children of women workers.
- **Cheap Public healthcare** was provided and model living quarters were made for workers.

However, the effect of all these measures was uneven as government resources were limited.

Stalinism and Collectivisation

The period of early planned economy of Soviet Russia brought with it some disasters and one such disaster was **collectivisation of agriculture**.

By 1927- 1928, the towns in Soviet Russia were facing an acute problem of grain supplies. The government fixed prices at which grain must be sold, but the peasants refused to sell their grain to government buyers at these prices.

Stalin headed the party after the death of Lenin and he introduced firm emergency.

Stalin believed the rich peasants and traders in the countryside were holding stocks in the hope of higher prices.

To stop the speculations and confiscate the supplies, party members toured the grain producing areas in 1928. They supervised enforced grain collections and raided the **Kulaks**[12].

After 1917, land had been handed over to the peasants. Due to the shortages of foodgrains, the decision was taken to collectivise farms. For the development of modern farms, it was necessary to eliminate Kulaks to take away land from peasants and to establish large state-controlled farms.

From 1929, the Communist Party forced all peasants to cultivate in collective farms (Kolkhoz). Peasants worked on lands and the profit of the collective farms was shared among them.

Peasants who opposed collectivisation destroyed their livestocks. Thus, between 1929 to 1931, the number of cattle decreased by one-third.

Peasants who opposed the collectivisation were severely punished and many were **deported**[13] and **exiled**[14]. Peasants resisted collectivisation, saying they were not rich or against socialism. They just did not want to work on collective farms. Stalin allowed some private cultivation, but was not supportive of it. However, production did not increase immediately due to the collectivisation programme.

The bad harvests of 1930-33 led to one of the most devastating famines in Soviet history in which over 4 million died.

Many within the party criticised the confusion in industrial production under the planned economy and the consequences of collectivisation.

Stalin and his sympathisers charged these critics with conspiracy against socialism. Many were forced to make false confessions. They faced torture and executions.

2.5 Global Influence of Russian Revolution and the USSR

Communist parties began to be formed around the world like Communist Party of Great Britain.

The Bolsheviks encouraged colonial people to follow their ideas. Many non-Russians participated in the Conference of the People of the East (1920). The Bolshevik founded *Comintern*, an international union of pro-Bolshevik socialist parties. Some non-Russians received education in the USSR's Communist University of the Workers of the East.

12 **Kulaks** The name for well-to-do-peasants.

13 **Deported** Forcibly removed from one's own country.

14 **Exiled** Forced to live away from one's own country.

By the 1950s, people in the USSR saw that the government did not follow the ideals of Russian Revolution.

The USSR had grown from a backward country to a great power. With progress in industries and agriculture, the poor were being fed. But citizens lost freedom as development came through strict policies.

By the time of Second World War, socialism received a global presence and admiration. By the end of the 20th century, the international reputation of the USSR as a socialist country had declined. However, the socialist ideas were rethought in a variety of different ways, in each country.

Writing About the Russian Revolution in India

The Russian Revolution inspired many Indians. By the mid-1920s, the Communist Party was formed in India. Its members were connected with the Soviet Communist Party.

Important Indian political and cultural figures took an interest in the Soviet experiment and visited Russia. Among them, prominent ones were **Jawaharlal Nehru** and **Rabindranath Tagore**, who wrote about Soviet Socialism.

In India, writings gave impressions of Soviet Russia. In Hindi, **RS Avasthi** wrote *Russian Revolution, Lenin, His Life and His Thoughts in 1920-21,* and *later The Red Revolution*. SD Vidyalankar wrote *The Rebirth of Russia* and *The Soviet State of Russia*. The writing were much written in Bengali, Marathi, Malayalam, Tamil and Telugu.

Try These

1. **Who nationalised the banks and industries in November 1917?**
2. **What was the Boleshevik secret police called?**
3. **In the Russian Civil War, the Bolsheviks and the socialist revolutionaries were represented by which colours?**
4. **Name two prominent Indians who wrote about Soviet Socialism.**

TIME LINE

Covering Major Events with their Time Periods in Chronological Order

Year	Important Events
1850-1880	Debates over socialism in Russia.
1898	Formation of the Russian Socialist Democratic Workers Party.
22nd Jan, 1905	Bloody Sunday: the Revolution of 1905 starts.
22nd - 27th Feb, 1917	February Revolution.
2nd March, 1917	Tsar abdicates.
24th Oct, 1917	Bolshevik uprising in Petrograd.
3rd March, 1918	Russia withdraws from First World War after signing Treaty of Brest-Litovsk with Germany.
1918-1920	Civil War in Russia.
1919	Formation of Comintern.
1929	Beginning of collectivisation in farming.

Note Russian followed the Julian Calendar until 1st February, 1918, then the country changed to Gregorian Calendar. The Gregorian dates are 13 days ahead of the Julian dates.

Mind Map

SOCIALISM IN EUROPE AND THE RUSSIAN REVOLUTION

Economy and Society
- Industries were few in number.
- Workers were divided on the basis of skill as a social group.
- Women made up about 31% of the factory labour force by 1914.

The First World War and the Russian Empire
- Broke out in 1914 between two European alliances-Germany, Austria and Turkey (the Central Powers), and France, Britain and Russia (later Italy and Romania).
- Russia suffered shocking defeats along with heavy casualties in the War.
- Russian armies lost badly in Germany and Austria between 1914 and 1916.

The Revolution of October (1917)
- Lenin persuaded the Petrograd Soviet and the Bolshevik Party to agree to a socialist seizure of power.
- To organise the seizure, Military Revolutionary Committee was appointed by the Soviet under Leon Trotskii.

Actions
- Demonstrating workers crossed from the factory quarters to the centre of the capital-the Nevskii Prospekt.
- Curfew was imposed by the government, to restrict the demonstrators, cavalry and the police was called out.

The Russian Empire (1914)
- Tsar Nicholas II ruled Russia and its empire.
- Russian Empire included territory around Moscow present day Finland, Latvia, Estonia, parts of Poland, Ukraine and Belarus.

The February Revolution in Petrograd
- In February 1917, there were food shortages in the workers' quarters in Petrograd which led to a strike on 22nd February in many factories.

The Russian Revolution

Outcomes
- Tsar resigned the throne on the advice of the military commanders on 2nd March, 1917.
- Soviet leaders and Duma leaders formed a provisional government to run the country.
- A Constituent Assembly was elected on the basis of Universal Adult Suffrage in Russia.

Socialism in Russia
- The Russian Social Democratic Workers Party was founded in 1898 by socialists who respected Marx's ideas.
- Socialists in the country-side formed the Socialist Revolutionary Party in 1900.
- The Social Democratic Party was later divided into two wings, the Bolsheviks and the Mensheviks.

The Age of Social Changes
- After French Revolution, several groups emerged in Europe, some of which were conservatives, and others were liberals or radicals.
- Liberals wanted a nation which tolerated all religions.
- Radicals wanted a nation in which government was based on the majority of country's population.
- Conservatives were opposed to radicals and liberals.

Global Influence of Russian Revolution and the USSR
- Communist parties began to be formed around the world like Communist Party of Great Britain.
- The Bolsheviks encouraged Colonial people to follow their ideas.
- The Bolsheviks founded Comintern, an International Union of Pro-Bolshevik socialist parties.

The 1905 Revolution
- In 1904, price of essential goods rose so quickly that real wages of the workers declined by 20%.
- Tsar allowed the creation of an elected consultative Parliament or Duma.
- Over 100 workers were killed and about 300 were wounded in the attack by the police and the Cossacks over the procession of workers at the Winter Palace. This incident was known as Bloody Sunday.

Changes after October
- The Bolsheviks nationalised the banks and the industries in November 1917.
- The Bolshevik Party was renamed as the Russian Communist Party.
- The Bolsheviks were totally opposed to private property.

Stalinism and Collectivisation
- From 1929, the Communist Party forced all peasants to cultivate in collective farms (Kolkhoz).
- Peasants who opposed the collectivisation were severely punished and many were deported and exiled.

The Civil War
The pro-Tsarists and the Socialist Revolutionaries fought a Civil War with Bolshevik troops during 1918 and 1919.

Making a Socialist Society
- An extended schooling system developed.
- Creches were established in factories.
- Cheap Public Healthcare was provided.

NCERT FOLDER

Covering Intext Questions and Exercises of NCERT

INTEXT QUESTIONS

Q.1 List two differences between the capitalist and socialist ideas of private property.

Ans. The differences between capitalist and socialist ideas of private property were

Capitalist Ideas	Socialist Ideas
Capitalists were owners of the industries in which they have invested capital. They believe in private property and a class-based society.	Socialists think that all property and means of production should be socially controlled. They believe in a classless society.
Capitalists believe that the profit should be enjoyed by the owners of the industry.	Socialists believe that the profits are the result of the workers' labour, so the workers deserve a share.

Q.2 Why were there revolutionary disturbances in Russia in 1905? What were the demands of the revolutionaries?

Ans. The causes of the revolutionary disturbances in Russia in 1905 were

- Russia's defeat in the Russo-Japanese War of 1904 due to the poorly organised Russian army.
- The prices of essential commodities rose, so that real wages declined by 20 per cent.
- Workers were dismissed at the Putilov Iron Works.

The revolutionaries demanded a reduction in daily working hours to eight, increase in wages and improvement in working conditions.

Q.3 Why did people in Central Asia respond to the Russian Revolution in different ways?

Ans. The people in Central Asia responded enthusiastically to the February 1917 Revolution because it freed them from the oppression of the Tsar's reign and they became masters of their land again. They expected to regain their autonomy.

However, they responded negatively to the October Revolution, as it brought violence, robbery, extra taxes and another dictatorial power to rule over them. They feared now that their autonomy would be lost.

Q.4 Compare the passages written by Shaukat Usmani and Rabindranath Tagore. Read them in relation to Sources C, D and E and answer the following questions

(a) What did Indians find impressive about the USSR?

(b) What did the writers fail to notice?

Source F

An Indian arrives in Soviet Russia in 1920

For the first time in our lives, we were seeing Europeans mixing freely with Asians. On seeing the Russians mingling freely with the rest of the people of the country, we were convinced that we had come to a land of real equality.

We saw freedom in its true light. In spite of their poverty, imposed by the counter-revolutionaries and the imperialists, the people were more jovial and satisfied than ever before. The revolution had instilled confidence and fearlessness in them. The real brotherhood of mankind would be seen here among these people of fifty different nationalities. No barriers of caste or religion hindered them from mixing freely with one another. Every soul was transformed into an orator. One could see a worker, a peasant or a soldier haranguing like a professional lecturer.'

Shaukat Usmani, *Historic Trips of a Revolutionary*

Source G

Rabindranath Tagore wrote from Russia in 1930

'Moscow appears much less clean than the other European capitals. None of those hurrying along the streets look smart. The whole place belongs to the workers ... Here the masses have not in the least been put in the shade by the gentlemen ... those who lived in the background for ages have come forward in the open today ... I thought of the peasants and workers in my own country. It all seemed like the work of the Genii in the Arabian Nights. [here] only a decade ago, they were as illiterate, helpless and hungry as our own masses ... Who could be more astonished than an unfortunate Indian like myself to see how they had removed the mountain of ignorance and helplessness in these few years.'

Ans. (a) Indians were impressed by the fact that all persons in Russia were treated equally. In spite of them, not being very prosperous, they were happily going about their work. Asians and Europeans mingled freely in Russia, whereas it was unthinkable in India at that time.

(b) The two writers failed to notice that essentially the people were not free to do as they liked. The Bolsheviks ruled like dictators and followed repressive policies to develop the nation quickly. The hard lives and poor working conditions of the people went unnoticed by these writers.

EXERCISE

Q.1 What were the social, economic and political conditions in Russia before 1905?

Ans. The social, economic and political conditions in Russia before 1905 were

- **Social Conditions** Russian society was divided into three classes: the clergy, nobility and the working class. Slavery was abolished in 1861, but the peasants, who constituted 85 per cent of the population, had to pay heavy taxes for small holdings.
- **Economic Conditions** After industrialisation, many factories were set up by industrialists. The wages were minimum and the working hours were sometimes 15 hours a day. The condition of the workers was miserable. The state treasury was bankrupt due to heavy expenditure.
- **Political Conditions** Under the autocratic rule of Tsar Nicholas II, the Russian empire was vast and feudal. The disastrous defeat of Russia in the Russo-Japanese War of 1904 had eroded the prestige of Tsar Nicholas II.

Q.2 In what ways was the working population in Russia different from other countries in Europe, before 1917?

Ans. The working population in Russia was different from that of those in other countries in Europe before 1917 in the following ways

- About 85 per cent of Russians were agriculturists. Whereas in France and Germany, the farmers were between 40 per cent and 50 per cent.
- The cultivators in Russia produced for the markets as well as for their own needs. Industrialisation started late in Russia and industries were only found in small pockets. Workers were a divided social group and maintained strong links with the villages they had come from. Metal workers considered themselves aristocrats among other workers. In Russia, sometimes the working hours for workers were 15 hours as compared to 10 or 12 hours in Europe. On the other hand, in Europe, the Industrial Revolution changed a mainly rural society into an urban one.
- In France, during French Revolution, the French peasants respected nobles and also fought for them. But in Russia, peasants wanted the land of the nobles. They refused to pay rent and even murdered landlords.
- In Russia, peasants had pooled their land together and divided the profits according to the family needs. In other parts of world, agriculture was done individually by the peasants.

Q.3 Why did the Tsarist autocracy collapse in 1917?

Ans. The Tsarist autocracy collapsed in 1917 due to social, economic and political reasons as follows

- **Social Reasons** In the First World War, the defeat of the Russian army was shocking and demoralising there were over 7 million casualties and 3 million refugees by 1917. The rest of the population became hostile to the Tsar.
- **Economic Reasons** There were labour shortages due to the participation of able-bodied men in the war, which led to the shut down of many small factories. Moreover, large quantities of grain were sent to feed the army. For the people in cities, bread and flour became expensive and scarce. This scarcity led to riots at bread shops. People became very dissatisfied with the policies of the Tsar.
- **Political Reasons** Tsar Nicholas II was an autocratic, inefficient and weak ruler who believed in the divine rights of the king. The bureaucracy got special rights and privileges, but the general public got none. Moreover, the Tsar had built a vast empire and imposed Russian language and culture on diverse nationalities. A large section of the Russian empire became hostile to the Tsar and his corrupt bureaucracy. All these factors led to discredit of the government and brought about the end of Tsarist autocracy.

Q.4 Make two lists : One with the main events and the effects of the February Revolution and the other with the main events and effects of the October Revolution. Write a paragraph on who was involved in each and who were the leaders and what was the impact of each on Soviet history.

Ans. Events of the February Revolution

- **22nd February, 1917** Lockout of a factory on the right bank of the Neva river. The next day, the workers of 50 factories went on strike in sympathy.
- **24th and 25th February** Demonstrators came back on the streets and were dispersed by imposing curfew.
- **25th February** The government suspended the Duma. Politicians criticised the measure.
- **26th February** Demonstrators returned in force to the streets.
- **27th February** Workers looted the Police Headquarters.
- **2nd March** The Tsar gave up his throne. Soviet leaders and Duma leaders formed a Provincial Government to run the country.

  No political party was actively organising the February Revolution. Men and women workers were involved in this movement who were supported by the soldiers.

Effects of the February Revolution

- Restriction on public meetings and associations were removed.
- Soviets were set up everywhere, but no common system of election was followed.
- In industrial areas, factory committees were formed which began questioning the way industrialists ran their factories.
- Trade unions grew in number.

- Soldiers' committees were formed in the army.
- Provisional Government's power reduced and Bolshevik influences grew.
- The Bolsheviks were repressed.
- Land committee was formed, peasants seized land between July and September 1917 by the encouragement of the socialist revolutionaries.

Events and Effects of the October Revolution

- **16th October, 1917** Lenin became the leader and he persuaded the Petrograd Soviet and the Bolshevik Party to agree to a socialist seizure of power. It led to the formation of a Military Revolutionary Committee for seizure of power.
- **24th October** Uprising began on 24th October. The buildings of two Bolshevik newspapers were seized by the military men loyal to the government. On the same day, pro-government troops were sent to take over telephone and telegraph offices and protect the Winter Palace.

  Responding to the government's action, the Military Revolutionary Committee seized the government offices and arrested the ministers.

  The navy played a significant role in the assault on the Winter Palace. The revolutionaries took over different military points.

Q.5 What were the main changes brought about by the Bolsheviks immediately after the October Revolution?

Ans. The changes brought by the Bolsheviks after October Revolution were

- The Bolsheviks opposed private properties; thus they nationalised most industries and banks.
- Lands of the clergy and nobility were seized and land was declared state property.
- In cities, the large houses were partitioned to accommodate other families.
- The use of old titles of aristocracy was banned. To assert the social change, new uniforms, e.g., Soviet hat, were designed for the army and the officials.
- The Bolshevik Party renamed itself as the Russian Communist Party. Russia became a one-party state.
- All Russian Congress of Soviets became the Parliament of the country. Trade unions were kept under party control.
- The secret police kept vigilance on citizens and punished those who criticised the Bolsheviks.

Q.6 Write a few lines to show what you know about

- **Kulaks**
- **The Duma**
- **Women Workers between 1900 and 1930**
- **The Liberals**
- **Stalin's Collectivisation Programme**

Ans. **Kulaks** Kulak is the Russian name for well-to-do peasants. In 1927-1928, Stalin took the decision to develop modern farms and run them along industrial lines. For this purpose, it was necessary to eliminate Kulaks. Many Kulaks' properties were raided.

Under Stalin's Collectivisation Programme, land of Kulaks was taken away and converted into large modern farms. This programme was severely resisted by the Kulaks. Many of them destroyed their livestock. Those who resisted collectivisation were punished; many Kulaks were deported and exiled.

The Duma It was the elected consultative Parliament set up after the Revolution of 1905.

Its members were charged with the responsibility of making laws. The Tsar dismissed the first Duma within 75 days and re-elected the second Duma within 3 months.

The Tsar did not want any questioning of his power.
He changed the voting laws and packed the third Duma with conservative politicians. Finally, in February 1917, the Duma was suspended. Many members of the Duma became a part of the Provisional Government.

Women Workers between 1900 and 1930 In Russia, the women workers constituted 31 per cent of the factory labour force. They were paid less than their men counterparts. In most of the factories, they were paid between half and three-quarters of a men's wage. During the February Revolution (23rd February, 1917), women led the way to strikes in many factories.

The Liberals One of the groups which looked to change society were the liberals. They were opposed to the uncontrolled power of the dynastic rulers. They preferred religious tolerance and wanted to safeguard individual rights. They favoured parliamentary system of government and an independent judiciary.

They did not believe in universal adult franchise.
They wanted voting rights to be restricted to men of property only.

Stalin's Collectivisation Programme

It was started in 1927-1928, when Soviet Russia was facing an acute problem of grain supplies. The peasants refused to sell the grains at the price fixed by the government. Stalin believed that the peasants had surplus grain, but were holding it back, expecting higher prices. So, he introduced the concept of collective farms (kolkhoz). To develop these farms, it was necessary to eliminate Kulaks, take away land from peasants and establish state-controlled large farms.

From 1929, all peasants were forced to work in kolkhoz. The kolkhoz profit was shared by all the peasants who worked on the land. Those who resisted collectivisation were severely punished. Stalin's government allowed some independent cultivation, but treated such peasants unsympathetically.

REVIEW EXERCISE

Including Competency Based Questions

Part I

Multiple Choice Questions (MCQs)

1. Suffragette Movement means a movement to give women the right to

(a) vote (b) property
(c) equality (d) None of these

2. According to Karl Marx, what characterised an industrial society?

(a) Capitalism (b) Feudalism
(c) Socialism (d) Communism

3. They felt only men with property should have the vote and women should not have the vote. Who were they?

(a) Democrats (b) Radicals
(c) Liberals (d) Conservatives

4. Who thought that private property is the root of all social ills of the time?

(a) Socialists (b) Democrats
(c) Liberals (d) None of these

5. Who was Robert Owen?

(a) A leading English manufacturer
(b) A socialist who believed in the idea of cooperatives
(c) Both (a) and (b)
(d) None of the above

6. At the beginning of the 20th century, the vast majority of Russia's people was

(a) agriculturists (b) industrialists
(c) teachers (d) lawyers

7. Prominent industrial area (s) in Russia was/were

(a) Moscow (b) St Petersberg
(c) Petrograd (d) Both (a) and (b)

8. When was Russia's railway network extended?

(a) In 1850s (b) In 1890s
(c) In 1900s (d) In 1920s

9. When was the Russian Social Democratic Workers' Party founded?

(a) In 1898 (b) In 1895
(c) In 1890 (d) In 1910

10. When did the USSR socialism become a global face and world stature?

(a) At the time of the outbreak of the Second World War.
(b) At the time of the First World War.
(c) At the time of the Civil War.
(d) None of the above

11. Consider the following statements and choose the right one.

(a) Jadidists were the Muslim scholars within the Russian empire.
(b) Jadidists were the Muslim landlords within the Russian empire.
(c) Jadidists were the Sufi philosophers within the Russian empire.
(d) Jadidists were the Muslim reformers within the Russian empire.

12. Consider the following statements and choose the right one.

(a) Kulaks are rich farmers of Russia
(b) Kulaks are poor farmers of Russia
(c) Kulaks are workers of Russia
(d) Kulaks are metal workers of Russia

13. Find the incorrect option.

(a) Robert Owen was a leading French manufacturer.
(b) Robert Owen built a cooperative community called 'New Harmony' in Indiana (USA).
(c) Louis Blanc wanted the government to encourage cooperative.
(d) Louis Blanc wanted to replace capitalist enterprises.

14. Find the incorrect option.

(a) The First World War had a severe impact on industry of Russia.
(b By 1917, railway lines began to break down in Russia.
(c) Able-bodied men were called up to the war.
(d) For the people in the cities of Russia, bread and flour became scarce.

15. In 1914, Tsar Nicholas II ruled Russia and its empire. The Russian Empire included territory around Moscow, present day Finland Latvia, Lithunia, Estonia, parts of Poland, Ukraine and Belarus. How was the economy and society during the Tsar Nicholas II reign? Competency Based

(a) Industries were very few in number, prominent industrial areas were St Petersburg and Moscow.
(b) Russia was a major importer of grain in the Empire.
(c) Many factories were set up in the 1790's.
(d) Most of the industries were government owned.

16. During the revolution of 1905, liberals wanted to end the autocratic state of affairs. They joined hands with social democrats and socialist revolutionaries worked with peasants and workers to demand a Constitution.

One of the most likely reasons responsible for the 1905 revolution was

(a) In 1903, industrial action was introduced.
(b) In 1904, prices of essential goods declined so quickly.
(c) Real wages of the workers decreased by 20 per cent.
(d) No members of the Putilov Iron works were dismissed.

17. 'Some Russian socialists felt that the Russian peasant custom of dividing land periodically made them natural socialists. So peasants, not workers, would be the main force of the revolution, and Russia could become socialist more quickly than other countries. Socialists were active in the countryside through the late 19th century. They formed the Socialist Revolutionary Party in 1900.'

The main difference between Socialist Revolutionaries and Social Democrats regarding the peasantry was **Competency Based**

(a) Socialist Revolutionaries believed peasants wouldn't need a revolution, while Social Democrats believed they would.
(b) Socialist Revolutionaries focused on land redistribution, while Social Democrats focused on worker's rights.
(c) Socialist Revolutionaries viewed peasants as naturally socialist, while Social Democrats saw them as a diverse group.
(d) Socialist Revolutionaries advocated for violent revolution, while Social Democrats preferred peaceful means.

18. 'Perhaps one of the most far-reaching visions of how society should be structured was socialism. By the mid - 19th century in Europe, socialism was a well-known body of ideas that attracted widespread attention.'

Choose the correct option about the Coming of Socialism in Europe. **Competency Based**

(a) Socialists were against private property, and saw it as the root of all social ills of the time.
(b) Marx argued that industrial society was not 'capitalist'.
(c) Socialists felt that cooperatives could be built on a wide scale only through individual initiative.
(d) Cooperatives were to be associations of people who produced goods alone and keep the profits with himself.

19. Rapid construction led to poor working conditions for workers. In Magnitogrosk, a steel plant was constructed in three years. Workers did not have even basic facilities of toilet, health care, etc.

Which measure was taken to improve status of workers ?

(a) An extended schooling system was developed and arrangement were made for factory workers and peasants to enter universities.
(b) Costly Public healthcare was provided.
(c) No model living quarters were made for workers.
(d) Creches (day boarding) were not established in factories for the children of women workers.

20. Arrange the following in sequence.

I. Formation of Comintern
II. Formation of the Russian Social Democratic Workers Party
III. Beginning of Collectivisation

(a) II, I, III
(b) I, II, III
(c) III, II, I
(d) II, III, I

21. Consider the statements given below and choose the correct answer.

Statement I Socialists took over the government in Russia through the October Revolution of 1917.

Statement II The fall of monarchy in February 1917 and the events of October are normally called the Russian Revolution.

Codes

(a) Statement I is correct and II is incorrect.
(b) Statement I is incorrect and II is correct
(c) Both I and II are incorrect
(d) Both I and II are correct

22. During the Industrial Revolution, many changes came in the society and economy. What were these changes?

I. Women and children were not working in factories.
II. Unemployment was not common due to high demand for industrial goods.
III. New cities, new industrial regions and new railway lines were developed.
IV. Working hours were often long and wages were poor.

Codes

(a) Only I
(b) Both III and IV
(c) Both I and II
(d) Only II

23. The incident known as Bloody Sunday started a series of events that became known as 1905 revolution. These events were

I. Trend of strikes spread all over the country.
II. Universities closed down when students complained about the lack of civil liberties.
III. Doctors, lawyers, engineers and other middle-class workers established the Union of Unions and demanded a Constituent Assembly.
IV. A large number of trade unions and factory committees consisted of factory workers also existed for short time.

Codes

(a) Statements I and II are appropriate.
(b) Statements I, II and III are appropriate.
(c) All the statements are appropriate.
(d) Only statement IV is appropriate.

24. **Consider the statements about 'the February Revolution in Petrograd' and choose the correct answer.** Competency Based

Statement I On 22nd February, a lockout took place at a factory. This led to protests and strikes against the factory joined by women. This day came to be known as International Women's Day .

Statement II In February 1917, there was acute shortage of food in Russia which made the life of workers very difficult. Parliamentarians opposed the Tsar's desire to dissolve the Duma.

Codes

(a) Statement I is correct and II is incorrect.
(b) Statement I is incorrect and II is correct
(c) Both I and II are incorrect
(d) Both I and II are correct

Answers

1. (a)	2. (a)	3. (c)	4. (a)	5. (c)
6. (a)	7. (d)	8. (b)	9. (a)	10. (a)
11. (d)	12. (a)	13. (a)	14. (b)	15. (a)
16. (c)	17. (c)	18. (a)	19. (a)	20. (a)
21. (d)	22. (b)	23. (c)	24. (d)	

Match the Following

1.

	List I		List II
A	Karl Marx	1	Leader of Bolshevik Party
B	Lenin	2	Tsar of Russia
C	Stalin	3	Father of Communism
D	Nicholas II	4	Collectivisation Programme

Codes

	A	B	C	D		A	B	C	D
(a)	1	2	3	4	(b)	3	1	4	2
(c)	2	3	4	1	(d)	4	3	2	1

2.

	List I		List II
A	Bloody Sunday	1	1914
B	World War	2	1918-20
C	Civil War in Russia	3	1905
D	April Theses	4	April, 1917

Codes

	A	B	C	D		A	B	C	D
(a)	1	2	3	4	(b)	1	4	3	2
(c)	3	1	2	4	(d)	2	1	4	3

Ans. 1. (b) 2. (c)

Assertion-Reason

1. **Assertion** (A) The First World War on the 'Eastern front' differed from that on the 'Western front'.

Reason (R) The soldiers of Russia did not wish to fight this war.

Codes

(a) Both A and R are true and R is the correct explanation of A
(b) Both A and R are true, but R is not the correct explanation of A
(c) A is true, but R is false
(d) A is false, but R is true

2. **Assertion** (A) Russia was a major exporter of grain.

Reason (R) About 85 per cent of Russian's population was agriculturalists and produced for the market as well as for their own needs.

Codes

(a) Both A and R are true and R is the correct explanation of A
(b) Both A and R are true, but R is not the correct explanation of A
(c) A is true, but R is false
(d) A is false, but R is true

3. **Assertion** (A) The Russian Social Democratic Workers Party was operating as an illegal organisation.

Reason (R) All political parties were illegal in Russia before 1914, due to government policing.

Codes

(a) Both A and R are true and R is the correct explanation of A
(b) Both A and R are true, but R is not the correct explanation of A
(c) A is true, but R is false
(d) A is false, but R is true

4. **Assertion** (A) In other parts of the world new ideas about individual rights and who controlled social power began to been discussed.

Reason (R) The French Revolution opened up the possibility of creating a dramatic change in the way in which society was structured.

Codes

(a) Both A and R are true and R is the correct explanation of A
(b) Both A and R are true, but R is not the correct explanation of A
(c) A is true, but R is false
(d) A is false, but R is true

5. **Assertion** (A) Industrialisation brought men, women and children to factories.

Reason (R) Work hours were often long and wages were poor.

Codes

(a) Both A and R are true and R is the correct explanation of A
(b) Both A and R are true, but R is not the correct explanation of A
(c) A is true, but R is false
(d) A is false, but R is true

Ans. 1. (b) Both A and R are true, but R is not the correct explanation of A
2. (a) Both A and R are true and R is the correct explanation of A
3. (a) Both A and R are true and R is the correct explanation of A
4. (a) Both A and R are true and R is the correct explanation of A
5. (a) Both A and R are true and R is the correct explanation of A

Picture Based Questions

1. Identify the personality and name the famous programme introduced by him.

(a) Joseph Stalin, Collectivisation Programme
(b) V Lenin, Commune (mir) Programme
(c) Karl Marx, Dictatorship of Proletariat
(d) F Engels, Communism

2. Name the typical Soviet hat wore by the soldier in the picture.

(a) Budeonovka (b) Fedora
(c) Tril by (d) Snapback

3. What event does the given image depict?

(a) The French Revolution
(b) The Paris Commune of 1871
(c) The signing of the Treaty of Versailles
(d) Napoleon's coronation

Ans. 1. (a) Joseph Stalin, Collectivisation Programme
2. (a) Budeonovka
3. (b) The Paris Commune of 1871

Case Based Question

1. Read the source given below and answer the questions that follow.

Socialists had different visions of the future. Some believed in the idea of cooperatives. Robert Owen (1771-1858), a leading English manufacturer, sought to build a cooperative community called New Harmony in Indiana (USA). Other socialists felt that cooperatives could not be built on a wide scale only through individual initiative: they demanded that governments encourage cooperatives. In France, for instance, Louis Blanc (1813-1882) wanted the government to encourage cooperatives and replace capitalist enterprises. These cooperatives were to be associations of people who produced goods together and divided the profits according to the work done by members. Karl Marx (1818-1883) and Friedrich Engels (1820-1895) added other ideas to this body of arguments. Marx argued that industrial society was 'capitalist'. Capitalists owned the capital invested in factories, and the profit of capitalists was produced by workers.

(i) How did some socialists view the potential of cooperatives?
(a) They believed cooperatives could only be successful on a small scale, led by individuals like Robert Owen.
(b) They considered cooperatives a viable alternative to capitalist enterprises and advocated for government support.
(c) They saw cooperatives as an unrealistic ideal impractical in the real world.
(d) They felt government involvement would hinder the organic growth of cooperative communities.

(ii) What was the core idea of Louis Blanc's proposal for French cooperatives?
(a) They would be worker-owned and operated, sharing profits based on individual contributions.
(b) They would receive financial incentives from the government to compete with capitalist businesses.
(c) They would function as state-controlled enterprises, eliminating private ownership entirely.
(d) They would focus on social welfare and community development rather than profit generation.

(iii) How did Karl Marx and Friedrich Engels differ from earlier socialists' views on cooperatives?

(a) They embraced cooperatives as the primary pathway to a socialist society.

(b) They criticised cooperatives as insufficient and emphasised the need for broader systemic change.

(c) They believed cooperatives could function effectively within a capitalist framework.

(d) They saw cooperatives as irrelevant to achieving their socialist goals.

(iv) What key takeaway can we draw from this passage about socialist visions of the future?

(a) There was a single, unified socialist vision with no internal disagreements.

(b) Socialistic ideas evolved over time, incorporating diverse perspectives on economic structures.

(c) Cooperatives were universally considered the ideal model for a socialist future.

(d) Government intervention was universally rejected by socialists in favor of purely private initiatives.

Ans. (i) (b) They considered cooperatives a viable alternative to capitalist enterprises and advocated for government support.

(ii) (a) They would be worker-owned and operated, sharing profits based on individual contributions.

(iii) (b) They criticised cooperatives as insufficient and emphasised the need for broader systemic change.

(iv) (b) Socialistic ideas evolved over time, incorporating diverse perspectives on economic structures.

Part II

Very Short Answer Type Questions

1. What were the views of the liberals in 19th century Europe regarding Universal Adult Franchise?

Ans. The liberals were opposed to Universal Adult Franchise. They felt that only men of property should have the right to vote. They also did not want the vote for women.

2. Who opposed the ideas of both liberals and radicals?

Ans. Conservatives opposed the ideas of both liberals and radicals.

3. What were conservatives views on change in the society?

Ans. By the 19th century, conservatives wanted a slow change in society. They believed the change should be done by respecting the past.

4. How did the revolutionaries originate in the year 1815?

Ans. In France, Italy, Germany and Russia, some nationalist liberals and radicals became revolutionaries. They worked to overthrow existing monarchs.

5. Name the ruler of Russia at the start of the First World War.

Ans. Tsar Nicholas II was the ruler of Russia at the start of the First World War.

6. Which group of workers were regarded as aristocrats among workers?

Ans. The metal-workers were regarded as aristocrats among workers.

7. Mention the period of Civil War in Russia.

Ans. The period of Civil War in Russia was 1918-1920.

8. In the context of Russia, what was *'kolkhoz'*?

Ans. 'Kolkhoz' was the collective farm in Russia.

9. The event 'Bloody Sunday' was later on called by what name?

Ans. It was called as the 1905 Revolution.

10. After 1905, which elected representative body was formed in Russia?

Ans. The elected representative body formed in Russia after 1905 was the Duma.

11. What was the difference between Lenin's and the Mensheviks, views on the Bolshevik party?

Ans. Lenin believed the party should be disciplined and controlled, while the Mensheviks thought the party should be open to all, like in Germany.

12. All political parties were illegal in Russia before 1914. The Russian Social Democratic Workers Party was founded in 1898 by socialists who respected Marx's ideas. Due to government policies, the party was operated secretly as an illegal organisation.

What was the role of the Russian Social Democratic Workers Party in the political landscape of Russia before 1914? Competency Based

Ans. The Russian Social Democratic Workers Party played a significant role in mobilising workers and organising strikes, despite being an illegal organisation due to government policies. They respected Marx's ideas and even started their own newspaper.

13. In the beginning of 20th century, Russia was still an autocracy and the Tsar was not responsible to the Parliament. During the revolution of 1905, liberals wanted to end this state of affairs.

(i) Who were the major participants in the 1905 revolution and what were their demands?

(ii) What led to the revolution of 1905 in Russia? Competency Based

Ans. (i) The major participants were liberals, social democrats and socialist revolutionaries. They demanded a Constitution and joined forces with peasants, workers, nationalists and Jadidists.

(ii) The 1905, revolution was mainly caused by rising prices of essential goods, reduction in real wages by 20%, and dismissal of workers at the Putilov Iron works.

14. 'When the procession of workers led by Father Gapon reached the Winter Palace it was attacked by the police and the Cossacks. Over 100 workers were killed and about 300 wounded. The incident, known as Bloody Sunday.'

How did the actions of Tsarist troops and authorities contribute to the bloodshed?

Ans. On Bloody Sunday, the Tsar's troops mistakenly fired at peaceful protesters, turning it into a violent event. The soldiers' fear and the authorities' lack of control contributed to the bloodshed.

Short Answer Type Questions

1. Who were the socialists in 19th century Europe? What kind of society did they envisage?

Ans. In the 19th century Europe, socialists were those who were against private property and saw it as the root of all social evils. They believed in the idea of cooperatives. In cooperatives, people made associations and produced goods together. The profits of the business were divided among all members of the association.

However, different socialists had different views regarding the society. Robert Owen, one of the founders of socialism, suggested that cooperatives should be built on individual initiative.

Other socialists like Louis Blanc wanted the government to encourage cooperatives and replace capitalist enterprises. These cooperatives were the associations of people who produced goods together and divided the profit according to their work.

2. Explain the concept of Karl Marx about socialist society.

Ans. Karl Marx (1818-1883) believed that the industrial society was capitalist. Capitalist owned the capital invested in factories and the profit of capitalists was produced by workers.

The conditions of workers could not improve till the profit was accumulated by private capitalists. He believed that to remove capitalism, workers had to construct a radically socialist society in which all property would be socially controlled. This would be a communist society. He wanted the whole society to have common control over the means of production.

3. Describe the economic condition of Russia before 1905.

Ans. The economic condition of Russia before 1905 is described below

- At the beginning of the 20th century, about 85 per cent of the Russian population was agriculturist, which was much higher than other European countries.
- Industry in Russia was developed in some pockets like St Petersburg and Moscow. Large factories existed alongside craft workshops.
- Many factories were set up in the 1890s due to the extension of the railway network and the increase in foreign investment. Coal, iron and steel production increased.

4. Describe the conditions of the workers under the Tsar in Russia.

Or **Describe any three points regarding the condition of workers in Russia in the beginning of the 20th century.**

Or **Explain the conditions of workers in Russia before 1917.**

Ans. The following points state the conditions of workers under the Tsar in Russia before 1917

- They worked in craft units and small workshops, sometimes, working hours were 15 hours, compared with 10-12 hours in big factories.
- Workers were divided into different social groups. Some had strong links with native villages, other permanently settled in towns.
- Workers were divided according to their skills. Metal workers were considered aristocrats among other workers.
- Women consisted of 31 per cent of the factory labour force and they were paid less than men.
- Some workers formed associations to help members in time of unemployment or financial crisis. But, they were few in numbers.

5. What actions did the Tsar take after the 1905 Revolution regarding political activity and the Duma?

Ans. After the 1905 Revolution, the Tsar allowed the creation of a consultative Parliament, the Duma. However, he quickly dismissed the first Duma within 75 days and the second Duma within three months, as he did not want any challenge to his authority. Most trade unions and factory committees, initially active, were declared illegal and worked unofficially. The Tsar changed the voting rules and filled the third Duma with conservative politicians, keeping out liberals and revolutionaries to maintain control over the government.

6. Describe the main events which led to the February Revolution in Petrograd.

Ans. The main events which led to the February Revolution in Petrograd were

- On 22nd February, a lockout took place at a factory on the right bank of the river Neva in Petrograd.
- On 23rd February, workers in fifty factories called a strike in sympathy. In many factories, women led the strikes.
- Government imposed a curfew, causing the demonstrators to disperse, but they came back on the 24th and 25th.
- On the 25th February, the Tsar suspended the Duma. This caused widespread anger. A delegation went to see the Tsar. Tsar resigned on the advise of the Military commanders on 2nd March.
- Soviet leaders and Duma leaders formed a Provisional Government to run the country.

7. Describe the incident known as 'Bloody Sunday'. State any two events after the Bloody Sunday which led to the Revolution of 1905 in Russia.

Ans. Bloody Sunday occurred in Russia on 22nd January, 1905. On this day, the workers of Russia, led by Father Gapon, reached the Winter Palace of the Tsar to present a petition. But they were fired at indiscriminately by police and the Cossacks, resulting in the death of more than 100 workers and about 300 wounded. This incident led to series of events, known as the 1905 Revolution.

Two important events which led to the Revolution of 1905 in Russia were

- Strikes took all over the country and universities of Russia were closed down when student bodies staged walkouts, complaining about the lack of civil liberties.
- Lawyers, doctors, engineers, middle-class workers established a Union of Unions and demanded a Constituent Assembly.

8. Describe the events during the First World War.

Ans. The following events took place during the First World War

- In Russia, the First World War war was initially popular and the policies of Tsar Nicholas II were supported by the people.
- The First World War on the Eastern front differed from that on the Western front. In the West, armies fought from trenches, but in the East, armies moved a good deal and fought battles leaving large casualties.
- Russia's army lost badly in Germany and Austria between 1914 and 1916. There were over 7 million casualties by 1917. This defeat shocked and demoralised Russian army.
- As the German armies moved forward, the Russian army destroyed crops and buildings to prevent the enemy from being able to live off the land. The situation discredited the Russian Government and the Tsar. The Russian soldiers did not wish to fight such a war.

9. State any three effects of the First World War on the Russian economy.

Ans. The effects of the First World War on the Russian economy were

(i) Russia had few industries and the country was cut off from other supplies of industrial goods by German control of the Baltic Sea.

(ii) Industrial equipment disintegrated more rapidly in Russia than elsewhere in Europe. By 1916, railway lines began to break down.

(iii) Able-bodied men were sent to fight the war. Thus, labour shortages resulted in shutting down of the industries and small workshops producing essentials.

10. State any three measures taken by the Provisional Government to suppress the Bolshevik influence.

Ans. As the Provisional Government realised that its power was reducing and Bolshevik influence growing, it decided to take the following measures

(i) It resisted attempts by workers to run factories and began arresting leaders.

(ii) Popular demonstrations staged by the Bolsheviks were strongly repressed. Many Bolshevik leaders had to go into hiding or flee.

(iii) Military men loyal to the Provisional Government seized the buildings of two Bolshevik newspapers.

11. What was the disagreement between Socialist revolutionaries and Social Democrats regarding peasants in Russia?

Ans. Some Russian socialists believed that the peasant custom of dividing land made them natural socialists, and that peasants, not workers, would lead the revolution. They thought Russia could become socialist quickly. The Socialist Revolutionary Party, formed in 1900, fought for peasants' rights and demanded the transfer of noble lands to peasants. However, Social Democrats, led by Lenin, disagreed. Lenin argued that peasants were not a unified group, as some were poor while others were rich or employed workers, making them unsuitable for a unified socialist movement.

12. Read the statements given below regarding the Russian Revolution.

Statement 1 (S1) In 1914, Tsar Nicholas II ruled Russia and its empire.

Statement 2 (S2) About 85 per cent of the Russian empire's population earned their living from agriculture.

Explain what trend do these statements - S1 and S2 - reflect in the Russian Revolution.

Ans. Statements 1 and 2 highlight the stark contrast between Russia's leadership and its majority population. While Tsar Nicholas II lived in luxury, about 85% of the people worked in farming, likely living in poverty and facing tough conditions. These struggling farmers were open to new ideas for change.

Their problems - like poverty, no voice in government, and desire for change - led to opposition against the Tsar's rule. This shows the big gap between the rich rulers and the poor farmers, which was a key reason for the revolution that ended the Tsar's rule.

13. What actions did workers in England and Germany take to improve their living and working conditions? Competency Based

Build the answer around these points

- **Formation of associations**
- **Establishment of funds**
- **Demands for reduced working hours**

Ans. Workers in England and Germany took following actions to improve their living and working conditions

Formation of associations Workers formed associations and trade unions to collectively advocate for their rights and interests.

Establishment of funds They set up funds within these associations to provide financial assistance to members during times of distress, such as unemployment or illness.

Demands for reduced working hours Workers demanded a reduction in the number of working hours to prevent overwork and exhaustion.

14. Read the statements given below regarding the changes that took place after the February Revolution in Petrograd.

Statement 1 (S1) The Worker's Movement spread throughout the summer.

Statement 2 (S2) Intense conflict grew between the Provisional Government and Bolsheviks.

Explain what trend do these statements - S1 and S2 - reflect in the February Revolution.

Ans. Statements 1 and 2 show a worrying change in Petrograd after February: from unity to increasing disagreements and tensions.

Statement 1 shows growing worker dissatisfaction in industrial area, factory committees were formed which began questioning the way industrialists ran their factories.

Statement 2 highlights the growing gap between the Provisional Government and the Bolsheviks, Lenin feared that the provisional government would establish a dictatorship. This disagreement led to conflict and instability. So, these statements show a shift from hope to hostility.

15. 'Nobles got their power and position through their services to the Tsar, not through local popularity. This was unlike France where, during the French Revolution in Brittany, peasants respected nobles and fought for them. In Russia, peasants wanted the land of the nobles to be given to them. Frequently, they refused to pay rent and even murdered landlords'. Analyse the contrasting relationship between peasants and nobles in Russia and Brittany (France) during their respective revolutions. Competency Based

Ans. In Brittany, France, peasants and nobles had a shared history and pride. During the revolution, some peasants even saved nobles from angry mobs. This was because they had common cultural bonds, there was no serfdom (peasants weren't forced to stay on the land), and they were influenced by Enlightenment ideas like freedom and equality.

In Russia, the relationship between nobles and peasants was very bad. The peasants had been serfs for centuries, which meant they had to work hard on the nobles' land for very little in return. The revolution was a chance for them to take land and get away from this unfair system. The violent killing of nobles showed how angry and desperate the peasants were for change.

Long Answer Type Questions

1. Explain any five socio-economic conditions of Russia at the beginning of the 20th century?

or **What type of an economy existed in Russia before the revolution?**

Ans. At the beginning of the 20th century, Russia was ruled by Tsar Nicholas II.

The socio-economic conditions of Russia at that time can be explained in the following ways

- 85 per cent of the Russian people were agriculturists. Cultivators produced for the market and for their own needs. Russia was a major exporter of grain.
- Industry was found in some specific areas. St Petersburg and Moscow were famous for industry. Large factories existed alongside craft workshops. In some areas, factory workers and craftmen were almost equal in number.
- Workers were a divided social group. Some had strong links with the villages, while others had settled in cities permanently.
- Despite divisions, workers did unite to strike work when they disagreed with the employers.
- Peasants had no respect towards nobility. They pooled their land together periodically and their commune (mir) divided it according to the needs of individual families.

2. What were the main causes of the civil war between the Bolsheviks and the Russian army, the non-Bolshevik socialist?

Ans. The main causes of the civil war between the Bolsheviks and the Russian army, the non-Bolshevik socialists were

- After the success of October Revolution, the Bolsheviks ordered land redistribution to the peasants. The Russian army began to break up. Soldiers deserted the army and wanted to go home for the redistribution of land.
- Non-Bolshevik socialists, liberals and supporters of autocracy condemned the Bolshevik uprising. All the leaders of these group moved to South Russia and organised their army to fight against the Bolsheviks. During 1918 and 1919, the Greens (Socialist revolutionaries) and the Whites (Pro-Tsarists) controlled most of the Russian empire.
- The Greens and Whites were backed by French, American, British and Japanese Troops. All these forces were worried at the growth of socialism in Russia.
- In many areas, Bolshevik colonists brutally massacred local nationalist in the name of defending socialism. In this situation, many were confused about the standpoint of the Bolsheviks.

3. Explain how a socialist society was established in Russia.

Ans. The Bolsheviks took the following measures to establish a socialist society in Russia

- The Bolsheviks nationalised industries and banks.
- Land was declared social property and peasants were allowed to seize the land of the nobility.
- Officials assessed how the economy could work and made Five Year Plans on its basis.
- Centralised planning led to economic growth. Industrial production increased and new factory cities established in Russia.
- An extended schooling system was developed. Arrangements were made for higher education for workers and peasants which helped them to enter universities.
- Cheap public healthcare was provided.
- Model living quarters were established for workers.
- Creches were established in factories for the children of women workers.

4. Explain the views of the socialists on private property with special emphasis on Karl Marx. Name the international body set up to spread and coordinate their efforts.

Ans. Socialists were against private property. They saw it as the root of all social evils.
Their views are stated below

- Socialists favoured ownership of property by society as a whole rather than single individually owned properties, thus attention would be paid to collective social interests.
- According to Marx in capitalism, factories were owned by the capitalists and the profit of capitalists was produced by workers. But the workers had to overthrow capitalism and the rule of private property.
- Marx suggested that to free themselves from capitalist exploitation, the workers had to construct a radically socialist society. In a socialist society, all property was socially controlled.
- Marx believed that workers would win in their conflict with capitalists and there should be 'dictatorship of the proletariat'. This communist society would be the natural society of the future.

To coordinate their efforts, socialists formed the international body, viz, the 'Second International.'

5. Explain the contribution of Lenin to the Russian Revolution.

Ans. Lenin was the leader of the Bolshevik Party. He was prepared to take desperate measures to make the revolution successful. The following points state his contribution in Russian Revolution

- On his return from exile in April 1917, he organised his party to take over the reigns of government, as the Mensheviks, running the provisional government, had lost popular support.
- In his 'April Theses', he put forward clear policies to end Russian participation in the war, transferring land to the tiller and nationalising banks.
- He implemented his policies to make Russia a truly socialist society till his death in 1924.

6. Read the information given below regarding Industrial Society and Social Change and answer the question that follows. **Competency Based**

It was a time of profound social and economic changes. It was a time when new cities came up and new industrialised regions developed, railways expanded and the Industrial Revolution occurred. Industrialisation brought men, women and children to factories. Work hours were often long and wages were poor. Unemployment was common, particularly during times of low demand for industrial goods. Housing and sanitation were problems since towns were growing rapidly. Liberals and radicals searched for solutions to these issues. Almost all industries were the property of individuals. Liberals and radicals themselves were often property owners and employers.

Analyse the passage in terms of its impact - negative and/or positive - on Industrial Society and Social Change.

Ans. **Positive Impacts** The passage suggests rapid industrialisation and the rise of new industries and regions. This would have led to economic growth, increased national wealth, and the creation of new jobs. The rise of railways and the Industrial Revolution represent innovations and technological advancements that would have improved transportation, communication, and production efficiency. The growth of new cities indicates increased opportunities for education, healthcare, and access to goods and services, potentially improving the quality of life for some.

Negative Impacts The passage highlights harsh working conditions for men, women, and children, characterised by long hours, low wages, and unemployment. This likely led to exploitation, poverty, and health issues for labourers. Rapid urban growth often meant poor housing, sanitation, and overcrowding, leading to disease and social problems. The ownership of industries by individuals and the prominence of property owners among liberals and radicals suggest a widening gap between the wealthy and the working class, potentially resulting in social unrest and political tensions.

The passage presents a mixed picture of industrialisation, highlighting both the potential for economic growth and technological advancement alongside the concerns of worker exploitation, social inequality, and urban problems.

7. How did the Bolsheviks influence socialism globally, and what challenges did the USSR face by the mid-20th century?

Ans. The Bolsheviks' rise to power in Russia inspired socialist movements across the world, leading to the formation of communist parties in many countries, such as the Communist Party of Great Britain. They promoted the idea of a workers' state and urged colonial nations to adopt their model. The Comintern, an international union of pro-Bolshevik socialist parties, and the 1920 Conference of the Peoples of the East spread revolutionary ideas globally.

The USSR became a hub for education, especially for people from colonised countries. However, by the 1950s, the USSR's government diverged from the ideals of the Russian Revolution. While the USSR became a great power with a developed economy, it restricted freedoms and used repressive methods. By the 20th century's end, socialism's global reputation declined, though its ideals remained respected and adapted in various countries.

In the 19th century, new political ideas, especially socialism, began to emerge as a response to the hardships caused by industrialisation and inequality. Socialism aimed to improve the lives of workers and promote equality. The Russian Revolution of 1917 was a key event where socialism transformed society, influencing the world in the 20th century.

8. 'News of the revolutionary uprising of 25th October, 1917, reached the village the following day and was greeted with enthusiasm; to the peasants it meant free land and an end to the war. ...The day the news arrived, the landowner's manor house was looted, his stock farms were 'goccupied' and his vast orchard was cut down and sold to the peasants for wood; all his far buildings were torn down and left in ruins while the land was distributed among the peasants who were prepared to live the new Soviet life'.

Source: Fedor Belov, The History of a Soviet Collective Farm

Analyse the October Revolution in terms of its impact - negative and /or positive. **Competency Based**

Ans. The October Revolution of 1917, a watershed moment in Russian history, carries a multifaceted legacy encompassing both positive and negative ramifications. Positively, the revolution signified the overthrow of the oppressive Tsarist regime, which had long suppressed dissent and perpetuated socioeconomic inequality. The establishment of a new government under the Bolsheviks indicates a revolutionary shift towards a society founded on principles of equality, worker empowerment, and social justice.

Economically, the revolution brought about significant changes with the nationalisation of industries, banks and land redistribution. The seizure of private property and its redistribution among the peasantry promised to alleviate landlessness and empower rural communities.

Negatively, the October Revolution also unleashed a wave of violence and instability. The subsequent Civil War, fought between the Bolshevik Red Army and various counter-revolutionary forces, resulted in widespread destruction, loss of life and societal upheaval. The brutality of the conflict inflicted immense suffering on civilians and increased economic hardships, plunging the country into chaos and turmoil.

Case Based Questions

1. Read the sources given below and answer the questions that follow.

Source A The Russian Communist Party

The Bolshevik Party was renamed the Russian Communist Party (Bolshevik). In November 1917, the Bolsheviks conducted the elections to the Constituent Assembly, but they failed to gain majority support. In January 1918, the assembly rejected Bolshevik measures and Lenin dismissed the assembly. Lenin believed that the All Russian Congress of Soviets was more democratic than an assembly elected in uncertain conditions.

(i) Lenin did not consider the Constituent Assembly as democratic. Explain.

Source B The Russia became a One-Party State

In March 1918, despite opposition by their political allies, the Bolsheviks made peace with Germany at Brest Litovsk. In the years that followed, the Bolsheviks became the only party to participate in the elections to the All Russian Congress of Soviets, which became the Parliament of the country. Russia became a one-party state. Trade unions were kept under party control. The secret police (called the Cheka first, and later OGPU and NKVD) punished those who criticised the Bolsheviks.

Many young writers and artists rallied to the party because it stood for socialism and for change. After October 1917, this led to experiments in the art and architecture. But many became disillusioned because of the censorhip the Party encouraged.

(ii) To what extent the Bolshevik Party was not appreciated by the Russian ? Give an example.

Source C The Changes brought by the Bolsheviks

The Bolsheviks were totally opposed to private property. Most industry and banks were nationalised in November 1917. This meant that the government took over ownership and management. Land was declared social property and peasants were allowed to seize the land of the nobility. In cities, Bolsheviks onforced the partition of large house according to family requirements. They banned the use of the old titles of aristocracy. To assert the change, new uniforms were designed for the army and officials, following a clothing competition organised in 1918–when the Soviet hat (*budeonovka*) was chosen.

(iii) To what extent did the Bolshevik Party introduce changes in economic front of Russia? Explain by giving examples.

Ans. (i) In Russia, the Constituent Assembly rejected the popular measures of the Bolsheviks. Under the leadership of Lenin, the Bolsheviks became popular in Russia, but they failed to gain majority support in the election to the Constituent Assembly. Lenin thought that the Constituent Assembly would became dictator as the Bolshevik had no strong representation in it.

(ii) The Bolsheviks became the only party to rule Russia. But, it was not appreciated by all Russians. The Bolshevik party also introduced censorship as control for all expressions. Many intellectuals thought that the Bolshevik Party controlled their freedom of expression, thus, they became disillusioned about the Bolshevik Party.

(iii) The Bolshevik Party introduced immense changes in economic front of Russia in the following ways

- They nationalised most of the industries and banks.
- They advised the peasants to grab lands from the landowners.
- They made the division of the large houses in cities according to the requirement of a family.

2. Read the source given below and answer the questions that follow.

On 16th October, 1917, Lenin persuaded the Petrograd Soviet and the Bolshevik Party to agree to a socialist seizure of power. A Military Revolutionary Committee was appointed by the Soviet under Leon Trotskii to organise the seizure. The date of the event was kept a secret. The uprising began on 24th October. Sensing trouble, Prime Minister Kerenskii had left the city to summon troops.

At dawn, military men loyal to the government seized the buildings of two Bolshevik newspapers. Pro-government troops were sent to take over telephone and telegraph offices and protect the Winter Palace. In a swift response, the Military Revolutionary Committee ordered its supporters to seize government offices and arrest ministers. Late in the day, the ship Aurora shelled the Winter Palace. Other vessels sailed down the Neva and took over various military points. By nightfall, the city was under the committee's control and the ministers had surrendered.

At a meeting of the All Russian Congress of Soviets in Petrograd, the majority approved the Bolshevik action. Uprisings took place in other cities. There was heavy fighting especially in Moscow but by December, the Bolsheviks controlled the Moscow-Petrograd area.

(i) The Military Revolutionary committee was appointed by the Soviet. Suggest the reason.

(ii) Infer the importance of the control of the Military Revolutionary Committee over the Petrograd city.

(iii) Why did Lenin make the Petrograd Soviet and the Bolshevik party to agree socialist seizure of power in Russia in October 1917?

Ans. (i) The Military Revolutionary committee was appointed by the Soviet under Leon Totskii to organise the socialist seizure of power in Russia.

(ii) The control of the Military Revolutionary Committee over Petrograd was crucial as it facilitated decisive actions such as seizing government offices, arresting ministers, and taking control of key points like the Winter Palace. This control ensured the success of the socialist seizure of power in the city.

(iii) Lenin feared that the Provisional Government would set-up a dictatorship in Russia. He wanted to arrange an uprising against the Government. Thus, he persuaded the Petrograd Soviet and the Bolshevik Party unitedly agree to a socialist seizure of power in Russia and both of them agreed to do that.

Map Based Questions

1. On the given outline map of world, locate the countries that were central powers in the First World War.

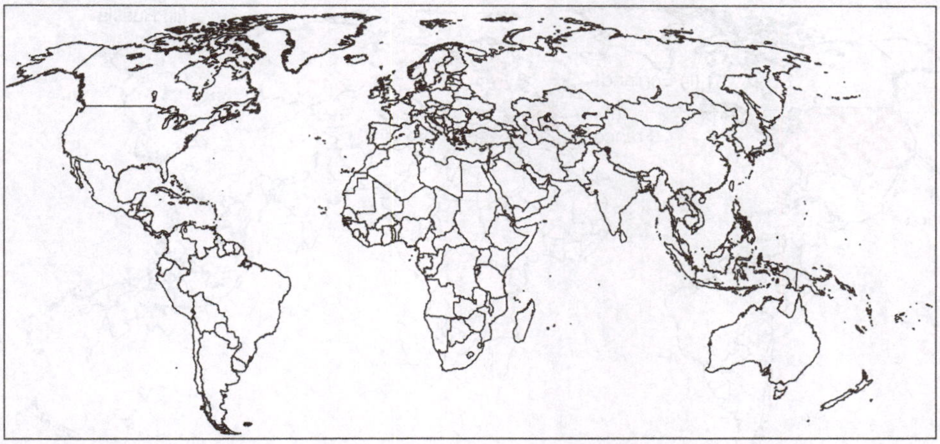

Ans. The Central Powers in the First World War were Germany, Austria-Hungary and Turkey.

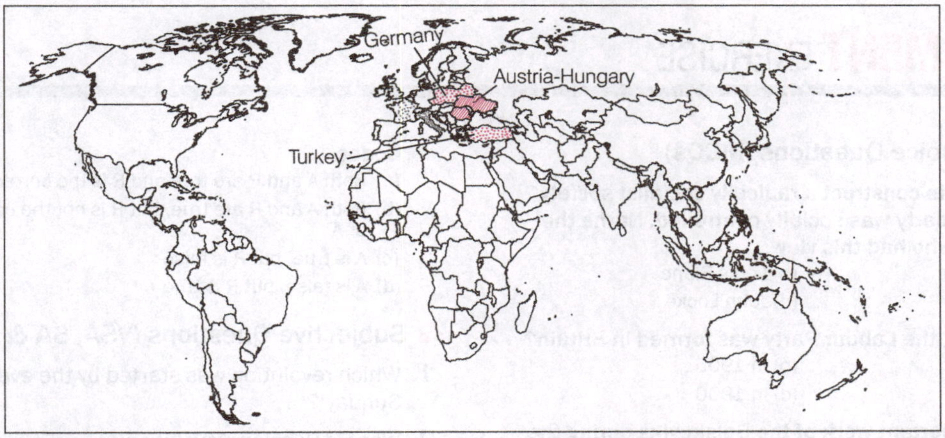

2. On the given outline map of the world, four features are marked. These are the countries that were Allied Powers in the First World War. Identify them.

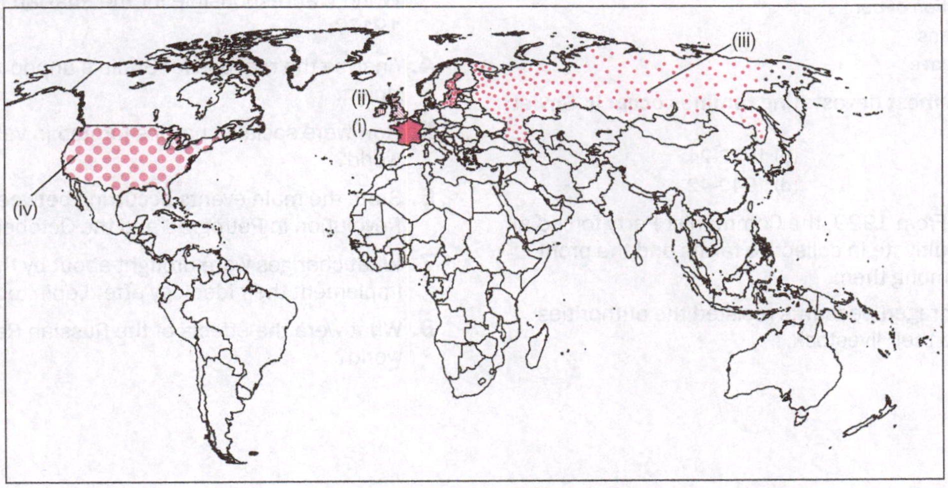

Ans. The countries marked on the above map are
(i) France (ii) England (iii) Russia (iv) America

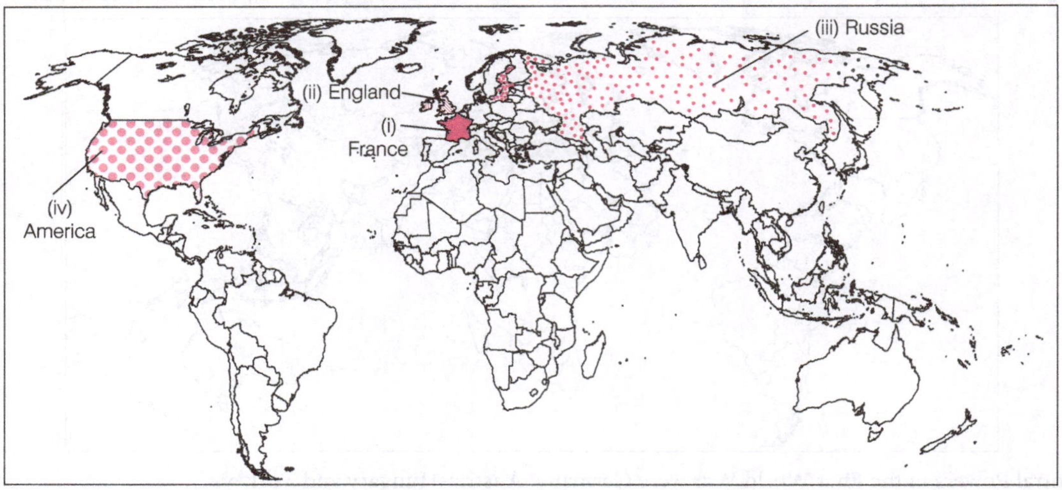

ASSESSMENT EXERCISE

Multiple Choice Questions (MCQs)

1. Workers had to construct a radically socialist society where all property was socially controlled. Name the philosopher who had this view.
(a) Robert Owen (b) Louis Blanc
(c) Karl Marx (d) John Locke

2. In which year, the Labour Party was formed in Britain?
(a) In 1904 (b) In 1905
(c) In 1902 (d) In 1900

3. The most important work of the Bolsheviks during the Civil War was
(a) nationalisation of industries
(b) nationalisation of banks
(c) five year plans
(d) All of the above

4. When did the most devastating famines occur in Soviet history?
(a) 1920-22 (b) 1922-24
(c) 1930-33 (d) 1940-42

5. Assertion (A) From 1929, the Communist Party forced all peasants to cultivate in collective farms and the profit was shared among them.

Reason (R) Enraged peasants resisted the authorities and destroyed their livestock.

Codes
(a) Both A and R are true and R is the correct explanation of A
(b) Both A and R are true, but R is not the correct explanation of A
(c) A is true, but R is false
(d) A is false, but R is true

Subjective Questions (VSA, SA & LA)

1. Which revolution was started by the event 'Bloody Sunday'?

2. What is Russian Revolution?

3. To what extent was Russian participation in the First World War responsible for the Russian Revolution in 1917?

4. Analyse the reasons for Stalin's unpopularity in the Soviet Union.

5. How were socialist parties formed in various parts of the world?

6. State the main events occurring between the February Revolution in Petrograd and the October Revolution.

7. What changes were brought about by the Bolsheviks to implement their ideology after Lenin took over?

8. What were the effects of the Russian Revolution on the world?

Nazism and the Rise of Hitler

CHAPTER 3

Nazism was a political ideology which flourished in Germany and influenced world politics. A genocidal war[1] started in Germany during the Second World War. It resulted in the mass killing of Europeans in different inhuman ways.

3.1 Birth of the Weimar Republic

Germany was a powerful empire in the early years of the 20th century. It fought the First World War (1914–1918) together with the Austrian empire and against the Allies (England, France and Russia).

At the first stage of war, Germany occupied France and Belgium. Later the Allies were strengthened by the US entry in 1917. They defeated Germany and the Central Powers in November, 1918.

The defeat of Imperial[2] Germany and the resigning of the emperor gave an opportunity to parliamentary parties to change German polity.

A National Assembly met at Weimar and established a democratic Constitution with a federal structure. Deputies were elected to the **Reichstag** or **German Parliament** on the basis of equal and universal votes cast by all adults including women.

This republic was not supported by the people of Germany largely because of the terms it was forced to accept after Germany's defeat in the First World War.

Peace Treaty of Versailles

The peace Treaty of Versailles with the Allies was harsh and humiliating peace. By signing the Peace Treaty of Versailles, Germany lost

- its overseas colonies, one-tenth of its population and 13 per cent of its territories.
- The War Guilt clause held Germany responsible for the war and damages the allied countries suffered.
- 75 per cent of its iron and 26 per cent of its coal to France, Poland, Denmark and Lithuania.
- £ 6 billion as compensation for war.
- Resource-rich **Rhineland** occupied by Allied armies.

The Allied powers removed military forces from Germany to weaken its power. They believed that Germany was responsible for the war and damages that Allied powers faced.

Many Germans held the new republic responsible for both defeat in the war and unfair Versailles treaty.

The Effects of the War

The First World War, both psychologically and financially affected Europe in the following ways

- Europe became a continent of debtors from creditors.
- Newly formed Weimar Republic was forced to pay a huge compensation.
- Socialists, Catholics and Democrats who supported the Weimar Republic were criticised and came to be known as **November Criminals** by the conservative nationalists.
- First World War left deep impact on European society and polity.
- After the First World War, soldiers were placed above civilians. Media glorified their trench life but in reality they lived miserable life in trenches[3]. They faced poisonous gas and enemy shelling. Their ranks reduced rapidly.
- Politicians and publicists put great stress on the need for men to be aggresive, strong and masculine.

---

1 Genocidal War It means killing on a large scale leading to destruction of large sections of people.

2 Imperial It means being connected with an empire.

3 Trench It means a long deep hole dug in the ground in which soldiers can be protected from enemy attacks.

- Aggressive war **propaganda**[4] and national honour gained public attention and support for conservative dictatorship grew.
- Democracy was a new and delicate idea that could not handle the problems and instabilities in Europe between the 2 world wars.

Political Radicalism and Economic Crisis

The birth of Weimar Republic coincided with revolutionary uprising of the **Spartacist League**. Spartacist League was based on the pattern of the Bolshevik Revolution in Russia. The people of Berlin demanded for Soviet-style governance.

The Weimar Republic suppressed the uprising of the Spartacist League with the help of the war organisation called the **Free Corps**. The Spartacists later founded the **Communist Party** of Germany. Thus, communist and socialists were unable to unite against Hitler and became incompatible enemies. Both revolutionaries and militant nationalists desired for radical solutions.

Political radicalisation was only increased by the economic crisis of 1923. Germany had fought the war largely on loans and had to pay war **reparations**[5] in gold. This resulted in depletion of gold reserves when resources were insufficient.

When Germany refused to pay in 1923, France occupied Germany's industrial area, the **Ruhr**, which was rich in coal.

Germany controlled the economic crisis by massive printing of paper currency. However, excess circulation of printed currency resulted in a sharp fall of the value of the **German mark**[6], due to which prices of goods increased. This crisis came to be known as **hyperinflation** in Germany.

The Americans introduced the **Dawes Plan** which helped Germany to overcome the crisis. The plan made changes in the terms of reparation to relieve the financial burden on Germans.

The Years of Depression

There was some economic stability in Germany between 1924 to 1928. In Germany, investment and industrial recovery were totally dependent on short term loans largely from the USA. However, this support from USA was withdrawn when the **Wall Street Exchange**[7] crashed in 1929. People were afraid of falling prices and rushed to sell their shares. On 24th October, 13 million shares were sold in a single day. This marked the beginning of the Great Depression.

Between 1929 and 1932, the national income of the USA fell by half. The effects of this recession in the US economy were felt all over the world. The German economy was severely hit by the economic crisis.

The main effects of recession on Germany were

- By 1932, industrial production was reduced to 40 per cent of 1929 level.
- Workers lost their jobs or their wages were reduced.
- The number of unemployed people increased to 6 million.
- On the streets of Germany, men started moving with **placards**[8] around their necks saying, 'Willing to do any work'.
- Unemployed youths played cards or simply sat at street corners, or desperately queued up at the local employment exchange.
- As there were no jobs, the youth involved in criminal activities and depression became common.
- The economic crisis created deep anxieties and fears in people.
- The savings of the middle classes, especially of salaried employees and pensioners, decreased when the currency lost its value.
- Every member of the society was affected by this economic crisis and was filled with the fear of **proletarianisation**[9].
- Unemployment weakened the **bargaining** power of the organised workers.
- Big businesses were in crisis.
- Peasants were affected by the sharp fall in agricultural prices.
- Women felt depressed as they could not feed their children properly.

The Weimar Constitution had some internal defects which made it unstable and vulnerable to dictatorship. It was impossible to get a majority for one single party due to proportional representation.

4 **Propaganda** It refers to an information used to promote a political cause or point of view.
5 **Reparations** It is the money that is paid by a country that has lost a war.
6 **German Mark** It was the Former currency of Germany.
7 **Wall Street Exchange** It is the name of the world's biggest stock exchange located in USA.
8 **Placards** It is printed or handwritten notice or sign for public display.
9 **Proletarianisation** It means to become impoverished (very poor) to the level of working classes.

Moreover, Article 48 gave the President the powers to impose emergency, suspend civil rights and rule by **decree.** Within a short time, Weimar Republic saw 20 different cabinets which lasted for 239 days. People lost confidence in the democratic parliamentary system, which did not offer any solutions to the problems.

Try These

1. **What proportion of its territories was lost by Germany under the Peace Treaty of Versailles?**
2. **Which plan of America helped Germany to overcome the Hyperinflation crisis?**
3. **Who founded the Communist Party of Germany?**
4. **In which year did Wall Street Exchange crash?**

3.2 Hitler's Rise to Power

Hitler was born in 1889 in Austria. Socio-economic and political conditions of Germany led to the rise of Hitler.

Hitler spent his youth in poverty. When the First World War broke out, he enrolled for the army, acted as a messenger in the front, and earned medals for bravery. The German defeat horrified him.

After Versailles Treaty, Hitler joined the **German Worker's Party** in 1919 which was later renamed as the **National Socialist German Workers' Party.** It was later came to be known as the **Nazi Party.**

In 1923, Hitler planned to seize control of Bavaria, for which he marched to Berlin and captured power. However, he was arrested, imprisoned for treason[10] and later released. As a result of economic crisis in Germany in 1929, Nazi propaganda gave hopes of a better future to the German people.

In 1928, the Nazi Party got only 2.6 per cent votes in the elections to the Reichstag, the German Parliament. But by 1932, it had become the largest party with 37 per cent votes. Hitler was a powerful speaker. His passionate speeches and promises inspired German people. He promised

- to build a strong nation, undo the injustice of the Versailles Treaty and restore the dignity of the German people.
- to create opportunities for unemployed people and secure future for the youth.
- to remove foreign influences and to resist all foreign conspiracies against Germany.

Hitler came up with a new style of politics. His party (Nazi) held big rallies and public meetings to demonstrate support for Hitler.

The Red banners with the **Swastika**, the Nazi salute and the ritualised rounds of applause after every speech were new developments at the time of Hitler.

Nazi propaganda regarded Hitler as a messiah[11], a saviour, who had arrived to help German people in a time of economic and political crisis.

The Destruction of Democracy

On 30th January, 1933, President **Hindenburg** offered the Chancellorship to Hitler. It was the highest position in the Cabinet of Ministers after gaining power.

After obtaining the power, Hitler started to destroy the structures of democratic rule. A mysterious fire broke out in the German Parliament in February and it gave an opportunity to Hitler to assume all his powers.

A **Fire Decree** was announced on 28th February, 1933. Under the decree various civic rights which were guaranteed by the Weimar Constitution were suspended like freedom of speech, press and assembly.

The communists were the main enemies of Hitler. Most of the communists were sent to newly established Concentration camps[12]. The suppression of the communist was severe in Hitler's regime.

On 3rd March, 1933, the famous Enabling Act was passed, which gave Hitler all powers to sideline Parliament and rule by decree. This act established dictatorship in Germany.

All political parties and trade unions (except the Nazi Party and its affiliates) were banned. The Nazi state established complete control over the economy, media, army and judiciary.

Special surveillance and security forces were created to control and order society in the ways that Nazis wanted. Apart from the already existing regular police in Green uniform and the SA or the Storm Troopers, the Nazi government introduced **Gestapo** (the secret state police), the **SS** (protection squads), **criminal police** and the **Security Service** (SD).

All these newly organised forces had extra-constitutional powers. It made the Nazi state as the most dreaded (fearful) **criminal state.**

People could be detained in Gestapo torture chambers, rounded up and sent to concentration camps, deported at will or arrested without any legal procedures.

10 Treason The crime of doing something that could cause danger to a country.
11 Messiah A leader who people believe will solve the problems of a country or the world.
12 Concentration Camps These referred to camps where people were isolated and detained without due process of law.

Economic Reconstruction

Hitler gave the responsibility of economic recovery to the economist **Hjalmar Schacht** who aimed at full production and full employment through a state-funded work-creation programme.

As a result, the famous German superhighways and the people's car, the Volkswagen, were made.

In foreign policy, Hitler acquired quick successes which were

- Hitler withdrew from the League of Nations in 1933 and reoccupied the Rhineland in 1936.
- In 1938, under the slogan, ***'One people, One empire and One leader'***, Austria and Germany were integrated by Hitler.
- In 1938, Hitler seized the German-speaking Sudentenland from Czechoslovakia and then took over the whole country. England supported this act of Hitler as it thought that Versailles Treaty was too harsh for Germany.

Schacht told Hitler not to spend too much on weapons since the state was in debt.

Hitler chose war to overcome economic crisis, as he thought that resources were to be accumulated through expansion of territory.

In September 1939, Germany invaded Poland and this started a war with France and England.

In September 1940, a **Tripartite Pact** was signed between Germany, Italy and Japan. It strengthened Hitler's international power.

By the end of 1940, Hitler became very powerful. **Puppet**[13] regimes which supported Hitler were established in a large part of Europe.

Hitler now moved to invade Eastern Europe. He wanted to ensure food supplies and living space for Germans.

Hitler attacked the Soviet Union in June, 1941. It was a historic mistake made by Hitler. The Soviet Red Army defeated Germany at Stalingrad and reached to Berlin. After that the Soviet army established their **hegemony**[14] over the Eastern Europe.

In the beginning of the Second World War, USA was not involved. It didn't want to face the same economic problems caused by World War 1. But staying out of the war was not possible for long. However, when Japan occupied French Indo- China and planned to attack USA naval bases in the Pacific Ocean, the USA entered the Second World War. Japan supported Hitler and bombed USA base at Pearl Harbour.

The Second World War ended in May 1945 with Hitler's defeat and the US dropping of the atomic bomb on Hiroshima in Japan.

3.3 The Nazi Worldview

Nazi ideology was similar to Hitler's worldview. According to this, there was no equality between people, but only a **racial hierarchy**[15] was present.

In this view, blond, blue-eyed placed, **Nordic German Aryans** were at the top, while Jews were at the lowest rank. All other coloured people were placed in between depending upon their external features.

Hitler's racism was borrowed from the ideas of **Charles Darwin** and **Herbert Spencer.** Darwin, a natural scientist tried to explain that plants and animals were created through the concept of evolution and natural selection.

Herbert Spencer introduced the idea of 'Survival of the Fittest'. According to this idea, only those species survived on Earth that could adapt themselves to changing climatic conditions.

These ideas were used by the racist thinkers and politicians to justify imperial rule over conquered people. The Nazi thinkers believed that the strongest race would survive and weak ones would perish.

According to them, the Aryan race was the finest and had to retain its purity, become stronger and dominate the world.

The other aspect of Hitler's ideology was related to the geopolitical concept of ***Lebensraum***, or living space.

He believed that new territories had to be acquired for settlement and to increase the area of the mother country.

This would increase the resources and power of German nation.

Hitler intended to extend German boundaries by moving Eastwards, to concentrate all Germans geographically in one place.

13 **Puppet** It refers to a person or group whose actions are controlled by another.

14 **Hegemony** It means control by one country over other countries.

15 **Racial hierarchy** It means people are organised into different level according to their race.

Establishment of the Racial State

Nazis wanted only a society of pure and healthy **Nordic German Aryans**[16]. They alone were considered as 'desirable', while other communities were classified as 'undesirable'. These 'undesirables' had no right to exist.

Jews, Gypsies and Blacks living in Nazi Germany were considered as racial inferiors who threatened the biological purity of the 'superior Aryan' race. They were widely **persecuted**[17].

Even Russians and Poles were tortured by the Nazi government. The captured civilians were being forced to work as slave labour.

In Nazi Germany, Jews were the worst sufferers. Jews had been **stereotyped**[18] as killers of Christ and **usurers**[19]. In medieval times, Jews could not own land. They earned a living through trade and moneylending. Jews lived in separately marked areas called **ghettos**[20].

Hitler's hatred of Jews was based on **pseudoscientific**[21] theories of race, which could be satisfied only through their total elimination.

From 1933 to 1938, the Nazis terrorised, **pauperised**[22] and segregated the Jews. From 1939-1945, the Nazis aimed to kill the Jews in gas chambers of Poland.

The Racial Utopia

The Nazis tried to realise their racial ideal through genocide. They divided the occupied Poland. Much of the North–Western Poland was made the part of Germany.

Poles were forced to leave their homes and properties, which were then occupied by Germans. Poles were deported to the other part called the **General Government**.

Members of the Polish intelligentsia were murdered in large numbers in order to keep the entire class of people under their control.

Polish children who looked like Aryans were examined by 'race experts' and if they passed the race tests, they were raised in German families. If they failed in these test, then they were sent to orphanages where most of them were perished.

Try These

1. **Who was the propounder of the theory- 'Survival of the Fittest'?**
2. **When did the Nazi Party become the largest party in Germany?**
3. **Which act helped to establish dictatorship in Germany?**
4. **In which year USA dropped atomic bombs on Hiroshima in Japan?**

3.4 Youth in Nazi Germany

Hitler believed that a strong Nazi Society could be established by teaching Nazi ideology to the children. A control over the child both inside and outside the school was required.

For this following measures were adopted

- All schools were cleansed and purified.
- Children and teachers who were Jews, the physically handicapped and Gypsies, were thrown out of schools.
- The school textbooks were rewritten. Germans and Jews could not sit and play together.
- Racial science was introduced to justify Nazi ideas of race.
- Stereotypes about Jews were popularised even through maths classes.
- Children were taught to be loyal, submissive, hate Jews and worship Hitler.
- Sports like boxing was introduced to encourage violence and aggression among children. Hitler thought that boxing could make children iron-hearted, strong and masculine.
- Youth organisations were made responsible for educating, German Youth in the 'Spirit of National Socialism.'
- Ten-year-old children had to join **Jungvolk**[23].
- In 1922, the **Youth League** of the Nazis was founded. After four years, it was renamed as Hitler Youth.
- At 14, all boys had to join the Nazi youth organisation-**Hitler Youth**. To control the youth, all other youth organisations were banned.

---

16 **Nordic German Aryans** It was a branch of those who were classified as Aryans. They lived in North European countries.
17 **Persecuted** It means systematic and organised punishment of those belonging to a group or religion.
18 **Stereotype** It means a fixed idea or image that many people have about a particular type of person, but which is not true in reality.
19 **Usurers** It refers to moneylender charging very high rate of interest.
20 **Ghettos** It refers to where people of the same race live, separately from the rest of the population.
21 **Pseudoscientific** It means falsely or mistakenly claimed or regarded as being based on scientific method.
22 **Pauperise** It refers to the act of making poor.
23 **Jungvolk** It was a Nazi youth group for children below 14 years of age.

- After a period of rigorous ideological and physical training, youth had to join the **Labour Service** at the age of 18. Then they had to serve in the armed forces and enter one of the Nazi organisations.

The Nazi Cult of Motherhood

In Nazi Germany, young people and even children, were repeatedly told that women were radically different from men. According to the Nazi ideology, the fight for equal rights for men and women, was quite wrong and it would destroy society.

Boys were taught to be aggressive, masculine and hardworking while girls were told to become good mothers and bring up pure-blooded Aryan children.

Women had to maintain the purity of the race, distance themselves from Jews, look after the home and teach Nazi ideology to their children.

In 1933, Hitler declared that the mother was the most important citizen, but all mothers were not equally treated. Those mothers who produced racially desirable children were awarded, given favoured treatment in hospitals, concessions in shops, theatres and even in the railways.

Honour crosses were given to encourage women to produce many children. Honour cross of bronze was given for producing four children, silver for producing six children and gold for producing eight or more children.

Aryan women who did not follow proper code of conduct were severely punished. Women who maintained contacts with Jews, Poles or Russians were punished or imprisoned. Many received jail sentences and lost civic honour for this criminal offence.

The Art of Propaganda

The Nazi regime used language and the media effectively to describe their activities. They never used the words 'kill' or 'murder' in their official communications.

Mass killings were called *special treatment*, *final solution* (for the Jews'), *euthanasia* (for the disabled), *selection* and *disinfection*.

'Evacuation' meant deporting people to gas chambers for killing them. The gas chambers were called **disinfection-areas**. They looked like bathrooms equipped with fake showerheads.

Media was carefully used to win support for the regime and popularise its worldview. Nazi ideas were spread through visual images, films, radio, posters, catchy slogans and leaflets. Socialists and liberals were represented as weak and degenerate and attacked as malicious foreign agents. Propaganda films were made to create hatred for Jews. The most infamous film was ***The Eternal Jew***.

In Nazi Germany, Orthodox Jews were **stereotyped** and marked. They were shown with flowing beards, wearing kaftans. However, in reality it was difficult to distinguish the German Jews from other German people.

Jews were referred to as vermin (insects), rats and pests. Their movements were compared to those of rodents.

3.5 Ordinary People and the Crimes against Humanity

Many ordinary people genuinely believed that only Nazism could bring prosperity and well-being for them . Some Germans opposed Nazism, but the large majority of Germans had no courage to protest.

Charlotte Beradt in her book **Third Reich of Dreams** described that Jews started believing the Nazi's stereotypes about them. The Nazi propaganda haunted the Jews and they were immensely suffered.

Knowledge about the Holocaust

World became aware about the Nazi atrocity (cruel and violent act) during the last year of its regime. The atrocities and sufferings that Jews had experienced during the Nazi killing operations are called the **Holocaust**.

People know about the Holocaust by the documents preserved by the Jews in many ghettos. The documents included diaries, notebook, created archives (the place where historical documents or records are stored), etc.

The Nazi leadership tried to destroy all these evidences when they started losing the war. Today many of the evidences of Holocaust are preserved in various memoirs, fiction, documentaries, poetry, memorials and museums of the world.

Try These

1. **In which year the 'Youth League of Nazis' was founded?**
2. **Which Nazi Youth Organisation consisted of all German boys of 14 to 18 years of age?**
3. **What was the name given to gas chambers by Nazis?**
4. **Name the most infamous film which was made to create hatred for Jews.**
5. **The book 'Third Reich of Dreams' was written by whom?**

Mind Map

NAZISM AND THE RISE OF HITLER

The Destruction of Democracy
- On 30th January, 1933, President Hindenburg offered the Chancellorship to Hitler which was the highest position in the Cabinet of Ministers.
- The Fire Decree was announced on 28th February, 1933.
- The Nazi government introduced Gestapo, the SS (the protection squads), Criminal Police and the Security Service.

Economic Reconstruction
- In September 1939, Germany invaded Poland and this started a war with France and England.
- In September 1940, a Tripartite Pact was signed between Germany, Italy and Japan. By the end of 1940, Hitler became very powerful.

Establishment of the Racial State
- Nazis wanted only a society of pure and healthy Nordic German Aryans.
- In Nazi Germany, Jews had been stereotyped as killers of Christ and Usurers.
- Jews lived in separately marked areas called Ghettos. From 1933 to 1938, the Nazis terrorised, pauperised and segregated the Jews.

The Racial Utopia
- The Nazis divided the occupied Poland, and much of the North-Western Poland was made part of the Germany.
- Poles were forced to leave their homes and properties, which were then occupied by Germans and deported to the other part called the General Government.

Ordinary People and the Crimes against Humanity
- Charlotte Beradt in her book Third Reich of Dreams described that Jews started believing the Nazi's stereotypes about them.
- The Nazi propaganda haunted the Jews and they suffered immensely.
- The atrocities and sufferings that Jews had experienced during the Nazi killing operations are called the Holocaust.

Hitler's Rise to Power
- Hitler joined the German Worker's Party in 1919 which was later renamed as the National Socialist German Workers' Party after Versailles Treaty.
- Nazi propaganda (false ideas) represented Hitler as a messiah, a saviour.

The Nazi Worldview
- Hitler's racism was borrowed from the ideas of Charles Darwin and Herbert Spencer.
- The other aspect of Hitler's ideology was related to the geopolitical concept of Lebensraum or living space.

The Nazi Cult of Motherhood
- According to the Nazi ideology, the fight for equal rights for men and women, was quite wrong and it would destroy society.
- Honour crosses were given to encourage women to produce many children.
- Women who maintained contact with Jews, Poles or Russians, were punished or imprisoned.

Birth of the Weimar Republic
- The defeat of Imperial Germany and the resignation of the emperor gave the parliamentary parties an opportunity to change the German polity.
- A National Assembly met at Weimar and established a democratic Constitution with a federal structure.

Youth in Nazi Germany
- Children and teachers who were Jews, the physically handicapped and Gypsies, were thrown out of schools.
- The school textbooks were rewritten. Germans and Jews could not sit and play together.
- Racial Science was introduced to justify Nazi ideas of race.
- In 1922, the Youth League of the Nazis was founded.

The Effects of the War
- Newly formed Weimar Republic was forced to pay a huge compensation.
- Socialists, Catholics and Democrats who supported the Weimar Republic were criticised and came to be known as November Criminals by the conservative nationalists.
- Europe became a continent of debtors from creditors.

Political Radicalism and Economic Crisis
- The Weimar Republic suppressed the uprising of the Spartacist League with the help of the war organisation called the Free Corps.
- The Spartacists later founded the Communist Party of Germany.
- Economic crisis in Germany came to be known as hyper-inflation.
- The Americans introduced the Dawes Plan which helped Germany to overcome the crisis.

The Years of Depression
- Workers lost their jobs or their wages were reduced.
- The youth involved in criminal activities and depression became common.
- Unemployment weakened the bargaining power of the organised workers.
- Peasants were affected by the major decline in agricultural prices.

The Art of Propaganda
- The Nazi regime used language and the media effectively to describe their activities.
- Mass killings were called special treatment, final solution, euthanasia, selection and disinfections.
- In Nazi Germany, Orthodox Jews were stereotyped and mocked.

NCERT FOLDER

Covering Intext Questions and Exercises of NCERT

INTEXT QUESTIONS

Q.1 Read Sources A and B and answer the questions that follow.

Source A

'For this Earth is not allotted to anyone nor is it presented to anyone as a gift. It is awarded by providence to people who in their hearts have the courage to conquer it, the strength to preserve it and the industry to put it to the plough... The primary right of this world is the right to life, so far as one possesses the strength for this. Hence on the basis of this right, a vigorous nation will always find ways of adapting its territory to its population size'. *Hitler, Secret Book, ed.* Telford Taylor.

Source B

'In an era when the Earth is gradually being divided up among states, some of which embrace almost entire continents, we cannot speak of a world power in connection with a formation whose political mother country is limited to the absurd area of five hundred kilometers'.

'Hitler, Mein Kampf, p. 644.

(a) What do they tell you about Hitler's imperial ambition?

Ans. The two texts tell that Hitler's imperial ambition was to expand the boundaries of Germany till wherever they could possibly reach. He believed that an aggressive nation will find methods to adjust its territory to its population's size.

In Source 'B', he was comparing Germany's size to that of Russia and wanted Germany to become a world power of similar size.

(b) What do you think Mahatma Gandhi would have said to Hitler about these ideas?

Ans. Mahatma Gandhi would have told Hitler to remove the idea of aggression against other nations from his mind, as violence begets violence.

Q.2 What does citizenship mean to you? Look at Chapters 1 and 3 and write 200 words on how the French Revolution and Nazism defined citizenship.

Ans. To me, citizenship means the right to live freely in the country of my birth or the country where I desire to live.

The French Revolution defined citizenship in a way which was different from way that Nazism defined it. The French people thought that all men have equal rights, as they are born equal.

The rights of a citizen include liberty, security, owning of property and resisting oppression. They also believed in the freedom of expression, whether verbal or in writing, art, etc.

They believed in the rule of law and that no one can be above it. However, the Nazi definition of citizenship was quite different. It was defined with the perspective of racial discrimination against all except the 'pure Aryan' Nordic race. So they said that Jews and other 'undesirable' people would not be considered as citizens of Germany. These people were given very harsh treatment like death in the gas chambers or were banished from Germany.

Q.3 What did the Nuremberg Laws mean to the 'undesirables' in Nazi Germany? What other legal measures were taken against them to make them feel unwanted?

Ans. Basically, the Nuremberg Laws meant that the 'undesirables' had no rights to live along with the other citizens. These included Jews, Gypsies, Blacks and other nationalities like Polish and Russian people.

These laws, promulgated in 1935, stated that

- Only persons of German or related-blood would be German citizens, enjoying the protection of the German empire.
- Marriages between Germans and the 'undesirables' were forbidden. Extramarital relations between them also became a crime.

Other legal measures included

- Boycott of Jewish businesses.
- Expulsion of Jews from government services.
- Seizing and forcible selling of the properties of Jews.

Q.4 Look at the figures and answer the following

GERMAN FARMER
YOU BELONG TO HITLER!
WHY?

The German farmer stands in between two great dangers today:
The one danger: American economic system - Big Capitalism!
The other is the Marxist economic system of Bolshevism.
Big Capitalism and Bolshevism work hand in hand:
they are born of Jewish thought
and serve the master plan of world Jewery.
Who alone can rescue the farmer from these dangers?
NATIONAL SOCIALISM.

From: *a Nazi leaflet, 1932.*

What do they tell us about Nazi propaganda? How are the Nazis trying to mobilise different sections of the population?

Ans. The first poster is addressed to the German farmer, while the second one is addressed to the German worker. This tells us that through this kind of propaganda, the Nazis were trying to win the support of the working classes.

The first poster is condemning the capitalists and the Bolsheviks because they are the enemies of Nazism. The second poster is telling the working class of the Germany to vote for Hitler who has fought on the front line in the First World War.

From these two poster we can assume that the Nazis are trying to mobilise different sections of people under their banner. These people include agriculturalists, workers and all pure Germans under the banner of Nazi Party.

Q.5 Write a one page history of Germany

(a) As a school child in Nazi Germany

(b) As a Jewish survivor of a concentration camp

(c) As a political opponent of the Nazi regime

Ans. (a) **As a School Child in Nazi Germany** I have been conditioned to behave in a particular manner since I was six years old. First I was given a flag to wave, to show my patriotism. I was told that men's and women's roles in life were totally different. We were told that the fight for equal rights of men and women was a thing of the past as it would destroy our society today. We boys were taught to be aggressive, masculine and iron hearted, while the girls were told that they had to become good mothers and rear pure-blooded Aryan children.

The girls had to maintain the purity of the race, distance themselves from Jews, look after the home and teach their children Nazi values.

I had to take an oath of loyalty to Hitler, proclaiming him as the saviour of the country.

I have been told that after finishing school, I will join the Hitler Youth Organisation. This will be followed by military service, which is compulsory.

(b) **As a Jewish Survivor of a Concentration Camp** Thanks to the Lord for saving my life. I am happy to have survived three years of torturous life in the concentration camp. Of course, I am now very weak and ill, but I am still alive. So many of my friends, relatives and even my family members died infront of my eyes due to the bad treatment in the camp. They were regularly beaten, left to starve and made to work in very harsh conditions. Many of them were sent to the gas chambers and I was always afraid of my turn coming next. Luckily, I have survived to tell this tale.

(c) **As a Political Opponent of the Nazi Regime** Since the Nazis have captured power, they are making life hell for all people who do not follow their doctrine. I do not understand what they will gain by trying to conquer other nations. The bombing by the British on our homes has killed many of my relatives and friends. Aggression on other countries will definitely cause war with them and we will also lose men and property in war. The way the Nazis are going about increasing their power, I feel, in the long run, we will lose out, as this war will make all other nations to go against us. I hope, Hitler sees sense and stops this war soon.

Q.6 Imagine that you are Helmuth. You have had many Jewish friends in school and do not believe that Jews are bad. Write a paragraph on what you would say to your father.

Ans. I would speak to my father like this

"Father, please do not behave badly with the Jews. Earlier, in my school Jewish children studied in my class and Spitz was a close friend of mine. You know him. He used to come to our home many times and both of us played together. That time, you did not say anything.

How has he suddenly become bad? Is it only because his parents are Jews? Now Spitz has been removed from our school and you do not allow him to come to our home. I think this is not fair for the Jews. You should not join hands with people who are telling bad things about Jews. It is spoiling our lives and we are losing many friends. I hope you will understand what I am trying to say and will do something about it."

EXERCISE

Q.1 Describe the problems faced by the Weimar Republic.

Ans. The problems faced by Weimar Republic were as follows

- The Weimar Republic was not treated well by the people because of the terms it was forced to accept the Treaty of Versailles at the end of the First World War. It was a harsh and humiliating treaty. By signing this treaty, the Republic carried the burden of war guilt and was financially being forced to pay compensation. It became very unpopular among Germans.
- Supporters of the Weimar Republic, i.e, Socialists, Catholics and Democrats were mockingly called the 'November Criminals' because they had accepted the humilating terms of the Versailles Treaty.
- The birth of the Weimar Republic coincided with the Russian Revolution. Soviets of workers and sailors were established in many cities. Most people were demanding Soviet-style governance.
- In the Weimar Republic, both the communists and socialists became enemies and could not unite against Hitler.
- The Weimar Republic faced economic crisis. USA withdrew its support when Wall Street Exchange crashed in 1929. Workers lost their jobs and were paid reduced wages. The number of unemployed touched 6 million. This created deep anxieties and fear among people.

Q.2 Discuss why Nazism became popular in Germany by 1930.

or What were the reasons for the rise of Nazism in Germany?

or Why did Nazism become popular in Germany by 1930? Explain.

Ans. Nazism became popular in Germany due to the following reasons

- The Treaty of Versailles imposed very humiliating terms on Germany and people began to think the Weimar Republic as responsible for that.
- There was political instability under the Weimar Republic within its short period, had 20 different Cabinets lasting on an average 239 days.
- Germany witnessed a grave economic crisis and Hitler promised the people to restore prosperity and peace.
- The communists in Germany tried to stage a revolution on the pattern of the Soviet Revolution of 1917 AD. The German capitalist supported Hitler's Nazi Party as the party was against Socialism.
- Hitler had a strong personality and mass appeal. He was a powerful speaker. His passion and words inspired people. Hitler devised a new style of politics which inspired the people of Germany.

Q.3 What are the peculiar features of Nazi thinking?

or Describe briefly five inhuman features of Nazi thinking.

Ans. The peculiar features of Nazi thinking were

- They believed that the strong should rule the world and the rest should accept their leadership.
- They believed in racial hierarchy, where the Nordic German Aryans were at the top and the Jews at the lowest rank.
- The Nazis believed that the Jews were their greatest enemies. So, the Jews were tortured and killed.
- From a very young age, children were indoctrinated both inside and outside school with the Nazi ideology of nationalism and war.
- The Nazis believed in the geopolitical concept of Lebensraum or living space, i.e. new territories had to be acquired for the German nation.
- Women were seen as only bearers of the Aryan culture and race.

Q.4 Explain why Nazi propaganda was effective in creating a hatred for Jews.

Ans. Nazi propaganda was effective in creating hatred for the Jews due to the following reasons

- Nazis successfully exploited the low position of the Jews in medieval times as there was a traditional Christian hatred against the Jews.
- The Jews lived separately in marked areas called Ghettos thus they became easy targets.
- The Nazis introduced the hatred theory against the Jews from the very beginning of the child's school life, so that they grew up with this hatred.
- Nazi ideas were spread through visual images, posters, slogans, leaflets, films etc. This propaganda worked on the minds and emotions of the German people.

Q.5 Explain what role women had in Nazi society. Return to Chapter 1 on the French Revolution. Write a paragraph comparing and contrasting the role of women in the two periods.

Ans. Role of women in Nazi society was dominated by the principles of a male-dominated society.

Hitler declared mother as the most important citizen. But this was limited to only Aryan women who produced racially desirable children, otherwise they would be punished.

Girls were taught that they had to became good mothers and maintain the purity of race. They must distance themselves from Jews, look after the home and teach their children Nazi values.

Differences between the French women and the Nazi women were

French Women	Nazi Women
In France women took an equal part in social political developments of their country. Many women played important role in the French Revolution.	In Nazi Germany women could not take part in democratic struggle as it was believed that it would destroy society.
In France most of the women had to work for a living along with their men.	In Nazi Germany women were not allowed to work along with men.
Women in France established their own political club and newspaper to express their views.	In Nazi Germany, no political clubs or organisations were allowed.
In France both men and women were treated equally.	In Nazi Germany women were considered to be the bearers of the Aryan culture and race.
In France women could not be forced to marry against their will. They had the rights to choose their partners.	In Germany women had to maintain the purity of race, they were not allowed to mix with the Jews.

Q.6 In what ways did the Nazi state seek to establish total control over its people?

or **State three ways in which Nazi state established total control over its people.**

Ans. The Nazi state established total control over its people in the following ways

- All political parties and trade unions were banned except the Nazi Party and its affiliates.
- The state established total control over the economy, media, army and judiciary.
- Germany became almost a police state. Special surveillance forces, security forces, secret state police (Gestapo) were created to control the society.
- The Nazi rule glorified war and chose the path of war as a way out of the economic crisis.
- Hitler introduced a massive programme of militarisation to enhance the military power of Germany and to restore its international honour and glory.

REVIEW EXERCISE

Including Competency Based Questions

Part I

Multiple Choice Questions (MCQs)

1. The Allied powers consisted of
(a) UK and France (b) USSR and USA
(c) Both (a) and (b) (d) None of these

2. Germany, Italy and Japan were jointly known as
(a) Allied powers (b) Axis powers
(c) Centralist powers (d) None of these

3. Goebbels was the .... minister in Hitler's regime.
(a) law (b) defence
(c) propaganda (d) None of these

4. Under the shadow of the Second World War, Germany had waged
(a) a genocidal war (b) a civil war
(c) a guerilla war (d) None of these

5. Find the incorrect option.
(a) In 1920 Hitler joins the German Worker's Party.
(b) In 1922 Nazi Youth League was founded.
(c) In 1933 the Enabling Act was passed
(d) In 1941 Germany attacks USSR.

6. What was/were the promise(s) given by Hitler?
(a) To build a strong nation
(b) Undo the injustice of the Versailles Treaty
(c) Restore the dignity of the German people
(d) All of the above

7. What was/were the speciality of Nuremberg Rally?
(a) It was held every year
(b) It demonstrated Nazi power
(c) It showed loyalty to Hitler
(d) All of the above

8. Nazi propaganda skillfully projected Hitler as a
(a) messiah (b) saviour
(c) Both (a) and (b) (d) None of these

9. Hitler's racism was borrowed from the views of
(a) Charles Darwin (b) Herbert Spencer
(c) John Locke (d) Both (a) and (b)

10. Nazis wanted only a society of pure and healthy
(a) Jews (b) Nordic German Aryans
(c) citizens (d) None of these

11. **Synagogue is the place of worship for people of**
(a) Buddhism (b) Jewish faith
(c) Christianity (d) None of these

12. **Who were regarded as the undesirable children in Nazi period?**
(a) Jews (b) Physically handicapped
(c) Gypsies (d) All of these

13. **Find the incorrect option.**
(a) Hitler's racism was borrowed from the ideas of Charles Darwin and Herbert Spencer.
(b) Mills idea of 'Survival of the Fittest' was accepted by Hitler.
(c) The Jews were regarded as the arch-enemies of the Aryans.
(d) Hitler believed that new territories had to be acquired for settlement.

14. **Which incident made Hitler furious?**
(a) German defeat in the First World War
(b) The Versailles Treaty
(c) Great Depression
(d) Both (a) and (b)

15. **Consider the following statements and choose the correct option.**
(a) Hitler was against the Versailles Treaty.
(b) Hitler became Chancellor in 1930.
(c) Hitler pulled out of the League of Nations in 1931.
(d) Germany reoccupied Rhineland in 1934.

16. **Consider the following statements and choose the correct option.**
(a) From 1930 to 1938, the Nazis terrorised, pauperised and segregated the Jews.
(b) Jungvolk was the Nazi Youth Group for children below 14 years of age.
(c) The Soviet Red Army inflicted a crushing and humiliating defeat on Germany at Berlin.
(d) In 1942, a Tripartite Pact was signed between Germany, Italy and Japan.

17. **'On 3rd March, 1933, the famous Enabling Act was passed, which gave Hitler all powers to sideline Parliament and rule by decree'**
Which statement accurately describes the main purpose of the Enabling Act? Competency Based
(a) It allowed Hitler to rule by decree, bypassing Parliament.
(b) It officially banned all political parties except the Nazi Party.
(c) Both (a) and (b)
(d) It strengthened the authority of the Weimar Republic and its democratic institutions.

18. **Many Gypsies and blacks living in Nazi Germany were considered as racial 'inferiors' who threatened the biological purity of the 'superior Aryan' race. They were widely persecuted.**
What were the long-term effects of the persecution of 'undesirable' communities in Nazi Germany? Competency Based
(a) It led to the establishment of a homogeneous society.
(b) It led to widespread global condemnation and the eventual downfall of Nazi Germany.
(c) It led to an increase in the popularity of Nazi ideology.
(d) It had no long-term effects.

19. **Arrange in sequence.**
I. Proclamation of the Weimar Republic
II. Germany invaded the USSR
III. Treaty of Versailles
Options
(a) I, II, III (b) II, I, III
(c) III, I, II (d) I, III, II

20. **Arrange in sequence.**
I. Mass murder of the Jews begins
II. Germany invaded Poland
III. Soviet troops Liberate Auschwitz
Options
(a) I, II, III (b) III, II, I
(c) II, I, III (d) II, III, I

21. **Arrange in sequence.**
I. The famous Enabling Act was passed
II. The Fire Decree suspended civic rights
III. Hitler was offered the Chancellorship
Options
(a) III, II, I (b) I, II, III
(c) III, I, II (d) II, I, III

22. **Which of the following statements accurately describes a "Birth of the Weimar Republic"?** Competency Based
I. A National Assembly met at Weimar and established a democratic Constitution with a federal structure.
II. Deputies were elected to the Reichstag, German Parliament on the basis of equal and universal votes cast by all adults including women.
III. At the first stage of war, Germany failed to occupy France and Belgium.
IV. The Allies were weaken by the US entry in 1917.
Options
(a) Only I (b) Only III
(c) Only IV (d) Both I and II

23. **By signing the Peace Treaty of Versailles, Germany lost**
I. £ 16 billion as compensation for war.
II. Resource-rich Rhineland was not occupied by Allied armies.
III. Its overseas colonies, one-tenth of its population and 13 per cent of its territories.

IV. 75 per cent of its iron and 26 per cent of its coal to France, Poland, Denmark and Lithuania.

Options

(a) Only I (b) Both III and IV
(c) Both I and II (d) Only II

24. Consider the statements given below and choose the correct answer. Competency Based

Statement I Germany was a powerful empire in the early years of the 20th century.

Statement II Germany fought the First World War (1914–1918) together with the Austrian empire and against the Allies (England, France and Russia).

Options

(a) Statement I is correct and Statement II is incorrect.
(b) Statement I is incorrect and Statement II is correct
(c) Both Statement I and II are incorrect
(d) Both Statement I and II are correct

25. Consider the statements given below and choose the correct answer. Competency Based

Statement I Political radicalisation was only increased by the economic crisis of 1923.

Statement II The Weimar Republic suppressed the uprising of the Spartacist League with the help of the war organisation called the Free Corps.

Options

(a) Statement I is correct and Statement II is incorrect.
(b) Statement I is incorrect and Statement II is correct
(c) Both Statements I and II are incorrect
(d) Both Statements I and II are correct

Answers

1. (c)	**2.** (b)	**3.** (c)	**4.** (a)	**5.** (a)
6. (d)	**7.** (d)	**8.** (c)	**9.** (d)	**10.** (b)
11. (b)	**12.** (d)	**13.** (b)	**14.** (d)	**15.** (a)
16. (b)	**17.** (c)	**18.** (b)	**19.** (d)	**20.** (c)
21. (a)	**22.** (d)	**23.** (b)	**24.** (d)	**25.** (d)

Match the Following

1.

List I		List II
A.	Great Depression	1. 1933
B.	Hitler became Chancellor	2. 1922
C	Nazi Youth League founded	3. 1929-32

Codes

	A	B	C		A	B	C
(a)	1	2	3	(b)	3	1	2
(c)	2	1	3	(d)	3	2	1

2.

List I		List II
A.	A German Parliament	1. Jungvolk
B.	Nazi Youth Groups for Children	2. Wall street
C.	Biggest Stock Exchange	3. Reichstag

Codes

	A	B	C		A	B	C
(a)	1	2	3	(b)	2	1	3
(c)	3	1	2	(d)	1	3	2

3.

List I		List II
A.	Lebensraum	1. Killing on large scale to destruct
B.	Genocidal	2. Become impoverished like working class
C.	Proletarianism	3 Living space

Codes

	A	B	C		A	B	C
(a)	3	1	2	(b)	1	2	3
(c)	2	1	3	(d)	2	3	1

Ans. 1. (b) 2. (c) 3. (a)

Assertion-Reason

1. Assertion (A) The US entered the Second World War.

Reason (R) Japan bombed the US naval base at Pearl Harbour.

Codes

(a) Both A and R are true and R is the correct explanation of A
(b) Both A and R are true, but R is not the correct explanation of A
(c) A is true, but R is false
(d) A is false, but R is true

2. Assertion (A) Nazi ideology was synonymous with Hitler's world view.

Reason (R) Hitler was inspired by the writings of Charles Darwin and Herbert Spencer.

Codes

(a) Both A and R are true and R is the correct explanation of A
(b) Both A and R are true but, R is not the correct explanation of A
(c) A is true, but R is false
(d) A is false, but R is true

3. Assertion (A) The German economy was the worst hit by the economic crisis.

Reason (R) By 1930, industrial production was reduced to 60 per cent of 1929 level.

Codes

(a) Both A and R are true and R is the correct explanation of A

(b) Both A and R are true, but R is not the correct explanation of A

(c) A is true, but R is false

(d) A is false, but R is true

4. Assertion (A) The tribunal sentenced only eleven Nazi leaders and many others were imprisoned for life.

Reason (R) After the Second World War, an International Military Tribunal at Nuremberg was setup to prosecute Nazi war criminals.

Codes

(a) Both A and R are true and R is the correct explanation of A

(b) Both A and R are true, but R is not the correct explanation of A

(c) A is true, but R is false

(d) A is false, but R is true

Codes

(a) Both A and R are true and R is the correct explanation of A

(b) Both A and R are true, but R is not the correct explanation of A

(c) A is true, but R is false

(d) A is false, but R is true

Ans. 1. (a) Both A and R are true and R is the correct explanation of A

2. (b) Both A and R are true, but R is not the correct explanation of A

3. (c) A is true, but R is false

4. (b) Both A and R are true, but R is not the correct explanation of A

Picture Based Questions

1. What does the picture suggest?

(a) Money is the God of Jews.

(b) To earn money Jews commit the greatest crime.

(c) Jews do not rest, until he becomes the king of money.

(d) All of the above

2. What do we know from this picture?

(a) Classroom in Germany depicting a lesson on racial Anti-Semitism.

(b) Classroom in Germany suggests the proper teaching process of German students.

(c) The student explains the numerical numbers.

(d) None of the above

3. Write about the incident that took place in this cartoon.

(a) Jewish students are expelled from school.

(b) Jewish students are expelled from school

(c) Racism is introduced in Nazi school

(d) Both (a) and (b)

4. What does this picture depict?

(a) Unemployed youth taking rest.

(b) Unemployed persons sleeping on the line.

(c) Unemployed person sleeping on the line during the Great Depression.

(d) None of the above

Ans. 1. (d) All of the above

2. (a) Classroom in Germany depicting a lesson on racial Anti-Semitism.

3. (d) Both (a) and (b)

4. (c) Unemployed person sleeping on the line during the Great Depression.

Case Based Question

1. Read the source given below and answer the questions that follow.

Jews remained the worst sufferers in Nazi Germany. Nazi hatred of Jews had a precursor in the traditional Christian hostility towards Jews. They had been stereotyped as killers of Christ and usurers. Until medieval times Jews were barred from owning land. They survived mainly through trade and moneylending. They lived in separately marked areas called ghettos. They were often persecuted through periodic organised violence and expulsion from the land. However, Hitler's hatred of Jews was based on pseudo scientific theories of race, which held that conversion was no solution to 'the Jewish problem'. It could be solved only through their total elimination.

(i) What was Hitler's solution to 'the Jewish problem'?

(a) Encouraging Jews to convert to Christianity.
(b) Encouraging Jews to leave Germany.
(c) Total elimination of Jews.
(d) Encouraging Jews to integrate into German society.

(ii) During which years did the Nazis primarily focus on terrorising, impoverishing, and segregating the Jews, ultimately forcing many to leave the country?

(a) 1939-1945 (b) 1933-1938
(c) 1945-1950 (d) 1920-1925

(iii) What was the primary occupation of Jews until medieval times?

(a) Land ownership (b) Trade and moneylending
(c) Agriculture (d) Politics

(iv) According to the passage, a key justification for Nazi persecution of certain groups was

(a) their political beliefs.
(b) their religious practices.
(c) their perceived racial inferiority.
(d) their economic status.

Ans. (i) (c) Total elimination of Jews.
(ii) (b) 1933-1938
(iii) (b) Trade and moneylending
(iv) (c) their perceived racial inferiority.

Part II

Very Short Answer Type Questions

1. What were the main groups targeted for mass murder by the Nazis during the Second World War?

Ans. The main groups targeted for mass murder by the Nazis included Jews, Gypsies, Polish civilians, Germans with disabilities and political opponents.

2. What was the work entrusted to the International War Tribunal set-up in Nuremberg after the war?

Ans. The work entrusted to the International War Tribunal in Nuremberg after the war was to prosecute Nazi War criminals for crime against peace and humanity.

3. How were the deputies of the Reichstag appointed?

Ans. The deputies of the Reichstag were elected on the basis of Universal Adult Franchise.

4. Who were mockingly called 'November Criminals'?

Ans. Those who supported the Weimar Republic, mainly Socialists, Catholics and Democrats, were mockingly called the 'November Criminals'.

5. What was the symbol of Nazi Party?

Ans. The Red banners with Swastika became the symbol of Nazi Party.

6. When was Hitler offered Chancellorship of Germany and by whom?

Ans. On 30th January, 1933, President Hindenburg was offered the Chancellorship, the highest position in the Cabinet of Ministers, to Hitler.

7. Which was the most feared security force of the Nazi state?

Ans. The Gestapo (secret state police) was the most feared security force of the Nazi state.

8. Which move of Hitler is said to be a historical blunder?

Ans. Hitler attacking the Soviet Union in June, 1941 is said to be a historic blunder.

9. What does the term 'Genocidal War' refer to?

Ans. The term 'Genocidal War' refers to the mass murder of selected groups of innocent civilians in Europe by Germany during the Second World War.

10. Which factors enabled the recast of Germany's political system after the First World War?

Ans. The factors which enabled the recast of German policy after the First World War were the defeat of Germany in the war and the abdication of the German emperor.

11. Name the author of the book *'Third Reich of Dreams'*.

Ans. Charlotte Beradt is the author of the book, *'Third Reich of Dreams'*.

12. Under the shadow of the Second World War, Germany had waged a genocidal war, which resulted in the mass murder of selected groups of innocent civilians of Europe.

Analyse the reason why the Nazis chose the method of gassing for mass murder during the Second World War. **Competency Based**

Ans. The Nazis used gassing as a method of mass murder during the Second World War due to its efficiency and the ability to kill large numbers of people simultaneously. This method was part of their systematic approach to the genocide.

13. The First World War had a big impact on Europe, both in terms of people's minds and money. From a continent of creditors, Europe turned into one of debtors. What was the effect of the war. **Competency Based**

Ans. The First World War had a profound impact on both the mindset and economy of Europe. The extensive destruction caused by the war resulted in substantial reconstruction expenses, transforming previously prosperous nations into ones burdened with debt.

14. In foreign policy, Hitler acquired quick successes. Many quick successes at home and abroad seemed to reverse the destiny of the country.

How did Hitler achieve quick successes in his foreign policy and what impact did they have on Germany? **Competency Based**

Ans. Hitler's foreign policy initiatives yielded rapid successes, reshaping Germany's destiny. For instance, in 1933, he withdrew Germany from the League of Nations, followed by the reoccupation of the Rhineland in 1936 and the annexation of Austria in 1938.

15. Nazis wanted only a society of pure and healthy Nordic German Aryans. They alone were considered as 'desirable', while other communities were classified as 'undesirable'.

(i) What was the Nazis' justification for persecuting these 'undesirable' communities?

(ii) How did the Nazis' racial policies impact the lives of those deemed 'inferior'? **Competency Based**

Ans. (i) Nazis justified the persecution of 'undesirable' communities by claiming that they threatened the biological purity of the 'superior Aryan' race.

(ii) The Nazi's racial policies impacted the lives of those deemed 'inferior' as they faced widespread discrimination and violence. Their basic rights were taken away and many were sent to concentration camps.

Short Answer Type Questions

1. State the verdict of the Nuremberg Tribunal. Why did the Allies avoid harsh punishment on Germany?

Ans. The Nuremberg Tribunal against Germany verdicted only eleven leading Nazis to death, others were imprisoned for life. This punishment of Nazis was less as compared to the brutality and crimes they had committed against the humanity.

Nazis murdered a number of groups, like Jews, Gypsies, Polish, Undesirable Germans, etc. Millions of people were killed by the Nazis in various killing centres of Auschwitz.

The Allies did not want to be harsh on Germany because they realised that the rise of Hitler and Nazi Germany was the result of the humiliation, Germany faced after the First World War.

2. Explain the impact of the First World War on European society and polity.

or **State any three effects of the First World War over Europe.**

or **First World War left deep imprint on European society and polity. Support the statement with three examples.**

or **Describe the effect of First World War on European society.**

Ans. The effects or impacts of First World War were as follows

(i) In society, soldiers were ranked higher than civilians. Trench life of the soldiers was glorified by the media.

(ii) Politicians laid great stress on the need for men to be aggressive and masculine.

(iii) Aggressive war propaganda and national honour occupied centre stage in the public sphere.

(iv) People's support grew for the recently established dictatorships.

(v) Democracy as a young and fragile idea could not survive in Europe between the two World Wars.

3. Explain the impact on Germany because of her refusal to pay war compensation in 1923.

Ans. The impacts of refusal to pay war compensation in 1923 on Germany were

- France occupied its leading industrial area, Ruhr, which was rich in coal.
- Germany retaliated with passive resistance and printed paper currency recklessly. With too much printed money in circulation, the value of the German mark fell drastically, causing the prices of goods to soar.

Eventually, the Americans helped Germany to recover from the crisis by reworking the terms of reparation to ease the financial burden on Germans.

4. What was the impact of the Great Depression on the US?

Ans. The impact of the Great Depression on the US were

- Values of shares dropped drastically and the national income of the USA fell by half.
- Hundreds of American banks, factories, mining companies and business firms went bankrupt.
- There was large scale unemployment, poverty and starvation in the country.
- The effects of this recession in the US economy were felt worldwide.

5. What were the promises made by Hitler to people of Germany?

or **State any three promises made by Adolf Hitler to the German society.**

Ans. The promises made by Hitler to people of Germany were

(i) He promised to build Germany into a strong nation.

(ii) He promised to undo the injustice and humiliation caused by the Treaty of Versailles and restore the dignity of the German people.

(iii) He promised employment for those looking for work.

(iv) He promised to secure the future of the youth.

(v) He promised to remove all foreign influence and resist all foreign conspiracies against Germany.

6. When was the Enabling Act passed in Germany? How did this act establish dictatorship of Hitler in Germany?

Ans. On 3rd March, 1933, the famous Enabling Act was passed. This Act established dictatorship in Germany in the following ways

- It gave Hitler all powers to sideline Parliament and rule by decree.
- All political parties and trade unions were banned in Germany, except the Nazi Party and its supporters.
- The new state machinery under Hitler established complete control over the Economy, Media, Army and Judiciary.
- Exclusive surveillance and security forces like the SS, SD, Gestapo and criminal police were created to control and mould society in the way that the Nazis wanted.

7. Explain any four points of Hitler's foreign policy. What did Schacht advise to Hitler?

or **Describe any three important points of Hitler's foreign policy.**

or **Describe Hitler's foreign policy before the Second World War.**

Ans. In foreign policy, Adolf Hitler took quick and successful steps. These were

(i) He pulled Germany out of the League of Nations in 1933.

(ii) Germany reoccupied the Rhineland in 1936.

(iii) He integrated Austria and Germany in 1938 under the slogan One people, One empire and One leader.

(iv) He then captured German-speaking Sudentenland from Czechoslovakia and later the entire country.

Schacht advised Hitler not to invest heavily on rearmament because the German state was still running on deficit financing.

8. Explain the impact of Hitler's attack on Soviet Union in June 1941.

Ans. Hittler wanted to achieve his long-term aim of conquering Eastern Europe. He also wanted to ensure food supplies and living space for Germans. Thus, he attacked Soviet Union in June, 1941.

This attack is regarded as a historical blunder of Germany. In this attack, Hitler exposed the German Western front to the British aerial bombing and Eastern front to the powerful Soviet Red Army.

The Soviet Red Army defeated Germany at Stalingrad badly. After this, the Soviet Red Army retreated German soldiers and they reached Berlin. Then Soviet Russia established its hegemony over the entire Eastern Europe for half a century.

9. List the communities which were classified as undesirable in Nazi Germany.

or **Mention the communities termed as 'desirable' and 'undesirable' by the Nazis.**

Ans. The communities which were classified as undesirable were

- The Jews, Gypsies and Blacks.
- Mentally or physically unfit persons.
- Poles and Russians.

The only community which was considered 'desirable' was pure and healthy Nordic Aryans who were considered superior to other races.

10. How were the Jews the worst sufferers in the Nazi government?

Ans. The Jews were considered the worst sufferers in Nazi Germany for the following reasons

- The Nazi stereotyped the Jews as killers of Christ and Usurers.
- In Nazi Germany, Jews lived in separately marked areas called ghettos. They were often persecuted through periodic organised violence and expulsion from the land.
- From 1933 to 1938, the Nazis terrorised, pauperised and segregated the Jews, compelling them to leave Germany.
- Hitler believed that 'the Jewish problem' could be solved only through total elimination. As a result, they were killed on a mass scale in gas chambers.

11. Explain any three points to prove that Nazi rule was barbarous.

Ans. The following points prove that Nazi rule was barbarous

- In Nazi Germany, only Nordic German Aryans were considered 'desirable'. Jews, Gypsies, Blacks, Russians and Polish people were considered undesirable.
- The Jews and Communists were tortured in concentration camps. Even 'undesirable children' were segregated and taken to the gas chambers.
- Special surveillance and security forces were created to control and carry out atrocities against the selected group of innocent people.

Extra-constitutional powers were given to these forces, which made the Nazi state as the most dreaded criminal state.

12. Explain the new education policy introduced by Hitler in Germany.

Ans. Hitler believed that Nazi society could be established only by teaching children Nazi ideology. Thus, he introduced a new education policy in Germany.

Its main components were

- Jew teachers were dismissed from the schools.
- Children were segregated - Germans and Jews could not sit together or play together.
- Undesirable children viz. Jews, the physically handicapped and Gypsies were thrown out of school.
- School textbooks were rewritten.
- Racial science was introduced to justify Nazi ideas of race.
- Stereotypes about Jews were popularised even through maths classes.
- Children were taught to be loyal and submissive, hate Jews and worship Hitler.
- Sports like boxing, which could make children iron-hearted, strong and masculine were introduced in schools.

13. Evaluate the use of media by the Nazis to popularise their ideology in Germany.

or **How was language and media used by Nazi regime to popularise their ideology?**

Ans. The Nazi regime used language and media with care to win support for the regime and popularise its worldviews. The following points state the use of media by the Nazis are

- Nazi ideas were spread through visual images, films, radio, posters, catchy slogans and leaflets.
- In posters, enemies of Germany were stereotyped, mocked and abused. Socialists and liberals were represented as weak and degenerate. They were criticised as malicious foreign agents.
- Propaganda films were produced to create hatred for Jews.
- Orthodox Jews were stereotyped and marked, being shown with flowing beards and wearing kaftans. They were referred to as vermin, rats and pests.
- Through media, Nazism worked on the minds of the people and turned their hatred at those marked as 'undesirable' by them.

14. Examine any three inherent defects in the Weimar Constitution.

or **Explain the inherent defects of the Weimar Constitution that made the republic unstable and vulnerable to dictatorship.**

or **State any three factors which made the Weimar Republic politically fragile.**

or **State three reasons of opposition to Weimar Republic by its own people.**

or **"Politically the Weimar was a fragile Republic." Explain this statement.**

Ans. The Weimar Constitution had following three inherent defects

(i) It was based on proportional representation, which made achieving a majority by one party virtually impossible. Only coalition governments ruled.

(ii) Existence of Article 48 in the Constitution, which gave the President the power to impose emergency, suspend civil rights and rule by decree.

(iii) Due to 20 different coalition governments being formed in 14 years, people lost confidence in the Democratic Parliamentary system, as it offered no solutions to their problems.

Thus, it can be concluded that politically the Weimar was a fragile republic.

15. How did the common people react to Nazism?

Ans. The common people reacted to Nazism in the following ways

(i) Many people saw the world through Nazi eyes. They felt hatred and anger when they saw someone who looked like a Jew. They marked the houses of Jews and reported about their suspicious neighbours.

(ii) Common men believed that Nazism would bring happiness and prosperity for them.

(iii) The large majority of Germans were passive onlookers, as they were scared to act or protest against Nazism. Many Germans organised active resistance to Nazism, braving police repression and death.

16. Nazis used chilling words as an art of propaganda. Justify.

Ans. The Nazis used chilling words as an art of their propaganda. They used deceptive (misleading) language with great effect. They never used the words 'kill' or 'murder' in their official communications.

The term 'special treatment', 'final solution' (for the Jews), 'euthanasia' (for the disabled), 'selection' and 'disinfection' were used. Gas chambers were labelled as 'disinfection area'.

'Evacuation meant departing people to gas chambers. These Nazi ideas were spread through visual images, films, radio, posters, catchy slogans and leaflets.

17. Discuss the most likely events which led to the Birth of the Weimar Republic **Competency Based**

Build the answer around these points

- **Peace Treaty of Versailles**
- **The Effect of war**
- **The years of depression**

Ans. The birth of the Weimar Republic was primarily influenced by several key events, each playing a crucial role in shaping the political landscape of post-war Germany.

Firstly, the Peace Treaty of Versailles, signed in 1919, significantly impacted the birth of the Weimar Republic. This treaty imposed harsh terms on Germany, including massive reparations payments, territorial losses and military restrictions.

Secondly, the devastating effects of World War I played a pivotal role in the emergence of the Weimar Republic. The war resulted in widespread destruction, loss of life and economic hardship. The war's aftermath left Germany in a state of turmoil, with social unrest and political instability gripping the nation.

Lastly, the years of depression following World War I increased challenges facing Germany and paved the way for the rise of the Weimar Republic. The economic downturn, along with hyperinflation and unemployment, plunged Germany into a deep crisis.

18. Read the statements given below regarding the Second World War. **Competency Based**

Statement 1 Hitler chose war to overcome economic crisis, as he thought that resources were to be accumulated through expansion of territory.

Statement 2 In September 1940, a Tripartite Pact was signed between Germany, Italy and Japan. It strengthened Hitler's international power.

Explain what trend do these statements - S1 and S2 - reflect in the Second World War.

Ans. The statements S1 and S2 highlight two key strategies during the Second World War.

Statement 1 shows Hitler's belief in territorial expansion as a solution to economic issues, reflecting the aggressive policies of the time.

Statement 2 indicates the formation of strategic alliances, like the Tripartite Pact between Germany, Italy and Japan, which were crucial in shaping the global dynamics during the war. These trends highlight the aggressive expansionism and power politics that marked this period.

Long Answer Type Questions

1. Explain any five measures adopted by Hitler to establish dictatorship in Germany.

Ans. On 30th January, 1933, Hitler became the Chancellor of Germany.

The five measures adopted by Hitler to establish dictatorship in Germany were

- Under his rule, the Fire Decree of 28th February, 1933 was passed, which indefinitely suspended civic rights like freedom of speech, press and assembly.
- The Communists were sent to the newly established concentration camps.
- The Socialists, Democrats and Catholics also were arrested and killed.
- On 3rd March, 1933, the famous Enabling Act was passed. This Act established dictatorship in Germany. It gave Hitler all powers to control over the economy, media, army and judiciary.
- All political parties and trade unions were banned. He controlled media, army and judiciary.

2. Describe the circumstances due to which Hitler came to power.

or **Discuss the factors contributing to the meteoric rise of Hitler.**

Ans. The factors contributing to the rise of Hitler were

(i) Hitler was a powerful orator. His speech could mesmerise the masses.

(ii) He promised to build a strong nation, undo the injustice of the Versailles Treaty and restore the dignity of the German people.

(iii) He assured employment for unemployed people and a secure future for the youth.

(iv) He promised to control all foreign influence and resist foreign conspiracies against Germany.

(v) He introduced a new style of politics. The Nazi Party held massive rallies and public meetings to demonstrate the support for Hitler and this massive mobilisation created a sense of unity among the German people.

(vi) Nazi propaganda skillfully projected Hitler as a messiah, a saviour and as someone who had arrived to save people from their distress.

(vii) Hitler came during such a period when the dignity and pride of German people were totally shattered due to the defeat in First World War followed by the humiliating Treaty of Versailles. The crisis in the economy, polity and society formed the background of Hitler's rise to power.

3. Describe the impact of Nazism on domestic and foreign policy of Germany.

Ans. Nazism impacted domestic policies of Germany as follows

- Hitler indefinitely suspended civic rights like freedom of speech, press and assembly.
- He sidelined Parliament and ruled by decree.
- All political parties and trade unions were banned except for the Nazi Party and its affiliates.
- The state established complete control over the economy, media, army and judiciary.
- Special security forces like Gestapo were created to control the citizens.

Nazism had great impact on Germany's foreign policy. The changes due to this were

- Germany pulled out of the League of Nations in 1933.
- Germany reoccupied the Rhineland (1936) and integrated Austria and Germany (1938) under the slogan, One people, One empire and One leader.
- Hitler occupied the Sudentenland province of Czechoslovakia and later took over the entire country.

4. State any five measures taken by the Nazis to create a pure German racial state.

or **Explain the Nazi idea of a racial state.**

or **Mention five steps adopted by the Nazis to establish a racial state.**

Ans. The five steps adopted by the Nazis to establish a racial state were

(i) Nazi ideology stated that the Nordic German Aryans were at the top and the Jews were located at the lowest rung of society.

(ii) The Jews, Gypsies and Blacks were regarded as racially impure and 'undesirable' and they were widely persecuted.

(iii) Under the Euthanasia programme, many Germans who were considered mentally or physically unfit, were sentenced to death.

(iv) Russians and Poles were considered as subhuman and captured civilians from Russia and Poland were forced to work as slave labour.

(v) From 1933 to 1938, the Nazis terrorised, pauperised and segregated the Jews, compelling them to leave Germany. From 1939 to 1945, a large number of them were killed in gas chambers in Poland.

5. Explain the meaning of Holocaust. How was it practised in Germany?

Ans. The atrocities and sufferings that the Jews had endured during the Nazi killing operations is known as the 'Holocaust' or 'destruction or slaughter on a mass scale'.

It was practised in Germany by the Nazis, using the following methods

- Physically eliminating all those who were seen as 'undesirable' (Jews, Gypsies, Blacks and other 'racially impure' people) by killing them in gas chambers by the use of poisonous gas.
- Making people from Poland and Russia as slave labour and imprisoned them in concentration camps.
- Jews were segregated (including Jewish children in school) and pauperised, forcing many of them to leave the country.
- Jews were victimised through the media by circulating pictures, films, slogans and leaflets. They were stereotyped, mocked, abused and described as evil.
- Jews were referred to as vermin, rats and pests. Their movements were compared to those of rodents.

6. Describe the reaction of the masses against Nazi barbarity.

Ans. The reaction of the masses against Nazi barbarity were

- Many organised active resistance against Nazi barbarity. They protested against police repression and even braved death in this resistance.
- The large majority of Germans, however, were passive onlookers and apathetic witnesses. They were too scared to act, to differ or to protest. They preferred to look away.
- Some historians observe that on the Jewish side, there was practically no resistance. In her book 'Third Reich of Dreams', Charlotte Beradt described that how Jews themselves began believing in the Nazi stereotypes about them. The stereotypical images publicised in the Nazi press haunted them.

7. Describe the effects of the Treaty of Versailles on Germany.

or **Discuss any three major clauses of the 'Treaty of Versailles'.**

or **The Treaty of Versailles sowed the seeds of the Second World War. Justify.**

or **"The Treaty of Versailles was humiliating on the Germans"—give three examples in support of this statement.**

or **Describe any five effects of the First World War on Germany.**

or **Explain any three effects of the First World War on Germany.**

Ans. The effects of the First World War and Treaty of Versailles on Germany were

(i) Financially, Germany suffered because the new Weimar Republic was made to pay compensation to the Allies for the war amounting to £6 billion.

(ii) Germany lost its overseas colonies, as they were annexed and distributed among the Allied Powers.

(iii) Germany was demilitarised to weaken its power.

(iv) Germany lost a tenth of its population, 13 per cent of its territories, 75 per cent of its iron and 26 per cent of its coal to France, Poland, Denmark and Lithuania.

(v) The Allied armies occupied the resource-rich Rhineland for much of the 1920s.

All these measures humiliated the Germans. To take revenge, Hitler annexed power in Germany and waged war against the Allies, thus sowing the seeds of the Second World War.

8. How were the ideas of Darwin and Herbert Spencer adopted by Hitler or Nazis?

Ans. Hitler's ideas of racism borrowed from thinkers like Charles Darwin and Herbert Spencer were

(i) Darwin was a natural scientist and Spencer was a biologist. Both of them tried to explain the creation of plants and animals through the concept of evolution and natural selection.

(ii) Spencer later added the idea of survival of the fittest. According to this idea, only those species survived on Earth that could adopt themselves to changing climatic conditions.

(iii) These ideas were used racist thinkers and politicians to justify imperial rule over conquered people.

(iv) The Nazi argument to accept this was the strongest race would survive and the weak ones would perish. The Aryan race was the finest. It had to retain its purity, become stronger to dominate the world.

9. Hitler considered men and women two different worlds. Explain.

or **How were women perceived in Nazi Germany? Explain**

Ans. According to Nazi ideology, women were radically different from men. Hitler believed that the fight for equal rights for men and women was wrong, as it would destroy the society.

His belief was implemented in the following measures

- While boys were taught to be aggressive, masculine and iron-hearted, girls were told to become good mothers and rear pure-blooded Aryan children.
- Girls had to maintain the purity of the race, distance themselves from Jews, look after the home and teach their children Nazi values.
- Women who bore racially undesirable children were punished and those who produced racially desirable children were awarded.
- The women who maintained contact with the Jews, Poles or Russians were severely punished.
- Boys on the other hand, learnt to worship war, glorify aggression and violence, condemn democracy and hate Jews and communists. At the age of 18, they had to serve in the armed forces and enter one of the Nazi organisations.

10. Read the information given below regarding The Racial Utopia and answer the question that follows.

Competency Based

'Under the shadow of war, the Nazis proceeded to realise their murderous, racial ideal. Genocide and war became two sides of the same coin. Occupied Poland was divided up. Much of North-Western Poland was annexed to Germany. Poles were forced to leave their homes and properties behind to be occupied by ethnic Germans brought in from occupied Europe. Poles were then herded like cattle in the other part called the General Government, the destination of all 'undesirables' of the empire. Members of the Polish intelligentsia were murdered in large numbers in order to keep the entire people intellectually and spiritually servile.'

Analyse the Racial Utopia in terms of its impact - negative and/or positive.

Ans. Hitler's vision of a 'Racial Utopia' had profound impacts on Germany, predominantly negative. Hitler's racial policies led to the Holocaust, resulting in the death of six million Jews. This horrific genocide is one of the darkest chapters in human history. Hitler's pursuit of racial purity contributed to the start of World War II, causing immense destruction and loss of life. Hitler's policies created deep divisions in society, fostering hatred and discrimination against those deemed racially inferior.

In terms of positive impacts, the atrocities committed during this period led to a global emphasis on human rights, culminating in the Universal Declaration of Human Rights in 1948. The need to prevent such atrocities led to increased international cooperation, resulting in the formation of the United Nations.

In conclusion, while Hitler's 'Racial Utopia' had devastating immediate impacts, it indirectly led to significant advancements in human rights and international cooperation in the long run. However, the cost was tragically high.

Case Based Question

1. Read the source given below and answer the questions that follow.

The years between 1924 and 1928 saw some stability. Yet this was built on sand. German investments and industrial recovery were totally dependent on short-term loans, largely from the USA. This support was withdrawn when the Wall Street

Exchange crashed in 1929. Fearing a fall in prices, people made frantic efforts to sell their shares. On one single day, 24 October, 13 million shares were sold. This was the start of the Great Economic Depression. Over the next three years, between 1929 and 1932, the national income of the USA fell by half. Factories were shut down, exports fell, farmers were badly hit and speculators withdrew their money from the market.

The effects of this recession in the US economy were felt worldwide. The German economy was the worst hit by the economic crisis. By 1932, industrial production was reduced to 40 per cent of the 1929 level. Workers lost their jobs or were paid reduced wages. The number of unemployed touched an unprecedented 6 million.

On the streets of Germany you could see men with playcards around their necks saying, 'Willing to do any work'. Unemployed youths played cards or simply sat at street corners or desperately queued up at the local employment exchange. As jobs disappeared, the youth took to criminal activities and total despair became commonplace.

(i) Given reason for the economic stability between 1924 and 1928 in Germany.

(ii) Suggest one example which is regarded as an indicator that Great Economic Depression has started.

(iii) Youth took to criminal activities in Germany. Explain the reason behind it.

Ans. (i) The economic stability between 1924 and 1928 in Germany was due to short-term loans given by the USA to boost up the economy of Germany mainly investment and industrial sector.

(ii) After the Wall Street Exchange crashed, on 24th October, 1929, on one day 13 million shares were sold. This was the beginning of Great Economic Depression.

(iii) The economic crisis in Germany led to widespread unemployment, with industrial production reduced to only 40% of its pre-crisis level. As jobs disappeared, many youths found themselves without employment opportunities. With limited options for earning a livelihood, some turned to criminal activities out of desperation.

Map Based Question

1. On an outline political map of world, locate the following major countries of Second World War.

(i) Axis Powers – Germany, Italy, Japan

(ii) Allied Powers – UK, France, Former USSR, USA

Ans.

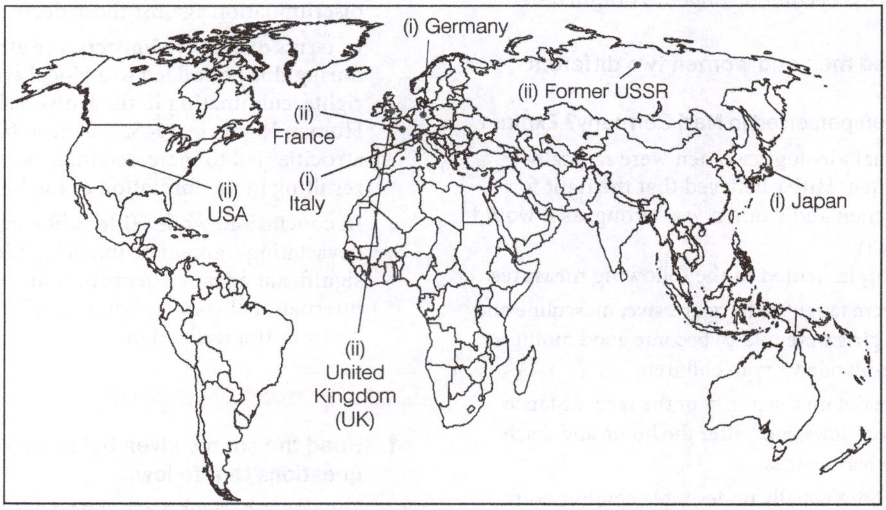

ASSESSMENT EXERCISE

Multiple Choice Questions (MCQs)

1. What is the name of the world's biggest stock exchange located in the USA?
(a) New York Exchange (b) Washington Exchange
(c) Lincoln Street Exchange (d) Wall Street Exchange

2. When was the famous Enabling Act passed?
(a) 30th February, 1930 (b) 3rd March, 1933
(c) 5th April, 1934 (d) None of the above

3. The Youth League of the Nazis was founded in ....
(a) 1920 (b) 1922 (c) 1925 (d) 1930

4. What was the main consequence of printing excessive paper currency in Germany in 1923?
(a) Increase in gold reserves
(b) Fall in value of German mark
(c) Economic stability
(d) None of the above

5. Match the following.

List I		List II
A. Hitler was born	1.	1923
B. Treaty of Versailles	2.	1919
C. France occupies Ruhr	3.	1889

Codes

	A	B	C
(a)	3	1	2
(b)	3	2	1
(c)	2	3	1
(d)	1	2	3

Subjective Questions (VSA, SA & LA)

1. Who were the Nordic German Aryans?

2. Under which slogan Austria and Germany were integrated by Hitler in 1938?

3. Compare and contrast the ideas of citizenship which existed in Nazi Germany with those of the French Revolution.

4. Explain by giving three reasons why Nazi propaganda isolated Jews from the rest of the Germans.

5. Describe the condition of the Polish people under Nazism.

6. Explain the steps taken by the Nazis to teach Nazi ideology to German children.

7. Explain the reactions of the common people to Nazism in Germany. Giving suitable reasons.

Forest Society and Colonialism

CHAPTER 4

Forests play a major role in enhancing the quality of environment. Forests provide us natural resources of economic and medicinal values. We get woods, tendu leaf, gum, honey, coffee, tea, rubber, different types of herbs, etc from forests. Due to growing population and rapid industrialisation, world's forest areas are disappearing at fast rate.

Between 1700 to 1995, during the period of industrialisation, 13.9 million sq km of forests or 9.3% of the world's total area was cleared for industrial uses, cultivation, pastures and fuel wood.

4.1 Deforestation

The disappearance of forests is referred to as deforestation. The process of deforestation began many centuries ago in India. Under colonial rule, it became more systematic and extensive.

Some of the causes of deforestation in India were

- **Land for Cultivation** About one-sixth of India's landmass was under cultivation in 1600. As the population increased with time, the demand for food increased. Cultivation was extended by clearing the forests.

  In the colonial period, cultivation expanded rapidly due to the following reasons

  - The British directly encouraged the production of commercial crops like jute, sugar, wheat and cotton. In 19th century, the demand of these crops increased in Europe where food grains were demanded to feed the growing urban population and raw materials were required for industrial production.
  - In the early 19th century, the colonial state thought forests were unproductive. To increase the income of the state, forests had to be cultivated.

    As a result, forests disappeared to a great extent and cultivation area rose by 6.7 million hectares between 1880 and 1920.

- **Timber Supply for Royal Navy** By the early 19th century, there was need for strong and durable timber supply for the Royal Navy ships in England.

  By the 1820s, to maintain the timber supply for Royal Navy, search parties were sent to explore the forest resources of India. Many trees in India were cut within a decade and huge quantity of timber was exported to England.

- **Sleepers on the Tracks** From 1860s, the railway network expanded rapidly. Wood was needed as a fuel to run rail engines (locomotives) and wooden sleepers[1] were required to hold the track together. To fulfil these needs of railway, forests were cut at large scale. The government gave out contracts to individuals to supply the required quantities of wood. These contractors began cutting trees indiscriminately. Forests around the railway tracks started disappearing.
- **Plantations** Large areas of natural forests were cleared to set up tea, coffee and rubber plantation to meet Europe's growing need for these commodities. The Colonial Government took over the forests and gave vast areas to European planters at cheap rates.

4.2 The Rise of Commercial Forestry

British were worried that the careless cutting of trees by traders and the use of forests by local people would destroy forests. So, the British Government appointed a German expert, **Dietrich Brandis** as the first Inspector-General of Forests in India.

Brandis realised that a proper system was needed for the conservation of forests. Rules had to be framed to prevent felling of trees and restriction for grazing so that forests could be preserved for timber production.

1 Sleepers These are Wooden planks laid across railway tracks.

Dietrich Brandis set up **the Indian Forest Service** in 1864 and helped to formulate the **Indian Forest Act of 1865**.

Under the Forest Act, forest officials surveyed the forests and planned how much of the plantation area was to be cut every year and replanted again.

The Forest Act of 1865, was amended twice, once in 1878 and then in 1927. The **Indian Forest Act 1878**, divided forest into three categories, reserved, protected and village forests. The best forests were called **Reserved Forests**[2]. Villagers could not take anything from these forests, even for their own use. For house building or fuel, they could take wood from protected or village forests.

Scientific Forestry

In scientific forestry, natural forests which had lots of different types of trees were cut down and in their place, one type of new trees was planted in straight rows. This is known as plantation.

The first forest research institute, **Imperial Forest Research Institute** was set up at Dehradun in 1906. The institute taught the system of Scientific Forestry.

Effect on Lives of People

After the implementation of the Forest Act, forest people and villagers experienced extreme hardships. Most of the traditional activities of forest communities like cutting wood for homes, collection of fuel wood, grazing the cattles, collecting fruits and roots, hunting and fishing, all were made illegal by the Act.

People were forced to steal wood from forests. Forest guards started to take bribes from local people if they were caught while stealing wood from forest.

It was also common for police constables and forest guards to harass people by demanding free food from them.

Use of Forest for People

- Villagers wanted forests to satisfy their different needs like, fuel, fodder, leaves.
- Foresters wanted trees which were suitable for building ships or railways. Thus, particular species like *teak* and *sal* were planted and others were cut.
- People use roots, leaves, fruits, tubers, flowers of different trees and plants for foods.
  - Herbs are used for medicine. Wood is also used for agricultural implements, like yokes and ploughs, bamboo is used for making fences, baskets and umbrellas.
- Dried scooped-out gourd can be used as a portable water bottle.
- Leaves can be stitched together to make disposable plates and cups.
- The **siadi** (Bauhinia Vahlii) creeper can be used to make ropes.
- The thorny bark of the **semur** (silk-cotton) tree is used to grind vegetables.
- Oil for cooking and to light lamps can be extracted from the fruit of mahua (*Madhuca indica*) tree.

KNOWLEDGE PLUS The sale of tendu leaves is a major source of income for a large section of people living in forests. Each bundle contains approximately 50 leaves. Women, children and oldmen are mainly involved in the collection.

Effect of Forest Rules on Cultivation

The major impact of forest laws was the ban on **shifting cultivation** or swidden agriculture.

This is a traditional agricultural practice in many parts of Asia, Africa and South America.

The shifting cultivation has many local names, like

- lading in South East Asia,
- milpa in Central America
- chitemene or tavy in Africa
- chena in Sri Lanka.

In India also it has many local names like dhya, penda, bewar, nevad, jhum, podu, khandad, kumri, etc.

In shifting cultivation, parts of the forest are cut and burnt in rotation. Seeds are sown in ashes after the first monsoon rain and the crops are harvested by October-November.

Such plots are cultivated for a couple of years and then left fallow for 12 to 18 years for the forest to grow back. A mixture of crops is grown on these plots. In central India and Africa it could be millets, in Brazil manioc and in other parts of Latin America maize and beans.

European foresters regarded the practice of shifting Cultivation as harmful for the forests. When a forest was burnt, there was a danger of spreading flames and burning valuable timbers.

Shifting cultivation made it more difficult for the government to calculate taxes. Therefore, British Government banned Shifting Cultivation.

2 **Reserved Forests** These were the forests which produced commercially valuable timber. No pastoralist was allowed access to these forests.

As a result, many communities were forcibly displaced from their homes. Some of them had to change their occupations, while some revolted against the law.

KNOWLEDGE PLUS Taungya Cultivation was a system adopted by the farmers in Burma. In this method, men-made holes in the soil using long bamboo poles with iron tips. The women sowed paddy in each holes.

Prohibition on Hunting after Forest Act

Before the forest laws, many people who lived in or near forests had survived by hunting small animals. This was prohibited by the new forest law.

The Forest law deprived the forest dwellers of their customary rights to hunt. Those who were caught hunting were punished. This illegal hunting was termed as **poaching**[3] by colonisers.

The Britishers believed that by killing dangerous animals, they would civilise India. As a result under colonial rule, the scale of hunting increased largely and as a result many animals became almost extinct.

A large number of wild animals were killed between 1875-1925. The Britishers gave rewards for the killings of tigers, wolves and other large animals so that there would be no threat to cultivators.

Initially, certain areas of forests were reserved for hunting. Later, environmentalists and conservators began to argue that all these species of animals needed to be protected and not killed.

New Trades, New Employments and New Services

Due to control of forest department on forests, some people suffered in many ways but some people benefitted from the new opportunities that had opened up in trade. This happened not only in India but in the whole world.

For example, due to growing demand of rubber, Mundurucu people of Brazilian Amazon began to collect **latex**[4] from wild rubber trees for supplying to traders.

In India, trade in forest product was a regular practice from medieval period. Adivasi communities traded elephants, hides (skin), horns, silk cocoons, ivory, bamboo, spices, fibres, grasses, gums and resins.

After the arrival of Britishers, the trade for forest products was completely regulated. British government gave sole right to large European trading firms to trade in forest products of particular areas. Grazing and hunting by local people were restricted.

In this process, many pastoralist and nomadic communities of Madras Presidency like the *Korava*, *Karacha* and *Yerukula* lost their livelihoods. Some of them began to be called **Criminal Tribes** and were forced to work in factories, mines and plantations under government supervision.

New opportunities in trade of forest products did not improve the life of the forest people. Forest communities like *Santhals, Oraons* (Jharkhand) and *Gonds* (Chhattisgarh) were recruited to work on tea plantations in Assam. Their wages were low and working conditions were very bad. They could not return easily to their home villages from where they had been recruited.

Try These

1. **Which decade witnessed rapid expansion of the railways network in India?**
2. **Which trees were promoted for building ships or railways by the colonial government?**
3. **In which country Taungya cultivation system was adopted by the farmers?**
4. **By which name shifting cultivation is known in Central America?**
5. **Santhals and Oraons are forest communities from which state?**

4.3 Rebellion in the Forest

In many parts of India and the world, forest communities rebelled against the changes that were being imposed on them.

In India, **Siddhu** and **Kanu** of Santhal Paraganas, **Birsa Munda** of Chhota Nagpur and **Alluri Sitarama Raju** of Andhra Pradesh revolted against the new forest policy.

The People of Bastar

Bastar is located in the Southernmost part of Chhattisgarh and borders of Andhra Pradesh, Orissa and Maharashtra.

The central part of Bastar is on a plateau. Chhattisgarh plain is in its North and Godavari Plain is in its South. The river Indrawati flows East to West across Bastar.

A number of different communities like **Maria** *and* **Muria Gonds, Dhurwas, Bhatras** and **Halbas**, live in Bastar. The people of Bastar speak different languages, but share common customs and beliefs.

3 Poaching It is an illegal hunting or capturing of wild animals.
4 Latex It is a milky fluid found in many plants.

The people believe that each village is given its land by the Earth and they make some offerings to the Earth at each agricultural festival. Further, they show respect to the spirits of river, forest and mountain.

The local people control all the natural resources within their boundary. If people from a particular village want to take some wood from another village, they pay a small fee called ***devsari***, ***dand*** or ***man*** in exchange.

Some villages also protect their forests by engaging watchmen and each household contributes some grain to pay them.

The Fears of the People

In 1905, the proposal of the Colonial Government to reserve two-third of the forest and stop shifting cultivation, hunting and collection of forest produce caused tension among the people of Bastar.

Some villages were allowed to stay in the reserved forests on the condition that they worked free for the forest department in cutting and transporting trees and protecting the forest from fires. These villages came to be known as **forest villages.**

This caused large-scale displacement and suffering of the people. Villagers had been suffering from increased land rents and frequent demands for free labour and goods by colonial officials. Two famine, one in 1899-1900 and another in 1907-1908 further worsened the condition of people.

The initiative to discuss these issues was taken by the Dhurwas of the Kanger forest, from where reservation of the forest took place.

Gunda Dhur from village Nethanar led the movement. In 1910, messages like mango boughs, a lump of Earth, chillies and arrows were circulated to invite villagers to rebel against the British.

People of Bastar attacked and looted houses, traders, police stations, schools, etc which were associated with the colonial state and its oppressive laws. The grain was redistributed. The British sent troops to suppress the rebellion.

The Adivasi leaders tried to negotiate but the Britishers entered the villages and punished the villagers who took part in the rebellion. As a result, people fled into the forests.

The British troops controlled the revolt after three months but not able to capture Gunda Dhur. After the revolt, work on reservation was temporarily suspended. The area to be reserved was reduced to roughly half of that planned before 1910.

After independence, the same practice of keeping people out of the forests and reserving them for industrial use continued.

KNOWLEDGE PLUS In the 1970s, the World Bank proposed that 4600 hectares of natural sal forest should be replaced by tropical pine to provide pulp for the paper industry. But after the protests by local environmentalists the project was stopped.

4.4 Forest Transformations in Java

There were many similarities in the laws for forest control in India and Indonesia. Java is a **famous rice producing island of Indonesia**. In past years, it was mostly covered with teak forests.

The colonial power in Indonesia were the Dutch and they wanted timber from Java to build ships. There were many villages in fertile plain. Moreover, many communities lived in the mountains and practiced shifting cultivation.

The Woodcutters of Java

The **Kalangs** of Java were a community of skilled forest cutters and shifting cultivators. They were so valuable that in 1755 when the mataram kingdom of Java split, the 6000 Kalang families were equally divided between the two kingdoms. Without their expertise, it would have been difficult to harvest teak and for the kings to build their palaces.

When the Dutch began to gain control over the forests in the 18th century, they tried to make the Kalangs work under them.

In 1770, the Kalangs resisted by attacking a Dutch fort at Joana, but their uprising was suppressed.

Dutch Scientific Forestry

In the 19th century, the Dutch enacted forest laws in Java, restricting villagers' access to forests. This law permitted use of forest wood only for specified purposes from specific forests under close supervision.

Villagers were punished for grazing cattle, transporting wood without a permit or travelling on forest roads with horse carts or cattle.

The forest service was introduced to manage trees for railways and shipbuilding, just like India.

In 1882, 280,000 sleepers were exported from Java. However, all this required labour to cut the trees, transport the logs and prepare the sleepers.

The Dutch imposed rents on land being cultivated in the forest. It exempted some villages from these rents if the villages worked collectively to provide free labour and buffaloes for cutting and transporting timber. This was known as the **Blandongdiensten System**.

Later, instead of rent exemption, forest villagers were given small wages, and their right to cultivate forest land was restricted.

Samin's Challenge

Around 1890, **Surontiko Samin** of Randublatung village (a teak forest village) started a movement against the state ownership of the forest.

He argued that state could not own forest as it had not created the wind, water, Earth and wood. By 1907, 3000 families were following his ideas.

Some of the Saminists protested by lying down on their land when the Dutch came to survey it, while others refused to pay taxes, fines or perform labour.

War and Deforestation

The First and Second World War had a devastating effect on the forests of India and other colonies. In India, at this time, the Forest Department was cutting trees freely to meet British war needs.

Before Japanese dominance, in Java, the Dutch followed a **Scorched Earth Policy.** By following this policy, Dutch destroyed sawmills and burned huge piles of giant teak logs, so that the Japanese could not utilise them.

Due to this, the Japanese exploited the forests recklessly for their own interests. Many villagers used this opportunity to expand cultivation in the forest.

After the war, it became difficult for the Indonesian forest service to get this land back. This situation was same as that of India, where people's need for agricultural land conflicted with the forest department's desire to control the land and exclude people from it.

New Developments in Forestry

Since the 1980s, governments across Asia and Africa found that scientific forestry and the policy of keeping forest communities away from forests has resulted in many conflicts.

The new developments in forestry are

- Conservation of forests became more important than collecting timber.
- The government recognised that to conserve forest, the people who live near the forests must be involved.
- In India, villagers protected the dense forests as they considered these as sacred groves[5], known as *sarnas*, *devarakudu*, *kan*, *rai*, etc.
- Some villagers started guarding their own forests, instead of depending on the forest guards.
- Local forest communities and environmentalists started thinking of different forms of forest management.

Try These

1. **Name the forest which the Dhurwas were associated with.**
2. **Name the famous rice producing island of Indonesia.**
3. **Who headed the Saminist Movement?**
4. **In which year the Kalangs resisted by attacking a Dutch fort at Joana?**
5. **Surontiko Samin started a movement against whom?**

TIME LINE | Covering Major Events with their Time Periods in Chronological Order

Period	Important Events
1755	The Mataram kingdom of Java split into two kingdoms.
1770	The Kalangas rose in rebellion against the Dutch but were suppressed.
Early 19th century	Colonial powers started exploiting forest as they considered it to be unproductive.
1860s	Rapid expansion of railway network.
1864	Brandis set up Indian Forest Service.
1865	Enactment of Indian Forest Act.
1878	Indian Forest Act divided forest into three categories, reserved, protected and village forest.
1890	Surontiko Samin of Randublatung village questioned state ownership of forest.
1899-1900	First terrible famine
1906	Imperial Forest Research Institute was set up.
1907-1908	Second terrible famine.
1980s	Government across Asia and Africa recognised importance of scientific forestry and conservation through participation of communities.

5 Sacred Groves These are small group of trees that have some religious importance to a particular culture.

Mind Map

FOREST SOCIETY AND COLONIALISM

The Fears of the People
- In 1905, the proposal of the Colonial Government to reserve two-third of the forest and stop shifting cultivation, hunting and collection of forest produce, caused tension among the people of Bastar.
- Some villages were allowed to stay in reserved forests on the condition that they worked free for forest department. These came to be known as 'Forest Villages'. People of other villages were displaced.
- People began to gather and discuss these issues, and gradually it led to rebellion in 1910. The British sent troops to suppress the rebellion.
- The Adivasi leaders tried to negotiate but the Britishers punished the villagers who took part in rebellion.

Rebellion in the Forest
In many parts of India like, Siddhu and Kanu of Santhal Paraganas, Birsa Munda of Chhota Nagpur and Alluri Sitarama Raju of Andhra Pradesh revolted against the changes that were imposed on them.

The People of Bastar
- A number of different communities like Maria and Muria Gonds, Dhurwas, Bhatras and Halbas, live in Bastar.
- If people from a particular village wanted to take some wood from another village. they paid a small fee called devsari, dand or man in exchange.

Deforestation
The causes of deforestation were
- Land for cultivation was increased due to the increase in population and demand for food.
- The spread of railways from the 1850s created a demand for wood.
- Large areas of natural forests were cleared to make way for tea, coffee and rubber plantations to meet Europe's growing need.

The Rise of Commercial Forestry
- Dietrich Brandis was appointed as the first Inspector General of Forests in India.
- Dietrich Brandis setup the Indian Forest Service in 1864 and helped to formulate the Indian Forest Act of 1865.

Effect of Forest Rules on Cultivation
- Major impact of forest laws was ban on shifting cultivation.
- Other names of shifting cultivation are
  - Lading in South East Asia
  - Milpa in Central America
  - Chitmene or tavy in Africa
  - Chena is Sri Lanka

The Woodcutters of Java
The Kalangs of Java were a community of skilled forest cutters and shifting cultivators.

Forest Transformations in Java
Java is a famous rice producing island of Indonesia.

War and Deforestation
- The First World War and the Second World War had a major impact on forests.
- The Dutch followed 'a Scorched Earth' Policy. It destroyed sawmills and burned huge piles of giant teak logs.
- The Japanese exploited the forests recklessly for their own war industries.

Prohibition on Hunting
- The forest laws deprived the forest dwellers of their customary rights to hunt.
- The illegal hunting was termed as poaching by colonisers and those who were caught hunting were punished.

New Trades, New Employments and New Services
- Due to demand of rubber, Mundurucau people of Brazilian Amazon began to collect latex from wild rubber trees for supplying to traders.
- Forest communities like Santhals, Oraons and Gonds were recruited to work on tea plantations in Assam.

New Development in Forestry
Conservation of forests became more important than collecting timber.

Effect on Lives of People
Cutting wood for homes, collection of fuel wood grazing the cattles, collecting fruits and roots, hunting and fishing, all were made illegal by the Indian Forest Act.

Dutch Scientific Forestry
In the 19th century, the Dutch enacted forest laws in Java, restricting villagers' access to forests.

Samin's Challenge
Around 1890, Surontiko Samin of Randublatung village started a movement against the state ownership to the forest.

NCERT FOLDER

Covering Intext Questions and Exercises of NCERT

INTEXT QUESTIONS

Q.1 Each mile of railway track required between 1760 and 2000 sleepers. If one average sized tree yields 3 to 5 sleepers for a 3 metre wide broad gauge track, calculate approximately how many trees would have to be cut to lay one mile of track.

Ans. Average number of sleepers required per mile

$$= \frac{1760 + 2000}{2} = 1880 \text{ sleepers}$$

Average number of sleepers obtained from one tree = 4

Therefore, approximate number of trees to be cut

$$= \frac{1880}{4} = 470 \text{ trees}$$

Q.2 If you were in the Government of India in 1862, responsible for supplying the railways with sleepers and fuel on such a large-scale, what were the steps you would have taken?

Ans. If I were in Government of India in 1862 and responsible for supplying the railway with sleepers and fuel, I would have taken the following steps

(i) In areas where trees are cut for making sleepers, plant similar nature of trees to those that are cut, so that the forest cover is maintained.

(ii) Try to increase coal mining and supply this to the railways as fuel instead of wood for running the steam engines.

(iii) Limit the cutting of trees by the natives of the forest to only what they personally require and not allow them to trade in wood.

(iv) Prevent poachers from entering the forests to cut wood illegally.

EXERCISE

Q.1 Have there been changes in forest areas where you live? Find out what these changes are and why they have happened.

Ans. There have been a number of changes in forest areas around my locality. These are as follows

- Entry to forest areas is restricted and the Forest Department has posted guards to check any illegal entry.
- Although, the number of trees in the forest has increased, but reduction of rainfall in recent years has stunted the growth of trees.
- The Adivasi villagers living inside the forest areas are gradually leaving their traditional occupations and migrating to the towns for education and jobs.
- A number of wild animals like tigers and elephants are sometimes seen on the edges of the forest, but they do not venture out for fear of being killed by human beings. Earlier the tigers used to come into the nearby villages and take away animals and small children at night.
- The smuggling of ivory and skin of tiger has been almost controlled.

Q.2 Discuss how the changes in forest management in the colonial period affected the following groups of people.

(a) Shifting Cultivators

(b) Nomadic and Pastoralist Communities

(c) Firms trading in timber/forest Produce

(d) Plantation Owners

(e) Kings/British officials engaged in Shikar (hunting)

Ans. Effects of changes in forest management in colonial period were

(a) **Shifting Cultivators** European foresters regarded shifting cultivation as harmful for the forests. The government banned shifting cultivation.

Many communities were forcibly displaced from their homes in the forests. Some had to change occupations, while some resisted through large and small rebellions.

(b) **Nomadic and Pastoralist Communities** The forest laws deprived people of their customary rights and that meant severe hardship for the Nomadic and Pastoralist communities.

They could not cut wood for their houses, could not graze their cattle or collect fruits and roots. Hunting and fishing became illegal.

Many Pastoralist and Nomadic communities like the Korava, Karacha and Yerukula of the Madras Presidency lost their livelihoods.

Some of the Nomadic communities began to be called 'Criminal Tribes' and were forced to work instead in factories, mines and plantations under government supervision. They were also recruited to work in plantations. Their wages were low and conditions of work were very bad.

(c) **Firms Trading in Timber/Forest Produce** By the early 19th century, oak forests in England were disappearing. This created a problem of timber supply for the Royal Navy. By the 1820s, search parties were sent to explore the forest resources in India. Trees were cut on a massive scale and large quantities of timber were being exported from India. The Colonial Government took over the forests and gave vast areas to European planters at cheap rates.

The British Government gave many large European trading firms the sole right to trade in the forest products of particular areas. The government gave contracts to contractors, who cut trees indiscriminately and made huge profits.

(d) **Plantation Owners** Large areas of natural forests were also cleared to make way for tea, coffee and rubber plantations to meet Europe's growing need for these commodities.

The Colonial Government took over the forests and gave vast areas to European planters at cheap rates. These areas were enclosed and cleared of forests and planted with tea or coffee. Communities like Santhals and Oraons from Jharkhand and Gonds from Chhattisgarh were recruited to work on tea plantation in Assam. Their wages were low and conditions of work were very bad. The plantation owners, under the protection and rights given by the British Government, made huge profits.

(e) **Kings/British Officials Engaged in Shikar or Hunting** Under colonial rule, the scale of hunting increased to such an extent that various species became almost extinct. The British saw large animals as signs of a wild, primitive and savage society. They believed that by killing dangerous animals, the British would civilise India.

The British gave rewards for the killing of tigers, wolves and other large animals on the grounds that they posed a threat to cultivators.

The Maharaja of Sarguja alone shot–1157 tigers and 2000 leopards upto 1957. A British Administrator George Yule killed 400 tigers.

Over 80000 tigers, 150000 leopards and 200000 wolves were killed for reward between 1875 and 1925. Initially, certain areas of the forests were reserved for hunting.

Q.3 What were the similarities between colonial management of the forests in Bastar and Java?

Ans. Forest management of Bastar in India was in the hands of the British and in Java, it was in the hands of the Dutch.

The similarities between these two were as follows

- The Dutch, like the British, wanted timber to build ships and to make sleepers for railway tracks.
- Both the British and the Dutch enacted forest laws to control the forests and put restrictions on the customary rights of the local people. They were prevented from entering the forests, they could not graze cattle or cut wood or take forest produce without permission.
- The British and the Dutch introduced scientific forestry. Both the governments banned shifting cultivation.
- Some villagers in Bastar were allowed to stay in the forests on the condition that their people would provide free labour for the Forest Department in cutting and transportation of trees and protecting the forests from fire.
- Similarly in Java, the Dutch imposed rents on the cultivated land in the forests. Some villages were exempted if they collectively provided free labour and buffaloes for cutting and transporting timber. This system was known as the 'Blandongdiensten System'.
- When the exploitation by the British in Bastar and the Dutch in Java became too much, the forest communities in Bastar and Java revolted under Gunda Dhur and Surontiko Samin respectively. Both the revolts were crushed by the colonial powers.

Q.4. Between 1880 and 1920, forest cover in the Indian subcontinent declined by 9.7 million hectare, from 108.6 million hectare to 98.9 million hectare. Discuss the role of the following factors in this decline.

(a) Railways
(b) Ship Building
(c) Agricultural Expansion
(d) Commercial Farming of Trees
(e) Tea/Coffee Plantations
(f) Adivasis and Other Peasant Users

Ans. (a) **Railways** The spread of railways from the 1850s created a new demand. Railways were essential for colonial trade and for the movement of imperial troops. To run locomotives, wood was needed as fuel and to lay railway lines, sleepers were essential to hold the tracks together. Each mile of railway track required between 1760 and 2000 sleepers.

From the 1860s, the railway network expanded rapidly. As the length of the railway tracks expanded, a very large number of trees were felled.

As early as the 1850s, in the Madras Presidency alone 35000 trees were cut annually for sleepers. Forests around the railway tracks started disappearing very fast.

(b) **Ship Building** By the early 19th century, Oak forests in England were disappearing. This created a problem of timber supply from the Royal Navy. English ships could not be built without a regular supply of strong and durable timber.

Imperial power could not be protected without ships. Therefore by the 1820s, search parties were sent to explore the forest resources of India.

Within a decade trees were being felled on a massive scale and vast quantities of timber were being exported, leading to disappearance of forests.

(c) **Agricultural Expansion** As population increased, the demand for food went up. Peasants extended the boundaries of cultivation by clearing forests. In the early 19th century, the colonial state thought that the forests were unproductive.

They were considered to be wilderness that had to be brought under cultivation so, that the land could yield agricultural products and revenue and enhance the income of the state.

Thus, between 1880 and 1920, cultivated area rose by 6.7 million hectares by clearing the forests. The demand for commercial crops like jute, sugar, wheat, cotton and raw material for industries increased.

Therefore, the British encouraged expansion of cultivation by clearing forests, leading to decline in forest cover.

(d) **Commercial Farming of Trees** In commercial farming, natural forests which had lots of different types of trees were cut down. In their place one type of trees were planted in straight rows. This is called a plantation.

To promote plantation farming or commercial farming, different varieties of trees were cut down leading to loss of many species and loss of forest cover when the trees were cut for commercial use.

(e) **Tea/Coffee Plantation** Large areas of natural forests were also cleared to make way for tea, coffee and rubber plantations to meet Europe's growing need for these commodities. The Colonial Government took over the forests and gave vast areas to European planters at cheap rates.

These areas were enclosed and forests were cleared and planted with tea or coffee. Plantations were large in area leading to loss of large forest areas.

(f) **Adivasis and other Peasant Users** As in most parts of the world, shifting cultivation was done by the Adivasis and other peasant communities, in India also it was practiced.

In shifting cultivation, parts of the forest area are cut and burnt in rotation.

Seeds were sown in the ashes after the first monsoon rains and the crop was harvested by October-November.

When fertility decreased, the process was repeated at another location. This led to a large loss of forests.

Note In the examination, this question will not be asked completely, only its one or two sub-parts will be asked.

Q.5 Why are forests affected by wars?

Ans. Forests are affected by wars because

- Forest products are used for fulfilling various needs and requirements during war. In the case of India, during the First World War and the Second World War, the Forest Department was cutting trees freely to meet British war needs.
- During the Second World War in Java just before the Japanese occupied the region, the Dutch followed a Scorched Earth Policy, destroying sawmills and burning huge piles of giant teak logs, so that they did not fall into Japanese hands.
- The Japanese exploited the forests recklessly for their war industries, forcing villagers to cut down forests. Many villagers took this opportunity to expand cultivation in the forests. Thus, wars also led to destruction of forests.

REVIEW EXERCISE

Including Competency Based Questions

Part I

Multiple Choice Questions (MCQs)

1. Which of the following correctly defines deforestation?

(a) The disappearance of forests
(b) Unplanned cutting of trees
(c) Cutting trees for agriculture
(d) All of the above

2. How much India's landmass was under cultivation in 1600?

(a) One-third (b) One-fourth (c) One-sixth (d) One-tenth

3. Which transport system was most essential for colonial trade and movement of goods?

(a) Roadways (b) Waterways
(c) Railways (d) None of these

4. Which act was passed in 1865?
(a) Indian Forest Act
(b) Tribal Rehabilitation Act
(c) Forest Protection Act
(d) None of the above

5. Where was the Imperial Forest Research Institute set up in 1906?
(a) New Delhi (b) Bombay
(c) Dehradun (d) Mussoorie

6. Which species of trees are suited for building ships and railways?
(a) Teak (b) Mahogany
(c) Sal (d) Both (a) and (c)

7. What is local name of Madhuca indica?
(a) Mahua (b) Deodar
(c) Hyperion (d) Methuselah

8. In forest, a dried scooped-out gourd was used as
(a) a utensil (b) portable water bottle
(c) container (d) None of these

9. Oils from the Mahua trees are used for
(a) cooking foods (b) lighting lamps
(c) hair oil (d) Both (a) and (b)

10. Where is Bastar located?
(a) Southernmost part of Chhattisgarh
(b) Northernmost part of Madhya Pradesh
(c) Easternmost part of Chhattisgarh
(d) None of the above

11. Which tribal community (s) is/are living in Bastar?
(a) Maria and Muria Gonds
(b) Dhurwas
(c) Bhatras and Halbas
(d) All of the above

12. What is common in different tribal communities of Bastar?
(a) Customs (b) Beliefs
(c) Language (d) Both (a) and (b)

13. In which year did the Bastar rebellion take place?
(a) 1910 (b) 1912 (c) 1915 (d) 1920

14. Adivasis were hired by the forest department to cut trees, and make smooth planks which would serve as sleepers for the railways. At the same time, they were not allowed to cut these trees to build their own houses. **Competency Based**

What does the above paragraph highlights?
(a) The environmental benefits of Adivasi forest management practices.
(b) The potential conflict between economic development and traditional ways of life.
(c) The unfair treatment of Adivasis by the forest department.
(d) All of the above

15. Dietrich Brandis set up the Indian Forest Service in 1864 and helped to formulate the Indian Forest Act of 1865. Under the Forest Act, forest officials surveyed the forests and planned how much of the plantation area was to be cut every year and replanted again.

The main purpose of the Forest Act of 1865 was to **Competency Based**
(a) protect endangered species in Indian forests.
(b) promote sustainable forestry practices.
(c) increase revenue from timber exports.
(d) grant local communities control over forest resources.

16. Most of the traditional activities of forest communities like cutting wood for homes, collection of fuel wood, grazing the cattles, collecting fruits and roots, hunting and fishing, all were made illegal by the Act.

The main consequence of these restrictions on forest communities was **Competency Based**
(a) Improved forest conservation due to reduced resource use.
(b) Widespread acceptance of the Act due to its environmental benefits.
(c) Economic hardship and cultural disruption for traditional communities.
(d) None of the above

17. Choose the best explanation for why European foresters found shifting cultivation problematic.
(a) They prioritised biodiversity and believed fire disrupts the delicate balance of forest ecosystems.
(b) They valued aesthetic beauty and saw charred trees as unsightly and detrimental to the forest's visual appeal.
(c) They focused on maximising timber production and feared the loss of potential timber due to uncontrolled burns.
(d) They were concerned about soil erosion and believed shifting cultivation leads to rapid land degradation.

18. Which of the following statements accurately describes the colonial state's view of forests in the early nineteenth century?
(a) They valued forests for their aesthetic beauty and recreational potential.
(b) They recognised the essential role of forests in maintaining environmental balance.
(c) They considered forests unproductive wilderness suitable for conversion to farmland.
(d) They promoted sustainable forest management practices for long-term resource utilisation.

19. Arrange in sequence.
I. The Kalangas rose in rebellion against the Dutch, but were suppressed.
II. The population of Java was estimated as 3.4 million.
III. The Mataram Kingdom of Java split into two kingdoms.

Codes
(a) II, III, I (b) I, II, III (c) III, II, I (d) I, III, II

20. **Arrange in sequence.**

I. Imperial Forest Research Institute was set up.
II. Enactment of Indian Forest Act.
III. Indian Forest Act divided forests into three categories.
IV. Indian Forest Service was set up.

Codes

(a) IV, II, III, I (b) IV, III, II, I
(c) II, I, III, IV (d) I, IV, III, II

21. **Which of the following statements accurately describes the causes of deforestation in India?** **Competency Based**

I. The need for wood for industrial uses, such as construction and furniture making.
II. Rapid population growth leading to increased demand for land for agriculture and settlements.
III. Inefficient management of forest resources and lack of sustainable practices.
IV. Legacy of deforestation practices implemented during the colonial era.

Codes

(a) Only I and II (b) Only III and IV
(c) Only II and IV (d) All of these

22. **Which of the following statements accurately describes the factors contributing to the increase in cultivated land in India?**

I. Increased demand for food due to population growth.
II. Introduction of new agricultural technologies and crop varieties during the colonial period.
III. Expansion of commercial agriculture for cash crops like cotton and indigo.
IV. Government policies promoting land reclamation and irrigation projects.

Codes

(a) Only I and II (b) Only III and IV
(c) Only I and III (d) All of these

23. **Consider the statements given below and choose the correct answer.** **Competency Based**

Statement I The deforestation rate during the industrialisation period (1700-1995) was relatively slow and gradual.

Statement II The industrialisation period witnessed the clearing of 13.9 million sq km of forests, representing 9.3% of the world's total area.

Codes

(a) Statement I is correct and II is incorrect.
(b) Statement I is incorrect and II is correct
(c) Both I and II are incorrect
(d) Both I and II are correct

24. **Consider the statements about England's timber shortage and imperial power and choose the correct answer.** **Competency Based**

Statement I The depletion of English oak forests was the only factor responsible for England's search for alternative timber sources in the 1820s.

Statement II England's imperial power relied on a strong navy, and English ships could be built only with a regular supply of strong and durable timber.

Codes

(a) Statement I is correct and II is incorrect
(b) Statement I is incorrect and II is correct
(c) Both I and II are incorrect
(d) Both I and II are correct

25. **People of Bastar rebelled against the charges imposed on them. Which statement about Bastar is correct?**

I. Bastar is situated in the Southernmost part of Chhattisgarh.
II. The Godavari plain lies to the North of Bastar.
III. The Central part of Bastar is a plateau with plains on either side.
IV. The people of Bastar have the same language despite belonging to different communities.

Codes

(a) Only statements I and II are appropriate.
(b) Statements I and III are appropriate.
(c) Statements I and III are IV are appropriate.
(d) Statements I, II and III are appropriate.

Answers

1. (d)	**2.** (c)	**3.** (c)	**4.** (a)	**5.** (c)
6. (d)	**7.** (a)	**8.** (b)	**9.** (d)	**10.** (a)
11. (d)	**12.** (d)	**13.** (a)	**14.** (d)	**15.** (b)
16. (c)	**17.** (c)	**18.** (c)	**19.** (a)	**20.** (a)
21. (d)	**22.** (d)	**23.** (b)	**24.** (b)	**25.** (b)

Match the Following

1.

List I	List II
A. Dietrich Brandis	1. Revolutionary of Java
B. George Yule	2. First Inspector General of Forests in India
C. Surantiko Samin	3. British Administrators

Codes

	A	B	C		A	B	C
(a)	3	2	1	(b)	2	1	3
(c)	2	3	1	(d)	1	2	3

2.

List I	List II
A. The Mataram kingdom of Java split into two kingdoms	1. 1770
B. The Kalangas rose in rebellion against the Dutch	2. 1865
C. Indian Forest Act introduced	3. 1755

Codes

	A	B	C		A	B	C
(a)	3	1	2	(b)	2	1	3
(c)	1	2	3	(d)	3	2	1

Ans. 1. (c) 2. (a)

Assertion-Reason

1. Assertion (A) Many pastoralists and nomadic communities were labelled as 'criminal tribes,'

Reason (R) Grazing and hunting in forests were restricted by the Britishers.

Codes

(a) Both A and R are true and R is the correct explanation of A

(b) Both A and R are true, but R is not the correct explanation of A

(c) A is true, but R is false

(d) A is false, but R is true

2. Assertion (A) The Kalangas of Java were a community of skilled forest cutters and shifting cultivations.

Reason (R) 6000 Kalanga families were equally divided between the two kingdoms.

Codes

(a) Both A and R are true and R is the correct explanation of A

(b) Both A and R are true, but R is not the correct explanation of A

(c) A is true, but R is false

(d) A is false, but R is true

3. Assertion (A) Villages in Bastar protect their forests by employing watchmen and contributing grain to pay them.

Reason (R) The people of Bastar have a strong connection to their natural surroundings showing respect to entities like the Earth, river, forest and mountain, and managing their resources sustainably.

Codes

(a) Both A and R are true and R is the correct explanation of A

(b) Both A and R are true, but R is not the correct explanation of A

(c) A is true, but R is false

(d) A is false, but R is true

4. Assertion (A) Control of forests by the Forest Department resulted in both disadvantages for some local communities and benefits for others due to new trade opportunities.

Reason (R) This phenomenon, observed globally, is exemplified by the Munducucu people of Brazil experiencing hardship as a result of stagnant rubber demand.

Codes

(a) Both A and R are true and R is the correct explanation of A

(b) Both A and R are true, but R is not the correct explanation of A

(c) A is true, but R is false

(d) A is false, but R is true

Ans. 1. (b) Both A and R are true, but R is not the correct explanation of A

2. (b) Both A and R are true, but R is not the correct explanation of A

3. (a) Both A and R are true and R is the correct explanation of A

4. (c) A is true, but R is false

Picture Based Questions

1. Name the system of cultivation and the country which adopted this system.

(a) Burma, Taungya Cultivation

(b) Thailand, Taungya Cultivation

(c) Java, Shifting Cultivation

(d) India, Shifting Cultivation

2. What is being depicted in the picture taken in Bastar in 1910?

(a) A market place
(b) A tribal camp
(c) An army camp
(d) A religious ceremony

3. Given below is the image of Bamboo rafts being floated down the Kassalong river, Chittagong Hill Tracts.

Which of the following impacts is shown in the picture?

(a) Plantation (b) Deforestation
(c) Soil Erosion (d) Flood

Ans. 1. (a) Burma, Taungya Cultivation
2. (c) An army camp
3. (b) Deforestation

Case Based Question

1. Read the source given below and answer the questions that follow.

In the early 19th century, the colonial state thought that forests were unproductive. They were considered to be wilderness that had to be brought under cultivation so that the land could yield agricultural products and revenue, and enhance the income of the state. So between 1880 and 1920, cultivated area rose by 6.7 million hectares. We always see the expansion of cultivation as a sign of progress. But we should not forget that for land to be brought under the plough, forests have to be cleared. By the early 19th century, oak forests in England were disappearing. This created a problem of timber supply for the Royal Navy.

(i) The main reason that the colonial state considered forests unproductive was

(a) lack of knowledge about sustainable forestry practices.
(b) the belief that only agriculture generated revenue.
(c) pressure from local communities to convert forests to farms.
(d) the presence of wild animals posing a threat to agriculture.

(ii) The increase in cultivated area between 1880 and 1920 most likely resulted in

(a) enhanced biodiversity and wildlife habitat.
(b) reduced dependence on imported timber.
(c) increased soil erosion and environmental damage.
(d) None of the above

(iii) The disappearance of oak forests in England was primarily caused by

(a) natural disasters like wildfires or disease outbreaks
(b) increased demand for agricultural land for food production.
(c) excessive hunting practices leading to ecological imbalance.
(d) demand for timber by the Royal Navy for shipbuilding.

(iv) The primary reason for the colonial state cleared the forests was

(a) to create wilderness reserves for wildlife.
(b) to increase agricultural land and generate revenue.
(c) to provide recreational activities for the population.
(d) All of the above

Ans. (i) (b) the belief that only agriculture generated revenue.
(ii) (c) increased soil erosion and environmental damage.
(iii) (d) demand for timber by the Royal Navy for shipbuilding.
(iv) (b) to increase agricultural land and generate revenue.

Part II

Very Short Answer Type Questions

1. Name at least six items around you which come from forests.

Ans. Some items around me which come from forests are paper in books, wood for desks and tables, dyes that colour my cloth, honey, coffee, tea, oil, tannin, etc.

2. What were the wooden planks laid down across railway tracks to hold tracks in a position called?

Ans. The wooden planks laid down across railway tracks to hold tracks in a position are called sleepers.

3. How many sleepers were required for each mile of railway track?

Ans. Each mile of railway track required between 1760 to 2000 sleepers.

4. How was Siadi creeper utilised?

Ans. Siadi creeper was utilised to make ropes.

5. Who were some of the tribal leaders of rebellions against British imposition in India?

Ans. Siddhu and Kanu in the Santhal Parganas, Birsa Munda of Chhotanagpur, and Alluri Sitarama Raju of Andhra Pradesh were some of the tribal leaders of rebellions against British imposition in India.

6. When was Forest Act, 1865 amended?

Ans. Forest Act, 1865 was amended twice, once in 1878 and then in 1927.

7. When was Bastar divided into three districts?

Ans. Bastar was divided into three districts, Kanker, Bastar and Dantewada in 1998.

8. From which tree, latex can be collected?

Ans. Latex can be collected from a rubber tree.

9. In 1905, the proposal of the Colonial Government caused tension among the people of Bastar. Some villagers were allowed to stay in the reserved forests on the condition that their people worked free for the forest department in cutting and transporting trees and protecting the forest from fire. Competency Based
What were the main reasons for the tension among the people of Bastar in 1905?

Ans. The main reasons for tension among the people of Bastar in 1905 were

- The colonial government proposed to reserve two-thirds of the forest, restricting shifting cultivation, hunting, and collection of forest produce. This caused worry among the people of Bastar.
- Villagers suffered from increased land rents, severe famine in 1899-1900 and 1907-1908 and faced oppression under colonial laws.

10. The Adivasi leaders tried to negotiate but the Britishers entered the villages and punished the villagers who took part in the rebellion. As a result, people fled into the forests.The British troops controlled the revolt after three months but not able to capture Gunda Dhur.
What can we infer about the impact of the rebellion on the relationship between the Adivasi communities and the British colonial government? Competency Based

Ans. We can infer that the rebellion had a negative impact on the relationship between the Adivasi communities and the British colonial government. The British troops were able to control the revolt but not able to capture Gunda Dhur. After the revolt, work on reservation was temporarily suspended, and the area to be reserved was reduced to roughly half of that planned before 1910.

11. The spread of railways from the 1850s created a new demand. Railways were essential for colonial trade and for the movement of imperial troops. To run locomotives, wood was needed as fuel, and to lay railway lines sleepers were essential to hold the tracks together.
How did the expansion of the railway network in India impact the surrounding environment, particularly in terms of deforestation?

Ans. The expansion of the railway network in India led to significant environmental consequences, particularly deforestation. By the 1850s, the Madras Presidency alone witnessed the felling of approximately 35,000 trees annually for sleepers, with contractors cutting trees indiscriminately. Consequently, as the railway tracks spread, forests surrounding them rapidly disappeared.

12. Large areas of natural forests were cleared to make way for tea, coffee and rubber plantations to meet Europe's growing need for these commodities. The colonial government took over the forests, and gave vast areas to European planters at cheap rates.
How did the British gave boost to plantation farming? Mention with example.

Ans. The British gave a boost to plantation farming by clearing large areas of natural forests to make way for tea, coffee and rubber plantations to meet Europe's growing need for these commodities.
For example, the extraction of rubber in the Putumayo region of the Amazon by the Peruvian Rubber Company.

13. The Kalangs of Java were a community of skilled forest cutters and shifting cultivators. They were so valuable that in 1755 when the Mataram kingdom of Java split, the 6,000 Kalang families were equally divided between the two kingdoms.
Which right was being violated in the above instance of struggle between tribe and British? Competency Based

Ans. Forest right was being violated in the above instance of struggle between Kalang tribe and British. The Kalangs were divided between two kingdoms and forced to work under the Dutch colonisers, who exploited their labour and resources.

Short Answer Type Questions

1. 'The expansion of cultivation is a sign of progress'. Do you agree with the statement? Justify your answer with arguments.

or **Explain any five reasons for the expansion of cultivation by the colonial rulers in India.**

Ans. In the colonial period, cultivation expanded for a variety of reasons. These are

(i) In Europe, foodgrains were needed to feed the growing urban population. The demand for wheat increased largely in the 19th century.
(ii) The colonial rulers considered the expansion of cultivation as a sign of progress.
(iii) The British government directly encouraged the production of commercial crops, like jute, sugar, wheat and cotton to get more profit.
(iv) Europe needed raw materials for industrial production.
(v) In the early 19th century, the colonial state thought that forests were unproductive so forests had to be brought under cultivation and land could yield agricultural products and revenue. In this way, the income of the state enhanced.

Thus, it can be concluded that expansion of cultivation is a sign of progress.

2. "The ship industry of England was also responsible for deforestation in India". Give one reason.

Ans. The ship industry of England was also responsible for deforestation in India because in the early 19th century, oak forests in England were disappearing due to the high demand. It created a problem of further timber supply for the Royal Navy of England which needed strong and durable timber to build ships.

As a result of this, the Britishers started exploring Indian forests for timber supply. Within a decade trees were cut on a large scale from Indian Forests and exported to England. Gradually, Indian forests started disappearing due to large scale export of timber for building ships.

3. When and why did the forests around railway tracks start disappearing very fast? Explain.

or **Why did forests around railway tracks in India start disappearing after 1860?**

Ans. The forests around railway tracks in India started disappearing rapidly after 1860 due to the increased demand for wood caused by the expansion of the railway network.

Railways became essential for colonial trade and the movement of imperial troops, leading to a surge in railway construction. Wood was required as fuel for locomotives, and sleepers were necessary to hold the tracks together, with each mile of railway track needing between 1,760 and 2,000 sleepers.

The expansion of the railway network from the 1860s onwards resulted in a significant increase in the number of trees being felled to meet the demand for sleepers and fuel. Government contracts were given to individuals to supply the required quantities of wood, leading to indiscriminate cutting of trees by contractors, which accelerated the disappearance of forests around railway tracks.

4. Explain any four ideas of Dietrich Brandis for the management of forests in India during the British period.

or **Who was Dietrich Brandis? Explain his achievement in India.**

Ans. Dietrich Brandis, a German expert, was appointed the first Inspector-General of Forests in India. His ideas and achievements for the management of forests are stated in the points below

- He formulated new forest legislation and helped to establish research and training institutions. The Imperial Forest Research Institute at Dehradun was founded by him in 1906.
- He set up the Indian Forest Service (IFS) in 1864 and helped to formulate the Indian Forest Act of 1865.
- He took an interest in the forest flora of North-West and Central India and Indian trees.
- He was among the earliest expert in India to formally link forest protection with local people.

5. What were the defects of 'Scientific Forestry' technique?

or **Describe the defects in the techniques of 'Scientific Forestry'.**

Ans. In 1906, the Imperial Forest Research Institute was set up at Dehradun and 'Scientific Forestry' was introduced in India. But ecologists believe that this system is not scientific at all and has many defects.

The defects in the techniques of 'scientific forestry were

- In this system, natural forest diversity was harmed because different types of trees were cut down.
- This system advocated only those trees in forests which provided timber. It snatched the different needs of forest dwellers.

  The forest dwellers wanted a mixture of species of trees for their fuel, fodder and food.
- It also affected the ecological balance, as multi- species forest gradually got converted into plantation.

6. Why did the Colonial Government start commercial forestry in India? Give any three reasons.

Ans. The British Colonial Government started commercial forestry in India due to following reasons

(i) By the early 19th century, oak forests in England were disappearing. The colonial government needed timber supply for the Royal navy and railways which were essential for the movement of imperial troops and commercial trade.

(ii) The Colonial Government took over the forests in India and gave vast areas to European planters at cheap rates. These areas were enclosed and planted with tea and coffee.

(iii) The British government was worried about the reckless use of forests by the local people.

British needed trees that could provide hard wood and were tall and straight. So, particular species like *teak* and *sal* trees were promoted by them. Thus, commercial forestry was started by the Britishers and Indian Forest Act was passed in 1865.

7. What are the local names of shifting cultivation in South East Asia, Central America and Sri Lanka? Describe any three features of shifting cultivation.

Ans. Shifting cultivation is a traditional agricultural practice in many parts of Asia, Africa and South America.

It has different local names in different areas, *viz.*,

- In South-East Asia it is known as lading.
- In Central America it is known as milpa.
- In Africa it is known as chitemene or tavy.
- In Sri Lanka it is known as chena

The main features of shifting cultivation are

(i) Parts of forest are cut and burnt in rotation.

(ii) Seeds are sown in the ashes after the first monsoon rains and the crop is harvested by October-November.

(iii) A mixture of crops is grown on such plots for a couple of years and then left fallow for 12 to 18 years for the forest to grow back.

8. Under colonial rule, why did the scale of hunting increase to such an extent that various species became almost extinct?

Ans. Under British rule, the scale of hunting increased to such an extent that various species became almost extinct. The reasons behind this condition were

- The British saw large animals as signs of a wild, primitive and savage society.
- They believed that by killing dangerous animals the British would civilise India.
- They gave rewards for the killing of tigers, wolves and other large animals on the grounds that they posed a threat to cultivators.
- Certain areas of forests were reserved for hunting.

9. Who worked as plantation workers and what were the working conditions?

Ans. The British Government recruited tribals like Santhals, Oraons (Jharkhand) and Gonds (Chattisgarh) as plantation workers.

The working condition of plantation workers were

- Plantation workers were getting low wages.
- They did not receive any social security benefit.
- They were not allowed to go to their native place.

10. How did the rebellion of the people of Bastar take place against the British?

Ans. The rebellion of the people of Bastar took place in the following ways

- Initiative of Rebellion was taken by Dhurwas of the Kanger forest to organise people. It is said that many people protested under leadership of Gunda Dhur.
- They looted Bazaars, houses of officials and traders, schools and police stations were burnt and robbed and grains were redistributed among the people.
- They attacked anyone who were in some way or other associated with colonial state and its oppressive laws.

11. What were the beliefs of people of Bastar?

Ans. There were different communities, *viz*, Maria and Muria Gonds, Dhurwa, Bhatras and Halbas who lived in Bastar. All of them shared common beliefs and customs.

Their beliefs were

- They believed that each village was given its land by the Earth. In return the villagers had to look after the Earth by making some offerings at each agricultural festival.
- The villagers believed and show respect to the spirits of the river, the forest and the mountain.
- The villagers looked after all the natural resources within the boundaries of their village as their duty.

12. What new developments have occurred in forestry in Asia and Africa in recent times?

Ans. New developments which have occurred in Asia and Africa in recent times are

- Asian and African Governments introduced social forestry and the policy of keeping forest communities away from forests. Conservation of forests rather than collecting timber was their primary aim.
- In order to preserve the forests, the government realised that the involvement of people living near the forests is must. Infact, across India from Mizoram to Kerala dense forests have survived only because villagers protected them in sacred groves known as Sarnas, Devarakudu, Kan, Rai, etc.
- Some villagers protected their own forest with each household taking it in turns instead of leaving it to forest guards.

13. Discuss the most likely impact if India operated without Forest Act. **Competency Based**

Build the answer around these points

- **Indian Forest Service**
- **Sustainable management**
- **Three categories of forest**

Ans. If India operated without the Forest Act, the following impacts would likely occur

- The Forest Act established the Indian Forest Service, without this service, there would be a lack of trained professionals dedicated to forest management and conservation.
- The Forest Act provided guidelines for the sustainable management of forests, including regulations on logging and conservation practices. Without these regulations, forests would be at risk of overexploitation and degradation, leading to loss of biodiversity, soil erosion, and other environmental issues.
- The Forest Act of 1878 categorised forests into reserved, protected, and village forests, with reserved forests receiving the highest level of protection. Without this categorisation and the accompanying regulations, there would be no formal distinction between different types of forests, potentially leading to the neglect or overuse of valuable forest ecosystems.

14. Read the statements given below regarding shifting cultivation.

Statement I Parts of the forest are cut and burnt in rotation.

Statement II European foresters regarded this practice as harmful.

Explain what trend do these statements - S1 and S2 - reflect in the agricultural sector in India. **Competency Based**

Ans. **Statement I** reflects the traditional practice of shifting cultivation, where farmers clear small portions of forest land by cutting down trees and burning the vegetation to create space for cultivation. This method has been practiced for centuries by indigenous communities in various parts of India.

Statement II reflects European foresters, representing modern scientific perspectives, who viewed shifting cultivation as harmful to the environment and unsustainable in the long term. They criticised this practice for its contribution to deforestation, soil erosion, loss of biodiversity, and inefficiency in land and resource use, and advocated for alternative, more sustainable farming methods.

15. Siddhu and Kanu fought from the same place, Santhal Parganas. Why did they organise revolt against British. What do you think? Write the significance of the revolt.

Ans. Siddhu and Kanu were the leaders of the Santhal rebellion, which was an uprising of the Santhal tribe against the British colonial rule and the zamindari system in 1855-56.

They organised the revolt because they were exploited by the British, the zamindars, the moneylenders, and the local non-tribals, who took away their lands, resources, and rights.

The significance of this revolt was that it was one of the earliest and largest tribal rebellions in India. It inspired other tribal and peasant movements in India, such as the Munda rebellion, etc. It highlighted the aspirations of the tribal communities in India.

16. After Independence, the same practice of keeping people out of the forests and reserving them for industrial use continued. In the 1970s, the World Bank proposed that 4,600 hectares of natural Sal forest should be replaced by tropical pine to provide pulp for the paper industry.

Why do you think forestry is becoming so popular in India? Substantiate your answer giving any three reasons. **Competency Based**

Ans. Forestry is becoming increasingly popular in India due to several compelling reasons

- Forestry serves as a significant rural industry, supporting the livelihoods of millions of people. Forest products such as timber, Non-timber Forest Produce (NTFP) and medicinal plants provide income to forest-dependent communities.
- Forests are recognised as a potential source of renewable energy, which is crucial for reducing dependence on fossil fuels.
- India faces challenges related to soil erosion and desertification in many regions.. By planting trees and restoring degraded lands, forestry contributes to soil conservation, water retention and overall improvement in soil health.

Long Answer Type Questions

1. How did the British exploit the forests resource of India for their economic development?

Ans. The British exploited the forests resources of India for their economic development in the following ways

- By the early 19th century, oak forests in England were disappearing, British needed timber supply for their Royal Navy and they sent search parties to explore forest resources of India in 1820. Within a decade vast quantities of timber were being exported from India.
- Britishers also needed the expansion of railways for their colonial trade. To run locomotives, they needed wood and also for railway tracks they needed timber supply. They met these needs by exploiting forest resources of India.
- Large areas of natural forests were cleared to make way for tea, coffee and rubber plantations to meet Europe's growing need for these commodities. For this purpose, the Colonial Government took over the forests and gave vast areas to European planters at cheap rates.
- In the colonial period, cultivation expanded rapidly. The British directly encouraged the production of commercial crops like jute, sugar wheat and cotton. These crops were demanded for the consumption of urban population and also for the raw materials needed in industrial production.
- The colonial power thought that forests were unproductive, so they tried to expand agriculture by clearing forests which would enhance the revenue of the state. Between 1880 and 1920, cultivated area in India rose by 6.7 million hectares.

2. Why and how were plantations started in Colonial India?

Ans. Plantations started in colonial India due to the following reasons

- The colonial power thought the forests as unproductive.
- There was a demand for raw materials for industrial production in England in the 19th century.
- The Britishers wanted to enhance the revenue from lands by transforming the forests into agricultural land.
- The colonial government wanted to control the misuse of forest by local people as in shifting cultivation.

The plantations were started in the following ways

- To start plantation industry government gave vast areas of forest to contractors and European planters at cheap rates.
- The European planters started reckless felling of trees to make way for tea, coffee and rubber plantations.
- The British Government appointed German expert Dietrich Brandis as first inspector General of Forest. He recommended formation of rules and regulation of Forest Management and helped to formulate Indian Forest Act, 1865.
- Scientific forestry was introduced when forest was cleared for plantation.

3. How did the Forest Act affect the lives of foresters and villagers?

or **How did Forest Act mean severe hardship for villagers across the country? Explain.**

or **How far do you agree that Forest Act affected the lives of villagers?**

Ans. The 1878 Forest Act divided forests in India into three categories: reserved, protected and village forests.

The following points show the effect of Forest Act on the lives of foresters and villagers

- Villagers wanted forests with a mixture of species to satisfy different needs–fuel, fodder and leaves. Villagers could not take anything from 'reserved' forests. For house building or fuel, they could take wood from protected or village forests.
- On the other hand, forest department needed trees that could provide hard, tall and straight woods for commercial use. So, they encouraged to plant only teak and sal and other trees should be cut.
- In forest areas, people use forest products roots, leaves, fruits, tuber, etc. Almost everything is available in the forest for their livelihood.
- The Forest Act meant severe hardship for them. All their everyday practices of cutting wood for their houses, grazing their cattle, collecting fruits and roots, hunting and fishing became illegal.
- Villagers were forced to steal wood and if they were caught, they were at the mercy of the forest-guards, who even claimed bribe from them.
- Women who collected fuelwood were scared of the forest guards. It became common practice for police constables and forest guards to harass villagers by demanding free food for themselves.

Thus, it can be concluded that the forest act brought severe hardship for villagers across the country.

4. Explain how did the lives of forest-dwellers change after the forest department took over control of the forests? Mention any five points.

Ans. The forest department took control of the forests by introducing the Forest Act of 1865 and 1878.

The life of forest-dwellers changed after the act in the following ways

- After this act, some people benefitted from the new opportunities, they left their traditional occupations and started trading in forest products.
- The British Government took total control of the trade in forest products. They gave many large European trading firms the sole right to trade in the forest products of particular areas.
- Grazing and hunting by local people were restricted. Many pastoralist and nomadic communities like the Korava, Karacha, Yerukula of Madras Presidency and Banjaras lost their livelihoods.
- Some tribals were branded as 'criminal tribes' and they lost their old occupations and were forced to work in factories, mines and plantation under government supervision and were offered a very low wage. In this way, the lives offorest- dwellers were completely changed after the forest department took over control of the forests.

5. What is Swidden agriculture? Where is it practiced? Describe its main features.

Ans. Swidden agriculture or shifting cultivation is a traditional agricultural practice where cultivators used to cut certain parts of the forest in rotation. Then they burn the trees and sow seeds in ashes after the monsoon rains.

It is practiced in many parts of Asia, Africa and South America. It has many local names like lading in South-East Asia, milpa in Central America, chitemene or tavy in Africa, chena in Sri Lanka.

In India, dhya, penda, bewar, nevad, jhum, podu, khandad and kumri are some of the local terms for swidden agriculture.

Main features of Swidden agriculture are

- Seeds are sown in the ashes after the first monsoon rains.
- The crop is harvested in October-November.
- These crops are cultivated for couple of years and then, they are left fallow for 12 to 18 years to allow the forest to grow back.
- A mixture of crops is grown on the plots.

6. Why did the people of Bastar rise in revolt against the British? Explain.

or **How did the people of Bastar react against the British forest policies? What were its consequences?**

Ans. The people of Bastar rose in revolt due to the following reasons

- When the colonial power proposed to reserve two-thirds of the forest in 1905 and stop shifting cultivation, hunting and collection of forest product, the people of Bastar became worried.
- Some people of Bastar were allowed to stay in 'forest villages' on the condition that they worked for the forest department and protected the forest from fires. Other people were displaced without any notice or compensation.
- For long the villagers had been suffering from increased land rents and frequent demands for free labour and goods by colonial officials.
- Moreover, there were two terrible famines, one in 1899-1900 and other in 1907-1908. This made the condition of people of Bastar worse therefore they rose in revolt.

In this revolt, the rebels looted the Bazaars, the houses of officials and traders. Schools and police stations were burnt and robbed and grains were redistributed.

The consequences of the revolt were

- The British troops suppressed the rebellion. Adivasis fled into jungles, their leader Gunda Dhur could not be captured.
- In a major victory for the rebels, work on reservation was temporarily suspended and the area to be reserved was reduced to roughly half of that planned before 1910.

7. Why were the Kalangas of Java considered an important community? What compelled them to rebel against the Dutch and to what extent?

Ans. Kalangas community of Java were very important due to their expertise in forest cutting and shifting cultivation. Their importance could be realised by the fact that they were divided into two parts when Mataram Kingdom of Java was split into two parts.

Without their expertise, harvesting teak and building palaces were impossible. The Kalangas rebelled against Dutch for the following reasons

- Dutch introduced forest laws to restrict villager's access to forest. Forest laws specified that wood could be only used for making river boats and houses.
- Villagers were punished for grazing cattle or transporting wood without a permit.
- Imposition of rents on land being cultivated which was later exempted on condition of free supply of labour and buffaloes.

The Kalangas in 1770 revolted against the Dutch. But their revolt was not successful as they were brutally suppressed by the Dutch forces.

8. Describe the Saminist Movement in Indonesia.

Ans. The Saminist Movement started in the last decade of the 19th century in Java. Surontiko Samin of Randublatung village, a teak forest village headed this movement. The reason of this movement was that the Dutch government forced the farmers to pay taxes on land and restricted villagers' access to forest by enacting the Forest Law in Java.

This movement was started when Samin questioned state ownership of the forest. He argued that the state had not created the wind, water, Earth and wood, so it could not own it. By 1907, three thousand families started following the ideas of Samin. Some of the rebels in this movement protested by lying down on their land, when the Dutch came to survey the land. Some even refused to pay taxes or fines or perform free labour.

9. Read the information given below regarding Dutch Forest Laws and answer the question that follows.

In the 19th century, the Dutch enacted forest laws in Java, restricting villagers' access to forests. This law permitted use of forest wood only for specified purposes from specific forests under close supervision. Villagers were punished for grazing cattle, transporting wood without a permit or travelling on forest roads with horse carts or cattle. In 1882, 280,000 sleepers were exported from Java. However, all this required labour to cut the trees, transport the logs and prepare the sleepers. The Dutch imposed rents on land being cultivated in the forest.

Analyse the result of Dutch Forest Laws in terms of its impact-negative and/or positive-on forest people, British and the forest. Competency Based

Ans. The Dutch Law enacted in 19th century allows forest use only for very specific purposes which affected forest people, forest and the British hardly in the following ways

- The law limited the forest resources for forest people which were earlier used for collecting firewood, grazing cattle and shifting cultivation.
- This law limited their livelihood options and increased dependence on the british people.This law forced them to work as a forced labour.
- British people now had to pay higher than earlier for timber resource for their railway project. The focus on commercial timber extraction led to rapid deforestation, exceeding sustainable levels. This caused soil erosion, loss of biodiversity and disruption of ecological balance.

The positive impacts were

- Villagers received income through participation in the forestry industry, though underpaid.

- As forest access was restricted and the laws prevented uncontrolled deforestation by local communities compared to pre-colonial times. The forest law provide conservation of forest resource to some extent.
- The laws ensured a steady supply of high-quality teak for British infrastructure projects. Also, it provided them forced labour for their work at very low wage.

10. A think-tank has been given the task to design an outline to measure how world war caused deforestation during colonial period. Competency Based

Discuss the key indicators that the think-tank should consider while designing this outline.

Ans. The first and second world war was one of the major reasons for deforestation in India and other colonies in the following ways

- **Increased Timber Extraction** Colonial powers like the British intensified timber extraction during wartime for building infrastructure.
- **Scorched Earth Policies** Dutch tactics in Java during World War II, aimed at resource denial, led to deliberate burning of timber resources, worsening deforestation.
- **Impact of Japanese Occupation** Japanese exploitation of remaining forests in occupied colonies increased deforestation and environmental degradation.
- **Post-War Impact and Land Conflicts** Wartime disruptions enabled local expansion into forested areas Post-World War II, sparking conflicts with forest departments, perpetuating deforestation.
- **Legacy of Colonial Forest Management** Prioritisation of commercial extraction over sustainability by colonial forest management fueled ongoing exploitation and deforestation, highlighting the enduring impact of colonialism on forests.

Case Based Questions

1. Read the sources given below and answer the questions that follow.

Source A New laws for the people of Bastar

When the colonial government proposed to reserve two-thirds of the forest in 1905, and stop shifting cultivation, hunting and collection of forest produce, the people of Bastar were very worried. Some villages were allowed to stay on in the reserved forests on the condition that they worked free for the forest department in cutting and transporting trees, and protecting the forest from fires.

Subsequently, these came to be known as 'forest villages'. People of other villages were displaced without any notice or compensation. For long, villagers had been suffering from increased land rents and frequent demands for free labour and goods by colonial officials. Then came the terrible famines, in 1899-1900 and again in 1907-1908. Reservations proved to be the last straw.

(i) Evaluate the causes of suffering of the villagers of Bastar during the British rule.

Source B Rebellion started in Bastar

People began to gather and discuss these issues in their village councils, in bazaars and at festivals or wherever the headmen and priests of several villages were assembled. The initiative was taken by the Dhurwas of the Kanger forest, where reservation first took place. Although, there was no single leader, many people speak of Gunda Dhur, from village Nethanar, as an important figure in the movement. In 1910, mango boughs, a lump of Earth, chillies and arrows, began circulating between villages.

These were actually messages inviting villagers to rebel against the British. Every village contributed something to the rebellion expenses. Bazaars were looted, the houses of officials and traders, schools and police stations were burnt and robbed, and grain redistributed.

Most of those who were attacked were in some way associated with the colonial state and its oppressive laws.

(ii) To what extent the messages which were sent to villagers to rebel against the British inspired the villagers.

Source C Victory for the Rebels

The British sent troops to suppress the rebellion. The adivasi leaders tried to negotiate, but the British surrounded their camps and fired upon them. After that they marched through the villages flogging and punishing those who had taken part in the rebellion. Most villages were deserted as people fled into the jungles. It took three months (February-May) for the British to regain control.

However, they never managed to capture Gunda Dhur. In a major victory for the rebels, work on reservation was temporarily suspended, and the area to be reserved was reduced to roughly half of that planned before 1910.

(iii) The rebels were victorious even after they suppressed. Explain this in context of Bastar rebellion.

Ans. (i) During the British rule, people of Bastar suffered from the following causes

- Increased land rents.
- Frequent demands for free labour and goods by colonial officials.
- Two terrible famines, one in 1899-1900 and another in 1907-1908.

(ii) The messages that were sent to villagers of Bastar to rebel against the British include mango boughs, a lump of Earth, chillies and arrows, etc. After getting these, people started to unite and revolt against the British in Bastar.

(iii) The rebels were some how victorious because their leader Gunda Dhur was not captured and the Britishers were forced to suspend the work on reservation and the area to be reserved was reduced to half.

2. Read the source given below and answer the questions that follow.

One of the major impacts of European colonialism was on the practice of shifting cultivation or swidden agriculture. This is a traditional agricultural practice in many parts of Asia, Africa and South America. It has many local names such as lading in Southeast Asia, milpa in Central America, chitemene or tavy in Africa, and chena in Sri Lanka. In India, dhya, penda, bewar, nevad, jhum, podu, khandad and kumri are some of the local terms for swidden agriculture. In shifting cultivation, parts of the forest are cut and burnt in rotation.

Seeds are sown in the ashes after the first monsoon rains, and the crop is harvested by October-November. Such plots are cultivated for a couple of years and then left fallow for 12 to 18 years for the forest to grow back. A mixture of crops is grown on these plots. In central India and Africa it could be millets, in Brazil manioc and in other parts of Latin America maize and beans.

European foresters regarded this practice as harmful for the forests. They felt that land which was used for cultivation every few years could not grow trees for railway timber.

When a forest was burnt, there was the added danger of the flames spreading and burning valuable timber.

(i) Shifting cultivation is a traditional practice in many parts of the world. Explain.

(ii) How do you justify the name of agricultural practice 'shifting cultivation'?

(iii) European foresters thought shifting cultivation as harmful for the forests. Given reasons.

Ans. (i) Shifting cultivation is a traditional practice of agriculture where parts of land are cultivated for a period of time, then left fallow for sometime and cultivation is done in another land. This method is practiced in many parts of Asia, Africa and South America. This shifting cultivation is a popular way of cultivation in world.

(ii) In shifting or Swidden cultivation, an area of ground is cleared for vegetation and cultivated for a few years and then abandoned for a new area until its fertility has been naturally restored.

Sometimes land is left for 12 to 18 years for the forest to grow back. After the land restores its fertility, the agricultural process is again started on this land. Thus, this process of agriculture in known as shifting cultivation.

(iii) European foresters regarded Shifting Cultivation as harmful for the forests for the following reasons

- They felt that land which was used for cultivation every few years could not grow trees for railway timber.
- When a forest was burnt, there was a danger of the flames spreading and burning valuable timber.
- Shifting cultivation also made it harder for the government to calculate taxes.

ASSESSMENT EXERCISE

Multiple Choice Questions (MCQs)

1. Who is the author of the book 'The Forest of India'?

(a) Dietrich Brandis (b) EP Stebbing

(c) Michael Taussig (d) None of these

2. In the colonial period, which animal was used to lift heavy timber?

(a) Buffalo (b) Cow

(c) Elephant (d) None of these

3. Match the following.

List I	List II
A. The Indian Forest Service	1. 1906
B. The Indian Forest Act	2. 1864
C. Imperial Forest Research Institute	3. 1865

Codes

	A	B	C		A	B	C
(a)	2	3	1	(b)	1	2	3
(c)	3	2	1	(d)	2	1	3

4. **Assertion** (A) The Forest Act meant severe hardship for villagers across the country.

Reason (R) Foresters and villagers had very different ideas of what a good forest should look like.

Codes

(a) Both A and R are true and R is the correct explanation of A

(b) Both A and R are true, but R is not the correct explanation of A

(c) A is true, but R is false

(d) A is false, but R is true

Subjective Questions (VSA, SA & LA)

1. What was the major source of income for many people living in forests?

2. Name the colonial power which ruled Java.

3. What was a good forest according to villagers? How did they benefit from it?

4. What do you mean by Devsari?

5. Explain 'Scorched Earth Policy'.

6. How did life change in India after the forest department took control of forests?

7. Why were the forests important to the villagers?

8. What was the impact of regulation of trade in forest products by British Government in India?

9. Give an account of colonial management of forests in Bastar and Java.

Pastoralists in the Modern World

CHAPTER 5

Pastoralism is a way of keeping animals such as goats, sheep, camels and cattle. It involves moving from one place to another in search of water and food. Pastoralism has been in practice in societies like India and Africa for years.

5.1 Pastoral Nomads and their Movements

Nomads are people who do not live in one place, but move from one area to another to earn their living.

Pastoral Communities in the Mountains

Gujjar Bakarwals, Gaddi Shepherds, Bhotiyas, Sherpas and Kinnauris are pastoral communities found in the mountains.

Gujjar Bakarwals

Gujjar Bakarwals migrated and settled in **Jammu and Kashmir** in the 19th century in search of pastures for their goat and sheep.

They move annually between their summer and winter grazing grounds in groups known as ***kafila***.

In winter, when the mountains were covered with snow, they lived with their herds in the low hills of **Siwalik range**. Here, the dry scrub forests provided pastures for their herds.

In summer (by the end of April), they crossed the Pir Panjal passes and entered Kashmir valley. The snow melted and the mountainsides were lush and green. The variety of sprouted grass here provided rich nutritious food for their animals.

By the end of September, they used to start moving again for their downward journey.

The Gujjar cattle herders live in the **mandaps**, made of ringal (a hill bamboo) and grass from the Bugyals[1].

The mandaps were also used as work places. Here, they used to make ghee which they sold. These mandaps are situated at a height of about 10,000 to 11,000 feet, as buffaloes can not climb any higher.

Further to the East in Garhwal and Kumaon, the Gujjar cattle herders came down to the dry forests of the **Bhabar** in the winter and went up to the high meadows-the Bugyals in summer.

Many of these people were originally from Jammu and came to the UP hills in the 19th century in search of good pastures.

Gaddi Shepherds

This a pastoral community of **Himachal Pradesh**. It had a similar cycle of seasonal movements like Gujjar Bakarwals.

During winter, Gaddi Shepherds grazed their flocks in scrub forests of the low hills of Siwalik range. By April, they moved North and spent the summer in **Lahul** and **Spiti**.

When the snow melted and the high passes were clear they moved onto higher mountain meadows (*dhars*).

By September, they began their return movement. On the way, they stopped once again in the villages of Lahul and Spiti, to reap their summer harvest and sow their winter crop. Further down, they stopped to shear their sheep. The sheep are bathed and cleaned before wool is cut.

Uhl valley near Palampur in Himachal Pradesh is one of the areas where shearing of wool is done. Then, they further moved to their winter base i.e. the Siwalik hills.

In April, they began their march once again with their cattle to the summer meadows.

Bhotiyas, Sherpas and Kinnauris

Many pastoralists of Himalayas like the Bhotiyas, Sherpas and Kinnauris also follow Cyclic movement between summers and winters in search of pastures.

They all had to adjust to seasonal changes and make proper use of available pastures.

1 Bugyals These are vast natural pastures on the high mountains, above 12,000 feet. They are under snow in the winter and come to life after April.

When the pastures exhausted or became unusable in one place, they moved their herds and flock to new areas. This continuous movement of the pastoralists allowed the pastures to recover and prevented their overuse.

On the Plateaus, Plains and Deserts

Pastoralists were also found in the plateaus, plains and deserts of India.

Dhangars, Gollas, Kurumas, Kurubas, Banjaras, Raikas and Maldharis are the pastoral communities found in the plateaus, plains and deserts of India.

Dhangars

Dhangars were an important pastoral community of **Maharashtra**. In the early 20th century, their population in this region was more about 4,67,000. They were mainly shepherds, blanket weavers and buffalo herders.

The Dhangar shepherds stayed in the Central Plateau of Maharashtra during the monsoon. This was a semi-arid region with low rainfall and poor soil which was covered with thorny scrub. Dry crops like bajra were sown here.

In the monsoon, Central Plateau tract become a vast grazing ground for their cattle.

By October, the Dhangars harvested the bajra and started to move towards Konkan in West. Here, they were welcomed by the Konkani peasants.

After the harvest of **kharif**[2] crop, the fields had to be fertilised and made ready for the **rabi**[3] harvest. Dhangar cattle manured the fields and fed on the **stubble**[4].

The Konkani peasants also gave supplies of rice to the shepherds when they returned back on the onset of monsoon. The sheep couldn't tolerate the wet monsoon conditions.

The Gollas, Kurumas and Kurubas

These are important Pastoral communities of the dry Central Plateau of **Karnataka** and **Andhra Pradesh**. The Gollas herded cattle. The Kurumas and Kurubas reared sheep and goats, and sold woven blankets.

These pastoralists lived near the forests, cultivated small patches of land, engaged in a variety of small trades and took care of their herds.

The movement of these pastoralists depended on monsoon and dry season. In the dry season, they moved to the coastal areas and left when the rains came.

Only buffaloes liked the swampy, wet conditions of the coastal areas during the monsoon months. Other herds were shifted to the dry plateau at this time.

Banjaras

They were an important group of graziers, which were found in the villages of **Uttar Pradesh, Punjab, Rajasthan, Madhya Pradesh** and **Maharashtra**.

In search of good pasture land for their cattle, they moved over long distances. They sold their plough cattle and other goods to villagers in exchange of grain and fodder.

Raikas

They lived in the deserts of **Rajasthan**. Due to the small and uncertain rainfall, harvest was irregular in this region. So, they combined cultivation with pastoralism.

During the monsoon, the Raikas of Barmer, Jaisalmer, Jodhpur and Bikaner stayed in their home villages where pasture was available.

By October, they moved out in search of other pastures and water and returned again during the next monsoon.

One group of Raikas were known as **Maru Raikas** who herded camels and another group reared sheep and goat. The settlement of Maru Raikas is called a **dhandi**.

Factors that Contributed to Movement of Pastoralists

- Pastoralists had to judge how long the herds could stay in one area and know where they could find water and pasture.
- They needed to calculate the timing of their movements and ensure that they could move through different territories.
- They had to set up a relationship with farmers on the way, so that the herds could graze in harvested fields and manure the soil.
- They combined a range of different activities *viz*, cultivation, trade and herding to make their living.

Try These

1 **Gaddi shepherds belong to which state?**
2 **Name the pastoral community from Maharashtra.**
3 **Name a pastoral community of the dry Central Plateau of Karnataka and Andhra Pradesh.**
4 **Which group of Raikas tribe herded camels?**

2 **Kharif** It is autumn crop, usually harvested between September and October.
3 **Rabi** It is spring crop, usually harvested after March.
4 **Stubble** It is the lower end of grain stalks left in the ground after harvesting.

5.2 Colonial Rule and Pastoral Life

Under colonial rule the life of pastoralists changed dramatically. The Colonial Government made different laws for pastoralists.

Their grazing grounds shrank, movements were regulated, they had to pay high tax, their agricultural stock declined and their trades and crafts were affected adversely.

Wasteland Rules

Land revenue was one of the main sources of finance for the colonial state. So they wanted to transform all grazing lands into cultivated farms to increase land revenue.

Land was also required to increase production of wheat, cotton, jute and other agricultural products that England needed.

For colonial officials all uncultivated land was unproductive, it produced neither revenue nor agricultural produce. It was seen as **waste land** that needed to be brought under cultivation.

From the mid-19th century, wasteland rules were enacted in various parts of our country. According to these rules, uncultivated lands were taken over and given to selected individuals who were given different concessions for settlement. Some were even made village headmen. In most areas, the lands which were taken over were the grazing lands used by the pastoralists.

Forest Acts

The Forest Acts made by the British Government changed the lives of pastoralists. Some forests which produced commercially valuable timber like *deodar* or *sal* were declared as **reserved.** In the reserved forests, no pastoralist was allowed.

Other forests were considered as **protected** where some customary grazing rights of pastoralists were granted, but their movements were strictly restricted.

The colonial officials thought that grazing destroyed the saplings and shoots which prevented new trees from growing.

The Forest Acts changed the lives of pastoralists. They were now prevented from entering many forests where they used to find valuable forage[5] for their cattle.

In the areas where they were allowed to enter, their movements were regulated. They needed a permit for entry. The timing of their entry and departure was specified and the number of days they could spend in the forest was limited.

They couldn't stay in the area even if there was enough food, and they had to move because the permits from the forest department controlled their lives with fines for staying too long.

Criminal Tribes Act

British officials were very suspicious of nomadic people. They wanted to rule over a settled population which could be easily identified and controlled. Those who were settled were seen as peaceable and law abiding; those who were nomadic were considered to be criminal.

In 1871, the British Government in India passed the Criminal Tribes Act. This act classified communities of craftsmen, traders and pastoralists as **Criminal Tribes.**

As a result of this Act, these communities were expected to live only in notified village settlements and they were not allowed to move without a permit.

Imposition of Grazing Tax

To expand the revenue income, the Colonial Government imposed the tax on land, canal water, on salt and on trade goods.

In the mid-19th century, **Grazing Tax** was introduced by British Government in most pastoral lands of India.

In order to increase income, the government imposed tax even on animals. The tax on the cattle was increased and the system of collection was made increasingly efficient.

In the decades between the 1850s and 1880s, the right to collect the tax was given to contractors. By the 1880s, the government began collecting taxes directly from the pastoralists. To enter a grazing tract, the cattle herder had to show his pass and pay the tax. The number of cattle heads he had and the amount of tax he paid was entered on the pass.

Effects of Colonial Changes on the Lives of Pastoralists

- There was serious shortage of pastures as grazing lands were turned into cultivable land.
- The shepherds and cattle herds could no longer freely graze their cattle in the forests.
- As pasture lands were converted into cultivated land, the existing animal stock had to feed on remaining grazing land.
- Nomadic people had to move frequently from one place to another in search of pastures.
- Animal stock was declined as underfed cattle died in large numbers during scarcities and famines.

5 Forag It refers to plants that are grown for horses and cows.

Ways by which Pastoralists Cope with Changes

- Some pastoralists reduced the number of cattle in their herds, since there was not enough pasture to feed large numbers.
- Some pastoralists discovered new pastures when movement to old grazing grounds became difficult.
- After 1947, the camel and sheep herding Raikas, could no longer move into Sindh (Pakistan) and graze their camels on the banks of the Indus. In recent year, they have been migrating to Haryana where sheep can graze on agricultural fields after the harvests are cut.
- Some richer pastoralists began buying land and settling down, giving up their nomadic life.
- Many poor pastoralists borrowed money from moneylenders to survive. Some of them became labourers, working on fields or in small towns.
- Pastoralists have not only survived but have also increased in number in recent years. When grazing lands were closed, they adapted by changing their routes, keeping smaller herds, finding other sources of income, and adjusting to modern life. Many ecologists believe that in dry areas and mountains, pastoralism remains the most suitable way of living.

Try These

1. **By which act many pastoral communities were classified as criminal tribes?**
2. **From which century wasteland rules were enacted in our country?**
3. **The Forest Act made by the British changed the life of whom?**
4. **Which forests are producing 'deodar' or 'sal'?**
5. **Which act classified communities of craftsmen, traders and pastoralists as Criminal Tribes?**

5.3 Pastoralism in Africa

Africa is a country where over half the world's pastoral population lives. Even now, over 22 million Africans depend on some forms of pastoral activities for their livelihood.

The different pastoral communities of Africa are *Bedouins, Berbers, Maasai, Somali, Boran* and *Turkana*. Most of them lived in semi arid grasslands where rainfed agriculture is difficult.

Pastoralists of Africa raise cattle, camels, goats, sheep and donkeys. They sell milk, meat, animal skin and wool. Some of them earn through trade and transport. Others did a variety of odd jobs to supplements their small earning from pastoralism.

Like pastoralists in India, the lives of African pastoralists have changed dramatically over the colonial and post-colonial periods.

Maasai Community

The Maasai cattle herders live primarily in East Africa in Southern Kenya and Tanzania.

The Maasai are nomadic and pastoral people who depend on milk and meat for subsistence.

The title Maasai derives from the word 'Maa'. Maa-sai means 'My People'. Maasai believed that tilling the land for crop farming is a crime against nature.

Effect of Colonial Rule on Maasai Community

- Massais lost their grazing lands. Before colonial rules, Maasailand stretched over a vast area from North Kenya to the steppes of Northern Tanzania. In the late 19th century, European imperial powers divided the region into different colonies.
  After colonial rule, best grazing lands of Maasai community were gradually taken over for white settlement and the Maasai were pushed into a small area in South Kenya and North Tanzania.
- From the late 19th century, the British Colonial Government in East Africa also encouraged local peasant communities to expand cultivation. As cultivation expanded, pasturelands were turned into cultivated fields. The Maasai community lost about 60% of their land and were confined to an arid zone with uncertain rainfall and poor pastures.
- In 1885, Maasailand was cut into half with an International boundary between British Kenya and German Tanganyika.
  Large areas of grazing land were turned into game reserve like the Maasai Mara and Samburu National Park in Kenya and Serengeti Park in Tanzania.

The effects of turning grazing lands into cultivated field and the Maasais losing their lands were as follows

- Without grass of pasture lands, livestock (cattle, goats and sheep) were malnourished, which meant less food available for Maasai people and their families.
- The loss of finest grazing lands and water resources created a serious problem for the pastoralists to feed their cattle.
- The Kilimanjaro Water Project cuts through the communities of the area near Amboseli National Park but the villagers are barred from using the water for irrigation or for livestock.

The Borders are Closed

In late 19th century, Colonial Government began imposing various restriction on the movements of pastoralists in Africa.

Pastoral groups were forced to live within the boundaries of special reserves. They were not allowed to move out with their stock without special permits.

It was difficult to get permits without trouble and harassment. Those found guilty of disobeying the rules were severely punished. They were not even allowed to trade and enter the markets in white areas.

In many places, pastoralists were banned from trading. White settlers and European colonists saw them as dangerous and uncivilised. However, they could not completely avoid contact because they needed black workers to dig mines, build roads, and develop towns.

These restrictions adversely affected both their pastoral and trading activities. Earlier, pastoralists looked after animal herds as well as traded in various products. However, during colonial trade, pastoralists could do trading but they were subject to various restrictions.

Effects of Drought

Drought affects the life of pastoralists everywhere. That is why, traditionally, pastoralists moved from one place to other. This allowed them to survive bad times and avoid crises due to insufficient rains.

From the colonial period, Maasai were bound to a fixed area. They were cut off from the best grazing lands and forced to live within a semi-arid tract that was prone to frequent droughts.

As a result large numbers of Maasai cattle died of starvation and disease. There was a severe decline of the animal stock of Maasais. Over half of the cattle in the Maasai reserves died after two years of serious drought i.e. 1933 and 1934.

Not All Were Equally Affected

In pre-colonial times Maasai society was divided into two social categories-**elders** and **warriors**.

The Elders formed the ruling group and met in periodic councils to decide on the affairs of the community and settle disputes.

The Warriors consisted of young people, mainly responsible for the protection of the tribe. The Warriors defended the community and organised cattle raids. They were under the authority of elders.

Raiding was important in a society where cattle was wealth. It is through raids that power of different pastoral groups are asserted. The young man proved their manliness by capturing the cattle of other pastoral groups.

To administer the Maasai tribe, the Britishers took a series of measures. They appointed Chiefs of different sub-groups of Maasai, who were responsible for the affairs of the tribe.

The British imposed various restrictions on raiding and warfare. Thus, the traditional authority of both Elders and Warriors was negatively affected.

The chiefs appointed by the Colonial Government accumulated wealth over time. They started to live in towns and involved in trades. Their family stayed back in villages to look after lands and animals.

The chiefs managed to survive the destructions of war and drought, as they had both pastoral and non-pastoral income.

The poor pastoralists did not have the resources to survive in bad times. In times of war and famine, they lost nearly everything. They had to look for work in towns. Some used to work as charcoal burners and others did odd jobs to earn their living. The lucky could get more regular work in road or building construction.

The social change in Maasai society happened at two levels.

(i) First, the traditional difference based on age between the Elders and Warriors was disturbed.

(ii) Second, a new distinction between the wealthy and poor pastoralists was developed.

Rituals to become Maasai Warrior

Maasai young men go through an elaborate ritual before they become warriors. They must travel throughout the section's region for about four months, ending with an event where they started to live in house surrounded with some land for cultivation and became a raider who captured cattle of other groups.

During the ceremony, boys dress in loose clothing and dance non-stop throughout the day. This ceremony is the transition into a new age. Girls are not required to go through such a ritual.

Conclusion

Pastoral communities in different parts of the world are affected in a variety of different ways by changes in the modern world. New laws and new borders affect the patterns of their movement.

Pastoralists adapt to these new changes in the following ways

- They change the path of their annual movement.
- They reduce their cattle numbers.
- They pressurise for rights to enter new areas.
- They exert political pressure on the government for relief, subsidy and other forms of support.
- They demand a right in the management of forests and water resources.

According to environmentalists and economists, pastoral nomadism is a form of life that is perfectly suited to many hilly and dry regions of the world.

Try These

1. **Name some pastoral communities of Africa.**
2. **Which area was regarded as Maasai land before colonial rule?**
3. **Where did the Maasai cattle herders live?**
4. **In pre-colonial period, the Maasai society was divided into how many categories?**

TIME LINE

Covering Major Events with their Time Periods in Chronological Order

Year/Period	Event
In 19th century	Gujjar Bakarwals migrated to Jammu and Kashmir in search of pastures. Gaddi shepherds from Jammu and Kashmir came up to hills.
In mid-19th century	Grazing Tax was introduced.
1850s	Right to collect tax auctioned out to contractors.
1871	British Government in India passed the Criminal Tribes Act.
1885	Maasailand was cut into half with an International boundary between British Kenya and German Tanganyika.
1919	Tanganyika came under British rule.
1928	Report of Royal Commission on agriculture.
1933-34	Severe drought in Maasailand.
1947	Raikas could not move to Sindh anymore after independence so migrated to Haryana.
1961	Tanganyika attained independence.
1964	Tanganyika united with Zanzibar to form Tanzania.

Mind Map

PASTORALISTS IN THE MODERN WORLD

Colonial Rule and Pastoral Life
The Colonial Government made different laws for pastoralists.

Effects of Laws
- Shortage of Pastures
- Cattle herds could not graze freely
- Animal Stock declined

Colonial Laws

Criminal Tribes Act
Criminal Tribes Act classified communities of traders, craftsmen and pastoralists as Criminal Tribes.

Waste Land Rules
- Wasteland needed to be brought under cultivation.
- Uncultivated lands were taken over and given to selected individuals who were given different concessions for settlement.

Forest Acts

Reserved Forests
In the reserved forests, no pastoralist was allowed.

Protected Forests
In the protected forests, customary grazing rights of pastoral were granted, but their movements were strictly restricted.

Pastoralism in Africa
- The different pastoral communities of Africa are Bedouins, Berbers, Maasai, Somali, Boran and Turkana.
- Pastoralists of Africa raise cattle, camels, goats and sheep.

The Borders are Closed
- Pastoral groups were forced to live within the boundaries of special reserves.
- They were not allowed to move out with their stock without permits.

Effects of Drought
- Maasais were cut-off from the best grazing lands and forced to live within a semi-arid tract that was prone to frequent droughts.
- Many Maasai cattle died.

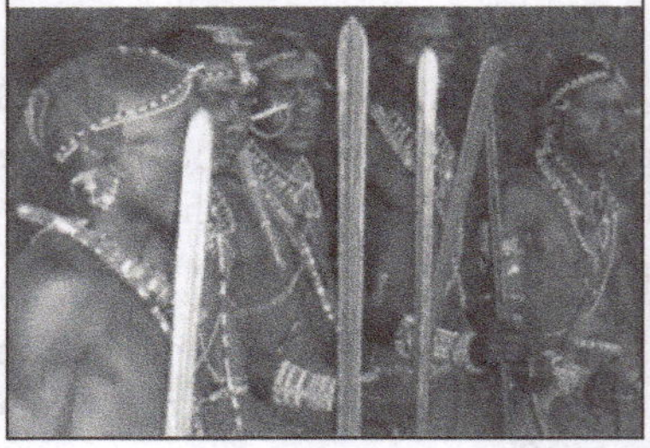

Not All were Equally Affected
- Maasai society was divided into two social categories- elders and warriors.
- The elders formed the ruling group and met in periodic councils to decide on the affairs of the community and settle disputes.
- The warriors consisted of young people responsible for the protection of the tribe.

Pastoral Nomads and their Movements

Pastoral Communities on the Plateaus, Plains and Deserts

Raikas
- They lived in the deserts of Rajasthan.
- A group of Raikas known as Maru Raikas herded camels and other group reared sheep and goat.
- Settlement of Maru Raikas is called a dhandi.

Dhangars
- This is a pastoral community of Maharashtra.
- They were mainly shepherds, blanket weavers and buffalo herders.

Banjaras
- They were an important group of graziers.
- They are found in Uttar Pradesh, Punjab, Rajasthan, Madhya Pradesh and Maharashtra.

The Gollas, Kurumas and Kurubas
- These are pastoral communities of the dry central plateau of Karnataka and Andhra Pradesh.
- The Gollas herded cattle.

The Kurumas and Kurubas reared sheep and goats, and sold woven blankets.

Pastoral Communities in the Mountains

Gujjar Bakarwals
- They migrated and settled in Jammu and Kashmir in the 19th century in search of pastures for their goat and sheep.
- They moved annually between their summer and winter grazing grounds in groups known as kafila.

Gaddi Shepherds
- This is a pastoral community of Himachal Pradesh.
- During winter, Gaddi Shepherds grazed their flocks in scrub forests of Shiwalik range.
- They spent the summer in Lahaul and Spiti.

Bhotiyas, Sherpas and Kinnauris
- They followed the cyclic movement between summer and winter in search of pastures.
- They had to adjust to seasonal changes and make proper use of available pastures.

NCERT FOLDER

Covering Intext Questions and Exercises of NCERT

INTEXT QUESTION

Q.1 Write a comment on the closure of the forests to grazing from the standpoint of
(a) A forester (b) A pastoralist

Ans. (a) **A forester** As a forester's duty is to ensure the conservation of forests, it is good that the forests have been closed for grazing. This will ensure proper growth of the vegetation and trees, so that the forest wealth will be maintained.

(b) **A pastoralist** Earlier our animals were grazing in the forest areas, where vegetation was plentiful. Now, as the forests are restricted for grazing, our animals have to be taken far away to find grass and vegetation for food. This has caused a lot of inconvenience, as managing our flock has become more difficult.

EXERCISE

Q.1 Imagine that it is 1950 and you are a 60 years old Raika herder living in post-independence India. You are telling your grand-daughter about the changes which have taken place in your lifestyle after independence. What would you say?

Ans. After the independence, our life has changed a lot. Since now, there is not enough pasture for our animals to feed, we had to reduce the number of cattle in our herds.

We also had to change our grazing ground as we were not allowed to go to Sindh and graze our camels on the banks of the river Indus because it is now a part of Pakistan. The political boundary between India and Pakistan prevented us to go there.

Then, we have found an alternative grazing ground in Haryana. In recent years, our cattle go there and can graze on agricultural fields after the harvests are cut. The animals also fertilise the soil with manure from their excreta.

Your father did not like a herder's life and decided to become a farmer. I gave him some money to buy a land and he bought the land. We built our present house in this land and your father is now cultivating foodgrains in the remaining parts of the land.

Now, we became a farmer community.

I think you will have a much better life than what your father had. I hope you will be serious about your studies and do well in your life. Your father tries to give you all the facilities which he did not get. You must respect his sacrifice and try to achieve something in your life.

Q.2 Imagine that you have been asked by a famous magazine to write an article about the life and customs of the Maasai in pre-colonial Africa. Write the article, giving it an interesting title.

Ans. Peculiarities of Maasai Culture

The word Maasai means 'My People' ('Maa' means 'My' and 'Sai' means 'People' in their language). They are traditionally nomadic people. Their society is divided into two parts–Elders and Warriors.

The Elders belong to the higher age group and decide on the affairs of the community by meeting as a group and also settle disputes. The Warriors are the younger group who were responsible for the protection of the tribes. They also organise cattle raids when it is required. Since, cattle are their wealth, these raids assume importance, as in this way, they are able to assert their power over other pastoral groups. However, the Warriors are subject to the authority of the Elders.

Q.3 Find out more about the life of some of the pastoral communities marked in figures A and B.

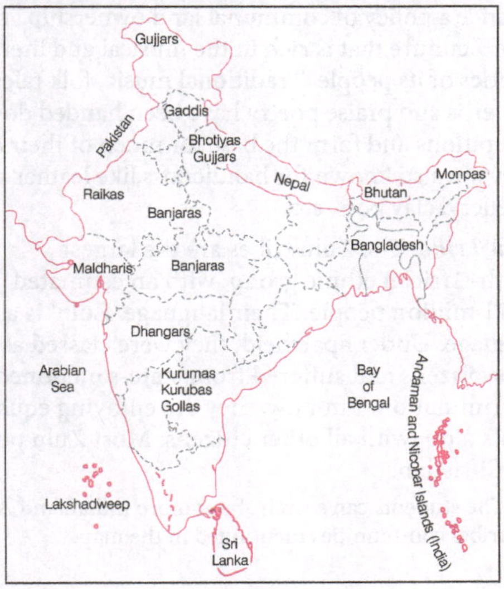

• Figure A

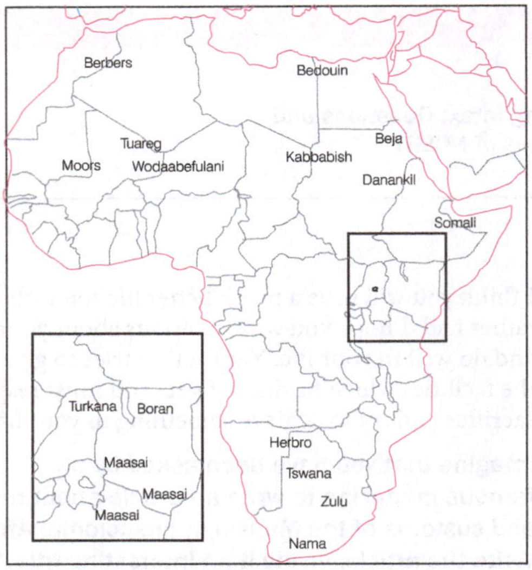

• Figure B

Ans. **Figure A** (Indian Tribes)

Maldharis They are nomadic tribal herdsmen who live in the Gujarat state of India. The literal meaning of Maldhari is 'owner of animal stock'. They are notable as the traditional dairymen of the region and once supplied milk and cheese to the palaces of Rajas.

Monpas They live in Arunachal Pradesh. They are also one of the 56 officially recognised ethnic groups in China. Their language belongs to the Tibeto-Burman family and is written in Tibetan script. There are six sub-groups of Monpas. They adopted Tibetan Buddhism.

Figure B (African Tribes)

Nama Tribe They are an African ethnic group of South Africa, Namibia and Botswana. In general, the Nama practice a policy of communal land ownership. The Nama have a culture that is rich in the musical and literary abilities of its people. Traditional music, folk tales, proverbs and praise poetry have been handed down for generations and form the base for much of their culture. They are also known for handicrafts like leather work, jewellery, clay pots, etc.

Zulu Tribe The Zulu tribes are the largest South-African ethnic group, with an estimated 10-11 million people. Their language 'Zulu' is a Bantu language. Under apartheid, they were classed as third class citizens and suffered from state-sanctioned discrimination. But now, they are enjoying equal rights alongwith all other citizens. Most Zulu people are Christian.

Note The students can search about more Indian and African tribal communities mentioned in the map.

Q.4 Explain why nomadic tribes need to move from one place to another. What are the advantages to the environment of this continuous movement?

Ans. Nomads are people who do not live in one place but move from one area to another to earn their living. They have to move from one place to another as their main occupation is cattle rearing for which they need availability of water and pastures for grazing their animals.

When the pastures get depleted, they move to another place with their animals, looking for pasture and water. When the water and pastures get depleted, they move again and keep repeating the cycle.

Advantages to the Environment of Continuous Movement

- The movement of the nomads allows the pasture to regrow and recover.
- It helps to protect the ecology.
- It prevents the overuse of pastures.

Q.5 Discuss why the Colonial Government in India brought in the following laws. In each case, explain how the law changed the lives of the pastoralists.

(a) Wasteland Rules **(b) Forest Acts**
(c) Criminal Tribes Act **(d) Grazing Tax**

Ans. (a) **Wasteland Rules** According to these rules, all uncultivated land is considered as wasteland. To the colonial officials, all uncultivated land appeared to be unproductive. Therefore, grazing lands were also considered as wastelands as they produced neither revenue nor agricultural produce. The Colonial Government wanted to bring the grazing lands under cultivation so that they could get revenue and agricultural goods from this land.

Effects of the Wasteland Rules According to Wasteland Rules, the uncultivated lands were taken over and given to select individuals who were granted concessions and encouraged to settle these lands. Therefore, expansion of cultivation inevitably meant the decline of pastures and created problems and hardships for the pastoralists.

(b) **Forest Acts** Through the Forest Acts, the forests were divided into two categories: Reserved Forests and Protected Forests.

Effects of the Forest Acts Pastoralists could no longer remain in an area even if forage was available. They could enter only by getting a permit for entry. If they overstayed the specified period of time, they were liable to fines. Their lives became difficult and full of hardships. Their traditional rights were severely restricted.

(c) **Criminal Tribes Act** In 1871, the Colonial Government passed the Criminal Tribes Act. By this act, many communities of craftsmen, traders and pastoralists were classified as Criminal Tribes. They were stated to be criminal by nature and birth.

Effects of Criminal Tribes Act After this act was enforced, nomadic communities were expected to live only in notified village settlements. They were not allowed to move out without a permit. The village police kept a continuous watch on them. They could no longer move from one place to another.

(d) **Grazing Tax** The Grazing Tax in India was introduced by the Colonial Government in the mid-19th century. Pastoralists had to pay tax on every animal they grazed on the pastures. The tax per head of cattle went up rapidly and the system of collection was made increasingly efficient.

Effects of the Grazing Tax To enter a grazing tract, pastoralists had to show the pass and pay the tax. Pastoralists had to pay tax on every animal they grazed on the pastures. The tax went up rapidly. So, the economic hardship of the pastoralists increased.

Q.6 Give reasons to explain why the Maasai community lost their grazing lands.

Ans. The Maasai tribes lost their grazing land because

- European countries tried to possess territories in Africa and sliced up the region into different colonies. In 1885, Maasailand was cut into half with an international boundary between British Kenya and German Tanganyika.
- The grazing lands were taken over for white settlement and the Maasais were pushed into a small area in South Kenya and North Tanganyika. The Maasais lost about 60% of their pre-colonial lands.
- Encouragement was given by the British Colonial Government in East Africa to peasant communities to expand cultivation and pasture lands were converted into cultivated fields.
- Large areas of grazing land were also turned into game reserves like the Maasai Mara and Samburu National Park in Kenya and Serengeti Park in Tanzania. Pastoralists were not allowed to enter these reserves.

Q.7 There are many similarities in the way in which the modern world forced changes in the lives of pastoral communities in India and East Africa. Write about any two examples of changes which were similar for Indian pastoralists and the Maasai herders.

Ans. Following are the similarities between Indian pastoralists and Maasai herders

- Both India and East Africa were under the control and dominance of the European colonial powers with similar intentions and objectives. In both places, the pastoral communities lost their pasture land because the colonial powers took control of these pastures and brought them under cultivation.
- Both in India and East Africa, forest laws were made and the pastoralists were not permitted to use the forests for grazing their animals or taking out forest produce. The mobility of the pastoralists was severely restricted whereby fodder was in short supply and feeding the cattle became a persistent problem. Many of them were thereby forced to give up their old mode of occupation.
- Both in India and Africa, Grazing Tax was imposed on the pastoralists. All these created a lot of hardship for the pastoral communities of India and Africa.

Two example of changes which were similar for Indian pastoralists and the Maasai herders are

(i) Both the pastoralists took other professions to survive, e.g. wage labourers.

(ii) Both the pastoralist lost their cattle due to the Forest Acts.

REVIEW EXERCISE

Including Competency Based Questions

Part I

Multiple Choice Questions (MCQs)

1. Who are the pastoral nomadic communities of Jammu and Kashmir?

(a) Gujjar Bakarwals (b) Gaddi shepherds
(c) Bhotiyas (d) Sherpas

2. The Gujjar Bakarwals begin their Northern march for the summer grazing ground in the month of April. How do they begin their journey?

(a) By forming 'Kafila' (b) By forming 'Dangal'
(c) By forming 'large group' (d) None of these

3. What is a mandap?
(a) Living place and work place of Gujjar cattle herders
(b) Gaddi shepherd's work place
(c) Sherpa's work place
(d) None of the above

4. Define the Bugyal.
(a) A dry forest area
(b) Vast meadows in the high mountains
(c) High mountains in desert
(d) None of the above

5. Bhabar is a dry forested area below the foothills of
(a) Jammu and Kashmir (b) Himachal Pradesh
(c) Garhwal and Kumaun (d) None of these

6. The continuous movement of the pastoral community helps in
(a) recovery of pasture
(b) commercial activity
(c) reduction in demand of houses
(d) None of the above

7. Nomadic tribes need to move from one place to another because of
(a) because of seasonal changes
(b) in search of pastures
(c) to maintain ecological balance
(d) All of the above

8. The Dhangar shepherds stayed in the Central Plateau of Maharashtra during the
(a) winter (b) summer
(c) monsoon (d) autumn

9. Rights that people used by custom and tradition is known as
(a) formal rights (b) customary rights
(c) social rights (d) personal rights

10. To colonial officials, all uncultivated land appeared to be
(a) unproductive (b) wastage
(c) barren (d) None of these

11. Forests which produced commercially valuable timber like deodar or sal were declared
(a) protected (b) commercial
(c) reserved (d) None of these

12. British officials were suspicious of
(a) mobile craftsmen
(b) traders who hawked their goods in villages
(c) pastoralists
(d) All of the above

13. When did the Colonial Government in India passed the Criminal Tribes Act?
(a) 1850 (b) 1871
(c) 1875 (d) 1890

14. Consider the statements and choose the incorrect option.
(a) The Raikas combined cultivation with pastoralism.
(b) During monsoons, the Raikas stayed in their home villages, where pasture was available.
(c) The Maru Raikas herded camels, sheep and goat.
(d) The settlements of Maru Raikas were known as Mandaps.

15. Identify the pastoral community with the help of following information. Competency Based
- **This is a pastoral community of Himachal Pradesh.**
- **During winter, they grazed their flocks in scrub forests of the low hills of Shiwalik range.**
- **It performs a similar cycle of seasonal movements like Gujjar Bakarwals.**

Options
(a) Gaddi Shepherds (b) Dhangars
(c) Banjaras (d) Maldharis

16. Pastoralists operated not only in the mountains but also in the plateaus, plains and deserts of India. Which of the following examples represent pastoralists?
(a) Dhangars (b) Rabari (c) Todas (d) Sherpas

17. This pattern of cyclical movement between summer and winter pastures was typical of many pastoral communities of the Himalayas, including the Bhotiyas, Sherpas and Kinnauris. All of them had to adjust to seasonal changes and make effective use of available pastures in different places.
Which of the following most likely will describe the potential challenge faced by these Himalayan pastoral communities? Competency Based
(a) Difficulty in maintaining strong social bonds within the community due to constant movement.
(b) Increased risk of exposure to natural disasters in both summer and winter locations.
(c) Competition for resources with other nomadic groups encountered during migration routes.
(d) Overgrazing and depletion of vegetation in both summer and winter pastures due to repeated use.

18. Pastoralists faced a lot of changes due to changes in their pastoral land.
Which of the following best describes the primary consequence of shrinking pasturelands under agricultural expansion?
(a) Increased conflicts between pastoralists and farmers over land use.
(b) Reduced income due to decreased livestock productivity.
(c) Loss of traditional migration routes and cultural practices.
(d) Difficulty in finding suitable water sources for livestock.

19. **Banjaras were yet another well-known group of graziers. They were to be found in the villages of Uttar Pradesh, Punjab, Rajasthan, Madhya Pradesh and Maharashtra. In search of good pastureland for their cattle, they moved over long distances, selling plough cattle and other goods to villagers in exchange for grain and fodder.**

What can be inferred about the relationship between Banjaras and other communities?

(a) They primarily interacted with other nomadic groups for trade and social exchange.

(b) They maintained a strictly bartering system and rarely engaged in monetary transactions.

(c) They developed mutually beneficial relationships with villagers for exchanging goods and services.

(d) They faced discrimination and social exclusion due to their nomadic way of life.

20. **Under colonial rule, the life of pastoralists changed dramatically. Their grazing grounds shrank, their movements were regulated, and the revenue they had to pay increased. Their agricultural stock declined and their trades and crafts were adversely affected.**

Which statement best describes the primary consequence of shrinking grazing grounds for pastoral communities under colonial rule? **Competency Based**

(a) Increased reliance on agriculture and settled life.

(b) Difficulty in finding suitable seasonal pastures for their livestock.

(c) Reduced income due to decreased trade with other communities.

(d) Loss of cultural traditions associated with nomadic lifestyles.

21. **Dhangars were an important pastoral community of Maharashtra.**

What did the Dhangars receive from the Konkani peasants in exchange for their services?

I. Gold and precious metals.

II. Tools and agricultural equipment.

III. Supplies of rice for their journey.

IV. Shelter and access to markets.

Codes

(a) Only III (b) Both I and II

(c) Both III and IV (d) Only IV

22. **Consider the statements given below and choose the correct answer.**

Statement I The survival of these pastoral groups depended solely on their ability to herd livestock.

Statement II Their success and sustainability involved managing various factors and adapting to different environment.

Codes

(a) Statement I is correct and II is incorrect.

(b) Statement I is incorrect and II is correct.

(c) Both I and II are incorrect.

(d) Both I and II are correct.

Answers

1. (a)	**2.** (a)	**3.** (a)	**4.** (b)	**5.** (c)
6. (a)	**7.** (b)	**8.** (c)	**9.** (b)	**10.** (a)
11. (c)	**12.** (d)	**13.** (b)	**14.** (d)	**15.** (a)
16. (a)	**17.** (d)	**18.** (b)	**19.** (c)	**20.** (b)
21. (a)	**22.** (d)			

Match the Following

1.

	List I		List II
A.	Work place for Gujjar	1.	Dhars
B.	A hill bamboo	2.	Mandap
C.	High meadows	3.	Ringal

Codes

	A	B	C		A	B	C
(a)	1	2	3	(b)	2	3	1
(c)	2	1	3	(d)	3	2	1

2.

	List I		List II
A.	A dry forested area below the foot hills of Garhwal and Kumaon	1.	Bhabar
B.	Vast meadows in the high mountains	2.	Stubble
C.	Lower ends of grain stalks left in the ground after harvesting	3.	Bugyal

Codes

	A	B	C		A	B	C
(a)	1	3	2	(b)	3	1	2
(c)	2	1	3	(d)	2	3	1

3.

List I	List II
A. Maasailand was cut in to half	1. 1919
B. Tanganyika came under British control	2. 1964
C. Formation of Tanzania	3. 1885

Codes

	A	B	C		A	B	C
(a)	1	2	3	(b)	3	2	1
(c)	3	1	2	(d)	2	1	3

Ans. 1. (b) 2. (a) 3. (c)

Assertion-Reason

1. Assertion (A) No pastoralists are allowed to access 'reserved forests'.

Reason (R) 'Reserved forests' produces commercially valuable timber, viz, deodar, sal, etc.

Codes

(a) Both A and R are true and R is the correct explanation of A
(b) Both A and R are true, but R is not the correct explanation of A
(c) A is true, but R is false
(d) A is false, but R is true

2. Assertion (A) The British Colonial Government in East Africa encouraged a local peasant communities to expand cultivation.

Reason (R) Large areas of grazing land were turned into game reserves like the Maasai Mara and Samburu National Park.

Codes

(a) Both A and R are true and R is the correct explanation of A
(b) Both A and R are true, but R is not the correct explanation of A
(c) A is true, but R is false
(d) A is false, but R is true

3. Assertion (A) Raikas lived in the deserts of Rajasthan.

Reason (R) One group of Raikas known as the Maru Raikas which herded camels and another group reared sheep and goat.

Codes

(a) Both A and R are true and R is the correct explanation of A
(b) Both A and R are true, but R is not the correct explanation of A
(c) A is true, but R is false
(d) A is false, but R is true

4. Assertion (A) Through Forest Acts, some forests which produced commercially valuable timber like deodar or sal were declared 'Reserved'.

Reason (R) Pastoralist were allowed access to these forests.

Codes

(a) Both A and R are true and R is the correct explanation of A
(b) Both A and R are true, but R is not the correct explanation of A
(c) A is true, but R is false
(d) A is false, but R is true

5. Assertion (A) British officials distrusted mobile craftsmen and traders who hawked their goods in villages.

Reason (R) British officials wanted the rural people to live in villages, in fixed places with fixed rights on particular fields.

Codes

(a) Both A and R are true and R is the correct explanation of A
(b) Both A and R are true, but R is not the correct explanation of A
(c) A is true, but R is false
(d) A is false, but R is true

Ans. 1. (a) Both A and R are true and R is the correct explanation of A
2. (b) Both A and R are true, but R is not the correct explanation of A
3. (b) Both A and R are true, but R is not the correct explanation of A
4. (c) A is true, but R is false
5. (b) Both A and R are true, but R is not the correct explanation of A

Picture Based Questions

1. Identify the pastoralist and name their settlements.

(a) Gujjar Bakarwals, Mandap (b) Gaddi Shepherds, Mandap
(c) Bhotiyas, Kafila (d) Sherpas, Kafila

2. Identify the pastoralist of Rajasthan from the image given below.

(a) Banzaras (b) Kurumas
(c) Maru Raikas (d) Raikas

3. Identify the pastoralist in the picture given below.

(a) Maasai of Africa (b) Zulu of Africa
(c) Somali of Africa (d) Kabbabish of Africa

4. Observe the map given below showing the location of pastoral communities.

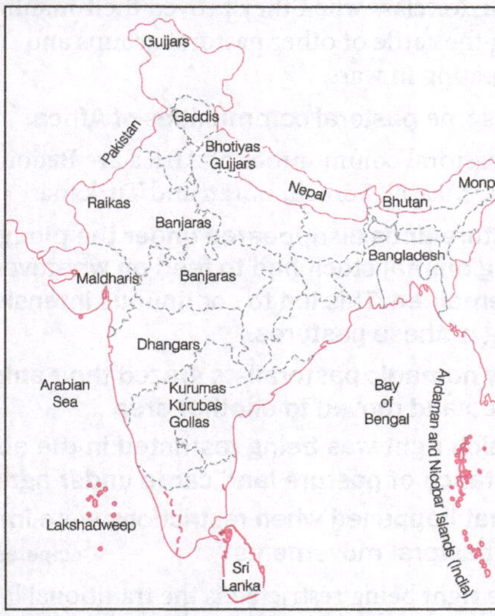

Pastoralists had been an important part of society like Africa and India. Accordingly, which of the following pastoralists marked on the map is most likely to sell woven blankets made of sheep and goats? Competency Based

(a) Kurumas (b) Banjaras
(c) Dhangars (d) Maldharis

5. Given above is the painting of Gaddi sheep being sheared.

Which of the following best describes about the Gaddi shepherds' lifestyle?

(a) They primarily specialise in sheep and goat herding compared to cattle due to the terrain.

(b) They have adapted to seasonal variations in resource availability through their cyclical movement.

(c) They have a permanent settlement in the Siwalik hills and only take their flocks to Lahaul and Spiti for short periods.

(d) They rely heavily on agriculture and cultivation in addition to animal husbandry.

Ans. 1. (a) Gujjar Bakarwals, Mandap

2. (c) Maru Raikas

3. (a) Maasai of Africa

4. (a) Kurumas

5. (b) They have adapted to seasonal variations in resource availability through their cyclical movement.

Case Based Question

1. Read the source given below and answer the questions that follow.

To expand its revenue income, the colonial government looked for every possible source of taxation. So tax was imposed on land, on canal water, on salt, on trade goods, and even on animals. Pastoralists had to pay tax on every animal they grazed on the pastures. In most pastoral tracts of India, grazing tax was introduced in the mid-19th century. The tax per head of cattle went up rapidly and the system of collection was made increasingly efficient. In the decades between the 1850s, and 1880s, the right to collect the tax was auctioned out to contractors. These contractors tried to extract as high a tax as they could to recover the money they had paid to the state and earn as much profit as they could within the year.

(i) What was the primary motive behind the colonial government's imposition of grazing tax?

(a) To encourage pastoral settlement and agricultural development.

(b) To increase the land revenue collected from pastoral communities.

(c) To generate additional income for the state through direct taxation.

(d) To control the movement and activities of nomadic pastoralists.

(ii) What was the purpose of shifting from contractor-based to direct tax collection in the 1880s?

(a) Improving the tax burden for pastoralists by streamlining the collection process.

(b) Solving concerns about corruption and exploitation by contractors.

(c) Allowing the government to exert greater control over the movement and resource access of pastoral communities.

(d) All of the above

(iii) Identify the statement that accurately reflects the impact of colonial taxation on pastoral communities.

(a) It disrupted traditional grazing patterns and resource access practices.

(b) It did not imposed a significant financial burden on pastoralists, often exceeding their animal's market value.

(c) It had not contributed to the sedentarisation of some pastoral communities, pushing them towards alternative livelihoods.

(d) It had not fostered resentment and resistance among pastoral groups, sometimes leading to protests and uprisings.

Ans. (i) (b) To increase the land revenue collected from pastoral communities.

(ii) (d) All of the above

(iii) (a) It disrupted traditional grazing patterns and resource access practices.

Part II

Very Short Answer Type Questions

1. How do you define nomadic pastoralists?

Ans. Nomadic pastoralists are people who move from one place to another with their herds to earn a living.

2. What do you mean by the term 'Kafila'?

Ans. *Kafila* is a group of people of several household, who move together in the journey.

3. Name the state from which Gaddi shepherds hail.

Ans. Gaddi shepherds hail from the state of Himachal Pradesh.

4. Name some pastoral communities of the Himalayas.

Ans. Bhotiyas, Gujjar Bakarwals, Gaddi and Kinnauris are some pastoral communities of the Himalayas.

5. In which state Dhangars are found?

Ans. Dhangars are an important pastoral community of Maharashtra.

6. The Kharif crops are harvested in which months?

Ans. The Kharif crops are harvested between September and October.

7. What is rabi crop?

Ans. The spring crop, usually harvested after March is known as rabi crop.

8. What do you mean by stubble?

Ans. Lower ends of grain stalks left in the ground after harvesting is known as stubble.

9. Name any three states where Banjaras were found.

Ans. Banjaras are nomadic herders found in Uttar Pradesh, Punjab and Rajasthan.

10. Who are known as Raikas?

Ans. The Raikas are a pastoral community of Rajasthan.

11. Which tax was imposed by British colonists on pastoralists?

Ans. Grazing Tax was imposed by colonists on pastoralists.

12. How could Maasai warriors prove their manliness?

Ans. Massai young men came to be recognised as members of the Warrior class when they proved their manliness by raiding the cattle of other pastoral groups and participating in wars.

13. Name some pastoral communities of Africa.

Ans. Some pastoral communities of Africa are Bedouins, Berbers, Maasai, Somali, Boran and Turkana.

14. As pasturelands disappeared under the plough, the existing animal stock had to feed on whatever grazing land remained. This led to continuous intensive grazing of these pastures.

Usually nomadic pastoralists grazed their animals in one area and moved to another area....

(i) Which right was being restricted in the above instance of pasture land came under agriculture?

(ii) What happened when restrictions were imposed on pastoral movements? **Competency Based**

Ans. (i) The right being restricted is the traditional land-use and resource access rights of nomadic pastoral communities.

(ii) When restrictions were imposed on pastoral movements, limited grazing lands were extensively used, leading to a decline in the pasture quality. Land could not restore naturally because of increased pressure.

15. Bhushan read in a magazine that in pre- colonial period the maasai tribe was affected by the division of elders and warriors. He asked his teacher.

How did the division between elders and warriors impact Maasai society during the pre-colonial period?

Ans. The division between elders and warriors played a significant role in Maasai society's structure and function. Elders formed the ruling class, met in cyclic councils to decide on the affairs of the community and resolve disputes. On the other hand, warriors were responsible for defense and organising cattle raids, which were crucial for asserting power and accumulating wealth.

Short Answer Type Questions

1. Explain the annual movement of the Gujjar Bakarwals.

Ans. The Gujjar Bakarwals of Jammu and Kashmir are great herders of goat and sheep.

The annual movement of these herders is discussed below

- In winter, they live with their herds in the low hills of the Shiwalik range. The dry scrub forests provide good grazing grounds for their herds.
- In summer, they cross the Pir Panjal passes and enter the Kashmir valley. They graze their cattle on the lush green mountain sides, covered with a variety of grasses.
- At the onset of winter, the Bakarwals move again back to their winter pastures.

2. Where did the Gaddi shepherds live? Describe the seasonal movement of the Gaddis.

Ans. The Gaddi shepherds of Himachal Pradesh spend their winter in the low hills of Shiwalik range, grazing their flocks in the scrub forests.

The seasonal movement of the Gaddis are

- By April, they moved North and spent the summer in Lahul and Spiti. When the snow melted and the high passes were clear, many of them moved onto higher mountain meadows.
- By September, they began their return movement. On the way, they stopped in the villages on Lahul and Spiti, reaping their summer harvest and sowing their winter crops. Then, they descended with their flock to their winter grazing ground on Shiwalik hills.
- Next April, again they start their march with their animals, to the summer meadows.

3. What is the difference between the annual movement of the Gollas of Karnataka and Andhra Pradesh from the Gujjar Bakarwals of Jammu and Kashmir?

Ans. The movement of Gollas of Andhra Pradesh and Karnataka revolve around the arrival and departure of monsoon. In the dry season, they move to the coastal tracts and leave when the rains come.
On the other hand, the movement of the Gujjar Bakarwals revolve around cold and hot seasons. During winters, when high mountains are covered with snow they move to low hills and in summer, they once again move towards the high altitudes.

4. Who were Dhangars and what were their occupations? Why were they continuously on the move? Explain how the pattern of cyclical movement of Dhangars defined by the changing weather.

Ans. Dhangars were an important pastoral community of Maharashtra. Most of the Dhangars were shepherds, blanket and wool weavers and still others were buffalo herders.

They were continuously on the move in search of pasture for their cattle.

Their pattern of cyclical movement according to changing weather is discussed below

- They stayed in the Central plateau of Maharashtra during the monsoon. This was a semi-arid region with low rainfall and poor soil, only bajra could be grown here. In the monsoon, this tract became a vast grazing ground for their cattle.
- By October, the Dhangars harvested their bajra and started on their move and reached Konkan. Their cattle manured the fields and fed on the stubble.
- With the onset of monsoon, they returned back to their own settlement in dry plateau.

5. (a) Who were the Banjaras and name any two states where they were found ?

(b) Name a pastoral community of Rajasthan. Why did they combine both cultivation and pastoralism as means of profession?

Ans. (a) Banjaras were nomadic people who used to move from one region to another in search of good pasture land for their cattle. They moved over long distances, selling plough cattle and other goods to villagers. They were found in Uttar Pradesh, Punjab, Rajasthan, Madhya Pradesh and Maharashtra.

(b) A pastoral community of Rajasthan were the Raikas. The uncertainty and meagre rainfall in the desert region led to fluctuating harvests. This situation forced the Raikas to combine both cultivation and pastoralism as means of profession.

6. Describe the life of Raikas Community of Rajasthan.

Ans. The Raikas were found in the deserts of Rajasthan. The rainfall in the region was uncertain and poor. Hence, the Raikas combined cultivation with pastoralism.
During the monsoons, the Raikas of Barmer, Jaisalmer, Jodhpur and Bikaner stayed in their home villages, where pasture was available.
By October, when these grazing grounds were dry, they moved out in search of other pasture and water and returned again during the next monsoon.

One group of Raikas, known as the Maru (desert) Raikas, herded camels and another group reared sheep and goat. They mainly lived in Thar desert near Jaisalmer and their settlement is known as 'dhandi'.

7. How did colonial policies, such as the expansion of cultivation and Forest Acts, significantly impact the livelihoods of pastoralists in India during the nineteenth century?

Ans. Colonial policies during the nineteenth century impacted the livelihoods of pastoralists in the following ways

- The British administration sought to convert grazing lands into cultivated farms to boost revenue, leading to the shrinkage of grazing grounds for pastoralists.
- Additionally, Forest Acts restricted pastoralists' access to forests, further limiting their pasture options and disrupting their traditional migratory patterns. These policies resulted in a decline in agricultural stock, as pastoralists faced reduced grazing areas and increased regulations on movement.
- Moreover, the imposition of taxes on animals grazed on pastures increased their economic burdens, contributing to indebtedness and deteriorating livestock quality.

8. Why did the British introduced 'Wasteland Rules'? Explain.

Ans. The British introduced wasteland rules, as they believed that all uncultivated land was unproductive. It produced neither revenue nor agricultural produce. It was seen as 'wasteland' that needed to be brought under cultivation.

From the mid-19th century, Wasteland Rules were enacted in various parts of our country. By these rules, uncultivated lands were taken over and given to selected individuals. These individuals were granted various concessions and encouraged to settle on these lands. Some of them were made headmen of villages in the newly cleared areas.

Wastelands gradually transformed into cultivated lands. The Colonial Government imposed tax on these lands and earned revenue from these lands.

9. (a) Why did the British Government classify forests as 'Reserved forests' and 'Protected forests'?
(b) Distinguish between 'Reserved forests' and 'Protected forests'.

Ans. (a) The British Government classified forests as 'Reserved' and 'Protected' under the Forest Act. The reason for this was that the Britishers believed that grazing destroyed the saplings and young shoots of trees and it further prevented new trees from growing.

(b) The following points distinguish Reserved forests from Protected forests

Reserved Forests	Protected Forests
Reserved forests were the forests which produced commercially valuable timber, like deodar and sal.	Protected forests were the forests which produced non-commercial wood.
No pastoralist was allowed an access to the reserved forests.	In the protected forests, some customary grazing rights of pastoralists were granted, but their movements were severely restricted.

10. Mention three ways in which colonialism affected the lives of the pastoralists in India.

Ans. Under Colonial rule, the lives of the pastoralists in India changed dramatically. The following points state effect of Colonial rule on pastoralists

(i) The grazing grounds of pastoralists shrank.
(ii) Their movement was regulated and they had to pay taxes for each animal.
(iii) Their agricultural stock declined and their trades and crafts were adversely affected.

11. What factors had to be kept in mind by the pastoralists in order to survive?

Ans. In order to survive, the pastoralists took the following steps

- They had to judge how long the herds could stay in one area and know where could they find water and pasture.
- They needed to calculate the timing of their movements and ensure the path from where they could move through different territories.
- They also had to develop a relationship with farmers on the way so that the herds could graze in harvested fields in turn providing manure to the soil.
- They had to combine a range of different activities like cultivation, trade and herding to make their living.

12. How did drought affect the life of pastoralists?

Ans. Drought affects the life of pastoralists everywhere in the following ways

- Drought affects pastoralists by causing pastures to dry up, leading to a scarcity of forage for their cattle.
- During the colonial period, some pastoralist communities like the Maasai were confined to fixed areas, restricting their ability to search for pastures during droughts.
- Without the ability to shift their cattle to areas with sufficient forage, large numbers of cattle died of starvation and disease during severe droughts.
- An enquiry in 1930 revealed a significant loss of livestock among the Maasai, with over half of their cattle dying in just two years of severe drought in 1933 and 1934.

13. Describe any three features of the life of African pastoralists.

Ans. The three features of the life of African pastoralists are

(i) Some important pastoral communities of Africa include Bedouins, Berbers, Maasai, Somali, Boran and Turkana, etc. Most of them live in the semi-arid grasslands or arid deserts where rainfed agriculture is difficult.

(ii) They raise cattle, camels, goats, sheep and donkey. Their main occupation is selling milk, meat, animal skin and wool.

(iii) They also earn through trade and transport, some types of agricultural activities and also variety of odd jobs. By doing all these jobs, the pastoralists try to supplement their meagre and uncertain earnings from pastoralism.

14. Why did the cattle stock of the Maasai's decrease under colonial rule?

Ans. The cattle stock of the Maasai decreased under colonial rule for the following reasons

- In the 19th century, Maasai tribes could move over vast areas in search of pastures. From the late 19th century, the Colonial Government began imposing various restrictions on their mobility. The Maasais were bound down to a fixed area.
- They were cut off from the best grazing lands and forced to live within a semi-arid tract prone to frequent droughts. Since, they could not shift their cattle to places where pastures were available, large numbers of Maasai cattle died of starvation and disease.
- As the area of grazing lands decreased, the adverse effect of the drought increased. In just 2 years of severe drought 1933 and 1934, over half of the cattle of Maasai tribes died.

15. What role did the permits issued by the Colonial Government play in the lives of the African pastoral groups?

Ans. The permits issued by the colonical government played a significant role in lives of the African pastoralists in the following ways

- The pastoralists were not allowed to move out with their stock without special permits. It was difficult to get permits without trouble and harrassment.
- The permits specified the periods in which they could legally stay within a forest. If they overstayed, they were liable to fines.
- Further in many regions, pastoralists were prohibited from participating in any form of trade.

16. Discuss the most likely impact of the colonial government in Africa imposing various restrictions on pastoral communities. **Competency Based**

Build the answer around these points

- **Traditional governance**
- **Forced labour**
- **Reserve forest**

Ans. The colonial government in Africa implemented a series of restrictions that significantly impacted pastoral communities and their way of life in the following ways

- The imposition of restrictions eroded traditional governance structures within pastoral communities. Decisions that were historically made internally were now dictated by external authorities, stripping pastoralists of their autonomy and cultural authority.
- Pastoralists were forced into low-wage labour for colonial infrastructure projects, exploiting their skills and traditional knowledge. This forced labour further strengthened power imbalances and societal inequalities, as pastoralists were underpaid and subjected to unfair treatment.
- Pastoralists were confined to reserves, depriving them of access to vast grazing areas essential for their nomadic lifestyle and livestock survival. The loss of grazing land disrupted centuries-old migratory patterns, leading to overcrowding and overgrazing in limited areas, exacerbating environmental degradation and livestock mortality.

17. Read the statements given below regarding Nomads.

Statement 1 (S1) During drought cattle are likely to starve unless they can be moved to areas where forage is available.

Statement 2 (S2) Pastoralists are nomadic which allows them to survive bad times and avoid crises.

Explain what trend these statements - S1 and S2 - reflect in the nomadic culture. **Competency Based**

Ans. The trend reflected in statements S1 and S2 regarding nomadic culture is the adaptive resilience inherent in nomadic lifestyles.

Statement 1 (S1) highlights the necessity for mobility in nomadic cultures, especially during times of drought or scarcity. The ability to move cattle to areas with available forage is crucial for their survival. This reflects the practical aspect of nomadic culture, where mobility is not just a tradition but a survival strategy.

Statement 2 (S2) emphasises the role of nomadism in mitigating crises and surviving adverse conditions. Nomadic lifestyles allow pastoralists to adapt to changing environmental conditions by relocating to areas with better resources. This illustrates the adaptibility ingrained in nomadic cultures, as they have developed practices and traditions that enable them to navigate challenging circumstances.

Long Answer Type Questions

1. How did the pasture lands decline in India? Describe the impact of the shortage of pasture land on the lives of pastoralists.

Ans. The pasture lands declined in India in the following ways

- The British Government considered all uncultivated land as unproductive. They wanted to transform all grazing lands into cultivated farms. Land revenue was the main source of its finance. So, to increase its revenue, the British Government brought the pastures under cultivation.

- The Colonial Government passed the 'Wasteland Rules'. By these rules, uncultivated lands were taken over and given to selected individuals for cultivation which further led to decrease in pasture lands.
- By the mid-19th century, various Forest Acts were implemented in the different provinces of India. This also led to decline in pasture lands as by these acts, forests were classified as 'Reserved' and 'Protected'.
- No pastoralist was allowed to access to the 'Reserved' forests. In 'Protected' forest, some customary grazing rights of pastoralists were granted but their movement was severely restricted.

The decline of pasture lands had a deep impact on the life of pastoralists in following ways

- They were expected to live only in notified village settlements.
- The village police was to keep strict watch on them.
- They reduced the number of cattle in their herd.
- Some richer pastoralists bought land and settled down and gave up their nomadic life. The poor pastoralists became labourers working on fields or in small towns.

2. What are some of the problems that pastoralists face in the modern world? How have these groups adapted to the new times?

Ans. The problems faced by the pastoralists in modern world are

- In the modern world, the life of pastoralists changed largely. Their grazing grounds shrank, their movements were regulated and the revenue they had to pay was increased.
- Colonial powers thought all uncultivated land as unproductive. Thus, Wasteland Rules were enacted and by these rules uncultivated lands were taken over and used for cultivation. The expansion of cultivation led to the decline of pastures for the cattle.
- Various Forests Acts prevented the pastoralists from entering many forests that had provided forage for their cattle. Even they had to pay taxes on every animal they grazed.

The pastoralist have adapted the new times in the following ways

- Some reduced the number of cattle in their herds as there was not enough pasture to feed them.
- Others changed their path by discovering new pastures, as movement to old grazing grounds became difficult.
- Some rich pastoralists bought land and settled down and gave up their nomadic life.
- Some became settled peasants by cultivating land and others became trader. Many poor pastoralists became labourers by working in fields or in small towns.

3. How did restrictions on pasture lands affect the animal stock?

Ans. The restrictions on pasture lands affected the animal stock in the following ways

- The Forest Act changed the lives of pastoralists to a great extent. The pastoralists were now prevented from entering many forests that provided valuable forage for their cattle in earlier times.
- The pastoralists needed a permit for entry in the forests. In most pastoral tracts of India, Grazing Tax was imposed. The timing of their entry and departure was specified and the number of days they could spend was also limited. The number of cattle and the amount of tax were entered on the pass.
- The pastoralist could no longer remain in the areas, even if forage was available sufficiently. They had to move according to the time limit mentioned in their permit. If they overstayed they had to give fines.
- The over restriction of the movement of pastoralists created a shortage of forage for animals and the deterioration of animal stock. Underfed cattle died in large numbers during scarcities and famines.

4. Explain the main provisions of the Forest and Criminal Tribes Acts. How did they affect the life of the pastoralists?

Ans. The main provisions of Forest Act were

- Some forests which produced commercially valuable timber like deodar or sal were declared 'Reserved' and no pastoralist was allowed to these forest.
- Other forests were classified as 'Protected' where some customary grazing rights of Pastoralists were granted. But their movement was strictly restricted by providing permits where the timings of entry and departure were mentioned. The Pastoralist had to follow this rule.

The Criminal Tribe Act had following provisions

- Many communities of craftsmen, traders and pastoralist were classified as Criminal Tribes.
- They were stated to be criminal by nature and birth.
- They were expected to live only in notified village settlements and not allowed to move without permit.
- The village police was to keep strict watch on them.

Impact of these acts on lives of pastoralists were as follows

- The above acts lead to serious shortage of pastures.
- Movement of cattle herders and shepherds was restricted so they had to feed on limited available stock.
- Nomadic people had to continuously shift their places to suit the colonial rule and could not find enough pastures for their cattle.

- Continuous use of same land for pasture, (as their movement was restricted), lead to deterioration of quality of pasture. Underfed cattle died in large number which affected the livelihood of pastoralist.

5. What motivated the British Government to issue permit to Maasai herders? Describe the sudden change in the lives of pastoralist?

Ans. The British government issued permit to the Maasai tribes for the following reasons

- The British colonisers thought pastureland as unproductive and waste land. So, they encouraged the local peasant communities to expand cultivation. Expansion of cultivation resulted into more revenue for the colonisers.
- The British colonisers thought pastoralists as dangerous and savage and tried to minimise all contact with them.

Thus, Maasai were not allowed to move out without special permits. It was difficult to get permit and if they were found guilty of disobeying the rules, they were strictly punished.

The permit system affected the lives of pastoralist in following ways

- Grazing land was reduced and feeding cattle became very difficult.
- Underfed cattle died which had negative impact on livelihood of Maasai herders.
- They also lost valuable water resources for themselves and their cattle.
- They were sometimes imprisoned without valid reasons.
- Restriction on their movement or entry to white areas not only affected their freedom of movement, but also their livelihood.
- Maasai herders were expected to confine within semi-arid drought-prone area and frequent drought reduced the size of their cattle.

6. 'Pastoralists were not allowed to enter the markets in white areas'. Explain its impact on the pastoralists of Africa.

Ans. From the late 19th century, the British colonisers started to impose various restrictions on the mobility of the pastoralists of Africa. They were not allowed to enter the markets in white areas.

The impact of this restriction on the Pastoralists were

- The pastoralists were prohibited from participating in any form of trade. This severely affected their economic conditions.
- White settlers and European colonists saw pastoralists as dangerous and primitive. They tried to minimise all contact with the tribes. This severely affected the pastoral and trading activities of them.
- The poor pastoralists did not have the resource to survive in bad times. They had to take odd jobs like charcoal burners, daily labourers in roads and building construction. Thus, white colonists needed black labours to bore mines, build roads and towns. They had to depend on pastoral community automatically.

7. Read the information given below regarding grazing land and answer the question that follows.

In the 19th century, African pastoralists could move over vast areas in search of pastures. When the pastures were exhausted in one place they moved to a different area to graze their cattle. From the late 19th century, the colonial government began imposing various restrictions on their mobility. Like the Maasai, other pastoral groups were also forced to live within the confines of special reserves. The boundaries of these reserves became the limits within which they could now move. They were not allowed to move out with their stock without special permits.

Analyse the circumstances that forced tribals to abandon their land in terms of its impact - negative and/or positive - on economic growth, the environment and the sustainable development.

Competency Based

Ans. The colonial restrictions on African pastoralists' mobility had significant impacts in both negative and positive ways which are discussed below

Negative Impacts are

- **Economic Disruption** The restrictions imposed by the colonial government on the mobility of African pastoralists disrupted their traditional livelihood practices. Forced confinement to special reserves limited their access to grazing lands, leading to economic hardships as their ability to sustain livestock herds diminished.
- **Environmental Degradation** Confining pastoralists to limited grazing reserves resulted in overgrazing and land degradation within these areas. Without the ability to rotate grazing lands, the environmental carrying capacity of the reserves was exceeded, leading to soil erosion, loss of vegetation, and degradation of water sources.

Positive Impacts are

- **Conservation Efforts** The confinement of pastoralists to reserves may have unintentionally contributed to the preservation of certain ecosystems and biodiversity hotspots. By limiting human activities such as grazing and settlement, these reserves could serve as protected areas, allowing for the conservation of natural habitats and wildlife populations.

- **Development of Sustainable Land Use Practices** The restrictions imposed on pastoral mobility may have lead to the adoption of more sustainable land management practices within the reserves. Pastoralists, constrained by limited grazing areas, may have implemented rotational grazing schemes and other conservation measures to ensure the long-term viability of the land for livestock rearing.

Case Based Questions

1. Read the sources given below and answer the questions that follow.

Source A Dhangars, an Important Pastoralist

Dhangars were an important pastoral community of Maharashtra. In the early 20th century, their population in this region was estimated to be 4,67,000. Most of them were shepherds, some were blanket weavers, and still others were buffalo herders. The Dhangar shepherds stayed in the Central plateau of Maharashtra during the monsoon. This was a semi-arid region with low rainfall and poor soil. It was covered with thorny scrub. Nothing but dry crops like bajra could be sown here: In the monsoon, this tract became a vast grazing ground for the Dhangar flocks. By October, the Dhangars harvested their bajra and started on their move West.

(i) Evaluate the effectiveness of the factor which influences the movement of Dhangars.

Source B The Kurumas and Kurubas Pastoralists

In Karnataka and Andhra Pradesh, again, the dry central plateau was covered with stone and grass, inhabited by cattle, goat and sheep herders. The Gollas herded cattle. The Kurumas and Kurubas reared sheep and goats and sold woven blankets. They lived near the woods, cultivated small patches of land, engaged in a variety of petty trades and took care of their herds.

Unlike the mountain pastoralists, it was not the cold and the snow that defined the seasonal rhythms of their movement: rather it was the alternation of the monsoon and dry season. In the dry season, they moved to the coastal tracts and left when the rains came.

Only buffaloes liked the swampy, wet conditions of the coastal areas during the monsoon months. Other herds had to be shifted to the dry plateau at this time.

(ii) To what extent the occupation of the pastoralists of central plateau was influenced by the climate of the region?

Source C Banzaras and their lifestyle

Banjaras were yet another well-known group of graziers. They were to be found in the villages of Uttar Pradesh, Punjab, Rajasthan, Madhya Pradesh and Maharashtra. In search of good pastureland for their cattle, they moved over long distances, selling plough cattle and other goods to villagers in exchange for grain and fodder.

In the deserts of Rajasthan lived the Raikas. The rainfall in the region was meagre and uncertain. On cultivated land, harvests fluctuated every year. Over vast stretches no crop could be grown. So the Raikas combined cultivation with pastoralism. During the monsoons, the Raikas of Barmer, Jaisalmer, Jodhpur and Bikaner stayed in their home villages, where pasture was available. By October, when these grazing grounds were dry and exhausted, they moved out in search of other pasture and water and returned again during the next monsoon.

One group or Raikas–known as the Maru (desert) Raikas-herded camels and another group reared sheep and goat.

(iii) How did the Banjaras and Raikas adapt their livelihood strategies to cope with environmental challenges and fluctuations in resource availability?

Ans. (i) The factor which influences the movement of the Dhangars is the onset of the monsoon. They stayed in the semi-arid region of the central plateau. During monsoon, this region became a grazing ground for the cattle and the Dhangars stayed there. By October, the Dhangars went to the Konkan and coastal area with their cattles and they left the Konkan and coastal area with the onset of monsoon and returned back to the dry central plateau of Maharashtra.

(ii) In the dry Central plateau of South India, viz in Karnataka and Andhra Pradesh, pastoralists like the Gollas, the Kurumas and the Kurubas live. They reared sheep and goat. They lived near the woods. They cultivated small patches of land. There was a little scope for them to cultivate in large scale as the area was dry. They also engaged in a variety of petty trades, viz, selling woven blankets.

(iii) The Banjaras in regions like Uttar Pradesh, Punjab, Rajasthan, Madhya Pradesh, and Maharashtra, roamed extensively for pastureland. They engaged in trade, exchanging plough cattle and other goods for grain and fodder, demonstrating a flexible approach to resource acquisition.

Raikas in Rajasthan's desert balanced farming and herding, staying home during monsoons and venturing out in dry seasons. This adaptation allowed them to optimise resource utilisation and sustain their livelihoods amidst environmental variability.

2. Read the source given below and answer the questions that follow.

Pastoralists reacted to these changes in a variety of ways. Some produced the number of cattle in their herds, since there was not enough pasture to feed large numbers. Others discovered new pastures when movement to old grazing grounds became difficult. After 1947, the camel and sheep herding Raikas, for instance, could no longer move into Sindh and graze their camels on the banks of the Indus, as they had done earlier. The new political boundaries between India and Pakistan stopped their movement. So, they had to find new places to go. In recent years, they have been migrating to Haryana where sheep can graze on agricultural fields after the harvests are cut. This is the time that the fields need manure that the animals provide.

Over the years, some richer pastoralists began buying land and settling down, giving up their nomadic life. Some became settled peasants cultivating land, others took to more extensive trading. Many poor Pastoralists, on the other hand, borrowed money from money lenders to survive.

At times, they lost their cattle and sheep and became labourers, working on fields or in small towns. Yet, pastoralists not only continue to survive, in many regions. Their numbers have expanded over recent decades.

When, pasturelands in one place was closed to them, they changed the direction of their movement, reduced the size of the herd, combined pastoral activity with other forms of income and adapted to the changes in the modern world.

Many ecologists believe that in dry regions and in the mountains, pastoralism is still ecologically the most viable form of life.

(i) The pastoralists changed their life after the implementation of the Forest Acts in India. Explain by giving example.

(ii) After the partition, the life of some pastoralists changed. Justify.

(iii) Inspite of the implementation of the Forests Act, the number of pastoralists have increased in recent times. Explain.

Ans. (i) The implementation of Forest Acts in India changed pastoralists' traditional practices. Closed pasturelands prompted them to adjust movement, reduce herds, and seek alternative incomes like agriculture or trading. Financial strains led some to borrow from moneylenders. Despite challenges, pastoralists resiliently adapted to governmental restrictions, finding ways to sustain themselves.

(ii) After the partition, the life of some pastoralists are changed in the following ways

(a) Some pastoralists had to change their path for pastureland. For example, Raika pastoralists could not go to Sindh as it became a part of Pakistan. Thus, instead of going there they had to go to Haryana for grazing land.

(b) Some pastoralists became wage labourers, after the scarcity of pasture land.

(iii) Inspite of the implementation of the Forest Act, the number of pastoralists have increased in recent times. This can be explained in the following ways

- The Pastoralists changed their direction of movement, reduced the size of the herd.
- Sometimes, they combined pastoral activity with other forms of profession.

In this way, by adapting new changes in the modern world the Pastoralists not only survive but also increase their number.

ASSESSMENT EXERCISE

Multiple Choice Questions (MCQs)

1. After partition, where do the Raikas go for grazing cattle instead of Sindh?
(a) Himachal Pradesh
(b) Maharashtra
(c) Haryana
(d) Gujarat

2. Where is Serengeti National Park located?
(a) Kenya
(b) Tanzania
(c) Uganda
(d) Somalia

3. What are two main social categories of Maasai society?
(a) Elders and warriors
(b) Elders and youngers
(c) Rich and poor
(d) High caste and low caste

4. Match the following.

List I	List II
A. Gujjar Bakarwals	1. Rajasthan
B. Gaddi Shepherds	2. Himachal Pradesh
C. Banjaras	3. Jammu and Kashmir

Codes

	A	B	C		A	B	C
(a)	3	2	1	(b)	1	2	3
(c)	3	1	2	(d)	2	3	1

5. **Assertion** (A) Gujjar Bakarwals of Jammu and Kashmir are great herders of goat and sheep.

Reason (R) They migrated to this region in the 19th century in search of pastures for their animals.

Codes
(a) Both A and R are true and R is the correct explanation of A
(b) Both A and R are true, but R is not the correct explanation of A
(c) A is true, but R is false
(d) A is false, but R is true

Subjective Questions (VSA, SA & LA)

1. Why is the Raika community considered both pastoralist and cultivator?

2. Why did pastoral communities move from place to place?

3. What term is given to the dry forested area of Kumaon and Garhwal?

4. What are 'protected forests'?

5. What does the word 'Maasai' mean? Where are they found?

6. What restrictions were imposed by the Colonial Government on the African pastoralists?

7. Who are Gujjar Bakarwals and Gaddis? What are the similarities between them?

8. State any five ways in which the various laws passed by the British affected the Indian pastoralists.

9. Why did the pastoral nomads give up their traditional livelihood practices? Give any five reasons.

CHAPTER 1

India : Size and Location

India is a vast nation. It refers to one of the world's ancient civilisations. Over the past 50 years, it has made significant socio-economic growth. India has made remarkable progress in the field of agriculture, industry, technology and over all economic development.

1.1 Location

India is a vast country located in the **Northern hemisphere.** Its mainland extends between latitudes[1] 8°4' N and 37°6' N and longitudes[2] 68°7' E and 97°25' E. India is divided into almost two equal parts by the Tropic of Cancer[3] (23° 30′ N) which passes through the States of Gujarat, Rajasthan, Madhya Pradesh, Chhattisgarh, Jharkhand, West Bengal, Tripura and Mizoram.

Andaman and **Nicobar** islands are situated in South-East of mainland in the Bay of Bengal. **Lakshadweep** islands are situated in South-West of mainland in the Arabian Sea. These are the two groups of islands belonging to India.

Note The Southernmost point of the Indian Union, 'Indira Point', got submerged under the sea water in 2004 during the Tsunami.

Size and Extent

Area of India is 3.28 million sq km which occupies 2.4% of the total geographical area of the world.

India is the **seventh largest country** of the world, after Russia, Canada, USA, China, Brazil and Australia. India has a land boundary of about 15200 km.

The total length of coastline[4] of the mainland including Andaman and Nicobar and Lakshadweep islands is about 7516.6 km.

India is bounded by young fold mountains[5] in the North-West, North and North-East.

India's landmass begins to taper (forms a cone shape) from the South of about 22° North latitude. It extends towards the Indian ocean and divides it into Arabian sea in West and the Bay of Bengal in East.

The latitudinal and longitudinal extent of the mainland is about 30° but the East-West extent appears smaller than the North-South extent.

The North-South distance is 3214 km while the East-West distance is 2933 km.

There is a time lag of almost two hours from Gujarat in the West to Arunachal Pradesh in the East. Hence, time along the Standard Meridian[6] of India (82°30' E) passing through Mirzapur (in Uttar Pradesh) is taken as Indian Standard Time[7] (IST) for the whole country.

The latitudinal extent influences the duration of day and night as one moves from South to North.

1 **Latitudes** The positions North or South of the equator, measured from 0° to 90°, they run horizontally.
2 **Longitudes** The position on the Earth's surface to the East or West of the Greenwich near London in England, they run vertically.
3 **Tropic of Cancer** A latitude at 23°30′N. South of this is considered the tropical zone and North is sub-tropical.
4 **Coastline** A line that forms the boundary between the land and the ocean or a sea where land meets the sea or ocean.
5 **Fold Mountains** Mountains which develop when two tectonic plates come together causing compression, resulting in folding of rocks.
6 **Standard Meridian** The longitude which passes through a country/region which is used to fix the standard time for that country/region.
7 **Indian Standard Time (IST)** This is local time of the longitude 82°30′ East, taken as the time for the whole of India. This is five-and-a-half hours ahead of Greenwich Mean Time (GMT).

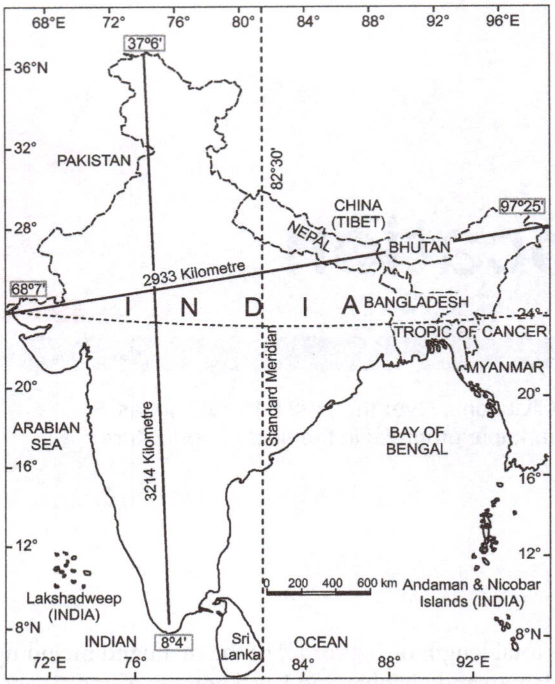

• India : Extent and Standard Meridian

1.2 India and the World

India is centrally located between the East and the West Asia. India is a Southward extension of the Asian continent.

The Trans Indian Ocean routes, which connect the countries of Europe in the West and the countries of East Asia, provide a strategic Central location to India.

The Deccan Peninsula extends towards the Indian ocean, helping India to establish close contact with West Asia, Africa and Europe from the Western coast and with South-East and East Asia from the Eastern coast.

India has the **longest coastline** on the Indian ocean as compared to other countries. Due to this reason, the Indian ocean is named after India.

KNOWLEDGE PLUS Due to the opening of Suez Canal in 1869, India's distance from Europe has been reduced by 7000 km.

India's Contact with the World

India's contacts with the world have continued through the ages, but its relationships through the land routes are much older than its maritime[8] contacts.

The various passes across the mountains in the North have provided passages to the ancient travellers while oceans restricted such interactions for a long time.

Some examples of how these routes have contributed in the exchange of ideas and commodities since ancient times are

- The ideas of the *Upanishads* and the *Ramayana*, the stories of the *Panchtantra*, Indian numerals and decimal system have reached many parts of the world.
- **Spices, muslin** and other merchandise were taken from India to different countries.
- The influence of Greek sculpture and the architectural style of domes and minarets from West Asia can be seen in many parts of India.

1.3 India's Neighbours

India has an important strategic position in South Asia. It has 28 states and 8 Union Territories. It has strong geographical and historical links with its neighbours.

India shares its land boundaries with **Pakistan** and **Afghanistan** in the North-West, **China (Tibet), Nepal** and **Bhutan** in the North, and **Myanmar** and **Bangladesh** in the East.

Two island countries, **Sri Lanka** and **Maldives,** lie to the South of India across the Indian ocean.

India and Sri Lanka are separated by a narrow channel of sea formed by the **Palk Strait** and **Gulf of Mannar.** Maldives lie to the South of Lakshadweep Islands.

KNOWLEDGE PLUS Before 1947, there were two types of states in India–the provinces and the princely states. Provinces were directly ruled by British officials. Princely states were ruled by local rulers who accepted the sovereignity of British rulers.

Try These

1. **Which type of mountains bounded India in the North-West, North and North-East?**
2. **What is the time lag between Gujarat and Arunachal Pradesh?**
3. **This strait separates India and Sri Lanka. Name the strait.**
4. **Which countries are included in the Indian subcontinent?**

8 **Maritime** Maritime refers to anything related to the ocean, sea and rivers.

Mind Map

INDIA : SIZE AND LOCATION

Location

- India is located in the Northern Hemisphere.
- It extends between 8°4' N and 37°6' N latitudes and 68°7' E and 97°25' E longitudes.
- It is divided into two equal parts by the Tropic of Cancer.

India's Neighbours

- India shares it land boundaries with Pakistan and Afghanistan in the North-West; China, Nepal and Bhutan in the North; and Myanmar and Bangladesh in the East.
- Two island countries Sri Lanka and Maldives lie to the South of India across the Indian Ocean.

India and the World

- India is centrally located between the East and the West Asia.
- The Trans-Indian Ocean routes connect the countries of Europe in the West and the countries of East Asia.
- The Deccan Peninsula connects India with West Asia, Africa and Europe from the Western Coast and with South-East and East Asia from the Eastern Coast.

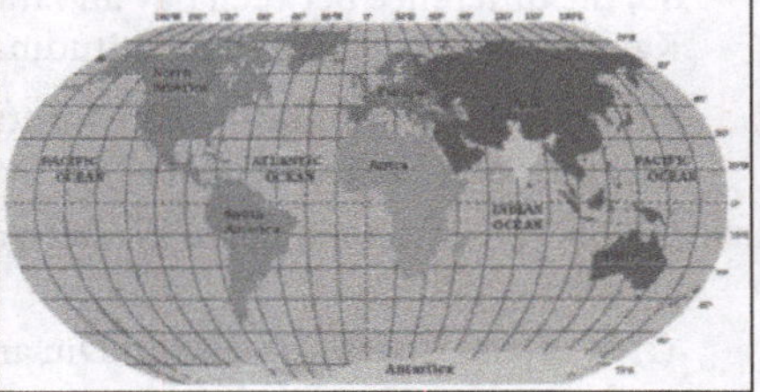

Size and Extent

- The area of India is 3.28 million sq km which occupies 2.4% of the total geographical area.
- It has a land boundary of 15200 km.
- The total length of its coastline is 7516.6 km.
- It extends towards the Indian Ocean and divides it into Arabian Sea in West and the Bay of Bengal in East.

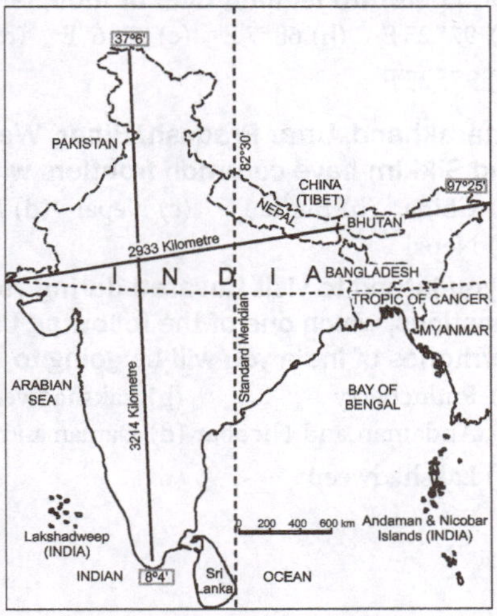

India's Contact with the World

- The ideas of Upanishads and the Ramayana, the stories of the Panchatantra, Indian numerals and decimal system have reached many parts of the world.
- Spices, Muslin and other merchandise were taken from India to different countries.

NCERT FOLDER

Covering Intext Questions and Exercises of NCERT

INTEXT QUESTIONS

Q.1 Why 82°30'E has been selected as the Standard Meridian of India?

Ans. 82°30'E is selected as the standard meridian of India because there is a time lag of 2 hours from the extreme East (Arunachal Pradesh) to the extreme West (Gujarat) of India.

To avoid confusions and difficulties arising out of local time differences, a meridian that is centrally located is chosen. This meridian in India is at 82° 30' E which passes through Mirzapur in Uttar Pradesh. It is also known as Standard Meridian of India.

Q.2 Why is the difference between day and night durations hardly felt at Kanyakumari, but not so in Kashmir?

Ans. The difference of day and night is hardly felt in Kanyakumari because it lies South of the Tropic of Cancer, closer to the equator. As equator receives direct Sun rays, there is not much difference in day and night there.

On the other hand, Kashmir lies North of the Tropic of Cancer, far from the equator. There is significant difference of 4-5 hours between day and night. Sun rays are not direct they are slanting here.

So, the difference between day and night in Kashmir and Kanyakumari is due to their latitudinal location.

Q.3 Find out the number of Union Territories along the Western and Eastern coasts.

Ans. Union Territories along the Western and Eastern coasts are given below

(i) **Western Coast** Daman and Diu and Dadra and Nagar Haveli, and Lakshadweep.

(ii) **Eastern Coast** Puducherry, Andaman and Nicobar islands.

Q.4 Find out area-wise which is the smallest and which is the largest state.

Ans. Smallest and Largest states as per area are as follows

(i) **Largest State** Rajasthan (342239 sq km)

(ii) **Smallest State** Goa (3702 sq km)

Q.5 Find out the states which do not have an international border or lie on the coast.

Ans. States which do not have international border or lie on the coast are Haryana, Jharkhand, Madhya Pradesh, Telangana and Chhattisgarh.

Q.6 Classify the states into four groups each having common frontiers with

(i) Pakistan **(ii) China**
(iii) Myanmar **(iv) Bangladesh**

Ans. States having common frontiers with

(i) **Pakistan** Gujarat, Rajasthan, Punjab and the UTs of Jammu and Kashmir and Ladakh

(ii) **China** Himachal Pradesh, Uttarakhand, Sikkim, Arunachal Pradesh and the UT of Ladakh

(iii) **Myanmar** Manipur, Nagaland, Arunachal Pradesh and Mizoram

(iv) **Bangladesh** West Bengal, Assam, Meghalaya, Tripura and Mizoram

EXERCISE

Q.1 Choose the right answer from the four alternatives given below.

(i) The Tropic of Cancer does not pass through

(a) Rajasthan (b) Odisha
(c) Chhattisgarh (d) Tripura

Ans. (b) Odisha

(ii) The Easternmost longitude of India is

(a) 97°25'E (b) 68°7'E (c) 77°6 'E (d) 82°32'E

Ans. (a) 97°25'E

(iii) Uttarakhand, Uttar Pradesh, Bihar, West Bengal and Sikkim have common frontiers with

(a) China (b) Bhutan (c) Nepal (d) Myanmar

Ans. (c) Nepal

(iv) If you intend to visit Kavarati during your summer vacations, which one of the following Union Territories of India you will be going to

(a) Puducherry (b) Lakshadweep
(c) Andaman and Nicobar (d) Daman and Diu

Ans. (b) Lakshadweep

(v) **My friend hails from a country which does not share land boundary with India. Identify the country.**

(a) Bhutan (b) Tajikistan

(c) Bangladesh (d) Nepal

Ans. (b) Tajikistan

Q.2 Answer the following questions briefly.

(i) **Name the group of islands lying in the Arabian sea.**

Ans. Lakshadweep islands lie in the Arabian sea.

(ii) **Name the countries which are larger than India.**

Ans. Russia, Canada, USA, China, Brazil and Australia are the countries larger than India.

(iii) **Which island group of India lies to its South-East?**

Ans. Andaman and Nicobar islands lies to the South-East of India.

(iv) **Which island countries are our Southern neighbours?**

Ans. Sri Lanka and Maldives are the two island countries that are the Southern neighbours of India.

Q.3 The Sun rises two hours earlier in Arunachal Pradesh as compared to Gujarat in the West, but the watches show the same time. How does this happen?

Ans. The Sun rises two hours earlier in Arunachal Pradesh as compared to Gujarat in the West, but the watches show the same time because the time along the Standard Meridian of India (82°30′ E) passing through Mirzapur in Uttar Pradesh is taken as the standard time for the whole country.

Q.4 The central location of India at the head of the Indian Ocean is considered of great significance. Why?

Ans. The central location of India at the head of the Indian ocean is of great significance due to the following reasons

- Sea trade links could be established with countries of East Africa, West Asia, Europe, East and South East Asia.
- Central location at the head of the Indian Ocean, gave India an easy access to the outside world from all areas.
- It also ensured that people coming from outside India could enter India through sea route.
- It has given India a distinct climate than the rest of the Asian Continent.

MAP SKILLS

Q.5 Identify the following with the help of map reading.

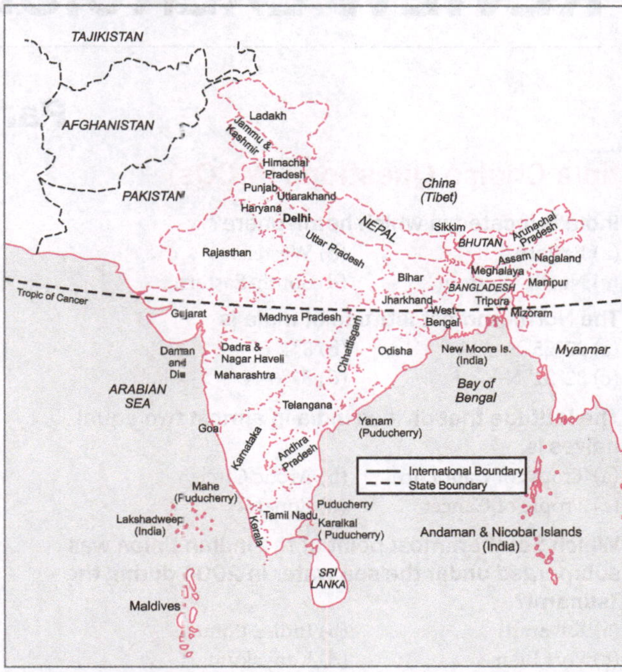

(i) **The island groups of India lying in the Arabian Sea and the Bay of Bengal.**

Ans. Lakshadweep islands lie in the Arabian sea and Andaman and Nicobar islands lie in the Bay of Bengal.

(ii) **The countries constituting the Indian subcontinent.**

Ans. India, Pakistan, Nepal, Bhutan, Bangladesh, Sri Lanka and Maldives.

(iii) **The states through which the Tropic of Cancer passes.**

Ans. Gujarat, Rajasthan, Madhya Pradesh, Chhattisgarh, Jharkhand, West Bengal, Tripura and Mizoram.

(iv) **The Northernmost latitude in degrees.**

Ans. 37°6′N

(v) **The Southernmost latitude of the Indian mainland in degrees.**

Ans. 8°4′N

(vi) **The Eastern and the Westernmost longitude in degrees.**

Ans. 68° 7′ E and 97° 25′ E

(vii) **The place situated on the three seas.**

Ans. Kanyakumari

(viii) **The strait separating Sri Lanka from India.**

Ans. Palk Strait

(ix) **The Union Territories of India.**

Ans. Andaman and Nicobar islands, Chandigarh, Dadra and Nagar Haveli and Daman and Diu, Lakshadweep, Puducherry, Delhi, Ladakh and Jammu and Kashmir.

REVIEW EXERCISE

Including Competency Based Questions

Part I

Multiple Choice Questions (MCQs)

1. India is located in which hemisphere?

(a) Eastern (b) Western
(c) North-Western (d) South-Eastern

2. The Northernmost latitude of India is

(a) 97°25' E (b) 8°4' E
(c) 82°32' N (d) 37°6' N

3. The latitude that divides India in almost two equal halves is

(a) Tropic of Capricorn (b) Arctic Circle
(c) Tropic of Cancer (d) Equator

4. Which Southernmost point of the Indian Union was submerged under the sea water in 2004 during the Tsunami?

(a) Kavaratti (b) Indira Point
(c) Port Blair (d) Kanyakumari

5. The latitudinal as well as longitudinal extent of the Indian mainland is about .... both ways.

(a) 20° (b) 40° (c) 30° (d) 35°

6. India is a ...... extension of the Asian continent.

(a) Northward (b) Southward
(c) Eastward (d) Westward

7. The route where India has a strategic central location and which connects European countries to East Asian countries is the

(a) trans-Arabian sea route
(b) trans-Indian ocean route
(c) trans-Bay of Bengal route
(d) None of the above

8. Which of the following countries has longest coastline along the Indian Ocean?

(a) Myanmar (b) Pakistan
(c) Bangladesh (d) India

9. India's contact with the world have continued through ages. Which is the oldest way of India's connection with the world?

(a) Air route (b) Sea route
(c) Land route (d) All of these

10. India does not share boundaries with which of the following countries?

(a) Bangladesh (b) Thailand
(c) Nepal (d) Myanmar

11. Which of the following statements best explains India's historical connections with the world?

(a) India's maritime contacts were older than its land routes.
(b) The mountain passes in the North facilitated early interactions, while oceans initialy restricted them.
(c) India's contact with the world was entirely based on trade, with no cultural exchange.
(d) The architectural styles in India remained unaffected by external influences.

12. Find the incorrect match.

(a) West Bengal – Border with Bangladesh
(b) Gujarat – Border with Pakistan
(c) Bihar – Border with China
(d) Uttarakhand – Border with Nepal

13. South of about 22° North latitude, it begins to taper and extends towards the Indian Ocean, dividing it into two seas, the Arabian Sea on the West and the Bay of Bengal on its East.

What geographical feature is responsible for dividing the Indian Ocean into Arabian Sea and Bay of Bengal?

(a) Mountain range (b) River delta
(c) Plateau (d) Plate boundary

14. Identify which statement best describes India's territorial extent of India. Choose from the appropriate statements among the following options

I. Extensive landmass with a moderate coastline.
II. Smaller landmass with a remarkably long coastline.
III. Large country with significant land and sea borders.
IV. Primarily an island nation with limited land boundaries.

Options

(a) Statements I and II are appropriate
(b) Statements I, II and III are appropriate
(c) All the statements are appropriate
(d) Only statement III is appropriate

15. Consider the statements given below and choose the correct answer.

Statement I From Gujarat to Arunachal Pradesh, there is a time lag of two hours.

Statement II The latitudinal extent influences the duration of day and night, as one moves from South to North.

Options

(a) Statement I is correct and statement II is incorrect
(b) Statement I is incorrect and statement II is correct
(c) Both statements I and II are incorrect
(d) Both statements I and II are correct

Answers

1. (a)	2. (d)	3. (c)	4. (b)	5. (c)
6. (b)	7. (b)	8. (d)	9. (c)	10. (b)
11. (b)	12. (c)	13. (c)	14. (d)	15. (d)

Match the Following

1.

List I	List II
A. Rajasthan	1. Tropic of Cancer passes through it
B. Andhra Pradesh	2. Located on West coast
C. Kerala	3. Located on East coast
D. Meghalaya	4. North of the Tropic of Cancer

Codes

	A	B	C	D		A	B	C	D
(a)	4	3	2	1	(b)	1	3	2	4
(c)	4	1	2	3	(d)	3	4	1	2

Ans. (b)

Assertion-Reason

1. Assertion (A) India is divided into two equal halves.

Reason (R) The Tropic of Cancer passes almost through the centre of the mainland of India.

Codes

(a) Both A and R are true and R is the correct explanation of A
(b) Both A and R are true, but R is not the correct explanation of A
(c) A is true, but R is false
(d) A is false, but R is true

2. Assertion (A) The longitudinal extent of India appears to be smaller than latitudinal extent of India.

Reason (R) The time difference of two hours between Arunachal Pradesh and Gujarat highlights the effect of longitudinal extent.

Codes

(a) Both A and R are true and R is the correct explanation of A
(b) Both A and R are true, but R is not the correct explanation of A
(c) A is true, but R is false
(d) A is false, but R is true

3. Assertion (A) India occupies a major part of South Asia.

Reason (R) India is a southward extension of the Asian continent.

Codes

(a) Both A and R are true and R is the correct explanation of A
(b) Both A and R are true, but R is not the correct explanation of A
(c) A is true, but R is false
(d) A is false, but R is true

4. Assertion (A) The total length of the coastline of India's mainland, including Andaman and Nicobar and Lakshadweep, is less than half of its land boundary.

Reason (R) India's land boundary measures about 50200 km, significantly exceeding the total coastline length.

Codes

(a) Both A and R are true and R is the correct explanation of A
(b) Both A and R are true, but R is not the correct explanation of A
(c) A is true, but R is false
(d) A is false, but R is true

Ans. 1. (a) Both A and R are true and R is the correct explanation of A
2. (b) Both A and R are true and R is not the correct explanation of A
3. (b) Both A and R are true, but R is not the correct explanation of A
4. (c) A is true, but R is false

Picture Based Question

1. Look at the picture given below and answer the following question.

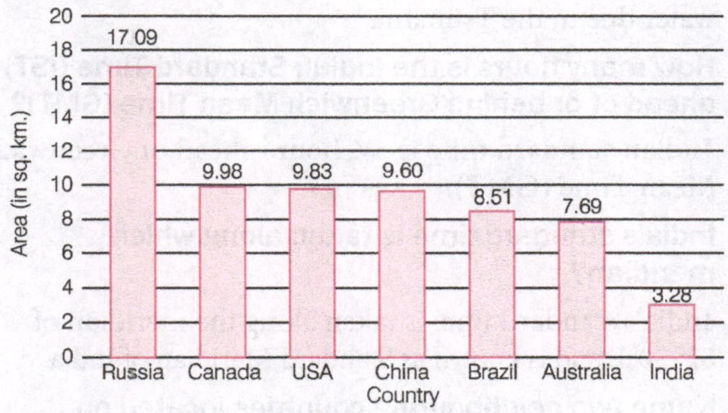

What does the above picture suggest?

(a) India is seventh largest country in terms of area.
(b) India is spread in 3.28 million sq kms of area.
(c) Russia is much larger in size than India.
(d) All of the above

Ans. (d) All of the above

Case Based Question

1. Read the source given below and answer the question that follow.

The Indian landmass has a Central location between the East and the West Asia. India is a Southward extension of the Asian continent. The trans-Indian ocean routes, which connect the countries of Europe in the West and the countries of East Asia, provide a strategic Central location to India. Note that the Deccan Peninsula protrudes into the Indian ocean, thus helping India to establish close contact with West Asia, Africa and Europe from the Western coast and with South-East and East Asia from the Eastern coast. No other country has a long coastline on the Indian Ocean as India has and indeed, it is India's eminent position in the Indian Ocean, which justifies the naming of an ocean after it.

(i) What is the total length of India's land boundary?
(a) 7516.6 km
(b) 15200 km
(c) 30200 km
(d) 50000 km

(ii) Which sea is located on the East side of India?
(a) Bay of Bengal
(b) Nicobar Sea
(c) Arabian Sea
(d) Andaman Sea

(iii) India's long coastline on the Indian Ocean allows it to
(a) gain dominance over landlocked nations.
(b) develop strong relationships with European countries.
(c) access important trade routes and resources.
(d) control the movement of ships in the region.

(iv) India's close contact with West Asia, Africa and Europe is facilitated by
(a) its proximity to the Mediterranean Sea.
(b) the development of landlocked trade routes.
(c) the presence of major ports on its Western coast.
(d) the construction of artificial canals.

Ans. (i) (b) 15200 km
(ii) (a) Bay of Bengal
(iii) (c) access important trade routes and resources.
(iv) (c) the presence of major ports on its Western coast.

Part II

Very Short Answer Type Questions

1. Why Indira point was submerged under sea water?

Ans. In the year 2004, Indira point got submerged under sea water due to the Tsunami.

2. How many hours is the Indian Standard Time (IST) ahead of or behind Greenwich Mean Time (GMT)?

Ans. Indian standard time is 5½ hours ahead of Greenwich Mean Time (GMT).

3. India's standard time is taken along which meridian?

Ans. India's standard time is taken along the meridian of 82° 30' E and is known as Standard Meridian of India.

4. Name two neighbouring countries located on North-West of India.

Ans. Afghanistan and Pakistan are located in North-West of India.

5. Which Union Territory of India has the least area?

Ans. The Union Territory of Lakshadweep has an area of only 32 sq km, which is the least among all the Union Territories.

6. India's contacts with the world were established first by which routes and why?

Ans. India's contacts with the world were established first by land routes because the various passes across the mountains in the North have provided passages to the ancient travellers, while the oceans restricted such passage for a long time.

7. Name the countries sharing a land boundary with India.

Ans. The countries sharing land boundary with India are Afghanistan, Bangladesh, Bhutan, China, Myanmar, Nepal and Pakistan.

8. Which waterway opened in 1869, reduced India's distance from Europe by 7000 km?

Ans. The opening of Suez Canal in 1869 reduced India's distance from Europe by 7000km.

9. Which Indian states border three countries?

Ans. The Indian states that border three countries are Sikkim, Arunachal Pradesh and West Bengal.

10. What is peninsula?

Ans. A peninsula is a piece of land that is almost entirely surrounded by water (from three sides) but is connected to the mainland on one side.

11. Define the term island.

Ans. An island is a piece of land that is surrounded by water (e.g. river, sea or ocean) on all sides.

12. 'India is the seventh largest country in the world'. Substantiate the statement with facts. Competency Based

Ans. India is the seventh largest country in the world. It has landmass area of 3.28 million sq. km. It accounts for about 2.4 percent of total geographical area of world.

13. India shares its land boundaries with Pakistan and Afghanistan in the North-West, China (Tibet), Nepal and Bhutan in the North and Myanmar and Bangladesh in the East. Our Southern neighbours across the sea consist of the two island countries.

(i) Which island countries are our Southern neighbours? Competency Based

(ii) How many States and Union Territories are there in India?

Ans. (i) The Maldives and Sri Lanka are the two island countries regarded as our Southern neighbours. Both Sri Lanka and the Maldives share a sea border with India.

(ii) There are 28 States and 8 Union Territories in India.

Short Answer Type Questions

1 Mention the latitudinal extent of India. Explain its significance.

Ans. The latitudinal extent of India is 8°4' N and 37°6'N. The significance of the latitudinal extent of India is as follows

- Latitudes determine the day light duration of a country.
- Due to India's latitudinal position, it is considered as a tropical country.
- The latitudinal extent of India influences the duration of day and night.

2. What do you understand by Indian Standard Time? Mention its importance.

Ans. Indian Standard Time refers to the time that is accepted all over India. It lies on the longitude of 82° 30' E and is known as Standard Meridian of India.
Its importance is as follows

- IST has enabled India to overcome the difference of two hours between its Easternmost and Westernmost regions.
- IST has prevented confusion arising out of differences in local time at each longitude in India. It has provided a uniform timing throughout the country.

3. What is the strategic significance of India's location in Asia?

Ans. The strategic significance of India's location in Asia is as follows

- It has made trade possible through land routes as India is located centrally between East and West Asia.
- It has made trade possible through sea routes as countries of East Africa, Europe and East Asia connect through Trans Indian Ocean routes.
- These routes have contributed in the exchange of ideas and commodities since ancient times.

4. Why is Indian ocean named after our country? Give three reasons.

or **Justify the naming of Indian ocean after India.**

Ans. Indian ocean is named after India due to its important features which are

(i) India has the longest coastline on the Indian ocean.

(ii) India has a central location between East and West Asia.

(iii) India's Southernmost extension, the Deccan Peninsula, extends towards the Indian ocean, which makes it significant to international trade done through the Indian ocean.

5. What is the longitudinal extent of India? What is its implication?

Ans. The longitudinal extent of India is 68°7' E to 97°25'E. Its implications are

- The longitudinal degrees provides East-West extent to India.
- The longitudinal extent provides time differences. In India there is a time gap of two hours from its extreme East to extreme West.
- Due to the longitudinal extent, India has chosen a meridian that is centrally located (82°30°' E) as its standard meridian.

6. What is a subcontinent? Why India and its adjacent countries are called Indian subcontinent?

Ans. A subcontinent is a distinctive geographical unit that stands out distinctively from rest of the continent. India and its adjacent countries together are called the Indian subcontinent because this region is different from other regions of Asia. The Himalayan mountains separate it from rest of Asia and provide a unique climate and natural vegetation.

The Deccan peninsula extends Southwards towards the Indian ocean which gives an eminent position to this subcontinent in the Indian ocean. Therefore, India and its adjacent countries are called as Indian subcontinent.

7. Explain why the cities of Mumbai and Chennai are able to see the noon Sun exactly over head twice a year, but Delhi never sees it exactly overhead?

Ans. The movement of the Sun towards North to South of the equator is within the two tropics. (i.e. the Tropic of Cancer and the Tropic of Capricorn).
All the places located within these two tropics are able to see the Sun overhead, twice a year. Mumbai and Chennai see noon Sun exactly over head twice a year as these cities lie in South of the Tropic of Cancer.
Delhi never sees the Sun exactly over head as it is located at 29°N latitude and is in North of the Tropic of Cancer. Areas of the Earth located North of Tropic of Cancer never experience the Sun directly over head. They lie in sub-tropical zone.

8. How many types of states were there in India before Independence? Briefly explain them.

Ans. There were two types of states in India before Independence i.e. the provinces and the princely states. These are discussed below

- **Provinces** These were ruled directly by British officials, who were appointed by the Viceroy.
- **Princely States** These were ruled by local, hereditary rulers, who acknowledged sovereignty in return for local autonomy.

9. Read the statements given below regarding India size and location.

Statement 1 India shares its land boundaries with Pakistan and Afghanistan in the North-West.

Statement 2 Our Southern neighbours across the sea consist of the two island countries, namely, Andaman and Nicobar and Lakshadweep.

Explain, which statement is incorrect and why?

Competency Based

Ans. Statement 2 is incorrect because the Southern neighbours across the sea consist of countries like Sri Lanka, Maldives and not the two Indian island territories, Andaman and Nicobar, and Lakshadweep. These island territories are part of India and are not separate countries. Andaman and Nicobar Islands is located in South-East of mainland in Bay of Bengal. The Lakshadweep islands is in South-West of mainland in Arabian Sea.

Long Answer Type Questions

1. Describe the location and size of India in three points each.

Ans. The location and size of India are discussed below

Location

(i) India lies entirely in the Northern hemisphere.

(ii) The mainland extends between latitudes 8°4' N and 37°6' N and longitudes 68°7' E and 97°25' E.

(iii) The Tropic of Cancer (23°30′ N) divides the country into almost two equal parts. Its Southern part is considered as the tropical zone and Northern is considered as the sub-tropical zone of India.

Size

(i) India is the seventh largest country in the World after Russia, Canada, USA, China, Brazil and Australia. The landmass of India has an area of 3.28 million sq km.

(ii) India's total area accounts for about 2.4 % of the total geographical area of the world.

(iii) India has a land boundary of about 15,200 km and the total length of coastline including Andaman and Nicobar and Lakshadweep islands is about 7,516.6 km.

2. India has a long coastline which is advantageous for India. Analyse.

Ans. India's long coastline is advantageous for India in the following ways

- Long coastline of India has provided a significant boost to its maritime trade. Almost 90% of India's international trade is done through sea.
- The Deccan Peninsula extends towards the Indian Ocean, thus helping India to establish close contact with West Asia, Africa and Europe from the Western coast and with South-East Asia and East Asia from the Eastern coast.
- The coastline is crucial for naval defense, safeguarding India's maritime interests.
- The sea routes passing through the Arabian sea and Bay of Bengal, provide easy connectivity to India in the West and the East Coasts.
- India has developed many ports on its Western and Eastern coasts to facilitate trade through sea.
- It provides vital access to marine resources, supporting fishing industries.

3. India is said to enjoy a strategic position with reference to international trade routes. In your view, which features provide India a strategic advantage?

Or **Explain the importance of India's location on the globe.**

Ans. India enjoys a strategic position due to the following reasons

- India is centrally located at the head of the Indian ocean due to which it is easily approachable from different directions.
- The Deccan Peninsula extends towards the Indian ocean and divides it into two seas i.e. Arabian sea and Bay of Bengal. Unlike other landlocked countries, India gets locational advantage of easy access through sea.
- India's long coastline helps in establishing trade links with East Asia, South-East Asia.
- India's long coastline on the West is useful in trade links with West Asia, Africa and Europe.
- Opening of Suez Canal reduced the sea route and the time taken to reach India from Europe. This worked favourably for India making it a centre for trade.

4. Ms. Geeta lives in Arunachal Pradesh with her family, but her sister Nita lives in Gujarat for the studies. Geeta called her sister at 4 am to ask if she saw the sunrise today, her sister said the Sun didn't rise yet here.

Explain, when Nita will be able to see sunrise in Gujarat and why? **Competency Based**

Ans. Nita in Gujarat would be able to see the sunrise at 6 am because Gujarat is located in the Western part of India, and the time zone is different from Arunachal Pradesh.

Arunachal Pradesh is situated in the Eastern part of India while Gujarat is in Western part. India extends to two time zones and as the Earth rotates from East to West, there is natural progression of time. Therefore, when Geeta called Nita at 4 am in Arunachal Pradesh, the Earth had not yet rotated enough to bring the sunrise to Gujarat. From Arunachal Pradesh, the Gujarat is situated at the 30° distance, 1°=4 min, so 30°=120 min. It means there is a time lag of two hours.

5. Read the information given below and answer the following question.

These routes have contributed in the exchange of ideas and commodities since ancient times. The ideas of the Upanishads and the Ramayana, the stories of Panchtantra, the Indian numerals and the decimal system thus could reach many parts of the world. The spices, muslin and other merchandise were taken from India to different countries. On the other hand, the influence of Greek sculpture, and the architectural styles of dome and minarets from West Asia can be seen in different parts of our country.

How did various mountain passes in the North contribute to ancient travellers and the exchange of ideas and commodities? **Competency Based**

Ans. Various mountain passes in Northern India served as essential paths for ancient trade and cultural exchanges. These natural routes facilitated the movement of goods, scholars, and traders, fostering interactions between India and neighbouring regions.

The passes played an important role in connecting India with Central Asia, enabling cross-cultural influences along the Silk Road. They contributed to the dissemination of Indian knowledge, including philosophical concepts from the Upanishad and stories like the Ramayana. Indian numerals and decimals system reached many parts of the world. Valuable goods like spices, muslin and other merchandise were carried from India to different countries.
The impact of Greek sculpture, and architectural styles of domes and minarets from West Asia are seen in various regions of India. It shows mixing of different cultural influences in India's architecture and art.

Case Based Questions

1. Read the sources given below and answer the questions that follow.

Source A India and the World

India's contacts with the World have continued through ages but her relationships through the land routes are much older than its maritime contacts. The various passes across the mountains in the North have provided passages to the ancient travellers, while the oceans restricted such interaction for a long time.

(i) In what way land routes helped India when oceans restricted its interaction?

Source B Location and Size

India is bounded by the young fold mountains in the North-west, North and North-East. South of about 22° North latitude, it begins to taper, and extends towards the Indian ocean, dividing it into two seas, the Arabian Sea on the West and the Bay of Bengal on the East.

(ii) Which geographical feature distinctly determines the location of India in the Indian ocean?

Source C India's Neighbours

India occupies an important strategic position in South Asia. India has 28 States and 8 Union Territories. India shares its land boundaries with Pakistan and Afghanistan in the North-West, China (Tibet), Nepal and Bhutan in the North and Myanmar and Bangladesh in the East. Our Southern neighbours across the sea consist of the two island countries.

(iii) India shares its land boundaries with many countries in North, East and West but not South. Why?

Ans. (i) Land routes helped India at the time when ocean routes were not developed. Land routes provided trade links and exchange of ideas from India to rest of the world and *vice-versa.*

(ii) The feature that distinctly determines India's location in the Indian ocean is the Deccan peninsula that begins to taper (forms a cone shape) from the South of 22° North latitude and extends towards the Indian ocean.

(iii) India does not share any land boundary in its South because there is presence of three water bodies and other countries are located far from it. The three water bodies are the Arabian Sea, Bay of Bengal and Indian Ocean which surround the Indian peninsula. However, there are two island countries across the sea.

2. Read the source given below and answer the questions that follow.

The Indian landmass has a central location between the East and the West Asia. India is a Southward extension of the Asian continent.
The trans Indian ocean routes, which connect the countries of Europe in the West and the countries of East Asia, provide a strategic central location to India.
Note that the Deccan Peninsula protrudes into the Indian ocean, thus helping India to establish close contact with West Asia, Africa and Europe from the Western coast and with Southeast and East Asia from the Eastern coast.

No other country has a long coastline on the Indian ocean as India has and indeed, it is India's eminent position in the Indian ocean, which justifies the naming of an ocean after it.

(i) How India benefits by its strategic location in Trans Indian Ocean routes?

(ii) How the protruding Deccan Peninsula helps India?

(iii) **Write two important facts that can be understood when an ocean is named after a country.**

Ans. (i) India lies mid way between the West and the East. The ships going in either direction in Indian ocean find India in central position and stop there.

(ii) The protruding Deccan Peninsula helps in the following ways

- The Deccan Peninsula provides India with a long coastline in East and West.
- The Deccan Peninsula also provide division of Indian ocean in two segments namely Arabian Sea and Bay of Bengal.

(iii) The two facts are

(a) It states that the country has a very prominent position in that oceanic region.

(b) It states that the country has a powerful presence in trade, commerce and exchange of ideas since ancient times.

Map Based Questions

1. On the map, locate and label the following with appropriate symbols.

(i) State with its capital Jaipur (ii) Capital of Bihar

(iii) The Standard Meridian of India

(iv) Tropic of Cancer

Ans.

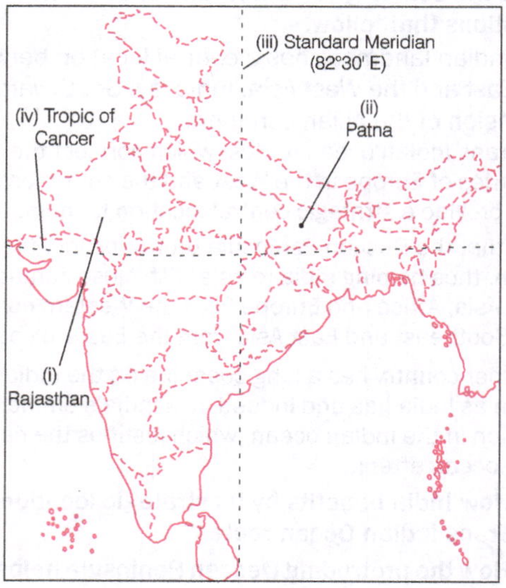

2. On the map of India, locate and label the following features with appropriate symbols.

(i) Capital of Odisha (ii) Capital of Gujarat

(iii) A state with its capital Bengaluru

(iv) A state with its capital Lucknow

(v) Capital of Haryana

Ans.

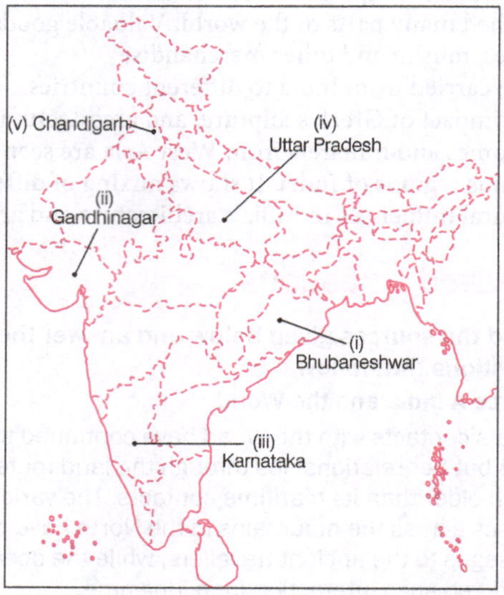

3. On the map of India, locate and label the neighbouring countries of India.

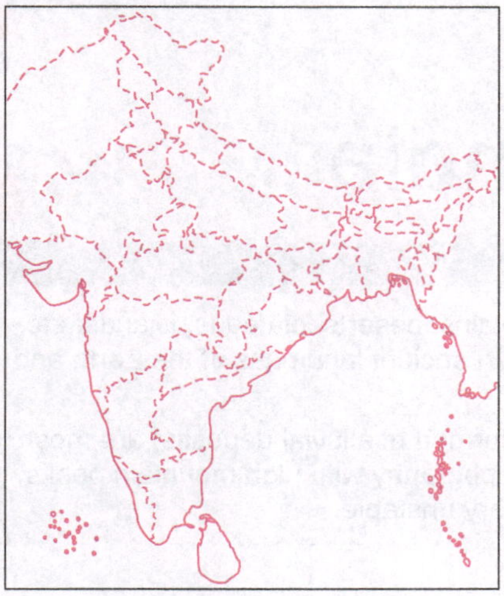

Ans.

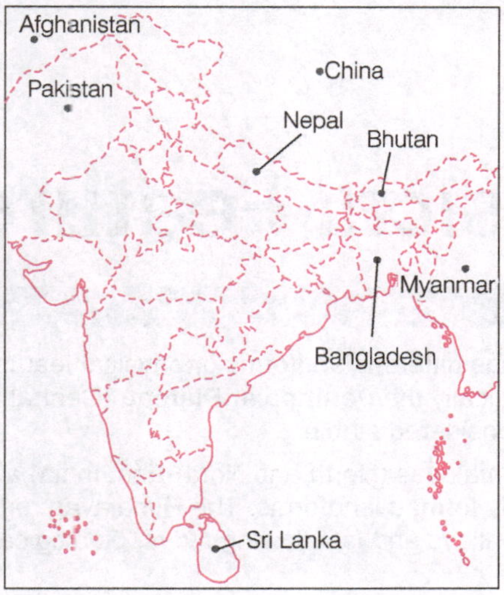

ASSESSMENT EXERCISE

Multiple Choice Questions (MCQs)

1. The North-South distance of India is
(a) 3214 km (b) 3333 km (c) 2933 km (d) 2565 km

2. Lakshadweep islands is situated South-West of Indian mainland in
(a) Arabian Sea (b) Bay of Bengal
(c) Indian Ocean (d) Andaman Sea

3. India does not share boundaries with which of the following countries?
(a) Bangladesh (b) Mauritius (c) Nepal (d) Myanmar

4. Which of the following countries is separated from India by a narrow channel of sea formed by the Palk strait and the Gulf of Mannar?
(a) Bangladesh (b) Myanmar (c) Sri Lanka (d) Maldives

5. Identify the incorrect statement with reference to Indian standard time.
(a) IST is also called Standard Meridian of India.
(b) IST passes through Mirzapur in Uttar pradesh.
(c) IST is applied to deal with the influence of latitudinal extent.
(d) IST Passes through 82°30′ E.

Subjective Questions (VSA, SA & LA)

1. Which Union Territory has its land borders touching two states in the Western part of India?

2. Name the states which have a common border with China.

3. What routes of trade replaced the 'Silk Route' in modern times? Why?

4. How has the opening of the Suez Canal benefitted India?

5. Why is the location of India at the head of the Indian ocean significant?

6. "Indian ocean is named after India." Justify the statement by three points.

7. How have the ancient and much older land routes contributed to exchange of ideas and goods?

8. What is the time lag between Arunachal Pradesh and Gujarat? How is a uniform time set at all places?

Physical Features of India

CHAPTER 2

India has different landforms or physical features like mountains, plains, deserts, plateaus, islands, etc. Geologically the **Peninsular Plateau** (Central and South India) is an ancient landmass of the Earth and was considered stable.

The Himalayas (North and North-East India) and Northern plains (formed of alluvial deposits) are most recently formed landforms. The Himalayan region has a youthful topography with high mountain peaks, deep valleys and fast flowing rivers. Geologically, Himalayas are very unstable.

2.1 Major Physiographic Divisions

The physical features of India can be grouped under the following physiographic divisions

1. The Himalayan Mountains
2. The Northern Plains
3. The Peninsular Plateau
4. The Indian Desert
5. The Coastal Plains
6. The Islands

1. The Himalayan Mountains

The Himalayas are geologically young and structurally **fold mountains**[1]. They form the highest and one of the most rugged mountain barriers in the world.

They stretch over the Northern borders of India. These mountain ranges run in West-East direction from the Indus to the Brahmaputra rivers.

They form an arc, covering a distance of about 2400 km. Their width varies from 400 km in Kashmir to 150 km in Arunachal Pradesh.

The altitudinal variations (differences in height) in Himalayas are greater in the Eastern half than those in the Western half.

The Himalayas consist of three parallel ranges in its longitudinal extent. They are **Himadri**, **Himachal** and **Shiwalik ranges**. A number of valleys lie between these ranges.

Himadri or Inner Himalayas or Great Himalayas

- It is the Northernmost range of the Himalayas.
- It is the most continuous range of the Himalayas consisting of highest peaks with an average height of 6000 m.
- It contains all the prominent Himalayan peaks like **Mount Everest, Kanchenjunga, Makalu,** etc.
- The Great Himalayas are covered with snow all round the year and a number of glaciers descend or move down from this range.
- The core of this part is composed of **granite**. The fold of Great Himalayas is asymmetrical in nature.

Some Highest Peaks of the Himalayas

Peak	Country	Height in metres
Mount Everest	Nepal	8848
Kanchenjunga	India	8598
Makalu	Nepal	8481
Dhaulagiri	Nepal	8172
Nanga Parbat	India	8126
Annapurna	Nepal	8078
Nanda Devi	India	7817
Kamet	India	7756
Namcha Barwa	India	7756
Gurla Mandhata	Nepal	7728

1 **Fold mountains** It refers to mountains formed by folding of layers in the upper part of Earth's crust.

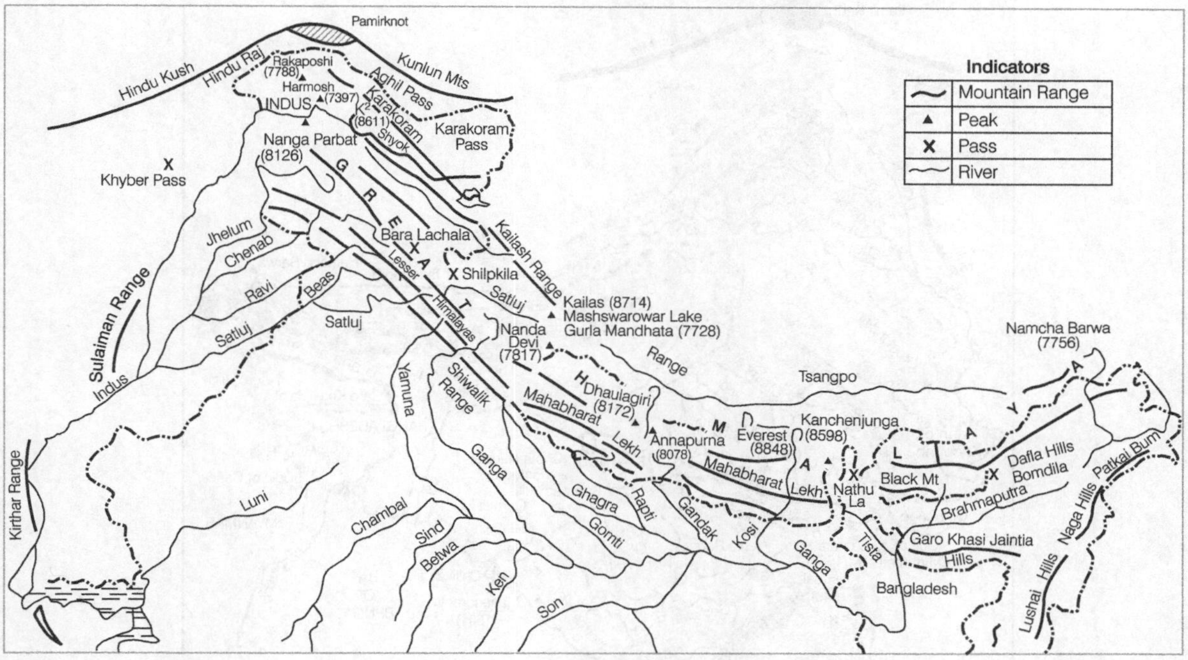

• The Himalayas

Himachal or Lesser Himalayas

- This range lies to the South of the Himadri and forms the most rugged mountain system.
- It is composed of highly compressed and altered rocks with height varying from 3700 to 4500 m.
- The average width of this range is 50 km. Important ranges are Pir Panjal (longest), Dhaula Dhar and Mahabharat.
- This range consists of valleys like Kashmir, Kangra, Kullu valley (in Himachal Pradesh) and well known hill stations like Mussoorie, Nainital, Ranikhet, etc.

Shiwalik

- This is the outermost range of the Himalayas with height varying between 900 and 1100 m.
- The average width of this range is 10 to 50 km. It is composed of coarse sediments brought down by rivers from the upper Himalayan ranges.
- Valleys of this range are covered with thick gravel (very small stones) and alluvium.
- Valleys lying between the Lesser Himalayas and Shiwaliks are known as **Duns** like **Dehra Dun, Kotli Dun** and **Patli Dun**.

Regional Division of Himalayas

Apart from the longitudinal division, the Himalayas are also divided from West to East on the basis of rivers valleys. These are Punjab, Kumaon, Nepal and Assam Himalayas.

In the West, the part of Himalayas lying between **Indus** and **Satluj rivers** has been traditionally known as **Punjab Himalayas**. However, from West to East, it is also known by regions like **Kashmir** and **Himachal Himalayas**.

The part of the Himalayas lying between **Satluj** and **Kali** rivers is known as **Kumaon Himalayas**.

The region between **Kali** and **Teesta** rivers is known as the **Nepal Himalayas**. The part lying between **Teesta** and **Dihang** rivers is known as **Assam Himalayas**.

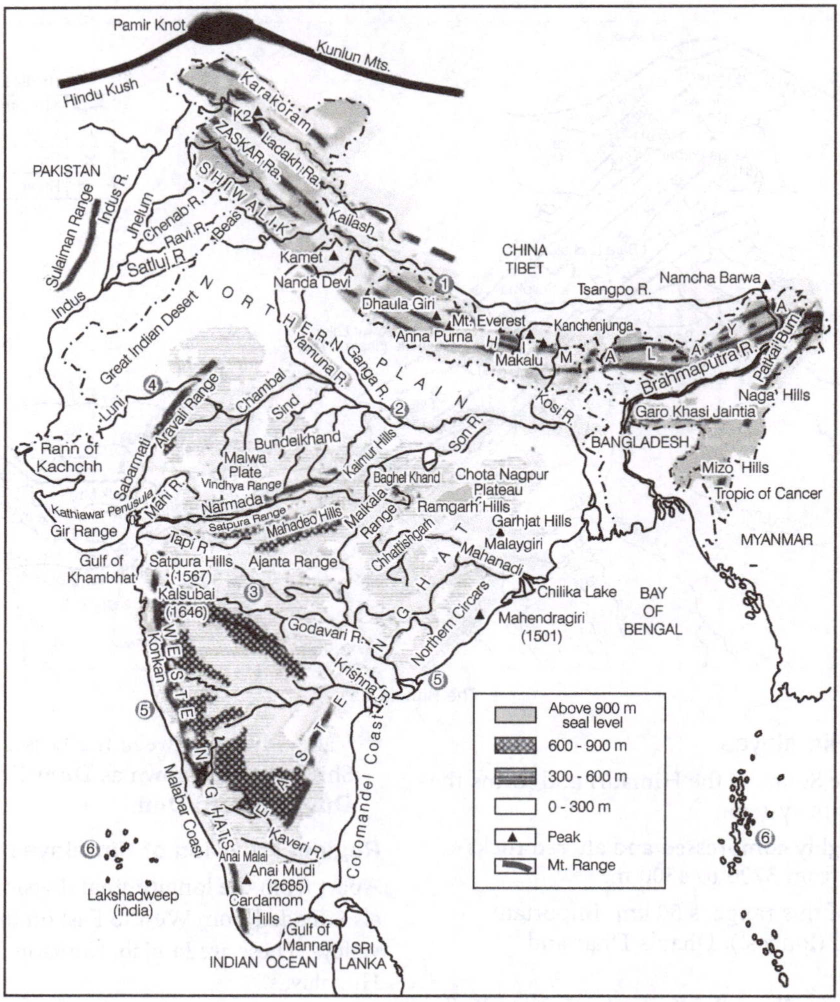

• Relief

Purvanchal or Eastern Range

The Himalayas in the Eastern part of India are known as **Purvanchal** or **Eastern Himalayas.**

The Brahmaputra river marks Easternmost boundary of the Himalayas. Beyond Dihang gorge[2], the Eastern Himalayan range turns South and spread along the Eastern boundary of India.

Purvanchal hills are mostly composed of strong sandstones which are sedimentary rocks and are covered with dense forest.

They mostly run as parallel ranges and valleys. The Purvanchal includes the Patkai hills, the Naga hills, the Manipur hills and the Mizo hills.

Try These

1. **It is an ancient and stable landmass of India. Identify.**
2. **Which is the highest peak of the Himalayas?**
3. **Between which two rivers is the Kumaon Himalayas situated?**
4. **Which river marks the Eastern most boundary of the Himalayas?**

2. The Northern Plains

These plains are formed by three river systems, *viz* the **Indus**, the **Ganga** and the **Brahmaputra**, along with their tributaries. These plains are composed of alluvial soil and spread over an area of 7 lakh sq km. These plains are about 2400 km long and between 240 to 320 km broad. These plains are densely populated.

2 Gorge It refers to narrow valley between hills or mountains with a river running through it.

The deposition of alluvium at the foothills of the Himalaya over million of years, formed this fertile plain.

These plains are agriculturally very productive part of India due to the fertile soil cover, adequate water supply, favourable climate and terrain.

Rivers from Northern mountains deposit a lot of silt. The gentle slope in lower course reduces the velocity of the rivers resulting in the formation of Riverine islands[3].

Majuli is the largest inhabited riverine island in the world and lies in the Brahmaputra river.

The rivers split into a number of channels in their lower courses due to deposition[4] of silt. These channels are called **Distributaries.**

Divisions of the Northern Plain

The three parts of the Northern plains are

(i) **Punjab Plain** It is the Western part of the plain. It is formed by the Indus and its many tributaries. The larger part of this plain lies in Pakistan.
The Indus and its tributaries—the **Jhelum**, the **Ravi**, the **Satluj**, the **Beas** and the **Chenab**, originate in the Himalayas. The Punjab plain is also dominated by doabs[5].

(ii) **Ganga Plain** It is the middle part of the plain. It extends from the Ghaggar river (in Haryana) to the Teesta river (in West Bengal) through the States of Haryana, Delhi, Uttar Pradesh, Bihar, partly Jharkhand and West Bengal.

(iii) **Brahmaputra Plain** It is the Eastern part of the plain lying in Assam.

KNOWLEDGE PLUS 'Doab' is made up of two words - 'do' meaning two and 'ab' meaning water. Similarly 'Punjab' is also made up of two words - 'Punj' meaning five and 'ab' meaning water.

Regions of the Northern Plain

The Northern plain is divided into four regions according to variation in relief feature which are as follows

(i) **Bhabar** After flowing down from the mountains, the rivers deposit pebbles in a narrow belt of about 8 to 16 km in width lying parallel to the slopes of the Shiwaliks known as bhabar belt. All the rivers disappear in bhabar belt.

(ii) **Terai** A wet, swampy and marshy region created by the streams and rivers in the South of bhabar belt, is known as terai.
Earlier, it was thickly forested region with a lot of wildlife, but now most of the forests have been cleared for agriculture land and to settle migrants from Pakistan after partition. **Dudhwa National Park** is located in this region.

(iii) **Bhangar** The largest part of the Northern plain consisting of older alluvium is known as bhangar. It lies above the flood plains of the rivers and presents a terrace like feature. It contains **calcareous** deposits (containing calcium) known as *kankars*.

(iv) **Khadar** The newer and younger deposits of the flood plain is known as khadar. The soil here is renewed whenever there is a flood (almost every year), so this area is fertile and best for intensive agriculture.

3. The Peninsular Plateau

This is a plateau composed of the old crystalline, igneous[6] and metamorphic rocks. It was formed due to the breaking up and drifting of Gondwana land[7].

Thus, it is a part of the oldest landmass. The plateau has broad and shallow valleys, and rising and rounded hills.

The Aravalli hills lie on the West and North-West margins of the Peninsular Plateau. These are highly eroded and broken hills. They extend from Gujarat to Delhi in South-West to North-East direction.

This plateau consists of two broad divisions which are

(i) Central Highlands

- This is the part lying North of the Narmada river, covering most of the Malwa plateau.
- It is surrounded by **Vindhyan range** which is bounded by Satpura range on the South and Aravallis on the North-West. In the West, it gradually merges with the sandy and rocky desert of Rajasthan.
- The Central highland slope from South-West to North-East, is indicated by the flow of Chambal, Sind, Betwa and Ken rivers. The highlands are wider in the West, but narrower in the East.
- Its Eastward extension are known as **Bundelkhand** and **Baghelkhand.**

3 Riverine Islands It refers to a landmass surrounded by river water that is located between two parallel rivers.
4 Deposition It is the geological process by which material is added to a landform or landmass.
5 Doabs It is a term used for tract of land lying between two confluent rivers.
6 Igneous rocks These rocks formed by cooling and solidification of magma or lava.
7 Gondwana Land It is the Southern part of the ancient super continent Pangaea with Angara land in the Northern part.

- The Chota Nagpur plateau lies in the further East of this highland and is drained by the Damodar river.

(ii) **Deccan Plateau**

- This triangular landmass lies to the South of the river Narmada. The broad base of the Satpura range is in North, while the **Mahadeo hills**, the **Kaimur hills** and the **Maikal range** are in its East.
- The Deccan plateau slopes gently West to East.
- The plateau extends to North-East and is generally known as the **Meghalaya Karbi-Anglong plateau** and **North Cachar hills.**
- It is separated from the Chota Nagpur plateau by a fault[8]. Three prominent hill ranges from its West to East are the **Garo**, the **Khasi** and the **Jaintia hills**.

Western and Eastern Ghats

These ghats mark the East and West edges of the Deccan plateau.

The Western Ghats (also called the Sahyadri range) lie parallel to the Western coast. They are higher than the Eastern Ghats.

The average elevation of Western Ghats is 900-1600 metres, while the average elevation of Eastern Ghats is 600 metres.

The Western Ghats are continuous ranges and can be crossed through passes like Thal, Bhor and Pal Ghats.

The Western Ghats cause orographic rain[9] when the rain-bearing moist monsoon winds strike the Western slopes of the ghats and rise up.

The height of the Western Ghats increases from North to South. **Anai Mudi** (2695 m) and **Doda Betta** (2637 m) are the highest peaks in the Western Ghats.

The famous hill stations of **Udagamandalam** (popularly known as **Ooty**) and **Kodaikanal** lie in the Western Ghats.

The Eastern Ghats stretch from the Mahanadi valley to the Nilgiris in the South. These Ghats are discontinuous and irregular and dissected by rivers flowing into the Bay of Bengal.

Mahendragiri (1501 m) is the highest peak **in the Eastern Ghats.** Shevroy hills and Javadi hills are located to the South-East of the Eastern Ghats.

The Nilgiri hills in Tamil Nadu lies at the junction of the Eastern and Western Ghats.

KNOWLEDGE PLUS The black soil area of Peninsular Plateau is known as Deccan Trap. The rocks here are igneous due to its volcanic orgin. Exposure of these rocks over time has led to the formation of black soil.

4. The Indian Desert

It lies towards the Western margins of the Aravalli hills. It consists of wave like sandy plain with sand dunes.

It receives less than 150 mm rainfall annually and has arid climate with low vegetation. Here streams appear only during the rainy season. **Luni** is the only large river in this region.

Crescent[10] shaped sand dunes called **Barchans** cover most of this desert. They can be seen in Jaisalmer. Longitudinal dunes[11] are mostly found near the Indo-Pakistan border.

5. The Coastal Plains

The Peninsular plateau is bordered by narrow coastal land running along the Arabian sea on the West and the Bay of Bengal on the East. These coastal lands are called coastal plains.

The Western coast which lies between the Western Ghats and Arabian Sea, is a narrow plain. It consists of three sections

(i) Northern part of the coast is called the **Konkan** (Mumbai-Goa).

(ii) Central stretch is called the **Kannad** plain.

(iii) Southern stretch is called the **Malabar coast**.

The plains, which lies along the Bay of Bengal are wide and level.

The Northern part of Eastern coastal plains is known as **Northern Circar** and the Southern part is known as **Coromandel coast**. Rivers like the Mahanadi, Godavari, Krishna and Kaveri have formed extensive deltas on this coast.

KNOWLEDGE PLUS Lake Chilika is the largest salt water lake in India which lies on the Eastern Coast of Odisha, South of the Mahanadi delta.

6. The Islands

India has two island groups. These are as follows

(i) **The Lakshadweep Islands Group** It lies close to the Malabar coast (Kerala). This is a group of small coral islands. Earlier, they were known as Laccadive, Minicoy and Amindive.

8 Fault It is a zone of fracture beween two blocks of rock.
9 Orographic rain Such rainfall occurs when moist air is forced to rise up the side of a mountain or plateau.
10 Crescent A thing which has the shape of a single curve that is broad in the centre and tapers to a point at each end.
11 Longitudinal dunes They are linear sand ridges that extend parallel to the direction of the dominant dune-building winds.

In 1973, these were named as Lakshadweep. They cover a small area of 32 sq km.

Kavaratti island is the administrative headquarters (capital) of Lakshadweep. In this group, the Pitti island has a bird sanctuary which is uninhabited.

KNOWLEDGE PLUS Coral polyps are tiny creatures that live together in groups. They like warm, clear water and create reefs by producing calcium carbonate. These reefs come in three types : **Barrier reefs, fringing reefs** and atolls[12]. The **Great Barrier Reef** of Australia is a good example of the first kind of coral reefs.

(ii) **The Andaman and Nicobar Islands** These are the chain of islands in Bay of Bengal extending from North to South. They are bigger in size and are more in number and scattered.

The entire group of islands is divided into two broad categories, the Andamans in the North and the Nicobars in the South.

These islands are believed to be an elevated portion of **submarine mountains**[13] and are of great strategic importance for the country.

India's only active volcano is found on Barren Island in the Andaman and Nicobar islands.

There is a great diversity of flora and fauna in this group of islands. These islands lie close to the equator and experience equatorial climate with thick forest cover.

Conclusion

After studying the physical features of India, following things can be concluded

- The mountains are the major sources of water and forest wealth.
- The Northern plains are the granaries of the country. Early civilisations started here.
- The plateau is a storehouse of minerals and has played an important role in industrialisation of the country.
- The coastal regions and island groups provide sites for fishing and port related activities.

Thus, the diverse physical features of India have immense future possibilities for development.

Try These

1. **Which river contributes to the formation of the Northern plains in India?**
2. **The wet, swampy region is created by rivers in the Northern Plain. Identify this region.**
3. **Which part of the Deccan Plateau is known as Deccan Trap?**
4. **It is the group of islands composed of small coral islands. Identify.**
5. **Which islands group enjoys equatorial climatic condition?**

12 **Atolls** Atolls are circular or horse shoe shaped coral reefs.

13 **Submarine mountains** Mountains rising from the ocean floor that do not reach to the water's surface (sea level) and thus, are not islands.

Mind Map

PHYSICAL FEATURES OF INDIA

Major Physiographic Division

The Islands

The Andaman and Nicobar Islands

- These are a chain of islands divided into the Andamans in the North and Nicobars in the South.
- These lie close to the equator and experience equatorial climate with thick forest cover.
- India's only active volcano is found on Barren Island.

The Lakshadweep Islands Group

- It lies close to the Malabar Coast.
- It is a group of small coral islands.
- These were named as Lakshadweep in 1973. Kavaratti island is the administrative headquarters of Lakshadweep.

The Coastal Plains

- The coastal lands running along the Arabian Sea on the West and the Bay of Bengal on the East are called Coastal Plains.
- The Western Coast lies between the Western Ghats and the Arabian Sea.
- The Northern Part of Coastal plains is known as Northern Circar and the Southern part is Coromandel Coast.
- Chilika Lake, the largest salt water lake lies on the Eastern Coast of Odisha.

The Northern Plains

- Formed by three river systems, the Indus, the Ganga and the Brahmaputra along with their tributaries.
- Majuli is the largest inhabited riverine island in this river.

Divisions of the Northern Plain

- Punjab Plain
- Ganga Plain
- Brahmaputra Plain

Regions of the Northern Plain

- Bhabar
- Terai
- Bhangar
- Khadar

The Indian Desert

- It lies towards the Western margins of the Aravalli hills.
- It receives less than 150mm of rainfall annually and has arid climate with low vegetation.
- Crescent-shaped sand dunes called Barchan cover most of this desert.
- Longitudinal dunes are found near the Indo-Pakistan border.

The Peninsular Plateau

- Composed of old crystalline, igneous and metamorphic rocks.
- Formed due to the breaking up and drifting of Gondwana land.
- Its Eastward extension is known as Bundelkhand and Baghelkhand.

Central Highlands

Surrounded by Vindhyan range which is bounded by Satpura range on the South and Aravallis on the North-West

Deccan Plateau

- It is also known as the Meghalaya Karbi-Anglong plateau and North Cachar hills.
- It is separated from the Chota Nagpur plateau by a fault.
- The hill ranges from West to East are the Garo, the Khasi and the Jaintia hills.

Western Ghats

- Average elevation is 900-1600 metres.
- Anai Mudi and Doda Betta are the highest peaks in the Western Ghats.

Eastern Ghats

- Average elevation is 600 metres.
- Mahendragiri is the highest peak in the Eastern Ghats.

The Himalayan Mountains

- The Himalayas are geologically young and structurally fold mountains.
- They stretch over Northern borders of India.
- They run in West-East direction from Indus to the Brahmaputra rivers.

Regional Division

- Punjab Himalayas
- Kumaon Himalayas
- Nepal Himalayas
- Assam Himalayas

Longitudinal Division

- Great Himalayas
- Lesser Himalayas
- Shiwalik

NCERT FOLDER

Covering Intext Questions and Exercises of NCERT

INTEXT QUESTIONS

Q.1 Find out the names of the glaciers and passes that lie in Great Himalayas.

Ans. Glaciers in the Great Himalayas are Siachen, Kolhai, Gangotri, Chaturangi, Satopanth, Nubra, Milam Kamet, Kharak, Bhagirathi and Pindari.

Passes in the Great Himalayas are Aghil, Karakoram, Bara Lacha, Bum La, Shipki La, Nathula and Bomdila.

Q.2 Find out the name of the states and UT's where highest peaks are located.

Ans. States and UT's where highest peaks are located are

- Jammu and Kashmir (Nanga Parbat)
- Sikkim (Kanchenjunga)
- Uttarakhand(Nanda Devi, Kamet)

Q.3 Find out the location of Mussoorie, Nainital, Ranikhet from your atlas and also name the state where they are located.

Ans. All these three towns are in the state of Uttarakhand in the range called Lesser Himalayas or Himachal.

EXERCISE

Q.1 Choose the right answer from the four alternatives given below.

(i) A landmass bounded by sea on three sides is referred to as

(a) Coast (b) Island
(c) Peninsula (d) None of these

Ans. (c) Peninsula

(ii) Mountain ranges in the Eastern part of India forming its boundary with Myanmar are collectively called

(a) Himachal (b) Uttarakhand
(c) Purvanchal (d) None of these

Ans. (c) Purvanchal

(iii) The Western coastal strip, South of Goa is referred to as

(a) Coromandel (b) Konkan
(c) Kannad (d) Northern Circar

Ans. (c) Kannad

(iv) The highest peak in the Eastern Ghats is

(a) Anai Mudi (b) Kanchenjunga
(c) Mahendragiri (d) Khasi

Ans (c) Mahendragiri

Q.2 Answer the following questions briefly.

(i) What is the Bhabar?

Ans. Bhabar is a narrow belt of plain land which is about 8 to 16 km wide. It is covered with pebbles deposited by the rivers and lies parallel to the foothills of the Shiwaliks.

(ii) Name the three major divisions of the Himalayas from North to South.

Ans. The three major divisions of the Himalayas from North to South are

(a) The Great or Inner Himalayas or the Himadri
(b) Himachal or Lesser Himalayas
(c) Shiwaliks

(iii) Which plateau lies between the Aravalli and the Vindhyan ranges?

Ans. Malwa plateau lies between the Aravalli and the Vindhya ranges.

(iv) Name the island group of India having coral origin.

Ans. Lakshadweep is the island group of India which has the coral origin on the Arabian Sea.

Q.3 Distinguish between

(i) Bhangar and Khadar

(ii) Western Ghats and Eastern Ghats

Ans. (i) Differences between Bhangar and Khadar are

Bhangar	Khadar
It is a land covered with old alluvial soil.	It is a land covered with new alluvial soil.
It is found above the flood plains.	It is found near the rivers and in flood plains.
It is less fertile than khadar.	It is very fertile.
It contains calcareous deposits locally known as *Kankar*.	The soil is fine-grained.
It is not much suited for agriculture.	It is renewed almost every year and is suited for intensive cultivation.

(ii) Differences between the Eastern Ghats and the Western Ghats are

The Eastern Ghats	The Western Ghats
The Eastern Ghats mark the Eastern edge of the Deccan plateau.	The Western Ghats mark the Western edge of the Deccan plateau.

The Eastern Ghats	The Western Ghats
They are discontinuous and irregular and cut by rivers flowing into the Bay of Bengal.	They are continuous and can be crossed through passes only.
They lie parallel to the Eastern coast along the Bay of Bengal.	They lie parallel to the Western coast along the Arabian sea.
The highest peak is Mahendragiri with a height of 1501 m.	The highest peak is Anai Mudi with a height of 2695 m.
Their average height is 600 m.	Their average height is 900 m to 1600 m.

Q.4 Which are the major physiographic divisions of India? Contrast the relief of the Himalayan region with that of the Peninsular plateau.

Ans. The major physiographic divisions of India are
(i) The Himalayan Mountains
(ii) The Northern Plains (iii) The Peninsular Plateau
(iv) The Indian Desert (v) The Coastal Plains
(vi) The Islands

Contrast between the relief of the Himalayan region and the Peninsular plateau is given below

The Himalayan Region	The Peninsular Plateau
It is formed by folding process of the plates.	It is formed due to the breaking up and drifting of Gondwana land.
The Himalayas are made up of sedimentary rocks.	Plateau contains igneous and metamorphic rocks.
The Himalayas consist of high mountain peaks, deep valleys.	Peninsular plateau consists of round hills, shallow valleys.
Average height of Himalayas is 6000 m.	Average height of the plateau is 900 m.
The Himalayas are an unstable zone because of tectonic activity.	Considered to be one of the most stable land blocks.
Himalayas are the most recent new and younger landforms.	The Deccan plateau is one of the most ancient landmasses.
The Himalayas are rich in water resources and forest wealth.	The plateau is a storehouse of minerals.

Q.5 Give an account of the Northern Plains of India.

Ans. Northern plains were formed when a depression created by the upliftment of the Himalayan mountains gradually got filled by deposition of sediments brought down by rivers like the Indus, Ganga and Brahmaputra.

Their features are

- They spread over an area of 7 lakh sq km. The plains are about 2400 km long and about 240 km broad.
- These are very fertile as they get renewed every year with sediments.
- With their adequate water supply and favourable climate, these are agriculturally a very productive part of India and therefore, densely populated.

The Northern plains are broadly divided into three sections. These are

(i) **Punjab Plain** The Western part of the Northern plains is called the Punjab plain. It is formed by the Indus and its tributaries.

(ii) **Ganga Plain** It extends between the Ghaggar and the Teesta rivers. It is spread over the states of Haryana, Delhi, Uttar Pradesh, Bihar and West Bengal.

(iii) **Brahmaputra Plain** It lies to the East of the Ganga plains. It covers the areas of Assam and Arunachal Pradesh.

Q.6 Write short notes on the following.
(i) The Indian Desert
(ii) The Central Highlands
(iii) The Island Groups of India

Ans. (i) **The Indian Desert**

The Indian desert lies towards the West of the Aravalli hills. It is a sandy plain covered with sand-dunes. This region receives very low rainfall, below 150 mm per year. It has arid climate with low vegetation cover. Streams appear during the rainy season only. Luni is the only large river in this region. Barchans (crescent shaped dunes) cover the larger areas, but longitudinal dunes become more prominent near the Indo-Pakistan border.

(ii) **The Central Highlands**

The Peninsular plateau consists of two broad divisions, namely the Central Highlands and the Deccan plateau. The part of the Peninsular plateau lying to the North of the Narmada river, covering a major area of the Malwa plateau, is known as the Central Highlands. Central Highlands are surrounded by the Vindhya range in the South and by the Aravalli hills in the North-West. In the West, they gradually merge with the sandy and rocky desert of Rajasthan.

The flow of the rivers in this region, namely the Chambal, Sind, Betwa and Ken, is from South-West to North-East. The Central Highlands are wider in the West, but narrower in the East. The Eastward extensions of this plateau are locally known as Bundelkhand and Baghelkhand. The Chotanagpur plateau lies in the East of this plateau and is drained by the Damodar river.

(iii) **The Island Groups of India** India has two groups of islands, namely the Lakshadweep group and the Andaman and Nicobar group.

(a) **The Lakshadweep Islands Group** It lies close to the Malabar coast of Kerala. These are composed of small coral islands. Earlier, they were known as Laccadive, Minicoy and Amindive. In 1973, these were renamed as Lakshadweep. They cover a small area of 32 sq km.

Kavaratti is the administrative headquarters of Lakshadweep. These island groups have a great diversity of flora and fauna. The Pitti island, which is uninhabited, has a bird sanctuary.

(b) **Andaman and Nicobar Islands** The elongated chain of islands located in the Bay of Bengal extending from North to South are the Andaman and Nicobar islands. They are bigger in size and more numerous and scattered than the Lakshadweep islands.

These islands are of great strategic importance for the country. They have great diversity of flora and fauna. These islands lie close to the equator and experience equatorial climate.

MAP SKILLS

Q.7 On an outline map of India, show the following.

(i) **Mountain and Hill Ranges** The Karakoram, the Zaskar, the Patkai Bum, the Jaintia, the Vindhya range, the Aravalli and the Cardamom hills.

(ii) **Peaks** K2, Kanchenjunga, Nanga Parbat and the Anai Mudi.

(iii) **Plateaus** Chota Nagpur and Malwa

(iv) The Indian Desert, Western Ghats, Lakshadweep Islands.

Ans.

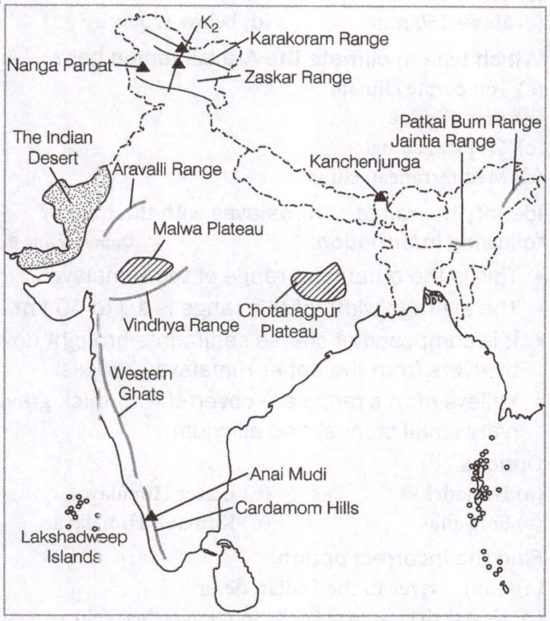

REVIEW EXERCISE

Including Competency Based Questions

Part I

Multiple Choice Questions (MCQs)

1. ...... are geographically young and structurally fold mountains that stretch over the Northern border of India.

(a) Aravallis (b) Vindhyas
(c) Himalayas (d) Cardamom Hills

2. In which direction, the Himalayan mountain ranges run from the Indus to the Brahmaputra?

(a) West-East (b) North-South
(c) East-West (d) North-East

3. Which of the following represents the loftiest and one of the most rugged mountain barriers of the world?

(a) Hindu Kush
(b) Sulaiman range
(c) Kunlun mountains
(d) Himalayan mountains

4. The Himalayan mountains form an arc and cover distance of

(a) 2400 km (b) 1500 km (c) 2700 km (d) 6000 km

5. The Himalayas consist of how many parallel ranges in their longitudinal extent?

(a) Three parallel ranges (b) Four parallel ranges
(c) Five parallel ranges (d) Six parallel ranges

6. The Northern plains have been formed by the interplay of how many river systems in India?

(a) Two (b) Three (c) Four (d) One

7. How much area is covered by the Northern plains?

(a) 3 lakh sq km (b) 5 lakh sq km
(c) 7 lakh sq km (d) 9 lakh sq km

8. Which of the following is agriculturally the most productive part of India ?

(a) Northern plains (b) Peninsular plateau
(c) Coastal plains (d) Indian desert

9. **The Indian Desert lies towards the Western margins of the**

(a) Shiwalik hills (b) Jaintia hills
(c) Aravali hills (d) Khasi hills

10. **The Aravali region annually receives rainfall**

(a) below 150 mm (b) below 125 mm
(c) above 150 mm (d) below 120 mm

11. **Which type of climate the Aravali region has?**

(a) Temperate climate
(b) Arid climate
(c) Tropical climate
(d) Mediterranean climate

12. **Identify the range of Himalayas with the help of following information.** **Competency Based**

- This is the outermost range of the Himalayas.
- The average width of this range is 10 to 50 km.
- It is composed of coarse sediments brought down by rivers from the upper Himalayan ranges.
- Valleys of this range are covered with thick gravel (very small stones) and alluvium.

Options

(a) Himadri (b) Lesser Himalayas
(c) Shiwaliks (d) Kumaon Himalayas

13. **Find the incorrect option.**

(a) Luni – river in the Indian desert
(b) Kaveri river – forms delta in the Northern circar
(c) Anai Mudi – Highest peak in the Western Ghat
(d) Baghelkhand – Eastward extension of the Central highlands.

14. **The Western Ghats and the Eastern Ghats mark the Western and the Eastern edges of the Deccan Plateau respectively. Western Ghats lie parallel to the Western coast.**

How do the Western Ghats contribute to the climate of that region ? **Competency Based**

(a) By forming plateaus
(b) By creating deserts
(c) By restricting rainfall
(d) By acting as a barrier to the rain-bearing winds

15. **The Western part of the Northern Plain is referred to as the Punjab plains. It is formed by the Indus and its tributaries, the larger part of this plain lies in Pakistan.**

The Northern Plain is broadly divided into how many parts? **Competency Based**

(a) 5 (b) 2 (c) 3 (d) 4

16. **Consider the following statements about Deccan Plateau and choose the correct option.**

I. Deccan Plateau has a triangular landmass.
II. Deccan Plateau lies South of the Narmada river.
III. Satpura range lies North of the Deccan Plateau.

Codes

(a) Only I (b) Only II
(c) I and II (d) All of these

17. **Which of the following statements accurately describes about the 'Shiwaliks'?** **Competency Based**

I. The Northern range of the Himalayas is called the Shiwaliks.
II. The outer-most range of the Himalayas is called the Shiwaliks.
III. This range consists of the famous Valley of Kashmir, the Kangra and Kullu Valley in Himachal Pradesh.
IV. The part of the Himalayas lying between Satluj and Kali rivers is known as Shiwaliks.

Options

(a) Only I (b) Only II
(c) Only IV (d) Both I and II

18. **Consider the following statements about Terai belt and choose the correct option.**

I. Terai is a wet, Swampy and marshy region.
II. Terai is created by the streams and rivers.
III. Terai lies in the South of Bhangar region of the Northern plains.

Codes

(a) Only I (b) Only II
(c) I and II (d) All of these

19. **Arrange the following regional divisions of the Himalayan-sequence from West to East direction.**

I. Kumaon Himalayas II. Nepal Himalayas
III. Punjab Himalayas IV. Assam Himalayas

Codes

(a) I, II, III, IV (b) IV, III, II, I
(c) III, I, II, IV (d) II, III, I, IV

20. **Arrange the following regions of the Northern Plains in sequence from North to South direction.**

I. Bhangar II. Terai III. Bhabar IV. Khadar

Codes

(a) III, II, I, IV (b) I, II, III, IV
(c) IV, III, II, I (d) III, IV, I, II

21. **Consider the statements given below and choose the correct option.** **Competency Based**

Statement I The Himalayas represent the loftiest and one of the most rugged mountain barriers of the world.

Statement II The Himalayas consist of three parallel ranges in its longitudinal extent.

Options

(a) Statement I is correct and II is incorrect
(b) Statement I is incorrect and II is correct
(c) Both I and II are incorrect
(d) Both I and II are correct

22. Identify in which regions Ganga Plain spreads. Choose from the appropriate statements among the following options **Competency Based**

I. It is spread over South India in Gujarat, Andhra Pradesh, Madhya Pradesh, Goa, partly Assam and East Bengal.

II. It is spread over North India in Haryana, Delhi, Uttar Pradesh, Bihar, partly Jharkhand and West Bengal.

III. It is spread over West India in Maharashtra, Goa, Sikkim, Tamil Nadu, partly Tripura and South Bengal.

IV. It is spread over Chandigarh, Ladakh, Himachal Pradesh, Telangana, partly Lakshadweep and Jammu and Kashmir.

Options

(a) Statements I and II are appropriate.
(b) Statements I, II and III are appropriate.
(c) All the statements are appropriate.
(d) Only statement II is appropriate.

Answers

1. (c)	**2.** (a)	**3.** (d)	**4.** (a)	**5.** (a)
6. (b)	**7.** (c)	**8.** (a)	**9.** (c)	**10.** (a)
11. (b)	**12.** (c)	**13.** (b)	**14.** (d)	**15.** (c)
16. (d)	**17.** (b)	**18.** (c)	**19.** (c)	**20.** (a)
21. (d)	**22.** (d)			

Match the Following

1.

List I	List II
A. Punjab Himalayas	1. Teesta-Dihang rivers
B. Nepal Himalayas	2. Satluj-Kali rivers
C. Assam Himalayas	3. Kali-Teesta rivers
D. Kumaon Himalayas	4. Indus-Satluj rivers

Codes

	A	B	C	D		A	B	C	D
(a)	4	1	3	2	(b)	4	3	2	1
(c)	4	3	1	2	(d)	3	4	2	1

2.

List I	List II
A. Makalu	1. 8078 m
B. Annapurna	2. 8481 m
C. Kanchenjunga	3. 8598 m
D Nanda Devi	4. 7817 m

Codes

	A	B	C	D		A	B	C	D
(a)	2	1	3	4	(b)	3	2	1	4
(c)	1	2	3	4	(d)	1	4	3	2

Ans. 1. (c) 2. (a)

Assertion-Reason

1. Assertion (A) The chambal, Sind, Betwa and Ken rivers flow from South-West to North-East.

Reason (R) The Central highland slopes from South-West to North-East direction.

Codes

(a) Both A and R are true and R is the correct explanation of A
(b) Both A and R are true, but R is not the correct explanation of A
(c) A is true, but R is false
(d) A is false, but R is true

2. Assertion (A) The Himalayas form the highest and the rugged mountains in the world.

Reason (R) The Mount Everest is the highest peak in the world lying in the Himalayas.

Codes

(a) Both A and R are true and R is the correct explanation of A
(b) Both A and R are true, but R is not the correct explanation of A
(c) A is true, but R is false
(d) A is false, but R is true

3. Assertion (A) The Eastern Ghats are discontinuous and irregular.

Reason (R) The Eastern Ghats are cut by rivers flowing into the Bay of Bengal.

Codes

(a) Both A and R are true and R is the correct explanation of A
(b) Both A and R are true, but R is not the correct explanation of A
(c) A is true, but R is false
(d) A is false, but R is true

4. Assertion (A) Himalayas is the most continuous range consisting of the loftiest peaks with an average height of 6,000 metres.

Reason (R) The Western part of the Northern Plain is referred to as the Punjab Plains.

Codes

(a) Both A and R are true and R is the correct explanation of A
(b) Both A and R are true, but R is not the correct explanation of A
(c) A is true, but R is false
(d) A is false, but R is true

5. Assertion (A) Besides longitudinal divisions, the Himalayas are also divided on the basis of regions from west to east, demarcated by rivers.

Reason (R) Each region has a distinct name based on the rivers surrounding it, like Kashmir and Himachal Himalayas between Indus and Satluj.

Codes

(a) Both A and R are true and R is the correct explanation of A

(b) Both A and R are true, but R is not the correct explanation of A

(c) A is true, but R is false

(d) A is false, but R is true

Ans. 1. (a) Both A and R are true and R is the correct explanation of A

2. (b) Both A and R are true, but R is not the correct explanation of A

3. (a) Both A and R are true and R is the correct explanation of A

4. (b) Both A and R are true, but R is not the correct explanation of A

5. (b) Both A and R are true, but R is not the correct explanation of A

Case Based Question

1. Read the given source and answer the questions that follow.

The Peninsular plateau is a table land composed of the old crystalline, igneous and metamorphic rocks. It was formed due to the breaking and drifting of the Gondwana land and thus, making it a part of the oldest landmass. The plateau has broad and shallow valleys and rounded hills. This plateau consists of two broad divisions, namely, the Central Highlands and the Deccan Plateau.

The part of the Peninsular plateau lying to the North of the Narmada river, covering a major area of the Malwa plateau, is known as the Central Highlands. The Vindhyan range is bounded by the Satpura range on the South and the Aravallis on the North-West. The further Westward extension gradually merges with the sandy and rocky desert of Rajasthan. The flow of the rivers draining this region, namely the Chambal, the Sind, the Betwa and the Ken is from South-West to North-East, thus indicating the slope. The Central Highlands are wider in the West but narrower in the East.

(i) The Deccan Plateau slopes gently in which direction?

(a) East (b) West (c) North (d) South

(ii) Which plateau is separated by a fault from the Chotanagpur Plateau?

(a) Deccan Plateau

(b) Meghalaya Plateau

(c) Karbi-Anglong Plateau

(d) None of the above

(iii) Which two mountain ranges mark the Western and Eastern edges of the Deccan Plateau?

(a) Himalayas and Aravalli

(b) Satpura and Vindhya

(c) Western Ghats and Eastern Ghats

(d) Karakoram and Zanskar

(iv) Which three hills ranges are found in the North-East, from West to East?

(a) Garo, Kaimur and Maikal

(b) Garo, Khasi and Jaintia

(c) Satpura, Vindhya and Karbi-Anglong

(d) Kaimur, Mahadev and Maikal

Ans. (i) (a) East

(ii) (a) Deccan Plateau

(iii) (c) Western Ghats and Eastern Ghats

(iv) (b) Garo, Khasi and Jaintia

Part II

Very Short Answer Type Questions

1. Which range of Himalayas is the most continuous range?

Ans. The Northernmost range which is also known as Himadri or Inner Himalayas, is the most continuous range of Himalayas.

2. Which is the largest mountain range of the Himachal or lesser Himalayas?

Ans. The Pir Panjal mountain range is the largest mountain range of the Himachal or lesser Himalayas.

3. Name the three prominent sub-ranges of the Himachal Himalayas.

Ans. The sub-ranges are named as Pir Panjal, Dhaula Dhar and Mahabharat.

4. Name the part of the Himalayas located between Kali and Satluj rivers.

Ans. The part of the Himalayas located between Kali and Satluj rivers is the Kumaon Himalayas.

5. State one characteristic of the Eastern Himalayas.

Ans. The Eastern mountain ranges of the Himalayas have higher altitudinal extent (height).

6. The Garo, Khasi and Jaintia hills lie in which region of the Himalayas?

Ans. The Garo, Khasi and Jaintia hills lie in the Eastern Himalayas region.

7. Which zone is known as Terai?

Ans. Terai is a zone of wet and marshy land located in the Northern plains.

8. Name the highest peak which lies in the Western Ghats.

Ans. Anai Mudi is the highest peak in Western Ghats. Its height is 2695 m.

9. Name the hills that lie at the junction of the Western and Eastern Ghats.

Ans. The Nilgiri hills in Tamil Nadu lie at the junction of the Eastern and Western Ghats.

10. Which part of the plateau contains black soil of volcanic origin?

Ans. The Western part of plateau known as the Deccan trap contains black soil of volcanic origin.

11. What do you understand by Deccan Trap?

Ans. The Deccan trap is the area made up of basaltic igneous rocks in peninsular India. Over the time, the rocks broke and formed the black soil.

12. Aravalli hills are located in the Western Ghats or the Eastern Ghats?

Ans. The Aravalli hills are neither in the Eastern nor in the Western Ghats, but they are located North to both the Ghats.

13. What are barchans? Where are they found?

Ans. Barchans are crescent shaped dunes which cover larger area of deserts. These are found in the Indian desert mainly in Jaisalmer and near Indo-Pakistan boundary.

14. What is the Southern part of the Western coastal plains known as?

Ans. The Southern part of the Western coastal plains is known as Malabar (mostly in Kerala).

15. What makes up the habitat in which coral polyps flourish?

Ans. Coral polyps flourish in a habitat consisting of shallow warm water which does not have mud. This kind of habitat is found in Lakshadweep.

16. The Western Ghats and the Eastern Ghats mark the Western and the Eastern edges of the Deccan Plateau respectively. Western Ghats lie parallel to the Western coast. They are continuous and can be crossed through passes only.

How do the Western Ghats influence the direction of moist winds? **Competency Based**

Ans. The Western Ghats influence the direction of moist winds by acting as a barrier to the rain-bearing winds from the Arabian Sea. As these winds approach the Western Ghats, they are forced to ascend along the slopes.

17. Andaman and Nicobar Islands are bigger in size and are more numerous and scattered. The entire group of islands is divided into two broad categories – The Andaman in the North and the Nicobar in the South.

What is the believed origin of Andaman and Nicobar Islands? **Competency Based**

Ans. The believed origin of the Andaman and Nicobar Islands is that they are an elevated portion of submarine mountains. This elongated chain of islands extends from North to South in the Bay of Bengal.

Short Answer Type Questions

1. State any three features of the Himalayan mountains.

Ans. Features of the Himalayan mountains are

(i) Himalayas stretch along the North and North East of India in an arc of over 2400 kms.

(ii) They are geologically newer and younger fold mountains of the Earth.

(iii) The Himalayan ranges have higher mountain peaks in the East than in the West.

2. Give a description of the Shiwaliks.

Ans. The outer most range or the foothills of the Himalayas is called the Shiwaliks. Its height varies between 900 and 1100 m. Its average width extends over 10-50 km.

They are composed of coarse sediments brought down by rivers from the main Himalayan ranges. The valleys in this range are covered with thick gravel and alluvium. The longitudinal valley lying between the lesser Himalaya and the Shiwaliks are known as 'Duns', with the names like Dehra Dun, Kotli Dun and Patli Dun.

3. Name the part of the Northern plains formed of older alluvium. Mention any two characteristic features of it.

Ans. The part of the Northern plains formed of older alluvium is known as *'bhangar'*.

Its two characteristic features are

(i) It lies above the flood plains of the rivers and presents a terrace like feature.

(ii) Its soil contains calcareous deposits locally known as *'kankar'*. It is not as agriculturally fertile as the part lying closer to the rivers because it does not get renewed every year.

4. Name the three sections into which the Northern plain has been divided. Write one feature of each.

Ans. The Northern plain is broadly divided into following three sections

(i) Punjab plain (ii) Ganga Plain (iii) Brahmaputra plain

Features of these sections are

(i) **Punjab Plain** It covers the Western part of Northern plains.

(ii) **Ganga Plain** It extends between Ganga and Teesta rivers.

(iii) **Brahmaputra Plain** It lies mostly in the state of Assam.

5. What are the differences between the Central Highlands and Deccan Plateau?

Ans. The differences between the Central Highlands and Deccan Plateau are

Feature	Central Highlands	Deccan Plateau
Location	North of the Narmada river	South of the Narmada river
Constituent parts and extensions	Malwa plateau, Bundelkhand, Baghelkhand and Chotanagpur plateau	Mahadeo, Kaimur and Maikal hills. Its Eastern extensions are Garo, Khasi, Jaintia, North Circar and Karbi- Anglong hills
Rivers	Chambal, Sind, Betwa and Ken	Mahanadi, Godavari, Krishna and Kaveri

6. Make a comparison between the Shiwalik and the Himachal Himalayas based on the following
(i) Composition (ii) Altitude

Ans. The comparison between the Shiwalik and Himachal Himalayas on the given basis are

Mountain Range	Composition	Altitude
Shiwalik	It is compose of unconsolidated sediments i.e. thick gravel and alluvium brought down by the Himalayan rivers.	It is the outermost range of the Himalayas with height varying between 900 and 1100 m.
Himachal Himalayas	It is compose of highly compressed and altered rocks.	It lies South of the Himadri with height varying from 3700 to 4500 m.

7. State any three differences between the Himadri range and Shiwalik range.

Ans. The differences between Himadri and Shiwalik ranges are

Feature	Himadri Range	Shiwalik Range
Location	This is the Northern most and innermost range of the Himalayas.	This is the outermost range of the Himalayas.
Altitude	The average altitude of this range is 6000 m.	The average altitude varies from 900 to 1100 m.
Composition	The core of this part of the Himalayas is composed of granite.	This range is composed of unconsolidated sediments brought down by rivers from the main Himalayan ranges.

8. How would you describe the topography of the Indian Desert? **Competency Based**

Build answer around these points
- **Landscape**
- **Nature**
- **Season**

Ans. The topography of the Indian desert is discussed below
- **Landscape** Indian desert's topography is characterised by a flat and arid landscape with scattered sand dunes and rocky terrain.
- **Nature** The region experiences the extreme temperatures, with not summers and relatively cooler winters.
- **Season** It experiences the scarcity of vegetation as the desert has a dry climate with minimal rainfall and limited water sources.

9. The Northern plains are generally described as flat land with no variations in its relief. It is not true. These vast plains also have diverse relief features. According to the variations in relief features, the Northern plains can be divided into four regions.
(i) What are the four regions into which the Northern plains are divided based on relief features?
(ii) How does the presence of diverse relief features challenge the typical description of the Northern plains? **Competency Based**

Ans. (i) The Northern Plains can be divided into four regions based on relief features as
- Bhabar, a narrow belt where rivers deposit pebbles.
- Terai, a wet and swampy region South of Bhabar and two distinct zones, bangar and khadar, each characterised by different soil attributes.

(ii) The presence of diverse relief features challenge the typical description of the Northern plains by highlighting that they are not uniformly flat. The existence of regions such as bhabar, terai, bangar and khadar reveals variations in elevation, soil characteristics and landforms within the Northern plains, disproving the misconception of a completely flat landscape.

10. Read the statements given below regarding physical features of India.
Statement 1 One of the distinct features of the Peninsular plateau is the black soil area known as Deccan Trap.
Statement 2 The Aravali Hills lie on the Western and North-Western margins of the Peninsular plateau.
Explain, which statement is correct and why? **Competency Based**

Ans. Both the statements are correct because the Deccan Traps are a distinct feature of the Peninsular Plateau. They are an extensive volcanic region formed by lava flows millions of years ago.
This volcanic activity resulted in the creation of fertile black soil regions in parts of Maharashtra, Madhya Pradesh, Gujarat, and Karnataka.
The Aravali Hills i.e on the Western and North-Western margins of the Peninsular Plateau. They are a fold mountain range, older than the Himalayas, and stretch for about 800 km, separating the Thar Desert from the fertile plains of Northern India.

Long Answer Type Questions

1. Name three longitudinal divisions of the Himalayas. State one characteristic feature of each.

***or* Name the three parallel ranges of the Himalayas. Write one main feature of each.**

***or* Give two characteristics of each of the following**

(i) The Great Himalayas

(ii) The Middle Himalayas

***or* Name the three major divisions of the Himalayas from North to South.**

Ans. The three longitudinal division of the Himalayas, in other words, the parallel ranges of the Himalayas are Himadri, Himachal and Shiwaliks.

(i) **Himadri/ Inner Himalayas /Great Himalayas**

- The Northernmost range is known as the Great or Inner Himalayas.
- It is the highest range with an average height of 6000 m.
- It contains all the prominent Himalayan peaks.
- The folds of Great Himalayas are asymmetrical in nature. The core of this part of the Himalayas is composed of granite.

(ii) **Himachal/ Lesser Himalayas / Middle Himalayas**

- It is known as the Himachal or Lesser Himalaya.
- It lies to the South of Himachal and forms the most rugged mountain system.
- The altitude varies between 3700 and 4500 m and the average width is 50 km.
- This range consists of the famous valley of Kashmir, the Kangra valley and Kullu valley in Himachal Pradesh.

(iii) **Shiwaliks /Outer Himalayas**

- The outermost range of the Himalayas is called Shiwaliks.
- The Shiwaliks extend over a width of 10 to 50 kms and have an altitude varying between 900 and 1100 m.
- This range is composed of unconsolidated sediments brought down by rivers from the main Himalayan ranges located farther North.
- The valleys are covered with thick gravel and alluvium.

2. Give an account of the four divisions of the Himalayas from West to East along with Purvanchal hills.

Ans. The divisions of the Himalayas from West to East are

(i) **Punjab Himalayas** The part lying between the Indus and Satluj rivers has been traditionally known as Punjab Himalayas, but it is regionally known as Kashmir and Himachal Himalayas.

(ii) **Kumaon Himalayas** The part lying between the Satluj and Kali rivers is known as Kumaon Himalayas.

(iii) **Nepal Himalayas** The part lying between the Kali and Teesta rivers is known as Nepal Himalayas.

(iv) **Assam Himalayas** The part lying between the Teesta and Dihang rivers is known as Assam Himalayas.

3. Describe the river systems of the Northern plains by giving their main features.

Ans. The three river systems in the Northern plains from West to East are the Indus systems, the Brahmaputra and the Ganga. There are discussed below

- **Indus River System** A large part of the Indus system lies in Pakistan. The Indus and its tributaries - Jhelum, Chenab, Ravi, Beas and Satluj originate in the Himalayas. This section of the plain is dominated by the doabs.
- **Ganges River System** The Ganga plain extends between the Ghaggar and Teesta rivers. It spreads over the States of Haryana, Delhi, Uttar Pradesh, Bihar, some part of Jharkhand and West Bengal. It has tributaries like the Yamuna, Gomati, Son, Gandak and Kosi.
- **The Brahmaputra River System** The Brahmaputra plain lies in Assam, where it is joined by its tributaries. These plains are comparatively narrow.

4. Give a brief explanation about important features of the Ganga plain.

***or* Write an account on the relief of the Ganga plain.**

Ans. The important features of the Ganga plain are

- The Ganga plain or basin forms the middle part of the Northern plains of India.
- It extends between the Ghaggar and Teesta rivers.
- It spreads over the states of Haryana, Delhi, Uttar Pradesh, Bihar, parts of Jharkhand and West Bengal.
- The Ganga plain is drained mostly in the Eastward direction by the Ganga and its major tributaries are the Yamuna, Gandak, Kosi, Son, etc.
- It slopes gently Eastwards and has high fertile soil. It is agriculturally the most important region of India.
- It is highly populated and has many major cities on its river banks.

5. Describe any five features of the Western coastal plains.

Ans. Five features of the Western coastal plains are

(i) These plains are sandwiched between the Western Ghats and the Arabian sea.

(ii) They are very narrow as compared to the Eastern coastal plains.

(iii) They consist of three sections, *Konkan* in the North, *Kannad* in the middle and *Malabar* in the South.

(iv) They have a number of ports because of the highly indented (not continuous) coastline.

(v) They get heavy rain during the monsoon due to the Western ghats causing orographic rain.

6. What are corals? Name and describe the island which is of coral origin.

***or* Write a short note on 'corals'.**

***or* What are corals? Describe the main features of the islands group which are of coral origin.**

Ans. Coral polyps are short-lived microscopic organisms which live in colonies. They flourish in shallow, mud free and warm waters. They secrete calcium carbonate.

The coral secretion and their skeletons form coral deposits known as reefs. They are mainly of three kinds

(i) **Barrier Reef** The Great Barrier Reef of Australia is a perfect example of the first kind of coral reef.

(ii) **Fringing Reef** 'Fringing reefs' are reefs that grow very close to the shore on mainland or high island (Continental shelf or volcanic mid-ocean island) coasts.

(iii) **Atolls** Atolls are circular or horse shoe-shaped coral reefs.

In India, Lakshadweep island is of coral origin. It covers a small area of 32 sq km. Kavaratti is the administrative headquarters of Lakshadweep. This island group has great diversity of flora and fauna.

7. How do the Himalayas play a vital role in the economic and cultural development of India?

Ans. The Himalayas play an important role in the economic and cultural development of India in the following ways

Economic Impact

- The Himalayas act as a barrier to the South-West monsoon winds. When they strike the Himalayas, they shed their moisture bringing much needed rainfall in the Northern parts of the country. Indian agriculture is immensely benefited by the monsoons.
- There are many hill stations in the Himalayan region like Shimla, Manali, Dharmshala, Nainital, etc. They are visited by tourists from all over the world, generating employment opportunities for the people.

Cultural Impact

- The Himalayas spread over vast regions running across various countries like India, Nepal, Bhutan, China, Pakistan, etc. This gives a common cultural background and provides scope for cultural exchange.
- The Himalayas also have shrines which are considered to be the abodes of Gods. Large number of pilgrims come to visit these sacred shrines.

8. 'The Indian landmass shows a great physical contrast.' Explain this statement.

Ans. India's landmass has great contrasts, this can be said by seeing the Peninsular plateau, the Himalayas and other landforms that exist in India.

The Peninsular plateau in the South is a very old landmass, whereas the Himalayas in the North are fairly new, the Himalayas and the Northern plains are unstable zones, whereas the Peninsular plateau is very stable.

While the Himalayas are composed of sedimentary and metamorphic rocks, the Northern plains are made of deposited alluvium and the Peninsular plateau is made up of igneous and metamorphic rocks.

Likewise, the Himalayas have lofty peaks and deep valleys, while the Deccan region has gently rising ranges and wide valleys. There exist vast sandy desert in the Western part of India. Thus, the Indian landmass shows a great physical contrast.

9. Name the two coastal strips that flank the Peninsular plateau. Distinguish the two by giving two characteristics of each.

Ans. The two coastal strips that flank the Peninsular plateau and differences between them are

Western Coastal Strip	Eastern Coastal Strip
It lies between the Western Ghats and the Arabian sea.	It lies between the Eastern Ghats and the Bay of Bengal.
It is a narrow plain consisting of three sections. The Northern part of the coast is called Konkan coast, the Central part is known as Kannad plain and Southern stretch is called the Malabar coast.	It is broader than the Western coastal plain. It consists of two main sections. In the Northern part, it is referred to as Northern Circar. In the Southern part, it is known as Coromandel coast.
The rivers flowing in this region are short and fast flowing. The major Westward flowing rivers are Narmada and Tapi.	The rivers flowing in this region are much longer and broader compared to the Western strip. The major rivers which make deltas are the Mahanadi, Godavari, Krishna and Kaveri.

10. Read the information about the Himalayas and answer the question that follows.

The Himalayas, geologically young and structurally fold mountains stretch over the Northern borders of India. These mountain ranges run in a West-East direction from the Indus to the Brahmaputra. The Himalaya consists of three parallel ranges in its longitudinal extent. A number of valleys lie between these ranges. The Northern-most range is known as the Great or Inner Himalayas or the Himadri.

How do regional names contribute to a better understanding of the diverse sections of the Himalayan mountain range? Discuss their significance in geographical and cultural contexts.

Ans. Regional names contribute to a better understanding of the diverse sections of the Himalayan mountain range by providing specific identifiers for different geographical and cultural contexts. These names help demarcate distinct regions based on features like river valleys, aiding in spatial recognition and navigation. Moreover, regional names offer insights into the unique cultural heritage, languages and traditions associated with each area, fostering a more comprehensive understanding of the complex diversity within the Himalayas.

In geographical contexts, regional names in the Himalayan mountain range hold significant importance as they serve as markers for specific sections, making navigation and spatial identification more accessible. These names demarcate distinct regions based on natural features like river valleys, aiding in the understanding of the topographical diversity within the Himalayas.

11. The Northern plains can be divided into four regions. The rivers, deposit pebbles in a narrow belt parallel to the slopes of the Shiwaliks. It is known as bhabar. South of this belt, the streams and rivers re-emerge and create a wet, swampy and marshy region known as terai. This was a thickly forested region full of wildlife.

What is the significance of the Terai region in the Northern plains, and how has it undergone changes over time? **Competency Based**

Ans. The Terai region in the Northern plains is ecologically significant for its rich biodiversity and dense forests. Its favourable conditions make it a crucial agricultural area, contributing significantly to India's food production.

Over time, it has undergone transformation due to human activities, including the clearing of forests for agriculture. The arrival of migrants post-partition contributed to increased human settlement, altering the landscape and land use patterns. These changes have posed challenges to wildlife conservation, as the original thickly forested region has been cleared and impacted the natural balance. The growing human settlements and development activities have tensed the delicate balance between human needs and environmental conservation.

These efforts and challenges promoted sustainable land management in the evolving terai region.

Case Based Questions

1. Read the sources given below and answer the questions that follow.

Source A The Peninsular Plateau

The Peninsular plateau is a table land composed of the old crystalline, igneous and metamorphic rocks.

It was formed due to the breaking and drifting of the Gondwana land and thus, making it a part of the oldest landmass.

(i) To what extent do you agree that the Peninsular plateau area is an old landmass?

Source B The Islands

The entire group of islands is divided into two broad categories – The Andaman in the North and the Nicobar in the South. It is believed that these islands are an elevated portion of submarine mountains. There is a great diversity of flora and fauna in this group of islands too.

(ii) Why there is a great diversity of flora and fauna in the island groups of India ?

Source C The Indian Desert

This region receives very low rainfall below 150 mm per year. It has arid climate with low vegetation cover. Streams appear during the rainy season. Soon after they disappear into the sand as they do not have enough water to reach the sea. Luni is the only large river in this region.

(iii) 'Streams appear during the rainy season' in the Indian Desert. Explain in brief.

Ans. (i) The Peninsular plateau region was formed by breaking and drifting of the Gondwana land. This took place many millions of years. Thus, it is a part of the oldest landmass.

(ii) There is a great diversity of flora and fauna in the island groups of India because they are located close to the equator and experience equatorial type of climate which support great diversity in flora and fauna.

(iii) Streams appear during the rainy season in the Indian desert. It is because this region has arid climate and vast expanse of sand. Rivers which flow here become underground due to presence of sand and have very small amount of water due to less rain i.e. 150 mm per year.

2. Read the source given below and answer the questions that follow.

A detailed account of the different physiographic units highlights the unique features of each region. It would, however, be clear that each region complements the other and makes the country richer in its natural resources.

The mountains are the major sources of water and forest wealth. The Northern plains are the granaries of the country. They provide the base for early civilisations. The plateau is a storehouse of minerals, which has played a crucial role in the industrialisation of the country.

The coastal region and island groups provide sites for fishing and port activities. Thus, the diverse physical features of the land have immense future possibilities of development.

(i) How are the coastal islands useful for India?

(ii) In what way the Himalayan mountains have become the major source of water?

(iii) What role plains and plateau play in India's development.

Ans. (i) The coastal islands are useful for India as they provide sites for fishing and port activities.

(ii) In the following ways, the Himalayan mountains have become major source of water

(a) The mountains block the way of monsoon winds causing rains in the Northern part of India.

(b) Melting of snow in the mountains give rise to rivers which are sources of water.

(iii) Plains and plateaus play an important role in India's development in the following ways

(a) The Northern plains provide fertile land that is most suitable for agriculture.

(b) The Peninsular plateau provides minerals that are needed by the industries.

Map Based Questions

1 (a) Three features are shown on the outline map of India. Identify these features and write their names on the lines marked on the map.

(i) A mountain range between the Narmada and Tapi rivers.

(ii) The highest peak in the Cardamom hills.

(iii) A mountain range North of the Satpura range.

(b) On the map, locate and label the following with appropriate symbols.

(i) A mountain range lying mostly in Rajasthan.

(ii) A plateau lying mostly in Jharkhand and Chhattisgarh.

(iii) A plateau in West-Central India.

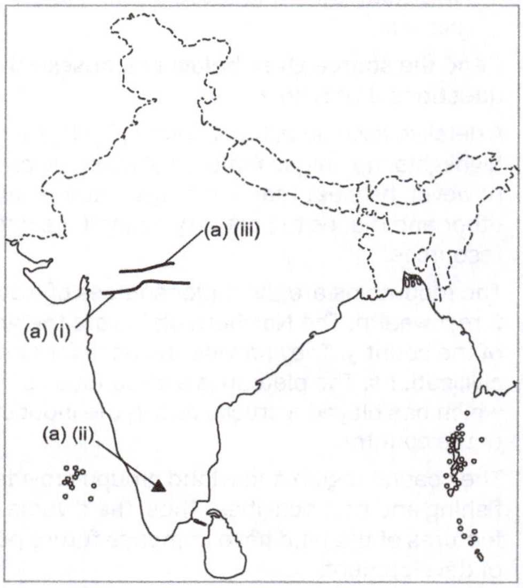

Ans.

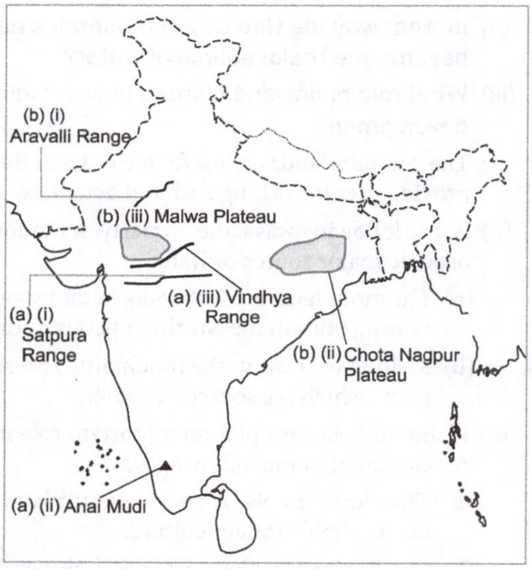

2 (a) Three features are shown on the outline map of India. Identify these features and write their names on the lines marked on the map.

(i) A mountain range in Uttarakhand.

(ii) The highest peak in the Himalayas in India.

(iii) Ghats which are continuous in nature.

(b) On the map, locate and label the following with appropriate symbols.

(i) A region of the Peninsular plateau which is triangular in shape.

(ii) K2 Mountain Peak

(iii) Ghats which are dissected in nature.

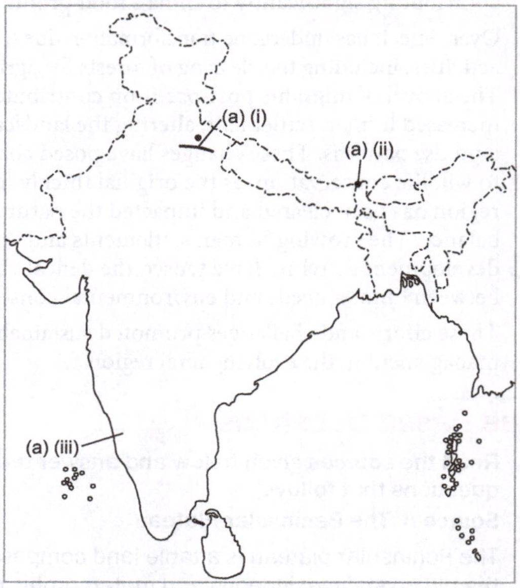

Ans.

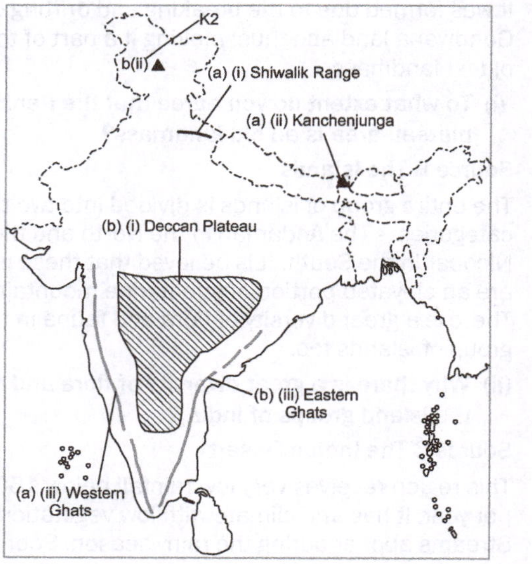

3 **On outline map of India locate and label the following features with appropriate symbols.**

(i) Konkan Coast (ii) Coromandel Coast
(iii) Malabar Coast (iv) Northern Circar
(v) Kannad plains

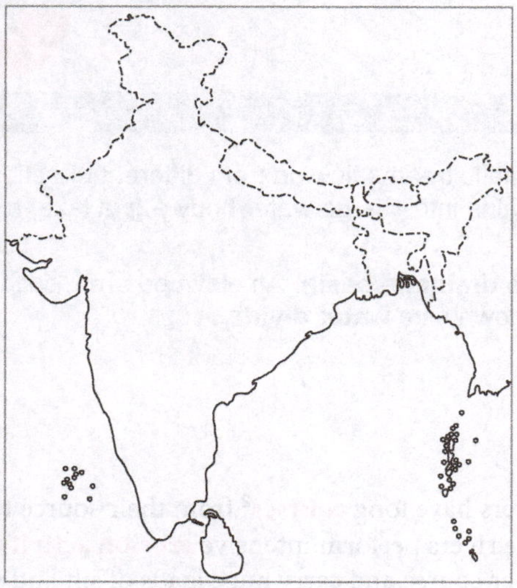

Ans.

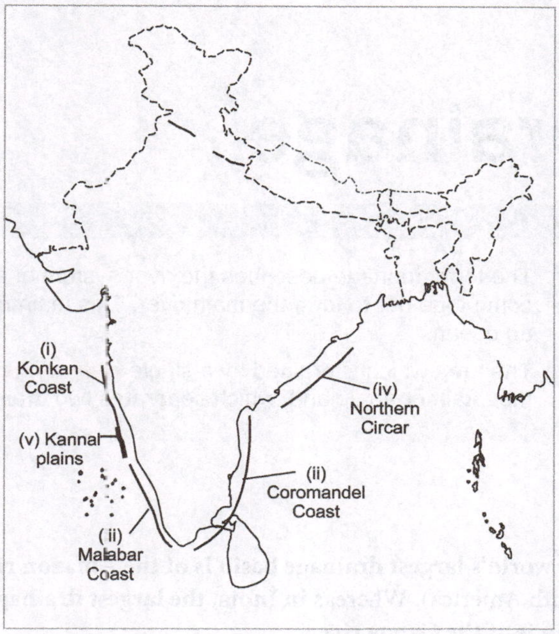

ASSESSMENT EXERCISE

Multiple Choice Questions (MCQs)

1. The outermost range of Himalayas is known by which of the following names?

(a) Inner Himalayas (b) Himadri
(c) Middle Himalayas (d) Shiwaliks

2. What is the name by which the Central stretch of the West coast is known?

(a) Konkan (b) Malabar coast
(c) Kannad plain (d) Coromandel coast

3. Consider the following statements

A. The Nilgiri hills are the junction point of the Eastern & Western Ghats.

B. Anai Mudi is the highest peak of the Eastern Ghats.

Options

(a) A is false but B is true (b) A is true but B is false
(c) Both A and B are true (d) Both A and B are false.

4. Match the following.

List I		List II	
A.	Terai	1.	Stones and pebbles
B.	Bhangar	2.	Intensive agriculture
C.	Bhabar	3.	Thickly forested
D.	Khadar	4.	Infertile

Codes

	A	B	C	D
(a)	3	4	1	2
(b)	3	2	1	4
(c)	1	2	3	4
(d)	1	4	3	2

Subjective Questions (VSA, SA & LA)

1. What are the physical features of the Northern plain? Name them.

2. Name the states where Kaimur hills, Javadi hills and Shevroy hills are located.

3. What are duns? Name some of them.

4. Give a description of the term 'fault' using an example from the Peninsular plateau.

5. Which features of desert restrict people to inhabit there?

6. Elucidate Khadar, Bhangar, Bhabar, Terai and Alluvium.

7. Why is India known as a country having all major geographical features of the world? Explain.

8. Give a brief account of Indian Coastal plains.

CHAPTER 3

Drainage

The term drainage describes the river system of an area. Many small streams flowing from different directions come together to form the main river. This main river ultimately drains into a large water body e.g. a lake, a sea or an ocean.

The area which is drained by a single river system[1] is known as a **drainage basin**. An elevated area, such as a mountain or an upland, which separates two drainage basins is known as a **water divide**.

The **world's largest drainage basin is of the Amazon river** (South America). Whereas **in India, the largest drainage basin is of the Ganga river**.

3.1 Drainage Systems in India

The drainage systems of India are mainly controlled by broad relief features of the subcontinent. Based on these features, the Indian rivers are divided into two major groups such as

- The Himalayan rivers
- The Peninsular rivers

Apart from originating from the two major physiographic regions of India, these two major groups are different from each other.

Both of these major groups are discussed below

1. The Himalayan Rivers

These rivers are mostly **perennial**, which means they have water throughout the year. These rivers receive water from rain as well as from melted snow from the high mountains. The **Indus** and the **Brahmaputra** are major Himalayan rivers. They originate from North of the mountain ranges. These rivers are long and joined by many large and important tributaries. They have cut through the mountains, making gorges.

These rivers have long courses[2] from their source to the sea. These rivers perform intensive erosion activity[3] in their upper course and carry huge loads of silt and sand. These rivers form meanders[4], Oxbow lakes[5] and other depositional features during their middle and lower courses in the floodplains. These rivers have well developed **deltas**.

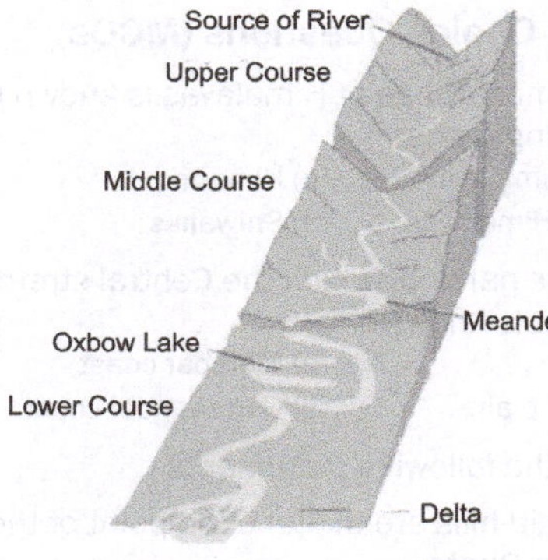

• Some Features Made by Rivers

A river along with its tributaries may be called as **river system**. The major river systems of the Himalayan rivers are

(i) The Indus river system

(ii) The Ganga river system

(iii) The Brahmaputra river system

---

1 River System It refers to a river alongwith its tributaries and distributaries.

2 Course It is the route or direction followed by a ship, road or river.

3 Erosion Activity It is the gradual destruction and removal of rock or soil in a particular area by rivers, the sea or the weather.

4 Meander It refers to a winding curve or bend of a river.

5 Oxbow Lake It is a crescent-shaped lake formed when a meander of a river or stream is cut off from the main channel.

The Indus River System

The Indus river originates from Tibet near Mansarowar lake. It flows Westwards and enters India in the **Ladakh** forming a gorge. Several **tributaries**[6], like Zaskar, Nubra, Shyok and Hunza join it in the Kashmir region.

The Indus flows through Baltistan and Gilgit and emerges from the mountains at Attock.

The Satluj, Beas, Ravi, Chenab and Jhelum join together the Indus river near Mithankot in Pakistan.

The Indus flows Southwards till it reaches the Arabian Sea East of Karachi part in Pakistan.

The Indus plain has a very gentle slope. It has a total length of 2900 km and it is one of the longest rivers of the world.

Its one-third basin is located in India in the Jammu and Kashmir, Ladakh, Himachal Pradesh and Punjab. The rest is in Pakistan.

KNOWLEDGE PLUS Indus Water Treaty was signed between India and Pakistan in 1960, India can utilise only 20% of water carried by the Indus River System. Punjab, Haryana and Southern and Western parts of Rajasthan use this water for irrigation.

The Ganga River System

The Ganga river originates from Gangotri **Glacier**[7], where it is known as **Bhagirathi**. It is joined by the Alaknanda river at Devaprayag in Uttarakhand. Its length is over 2500 km.

At Haridwar, the Ganga emerges from the mountains on to the plains. The Ganga is joined by many tributaries from the Himalayas. Few of these tributaries are major rivers such as the Yamuna, Ghaghara, Gandak and Kosi.

The river Yamuna originates from the Yamunotri glacier in the Himalayas. It flows parallel to the Ganga as a right bank tributary. It meets the Ganga at Allahabad (now Prayagraj).

The Ghaghara, the Gandak and the Kosi rise in the Nepal Himalayas. These rivers flood parts of the Northern plains each year. This causes widespread damage to life and property but also enrich the soil for agricultural use.

The Ganga's main tributaries which come from the Peninsular uplands are the Chambal, the Betwa and the Son. These rise from semi-arid areas, have shorter courses and do not carry much water in them.

The Ganga flows Eastwards till Farakka in West Bengal. This is the **Northernmost point** of the Ganga delta. Here it divides into two branches and forms a **distributary**[8] known as the **Bhagirathi-Hooghly** (also called Hugli), which flows Southwards through the deltaic plains into the Bay of Bengal.

The main stream of the Ganga flows Southwards into Bangladesh, where it is joined by the Brahmaputra. Further downstream, it is known as Meghna. This river flows into the Bay of Bengal.

The delta formed by the Ganga and the Brahmaputra rivers is known as the **Sundarban Delta**. It is the **world's largest** and fastest growing delta. It is also the home of Royal Bengal Tiger.

The Sundarban Delta derived its name from the Sundari tree which grows well in **marshland**[9].

Ambala is located on the water divide between the Indus and the Ganga river system. The plains from Ambala to the Sundarban stretch over nearly 1800 km but the fall in its slope is only 300 m. In simple terms, there is a fall of just one metre for every 6 km. Therefore, the river develops large meanders.

Namami Gange Programme

The Namami Gange Programme is an **Integrated Conservation Mission** approved as a flagship programme by the Union Government in June 2014. The objective of this programme is effective abatement (reduction) of pollution, conservation and rejuvenation of the national river Ganga.

The Brahmaputra River System

The Brahmaputra river originates in Tibet, East of Mansarowar lake, very close to the sources of the Indus and Satluj. It is slightly longer than the Indus and most of its course lies outside India.

It flows Eastward parallel to the Himalayas. On reaching the **Namcha Barwa mountain** (7757m), it takes a 'U' turn and enters India in Arunachal Pradesh through a gorge. Here, it is called **Dihang**.

It is joined by many tributaries like Dibang, Lohit, etc to form the Brahmaputra in Assam.

6 **Tributary** It is a river or stream flowing into a larger river or lake.
7 **Glacier** It is a huge mass of ice slowly flowing over a landmass, formed from compacted snow in an area where snow accumulation exceeds melting and sublimation.
8 **Distributary** It is a branch of a river that does not return to the main stream after leaving it.
9 **Marshland** It is an area of low-lying land that is usually saturated with water.

It carries very little silt and water in Tibet as it is a cold and dry area. Whereas in India, the Brahmaputra passes through a region of high rainfall (Assam) so, the river carries a large volume of water and considerable amount of silt.

It has a **braided channel**[10] in Assam and forms many riverine islands. **Majuli island**, the **world's largest riverine island** is formed by it.

Every year, Brahmaputra overflows its banks during the rainy season causing severe floods in Assam and Bangladesh.

Unlike other North Indian rivers, the Brahmaputra is marked by huge deposits of silt on its bed causing the riverbed to rise. The river also shifts its channel frequently.

KNOWLEDGE PLUS Brahmaputra is known as **Tsang Po** in Tibet and **Jamuna** in Bangladesh.

Try These

1. **Which river has the largest drainag basin in India?**
2. **Identify the major tributaries of the Ganga river system.**
3. **Name the world's largest and fastest growing delta that is the home of Royal Bengal Tiger.**
4. **This city is located at water divide between the Indus and the Ganga river system. Identify.**

2. The Peninsular Rivers

Most of these rivers are the seasonal rivers as their flow is dependent on rainfall. During the dry season, even the large rivers have reduced flow of water in their channels.

These rivers have shorter and shallower courses as compared to the Himalayan rivers.

Most Peninsular rivers originate in the Western Ghats and flow towards the Bay of Bengal, e.g. Mahanadi, Godavari, Krishna and Kaveri. These rivers make **deltas**[11] at their mouths.

The **Western Ghats** act as a main water divide in the Peninsular India. These Ghats run from North to South close to the Western coast.

The coastal plains between Western Ghats and the Arabian Sea are very narrow. Hence, the coastal rivers are short.

Some of the Peninsular rivers originate in the central highlands and flow towards the West.

There are numerous small streams flowing West of the Western Ghats. Tapi and Narmada are the only two long rivers which flow West and make **estuaries**[12]. The drainage basins of the Peninsular rivers are comparatively small in size.

The important basins of the Peninsular rivers are as follows

The Narmada Basin

The Narmada originates in the Amarkantak hills of Madhya Pradesh. It flows towards the West in a **rift valley**[13] formed due to faulting.

On its way to the sea, the Narmada creates many scenic locations. The **marble rocks** near Jabalpur, where the Narmada flows through a deep gorge is one such example. Another example is the Dhuadhar falls, where the river plunges (dive) over steep rocks.

All the tributaries of Narmada are very short in length. Most of its tributaries join the main stream at right angles.

The Narmada basin covers parts of Madhya Pradesh and Gujarat.

KNOWLEDGE PLUS The **Narmada River Conservation Mission** has been undertaken by the government of Madhya Pradesh by a scheme named **Namami Devi Narmade.**

The Tapi Basin

Tapi river originates in the Satpura ranges in the Betul district of Madhya Pradesh. It flows in a rift valley parallel to the Narmada river but it is much shorter in length. Its basin covers parts of Madhya Pradesh, Gujarat and Maharashtra.

The Godavari Basin

Godavari river originates from the slopes of the Western Ghats in the Nasik district of Maharashtra.

It is the **largest peninsular river** (about 1500 km) with the **largest drainage basin** and the **largest delta of the Peninsular rivers**. It is also known as **Dakshin Ganga** because of its length and the area it covers.

It has many tributaries such as Manjra, Wainganga and Penganga, Purna, Wardha and Pranhita.

10 **Braided Channel** It is a drainage channel in which bars and islands have been deposited and around which the river flows. Braiding occurs when the discharge fluctuates frequently or when the river cannot carry its full load.

11 **Deltas** These refers to triangular shaped alluvial deposits at the mouth of rivers where they enter the sea.

12 **Estuary** It is the tidal mouth of a large river, where the tide meets the stream.

13 **Rift Valley** It is a lowland region that forms where Earth's tectonic plates move apart.

The Godavari basin covers parts of Maharashtra (about 50%), Madhya Pradesh, Odisha and Andhra Pradesh. It drains into the Bay of Bengal.

The Mahanadi Basin

Mahanadi river originates in the highlands of Chhattisgarh. It flows through Odisha to reach the Bay of Bengal.

The length of the river is about 860 km. Its drainage basin is shared by Maharashtra, Chhattisgarh, Jharkhand and Odisha.

The Krishna Basin

Krishna river originates from the Western Ghats near Mahabaleshwar. It flows into the Bay of Bengal.

Its length is about 1400 km. Tungabhadra, Koyana, Ghatprabha, Musi and Bhima are some of its tributaries.

Its basin covers parts of Maharashtra, Karnataka and Andhra Pradesh.

The Kaveri Basin

Kaveri river originates in the Brahmagiri range of the Western Ghats. It flows into the Bay of Bengal South of Cuddalore in Tamil Nadu. The length of the river is about 760 km.

Its main tributaries are Amravati, Bhavani, Hemavati and Kabini. Its basin drains in the parts of Karnataka, Kerala and Tamil Nadu.

It makes the **second biggest waterfall** in India, known as **Shivasamudram**. The hydroelectric power generated from the falls is supplied to Mysuru, Bengaluru and the Kolar Gold Field.

KNOWLEDGE PLUS There are some other rivers which flow in the West and East direction. For example, the Sabarmati, Mahi, Bharathpuzha and Periyar are West flowing rivers, whereas the Damodar, Branmani, Baitarani and Subarnarekha are East flowing rivers.

Try These

1. **From which hills the Narmada river rises?**
2. **Which missions has been undertaken by the Government of Maharashtra under Namami Devi Narmde Scheme?**
3. **What is the length of Mahanadi river?**
4. **This is the largest Peninsular river. Identify the river.**

3.2 Lakes

India has many lakes which vary in size and characteristics. In India, most of the lakes are **permanent** while others are **seasonal** lakes.

Seasonal lakes contain water only during the rainy season. They can be found in the inland drainage basins[14] of semi-arid regions, e.g. the **Sambhar lake** (salt water lake) in Rajasthan.

Lakes in India are formed by different processes such as action of glaciers and ice sheets, by wind, river actions or human activities.

A meandering river across a flood plain forms **cut-offs** that later develop into **Ox-bow lakes**.

The Chilika, Pulicat and Kolleru lakes are examples of Spits[15] and bars[16] form lagoons[17] in coastal areas.

Freshwater lakes are formed when glaciers dig out (create) a basin, which is later filled with snowmelt. Most of the freshwater lakes are in the Himalayan region.

The **Wular lake** in Jammu and Kashmir is the result of tectonic activity. It is the **largest freshwater lake** in India.

The Dal lake, Nainital, Bhimtal, Loktak and Barapani are some other important freshwater lakes.

Apart from natural lakes, the damming of the rivers for the generation of hydel power has also led to the formation of lakes such as **Guru Gobind Sagar** (Bhakra Nangal Project), formed by damming the Satluj.

KNOWLEDGE PLUS Larger lakes are called the seas, like the Caspian Sea, the Dead Sea and the Aral Sea.

Importance of Lakes

- Lakes help to regulate the flow of a river. During heavy rainfall, it prevents flooding and during the dry season, it helps to maintain an even flow of water.
- It can also be used for developing hydel power. It moderates the climate of the surroundings, maintain the aquatic ecosystem, enhance natural beauty, helps develop tourism and provide recreation.
- Lakes which have saline water are used to produce salt, one such example is **Sambhar lake** of Rajasthan.

14 Inland Drainage Basin It refers to the point of land that absorbs water from rain or snow melt and drains downhill into a river, lake, reservoir, sea or ocean.
15 Spit It is a deposition bar or beach landform off coasts or lake shores.
16 Bar It is an elevated region of sediment in a river that has been deposited by the flow.
17 Lagoon It is a stretch of salt water separated from the sea by a low sandbank or coral reef.

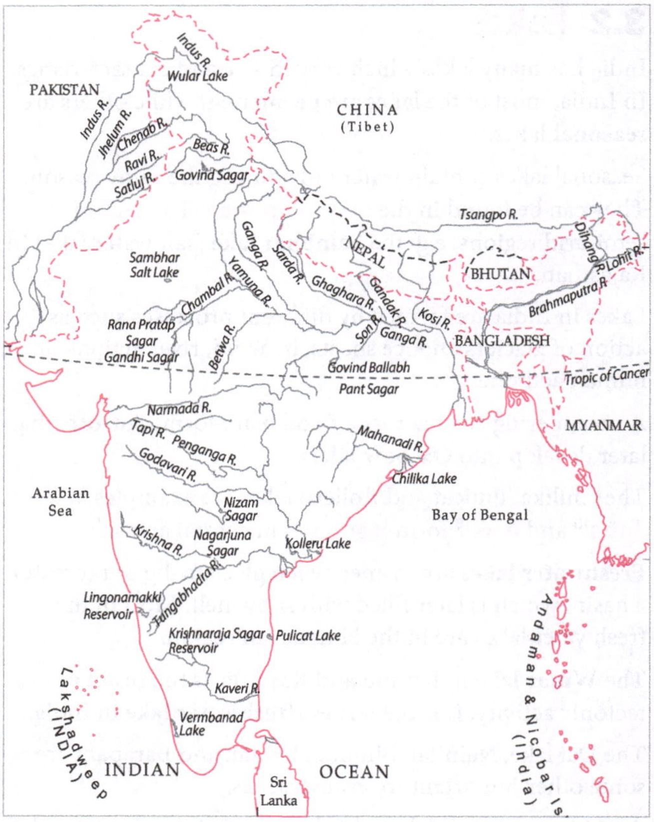

● Major rivers and lakes

3.3 Role of Rivers in the Economy

Rivers have fundamental importance throughout the human history. Water from rivers is a basic natural resource, essential for various human activities. Riverbanks have always attracted settlers from ancient times. Many of these have become big cities today.
Using rivers for irrigation, navigation, hydropower generation has a lot of economic and social significance for India.

This is also very important because agriculture is a major source of livelihood for a large section of the Indians.

KNOWLEDGE PLUS 71 per cent of the world's surface is covered with water, but 97 per cent of that is salt water. Of the 3 per cent that is available as freshwater, three quarters of it is trapped as ice.

3.4 Pollution of Rivers

The quality of river water is affected by the growing demands for domestic, municipal, industrial and agricultural use. So, to meet those growing demands, more river water is used and thus, reducing their volume of water.

When untreated sewage and industrial waste flow into river bodies, these greatly affect the quality of water and self-cleansing (self-purifying) capacity of rivers.

For example, in case of adequate stream flow the Ganga river has self cleansing capacity to absorb pollution loads with in 20 km of a large city. But it is not possible due to increasing urbanisation and industrialisation.

Thus, the pollution level of many rivers has gone up. Concern over rising pollution in many rivers has led to the launching of varies action plans to clean the rivers.

National River Conservation Plan (NRCP)

The river cleaning programme in the country was initiated with the launching of the **Ganga Action Plan** (GAP) in 1985. The Ganga Action Plan was expanded to cover other rivers under the National River Conservation Plan (NRCP), in the year 1995.

The objective of the NRCP is to improve the water quality of the rivers, which are major water sources in the country, through the implementation of pollution reduction.

Try These

1. **These lakes contain water only during rainy season. Identify them.**
2. **Which is the largest freshwater lake in India?**
3. **What per cent of the world's surface is covered with water?**
4. **Name the plan that was expanded to cover other rivers under the NRCP.**

Mind Map

DRAINAGE

Roles of Rivers in the Economy

- Water from rivers is a basic natural resource, essential for various human activities.
- Using rivers for irrigation, navigation, hydropower generation has a lot of economic and social significance for India.

Lakes

- In India, most of the lakes are permanent while others are seasonal lakes.
- Freshwater lakes are formed when glaciers dig out a basin which is later filled with snowmelt.
- Dal Lake, Nainital, Bhimtal, Loktak and Barapani are some freshwater lakes.
- Spits and bars form lagoons in coastal areas.

Pollution of Rivers

- The quality of river water is affected by the growing demands for domestic, municipal, industrial and agricultural use.
- When untreated sewage and industrial waste flow into river bodies, these affect the quality of water and self-cleansing capacity of rivers.

Features made by Rivers

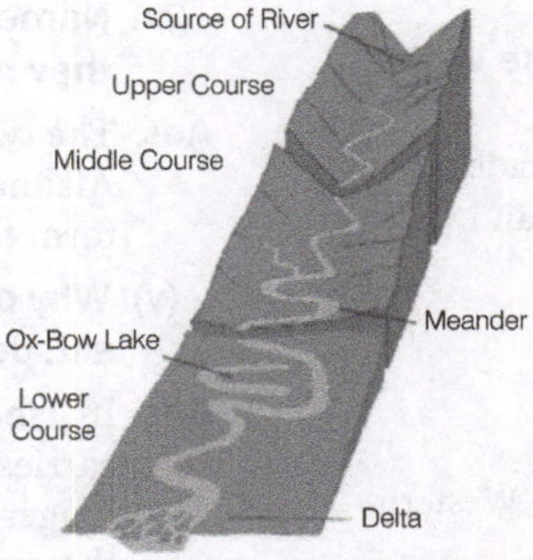

Peninsular Rivers

- Most rivers are seasonal.
- They have shorter and shallower courses as compared to Himalayan rivers.
- The Narmada Basin (Rises in the Amarkan-tak hills in Madhya Pradesh)
- The Tapi Basin (Rises in the Satpura Ranges in Madhya Pradesh)
- The Godavari Basin (Rises from the slopes of Western Ghats)
- The Mahanadi Basin (Rises in the highlands of Chhattisgarh)
- The Krishna Basin (Rises from a spring in Mahabaleshwar)
- The Kaveri Basin (Rises in the Brahmagiri range of Western Ghats)

Himalayan Rivers

- Rivers are perennial.
- These rivers form meanders, oxbow lakes and other depositional features during their middle and lower courses in the floodplains.

The Indus River System

- It originates from Tibet near Mansarowar.
- It flows Westwards and enter India in the Ladakh forming a Gorge.
- Its tributaries and Zaskar, Nubar, Shyok and Hunza.

The Ganga River System

- It originates from Gangotri glacier.
- Yamuna, Ghaghara, Kosi and Gandak are its tributaries.
- It flows Eastwards till Farakka in West Bengal.

The Brahmaputra River System

- It originates in Tibet, East of Mansarowar lake.
- It flows Eastward parallel to the Himalayas.
- Its tributaries are Dibang, Lohit, etc.

NCERT FOLDER

Covering Intext Questions and Exercises of NCERT

INTEXT QUESTIONS

Q.1 Which river has the largest basin in India?

Ans. The Ganga river has the largest basin in India.

Q.2 Find out the name of the biggest waterfall in India.

Ans. The biggest waterfall is the Kunchikal waterfall on the Varahi river in Shimoga district of Karnataka. Its height is 455 metres (1493 ft).

Q.3 Make a list of natural and artificial lakes with the help of the atlas.

Ans. **Natural lakes** are Wular lake, Dal lake, Nainital lake, Bhimtal lake, Loktak lake, Barapani lake, Chilika lake, Sambhar lake, Pulicat lake, Kolleru lake, Vembanad lake.

Artificial lakes are Gobind Sagar, Rana Pratap Sagar, Nizam Sagar, Nagarjuna Sagar, Hirakud.

EXERCISE

Q.1 Choose the right answer from the four alternatives given below.

(i) In which of the following states is the Wular lake located?

(a) Rajasthan (b) Uttar Pradesh
(c) Punjab (d) Jammu and Kashmir

Ans. (d) Jammu and Kashmir

(ii) The river Narmada has its source at

(a) Satpura (b) Brahmagiri
(c) Amarkantak (d) Slopes of the Western Ghats

Ans. (c) Amarkantak

(iii) Which one of the following lakes is a salt water lake?

(a) Sambhar (b) Dal
(c) Wular (d) Gobind Sagar

Ans. (a) Sambhar

(iv) Which one of the following is the longest river of the Peninsular India?

(a) Narmada (b) Krishna
(c) Godavari (d) Mahanadi

Ans. (c) Godavari

(v) Which one amongst the following rivers flows through a rift valley?

(a) Mahanadi (b) Tungabhadra
(c) Krishna (d) Tapi

Ans. (d) Tapi

Q.2 Answer the following questions briefly.

(i) What is meant by a water divide? Give an example.

Ans. The elevated area as a mountain or an upland, which separates two basins, is known as a water divide.

An example of water divide is the town of Ambala, which is located between the Indus and the Ganga.

(ii) Which is the largest river basin in India?

Ans. The Ganga basin is the largest river basin in India.

(iii) Where do the rivers Indus and Ganga have their origin?

Ans. The river Indus has its origin in Tibet near the Mansarowar lake. The river Ganga has its origin place at the Gangotri glacier. Both of them have their origin in the Himalayas.

(iv) Name the two headstreams of the Ganga. Where do they meet to form the Ganga?

Ans. The two headstreams of the Ganga are the Bhagirathi and Alaknanda. They meet at Devaprayag in Uttarakhand to form the Ganga.

(v) Why does the Brahmaputra in its Tibetan part have less silt, despite a longer course?

Ans. In Tibet, the river Brahmaputra, known as Tsangpo, carries a smaller volume of water and less silt despite a longer course because it is a cold and dry area. But in India, the river carries a large volume of water and considerable amount of silt because it passes through a region of high rainfall.

(vi) Which two Peninsular rivers flow through a trough?

Ans. Narmada and Tapi are the two Peninsular rivers that flow through a trough.

(vii) State some economic benefits of rivers and lakes.

Ans. Some economic benefits of lakes are

- They help to regulate the flow of rivers.
- They help to prevent flooding during rainy season.

- They can also be used for developing hydel power.
- They enhance natural beauty, help to develop tourism and provide recreation, e.g., Dal lake and Naini lake.
- Salt water lakes are sources for manufacturing edible salt.

Some economic benefits of rivers are

- They help to develop hydel power.
- They provide water for irrigation, drinking and other requirements.
- They also provide facility for navigation.
- They also provide water for fisheries and domestic use like washing, cooking so on.

Q.3 Below are given names of a few lakes of India. Group them under two categories, natural and created by human beings.

(a) Wular	(b) Dal
(c) Nainital	(d) Bhimtal
(e) Gobind Sagar	(f) Loktak
(g) Barapani	(h) Chilika
(i) Sambhar	(j) Rana Pratap Sagar
(k) Nizam Sagar	(l) Pulicat
(m) Nagarjuna Sagar	(n) Hirakud

Ans. **Natural lakes** Wular, Dal, Nainital, Bhimtal, Loktak, Barapani, Chilika, Sambhar and Pulicat.

Man-made lakes Gobind Sagar, Rana Pratap Sagar, Nizam Sagar, Nagarjuna Sagar and Hirakud.

Q.4 Discuss the significant difference between the Himalayan and the Peninsular rivers.

Ans. Differences between the Peninsular and Himalayan rivers are

Himalayan Rivers	Peninsular Rivers
They rise from glaciers or springs in high mountains.	They rise from plateaus and highlands.
They have well-developed deltas.	Those originating in the Central Highlands and flowing Westwards form estuaries, while those originating from the Western Ghats and flowing Eastwards form small deltas compare to Himalayan rivers.
They are perennial in nature due to originating from glaciers (flow throughout the year).	They are seasonal, as they only get water from rainfall (flow during a certain period).
Longer courses from their source to the mouth with high erosional activity in the upper course.	Shorter and shallower courses with very little erosional activity.
These rivers are good for agriculture, because these carry large quantity of silt and sand with them and deposit on the plains. Thus, renew the plains every year.	As these rivers do not bring much silt, there are no major plains. Only small delta regions have fertile lands for agriculture.
Their drainage basins are large.	Their drainage basins are small.
These are in young stage.	These are in mature stage.

Q.5 Compare the East flowing and the West flowing rivers of the Peninsular plateau.

Ans. Comparison between the East flowing and West flowing rivers of the Peninsular plateau is tabulated below

East Flowing Rivers	West Flowing Fivers
These rivers originate from the Western Ghats and flow Eastwards.	These rivers originate in the Central India and flow Westwards.
These rivers form deltas at their mouths.	These rivers form estuaries at their mouths.
They carry larger amount of water.	They carry a lesser amount of water.
These are the rivers which flow through shallow or mature valleys.	These are the rivers which flow through rift valleys.
Their tributaries are large in size.	Their tributaries are small in size as compared to the East flowing rivers.
They drain into the Bay of Bengal.	They drain into the Arabian Sea.
Examples are Mahanadi, the Godavari, the Krishna and the Kaveri.	Examples are the Narmada and the Tapi.

Q.6 Why are rivers important for the country's economy?

Ans. Rivers are important for the country's economy because water from the rivers is a basic natural resource and is essential for various human activities.

The importance of the rivers for the country's economy is stated in the points given below

- The rivers provide water for irrigation.
- They provide fertility to the soil.
- They are useful for navigation.
- They help to generate hydroelectricity.
- They help to develop tourism.
- They provide water for various domestic uses.
- They provide livelihood to fishermen.
- They help to moderate the climate and environment of nearby areas.
- The river banks have attracted settlers from ancient times and these settlements have now become big cities. It is due to the fertile nature of the river banks.

MAP SKILLS

Q.1 **(i) On an outline map of India mark and label the following rivers:**
Ganga, Satluj, Damodar, Krishna, Narmada, Tapi, Mahanadi and Brahmaputra.

(ii) On an outline map of India mark and label the following lakes.
Chilika, Sambhar, Wular, Pulicat, Kolleru.

Ans.

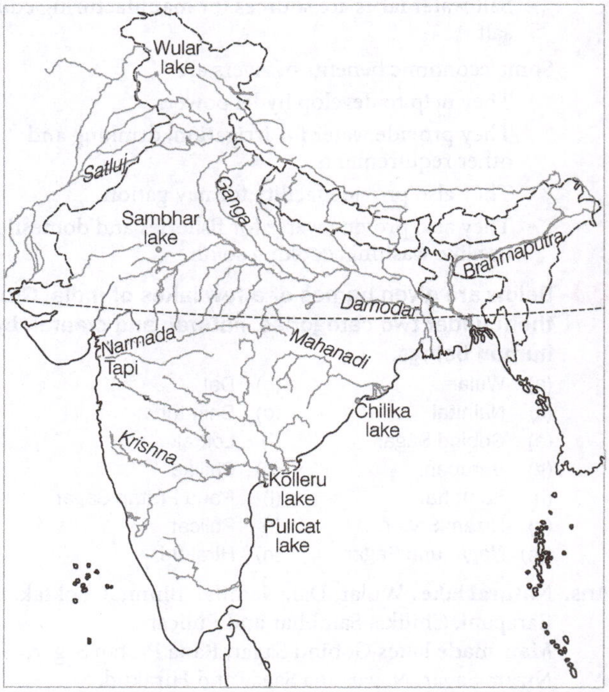

REVIEW EXERCISE

Including Competency Based Questions

Part I

Multiple Choice Questions (MCQs)

1. When an area is being drained by a single river system, it is called
(a) river system (b) drainage system
(c) drainage basin (d) river flow

2. Which of the following is the largest drainage basin of the world?
(a) Ganga basin (b) Brahmaputra basin
(c) Nile basin (d) Amazon basin

3. Indian rivers can be divided into how many groups?
(a) Two (b) Three
(c) Four (d) Five

4. Which is a tributary of Brahmaputra river?
(a) Kosi (b) Lohit
(c) Koyana (d) Musi

5. Which river rises in Tibet, near Mansarowar lake?
(a) Ganga (b) Brahmaputra
(c) Kaveri (d) Beas

6. The Indus flows Southwards eventually reaching the Arabian Sea near which city of Pakistan?
(a) Sindh (b) Islamabad
(c) Karachi (d) Lahore

7. The Himalayan rivers form ....
(a) Oxbow lakes (b) Meanders
(c) Depositional features (d) All of these

8. The rivers like the Mahanadi, the Godavari, the Krishna and the Kaveri flow in which of the following directions?
(a) Eastwards (b) Westwards
(c) Southwards (d) Northwards

9. Which of the following rivers flows in West direction and makes estuaries?
(a) Tapi (b) Ganga (c) Son (d) Krishna

10. Which river rises in the Amarkantak hills in Madhya Pradesh?
(a) Tapi (b) Krishna
(c) Kaveri (d) Narmada

11. Dal lake is located at which of the following places in India?
(a) Jammu (b) Kashmir
(c) Ladakh (d) Baramulla

12. A meandering river across a flood plain forms .... later develop into ....
(a) Cut-offs, Ox-bow (b) Ox-bow, Cut-offs
(c) Horse-shoe, Ox-bow (d) None of the above

13. Which of the following is the second biggest waterfall in India?
(a) Kunchikal Falls (b) Shivasamudram Falls
(c) Dudhsagar Falls (d) Nohkalikai Falls

14. The Wular lake in Jammu and Kashmir is the result of which of the following activities?
(a) Tectonic activity (b) Rainfall
(c) Human activity (d) None of these

15. The Dal lake, Bhimtal, Nainital, Loktak and Barapani are examples of which type of lakes?
(a) Natural salt water lakes
(b) Natural freshwater lakes
(c) Man-made freshwater lakes
(d) None of the above

16. Identify the river with the help of given information.
- The river originates in Tibet, East of Mansarowar Lake.
- It flows Eastward parallel to the Himalayas.
- Majuli Island, the world's largest riverine island is formed by it.
- It is known as Tsang Po in Tibet.

Options
(a) Indus (b) Sutlej
(c) The Ganga (d) The Brahmaputra

17. Arrange the following lakes in sequence from North to South direction.
1. Chilika Lake 2. Kolleru Lake
3. Sambhar Salt Lake 4. Pulicat Lake

Codes
(a) 1, 2, 3, 4 (b) 4, 3, 2, 1
(c) 3, 1, 2, 4 (d) 1, 4, 3, 2

18. Arrange the following rivers in sequence as per their length in ascending order.
1. Ganga river 2. Mahanadi river 3. Kaveri river

Codes
(a) 1, 3, 2 (b) 3, 2, 1 (c) 1, 2, 3 (d) 2, 3, 1

19. Find the incorrect option about Himalayan rivers.
(a) The Himalayan rivers are perennial in nature.
(b) The Himalayan rivers are long and joined by many large and important tributaries.
(c) These rivers do not have well developed deltas.
(d) These rivers perform intensive erosional activity in their upper course.

20. Find the incorrect option about peninsular rivers
(a) The Peninsular rivers are seasonal in nature.
(b) Due to the dry season, even the large peninsular rivers reduce the flow of water in their channel.
(c) Most of the Peninsular rivers orginate in the Western Ghats and flow towards the Arabian Sea.
(d) These rivers have shorter and shallower courses

21. Namami Gange will focus on pollution abatement interventions, namely interception and diversion and treatment of waste water flowing through open drains via bio-remediation/ appropriate in-situ treatment/ use of innovative technologies/ Sewage Treatment Plants (STPs)/ Effluent Treatment Plants (ETPs).

Source (edited) : The Economics Times

In which year, the Namami Gange Programme was approved by the Union Government? **Competency Based**
(a) 2015 (b) 2008 (c) 2010 (d) 2014

22. Which of the following statements accurately describes the 'Ganga River System'?
I. The length of the Ganga is over 4500 km.
II. It flows Eastwards parallel to the Himalayas.
III. The headwaters of the Ganga, called the 'Bhagirathi' is fed by the Gangotri Glacier and joined by the Alaknanda.
IV. At Haridwar, the Ganga emerges from the mountains on to the plains.

Codes
(a) Only I (b) Only II
(c) Only IV (d) Both III and IV

23. The major Himalayan Rivers are the Indus, the Ganga and the Brahmaputra. These rivers are long and are joined by many large and important tributaries. A river alongwith its tributaries may be called a river system.
Where does the river Indus originate? **Competency Based**
(a) Jammu and Kashmir
(b) Tibet, near lake Mansarowar
(c) Baltistan
(d) Attock

24. **Consider the statements given below and choose the correct answer.** **Competency Based**

Statement I Most of the Himalayan rivers are perennial.

Statement II The two major Himalayan rivers, the Indus and the Brahmaputra originate from the North of the mountain ranges.

Options

(a) Statement I is correct and II is incorrect
(b) Statement I is incorrect and II is correct
(c) Both I and II are incorrect
(d) Both I and II are correct

25. **Identify the length of the Godavari Basin and where it drains. Choose from the appropriate statements among the following options** **Competency Based**

I. Its length is about 2500 km. It drains into the Assam.
II. Its length is about 2000 km. It drains into the Kerala.
III. Its length is about 1500 km. It drains into the Bay of Bengal.
IV. Its length is about 3500 km. It drains into the Odisha.

Codes

(a) Statements I and II are appropriate
(b) Statements I, II and III are appropriate
(c) All the statements are appropriate
(d) Only statement III is appropriate

26. **Rita, Nita and Rina are preparing for the upcoming examination of Geography, and Rita asked a question to Nita and Rina that "Kaveri River rises from which ranges?". Nita said it rises from Amarkantak hills in Madhya Pradesh, but Rina said "No, it rises from the Western Ghats in the Nasik district of Maharashtra". Rita replied "You both are wrong, it actually rises ...." Complete Rita's statement .** **Competency Based**

(a) in the Brahmagiri range of the Western ghat, Kodagu district of Karnataka.
(b) in the Gir range in Western Gujarat state.
(c) in the Balaghat range in Western ghat, Maharashtra.
(d) in the Karakoram is a mountain range in the Kashmir region.

Answers

1. (c)	2. (d)	3. (a)	4. (b)	5. (b)
6. (c)	7. (d)	8. (a)	9. (a)	10. (d)
11. (b)	12. (a)	13. (b)	14. (a)	15. (b)
16. (d)	17. (c)	18. (b)	19. (c)	20. (c)
21. (d)	22. (d)	23. (b)	24. (d)	25. (d)
26. (a)				

Match the Following

1

List I (Rivers)	List II (Tributaries)
A. Kaveri	1. Yamuna
B. Ganga	2. Amravati
C. Brahmaputra	3. Manjra
D. Godavari	4. Dibang

Codes

	A	B	C	D		A	B	C	D
(a)	2	1	4	3	(b)	4	3	2	1
(c)	4	3	1	2	(d)	3	4	2	1

2

List I (Rivers)	List II (Total Length)
A. Mahanadi	1. 860 km
B. Ganga	2. 2500 km
C. Godavari	3. 1500 km
D. Kaveri	4. 760 km

Codes

	A	B	C	D		A	B	C	D
(a)	2	1	4	3	(b)	4	3	2	1
(c)	1	2	3	4	(d)	3	4	2	1

3

List I (Rivers)	List II (Originate From)
A. Narmada	1. Western ghats
B. Tapi	2. Satpura range
C. Godavari	3. Amarkantak hills
D. Mahanadi	4. Highlands of Chhattisgarh

Codes

	A	B	C	D		A	B	C	D
(a)	1	2	3	4	(b)	4	3	2	1
(c)	2	1	3	4	(d)	3	2	1	4

Answers

1. (a) **2.** (c) **3.** (d)

Assertion-Reason

1 **Assertion** (A) In Tibet, the Brahmaputra river, which is known as Tsango Po there, carries a smaller volume of water and less silt.

Reason (R) Tibet is a cold and dry area.

Codes

(a) Both A and R are true and R is the correct explanation of A
(b) Both A and R are true, but R is not the correct explanation of A
(c) A is true, but R is false
(d) A is false, but R is true

2 **Assertion** (A) The Chambal, the Betwa and the Son (tributaries of the Ganga) have shorter courses and do not carry much water in them.

Reason (R) These rivers rise from semi-arid areas.

Codes

(a) Both A and R are true and R is the correct explanation of A
(b) Both A and R are true, but R is not the correct explanation of A
(c) A is true, but R is false
(d) A is false, but R is true

3 Assertion (A) Ambala is a water divide.

Reason (R) Ambala is located between the Indus and the Ganga river system.

Codes

(a) Both A and R are true and R is the correct explanation of A
(b) Both A and R are true, but R is not the correct explanation of A
(c) A is true, but R is false
(d) A is false, but R is true

4 Assertion (A) The Western Ghats in Peninsular India form the main water divide.

Reason (R) Most of the major rivers in the Peninsula, such as the Mahanadi, the Godavari, the Krishna and the Kaveri, flow Eastwards and drain into the Bay of Bengal.

Codes

(a) Both A and R are true and R is the correct explanation of A
(b) Both A and R are true, but R is not the correct explanation of A
(c) A is true, but R is false
(d) A is false, but R is true

5 Assertion (A) The Narmada river flows towards the North in a rift valley formed due to faulting.

Reason (R) The 'Marble rocks' near Jabalpur and the 'Dhuadhar falls' are some of the picturesque locations created by the Narmada river on its way to the sea.

Codes

(a) Both A and R are true and R is the correct explanation of A
(b) Both A and R are true, but R is not the correct explanation of A
(c) A is true, but R is false
(d) A is false, but R is true

Ans. 1. (a) Both A and R are true and R is the correct explanation of A
2. (a) Both A and R are true and R is the correct explanation of A
3. (a) Both A and R are true and R is the correct explanation of A
4. (a) Both A and R are true and R is the correct explanation of A
5. (d) A is false, but R is true

Picture Based Question

1 Which one of the following options best signifies this image?

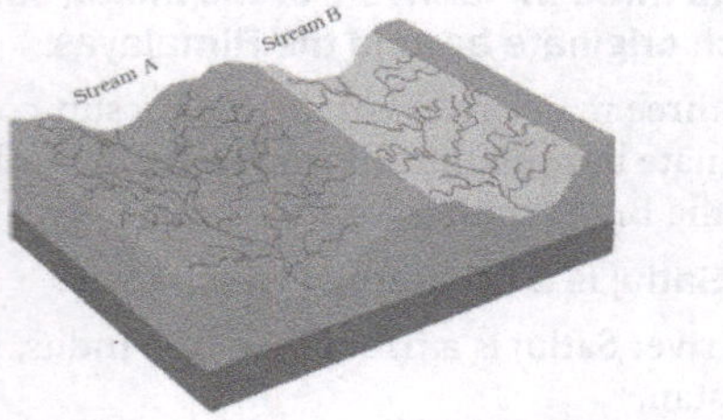

(a) River basin (b) Drainage basin
(c) Water divide (d) River system

Ans. (c) Water divide

Case Based Question

1. Read the source given below and answer the questions that follow.

India has many lakes. These differ from each other in the size and other characteristics. Most lakes are permanent; some contain water only during the rainy season, like the lakes in the basins of inland drainage of semi-arid regions. There are some of the lakes which are the result of the action of glaciers and ice sheets, while the others have been formed by wind, river action and human activities. A meandering river across a floodplain forms cut-offs that later develop into oxbow lakes. Spits and bars form lagoons in the coastal areas, e.g. the Chilika lake, the Pulicat lake, the Kolleru lake. Lakes in the region of inland drainage are sometimes seasonal; for example, the Sambhar lake in Rajasthan, which is a salt water lake. Its water is used for producing salt.

(i) Which lake in Jammu and Kashmir is the largest freshwater lake in India and is the result of tectonic activity?
(a) Wular lake (b) Dal lake (c) Bhimtal (d) Loktak

(ii) Which factor influences the size and characteristics of most lakes in India?
(a) Human activities (b) Rainy season
(c) Region of inland drainage
(d) Geologic processes

(iii) What is the primary source of water for most freshwater lakes in the Himalayas?
(a) Rainfall (b) River diversion
(c) Snowmelt (d) Underground springs

(iv) What is the primary origin of most freshwater lakes in the Himalayan region?
(a) Glacial origin (b) Wind action
(c) River action (d) Human activities

Ans. (i) (a) Wular lake (ii) (d) Geologic processes
(iii) (c) Snowmelt (iv) (a) Glacial origin

Part II

Very Short Answer Type Questions

1. Name three major rivers of the Indian sub-continent which originate beyond the Himalayas.

Ans. The three major rivers of the Indian sub-continent that originate beyond the Himalayas are the Indus, Ganga and the Brahmaputra.

2. The Satluj is a tributary of which river?

Ans. The river Satluj is a tributary of the Indus, joining it in Pakistan.

3. State the total length of the Indus river.

Ans. The total length of the Indus river is 2900 km.

4. Which of the rivers– Beas, Ghaghara, Indus and Yamuna rises from a glacier in Uttarakhand?

Ans. The Yamuna rises from the Yamunotri glacier in Uttarakhand.

5. What is the Sundarban famous for?

Ans. Sundarban is famous for being the home of the Royal Bengal Tiger.

6. Which river flows for the longest length in India?

Ans. The Ganga river flows for 2500 km in India which is the longest of all rivers flowing through it.

7. State any one important feature of the river Brahmaputra.

Ans. The river Brahmaputra has a braided channel in its entire length in Assam and forms many riverine islands.

8. Name five rivers rising in the Western Ghats.

Ans. The Godavari, the Krishna, the Kaveri, the Tungabhadra, the Ghatprabha are the five rivers rising in the Western Ghats.

9. Lakes are of great value to human beings. A lake helps to regulate the flow of a river. During heavy rainfall, it prevents flooding and during the dry season, it helps to maintain an even flow of water.

How can lakes be utilised for developing hydel power? **Competency Based**

Ans. Lakes can be utilised for developing hydel power through the construction of hydroelectric power plants. These plants typically involve building dams across rivers or lakes, creating reservoirs.

10. "The objective of the NRCP is to improve the water quality of the rivers, which are major water sources in the country, through the implementation of pollution abatement work".

Source (edited): India TV news

(i) When was the Ganga Action Plan (GAP) launched?

(ii) Why was the scope of the Ganga Action Plan expanded? **Competency Based**

Ans. (i) The Ganga Action Plan (GAP) was launched in 1985 with the goal of addressing pollution in the Ganges River, concluding its activities on 31st March, 2000.

(ii) The Ganga Action Plan was expanded to cover other rivers under the National River Conservation Plan (NRCP) in the year 1995.

Short Answer Type Questions

1. How do the Himalayan rivers perform erosional activities and form depositional features?

Ans. As the Himalayan rivers are perennial and have long courses, the regular flow of water in them performs intensive erosional activities in the upper part. The upper part has a steep slope. These rivers accumulate a lot of silt and sand.

When the Himalayan rivers reach the plains, the slope of the land is much less. This low slope flows down the rivers and make them deposit much of the silt they have accumulated.

Thus, the Himalayan rivers form depositional features like meanders, oxbow lakes, riverine islands and deltas in their lower courses.

2. Describe any three features of the Himalayan rivers.

or **Explain the main features of rivers originating from the Himalayas.**

Ans. Three features of the Himalayan rivers are

(i) Most of the Himalayan rivers are perennial. It means that they have water throughout the year.

(ii) The Himalayan rivers have long courses from their source to the sea. Many of them make spectacular gorges.

(iii) The Himalayan rivers perform intensive erosional activity in their upper courses and carry huge loads of silt and sand. Apart from this, they also form numerous depositional features like flood plains, river bluffs and levees (a ridge of sediment deposited naturally alongside a river by over flowing water).

3. Explain any three features of Peninsular rivers.

Ans. Three features of Peninsular rivers are

(i) A large number of Peninsular rivers are seasonal. It is because their flow depends on rainfall.
Thus, during summer season there is considerable reduction in their volume of water.

(ii) Peninsular rivers have short and shallow courses. They flow in straight and linear courses due to hard rocky bed and they lack in silt and sand.

(iii) Most of the Peninsular rivers originate in the Western Ghats and flow towards the Bay of Bengal.

4. Why are most of the Peninsular rivers draining into the Bay of Bengal? Give two reasons. Name two rivers draining into the Arabian Sea.

Ans. Most of the Peninsular rivers drain into the Bay of Bengal due to following reasons

(i) The Eastern Ghats are lower than the Western Ghats. These are discontinuous. Thus, allowing the rivers easy passage to the Bay of Bengal.

(ii) The Deccan plateau has a gentle slope towards the East. Thus, it gives easier passage in that direction.

The Narmada and the Tapi are two rivers draining into the Arabian Sea.

5. Describe the three main features of the Ganga river system.

Ans. The three main features of the Ganga river system are

(i) The length of the Ganga is over 2500 km. It is India's longest river.

(ii) It has a dendritic drainage pattern. It has many tributaries which join it from both North and South to form the Ganga river basin.

(iii) The Ganga river alongwith the Brahmaputra, forms the world's largest and fastest growing delta namely as the Sundarban delta.

6. In which state of India does river Brahmaputra have a braided channel in its entire length? Why does this river carry a larger volume of water and silt in India as compared to Tibet?

Ans. The river Brahmaputra rises in China (Tibet) East of the Mansarowar lake. It flows Eastwards and enters in India by taking a 'U' turn.

The river's braided channel can be seen mainly in Assam. It also forms many riverine Islands.

Reasons for carrying a larger volume of water and silt in India are

- The reason for carrying a larger volume of water and silt in India is due to mainly that it passes through a region of high rainfall.
- Besides, there is reduction in its velocity in this region.
- In Tibet, it is at young stage from where it is originated.
- But in India, it turns into mature and old stage thereby reducing its velocity of water. Thus, it gets overloaded with silt and sediments.

7. Describe any three important features of the Mahanadi basin.

Ans. Three important features of the Mahanadi basin are

(i) The river Mahanadi rises in the highlands of Chhattisgarh. It flows through Odisha to form a delta in the Bay of Bengal.

(ii) The Mahanadi basin covers parts of the states of Chhattisgarh, Jharkhand, Odisha and Maharashtra.

(iii) The length of the river is 860 km. Due to the devastating floods by it in the previous years, the Hirakud dam has been built on it forming the Hirakud reservoir.

8. (i) How are most of the freshwater lakes in the Himalayan region formed? Give two examples of freshwater lakes of this region.

(ii) How is Sambhar lake useful?

Ans. (i) Most of the freshwater lakes in the Himalayan region are formed as the result of glacial action and some are result of tectonic activity. They were formed when glaciers dug out a basin, which was later filled with snowmelt.

Examples of such lakes are Bhimtal, Nainital, Dal lake etc. India's largest freshwater lake is the Wular lake. It is the result of tectonic activity.

(ii) Sambhar lake is India's largest inland salt water lake. It is located in Rajasthan. It is useful as it is an important source of salt in India.

9. What are the causes of water pollution in rivers and lakes?

or **Explain any three causes of river pollution in India.**

Ans. The main causes of river pollution are

(i) Huge amounts of untreated sewage and industrial effluents are being emptied into the rivers and lakes. This has caused the water bodies to become highly polluted.

(ii) Human ashes (due to cremation near water bodies), dead animals and leaching out of nitrogen compounds from fertilised agricultural lands also increase the pollution.

(iii) Nutrient run-off in storm water from 'sheet flow' over an agricultural field or a forest is also another cause.

10. Make a comparison in tabular form between a delta and an estuary.

Ans. Comparison between a delta and an estuary is given below

Delta	Estuary
These are triangular deposits made by rivers at their mouths.	These are sharp edged mouths of rivers without any deposits.
These are formed in regions of low tides and coastal plains.	These are formed in regions of high tides and rift valleys.
These are agriculturally fertile lands.	These are not agriculturally fertile lands. But are the best fishing grounds of the world.
The rivers which form delta are the Ganga, the Krishna, the Godavari, and so on.	The rivers which form estuary are the Narmada and the Tapi.

11. Explain what life would be like if freshwater is not available.

Ans. If there is no freshwater available, then

- No activities of human beings or life would be possible.
- Sea water is salty and it cannot substitute for freshwater.
- No trees will be able to grow and no land based animals can survive.
- There will be no agricultural practices without freshwater, which will lead to widespread hunger.
- People would be forced to migrate in search of freshwater sources.

12. In what ways have rivers been of fundamental importance throughout human history?

Build answer around these points **Competency Based**

- **Cultures**
- **Industrial Activities**
- **Civilisations**

Ans. River have fundamental importance throughout human history in the following ways

Culture Significance Rivers have great cultural significance as they shape traditions, beliefs and ways of life.

Communities derive identity from rivers which connect people through travel, trade and settlement.

Rituals and celebrations centred around rivers further emphasise their cultural importance.

Industrial Activities Rivers power mills which use river energy to make electricity. Unfortunately rivers have also been used as dumping grounds for industrial waste.

Civilisation Growth Rivers play a fundamental role in nourishing civilisation, cultivating population growth and urban settlements.

13. The headwaters of the Ganga, called the 'Bhagirathi' are fed by the Gangotri Glacier and joined by the Alaknanda at Devprayag in Uttarakhand. The Ganga is joined by many tributaries from the Himalayas, a few of them being major rivers such as the Yamuna, the Ghaghara, the Gandak and the Kosi.

(i) What role do the tributaries Yamuna, Ghaghara, Gandak and Kosi play in enriching the soil for agriculture in the Northern plains?

(ii) What is the source of the river Yamuna and how does its flow contribute to the Ganga river system? **Competency Based**

Ans. (i) The tributaries Yamuna, Ghaghara, Gandak and Kosi play an important role in enriching the soil for agriculture in the Northern plains through annual flooding. These rivers bring nutrient-rich sediments and alluvium from the Himalayas, depositing them during floods.

(ii) The river Yamuna originates from the Yamunotri Glacier in the Himalayas.

It flows parallel to the Ganga and acts as a right bank tributary. The Yamuna meets the Ganga at Allahabad, contributing its flow to the Ganga river system.

14. Read the statements given below regarding Brahmaputra River System.

Statement 1 Brahmaputra river is slightly longer than the Indus and most of its course lies outside India.

Statement 2 The Brahmaputra has a braided channel in its entire length in Tripura and forms one riverine island.

Explain which statement is correct and how it reflects in the drainage system of India.

Ans. Only statement 1 is correct. The Brahmaputra is slightly longer than the Indus and a significant portion of its course lies outside India. The river originates in Tibet, flows through India and further downstream continues through Bangladesh.

The Brahmaputra's course reflects the international nature of river systems and drainage patterns, as it flows through multiple countries, impacting their ecosystems and contributing to regional water management challenges.

Statement II is incorrect because Brahmaputra does not lie completely in Tripura. It has a braided channel in its entire length in Assam and form many riverine islands such as Majuli, Umananda, Solmari, etc. Majuli is the world's largest riverine island formed by the Brahmaputra.

Long Answer Type Questions

1. How is Sundarban delta formed? Write some important features of this delta.

or **Give four characteristics of the Ganga-Brahmaputra delta.**

Ans. The Ganga's mainstream flows Southwards into Bangladesh and join the river Brahmaputra. This river further down stream comes to known as Meghna river. These rivers flow into the Bay of Bengal. The delta formed by these rivers is known as the Sundarban delta.

The four characteristics of the Sundarban or Ganga-Brahmaputra delta are

(i) It is the world's largest and fastest growing delta.

(ii) The Sundarban delta derived its name from the Sundari tree, which grows well in marshland.

(iii) It is among the most fertile regions in the world. With more than 130 million inhabitants, this belongs to the most densely populated areas in the world (1300 inhabitants/sq km).

(iv) It is also the home of Royal Bengal Tiger.

2. Name four East flowing peninsular rivers of India and explain any two of them.

Ans. Four East flowing peninsular rivers of India are the Mahanadi, the Godavari, the Krishna and the Kaveri.

Two peninsular rivers of India are explained below

(i) **The Godavari River** The Godavari is the largest peninsular river. It is about 1500 km long. It rises near Nasik from the slopes of the Western Ghats and forms a delta at the Bay of Bengal. Its drainage basin is the largest among all the peninsular rivers. Because of its length and the area it covers, it is also known as the 'Dakshin Ganga'.

(ii) **The Krishna River** The Krishna river rises from a spring near Mahabaleshwar. It flows for about 1400 km to form a delta in the Bay of Bengal. The rivers Tungabhadra, Koyana, Ghatprabha, Musi and Bhima are some of its tributaries. Its drainage basin is shared by Maharashtra, Karnataka, Telangana and Andhra Pradesh.

3. Explain the importance of salt water lakes in India with particular reference to Sambhar and Chilika lakes.

Ans. The importance of salt water lakes i.e. the Sambhar lake and the Chilika lake can be seen through the following points

The Sambhar Lake

- It is India's largest saline lake and has made Rajasthan the third largest salt producing state in India.
- It produces about 2 lakh tonnes of clean salt every year. Salt is produced by evaporation of brine.
- This lake is also recognised as a wetland of international importance because it is a key area for flamingos in winters and other birds that migrate from the Northern Asia.

The Chilika Lake

- Chilika lake in Odisha is the largest brackish water lake in India. It is the wintering ground for migratory birds of the Indian sub-continent.
- The lake is home to a number of threatened species of plants and animals. It is an ecosystem with large fishery resources sustaining 150000 fishermen living nearby.

4. What are the causes of river pollution? Suggest some ways to overcome them.

or **Suggest any three measures to control the river pollution.**

Ans. The causes of river pollution are

(i) **Untreated sewage** The discharge of untreated sewage into rivers is the single most important cause for pollution of rivers.

(ii) **Agricultural wastes** If a large amount of fertilisers or farm waste drains into a river, the concentration of nitrate and phosphate in the water increases, considerably.

(iii) **Industrial waste** Chemical waste products of industrial processes are sometimes discharged into rivers. These substances may enter the water in such high concentrations that fish and other animals are die immediately.

(iv) **Oil pollution** If oil enters a slow-moving river, it forms a rainbow coloured film over the entire surface. This prevents oxygen from entering the water. Thus, it causes death of many water organisms.

Ways to control water pollution are

(i) Various 'action plans' have been started to clean rivers, e.g., the Ganga Action Plan, the Yamuna Action Plan, etc.

(ii) Emphasis is ongoing for technologies reducing the wastage of water and promoting recycling, improvement of water quality, etc.

(iii) Measures are being taken to divert raw sewage of effluents flowing into the river to other locations for treatment and conversion into energy sources and chemicals.

5. Why is river water pollution considered as a significant danger? Explain.

Ans. Water pollution in rivers causes a significant danger to human health because human beings depend on rivers for many daily activities and necessities such as drinking water. Pollution introduces harmful bacteria, viruses, parasites and chemicals into the water. Consuming such water can lead to various waterborne diseases like cholera, typhoid, etc causing illness, deaths and economic burdens on healthcare systems.

Further, river water pollution affects the plants and other organisms living in it. It damages their individual species besides damaging their natural biological communities. It causes havoc to the ecological balance in the system. Less than 1% of the total water on the Earth is available as freshwater in lakes and rivers. As this needs to support the entire human population; any pollution to this miniscule amount of water poses a significant danger to human life as well as to the wildlife dependent on it.

6. "Rivers have been of fundamental importance throughout human history." How do rivers play an important in the economy of a country? Explain.

Ans. Rivers play an important role in the economy of a country in numerous ways which impact various sectors such as agriculture, industry, tourism, fisheries, etc.

The rivers are important for India's development. It is because India is mostly an agriculture based economy and river water is used for irrigation and hydro power generation. Multi-purpose dams provide all these features.

Rivers are also culturally and religiously significant for India. The Kumbh Mela (held every three years), is celebrated on the banks of major rivers. They also provide many tourist spots and places of religious significance for people to visit. Examples of such places are Haridwar, Prayag (Allahabad) and Varanasi.

7. Read the information about polluted river and answer the questions that follow. **Competency Based**

The growing domestic, municipal, industrial and agricultural demand for water from rivers naturally affects the quality of water. As a result, more and more water is being drained out of the rivers reducing their volume. On the other hand, a heavy load of untreated sewage and industrial effluents are emptied into the rivers. This affects not only the quality of water but also the self-cleansing capacity of the river.

(i) What are the causes of rising pollution levels in the Ganga river and other major rivers across India?

(ii) What concerns over rising pollution in rivers led to the initiation of various action plans for their cleanup?

Ans. (i) Urbanisation and industrialisation contribute to rising river pollution by increasing the discharge of untreated sewage and industrial effluents. Growing urban populations generate more wastewater, often untreated, which is released into rivers. Industrial activities release pollutants such as chemicals and heavy metals into water bodies.

Rapid urbanisation also leads to increased runoff of pollutants from paved surfaces into rivers. The expansion of industries and urban areas often outpaces the development of proper waste management infrastructure that increase the pollution of rivers.

(ii) Concerns over rising pollution in rivers led to the initiation of various action plans to address the environmental degradation and health risks associated with contaminated water. These action plans focus on improving water treatment, regulating industrial discharges, promoting sustainable practices and restoring river ecosystems to ensure the long-term health of rivers and the communities dependent on them.

8. The Ganga flows 2,500 km from the Himalayas to the Bay of Bengal. Its basin covers a quarter of India and houses more than 40 per cent of its 1.4 billion people. It accounts for more than one-quarter of national freshwater resources. Some 40 per cent of the country's economic output is produced here.

Source (edited) : Unep.org

Reflect on the overall impact of the Ganga's journey on the geographical, environmental and cultural landscapes of the regions it covers, from its origin to the Bay of Bengal. **Competency Based**

Ans. The Ganga's journey, from its origin in the Himalayas to its summit in the Bay of Bengal, has left a great impact on the geographical, environmental and cultural landscapes of the regions it traverses.

Over impact of the Ganga river is a follows

Geographical Landscape As the Ganga flows through the plains of North India, it creates a vast and fertile alluvial plain which provide ideal conditions for agriculture and settlement.

Environment Landscape The Ganga river ecosystem supports diverse flora and fauna but it faces problems such as pollution and habitat degradation. The Ganga basin plays an important role in sustaining agriculture, providing drinking water, etc. It also contributes to the fertility of the flood plains.

Cultural Landscape The Ganga highly influences the cultural landscape. It is highly sacred in Hindusim with pilgrimage sites i.e. Haridwar, Varanasi along its banks. Historic and contemporary settlements have also flourished along the Ganga.

Case Based Questions

1. Read the sources given below and answer the questions that follow.

Source A Drainage Systems in India

Most of the Himalayan rivers are perennial. It means that they have water throughout the year. These rivers receive water from rain as well as from melted snow from the lofty mountains. The two major Himalayan rivers, the Indus and the Brahmaputra originate from the North of the mountain ranges. They have cut through the mountains making gorges. The Himalayan rivers have long courses from their source to the sea.

(i) To what extent do you agree that the Himalayan rivers are perennial in nature? Give only one aspect.

Source B Drainage Systems in India

A large number of the Peninsular rivers are seasonal, as their flow is dependent on rainfall. During the dry season, even the large rivers have reduced flow of water in their channels. The Peninsular rivers have shorter and shallower courses as compared to their Himalayan counterparts. However, some of them originate in the central highlands and flow towards the West. Can you identify two such large rivers? Most of the rivers of peninsular India originate in the Western Ghats and flow towards the Bay of Bengal.

(ii) To what extent do you agree that the peninsular rivers have shorter and shallower courses as compared to their Himalayan counterparts?

Source C Role of Rivers in the Economy

Rivers have been of fundamental importance throughout the human history.
Water from rivers is a basic natural resource, essential for various human activities.
Therefore, riverbanks have attracted settlers from ancient times.

These settlements have now become big cities. Using rivers for irrigation, navigation, hydro-power generation is of special significance—particularly to a country like India, where agriculture is the major source of livelihood of the majority of its population.

(iii) Evaluate the importance of rivers.

Ans. (i) Yes, I agree with this statement that the Himalayan rivers are perennial in nature.

It is because these rivers receive water from rain as well as from melted snow from the lofty mountains.

(ii) Yes, I agree with this statement that the peninsular rivers have shorter and shallower course as compared to their Himalayan counter parts. It is because these rivers are dependent on rainfall and do not receive water from any other sources as the Himalayan rivers do.

(iii) The importance of rivers can be evaluated through the following points

- The rivers provide water for irrigation.
- The rivers sustain life. Due to this, the river banks have attracted settlers from ancient times and now these settlements have become big cities.
- The rivers are useful for navigation.
- They provide water for domestic use, like washing, cooking, drinking and so on.

2. Read the source given below and answer the questions that follow.

The Brahmaputra rises in Tibet East of Mansarowar lake very close to the sources of the Indus and the Satluj. It is slightly longer than the Indus and most of its course lies outside India. It flows Eastwards parallel to the Himalayas. On reaching the Namcha Barwa (7757 m), it takes a 'U' turn and enters India in Arunachal Pradesh through a gorge. Here, it is called the Dihang and it is joined by the Dibang, the Lohit, and many other tributaries to form the Brahmaputra in Assam.

In Tibet, the river carries a smaller volume of water and less silt as it is a cold and a dry area. In India, it passes through a region of high rainfall. Here, the river carries a large volume of water and considerable amount of silt.

The Brahmaputra has a braided channel in its entire length in Assam and forms many riverine islands. Every year during the rainy season, the river overflows its banks, causing widespread devastation due to floods in Assam and Bangladesh. Unlike other North Indian rivers, the Brahmaputra is marked by huge deposits of silt on its bed causing the river bed to rise. The river also shifts its channel frequently.

(i) How does the Brahmaputra river enter India?

(ii) Which situations make the Brahmaputra to carry smaller volume of water in Tibet and more water in India?

(iii) Evaluate the important features of the Brahmaputra river.

Ans. (i) The Brahmaputra river rises in Tibet, near the Mansarowar lake and flows Eastwards, parallel to the Himalayas. On reaching the Namcha Barwa, it takes a U-turn and enters India into Arunachal Pradesh through a deep gorge.

(ii) The following situations are responsible for this difference

- In Tibet, the Brahmaputra river carries a smaller volume of water and less silt. It is because of the reason that Tibet is a cold and dry area. Thus, it does not provide more water to the river.
- Whereas, when the Brahmaputra river enters India, it passes through a region of high rainfall. Thus, here the river carries a large volume of water and considerable amount of silt.

(iii) The important features of the Brahmaputra river are as under

- The Brahmaputra has its source in the Himalayas.
- It has a braided channel in its entire length in Assam and forms many riverine islands.
- Majuli is the world's largest reverine island formed by the Brahmaputra river.
- Every year during the rainy season, the river overflows its banks, causing widespread devastation due to floods in Assam and Bangladesh.
- Unlike other North Indian rivers, the Brahmaputra is marked by huge deposits of silt on its bed causing the riverbed to rise.
- The river also shifts its channel frequently.

Map Based Questions

1. (a) Two features are shown on the map of India. Identify these features and write their names on the lines marked on the map.

(i) A lake in Rajasthan from which salt is manufactured.

(ii) This river originates from the highlands of Chhattisgarh.

(b) On the map of India, locate and label the following with appropriate symbols:

(i) A salt water lake on the border between Andhra Pradesh and Tamil Nadu.

(ii) A lake in Odisha

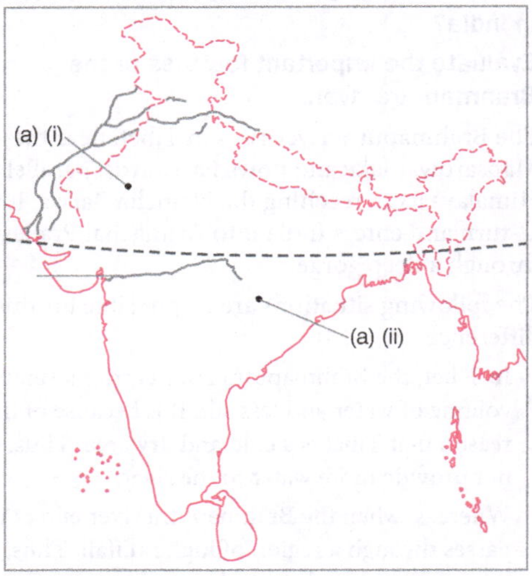

Ans.

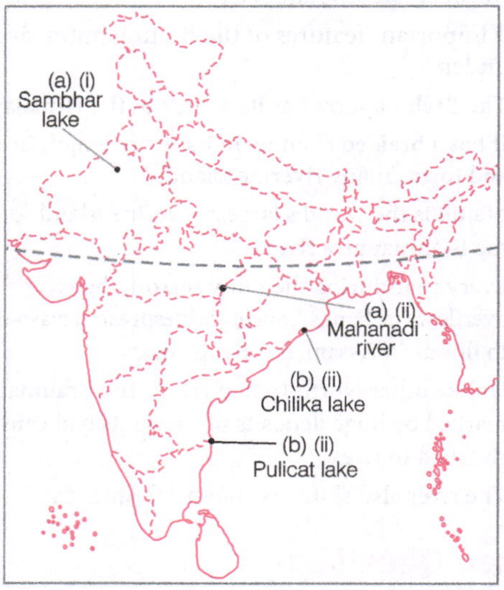

2. (a) Two features are shown on the outline map of India. Identify these features and write their names on the lines marked on the map.

(i) The river flowing North of the Tapi and having its estuary in the Gulf of Khambat.

(ii) This river flows through three countries.

(b) On the map of India, locate and label the following with appropriate symbols

(i) The river having the longest length in India.

(ii) This river flowing North of the Krishna has the largest river basin in South India.

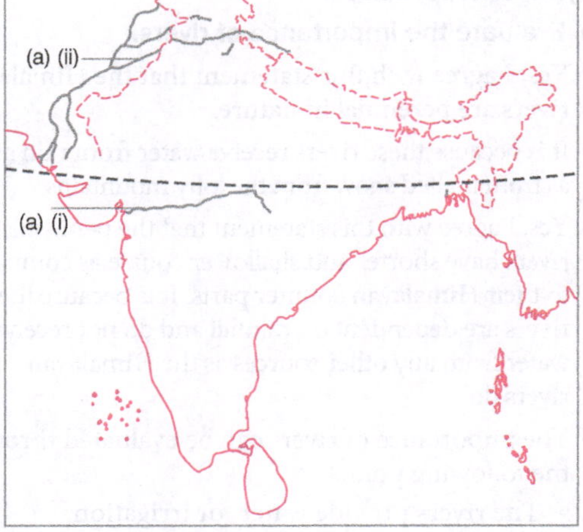

Ans.

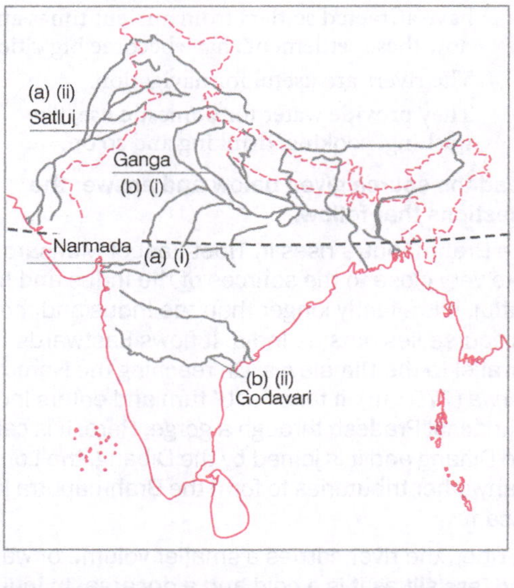

3 (a) Two features are shown on the outline map of India. Identify these features and write their names on the lines marked on the map.

(i) The largest freshwater lake in India.

(ii) A river rising in Tibet, near Lake Mansarowar.

(b) On the map of India, locate the following features and write their names on the lines marked on the map.

(i) The river rising in the Satpura ranges, in the Betul district of Madhya Pradesh.

(ii) The river drains parts of Karnataka, Kerala and Tamil Nadu.

(iii) The river rising from a spring near Mahabaleshwar

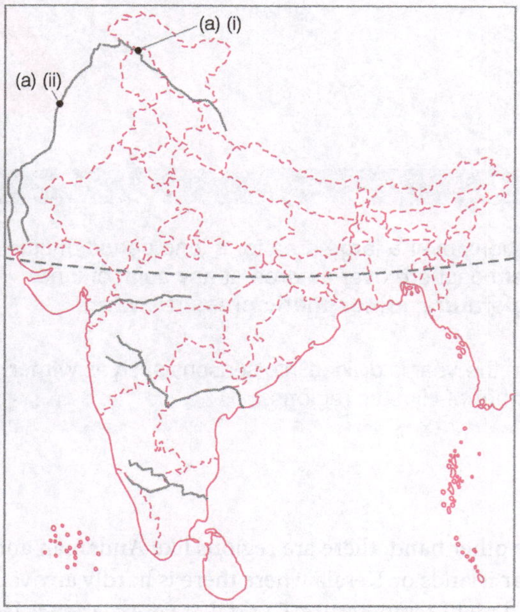

Ans.

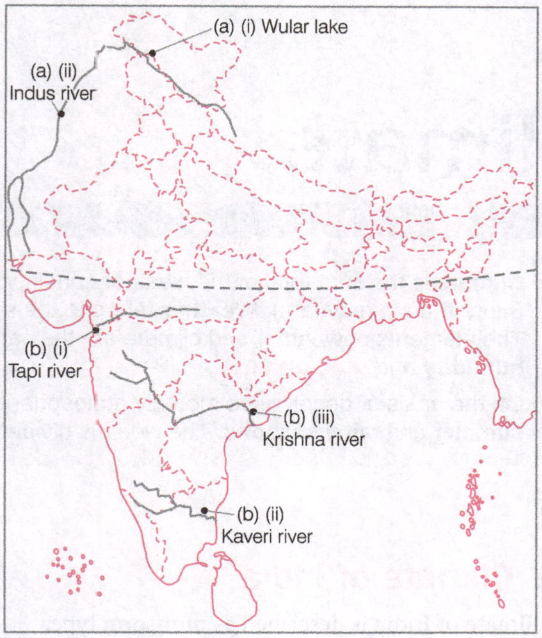

ASSESSMENT EXERCISE

Multiple Choice Questions (MCQs)

1. An upland separating two drainage basins is known as
(a) water divide (b) drainage basin
(c) river system (d) relief feature

2. The rivers perform intensive erosional activities in which course?
(a) Middle course (b) Upper course
(c) Lower course (d) All of these

3. At which place, the Ganga and Yamuna meet?
(a) Lucknow (b) Kanpur
(c) Allahabad (d) Aligarh

4. Find the incorrect option.
(a) The Godavari river from Betul district of Madhya Pradesh.
(b) It is the longest Peninsular river.
(c) The Godavari forms the largest delta of the Peninsular rivers.
(d) The Godavari basin covers parts of Maharashtra, Madhya Pradesh, Odisha and Andhra Pradesh.

5. Consider the following statements
A. Krishna river rises from Mahabaleshwar.
B. Musi and Bhima are its tributaries.
(a) A is false but B is true (b) Both A and B are true
(c) Both A and B are false (d) A is true but B is false

Subjective Questions (VSA, SA & LA)

1. Name the tributaries of the Ganga which flow from the Peninsular plateau.

2. The river Mahanadi rises from which state?

3. Identify the course of a river where meanders are formed.

4. Why are rivers considered lifeline of human civilisation? Explain any three reasons.

5. Name three main Himalayan river systems. Give two tributaries of each.

6. Describe any three important features of the Krishna river basin.

7. Which human activities have become the major threat to the Indian rivers? Suggest some measures to minimise them.

8. What is a lake? How are lakes formed? Explain the importance of lakes.

9. Describe the largest Peninsular West flowing river with regard to its source, flow and drainage basin.

CHAPTER 4

Climate

Climate is the sum total of the weather conditions and variations over a large area for a long period of time (more than thirty years). **Weather** refers to the state of the atmosphere over an area at any point of time. The elements of weather and climate are the same i.e. **temperature**, **atmospheric pressure**, **wind**, **humidity** and precipitation[1].

On the basis of generalised monthly atmospheric conditions, the year is divided into seasons such as **winter**, **summer** and **rainy seasons.** The world is divided into a number of climatic regions.

4.1 Climate of India

The climate of India is described as **monsoon** type. This type of climate is also found in South Asia and South-Eastern countries.

The word monsoon is derived from the Arabic word **mausim** which literally means season. 'Monsoon' refers to the seasonal reversal in the wind direction during a year.

There is an overall unity in the general climatic pattern in India but there are also some regional variations in climatic conditions within the country. The two important elements-temperature and precipitation are examined below

(i) Temperature

In India, there is great variation in the temperature of different parts of the country even in the same season.

For example, on a summer day the temperature in some parts of the **Rajasthan desert** may be 50°C but on the same day it will be around 20°C in **Pahalgam** in Jammu and Kashmir.

On a winter night, temperature at **Drass** in Jammu and Kashmir may be as low as minus 45°C. On the other hand, **Thiruvananthapuram** may have a temperature of 22°C.

In certain places there is a wide difference between day and night temperature. For example, in **Thar desert** the day temperature may rise upto 50°C and drops down to 15°C on the same night.

On the other hand, there are regions like Andaman and Nicobar islands or Kerala where there is hardly any variation in day and night temperature. Coastal areas experience less difference in temperature conditions.

(ii) Precipitation

There is variation in seasonal distribution, amount, types and forms of precipitation. For example, upper parts of Himalayas receive precipitation in the form of snow, while it rains over the rest of the country.

The **annual precipitation** varies from over 400 cm in Meghalaya to less than 10 cm in Ladakh and Western Rajasthan.

Most parts of the country receive rainfall from June to September, but the Tamil Nadu coast gets most of its rain during October and November.

Seasonal contrasts are more in the interior of the country. There is decrease in rainfall generally from East to West in the Northern Plains.

4.1 Climatic Controls

Permanent factors which govern the general nature of the climate of any location on the Earth are called factors of Climatic Controls.

There are six major controls of the climate of any place which are given below

(i) Latitude[2] Due to curvature[3] of the Earth, the amount of solar energy received varies with latitude. As a result, air temperature generally decreases from the equator towards the poles.

---

1 Precipitation A deposit of rain, hail, mist, sleet or snow on the Earth.

2 Latitude It is the angular distance of a location from the equator in North-South direction is called latitude.

3 Curvature It refers to the fact of being curved or the degree to which something is curved.

(ii) **Altitude**[4] With increase in altitude from the Earth surface, the temperature decreases and air becomes less dense. Therefore, hilly regions are cooler in summer.

(iii) **Pressure and Wind System** It depends on the latitude and altitude of a place. It influences the temperature and rainfall pattern of the area.

(iv) **Distance from the Sea** The sea exerts a moderating influence on the climate. As the distance from the sea increases, its moderating influence decreases leading to extreme weather conditions. This condition is known as **continentality** i.e. very hot during summers and very cold during winters.

(v) **Ocean Currents** Alongwith onshore winds, the ocean currents (warm or cold) affect the climate of the coastal areas. For example, cold onshore currents bring coolness in coastal areas and warm onshore currents bring warmth.

(vi) **Relief Features** High mountains act as a barrier for cold or hot wind. These high mountains may also cause precipitation if they are high enough and lie in the path of rain bearing winds. The **leeward side**[5] of mountains is relatively dry.

4.2 Factors Affecting India's Climate

Latitude

The Tropic of Cancer passes through the middle of the country from the Rann of Kachchh (West) to Mizoram (East).

It divides the country into almost two equal halves, the **tropical zone** which lies South of this line and the **sub-tropical zone** which lies North of this line. So, India's climate has characteristics of tropical as well as sub-tropical climates.

Altitude

Mountains in the North of India have an average height of about 6000 m. On the other hand, the vast coastal area of India has the maximum elevation of only about 30 m.

The Indian sub-continent experiences mild winters as compared to Central Asia because of the Himalayas which prevent the cold winds from entering the sub-continent.

Pressure and Winds

The climate and associated weather conditions in India are governed by the following atmospheric conditions

- Pressure and surface winds
- Upper air circulation
- Western cyclonic disturbances and tropical cyclones

India lies in the region of the North-Easterly winds. These winds originate from the sub-tropical high-pressure belt of the Northern hemisphere and blow over land during winters.

These winds blow Southwards and get deflected to the right due to the **Coriolis force** and move towards the equatorial-low pressure region.

The North-Easterly surface winds carry very little moisture as they originate and blow over land. Therefore, they bring no rain or very little rain.

The pressure and wind conditions over India are unique. During winter, there is a high-pressure area North of the Himalayas. This causes cold dry winds to blow from this area towards low-pressure areas over the oceans to the South.

In summer, a low-pressure area develops over interior Asia and over North-Western India. This causes a complete reversal of the direction of winds during summer.

Air moves from the high-pressure area over the Southern Indian Ocean in a South-Easterly direction. It crosses equator and turns right towards the low pressure region over the Indian subcontinent. These winds are known as the **South-West Monsoon winds.**

These winds blow over the warm oceans, gather large moisture and bring widespread rainfall over the mainland of India.

KNOWLEDGE PLUS Coriolis force is an apparent force caused by the Earth's rotation. The coriolis force is responsible for deflecting winds towards the right in the Northern hemisphere and towards the left in the Southern hemisphere. This is also known as **Ferrel's Law.**

Try These

1. **Name the type of climate found in India.**
2. **What are the 6 major controls of climate of any place?**
3. **Which region has wide fluctuation between day and night temperature?**
4. **This Indian state gets most of its rain in October and November. Identify.**

4 **Altitude** It refers to the height above the mean sea level.

5 **Leeward Side** It is the side of a mountain which receives less rainfall, as windward side already received much of its part.

4.3 The Seasons

The distinct seasonal pattern is an important characteristic of monsoon type of climate. The weather condition greatly change from one season to another and these changes are more noticeable in the interior parts of the country.

The coastal areas do not experience much variation in temperature though there is variation in rainfall pattern.

There are four seasons identified in India. These are

1. The Cold Weather Season (Winter)

The cold weather season (winter) begins from **mid-November** in the Northern India and stays till **February**. Clear sky, low temperatures, low humidity and weak variable winds are the characteristics of the weather during this period.

December and **January** are the coldest months in the Northern part of India. The temperature decreases from South to North. For example, the average temperature of Chennai, on the Eastern coast, is between 24°–25° C while in Northern plains, it ranges between 10°–15° C.

Features of Cold Weather Season

- Days are warm and nights are cold during this season. **Frost** is common in the North and snowfall is experienced in the high mountainous regions of the Himalayas.
- During this season, the North-East trade winds prevail over the country. They blow from land to sea and hence it is a dry season for most part of the country.
- Some amount of rainfall occurs on the Tamil Nadu coast from these winds as, here they blow from sea to land.
- In the Northern part of the country, a week high-pressure region develops, with light winds moving outwards from this area. These winds are influenced by the relief and blow through the Ganga valley from the West and the North-West.
- Over the Northern Plains, there is an inflow of **cyclonic disturbances** from the West and the North-West. These low-pressure systems have originated over the Mediterranean sea and Western Asia, and move into India alongwith the Westerly flow.
- The low pressure systems cause much-needed winter rains over the plains and snowfall in the mountains. The total amount of winter rainfall locally known as **Mahawat** is small, but they are important for the cultivation of 'rabi' crops.
- The peninsular region has a moderating effect from the sea and hence, there is hardly any seasonal change in temperature pattern during winters. The peninsular region does not have a well-defined cold season.

2. The Hot Weather Season (Summer)

The hot weather season (summer) in India lasts from March to May. This is due to the apparent Northward movement of the Sun.

Features of Hot Weather Season

- The influence of the shifting of heat belt can be seen from temperature recordings taken during March to May at different latitudes.
- In March, the **highest temperature** is about 38°C, recorded on **Deccan Plateau.** In April, temperature in Gujarat and Madhya Pradesh is around 42°C.
- In May, North-Western parts of the country experience temperature around 45°C and in peninsular India, the temperature remains lower due to the moderating influence of the oceans.
- The temperature of the Northern part of India rises and the atmospheric pressure falls.
- Towards the end of May, an extended low-pressure area develops which extends from Thar Desert in North-West to Patna and Chotanagpur plateau in the East and South-East. Circulation of air begins to appear around this **trough**[6].
- A strong, hot, gusty and dry wind, locally known as **Loo**, blows during this season over the North and North-Western India. Sometimes, they even continue until late in the evening. Direct exposure to loo may prove to be **fatal** (deadly).
- **Dust storms** are very common in the Northern India in the month of May. They bring temporary relief from the heat by lowering the temperature and may also cause light rain and cold breeze.

6 Trough It is a wide region of relatively low atmospheric pressure.

- Localised thunderstorms also occur during summer. They are associated with violentwinds, torrential down pours[7] and even hail[8]. Such thunderstorms are called **Kaal Baisakhi** in West Bengal.
- In the end of summer season, pre-monsoon showers are common. These are called **Mango Showers** which are common in **Kerala** and **Karnataka**. These help in the early ripening of the mango fruit.

3. Advancing Monsoon (Rainy Season)

The monsoon advances towards India during the early June as low pressure area over the Northern plains becomes stronger by early June. It attracts the South-East trade winds of the Southern hemisphere. These trade winds originate over the warm sub-tropical area of Southern ocean.

After crossing the equator, they blow in a South-Westerly direction and enter the Indian Peninsula as South-West monsoon.

As these winds blow over warm oceans, they bring abundant moisture to the sub-continent. These winds are strong and blow at an average velocity of 30 km per hour. They cover the entire sub-continent except extreme North-West in just one month. The South-West monsoon changes the Indian weather completely.

Features of Advancing Monsoon

- Early in the season, the windward side[9] of the Western Ghats receives very heavy rainfall, more than 250 cm. While the rain shadow area, the Deccan Plateau and parts of Madhya Pradesh also receive some amount of rainfall.
- The maximum rainfall of this season is received in the North-Eastern part of the country. **Mawsynram** in the Southern ranges of the Khasi hills receives the **highest average rainfall in the world.** Mawsynram is the wettest place on the Earth which is also famous for its stalagmite and stalactite caves.
- Rainfall in the Ganga valley decreases from the East to the West. Rajasthan and parts of Gujarat receive limited rainfall.
- The phenomenon associated with the moonsoon in India is its tendency to have 'breaks' in rainfall. It does not bring continuous rainfall rather it has **wet and dry spells.**
- In other words, the monsoon rains take place only for a few days at a time. They are interspersed (scattered) with rainless intervals. These breaks in monsoon are related to the movement of the monsoon trough.
- The **monsoon trough** and its axis keep on moving Northward or Southward and determines the spatial distribution of rainfall. When the axis of the trough lies over the plains, the region gets good rainfall.

  On the other hand, when the axis of trough lies closer to the Himalayas, the plains longer dry spells and widespread rains occur in the mountainous catchment areas of the Himalayan rivers. These heavy rains bring devastating floods causing damage to life and property in the plains.
- The frequency and intensity of **tropical depressions** determine amount and duration of the monsoon rains. These depressions form at the head of the **Bay of Bengal** and cross over to mainland. These depressions follow the axis of the 'monsoon trough of low pressure'.

Uncertainty of Monsoon

The monsoon is known for its uncertainties. The alternation of dry and wet spells differ in intensity, frequency and duration.

Monsoon causes heavy floods in one part and it may be responsible for causing drought in other regions. It is often irregular in its arrival and its retreat. Hence, it sometimes disturbs the farming schedule of millions of farmers all over the country.

4. Retreating/Post Monsoon Season (Transition Season)

The monsoon withdraws from the Northern plains by the beginning of October.

The months of October-November form a period of transition from hot rainy season to dry winter conditions.

During October-November, with the apparent movement of the Sun towards the South, the low pressure trough or monsoon trough become weak over the Northern plains.

It is gradually replaced by a high pressure system. The South-West monsoon winds become weaker and start withdrawing gradually.

Features of Retreating Monsoon

- The period of retreating monsoon marked by clear skies and rise in temperature.
- The day temperatures are high but nights are cool and pleasant.

7 Torrential Down pour It is any amount of rain that is considered especially heavy.
8 Hail It is a form of solid precipitation.
9 Windward Side It is the side or direction of a mountain from which the wind is blowing and pour its moisture in the form of heavy rain.

- Due to the high temperature and humidity, the weather becomes oppressive (harsh) during the day time. This phenomenon is known as **October heat**. In the second half of October, the temperature begins to fall rapidly in the Northern India.

Cyclonic Depression and Tropical Cyclone

The low pressure conditions over North-Western India, get shifted to the Bay of Bengal by early November. This shift is associated with the occurrence of **cyclonic depressions** which originate over the Andaman sea.

These cyclones generally cross the Eastern coast of India causing heavy and widespread rain. They often cause a lot of destruction. Sometimes, these cyclones arrive at the coasts of Odisha, West Bengal and Bangladesh.

These cyclones frequently strike the populated deltas of the Godavari, the Krishna and the Kaveri. The cyclones and depressions provide the majority rainfall to the **Coromandel Coast**.

4.4 Distribution of Rainfall

The parts of Western Coast and North-Eastern India receive over about 400 cm of rainfall annually. However, it is less than 60 cm in Western Rajasthan and adjoining parts of Gujarat, Haryana and Punjab.

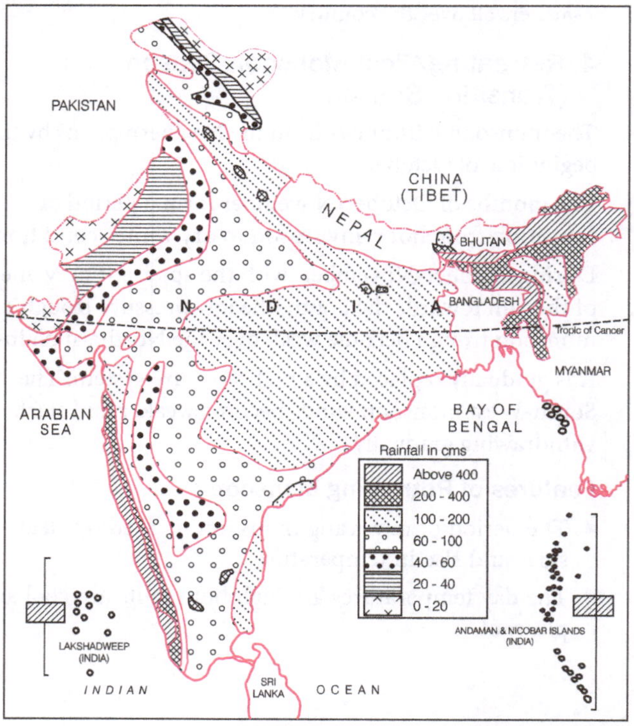

• Annual Rainfall

Rainfall is equally low in the interior of the Deccan Plateau and East of the Sahyadris. Another area of low precipitation is around Leh in Jammu and Kashmir.

The rest of the country receives moderate rainfall. Snowfall occurs only in the Himalayan region.

The annual rainfall is highly variable from year to year. Variability is high in the regions of low rainfall, such as parts of Rajasthan, Gujarat and the leeward side of the Western Ghats.

Areas of high rainfall are greatly affected by floods. On the other hand, areas which receive low rainfall are usually affected by drought like condition.

4.5 Monsoon as a Unifying Bond

The Northern India has uniformly higher temperatures than other areas on the same latitudes because the Himalayas protect it from the extremely cold Central Asian winds.

The Peninsular plateau has moderate temperatures due to the influence of the sea from three sides. Despite such moderating influences, there are great variations in the temperature conditions.

The seasonal alteration of wind systems and the associated weather conditions provide a rhythmic cycle of seasons. Even the uncertainties of rain and uneven distribution are usual characteristics of the monsoon.

The Indian landscape, its animals and plant life, agricultural activities and the life of the people, all revolve around the monsoon.

The monsoon provides the water to set agricultural activities in motion and hence, the arrival of the monsoon is awaited eagerly. The river valleys which carry this water also unite as single river valley unit.

Try These

1. **In which month the dust storms are common in North India?**
2. **What is the average temperature of Chennai during cold weather season?**
3. **Name any one region which receives low rainfall.**
4. **This area receives the highest rainfall in the world and is the wettest place on the Earth. Identify this area.**

Mind Map

CLIMATE

Climate of India
- The climate of India is described as Monsoon type.
- There is an overall unity in the general climatic pattern in India but there are also some regional variations in climatic conditions within the country.
- Two important elements are Temperature and Precipitation.

Monsoon as a Unifying Bond
- The peninsular plateau has moderate temperatures due to the influence of the sea from three sides.
- The seasonal alteration of wind systems and the associated weather conditions provide a rhythmic cycle of seasons.

Distribution of Rainfall
- The parts of Western Coast and North-Eastern India receive over about 400 cm of rainfall annually.
- The annual rainfall is less than 60 cm in Western Rajasthan and adjoining parts of Gujarat, Haryana and Punjab.
- Rainfall is equally low in the interior of the Deccan Plateau and East of the Sahyadris.

Climatic Controls
- Six major climatic controls are
  - (i) Latitude
  - (ii) Altitude
  - (iii) Pressure and Wind System
  - (iv) Distance from the Sea
  - (v) Ocean Currents
  - (vi) Relief Features

Pressure and Winds
- The climate and associated weather conditions in India are governed by pressure and surface winds, upper air circulation and Western cyclonic disturbances and tropical cyclones.
- India lies in the region of North-Easterly winds.
- These winds blow Southwards and get deflected due to the Coriolis force and move towards the equatorial-low pressure region.

The Seasons

The Cold Weather Season
- It begins from mid-November in the Northern India and stays till February.
- Days are warm and nights are cold.
- The North-East trade winds prevail over the country

Retreating/Post Monsoon Season
- The monsoon withdraws from the Northern plains by the beginning of October.
- The period of retreating monsoon is marked by clear skies and a rise in temperature.
- Due to the high temperature and humidity, the weather becomes oppressive during the day time which is known as October Heat.

Advancing Monsoon
- The low-pressure area over the Northern plains become stronger by early June.
- The Windward side of Western Ghats receives very heavy rainfall, more than 250 cm and, the rain shadow area, the Deccan Plateau and parts of Madhya Pradesh receive some amount of rainfall.
- Mawsynram receives the highest average rainfall in the world.
- Rainfall in the Ganga Valley decreases from the East to the West.
- Rajasthan and parts of Gujarat ‘eceive limited rainfall.

The Hot Weather Season
- It begins from March and stays till May.
- The temperature of the Northern part of India rises and the atmospheric pressure falls.
- Loo blows over the North and North-Western India.
- Dust Storms are common in Northern India in May.
- In the end of the summer season, pre-monsoon showers, called as Mango Showers, help in ripening of mango in Kerala and Karnataka.

Factor Affecting India's Climate

Latitude
- The Tropic of Cancer passes through the middle of the country from Rann of Kachchh to Mizoram.
- India's climate has characteristics of tropical as well as subtropical climates.

Altitude
- Mountains in the North India have an average height of 6000m.
- Coastal area has maximum elevation of 30m.

NCERT FOLDER

Covering Intext Questions and Exercises of NCERT

INTEXT QUESTIONS

Q.1 Why the houses in Rajasthan have thick walls and flat roofs?

Ans. The houses in Rajasthan have thick walls because in Rajasthan, the weather is very hot and there is less rainfall. So, the thick walls of the houses protect the people against the heat in summer and extreme cold in winter due to the desert. The flat roofs are easier to construct and as there is not much rainfall, water will collect on the rooftops.

Q.2 Why is it that the houses in the Tarai region and in Goa and Mangalore have sloping roofs?

Ans. The houses in the Tarai region, and in Goa and Mangalore have sloping roofs because they get heavy rain during the monsoon. When there are sloping roofs, the rain water can easily flow off towards the ground or to a receptive unit where water is collected instead of collecting on the rooftop.

Q.3 Why houses in Assam are built on stilts?

Ans. Houses in Assam are built on stilts because the state receives abundant rainfall due to which there are chances of floods. In case of flood, the water might get inside the houses if the houses are built on ground level. So in order to avoid flooding of houses, houses are built on stilts and above the ground level.

Q.4 Why most of the world's deserts are located in the Western margins of continents in the subtropics?

Ans. Most of the world's deserts are located in the Western margins of continents in the subtropics because the prevailing winds in the tropics are tropical easterly winds. These winds become dry by the time they reach the Western margins of the continents and so they bring no rainfall. Thus, the region becomes devoid of moisture which causes dry conditions leading to formation of deserts.

EXERCISE

Q.1 Choose the correct answer from the four alternatives given below

(i) Which one of the following places receives the highest rainfall in the world?

(a) Silchar (b) Mawsynram
(c) Cherrapunji (d) Guwahati

(ii) The wind blowing in the Northern plains in summers is known as

(a) Kaal Baisakhi (b) Loo
(c) Trade Winds (d) None of these

(iii) Which one of the following characterises the cold weather season in India?

(a) Warm days and warm nights
(b) Warm days and cold nights
(c) Cool days and cold nights
(d) Cool days and warm nights

Ans. (i) (b), (ii) (b), (iii) (b)

Q.2 Answer the following questions briefly.

(i) What are the controls affecting the climate of India?

Ans. The controls affecting the climate of India are latitude, altitude, pressure and wind system, distance from the sea, ocean currents and relief features.

(ii) Why does India have a monsoon type of climate?

Ans. India has monsoon type of climate. It is because of the occurence of the seasonal reversal of wind system and the strong influence of the monsoon winds over the sub-continent, which make Indian climate monsoon type.

(iii) Which part of India does experiences the highest diurnal range of temperature and why?

Ans. The highest diurnal range of temperature is experienced by the North-Western part of India comprising the Indian desert. This is because of the fact that sand (found in ample quantity in this region) gains and loses heat very quickly and it is located away from the sea.

(iv) Which winds account for rainfall along the Malabar coast?

Ans. The South-West monsoon winds (the Arabian sea branch) are responsible for rainfall along the Malabar coast.

(v) Define monsoon. What do you understand by 'break' in monsoon?

Ans. The word monsoon is derived from the Arabic word 'Mausim' which literally means season. 'Monsoon' refers to the seasonal reversal in the wind direction during a year.

Break in monsoon are related to the wet and dry spells during the monsoon rainfall. Monsoon in India does not bring continuous rainfall. The rains are interspersed (scattered) with rainless intervals. Such rainless intervals are called 'break' in monsoon. The breaks in monsoon are related to the movement of the monsoon trough. It is seen that when the axis of the monsoon trough lies over the Northern plains, the rainfall is heavier there. When this trough shifts towards the Himalayas, the plains are dry but the mountains receive heavy rainfall.

(vi) Why is the monsoon considered a unifying bond?

Ans. The monsoon is considered as a unifying bond because of the following reasons

- The presence of the Himalayan range in the North and ocean in the South have created a unique climatic condition over the Indian sub-continent.
- The seasonal alternation of wind system (i.e. monsoon) and the associated weather conditions provide a rhythmic cycle of seasons. Indian landscape, life style, agriculture, food habit, culture, etc. all revolve around these phenomena.
- By providing water to the agriculture and regulating the flow of water in river valleys (connecting different states), monsoon binds the whole country together.

Q.3 Why does the rainfall decrease from the East to the West in the Northern India?

Ans. There is a gradual decrease of rainfall from the East to the West in North India. The progressive decline of humidity of the winds is responsible for this. As the moisture bearing winds of the Bay of Bengal branch of the South-West monsoon move further and further inland, their moisture content decreases. As a result, there is a gradual decrease of rainfall from East to west direction.

Q.4 Give reasons as to why

(i) Seasonal reversal of wind direction takes place over the Indian sub-continent.

(ii) The bulk of rainfall in India is concentrated over a few months.

(iii) The Tamil Nadu coast receives winter rainfall.

(iv) The delta region of the Eastern coast is frequently struck by cyclones.

(v) Parts of Rajasthan, Gujarat and the leeward side of the Western Ghats are drought-prone.

Ans. (i) Seasonal reversal of wind direction takes place over the Indian sub-continent. This can be understood by the following points

(a) As there are different densities of land and water, so the rate of heating and cooling also varies. India is surrounded by water on three sides which gives special effect to the landmass. During summers, the Indian landmass becomes intensely heated than the surrounding seas. Thus, a low pressure region develops over the North-Western parts of the country. The nearby sea is cooler, thereby having higher pressure. So, the winds blow from sea to land in the form of monsoon winds.

(b) With the reversal in the direction of the surface winds, the monsoons withdraw from the Northern plains. This reversal occurs as the monsoon trough becomes weaker with the approach of winter months.

(c) During winters, a high pressure area develops North of the Himalayas. And cold dry winds blow from this high pressure region to the low pressure areas that develops over the oceans to the South.

(d) Thus, these differences in pressure conditions are responsible for a complete reversal of the direction of winds.

(ii) The bulk of rainfall in India is concentrated over a few months. It is because of the fact that Indian sub-continent largely receives rainfall from the South-West monsoon winds. These winds are highly characterised by the seasonal reversal of winds. These winds blow over the main land when it has intense low pressure region and the surrounding water body has high pressure region.
This ideal temperature and pressure condition develops in May month. Thus, rainfall occurs between June to September months for over 100 to 120 days approximately. After this period, the monsoon withdraws from India and rest of the year becomes practically dry except winters which receive low rainfall.

(iii) The Tamil Nadu coast receives winter rainfall due to North-East trade winds. This is because in this region these winds blow from sea (Bay of Bengal) to land, thereby carrying moisture alongwith them.

(iv) The delta region of the Eastern coast of India is frequently struck by cyclones. This is because the cyclonic depressions that originate over the Andaman sea are brought in by the sub-tropical Easterly Jet stream blowing over the peninsular India during the monoon as well as during the October to November period. The depression moves along East to West direction thus, hitting the Eastern coasts.

(v) Parts of Rajasthan, Gujarat and the leeward side of the Western Ghats are drought-prone due to the following reasons :

- Parts of Rajasthan are drought prone as they do not receive much rain because of the presence of Aravalli Range.

It is because this range lies parallel to the direction of the winds, which do not strike it and thus, do not cause any rain.

- Gujarat is a drought prone region which receives less rainfall. It is because there are no hills and mountain ranges to obstruct the rain-bearing winds.
- The leeward side of the Western Ghats receives less rainfall. It is because the rain bearing winds strike the windward side first (slopes facing the winds) and then proceed to the leeward side (opposite side of the windward side). Due to this fact, very little or no rainfall occurs on the leeward side of the Western Ghats and it became drought prone region.

Q.5 Describe the regional variations in the climatic conditions of India with the help of suitable examples.

Ans. The regional variation of the climatic conditions of India is mainly due to two factors, *viz*, temperature and precipitation (or rainfall). These two elements vary from place to place and season to season.

Temperature

During summer the temperature of desert area (e.g. parts of Rajasthan) crosses 50°C mark, on the other hand, hilly region (e.g. Pahalgam) has around 20°C temperature.

Similarly, the temperature of winter night at Drass (Jammu and Kashmir) is – 45°C whereas in coastal area (e.g. Thiruvananthapuram), it is about 22°C. The coastal region (e.g. Kerala) and island (e.g. Andaman and Nicobar) have uniform temperature throughout the year due to moderating effect of the sea.

Whereas the interior parts of India have continental climate as these are far from the sea.

Precipitation

In India, there is variation in the form, type, amount and seasonal distribution of rainfall from region to region. For example the precipitation is in the form of snowfall in the Himalayas, whereas it is in the form of rainfall in the rest of the country.

In the same season, Western Ghats and North-Eastern part of the country receive more than 200 cm rainfall (Meghalaya-400 cm), it is less than 10 cm in Ladakh and Western Rajasthan. Most parts of the country receives rainfall from June to September whereas the Tamil Nadu coast receives rainfall during October and November. There is gradual decrease of rainfall generally from East to West.

Q.6 Give an account of weather conditions and characteristics of the cold season.

Ans. The cold weather season begins from November in Northern India and stays till February. December and January are the coldest months in the Northern part of India.

The characteristics of cold season are as follows :

(i) The weather is normally marked by clear sky, low temperatures, low humidity and feeble, variable winds.

(ii) Days are warm and nights are cold. Frost is common in the North and higher slopes of the Himalayas experience snowfall.

(iii) During this season, the North-East trade winds blow from land to sea and hence, for most parts of the country, it is a dry season. Some amount of rainfall occurs on the Tamil Nadu coast from these winds as they blow there from sea to land.

(iv) A characteristic feature of the cold weather season over the Northern plains is the inflow of cyclonic disturbances from the West and the North-West. These low-pressure systems, originate over the Mediterranean Sea and Western Asia and move into India, along with Westerly flow.

(v) The peninsular region does not have a well-defined cold season. There is hardly any noticeable change in temperature pattern during winter due to the moderating influence of the sea.

Q.7 Give the characteristics and effects of the monsoon rainfall in India.

Ans. The characteristics of monsoon rainfall are :

- Its duration varies from 100-120 days (early June-mid September).
- Around the time of its arrival, there is sudden increase and continuous rainfall for several days, called as 'Burst of monsoon'.
- The monsoon takes place in wet and dry spells. The intervening rainless intervals are known as 'Breaks' in monsoon.
- Rainfall is unevenly distributed over the Indian mainland. Certain areas receive heavy rainfall while other areas receive scanty and low rainfall.

The effects of monsoon rainfall in India are :

- Indian agriculture is largely dependent upon the water from the monsoon rains, so most of the crops that need more water cultivated during this time.
- Monsoon rains recharge the water of the Southern Indian rivers.
- Due to the uneven distribution of rainfall across the country, there are some regions that are drought prone and some that are flood afflicted.
- The low or excessive rains have a negative impact upon crops.

The monsoon provides India with a distinct climatic pattern. Hence, in spite of the presence of great regional variations, it has a unifying influence upon the country and its people.

Q.8 **(i) Name two rainiest stations.**
(ii) Name two driest stations.
(iii) Name two stations with most equable climate.
(iv) Name two stations with most extreme climate.
(v) Name two stations influenced by both branches of the South-West monsoons.
(vi) Name two stations influenced by retreating and North-East monsoons.
(vii) Name the two hottest stations in the months of (a) February (b) April (c) May (d) June

Ans. (i) Shillong and Mumbai
(ii) Leh and Jodhpur
(iii) Thiruvananthapuram and Mumbai
(iv) Leh and Jodhpur
(v) Delhi and Punjab
(vi) Thiruvananthapuram and Chennai
(vii) (a) Febrauary : Thiruvananthapuram and Chennai
(b) April : Nagpur and Chennai
(c) May : Nagpur and Delhi / Jodhpur
(d) June : Jodhpur and Delhi

Q.9 **Now find out**
(i) Why are Thiruvananthapuram and Shillong rainier in June than in July?
(ii) Why is July rainier in Mumbai than in Thiruvananthapuram?
(iii) Why are South-West monsoons less rainy in Chennai?
(iv) Why is Shillong rainier than Kolkata?
(v) Why is Kolkata rainier in July than in June unlike Shillong which is rainier in June than in July?
(vi) Why does Delhi receive more rain than Jodhpur?

Ans. (i) They are rainier in June as the monsoon arrival occurs in both places in June. And the initial impact of the monsoon is an intense period of heavy rain.

(ii) July is rainier in Mumbai than in Thiruvananthapuram. It is because monsoon reaches Thiruvananthapuram by 1st of June and after giving initial showers the monsoon falls into a steady pattern of raining for at least a couple of hours most days.

By the time, monsoon reaches Mumbai (by 10th of June), it gets its maximum strength and obstructs by the Western Ghats and gives heavy rainfall for about a month and also during July month.

(iii) Chennai doesn't receive much rain during the South-West monsoon. It is because the Bay of Bengal branch of monsoon passes parallel to Tamil Nadu coast causing very little or no rainfall. Chennai gets most of its rainfall from the North-East monsoon from October to December.

(iv) Shillong is in a hilly area. The hills usually trap the monsoon winds. So that Shillong becomes rainier than Kolkata.

(v) Shillong is rainier in June than Kolkata because the monsoon reaches Shillong earlier than Kolkata (refer to the 'Advancing Monsoon' map in your textbook) and the initial impact is heavier than the later showers.

(vi) Delhi receives more rain than Jodhpur. It is because Delhi lies more East than Jodhpur and receives rainfall from the Bay of Bengal branch. This branch keeps on reducing its moisture as proceeds from East to West. By the time, this branch reaches further West, it looses its moisture and gives very few rainfall in Jodhpur.

On the other hand, Jodhpur is on the edge of the Thar desert and when monsoon winds reach there, most of their moisture is exhausted. Thus, Delhi receives more rain than Jodhpur.

Q.10 **Re-arrange the ten stations in two different sequences**
(i) According to their distance from the equator.
(ii) According to their altitude above mean sea-level.

Ans.

(i) Distance from the Equator	(ii) Altitude above Mean Sea Level
Leh (Farthest)	Leh
Delhi	Shillong
Jodhpur	Bengaluru
Shillong	Nagpur
Kolkata	Jodhpur
Nagpur	Delhi
Mumbai	Thiruvananthapuram
Chennai	Mumbai
Bengaluru	Chennai
Thiruvananthapuram (nearest)	Kolkata

Q.11 **Now think why**
(i) Thiruvananthapuram has equable climate?
(ii) Chennai has more rains only after the fury of monsoon is over in most parts of the country?
(iii) Jodhpur has a hot desert type of climate?
(iv) Leh has moderate precipitation almost throughout the year?
(v) While in Delhi and Jodhpur most of the rain is confined to nearly three months, in Thiruvananthapuram and Shillong it is almost nine months of the year?
(vi) In spite of these facts, see carefully if there are strong evidences to conclude that the monsoons still provide a very strong framework lending overall climatic unity to the whole country.

Ans. (i) Thiruvananthapuram has equable climate because of two reasons :

- It is situated on the sea coast. The moderating influence of the sea makes the climate equable.
- It is near to the equator. At the equator, all the seasons have similar temperatures and so this makes the climate equable.

(ii) Chennai gets most of its rainfall later than most other parts of the country because it receives most of its rainfall from the North-East monsoon or retreating monsoon which gives rains mostly from October to December. It receives very less or no rainfall from South-West monsoon like rest of the country.

(iii) Jodhpur has a hot desert type of climate because it is situated on the extreme North-Western part of India which is a desert and so, when the monsoon winds reach there, they exhaust their moisture.

(iv) Leh is a cold desert located in the mountains and because of its topographical location, it receives moderate precipitation almost throughout the year.

(v) Rains in Delhi and Jodhpur are confined to monsoon period only i.e. three months. It is because, these regions are located in the interior part of the country, which receives rainfall mostly from South-West monsoon.

Thiruvananthapuram receives rainfall almost nine months of the year because it lies on the sea coast and receives rainfall from both the South-West and North-East monsoons. Besides it receives rainfall due to local disturbances which pick up moisture from the sea.

Shillong also gets rainfall almost nine months of the year because it is in a hilly area and receives rain from the monsoon as well as from local disturbances which are trapped by the hills.

(vi) The seasonal alteration of the wind systems and the associated weather conditions provide a rhythmic cycle of seasons. Monsoon rains are unevenly distributed and typically uncertain.

The Indian landscape, plant and animal life, agriculture, the people and their festivities, all revolve around the monsoon.

All the Indian people eagerly await the arrival of the monsoon. It binds the whole country by providing water which sets all agricultural activities in motion. That is why, the monsoon is considered a unifying bond.

REVIEW EXERCISE

Including Competency Based Questions

Part I

Multiple Choice Questions (MCQs)

1. .... refers to the sum total of weather conditions and variations over a large area for a long period of time.

(a) Monsoon (b) Climate
(c) Weather (d) Environmental effects

2. Which among the following fluctuates very often even within a day?

(a) Weather (b) Climate
(c) Atmospheric conditions (d) Seasons

3. India has which type of climate?

(a) Monsoon (b) Oceanic
(c) Tundra (d) Tropical Savanna

4. What is the annual precipitation in the Indian state of Meghalaya?

(a) 300 cm (b) 350 cm (c) 400 cm (d) 450 cm

5. The most parts of the country receive rainfall in which of the following months ?

(a) June to September (b) April to July
(c) March to June (c) February to May

6. Which type of climate is characterised by a distinct seasonal pattern?

(a) Monsoon type of climate
(b) Tropical savanna type of climate
(c) Tundra type of climate
(d) Rainforest type of climate

7. The ...... areas do not experience much variation in temperature though there is variation in rainfall pattern.

(a) mountainous (b) plain
(c) coastal (d) None of these

8. How many seasons can be identified in India?

(a) Three (b) Four (c) Two (d) Five

9. Which of the following months are the coldest months in the Northern part of India?

(a) January and February (b) November and December
(c) December and January (d) September and October

10. During cold weather season, which wind prevails over the country?

(a) Monsoon wind (b) Westerlies wind
(c) North-East trade wind (d) North-West trade wind

11. Find the incorrect option.

(a) India lies in the region of the North-Easterly winds.
(b) These winds originate and blow over land during winter from the sub-tropical high-pressure belt of the Northern hemisphere.
(c) These winds blow Southwards and get deflected to the right due to the Coriolis force.
(d) Then these winds move towards the equatorial high-pressure region.

12. Which of the following statements defines Continentality?

(a) In Continentality summers are normal but Winters are very cold.
(b) In Continentality summers are very hot but Winters are mild.
(c) In Continentality summers are very hot and winters are very cold.
(d) In Continentality both summers and winters are mild.

13. There are six major controls of the climate of any place. They are latitude, altitude, pressure and wind system, distance from the sea (continentality), ocean currents and relief features.
The pressure and wind system of any area depends on which climate control factors? **Competency Based**

(a) Distance from the sea (b) Relief features
(c) Latitude and altitude (d) None of these

14. Tamil Nadu usually does not receive enough rain during monsoon, but this year, due to the formation of a weather system over South-West Bay of Bengal, Tamil Nadu has recorded a few good spells of rain.
When does the Tamil Nadu coast receive a significant portion of its rainfall? **Competency Based**

(a) June and July (b) August and September
(c) October and November (d) December and January

15. Arrange the following places according to their distance from the equator (from minimum to maximum).

I. Leh II. Delhi
III. Thiruvananthapuram IV. Shillong

Codes

(a) III, IV, II, I (b) IV, III, II, I
(c) I, II, III, IV (d) III, I, II, IV

16. Which of the following statements accurately describes about the "The Indian Monsoon"?

I. The climate of India is strongly influenced by monsoon winds.
II. The sailors who came to India in historic times were one of the first to have noticed the phenomenon of the monsoon.
III. The Mongols, who had also come to India as traders named this seasonal reversal of the wind system 'monsoon'.
IV. The monsoons are experienced in the tropical area roughly between 10° N and 10° S.

Codes

(a) Only I (b) Only II
(c) Only IV (d) Both I and II

17. Identify distribution of rainfall in India. Choose from the appropriate statements among the following options.

I. Parts of Western coast and North-Eastern India receive over about 400 cm of rainfall annually.
II. It is less than 60 cm in Western Rajasthan and adjoining parts of Gujarat.
III. Rainfall is equally low in the interior of the Deccan plateau.
IV. Variability is low in the regions of high rainfall such as parts of Delhi, Bihar and the leeward side of the Western ghats.

Codes

(a) Statements I and II are appropriate
(b) Statements I, II and III are appropriate
(c) All the statements are appropriate
(d) Only statement I is appropriate

18. Consider the statements given below and choose the correct answer. **Competency Based**

Statement I The cold weather season begins from mid-November in Northern India and stays till February.

Statement II The differential heating and cooling of land and water creates high pressure on the landmass of India while the ocean around experience comparatively low pressure.

Codes

(a) Statement I is correct and II is incorrect
(b) Statement I is incorrect and II is correct
(c) Both I and II are incorrect
(d) Both I and II are correct

Answers

1. (b)	2. (a)	3. (a)	4. (c)	5. (a)
6. (a)	7. (c)	8. (b)	9. (c)	10. (c)
11. (d)	12. (c)	13. (c)	14. (c)	15. (a)
16. (d)	17. (b)	18. (a)		

Match the Following

1.

	List-I (Seasons)	List-II (Duration)
A.	Cold Weather Season	1. Mid-November- February
B.	Hot Weather Season	2. March-May
C.	Advancing Monsoon Season	3. June-September
D.	Retreating/Post Monsoon Season	4. October-November

Codes

	A	B	C	D		A	B	C	D
(a)	1	2	3	4	(b)	1	3	2	4
(c)	4	3	1	2	(d)	4	3	2	1

Ans. (a)

Assertion-Reason

1. **Assertion** (A) India's climate has characteristics of tropical as well as sub-tropical climates.

Reason (R) The Tropic of Cancer passes through the middle of the country from the Rann of Kachchh in the West to Mizoram in the East.

Codes

(a) Both A and R are true and R is the correct explanation of A

(b) Both A and R are true, but R is not the correct explanation of A

(c) A is true, but R is false

(d) A is false, but R is true

2. **Assertion** (A) During retreating monsoon October heat is a common phenomenon.

Reason (R) High temperature and humidity is common during retreating monsoon. The weather becomes oppressive during the day time.

Codes

(a) Both A and R are the true and R is the correct explanation of A

(b) Both A and R are true, but R is not the correct explanation of A

(c) A is true, but R is false

(d) A is false, but R is true

3. **Assertion** (A) India has mountains to the North, which have an average height of about 6,000 metres.

Reason (R) India also has a vast coastal area where the maximum elevation is about 30 metres.

Codes

(a) Both A and R are the true and R is the correct explanation of A

(b) Both A and R are true, but R is not the correct explanation of A

(c) A is true, but R is false

(d) A is false, but R is true

4. **Assertion** (A) Due to the apparent Southward movement of the Sun, the global heat belt shifts Northwards.

Reason (R) In March, the highest temperature is about 38° Celsius, recorded on the Deccan plateau.

Codes

(a) Both A and R are the true and R is the correct explanation of A

(b) Both A and R are true, but R is not the correct explanation of A

(c) A is true, but R is false

(d) A is false, but R is true

Ans. 1. (a) Both A and R are the true and R is the correct explanation of A

2. (a) Both A and R are true and R is the correct explanation of A

3. (b) Both A and R are true, but R is not the correct explanation of A

4. (d) A is false, but R is true

Case Based Question

1. **Read the source given below and answer the questions that follow.**

During October-November, with the apparent movement of the Sun towards the South, the monsoon trough or the low-pressure trough over the Northern plains becomes weaker. This is gradually replaced by a high-pressure system. The South-West monsoon winds weaken and start withdrawing gradually. By the beginning of October, the monsoon withdraws from the Northern plains. The months of October-November form a period of transition from hot rainy season to dry winter conditions. The retreat of the monsoon is marked by clear skies and rise in temperature. While day temperatures are high, nights are cool and pleasant. The land is still moist. Owing to the conditions of high temperature and humidity, the weather becomes rather oppressive during the day.

(i) When does the mercury begin to fall rapidly in Northern India?

(a) Mid-November (b) Early October

(c) Late October (d) Late November

(ii) In which month does Delhi typically receive monsoon showers from the Bay of Bengal branch?

(a) March (b) April

(c) May (d) June

(iii) What is associated with the shift of low-pressure conditions to the Bay of Bengal?

(a) Winter

(b) Monsoon

(c) October heat

(d) Cyclonic depressions

(iv) What weather phenomenon influences the islands during the withdrawal of the monsoon?

(a) Tropical cyclones (b) Winter monsoon

(c) Heatwaves (d) None of these

Ans. (i) (a) Mid-November

(ii) (d) June

(iii) (c) October heat

(iv) (b) Winter monsoon

Part II

Very Short Answer Type Questions

1. Why does Thiruvananthapuram have a moderate climate?

Ans. Due to coastal location, Thiruvananthapuram has a moderate climate.

2. In which season does the rainfall in Ganga valley reduce from East to West?

Ans. Rainfall in Ganga valley reduces from East to West during the season of advancing monsoon.

3. Which force is responsible for the deflection of wind from its normal path?

Ans. The Coriolis force is responsible for the deflection of wind from its normal path.

4. Define the term 'Loo'.

Ans. 'Loo' are strong, gusty, hot, dry winds blowing during the day over the North and North-Western India in summer season.

5. In which season does the heat belt shift Northwards?

Ans. The heat belt shifts Northwards during the summer season.

6. Which part of India receives maximum rainfall during the rainy season?

Ans. The North-Eastern part of India receives maximum rainfall during the rainy season.

7. The phenomenon of 'October Heat' is the characteristic feature of which season?

Ans. The phenomenon of 'October Heat' occurs during the season of retreating monsoon.

8. The withdrawal of monsoon from North-West India marks the beginning of its retreat from the Indian subcontinent. Any delay in the monsoon's retreat means a longer rainy season, which can significantly impact agricultural production .... Competency Based
Source (edited): Hindustan Times

(i) Which crop production is impacted by monsoon rainfall in North-West India?

(ii) What unique factor contributes to the low rainfall around Leh in Jammu and Kashmir ?

Ans. (i) The Rabi crop production in North-West India is impacted by monsoon rainfall.

(ii) The low rainfall around Leh in Jammu and Kashmir is primarily influenced by its location in the rain shadow of the Himalayas.

9. The influence of the shifting of the heat belt can be seen clearly from temperature recordings taken during March-May at different latitudes. In March, the highest temperature is about 38° Celsius, recorded on the Deccan plateau.

What happens to temperature and air pressure in the Northern part of the country during the summer months? Competency Based

Ans. During the summer months, the Northern part of the country experiences rising temperatures and falling air pressure. This combination of increasing temperature and decreasing air pressure is a characteristic feature of the summer season in that region.

10. Despite an overall unity in the general pattern, there are perceptible regional variations in climatic conditions within the country.

Name two important elements used to examine climatic variations in India. Competency Based

Ans. Temperature and precipitation are two important elements used to analyse climatic variations in India.

Short Answer Type Questions

1. How do the following factors influence the climate of India?

(a) Latitude (b) Altitude (c) Distance from the sea

Ans. The factors which influence the climate of India are given below

(a) **Latitude** The Tropic of Cancer divides India into two equal halves. The region lying North to it has sub-tropical climate, whereas South to it has tropical climate.

(b) **Altitude** It means the height from the sea level. With increase in height from the Earth surface the temperature decreases and air becomes less dense. India has mountain ranges (the Himalayas) in the North with an average elevation of about 6000 m. The coastal areas as well as islands have maximum elevation of about 30m.

The Indian sub-continent experiences milder winters, as the Himalayas act as a barriers against the cold arctic winds and stop them to enter in India. The Himalayas also stop the South-West monsoon winds to escape from India and the whole Northern India experiences monsoon season.

(c) **Distance from the sea** The regions located near the sea have moderate climate and those lying away from it have extreme climate. This is due to moderating influence of ocean currents.

2. What is the Coriolis force? Describe briefly its effect on the world climate.

Ans. Coriolis Force

It is an apparent force caused by the Earth's rotation. It is responsible for deflecting winds towards the right in the Northern hemisphere and towards the left in the Southern hemisphere.

Effect of Coriolis Force on the World Climate

Under the effect of Coriolis force, the trade winds moving from sub-tropical high-pressure belts to equatorial low-pressure belts become North-East trade winds in the Northern hemisphere.

These trade winds become South-East trade winds in the Southern hemisphere. As a result, they bring heavy rainfall to the East coast, while the West coast remains dry.

3. State what is monsoon. How do monsoon winds act as a unifying bond for the Indian sub-continents?

Ans. The word 'monsoon' is derived from the Arabic word 'Mausim' which literally means season. It refers to the seasonal reversal in the wind direction during a year.

The monsoon unifies India by bringing seasonal rainfall essential for agriculture, rivers and livelihoods. Despite regional climatic variations, the entire nation eagerly awaits its arrival. It influences festivals, farming cycles and daily life. The monsoon finds diverse landscapes from North to South and East to West, ensuring water availability and sustaining the country's agricultural and economic activities.

4. Define 'Kal Baisakhi', 'Loo' and 'Mango Shower'. In which parts of India are they experienced?

Ans. **Kal Baisakhi** Kal Baisakhi are the local thunderstorms. These are associated with violent winds, torrential downpours, often accompanied by hail. They occur in West Bengal.

Loo Loo is a strong, gusty, hot, dry wind. It blows during the day over the North and North-Western India.

Mango Showers Mango showers are pre-monsoon showers. These help in the ripening of mangoes in coastal Kerala and Karnataka.

5. Why do the Western Ghats receive more rainfall than the Eastern Ghats? Explain briefly.

Ans. Western Ghats receive more rainfall than the Eastern Ghats because

(i) Western Ghats receive rainfall from the Arabian sea branch of the South-West monsoon winds. As these winds blow over warm oceans, they bring abundant moisture.

(ii) The Western Ghats do not allow the winds to cross over without shedding their moisture on the Western slopes so they receive more rainfall.

(iii) On the other hand, when these winds reach the Eastern Ghats, they are almost dry, so they receive less rainfall.

(iv) Another branch of South-West monsoon is the Bay of Bengal branch. This branch moves parallel to the Eastern Ghats. In this way, this region is located in an unfavourable position with reference to the monsoon winds.

6. Where is Mawsynram located? Why does Mawsynram receive the highest amount of rainfall?

Ans. Mawsynram is located in the Southern ranges of the Khasi hills in Meghalaya. It is located at a height of 1500 m above the sea level. It receives the highest average (annual 1140 cm) rainfall of the world.

Mawsynram receives the highest amount of rainfall because

- This place is enclosed by hills on three sides.
- The relief features give this place tunnel shaped location.
- The Bay of Bengal branch of the South-West monsoon is trapped in these hills. The winds of this branch try to get out of there, but are forced to pour down there extensively.

7. Explain any four features of advancing monsoon with reference to India.

Ans. The advancing monsoon prevails during the months of June, July, August and September.

The features of advancing monsoon are

(i) It brings a total change in weather conditions.

(ii) Early in the season of the advancing monsoon, the windward side of the Western Ghats receives very heavy rainfall. The maximum rainfall of this season occurs in the North-Eastern India.

(iii) It has wet and dry spells. The intervening dry period is called 'Breaks' in monsoon.

(iv) The monsoon is known for its uncertainties. The spatial distribution of rainfall is uneven.

8. Why does the North-West India receive rainfall during winters? Give any three reasons.

Ans. The North-West India receives rainfall during winters due to the following reasons

(i) The low-pressure systems originate over the Mediterranean sea and Western Asia during winter months.

(ii) These low-pressure systems which are also known as Western cyclonic disturbances, move into India alongwith the Westerly flow.

(iii) These Western disturbances cause winter rains in the North-Western India especially in Punjab, Haryana and Northern plains.

9. Why is the distribution of rainfall in India not uniform? Explain any three reasons.

Ans. The distribution of rainfall in India is not uniform. There is spatial and temporal variation of rainfall in India. Various factors contributed to this uneven distribution of rainfall in India.

They are

(i) **Relief** Relief factors (e.g. high mountains and hills) act as a barrier to rain bearing winds. When such winds collide with the high mountains, they cause orographic rainfall on the windward side. The leeward side on the other hand remains drier. E.g. due to the Western Ghats, the Western coastal plains get heavy rainfall.

(ii) **Distance from the Sea** (Continentality) As the distance from the sea increases, the moisture content of the wind decreases. So, the interior of landmass are much drier than those in the Coastal region.

(iii) **Direction of Wind** The regions lying in the direction of flow of wind are rainier than those not lying on its direction. E.g. Tamil Nadu coast which lies parallel to the Bay of Bangal branch does not get rainfall from the South-West monsoon.

10. "There is a great variation in the amount and type of precipitation in India." Justify the statement.

Ans. There is a wide variation not only in the forms and types of precipitation but also in its amount and the seasonal distribution such as

- In the upper parts of the Himalayas, precipitation occurs most likely in the form of snowfall. The rest of the country receives rainfall.
- Parts of Western coast and the North-Eastern India receives over about 400 cm of rainfall annually, e.g. Meghalaya.

  On the other hand, some regions like Ladakh, Western Rajasthan, parts of Gujarat and the leeward side of the Western Ghats receive rainfall less than 10 cm annually.

Thus, it can be concluded that there is a great variation in the amount and type of precipitation in India.

11. Why is it said that "Monsoon wind is known for its uncertainties"? Explain any four reasons.

Ans. Monsoon wind is known for its uncertainties because

(i) The movement of low-pressure trough controls the spatial distribution of rainfall.

(ii) The alteration of wet and dry spells varies in intensity, frequency and duration.

(iii) It sometimes causes heavy floods in one part, it may be responsible for drought in other.

(iv) It is often irregular in its arrival and retreat.

12. Study the following climatic data and answer the questions that follow.

Month	Temperature in (°C)	Rainfall in (cm)
January	14.4	2.5
February	16.7	1.5
March	23.3	1.3
April	30.0	1.0
May	33.2	1.8
June	33.3	7.4
July	30.0	19.3
August	29.4	17.8
September	28.9	11.9
October	25.6	1.3
November	19.4	0.2
December	15.6	1.0

(a) Name the rainiest month of the year. How much is the rainfall in this month?

(b) What is the annual range of temperature here?

(c) Name the hottest month and write the temperature.

Ans. (a) The rainiest month of the year is July. The rainfall in this month is 19.3 cm.

(b) The annual range of temperature is 33.3°C −14.4°C = 18.9°C

(c) The hottest month of the year is June and the temperature is 33.3°C.

13. Bring out any one similarity and four differences between climate and weather.

Ans. Similarity between climate and weather

Both weather and climate have the same elements. These elements are humidity, precipitation, temperature, wind and atmospheric pressure. Both indicate the atmospheric conditions of a region.

Differences between climate and weather

Climate	Weather
Climate refers to the sum total of weather conditions and variations over a large area for a long period of time.	Weather refers to the state of the atmosphere over an area at any point of time.
Climate is recorded for a longer period of time i.e. more than 30 years.	Weather data are recorded on daily basis i.e. a few hours or a few days.
Climate is referred to a large area.	Weather is referred to a particular area.
It is the collective effect of all the elements of it.	It is influenced by any one element of it. ie. humidity, pressure condition, temperature and so on.

14. Differentiate between the cold weather season and the hot weather season in India by explaining five distinctive features of each.

Ans. Differences between the cold weather season and the hot weather season are as follows

Cold Weather Season	Hot Weather Season
It begins from mid- November and lasts till February.	It begins from March and lasts till June.
The Northern India becomes a high pressure region, causing winds blowing outward.	The Northern India becomes a low pressure region, causing air circulation around it.
The temperature remains comparatively low during this season.	The temperature remains comparatively high during this season.
The days are short and warm, the nights are cold and long.	Days are hot and long, and nights are warm and short.
Important feature of this season is the Western cyclonic disturbances.	Important feature of this season is Loo.

15. By early June, the low-pressure condition over the Northern plains intensifies. It attracts, the trade winds of the Southern hemisphere. These South-East trade winds originate over the warm subtropical areas of the Southern oceans. **Competency Based**

(i) Where does the maximum rainfall during the South-West monsoon season occur in India?

(ii) What is the average velocity of the South-West monsoon winds? What is its significance?

Ans. (i) The maximum rainfall during the South-West monsoon season in India occurs in the North-Eastern part of the country. Mawsynram, located in the Southern ranges of the Khasi Hills, receives the highest average rainfall in the world during this monsoon season.

(ii) The South-West monsoon winds blow with an average velocity of 30 km per hour. These strong winds play a important role in carrying moisture across warm oceans, bringing substantial rainfall to the Indian subcontinent. The speed of these winds contributes to their effectiveness in covering the entire country in about a month during the monsoon season.

Long Answer Type Questions

1. Describe five characteristics/features of hot weather season in India.

Ans. India experiences the hot weather season from the month of March to May. During this season, there is apparent Northward movement of the sun.

The hot weather season has the following characteristics

(i) There is overall increase in temperature e.g. the temperature of the Northern plains is between 42-45℃ and in the Deccan plateau between 35-38℃.

(ii) An elongated low-pressure area develops from Thar Desert (in North-West) to Patna and Chota Nagpur plateau (in East and South-East) towards the end of May. From this low-pressure belt, the circulation of air begins.

(iii) In the Northern and North-Western plain, there is occurrence of 'Loo'- strong, hot, gusty, dry wind.

(iv) In the Northern India, there is common occurrence of dust storm in May.

(v) There is also occurrence of localised thunderstorms. These are associated with violent winds, torrential downpours, often accompanied by hailstorm at some places (e.g. West Bengal).

2. Describe various sources of rainfall other than monsoon that take place in India.

Ans. In India, apart from monsoons, the other sources of rainfall include

- Tropical cyclones bring heavy rainfall on the Eastern coast of India.
- Rainfall might occur for a brief time due to the formation of convective clouds. This is mostly in the interior landmass.
- Local water bodies create an impact on the pressure and wind system through evaporation causing rains to occur.
- Dust storms also reduce the temperature. These bring cool breeze and light rainfall in the Northern India.
- The Western disturbances coming from the West cause rainfall in the North and North-West of India during winter.

3. Study the table given below and answer the following questions.

Station	Latitude	Altitude
A	26°N	909 m
B	12°N	160 m

(a) What type of climate does station A have? Why?

(b) What type of climate does station B have? Why?

Ans. (a) The station A lies North of the Tropic of Cancer, so it is in sub-tropical zone. Due to its height from the sea level, it is a high altitude area. So, station A must have cold temperate climate. Here summer will be of very short duration and summer temperature would not be very high.

The precipitation might occur in the form of snowfall on its higher areas and for other parts, it may be rainfall. Temperature is cold in winter and warm in summer.

(b) The station B lies South of the Tropic of Cancer. Hence, it will have tropical climatic condition. Its height from sea level is also lesser than station A. The summer would be hot and rainy and of longer duration. In winter, it is dry and cold.

4. "India has diverse climatic conditions". Explain by giving two examples each of temperature and precipitation.

Or "India has diverse climatic conditions." Support this statement by giving three examples.

Or Describe the regional variations in climatic conditions of India with the help of suitable examples.

Ans. There is an overall unity in the general climatic pattern in India, however there are some perceptible regional variations in temperature and precipitation conditions. These variations are as under

Regional variation in temperature conditions

- In summer, the mercury occasionally touches 50°C in some parts of Rajasthan desert. On the other hand, it may be around 20°C in Pahalgam in Jammu and Kashmir.
- On a winter night, temperature at Drass in Jammu and Kashmir may be as low as –45°C. On the other hand, Thiruvananthapuram, may have a temperature of 22°C.
- Also there is a wide variation between day and night temperatures. E.g. in the Thar desert, the day temperature may rise up to 50°C and drop down to near 15°C the same night.
- On the other hand, there is hardly any difference in the day and night temperatures in the Andaman and Nicobar islands or in Kerala due to their location near to the sea/ocean.

Regional variation in precipitation conditions

- The annual precipitation varies from over 400 cm in Meghalaya to less than 10 cm in Ladakh and Western Rajasthan.
- Most parts of the country receive rainfall from June to September. But some parts like the Tamil Nadu coast gets a large portion of its rain during October and November.
- Precipitation is mostly in the form of snowfall in the upper parts of the Himalayas. On the other hand, the rest of the country experiences rainfall.
- Coastal areas experience less contrasts in temperature conditions. Seasonal contrasts are more in the interior of the country.
- There is decrease in rainfall generally from East to West in the Northern plains.

Thus, it can be concluded that India has diverse climatic conditions.

5. Evaluate spread of monsoon over the Indian sub-continent from Kerala to Jammu and Kashmir.

Ans. There is wide variation of amount, type and duration of monsoon in the Indian sub-continent.

Variation in amount of Monsoon Rainfall

- The Western coast (e.g. Kerala) and North-Eastern India receive very high rainfall (400 cm).
- Rainfall is less than 60 cm in Western Rajasthan, and adjoining parts of Gujarat, Haryana and Punjab.
- A third area of low precipitation (less than 20 cm) is around Leh in (Jammu and Kashmir).
- Rest of the country has moderate rainfall.

Variation in type of Precipitation

- In mountainous regions (parts of Jammu and Kashmir, Uttarakhand, etc.), there is snowfall.
- In the rest of the country, precipitation occurs in the form of rainfall.

Variation in duration of Monsoon

- The Kerala coast is the first hit by monsoon whereas Western Rajasthan and adjoining parts of Gujarat and Punjab are last to receive.
- The retreating of monsoon takes place first from the area where it reaches last (i.e. Rajasthan, Gujarat, Punjab plain) and finally to leave from the Eastern coast.

6. "Development of tropical cyclones is a distinguishing feature of monsoon". How do tropical cyclones affect the Indian Sub-continent?

Ans. Tropical cyclones are phenomena that occurs due to differences in pressure and temperature over land and ocean. It occurs during advancing monsoon as well as retreating monsoon (October-November).

The effects of tropical cyclones on Indian-subcontinent can be seen through the following points

- Tropical cyclones mostly affect the Eastern coastal regions of India.
- The thickly populated deltas of the Godavari, the Krishna and the Kaveri are frequently struck by tropical cyclones, which cause great damage to life and property.
- Torrential (abundant) rainfall (more than 30cm/h) associated with cyclones is another major cause of damages.
- Heavy rainfall is responsible for flood like situation in the coastal regions of India especially Eastern coast (Odisha, West Bengal and so on).
- Heavy rainfall from tropical cyclones is usually spread over wide area and cause large scale soil erosion and weakening of embankments.
- Tropical cyclones are also responsible for rising of sea level near the coasts. As a result, sea water inundates (overflow) low lying areas of coastal regions, drowning human beings and life stock and destroys everything on its way.

7. Distinguish between advancing monsoon and retreating monsoon.

Ans. The differences between advancing monsoon and retreating monsoon are as follows

Advancing Monsoon	Retreating Monsoon
Advancing monsoon falls between June-September.	Retreating monsoon falls between October and November.
It is a season of heavy rainfall.	It is a period of transition from hot rainy season to dry winter conditions.
The advance of monsoon is characterised by wet and dry spells of rainfall. The intervening spell of dryness is called 'Breaks' in monsoon.	The withdrawal of the monsoon is marked by clear skies and rise in temperature. The condition of high temperature and humidity leads to a phenomenon called 'October heat'.
During this season, most of the rainfall occurs by the South-West monsoon.	During this season, most of the rainfall is caused by the North-West monsoon and the tropical cyclones.
During this period, the low-pressure trough is strong. This trough attracts the South-West monsoon towards the Ganga plain.	As the low-pressure trough weakens, it is unable to draw the South-West monsoon. A high-pressure area develops in the North-West India. The North-West monsoon winds move from land towards the ocean.

8. Read the information and answer the question that follows.

Parts of Western coast and North-Eastern India receive over about 400 cm of rainfall annually.

However, it is less than 60 cm in Western Rajasthan and adjoining parts of Gujarat, Haryana and Punjab. Rainfall is equally low in the interior of the Deccan plateau, and East of the Sahyadris.

Which areas in India are considered drought-prone, and why? And what is the pattern of snowfall in India, and which region does it primarily affect?

Competency Based

Ans. Areas in India that are considered drought-prone include Western Rajasthan, parts of Gujarat, Haryana, Punjab, the interior of the Deccan plateau and the leeward side of the Western Ghats.

These regions are prone to drought due to factors such as low and erratic rainfall, high evaporation rates and the absence of reliable water sources.

The scarcity of precipitation, coupled with environmental and geographical conditions, makes these areas vulnerable to recurrent droughts, impacting agriculture, water resources and overall socio-economic stability.

The pattern of snowfall in India is primarily restricted to the Himalayan region. The Northern states of Jammu and Kashmir, Himachal Pradesh, Uttarakhand and parts of North-Eastern states experience significant snowfall during the winter months. The rest of the country generally does not experience widespread snowfall and the Himalayas play a important role in influencing this weather phenomenon in India.

9. The reason why the Eastern parts of India are receiving less than normal rainfall is the weather system that develops over the Bay of Bengal. Earlier, they used to travel in the North-West direction across North Odisha, Jharkhand, Bihar, Uttar Pradesh and reached Punjab across Delhi and Haryana.

Source (edited): Abp live **Competency Based**

(i) How are breaks in monsoon rainfall related to the movement of the monsoon trough?

(ii) Why does the rainfall decrease from the East to the West in Northern India?

Ans. (i) Breaks in monsoon rainfall are related to the movement of the monsoon trough, an extended low-pressure system. The trough's axis determines the spatial distribution of rainfall in India. When the axis lies over the plains, regions experience good rainfall, however, as the axis shifts closer to the Himalayas, dry spells occur in the plains. The dynamic movement of the monsoon trough significantly impacts the timing and duration of breaks in monsoon rainfall.

(ii) The rainfall decreases from East to West in Northern India because of the progressive decrease in the humidity of the winds. As the moisture- bearing winds of the Bay of Bengal branch of the South-West monsoon move further and further inland, they exhaust most of the moisture they carry along with them. This consequently leads to a gradual decrease in the amount of rainfall from East to West.

Case Based Question

1. Read the sources given below and answer the questions that follows

Source A Latitude

The Tropic of Cancer passes through the middle of the country from the Rann of Kuchchh in the West to Mizoram in the East. Almost half of the country, lying South of the Tropic of Cancer, belongs to the tropical areas. All the remaining area, North of the Tropic, lies in the sub-tropics. Therefore, India's climate has characteristics of tropical as well as subtropical climate.

(i) To what extent do you agree that India has characteristics of both tropical and sub-tropical climates? Give only one aspect?

Source B Altitude

India has mountains to the North, which have an average height of about 6000 metres. India also has a vast coastal areas where the maximum elevation is about 30 metres. The Himalyas prevent the cold winds from Central Asia from entering the subcontinent. It is because of these mountains that this subcontinent experiences comparatively milder winters as compared to Central Asia.

(ii) Evaluate the importance of the Himalayas in terms of its altitude.

Source C Pressure and Winds

The pressure and wind conditions over India are unique. During winter, there is a high-pressure area North of the Himalayas. Cold dry winds blow from this region to the low-pressure areas over the oceans to the South. In summer, a low-pressure area develops over interior Asia, as well as, over North-Western India.

This causes a complete reversal of the direction of winds during summer. Air moves from the high-pressure areas over the Southern Indian Ocean, in a South-Easterly direction, crosses the equator and turns right towards the low-pressure areas over the Indian subcontinent. These are known as the South-West Monsoon winds.

These winds blow over the warm oceans, gather moisture and bring widespread rainfall over the mainland of India.

(iii) To what extent do you agree that the pressure and wind conditions over India are unique?

Ans. (i) We can say that India has characteristics of both tropical and sub-tropical climates. The Tropic of Cancer passes through the middle of India. It divides the country into almost two equal halves as the trcpical zone (South of the Tropic of Cancer) and the Sub-tropical Zone (North of the Tropic of Cancer).

(ii) The importance of the Himalayas can be seen through the following point

- The Himalayas in the North of India have an average height of about 6000 m. The Himalayas prevent the cold winds from Central Asia from entering the sub-continent.
- Thus, is responsible for milder winters in India as compared to Central Asia.

(iii) The pressure and wind conditions over Indian are unique. This can be understood through the following points

- During winter, there is a high-pressure area North of the Himalayas. Cold dry winds blow from this region to the low-pressure areas over the oceans to the South.
- In summer , a low-pressure area develops over interior Asia, as well as, over North-Western India. This causes a complete reversal of the direction of winds during summer.

Map Based Question

1 On an outline map of India, show the following

(a) Area receiving highest rainfall

(b) Shade the areas receiving over 400 cm rainfall.

(c) The direction of South-West monsoon over India.

Ans.

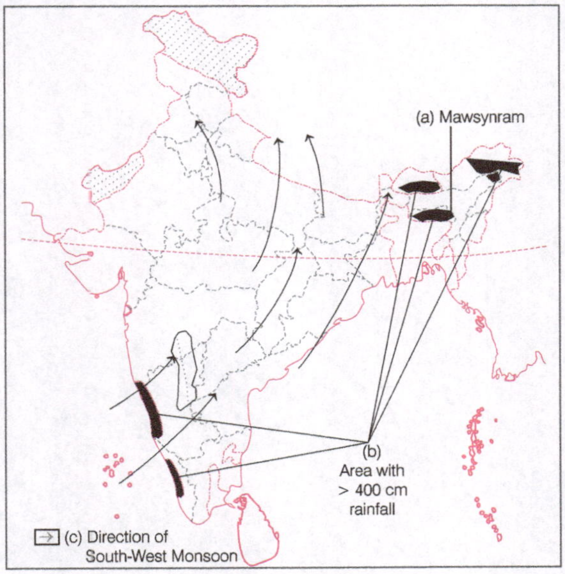

ASSESSMENT EXERCISE

Multiple Choice Questions (MCQs)

1. Which state of India gets large portion of its rainfall during the months of October and November?

(a) Himachal Pradesh (b) Punjab
(c) Tamil Nadu (d) Assam

2. **Assertion** (A) The Indian sub-continent experiences milder winters as compared to Central Asia.

Reason (R) The Himalayas prevent the cold winds of Central Asia from entering the sub-continent.

Codes

(a) A and R are true and R is the correct explanation of A
(b) A and R are true, but R is not the correct explanation of A
(c) A is true, but R is false
(d) A is false, but R is true

3. In which areas rainfall highly varies from year to year?

(a) North-Eastern India
(b) Western Rajasthan
(c) Leeward side of Western Ghat
(d) Northern India

4. Which place is famous for stalagmite and stalacite caves?

(a) Mawsynram (b) Guwahati
(c) Cherrapunji (d) Thiruvananthapuram

Subjective Questions (VSA, SA & LA)

1. Name the regions of India which receive less rainfall.

2. What is the primary cause for the horizontal motion of air over the earth's surface?

3. Which town among Lucknow, Mumbai, Amritsar and Nagpur has an equable temperature?

4. How will you differentiate between weather and climate?

5. Why do the Northern plains have higher range of temperatures than other areas of the world at the similar latitude as this region lies in the sub-tropical climatic belt? Give suitable reasons.

6. How does climate regulate the standard of living and food habits of people of the Indian sub-continent?

7. Give five reasons for the uneven distribution of rainfall in India.

8. Discuss the major climatic controls that controls the climate of any place.

9. Why pre monsoon showers in Kerala and Karnataka known as 'Mango Showers'?

CHAPTER 5

Natural Vegetation and Wildlife

India has varied types of **flora** and **fauna**. India is one of the twelve **mega bio-diversity countries** of the world. India has around 47,000 plant species and occupies tenth place in the world and fourth in Asia in plant diversity.

India has around 15,000 flowering plants which account for 6% of the world's total number of the flowering plants. India also has many non-flowering plants. For example, ferns, algae and fungi.

Natural vegetation is the plant community which has grown naturally without human help and has been left undisturbed over a long period of time. This is known as **virgin vegetation.** Thus, cultivated crops, fruits, orchards form part of vegetation but not natural vegetation.

Virgin vegetation are of two types as follows

(i) **Endemic or Indigenous Species** These plant species have originated in India.

(ii) **Exotic species** These plant species have originated outside India.

Types of Vegetation

India has the following major types of vegetation

1. Tropical Evergreen Forests
2. Tropical Deciduous Forests
3. Tropical Thorn Forests and Scrubs
4. Montane Forests
5. Mangrove Forests

KNOWLEDGE PLUS The term 'Flora' is used to denote plants of a particular region or period. Similarly, the species of animals are referred to as 'Fauna'.

1. Tropical Evergreen Forests

These forests are found in heavy rainfall areas where the rainfall is over 200 cm with a short dry season. These are also called **tropical rainforests.**

These forest cover the areas of Western ghats, island group of Lakshadweep, Andaman and Nicobar, upper parts of Assam and Tamil Nadu coast.

These forests have tall trees with height (up to 60 m) or above. The region of these forests remains warm and wet throughout the year leading to abundant vegetation of all kind – trees, shrubs and creepers.

The vegetation in these forests is **multilayered** in structure. These forests appear green throughout the year because there is no definite time for trees to shed their leaves.

Ebony, mahogany, cinchona, rubber and rosewood trees are commercially important trees of these forests.

Animals found in these forests include, elephants, monkey, lemur, deer. Apart from these birds, bats, sloth, scorpions and snails are also found here. One-horned rhinoceroses are found in the jungles of Assam and West Bengal.

2. Tropical Deciduous Forests

These forests are found where the annual rainfall is between 200 to 70 cm. These forests are most widespread forests of India. These forests are also called **monsoon forests.**

Trees of these forests shed their leaves for about 6 to 8 weeks in dry summer.

Lions, tigers, elephants, pigs and deer are common animals of these forests. Besides these, many varieties of birds, lizards, snakes and tortoises are found here.

On the basis of the availability of water, these forests are further divided into **moist and dry deciduous.**

Moist Deciduous Forests

- These forests area receive rainfall between 100 and 200 cm.
- These forests are found mostly in the Eastern part of the country such as North-Eastern states, West Odisha, Jharkhand, Chhattisgarh, along the foothills of Himalayas and the Eastern slopes (leeward side) of the Western Ghats.
- Teak (most dominant species), bamboo, sal, shisham, sandalwood, khair, kusum, arjun and mulberry trees are found in these forests. These are commercially important species.

Dry Deciduous Forests

- These forests receive rainfall between 70 and 100 cm.
- These forests are found in rainier parts of the Peninsular plateau and the plains of Uttar Pradesh and Bihar.
- There are open stretches in these forests in which teak, sal, peepal and neem trees grow.
- Many parts of these forests have been cleared for agricultural activities and for grazing.

3. Tropical Thorn Forests and Scrubs

These forests are found in areas where the annual rainfall is less than 70 cm. These forests are mostly found in North-Western part of the country including semi-arid areas of Gujarat, Rajasthan, Uttar Pradesh, Chhattisgarh, Haryana and Madhya Pradesh.

Trees in these forests are scattered and have long roots penetrating deep into the soil to get moisture.

The stems of the trees in these forests are **succulent**[1] to conserve water which help the trees to survive in arid climate.

Leaves of the trees in these forests are mostly thick and small to minimise **evaporation**[2].

These forests have scrubs and thorn forests in arid areas. Trees like acacia palms euphoria and cacti are the main plant species of these forests.

Fox, wolf, rats and mice, wild ass, horses, tiger, lion, camels and similar animals are found in these forests.

4. Montane Forests

These forests are found in mountainous areas of Jammu and Kashmir, Himachal Pradesh, Uttarakhand, Sikkim and Arunachal Pradesh.

In mountainous areas, the decrease in temperature with increasing altitude leads to the corresponding change in natural vegetation.

As a result, the natural vegetation belts are arranged in the same order as we find from the tropical to the tundra region.

Montane forests are distributed in the following ways based on altitude

- **Wet Temperate Forests** These forests are found at lower altitude between 1,000-2,000 m. Evergreen broad leaf trees such as oaks and chestnuts are mostly found here.
- **Temperate Forests** These forests are found at the altitude between 1,500-3,000 m. Here coniferous trees like pine, deodar, silver fir, spruce and cedar are found.

  These forests cover mostly the Southern slopes of the Himalayas, places having high altitude in Southern and North-East India.
- **Temperate Grasslands** These grasslands are found at higher elevations.
- **Alpine Vegetation** These vegetation are found above 3,600 m height in these forests. The common trees of these forests are silver fir, junipers, pines and birches. On the snow-line these forests get restricted/limited.

  Through shrubs and scrubs these forests merge into the Alpine grasslands which are used extensively for grazing by Nomadic tribes like the Gujjars and the Bakarwals.
- **Tundra Vegetation** Mosses and lichens are part of Tundra vegetation which are found at higher altitudes.

  Animals like Kashmir stag, spotted dear, wild sheep, jack rabbit, Tibetan antelope, yak, snow leopard, squirrels, shaggy horn wild ibex, bear and rare red panda, sheep and goats with thick hair are commonly found in these forests.

---

1 **Succulent** It refers to a plant having thick fleshy leaves adapted to storing water.

2 **Evaporation** It is the process by which water changes from liquid to a gas or vapour.

5. Mangrove Forests

These forests are found in coastal areas influenced by tides. Due to this fact, they are also called **tidal forests.** Dense mangroves are the common varieties in these forests and the roots of the mangroves are submerged under water.

These forests are found in the delta areas of the Ganga, Mahanadi, the Godavari, the Krishna and the Kaveri.

In the **Ganga-Brahmaputra delta, Sundari trees** are found. These provide durable hard timber. Other trees which grow here are palm, coconut, keora, agar, etc.

Royal Bengal Tiger is the famous animal found in these forests. Other animals found here include the snakes, turtles, gharials and crocodiles.

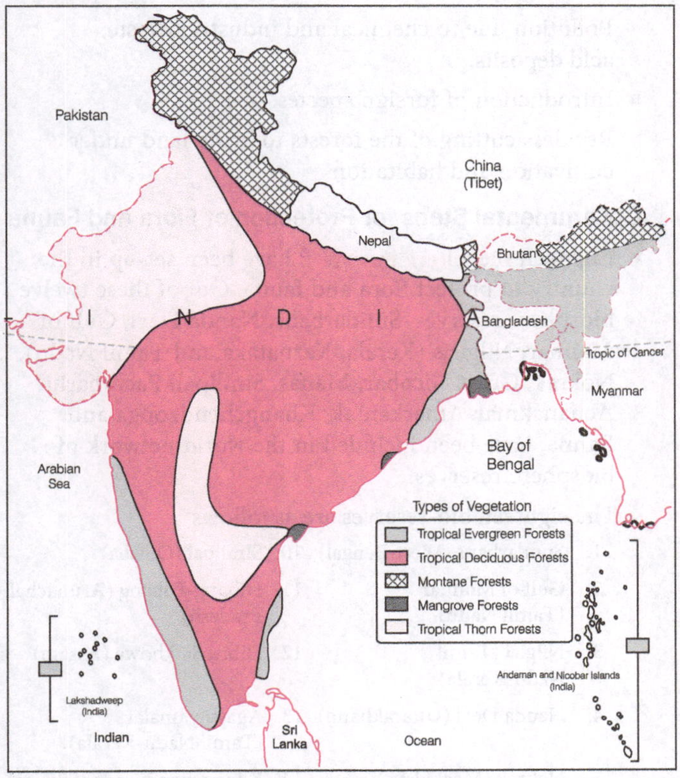

• Natural Vegetation of India

Medicinal Plant

India is known for its herbs and species from ancient times. About 2,000 plants have been described in Ayurveda and atleast 500 are in regular use. The **World Conservation Union's Red List** has named 352 medicinal plants of which 52 are critically threatened and 49 endangered.

The commonly used plants in India are given in the table below

Medicinal Plants	Features
Sarpagandha	It is used to treat blood pressure and found only in India.
Jamun	The juice from this ripe fruit is used to prepare vinegar, which is **carminative**[3] and **diuretic**[4] and has digestive properties. The powder of the seed is used for controlling diabetes.
Arjun	The fresh juice of its leaves is a cure for earache. It is also used to regulate blood pressure.
Babool	Its leaves are used as a cure for pain in the eye. Its gum is used as a tonic.
Neem	It has high antibiotic and antibacterial properties.
Tulsi	It is used to cure cough and cold.
Kachnar	It is used to cure asthma and ulcers. Its buds and roots are good for digestive problems.

Try These

1. **Give some examples of non-flowering plants.**
2. **Multilayered vegetation is occurred in which type of vegetation?**
3. **What is the dominant species of moist deciduous forest?**
4. **The fresh juice of this plant is a cure for earache. Identify the paint.**

3 **Carminative** It is a drug that relieves flatulence (gas in the gastrointestinal tract)
4 **Diuretic** They are medicines that help reduce fluid build up in the body.

5.2 Wildlife

India is rich in its fauna (animal life). India has approximately 90,000 animal species. The country has about 2,000 species of birds. They constitute 13% of the total world's stock.

There are 2,546 species of fish, which account for nearly 12% of the world's stock. It also have 5% to 8% of the world's amphibians, reptiles and mammals.

The existence of animals in our country varies from place to place.

The distribution of wildlife in India

- The elephants are found in the hot wet forests of Assam, Karnataka and Kerala.
- One-horned rhinoceroses are found in **swampy and marshy** lands of Assam and West Bengal.
- Wild ass and camels are found in arid areas of the Rann of Kachchh and the Thar desert, respectively.
- India is the only country in the world that has both tigers and lions. Natural habitat of the **Indian lion** is the **Gir Forest** in Gujarat. The Gir Forest is the last remaining habitat of the Asiatic lion.
- Tigers are found in the forests of Madhya Pradesh, the Sundarbans of West Bengal and the Himalayan region. Leopards too are important among animals of prey.
- The Himalayas have a range of animals, which can survive in extreme cold.
- Yak, the shaggy horned wild ox (weighing around 1 tonne), the Tibetan antelope, the bharal (blue sheep), wild sheep and the *kiang* (Tibetan wild ass) are found in freezing high altitudes in Ladakh.
- The ibex, bear, snow-leopard and rare red panda are found in certain areas.
- Turtles, crocodiles and gharials are found in the rivers, lakes and coastal areas. Gharial is the only representative of a variety of crocodile, found in the world today.
- Indian bison, *nilgai* (blue bull), *chousingha* (four horned antelope), gazel and different species of deer are some other animals found in India. It also has several species of monkeys.
- Peacocks, pheasants, ducks, parakeets, cranes and pigeons are some of the birds found in the forests and wetlands of the country.
- The wetlands of India are also home to many migratory birds such as siberian crane, flamingo, found in Rann of Kachchh.

Loss of Ecosystem

Every species has a role to play in the ecosystem, thus, its conservation is essential for environment.

Due to excessive exploitation of the plants and animal resources by human beings, the ecosystem has been disturbed. About 1,300 plant species are endangered and 20 species are extinct. There are also some animal species which are endangered and have become extinct .

The main causes of this threat to ecosystem are

- Hunting by greedy hunters for commercial purposes.
- Pollution due to chemical and industrial waste, acid deposits.
- Introduction of foreign species.
- Reckless cutting of the forests to bring land under cultivation and habitation.

Governmental Steps for Protection of Flora and Fauna

- Eighteen **biosphere reserves**[5] have been set-up in the country to protect flora and fauna. Out of these twelve biosphere reserves–Sundarbans, Nanda Devi, Gulf of Mannar, Nilgiris (Kerala, Karnataka and Tamil Nadu), Nokrek, Great Nicobar, Manas, Simlipal, Pachmarhi, Achanakmar-Amarkantak, Khangchendzonga and Panna, have been included in the world network of biosphere reserves.

  The eighteen bio-reserves are as follows

1. Sundarbans (West-Bengal)
2. Gulf of Mannar (Tamil Nadu)
3. Nilgiri (Tamil Nadu-Kerala)
4. Nanda Devi (Uttarakhand)
5. Nokrek (Meghalaya)
6. Great Nicobar (Andaman and Nicobar)
7. Manas (Assam)
8. Kachchh (Gujarat)
9. Seshachalam (Andhra Pradesh)
10. Simlipal (Odisha)
11. Dihang-Dibang (Arunachal Pradesh)
12. Dibru Saikhowa (Assam)
13. Agasthyamalai (Tamil Nadu-Kerala)
14. Khangchendzonga (Sikkim)
15. Pachmarhi (Madhya Pradesh)
16. Achanakmar-Amarkantak (Madhya Pradesh-Chhattisgarh
17. Cold Desert (Ladakh)
18. Panna (Madhya Pradesh)

5 Biosphere Reserves These are the areas where plant and animal species are protected. They are created so that this natural heritage can be transmitted to future generations.

- Financial and technical assistance is provided to many botanical gardens by the government since 1992.
- Many eco-developmental projects have been introduced such as **Project Tiger, Project Rhino, Project Great Indian Bustard**, etc.
- **Wildlife Protection Act** was implemented in 1972 in India.
- 103 **national parks**[6], 563 wildlife sanctuaries[7] and zoological gardens are set-up to take care of natural heritage.
- Inspite of all these steps, it is must to realise the importance of the natural ecosystem for our own survival. It is possible if indiscriminate destruction of natural environment is put to an immediate end.

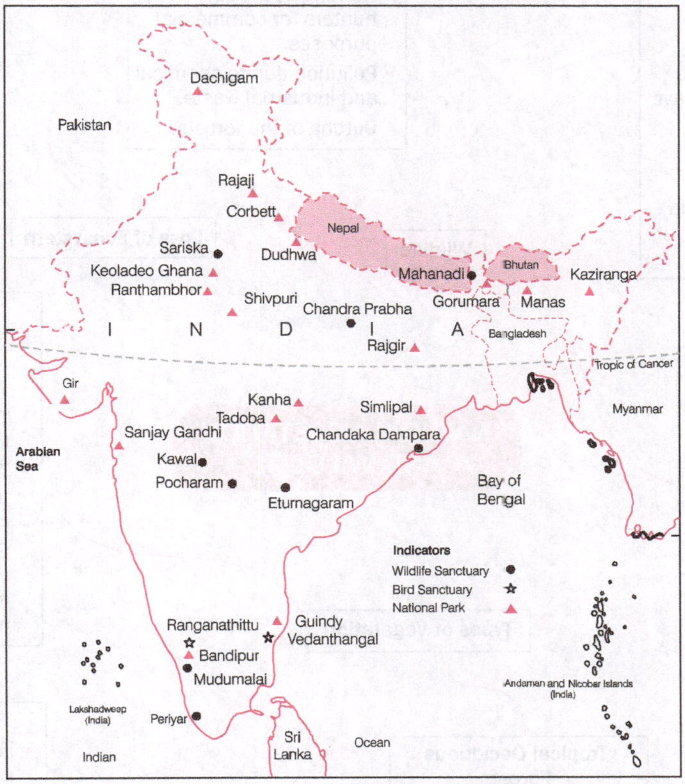

Try These

1. How many species of fishes are found in India?
2. What is the name of the only representative of a variety of crocodile, that is found in India?
3. When did Wildfife Protection Act implemented in India?
4. A migratory bird found at a place where the desert merges with the sea. Identify the bird.

6 National Park It is an area of country side, or occasionally sea or fresh water, protected by the state for the protection of wildlife.

7 Wildlife sanctuaries It is an area where animal habitats and their surroundings are protected from any sort of disturbance.

Mind Map

NATURAL VEGETATION AND WILDLIFE

Wildlife

Government Steps for Protection of Flora and Fauna

- Eighteen biosphere reserves have been setup.
- Project Tiger, Project Rhino and Project Great Indian Bustard have been introduced.
- Wildlife Protection Act was implemented in India.
- 103 national parks, 563 wildlife sanctuaries and zoological gardens parks are setup.

Distribution of Wildlife

- India is rich in its fauna.
- India has approximately 90000 animal species.
- The country has about 2000 species of birds.
- There are about 2546 species of fish.

Loss of Ecosystem

Causes

- Hunting by greedy hunters for commercial purposes.
- Pollution due to chemical and industrial waste.
- Cutting of the forests.

Effects

- 1300 plant species are endangered and 20 are extinct.
- A few animal species are endangered and some have become extinct.

Types of Vegetation

Tropical Thorn Forests

- Found in areas where the annual rainfall is less than 70cm.
- Trees are scattered and have long roots.
- These forests have scrubs and thorn forests in arid areas.
- Found in semi-arid areas of Gujarat, Rajasthan, Uttar Pradesh, Chhattisgarh, Haryana and MP. Euphoria and Cacti are found.

Tropical Evergreen Forests

- Found in areas where the rainfall is over 200 cm.
- Have tall trees with height up to 60m or above.
- One-horned rhinoceroses, snails, bats, sloth, etc are found.
- Ebony, Mahogany, Rubber and Rosewood are important trees.

Tropical Deciduous Forests

- Found in areas where the annual rainfall is between 200 to 70cm.
- Lions, tigers, pigs, birds, lizards, snakes, tortoises, elephants and deer are found.

Dry Deciduous Forests

- Receive rainfall between 70 and 100 cm.
- Found in the rainier parts of the Peninsular plateau and the plains of Uttar Pradesh and Bihar.
- Teak, sal, peepal and neem trees are found in these. forests

Moist Deciduous Forests

- Receive rainfall between 100 and 200 cm.
- Found in North-Eastern states, West Odisha, Jharkhand, Chhattisgarh, along the foothills of the Himalayas and the Eastern slopes of the Western Ghats.
- Teak, bamboo, sal, khair, kusum, sheesham and mulberry trees are found in these forests.

Mangrove Forests

- Found in the coastal areas influenced by tides.
- Sundari trees are found in the Ganga-Brahmaputra delta.
- Royal Bengal Tiger is found in these forests.
- Palm, Coconut, Keora, Agar, etc are found

Montane Forests

Found in the mountainous area of Jammu and Kashmir, Himachal Pradesh, Sikkim, Uttarakhand and Arunachal Pradesh

Wet Temperate Forests

Found at lower altitude between 1000-2000 m

Temperate Forests

Found at the altitude between 1500-3000 m

Tundra Vegetation

Found at higher altitudes

Alpine Vegetation

Found above 3600 m

Temperate Grasslands

Found at higher elevations

NCERT FOLDER

Covering Intext Questions and Exercises of NCERT

INTEXT QUESTION

Q.1. **(a) What will happen if plants and animals disappear from the Earth's surface?**

(b) Can human beings survive under such a situation?

(c) Why is bio-diversity necessary and why should it be conserved?

Ans. (a) If the plants and animals disappear from the Earth's surface, then the ecological balance will be disturbed. Without plants, there will be no oxygen available for breathing and after sometime everybody will die.

(b) No, human being can not survive in such a situation. It is because all plants and animals species including humans are interdependent.

(c) Bio-diversity is necessary as it is a fundamental part of the Earth's life support system. It encompasses the diversity of all living things, from human beings to microorganisms. It supports many basic natural services for humans, such as fresh water, fertile soil, clean air, pollination of flowers and crops, clean-up our wastes, etc.

Bio-diversity is needed to be conserved due to the following reasons

- It plays a vital role in regulating natural processes such as the growth of plants, the mating seasons of animals and even weather systems.
- It provides food for humans as about 80% of our food supply comes from just 20 kinds of plants and many kinds of animals are also used as food. Besides, medicines, building materials, fibres, dyes, gums, adhesives, rubber and oil, all are derived directly or indirectly from biological sources.
- It is directly involved in recycling nutrients, providing fertile soils and also gives leisure, cultural and aesthetic value to humans.

EXERCISE

Q.1 **Choose the right answer from the four alternatives given below.**

(i) To which one of the following types of vegetation does rubber belong to?

(a) Tundra

(b) Tidal

(c) Himalayan

(d) Tropical evergreen

Ans. (d) Tropical evergreen

(ii) Cinchona trees are found in the areas of rainfall more than

(a) 100 cm (b) 50 cm

(c) 70 cm (d) less than 50 cm

Ans. (a) 100 cm

(iii) In which of the following states is the Simlipal bio-reserve located?

(a) Punjab (b) Delhi (c) Odisha (d) West Bengal

Ans. (c) Odisha

(iv) Which one of the following bio-reserves of India is not included in the world network of bio-reserve?

(a) Manas (b) Nilgiri

(c) Gulf of Mannar (d) Nanda Devi

Ans. (a) Manas

Q.2 **Answer the following questions briefly.**

(i) What is a bio-reserve? Give two examples.

Ans. Bio-reserves are sites established by countries and recognised under UNESCO's Man and the Biosphere (MAB) and Programme. They are established to protect the flora and fauna of an area.

Two examples of bio-reserves are

(i) Nanda Devi located in Uttarakhand.

(ii) Gulf of Mannar located in Tamil Nadu.

(ii) Name two animals having habitat in tropical and montane type of vegetation.

Ans. Animals having habitat in Tropical type of vegetation are elephants, monkeys, rats, etc. Animals having habitat in montane type of vegetation are spotted deer, Kashmir stag, antelope and so on.

Q.3 **Distinguish between**

(i) Flora and fauna

Ans. Differences between flora and fauna are as follows

Flora	Fauna
The term 'flora' is used to denote plants species of a particular region or period.	The term 'fauna' is used to denote species of animals.
Flora remains at one place.	Fauna moves from one place to another.
About 47,000 plant species are found in India.	About 90,000 species of animals are found in India.
They make their food by photosynthesis.	They cannot make their own food. Herbivore animals are dependent on flora for food and some are dependent on other animals for food.

(ii) Tropical evergreen and deciduous forests.

Ans. Differences between tropical evergreen and deciduous forests are

Tropical Evergreen Forests	Tropical Deciduous Forests
They grow in areas of heavy rainfall, i.e., 200 cm and above.	They grow in areas receiving rainfall between 200 and 70 cm.
There is no definite time for trees to shed their leaves.	The trees shed their leaves for about 6 to 8 weeks in the dry summer.
Ebony, mahogany, rosewood, rubber and cinchona are the important trees of these forests.	Teak, bamboo, sal, shisham, sandalwood, khair, kusum, arjun, peepal and neem are the important trees of these forests.
Common animals found in these forests are elephants, monkeys, lemur, deer and the one-horned rhinoceros.	Common animals found in these forests are lion, tiger, deer and elephant.
Plenty of birds, bats, sloth, scorpions and snails are also found in these forests.	A huge variety of birds, lizards, snakes and tortoises are found in these forests.
These forests are found in areas of the Western Ghats and the island group of Lakshadweep, Andaman and Nicobar, upper parts of Assam and the Tamil Nadu coast.	These forests are found mostly in the Eastern part of India, North-Eastern states along the foothills of the Himalayas, Jharkhand, Odisha, Chhattisgarh, on the Eastern slopes of Western Ghats, Madhya Pradesh, Bihar and Uttar Pradesh.
These forests have a variety of vegetation such as tall trees, creepers, bushes etc.	These forests are divided into dry deciduous and moist deciduous forests.

Q.4 Name different types of vegetation found in India and describe the vegetation of high altitudes.

Ans. The different types of vegetation found in India are

- Tropical Evergreen or Rainforests
- Tropical Deciduous or Monsoon Forests
- Tropical Thorn Forests and Scrubs
- Montane Forests
- Mangrove Forests or Tidal Forests

The types of vegetation found at the high altitudes is montane forest. There is a succession of natural vegetation belts, as per successive change in altitude.

Altitudinal variation of montane forests are

- **Wet Temperate Forests** At lower altitude between 1,000-2,000 m, wet temperate forests are found. Evergreen broad leaf trees such as oaks and chestnuts are prominent here.
- **Temperate Forest** At the altitude between 1,500-3,000 m, temperate forests are found. Here coniferous trees like pine, deodar, silver fir, spruce and cedar are found. These forests cover mostly the Southern slopes of the Himalayas, places having high altitude in Southern and North-East India.
- **Temperate Grasslands** These are found at higher elevations. Alpine vegetation are found above 3,600 m height. The common trees of these forests are silver fir, junipers, pines and birches. On the snow- line these forests are not found. Through shrubs and scrubs these forests merge into the Alphine grasslands.
- **Alpine Grasslands** These grass are used extensively for grazing by Nomadic tribes like the Gujjars and the Bakarwals.
- **Tundra Vegetation** Mosses and lichens are part of Tundra vegetation which are found at higher altitudes.

Q.5 Quite a few species of plants and animals are endangered in India. Why?

Ans. Endangered species of plants and animals are those which face the danger of getting extinct. About 1300 plant species are endangered and 20 species are extinct.

The main causes for this endangerment of plants and animals species are

- Hunting by greedy hunters for commercial purposes.
- Pollution due to chemical and industrial wastes, acid deposits, etc.
- Increasing population.
- Reckless cutting of plants and trees to bring land under cultivation, expanding industrialisation and habitation, etc.
- Introduction of alien species causing imbalance in the ecosystem.

Q.6 Why has India a rich heritage of flora and fauna?

Ans. India has a rich heritage of flora and fauna due to following reasons

- **Different types of topography/relief** India has all the major physical features like mountains, plains, deserts, plateaus, island, etc. These relief features support different kinds of vegetation and a variety of wildlife.
- **Different types of Soil** The soils also vary from place to place. Different kinds of soils provide basis for different kinds of vegetation.
- **Climate** India has a varied climate from very dry to monsoon type and temperature ranges from very hot to cold which inhabits different kinds of flora and fauna.

REVIEW EXERCISE
Including Competency Based Questions

Part I

Multiple Choice Questions (MCQs)

1. ...... refers to a plant community which has grown naturally without any human aid.
(a) Formland (b) Natural vegetation
(c) National Park (d) None of these

2. Which type of forests are restricted to heavy rainfall areas of the Western Ghats and the island group of Lakshadweep and Andaman and Nicobar?
(a) Tropical deciduous forests
(b) Tropical evergreen forests
(c) Mangrove forests
(d) Montane forests

3. How much rainfall is being received by the tropical evergreen forests?
(a) 180 cm (b) 150 cm
(c) 200 cm (d) 300 cm

4. The trees of which of the following forests reach the height up to 60 metres or even above?
(a) Montane forests
(b) Mangrove forests
(c) Tropical deciduous forests
(d) Tropical evergreen forests

5. Some of the commercially important trees like ebony, mahogany, rosewood, rubber and cinchona are found in which of the following forests?
(a) Tropical evergreen forests
(b) Montane forests
(c) Mangrove forests
(d) Tropical deciduous forests

6. Which type of forest is also known as monsoon forest and spread over the region receiving rainfall between 200 cm and 70 cm?
(a) Tropical deciduous forests
(b) Tropical evergreen forests
(c) Tropical thorn forests and scrubs
(d) Mangrove forests

7. Which is a rare animal found in montane forests?
(a) Wild sheep (b) Yak
(c) Red panda (d) Tiger

8. The tropical dry deciduous forests are found in areas having rainfall between 100 cm and 70 cm. These forests are found in the rainier parts of the Peninsular plateau and the plains of Bihar and Uttar Pradesh.

Which animals are common in the Tropical dry deciduous forests? Competency Based
(a) Polar bears and penguins
(b) Lion, tiger, pig, deer, and elephant
(c) Kangaroos and koalas
(d) Giraffes and zebras

9. Sita was suffering from some bacterial infection. Her grandmother suggested her to eat the leaves of some medicinal plant. After taking it she started recovering from the infection. Name the medicinal plant.
(a) Mango (b) Bamboo
(c) Neem (d) Babool

10. Vegetation and wildlife are considered the valuable resources in the ecosystem. Plants give shelter to animals. Plants are the source of all food which the animals eat.

Source (edited): Untold Truth

What is the term for natural vegetation that have been left undisturbed for a long time?
(a) Orchards (b) Natural cultivation
(c) Virgin vegetation (d) Cultivated crops

11. Which among the following animals is a type of deer found in India?
I. Gazel II. Kashmir Stag
III. Chousingha

Codes
(a) I and II (b) Only III (c) I and III (d) All of these

12. Which of the following statements accurately describes about the natural vegetation?
I. Human intervention is necessary for the growth of natural vegetation.
II. It includes plant communities that have grown without human aid and remain undisturbed by human activities.
III. Cultivated crops and orchards form a significant part of natural vegetation.
IV. The term "virgin vegetation" refers to cultivated crops and fruits.

Codes
(a) Only I
(b) Only II
(c) Only IV
(d) Both I and II

13. **Consider the statements given below and choose the correct answer.** **Competency Based**

Statement I The mangrove tidal forests are found in the areas of coasts influenced by tides.

Statement II The deltas of the Ganga, the Mahanadi, the Krishna, the Godavari and the Kaveri are covered by mangrove forest.

Options

(a) Statement I is correct and II is incorrect
(b) Statement I is incorrect and II is correct
(c) Both I and II are incorrect
(d) Both I and II are correct

14. **Choose the appropriate statements regarding natural vegetation from the following statements.**

I. Wet temperate forests, with evergreen broad-leaf trees like oaks and chestnuts, are found between 1000 and 2000 m.

II. Tropical evergreen forests are found where the annual rainfall is between 200-70 cm.

III. The decrease in temperature with increasing altitude in mountainous areas leads to a corresponding change in natural vegetation.

Options

(a) Statements I and III are appropriate.
(b) Statements I, II and III are appropriate.
(c) All the statements are appropriate.
(d) Only statement I is appropriate.

15. **Arrange the following types of montane forests according to their altitude/elevation.**

I. Temperate forests - 500-3000
II. Alpine vegetation > 3600
III. Wet temperate forests - 1000-2000
IV. Temperate grasslands < 3600

Codes

(a) III, I, IV, II (b) IV, I, II, III
(c) I, II, III, IV (d) IV, I, III, II

16. **Identify the forest with the help of the following features.**

- These forests are found where the annual rainfall is between 200 to 70 cm.
- These forests are most abundant variety of forests in India.
- These forests are also called monsoon forests.
- Trees of these forests shed their leaves for about 6 to 8 weeks in dry summer.

Options

(a) Tropical Evergreen forests
(b) Tropical Deciduous forests
(c) Moist Deciduous forests
(d) Dry Deciduous forests

Answers

1. (b)	**2.** (b)	**3.** (c)	**4.** (d)	**5.** (a)
6. (a)	**7.** (c)	**8.** (b)	**9.** (c)	**10.** (c)
11. (d)	**12.** (b)	**13.** (d)	**14.** (a)	**15.** (a)
16. (b)				

Match the Following

1.

List I (Forests Types)	List II (Annual Rainfall)
A. Tropical Evergreen Forests	1. Less than 70 cm
B. Moist Deciduous Forests	2. 70 to 100 cm
C. Dry Deciduous Forest	3. 100 to 200 cm
D. Tropical Thorn Forests and Scrubs	4. More than 200 cm

Codes

	A	B	C	D		A	B	C	D
(a)	4	3	2	1	(b)	2	4	3	1
(c)	4	3	1	2	(d)	3	2	1	4

2.

List I (Forests types)	List II (Tree species)
A. Tropical Evergreen Forests	1. Ebony
B. Tropical Deciduous Forests	2. Teak
C. Thorn Forests and Scrub	3. Palms
D. Montane Forests	4. Pine

Codes

	A	B	C	D		A	B	C	D
(a)	1	2	3	4	(b)	4	3	2	1
(c)	3	4	1	2	(d)	1	4	3	2

Ans. 1. (a) 2. (a)

Picture Based Questions

1. **Which one of the following options best signifies the type of forests in the picture given below?**

(a) Tropical Evergreen Forest
(b) Tropical Deciduous Forests
(c) Tropical Thorn Forests and Scrubs
(d) Montane Forests

2. Which one of the following options best signifies the type of forests in the picture given below?

(a) Tropical Evergreen Forests (b) Mangrove Forests
(c) Montane Forests
(d) Tropical Deciduous Forests

3. The image given below is of tropical evergreen forests. These forests are restricted to heavy rainfall areas of the Western Ghats and the Island Groups of Lakshadweep, Andaman and Nicobar. The trees reach great heights up to 60 m or even above.

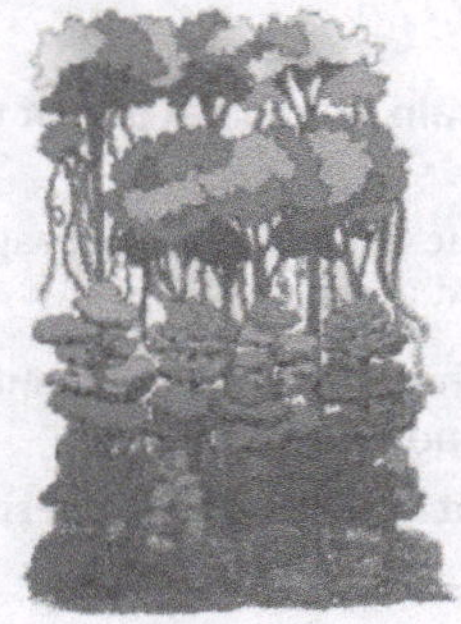

What is the unique feature regarding the shedding of leaves in these forests?

(a) Trees shed leaves in autumn
(b) Trees shed leaves in winter
(c) Trees shed leaves during the monsoon
(d) There is no definite time for trees to shed their leaves

Ans. 1. (d) Montane Forests
2. (b) Mangrove Forests
3. (d) There is no definite time for trees to shed their leaves.

Assertion-Reason

1. Assertion (A) In mountainous regions a variety of natural vegetation is found.
Reason (R) Temperature decreases with increase in altitude.

Codes
(a) Both A and R are true and R is the correct explanation of A
(b) Both A and R are true, but R is not the correct explanation of A
(c) A is true, but R is false
(d) A is false, but R is true

2. Assertion (A) Trees in Tropical Thorn Forests have long roots deep into the soil.
Reason (R) Long roots are helpful to get moisture from underground water.

Codes
(a) Both A and R are true and R is the correct explanation of A
(b) Both A and R are true, but R is not the correct explanation of A
(c) A is true, but R is false
(d) A is false, but R is true

3. Assertion (A) Montane forests cover mostly the Southern slopes of the Himalayas at high altitudes in Southern and North-East India.
Reason (R) At higher elevations, temperate grasslands are common, and at altitudes generally above 3,600 meters, temperate forests and grasslands give way to Alpine vegetation.

Codes
(a) Both A and R are true and R is the correct explanation of A
(b) Both A and R are true, but R is not the correct explanation of A
(c) A is true, but R is false
(d) A is false, but R is true

4. Assertion (A) Royal Bengal Tiger is the famous animal in Mangrove forests.
Reason (R) Mangroves are the common varieties with leaf of the plants submerged under soil.

Codes
(a) Both A and R are true and R is the correct explanation of A
(b) Both A and R are true, but R is not the correct explanation of A
(c) A is true, but R is false
(d) A is false, but R is true

Ans. 1. (a) Both A and R are true and R is the correct explanation of A
2. (a) Both A and R are true and R is the correct explanation of A
3. (d) A is false, but R is true
4. (c) A is true, but R is false

Case Based Question

1. Read the source given below and answer the questions that follow.

India is the only country in the world that has both tigers and lions. The natural habitat of the Indian lion is the Gir forest in Gujarat. Tigers are found in the forests of Madhya Pradesh, the Sundarbans of West Bengal and the Himalayan region. Leopards, too, are members of the cat family. They are important among animals of prey. The Himalayas harbour a hardy range of animals, which survive in extreme cold. Ladakh's freezing high altitudes are a home to yak, the shaggy horned wild ox weighing around one tonne, the Tibetan antelope, the bharal (blue sheep), wild sheep and the kiang (Tibetan wild ass). Furthermore, the ibex, bear, snow-leopard and rare red panda are found in certain pockets. In the rivers, lakes and coastal areas, turtles, crocodiles and gharials are found. The latter is the only representative of a variety of crocodile, found in the world today.

(i) In which Indian states elephants are found?
(a) Punjab and Haryana
(b) Gujarat and Rajasthan
(c) Madhya Pradesh and Chhattisgarh
(d) Assam, Karnataka and Kerala

(ii) Which of the following regions is the habitat for Indian bison, nilgai (blue bull), chousingha (four-horned antelope), gazel and different species of deer?
(a) Thar Desert
(b) Western Ghats
(c) Himalayan Mountains
(d) Rann of Kutch

(iii) When was the Wildlife Protection Act implemented in India?
(a) 1960 (b) 1972
(c) 1980 (d) 1990

(iv) What is the main threat to India's wildlife?
(a) Climate change
(b) Industrialisation
(c) Hunting
(d) Deforestation for agriculture

Ans. (i) (d) Assam, Karnataka and Kerala
(ii) (b) Western Ghats
(iii) (b) 1972
(iv) (c) Hunting

Part II

Very Short Answer Type Questions

1. Which plant out of algae, fungi, ferns and orchids is a flowering plants?

Ans. Only orchid is a flowering plant, while remaining are the non-flowering plants.

2. What are the climatic conditions of tropical evergreen forests?

Ans. The climatic conditions of tropical evergreen forests are high temperature and heavy rainfall (above 200 cm per year).

3. What kinds of commercially important trees are found in tropical evergreen forests?

Ans. The commercially important trees found in tropical evergreen forests are ebony, mahogany, rosewood, rubber and cinchona.

4. What kinds of forests are found in the areas with annual rainfall between 100 and 200 cm?

Ans. Tropical moist deciduous type of forests are found in the areas with annual rainfall between 100 and 200 cm.

5. What are the common animals found in thorn and scrub forests?

Ans. In thorn and scrub forests, the common animals found are rats, mice, rabbits, foxes, wolves, tigers, lions, wild ass, horses and camels.

6. Which trees out of coconut, cactus, acacia and cinchona are found in mangrove forests?

Ans. Only coconut trees are found in mangrove forests. Cactus and acacia are found in thorn forests, while cinchona trees are found in tropical evergreen forests.

7. What is the main medicinal use of the Sarpagandha plant?

Ans. The main medicinal use of the Sarpagandha plant is to treat high blood pressure.

8. Which medicinal plant has both anti-bacterial and anti-biotic properties?

Ans. The neem plant has both anti-bacterial and anti-biotic properties.

9. What is the term used for a species if it is introduced to another environment?

Ans. The term exotic species is used for a species if it is introduced to another environment.

10. Which biosphere reserves have been included in the world network of biosphere reserves?

Ans. The Sundarbans, Nanda Devi, Nilgiri, Nokrek, Great Nicobar, Manas, Similipal, Pachmarhi, Achanakmar-Amarkantak and Gulf of Mannar are the biosphere reserves which have been included in the world network of biosphere reserves.

11. Ravi visited Sundarban last week and learnt about the ecosystem of the region. When he returned his friend asked him which type of forest is found in delta region and name some flora that are found in the region? **Competency Based**

Ans. The delta regions of Ganga, Mahanadi, Krishna, Godawari and Kaveri are covered with mangrove forests. Flora of this region includes sundari, palm, coconut, keora and agar.

12. Tropical Evergreen Forests are found in the climatic region located between 5° to 10° North and South

latitudes. The tropical evergreen forests include Amazon basin, presently the largest Rainforest area in the world, Zaire (Congo) basin of Africa.......

Source (edited) : Untold Truth **Competency Based**

(i) In addition to the Western Ghats, which region in India is home to Tropical Evergreen Forests?

(ii) What is the vegetation structure in Tropical Evergreen Forests?

Ans. (i) Tropical Evergreen Forests are found in the upper part of Assam Tamil Nadu Coast and also in the Andaman Nicobar and Lakshadweep Island, contributing a rich biodiversity.

(ii) The vegetation structure in Tropical Evergreen Forests is characterised by a multilayered composition, including towering trees, shrubs and creeping plants.

Short Answer Type Questions

1. What is meant by vegetation? How much natural is the natural vegetation of India today?

Ans. Natural vegetation refers to a plant community which has grown naturally without human aid and has been left undisturbed by humans for a long time.

Today, natural vegetation has not been left natural anymore because of the following reasons

- Various new species of plants are raised in laboratories. These are planted to get better results.
- Human interference is continuously increasing day by day. This is deteriorating the quality of nature and is harmful for humans too.

2. Explain any three characteristics of tropical evergreen forests.

Ans. Three characteristics of tropical evergreen forests are

(i) The trees reach a great height upto 60 m or even above. Trees are tall, thick and have vigorous growth.

(ii) As the region is warm and wet throughout the year, it has a luxuriant vegetation of all kinds- trees, shrubs and creepers giving it a multilayered structure.

(iii) There is no definite time for trees to shed their leaves, as such these forests appear green all the year round.

3. In which region are the thorny forests and scrubs found in India? Mention any two characteristics of such type of vegetation.

Or **Explain any three features of the thorn forests and scrubs.**

Ans. Thorny forests and scrubs are found in the North-Western part of the country including semi-arid areas of Gujarat, Rajasthan, Madhya Pradesh, Chhattisgarh, Uttar Pradesh and Haryana.

Characteristics of the thorn forests and scrubs are as follows

(i) Trees are scattered and have long roots penetrating (pass into or through) deep into the soil in order to get moisture.

(ii) The stems are succulent (Juicy) to conserve water.

(iii) Leaves are mostly thick and small to minimise evaporation.

4. How has the vegetation of thorn forests adapted to the climate?

Ans. The thorn forests are found in the region with less than 70 cm rainfall.

The adaptive features of vegetation of thorn forests are

- Roots are long which can penetrate deep into the soil to get moisture.
- Stems are succulent to conserve water.
- Leaves are thick to minimise evaporation.

5. In which part of India, mangrove forests are found? Mention two characteristics of these forests.

or **Explain any three features of mangrove forests.**

Ans. Mangrove forests are found in the Ganga- Brahmaputra delta, Krishna, Kaveri, Godavari and Mahanadi delta.

Characteristics of these forests are as follows

(i) The mangrove forests are found in the areas of coast influenced by tides. Mud and Silt get accumulated on such coasts.

(ii) Roots of these plants remain sub-merged under water. Roots develop aerial root for sucking oxygen.

(iii) The tree species can tolerate high salt concentration.

6. Mention any four uses of biosphere reserve.

Ans. The four uses of biosphere reserves are

(i) In each bio-sphere reserve, the core aim is to preserve wildlife, the flora and the fauna in their natural forms.

(ii) The surrounding zone would be utilised for research and experimentation in developing forests and other products.

(iii) Biosphere reserves help to ensure the environmental, economic and social sustainability of the region, by encouraging wise use of natural and human resources.

(iv) They provide practical ways to resolve land use conflicts and to protect biological diversity.

7. How can community and government go hand in hand to protect the wildlife? Explain with examples.

Ans. The major threat to the wildlife is posed by the human being. Various human activities like hunting, pollution, cutting down of forests, etc have led to extinction of some of the wildlife. Through government initiatives, community can also support in conservation programme.

For example,

- Community can conduct awareness programme about wildlife preservation.

- Community can promise individual not to indulge in hunting or cutting down trees.
- Community can report to police if any one violates laws regarding wildlife is found.
- Stop buying products made by skins and horns of animals.

8. What are the differences between moist deciduous and dry deciduous forests?

Ans. Differences between moist deciduous and dry deciduous forests are as follows

Moist Deciduous Forests	Dry Deciduous Forests
They are found in areas with annual rainfall between 100 and 200 cm.	They are found in areas with annual rainfall between 70 and 100 cm.
Teak, bamboo, sal, shisham, sandalwood, khair, kusum, arjun and mulberry trees are found in these forests.	Teak, sal, neem and peepal trees are found in these forests.
These forests have not been cleared much.	Large areas of these forests have been cleared for cultivation and grazing.
They cover about 34% of India's forested area.	They cover about 30% of India's forested area.

9. How are thorn forests different from mangrove forests?

Ans. Thorn forests are different from mangrove forests in the following ways

Thorn Forests	Mangrove Forests
These are found in areas with annual rainfall less than 70 cm.	These are found in the delta regions of rivers and are not dependent on amount of rainfall.
Babool, kikar, palm, cactus and acacia trees/bushes are found here.	Sundari, palm, coconut, keora and agar trees are found here.
These are found in most of Rajasthan, Northern part of Gujarat and in some areas of Uttar Pradesh, Haryana and Deccan plateau.	These are found in the coastal delta regions (delta areas of rivers on the East coast of India).
They have lack of moisture.	These have adequate moisture as these are sub-merged under water.

10. Discuss why are tropical evergreen forests described as having a multilayered structure. Competency Based

Build answer around these points

- **Rainfall** • **Heights** • **Vegetation**

Ans. Tropical evergreen forest having a multilayered structure due to the abundant amount of rainfall receives by the forest about more than 200 cm that help in the growth of the vegetation at various heights. The trees reach the height up to 60 m and even more. It has a luxuriant vegetation of all kinds — trees, shrubs and creepers. Since the region is warm and wet throughout the year, it includes the forest floor, shrub layer, understory, canopy and emergent layer that give the forest a multilayered structure.

11. Read the statements given below.

Statement 1 (S1) Our country India is one of the 12 mega bio-diversity countries of the world with about 47,000 plant species.

Statement 2 (S2) India occupies tenth place in the world and fourth in Asia in plant diversity. There are about 15,000 flowering plants in India.

Explain, which statement is incorrect. Competency Based

Ans. Both statements (S1 and S2) are correct. India is one of the 12 mega bio-diversity countries globally, emphasising its significant diversity in various ecosystems. The country is home to about 47,000 plant species, showcasing a remarkable richness in flora.

India holds the tenth position globally and the fourth position in Asia in terms of plant diversity. The presence of approximately 15,000 flowering plant species contributes to this ranking, highlighting the abundance and variety of flowering plants in the country.

12. Some of the wetlands of India are popular with migratory birds. During winter, birds, such as Siberian Crane, come in large numbers. One such place favourable with birds is the Rann of Kutch.

What is the extraordinary sight described in the Rann of Kutch, where the desert merges with the sea? Competency Based

Ans The Rann of Kutch is a vast salt marsh located in the state of Gujarat, India, bordering the Arabian Sea. In the Rann of Kutch, an extraordinary sight occurs where the desert meets the sea. Many migratory birds such as siberian crane, flamingo found here during winter. Thousands of flamingos with their vibrant pink feathers flock to this location. Here, they build nest stack from salty mud and raise their young ones. This phenomenon of flamingos nesting amidst the desert merging with the sea is one of the many remarkable sights in India.

Long Answer Type Questions

1. "India is rich in its fauna." Explain the statement with example.

Ans. India is a vast country with variety of life forms. The various climatic and relief factors have contributed to its bio-diversity.

The richness of India's faunal (animal) species can be explained by following examples

- India has about 90,000 species of animals. It includes elephants, rhinoceros, wild ass, camel, yak, bisons, antelope, leopard, etc. It is also the only country in the world that has both tigers and lions.

- India also has colourful bird life. It has about 2000 species of birds. These include peacocks, pheasants, ducks, parakeets, cranes and pigeon.
- India has around 12% of world fish stock (about 2,546) which includes both fresh and marine water species.
- India has 5-8% of world's amphibians, reptiles and animals. The reptiles include turtles, crocodiles and gharials. Gharial is the only representative of a variety of crocodile, found in the world today.

Thus, we can conclude that India is rich in its fauna.

2. "The main reason for the dwindling wildlife resources in India is hunting by greedy hunters." Support the statement and suggest some steps to overcome this threat. **Competency Based**

Ans. India is rich in diverse heritage of floral and faunal life. This rich bio-diverssity is put under threat due to their excessive exploitation by human beings.

The ecological disturbance created by human has caused 1,300 plants species to become endangered and about 20 species to become extinct.

Quite a few animals species are also endangered and some have become extinct. The main reason for the dwindling wildlife resources in India is hunting by greedy hunters. The hunter kills valuable fauna like rhinoceros, tigers, etc. due to high demand for their products.

Steps that can be taken to stop these threats are

- Make people aware for the protection and conservation of wildlife. This can be done by making them to realise the importance of wildlife.
- Strict enforcement of laws and greater punishment and fines for violator of such laws.
- Inclusion of wild life conservation in school curriculum.
- Involving community in the process of conservation e.g., community forestry, social forestry, etc.
- Providing employment opportunities to local youth as tourist guide, forest guide, etc.
- Providing shares of forest products to the local community in return for their efforts in protection and conservation of wildlife.

3. Read the information given below and answer the question that follows.

In regions with less than 70 cm of rainfall, the natural vegetation consists of thorny trees and bushes. This type of vegetation is found in the North-Wwestern part of the country, including semi-arid areas of Gujarat, Rajasthan, Madhya Pradesh, Chhattisgarh, Uttar Pradesh and Haryana. Acacias, palms, euphorias and cacti are the main plant species.

Explain the specific adaptations of trees in thorn forests and scrubs to cope with arid conditions, including details about their roots, stems and leaves. How are these forests important to the local communities? **Competency Based**

Ans. In thorn forests and scrubs, trees have adapted to arid conditions by developing long and deep roots to access moisture from deeper soil layers. Their stems are succulent, storing water to endure extended periods of drought. Leaves are small, thick and reduced, minimising water loss through evaporation and conserving moisture. These adaptations collectively enable the trees to thrive in regions with less than 70 cm of rainfall, demonstrating resilience to arid environments in the North-Western part of India.

Thorn forests and scrubs are important for local communities as they provide grazing grounds for livestock, supporting pastoral livelihoods. The medicinal properties of many plant species in these forests contribute to traditional healthcare practices. The vegetation serves as an important source of fuel wood, meeting energy needs for cooking and heating in local households.

4. Tropical dry deciduous, tropical moist deciduous and tropical semi-evergreen forests, the three top-most dominant forest types in the country, shall be highly vulnerable to climate change.

Source (edited) : Weather

Despite both being classified as tropical forests, highlight the key differences between evergreen and deciduous forests in India. Consider aspects like climate, vegetation, wildlife and conservation challenges. **Competency Based**

Ans. The evergreen forest and deciduous forest are classified on the following aspects

Aspect	Evergreen Forests	Deciduous Forests
Climate	Constant warmth and heavy rainfall	Seasonal variation with dry summers and rainfall
Vegetation	Diverse, multilayered structure; trees remain green	Seasonal leaf shedding; dominated by teak, sal, bamboo
Wildlife	Elephants, lemurs, rhinoceroses	Lions, tigers, deer
Conservation Challenges	Logging threats, habitat fragmentation	Cultivation, grazing impacts

Case Based Question

1. Read the source given below and answer the questions that follow.

These are the most widespread forests of India. They are also called the monsoon forests and spread over the region receiving rainfall between 200 cm and 70 cm.

Trees of this forest type shed their leaves for about six to eight weeks in dry summer.

On the basis of the availability of water, these forests are further divided into moist and dry deciduous. The former is found in areas receiving rainfall between 200 and 100 cm. These forests exist, therefore, mostly in the

Eastern part of the country – North-Eastern states, along the foothills of the Himalayas, Jharkhand, West Odisha and Chhattisgarh and on the Eastern slopes of the Western Ghats.

Teak is the most dominant species of this forest. Bamboos, sal, shisham, sandalwood, khair kusum, arjun and mulberry are other commercially important species. The dry deciduous forests are found in areas having rainfall between 100 cm and 70 cm. These forests are found in the rainier parts of the Peninsular plateau and the plains of Bihar and Uttar Pradesh. There are open stretches, in which teak, sal, peepal and neem grow. A large part of this region has been cleared for cultivation and some parts are used for grazing. In these forests, the common animals found are lion, tiger, pig, deer and elephant. A huge variety of birds, lizards, snakes and tortoises are also found here.

(i) Why do tropical deciduous forests shed their leaves for about six to eight weeks in summer?

(ii) Why are moist deciduous forest found mostly in the Eastern part of India? Name the important species found in these forests.

(iii) Discuss the important features of dry deciduous forests.

Ans. (i) Tropical deciduous forests shed their leaves for about six to eight weeks in summer. It is because the weather is hot and dry during summer season (March and April). Due to high temperature the leaves get dried up and the lack of moisture causes the trees to shed their leaves for about six to eight weeks during March and April. Besides this, these forests are found in areas having prolonged dry season with heavy rainfall.

(ii) Moist deciduous forests are found mostly in the Eastern part of India because this region receives 100 to 200 cm annual average rainfall, which is suitable for such type of forests.

These regions are North-Eastern states, West Odisha, Jharkhand, Chhattisgarh, foothills of Himalayas and the Eastern slopes of the Western Ghats.

Important species of moist deciduous forests are

- Teak is the most dominant species of this forest.
- Other commercially important species are bamboos, sal, shisham, sandalwood, khair, kusum, arjun and mulberry.

(iii) Important features of dry deciduous forest are as follows

- These forests grow in annual rainfall areas between 70 to 100 cm .
- These forests are found in rainier parts of the Peninsular plateau and the plains of Uttar Pradesh and Bihar.

ASSESSMENT EXERCISE

Multiple Choice Questions (MCQs)

1. Which of the following plays a major role in enhancing the quality of environment?

(a) Rainfall (b) Forests (c) Fauna (d) None of these

2. A very large ecosystem on land having distinct type of vegetation and animal life is called

(a) natural vegetation (b) ecosystem

(c) biome (d) All of these

3. Match the following.

	List-I (Forest Types)		List-II (Characteristics)
A.	Tropical Evergreen Forests	1.	Appear green all the year round
B.	Tropical Deciduous Forest	2.	Shed leaves for six to eight weeks in summer.
C.	Tropical Thorn Forest and Scrubs	3.	Stems of trees are succulent to conserve water.
D.	Mangrove Forest	4.	Change in natural vegetation with height.

Codes

	A	B	C	D		A	B	C	D
(a)	1	2	3	4	(b)	2	3	1	4
(c)	4	3	2	1	(d)	3	2	4	1

4. Assertion (A) The Southern slopes of the Himalayas have thicker vegetation cover.

Reason (R) The Southern slopes to the Himalayas receive more rain and adequate amount of Sunlight.

Codes

(a) A and R are true and R is the correct explanation of A

(b) A and R are true, but R is not the correct explanation of A

(c) A is true, but R is false

(d) A is false, but R is true

Subjective Questions (VSA, SA & LA)

1. Give example of trees found in thorny and scrub vegetation.

2. Which type of vegetation is found in deltaic region? Give list of trees found there.

3. How virgin vegetation differs from natural vegetation?

4. Which vegetation is known as purely Indian vegetation?

5. Why does India have such a diverse variety of plant species and wildlife?

6. Explain any three features of montane forests.

7. Why do migratory birds travel to India in winter from thousands of kilometres away? Give reasons.

8. What are various steps taken by the Government of India to protect wildlife in India?

9. 'Tropical Evergreen Forests cannot be commercially exploited' why? Also give climatic conditions and distribution of these forests.

Population

CHAPTER 6

Population is an important element in social studies as people are the nation's most valuable resource. Human beings are important to develop the economy and society. They make resources and use them. Therefore, it is important to study population.

In India, the **census**[1] provides us with the information relating to the population of our country. The first census in India was done in 1872, but the first complete census was taken in 1881. The census is done every ten years in India. The Indian census is the most detailed source of demographic (relating to population), social and economic data.

6.1 India's Population Size and Distribution

The arrangement or spread of people of a country at different places is called population distribution.

As per 2011 Census, population of India is 1,210.6 million, which is 17.5 per cent of the total world population. It is unevenly distributed over the country's vast area of 3.28 million sq km, which is 2.4% of the world's area.

In India, the state of **Uttar Pradesh** with 199 million people has the **highest population** (about 16 per cent of the country's population) and Himalayan state **Sikkim** with 0.6 million people has the **lowest population** (about 0.05 per cent of the country's population).

Almost half of India's population lives in just five states comprising Uttar Pradesh, Maharashtra, Bihar, West Bengal and Andhra Pradesh.

Rajasthan which is the largest state in terms of area, accounts for only 5.5 % of the total population of India.

KNOWLEDGE PLUS Among Union Territories, Delhi has the highest (16.75 million) and Lakshadweep has the lowest (64,429) population.

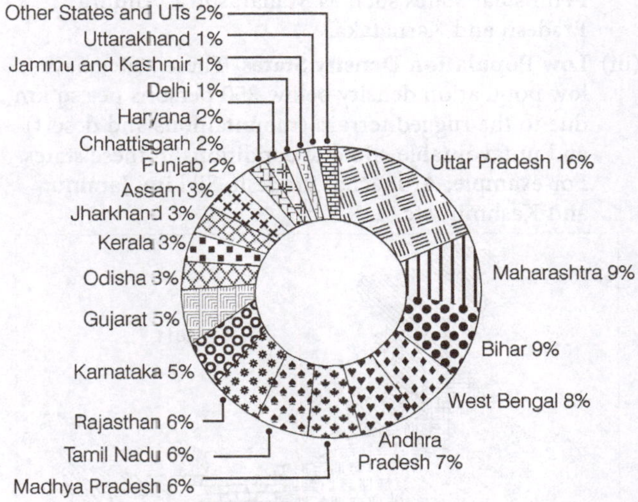

• Distribution of Population in India

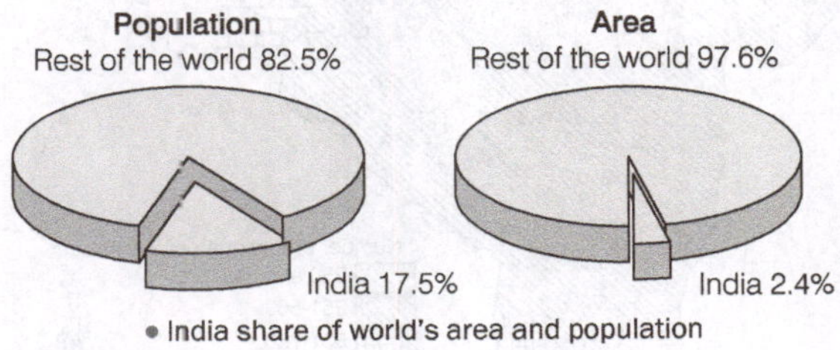

• India share of world's area and population

1 **Census** An official enumeration (numbering) of population done periodically.

India's Population Distribution by Density

The number of people living per unit area (sq km) is called population density of that area.

After Bangladesh and Japan, India is the third most densely populated country. India's population density in 2011 was 382 persons per sq km. Bihar has the highest density of 1102 persons per sq km and Arunachal Pradesh has the lowest density of 17 persons per sq km.

On the basis of population density, India is divided into three regions

(i) **High Population Density States** Flat plains with fertile soils and abundant rainfall are responsible for high population density in these States. For example, States of the Northern plains like Uttar Pradesh, Bihar, West Bengal and Kerala in the South.

(ii) **Moderate Population Density States** These states have moderate population density due to hilly dissected and rocky nature of terrain, moderate to low rainfall and shallow and less fertile soil. For example, Assam in the North-East and most of the Peninsular states such as Maharashtra, Andhra Pradesh and Karnataka.

(iii) **Low Population Density States** These states have low population density below 250 persons per sq km due to the rugged terrain (mountainous and desert) and unfavourable climatic conditions in these states. For example, Arunachal Pradesh, Sikkim, Jammu and Kashmir, etc.

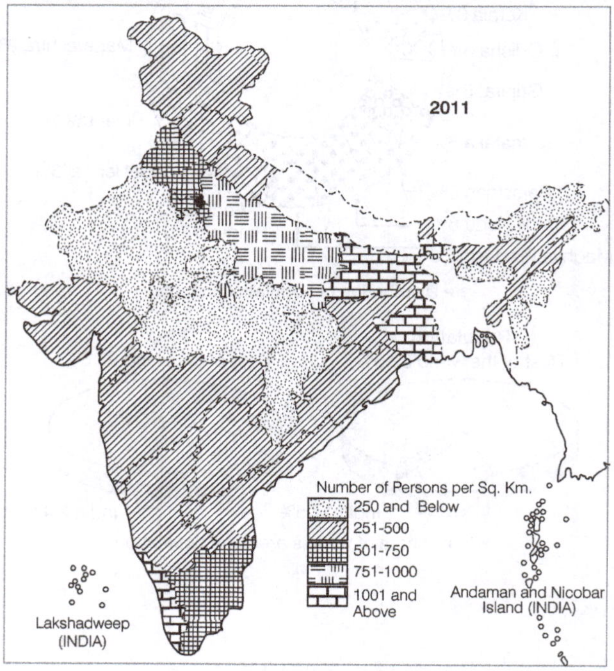

• Density of Population (Census 2011)

6.2 Population Growth

The change in the number of people of a country or state during a specific period of time is called growth of population.

Population growth is calculated at an interval of 10 years in India. The change in population growth can be expressed either in terms of absolute numbers or in terms of annual growth rate.

These are discussed below

- **Absolute Increase of Population** The absolute number of people added each year or in each decade is the magnitude of increase. It is obtained by simply subtracting the earlier population (e.g. that of 2001) from the later population (e.g. that of 2011).
- **Annual Growth Rate of Population** It is the rate at which the number of individuals in a population increase. It is studied in terms of per cent per annum. For example, a rate of increase of 2% per annum means that there was an increase of 2 persons for every 100 persons in the base population.

Population Growth in India Since Independence

India's population has increased from 361 million in 1951 to 1210 million in 2011.

There was a rapid increase in population from 361 million in 1951 to 683 million in 1981 due to continously increasing annual growth rate.

Since the year 1981, the rate of growth of population started declining gradually (2.22% in 1981 to 2.16% in 1991 and 1.97% in 2001). During this period, the birth rates declined rapidly.

Despite declining growth rate of population, 182 million people got added to the population from 1990-1999. This was the **largest annual addition of people** in Indian population.

India has a very large population and even when a low annual rate is applied to a very large population, it still leads to a large increase in the number of people.

India's increase in population every year is large enough to cancel or neutralise the effors to conserve the resources and environment. Though the declining trend of population growth is positive indicator of efforts of birth control, the total additions to population base continue to be large.

At this growth rate, India may overtake China in 2045 to become the most populous country in the world.

Processes of Population Change/Growth

The three processes that influence the change of population are birth rate, death rate and migration. The **natural increase** of population is determined by the difference between birth rates and death rates. It is also known as growth rate of population. The three processes are discussed below

- **Birth Rate** The number of live births per thousand persons in a year is called birth rate. In India, birth rate has been always higher than the death rate.
- **Death Rate** The number of deaths per thousand persons in a year is called death rate. In India, there has been a rapid decline in death rates which has led to increased rate of growth of the Indian population.

  Till 1980, high birth rates and declining death rates resulted into high rate of population growth. Since 1981, due to government efforts and increased awareness, the birth rate also started to decline, resulting in gradual decline in the population growth rate.
- **Migration** It is the movement of people across regions and territories. Migration can be **internal** (within the country) or **international** (between the countries).

  Internal migration does not change the population size of a country but it changes the population distribution of an area.

Migration Pattern in India

In India, most of the migrations have been from rural areas to urban areas. This is due to the following factors

- **Push Factors** These include poverty and unemployment in rural areas.
- **Pull Factors** These include increased employment opportunities and better living conditions in urban places.

Migration is an important factor contributing to population change. It changes the population size. It also changes the composition of population in urban and rural areas in terms of age and sex-composition.

Rural-urban migration has resulted in a continuous increase in the percentage of population in cities and towns. The urban population has increased from 17.29% of the total population in 1951 to 31.80% in 2011.

There has been a significant increase in the number of **million plus cities**[2] from 35 to 53 in just one decade, i.e. from 2001 to 2011.

Adolescent Population

Adolescents are generally those people who are in the age group of 10 to 19 years. They are the most important resource for the future.

In India, adolescents constitute a large percentage of population. The adolescent form about one-fifth of the total population of India.

The nutritional requirements of adolescents are much higher than those of a normal child or adult.

In India, the diet available to adolescents is inadequate in all nutrients. Poor nutrition may led to deficiencies and stunted (inferior quality) growth among the adolescents.

Many adolescent girls suffer from anaemia. Their problems have so far not received adequate attention in the process of development.

The adolescent girls have to be informed about the nutritional problem, through the spread of literacy and education.

National Population Policy

Family planning is regarded as an important way to improve individual health and welfare. Therefore, the Government of India initiated a Family Planning Programme in 1952.

This program aimed at promoting responsible and planned parenthood on a voluntary basis. In the year 2000, the government formulated the National Population Policy (NPP 2000), which had the following major objectives

- Providing a policy framework for giving free and compulsory school education up to 14 years of age.
- Reducing infant mortality rate to below 30 per 1000 live births.
- Achieving universal immunisation of children against all vaccine preventable diseases.
- Promoting delayed marriage for girls.
- Making family welfare a people-centered programme.

Try These

1. **The first complete census in India was held in which year?**
2. **What is the rank of India in the world in terms of population density?**
3. **It is the change in the number of inhabitants in a country during specific period. Identify the term.**
4. **Name two states where there are more females than the number of males.**
5. **What proportion of India's total population does the adolescent population represent?**

2 **Million Plus Cities** Cities in India with population of one million (10 Lakh) or more included in this category.

Mind Map

POPULATION

India's Population Distribution by Density

Population density is the number of people living per unit area (sq km).

Moderate Population Density States

- Assam, Maharashtra, Andhra Pradesh and Karnataka.
- These states have moderate population density due to hilly dissected and rocky nature of terrain, moderate to low rainfall, and shallow and less fertile soil.

High Population Density States

- Uttar Pradesh, Bihar, West Bengal and Kerala.
- These states have high population density due to flat plains with fertile soil and abundant rainfall.

Low Population Density States

- Arunachal Pradesh, Sikkim, Jammu and Kashmir.
- These states have low population density due to rugged terrain and unfavourable climatic conditions.

India's Population Size and Distribution

- According to the 2011 Census, population of India is 1210.6 million which is 17.5% of the total world population.
- In India, Uttar Pradesh has the highest population and Sikkim has the lowest population.

Population Growth in India since Independence

- India has a very large population and it has kept on increasing due to continuously increasing annual growth rate.
- India's increase in population is large enough to cancel or neutralise the effort to conserve the resources and the environment.

Processes of Population Change/Growth

- **Birth rate** Number of live births per thousand persons in a year.
- **Death Rate** Number of deaths per thousand persons in a year.
- **Migration** Movement of people across regions and territories. It can be internal (within the country) or International (between the countries).

Population Growth

- It is the change in the number of people of a country or state during a specific period of time.
- It is calculated at an interval of 10 years in India.
- Change in Population Growth can be expressed either in terms of absolute numbers or in terms of annual growth rate.

National Population Policy

- Providing a policy framework for giving free and compulsory school education up to 14 years of age.
- Reducing Infant Mortality rate to below 30 per 1000 live births.
- Promoting delayed marriage of girls.
- Making family welfare a people centered programme.

Adolescent Population

- Adolescents are those who are in the age group of 10-19 years.
- The adolescents form about one-fifth of the total population of India.

NCERT FOLDER

Covering Intext Questions and Exercises of NCERT

INTEXT QUESTIONS

Q.1 What could be the reason of uneven distribution of population in India?

Ans. The reason for uneven distribution of population are relief, climatic conditions, availability of resources, gender and age group divide.

Some of them are explained below

(i) **Relief** Mountains, deserts and plateaus are sparsely populated, due to rugged terrain and infertile soil. Plains are thickly populated due to flat features and availability of fertile soil.

(ii) **Climate** The region of high rainfall have very high population whereas regions of extreme climatic conditions like very cold, very hot and dry areas have sparse population.

Q.2 Consider the following table.

Years	Total Population (in millions)	Absolute Increase in the Decade (In million)	Annual Growth Rate (%)
1951	361.0	42.43	1.25
1961	439.2	78.15	1.96
1971	548.2	108.92	2.20
1981	683.3	135.17	2.22
1991	846.4	163.09	2.16
2001	1028.7	182.32	1.97
2011	1210.2	181.46	1.64

The above data reveals that despite the decline in growth rates, the number of people being added every decade is steadily increasing. Why?

Ans. The number of people added to the population are increasing every decade. This is because India has a very large population; when a low annual rate is applied to a very large population, it still leads to a large increase in the number of people. For example, when a low annual rate of 1.6% is supplied on 120 crore, it will lead to an increase of 1.2 crore people (1.6% of 120 crore). So, the number of people being added every decade is steadily increasing.

EXERCISE

Q.1 Choose the right answer from the four alternatives given below.

(i) Migrations change the number, distribution and composition of the population in

(a) the area of departure
(b) the area of arrival
(c) Both the area of departure and arrival
(d) None of the above

(ii) A large proportion of children in a population is a result of

(a) high birth rates (b) high life expectancies
(c) high death rates (d) more married couples

(iii) The magnitude of population growth refers to

(a) the total population of an area.
(b) the number of persons added each year.
(c) the rate at which the population increases.
(d) the number of females per thousand males.

(iv) According to the Census, a 'literate' person is one who

(a) can read and write his/her name.
(b) can read and write any language.
(c) is 7 years old and can read and write any one language with understanding.
(d) knows the 3'R's (Reading, Writing and Arithmetic)

Ans. (i) (c) (ii) (a) (iii) (b) (iv) (c)

Q.2 Answer the following questions briefly.

(i) Why is the rate of population growth in India declining since 1981?

Ans. The rate of population growth in India is declining since 1981 because the birth rates and death rates have declined rapidly in the following ways

- Improvement in female education and literacy has led to decline in birth rates.
- Better healthcare facilities have improved the life expectancy at birth. This helps in lowering the death rate.
- The positive effect of family planning programme, birth control measures and easy availability of contraceptives has led to decline in growth rate.

(ii) Discuss the major components of population growth.

Ans. Major components of population growth are

- **Birth Rate** It is the number of live births per thousand persons in a year. It is a major component of population growth. In India, birth rates have always been higher than death rates.
- **Death Rate** It is the number of deaths per thousand persons in a year. The main cause of growth of the population in India has been rapid decline in the death rate.
- **Migration** It is the movement of people across regions and territories. Internal migration only changes the distribution of population where as international migration changes both size and distribution of population.

(iii) Define age structure, death rate and birth rate.

Ans. **Age structure** It is the distribution of individuals a cross different age groups within a population at a specific time.

Death rate It is the number of deaths per thousand persons in a year.

Birth rate It is the number of live births per thousand persons in a year.

(iv) How is migration a determinant factor of population change?

Ans. Migration is a determinant factor of population change in the following ways

- Internal migration (within the country) changes the population distribution of a country.
- International migration (outside the country) changes composition as well as size of the population.
- In India, rural to urban migration has changed the size as well as the age-sex composition of urban and rural populations.

Q.3 Distinguish between population growth and population change.

Ans. The differences between population growth and population change is as follow

Population Growth	Population Change
Population growth always results due to change in the size of population.	Population change is any change that may result due to migration, death rates, birth rates and change in age composition and sex-ratio.
Without a change in population, population growth is not possible.	Even where there is no population growth, there may be a population change.
Internal migration does not lead to change in the population growth of a country.	Internal migration brings about a change in population of a country.
It can be expressed in terms of absolute number and in terms of the percentage change in a year.	It can be expressed in the number of individuals.

Q.4 What is the relation between occupational structure and development?

Ans. The distribution of the population according to the different types of occupations is referred to as the occupational structure of a population.

Occupations are generally classified as primary (agriculture, mining, fishing, etc) secondary (manufacturing industry, building and construction work, etc) and tertiary (transport, communications, banking, etc).

The relation between occupational structure and development is that the proportion of people working in different activities determines the economic development of a country.

Developed nations have a high proportion of people in secondary and tertiary activities. Developing countries have a higher proportion of their workforce engaged in primary activities.

In India about 50% of the population is engaged in agriculture (primary sector), 13% in secondary and 20% in tertiary sectors.

Q.5 What are the advantages of having a healthy population?

Ans. Health is an important component of population composition which effects the process of development. Some advantages of having a healthy population are

- A healthy populations makes full use of the natural resources provided by the environment.
- A healthy population develops the economy and society of a country.
- A healthy person is an asset to the country, is more productive and helps in the progress of the country.

Q.6 What are the significant features of the National Population Policy, 2000?

Ans. Significant features of National Population Policy, 2000 are

- Imparting free and compulsory school education upto 14 years of age.
- Reducing infant mortality rate to below 30 per 1000 live births.
- Achieving universal immunisation of children against all vaccine preventable diseases.
- Promoting delayed marriage for girls and strengthening legal measures to prevent child marriage.
- Making family welfare and people centered programmes.

REVIEW EXERCISE

Including Competency Based Questions

Part I

Multiple Choice Questions (MCQs)

1. India's population according to Census 2011 is

(a) 1601 million (b) 1210.6 million
(c) 1210.8 million (d) 988 million

2. Which state of India is the most populous state as per Census 2011?

(a) Madhya Pradesh (b) Arunachal Pradesh
(c) West Bengal (d) Uttar Pradesh

3. Which state of India has the least population as per Census 2011?

(a) West Bengal (b) Sikkim
(c) Madhya Pradesh (d) Uttarakhand

4. The uneven distribution of population can be better studied by which of the following concepts?

(a) Population growth
(b) Birth rate
(c) Growth rate
(d) Population density

5. Which among the following statements is incorrect?

(a) Population density of India in 2011 was 382 persons per sq km.
(b) Peninsular states have moderate population density in India.
(c) West Bengal is the most populous state in India.
(d) Bangladesh has high population density than India.

6. Which of the following factors are responsible for moderate population density in peninsular states of India?

(a) Hilly and rocky terrain (b) Moderate rainfall
(c) Shallow and less fertile soil (d) All of these

7. Which of the following states have moderate population density in India?

(i) Kerala **(ii) Assam**
(iii) Maharashtra **(iv) Andhra Pradesh**

(a) (i), (ii), (iii) and (iv) (b) (ii), (iii) and (iv)
(c) (i), (ii) and (iv) (d) (i), (ii) and (iii)

8. Which of the following is correctly arranged in terms of their population density (highest density to lowest density)?

(a) Assam, Kerala, Arunachal Pradesh
(b) Kerala, Assam, Arunachal Pradesh
(c) Assam, Arunachal Pradesh, Kerala
(d) Kerala, Arunachal Pradesh, Assam

9. What was the annual growth rate of population in the year 2011?

(a) 2.22% (b) 1.67% (c) 1.64% (d) 1.25%

10. What per cent of India's population live in urban areas?

(a) 16.2% (b) 31. 8% (c) 41 % (d) 12.3%

11. The 2011 Census data reveal that Uttar Pradesh with a population size of 199 million is the most populous state of India. Uttar Pradesh accounts for about 16 per cent of the country's population.

Which state despite being the largest in terms of area, has only 5.5% of India's total population?

Competency Based

(a) Uttar Pradesh (b) Maharashtra
(c) Rajasthan (d) West Bengal

12. Rachna was a part of the team who were conducting a census in 2011. She conducted census in Assam.

What is true regarding Assam's demographic statistics?

Competency Based

(a) higher population densities
(b) higher birth rate
(c) lower population densities
(d) moderate population densities

13. India has the largest adolescent population in the world. India stands to benefit socially, politically and economically if this large number of adolescents are safe, healthy, educated and equipped with information and life skills to support the country's continued development.

Source (edited): Unicef

What is a common health issue among a large number of adolescent girls in India?

(a) Obesity (b) Diabetes (c) Anaemia (d) Hypertension

14. Consider the statements given below and choose the correct answer.

Competency Based

Statement I The numbers, distribution and composition of the population are constantly stable.

Statement II Assam and most of the Peninsular states have moderate population densities.

Options

(a) Statement I is correct and II is incorrect
(b) Statement I is incorrect and II is correct
(c) Both I and II are incorrect
(d) Both I and II are correct

15. Which of the following statements accurately describes population density in India?

I. The population density of India in 2011 was 382 persons per sq km.

II. India is one of the least densely populated countries of the world.

III. The population density of India in 2011 was 682 persons per sq km.

IV. Population density is calculated as the number of persons per km area.

Codes

(a) Only I (b) Only II

(c) Only IV (d) Both I and II

Answers

1. (b)	2. (d)	3. (b)	4. (d)	5. (c)
6. (d)	7. (b)	8. (b)	9. (c)	10. (b)
11. (c)	12. (d)	13. (c)	14. (b)	15. (a)

Assertion-Reason

1. Assertion (A) Some states have population densities below 250 persons per square km.

Reason (R) The hilly, dissected and rocky nature of the terrain, along with moderate to low rainfall and shallow, less fertile soils, influences population densities in these areas.

Codes

(a) Both A and R true and R is the correct explanation of A

(b) Both A and R are true, but R is not the correct explanation of A

(c) A is true, but R is false

(d) A is false, but R is true

2. Assertion (A) The Northern plains and Kerala in the South have high to very high population densities.

Reason (R) These regions have flat plains with fertile soils and abundant rainfall.

Codes

(a) Both A and R true and R is the correct explanation of A

(b) Both A and R are true, but R is not the correct explanation of A

(c) A is true, but R is false

(d) A is false, but R is true

3. Assertion (A) Population growth is influenced by the interaction of births, deaths and migrations.

Reason (R) The three processes i.e. State, Economy, and Governments constantly change the numbers, distribution and composition of the population.

Codes

(a) Both A and R true and R is the correct explanation of A

(b) Both A and R are true, but R is not the correct explanation of A

(c) A is true, but R is false

(d) A is false, but R is true

4. Assertion (A) The rate of population increase is expressed in terms of percentage change per year.

Reason (R) Absolute increase is obtained by subtracting the earlier population from the later population.

Codes

(a) Both A and R true and R is the correct explanation of A

(b) Both A and R are true, but R is not the correct explanation of A

(c) A is true, but R is false

(d) A is false, but R is true

5. Assertion (A) Population growth refers to the change in the number of inhabitants of a state during a specific period of time.

Reason (R) The interaction of births, deaths and migrations influences the dynamic nature of population change.

Codes

(a) Both A and R true and R is the correct explanation of A

(b) Both A and R are true, but R is not the correct explanation of A

(c) A is true, but R is false

(d) A is false, but R is true

Ans. **1.** (a) Both A and R true and R is the correct explanation of A

2. (a) Both A and R true and R is the correct explanation of A

3. (c) A is true, but R is false

4. (b) Both A and R are true, but R is not the correct explanation of A

5. (b) Both A and R are true, but R is not the correct explanation of A

Case Based Question

1. Read the source given below and answer the questions that follow.

Growth of population refers to the change in the number of inhabitants of a country/territory during a specific period of time, say during the last 10 years. Such a change can be expressed in two ways: in terms of absolute numbers and in terms of percentage change per year. The absolute numbers added each year or decade is the magnitude of increase. It is obtained by simply subtracting the earlier population (e.g. that of 2001) from the later population (e.g. that of 2011). It is referred to as the absolute increase. The rate or the pace of population increase is the other important aspect. It is studied in per cent per annum, e.g. a rate of increase of 2 per cent per annum means that in a given year, there was an increase of two persons for every 100 persons in the base population. This is referred to as the annual growth rate.

(i) What factor contribute(s) to change in the population composition of a specific area?
(a) Birth rate decline
(b) Death rate decline
(c) External Migration
(d) All of the above

(ii) When did the rate of population growth in India start declining?
(a) 1951 (b) 1981
(c) 2001 (d) 2011

(iii) What is the main challenge posed by India's large population?
(a) High unemployment rate
(b) Difficulty in achieving economic development
(c) Strain on resource use and environment
(d) All of the above

(iv) What factor contributed to the large absolute increase in population in the 1990s?
(a) Rapidly declining death rates
(b) Steadily increasing growth rate
(c) Increasing birth rates
(d) Consistent efforts of birth control

Ans. (i) (d) All of the above
(ii) (b) 1981
(iii) (d) All of the above
(iv) (c) Increasing birth rates

Part II

Very Short Answer Type Questions

1. When was the first census held in India?

Ans. The first census in India (on a limited scale) was held in 1872. The first complete census was held in 1881 and since then, it has been subsequently held every 10 years.

2. Almost 50% of India's population lives in five states. Name them.

Ans. Almost 50% of India's population lives in the five states of Uttar Pradesh, Maharashtra, Bihar, West Bengal and Andhra Pradesh.

3. Which are the most populated and least populated states in India?

Ans. The most populated state in India is Uttar Pradesh and least populated is Sikkim.

4. Why there is moderate density of population in the peninsular states of India?

Ans. The peninsular states have moderate density of population because the land is uneven, hilly and rocky, rainfall is moderate and soil is shallow and less fertile.

5. What is the major reason for the state of Kerala having a very high population density?

Ans. Kerala has a very high population density because it has a fertile soil and gets abundant rainfall, thus resulting in good prospects for agriculture.

6. What kind of migration does not change the size of the population in a country?

Ans. Internal migration from one city to another or from rural areas to urban areas within a country does not change the size of the population in the country.

7. What kind of migration leads to changes in the distribution of population within a country?

Ans. Internal migration leads to changes in the distribution of population within a country.

8. When did the National Population Policy came into effect?

Ans. The National Population Policy came into effect in the year 2000.

9. Growth of population can be expressed in two ways in terms of absolute numbers and in terms of percentage change per year.
How is the magnitude of increase expressed in terms of population growth? Competency Based

Ans. The magnitude of increase in population growth is expressed through the concept of absolute numbers added each year or decade. It is calculated by subtracting the earlier population figure from the later population figure, providing a numerical representation of the population change during a specific period.

10. The population, which accounts for world's 17.5 per cent population, comprises 623.7 million males and 586.5 million females, said a provisional 2011 Census report. China is the most populous nation accounting for ....
Source (edited): Economics Times
What significant demographic change is predicted for India in relation to China by 2045? Competency Based

Ans. The significant demographic change predicted for India in relation to China by 2045 is the possibility of India overtaking China to become the most populous country in the world.

Short Answer Type Questions

1 What do you mean by 'Census'? After how many years is it prepared in India?

Ans. A census is an official enumeration (numbering) of the population of a country which is done periodically. It provides with the number of people, their distribution, age-sex composition, occupational structure, literacy levels, etc.

In India, the first complete census was held in 1882. Since then, it is done regularly every 10 years in India.

2. How is population density calculated? Where does India stand as compared to other countries with respect to population density?

Ans. The population density is calculated as the number of persons per unit of area.

India's status in terms of population density with respect to other countries is discussed below

- India is the third most densely populated country in the world after Bangladesh and Japan.
- India is one of the most densely populated countries in the world. As per Census 2011 report, the population density of India was 382 persons per sq km.
- Due to variation in climatic condition, economic opportunities and other geographic factors. India has very uneven distribution of population ranging from 1102 persons/sq km in Bihar to only 17 persons/sq km in Arunachal Pradesh.

3. Describe the three different population density regions of India.

Ans. The three population density regions in India are

(i) **High Population Density Region** It has a population density greater than 500 persons per sq km. It consists of the States of Uttar Pradesh, Bihar, West Bengal in the Northern Plains and Kerala in the South.

(ii) **Moderate Density Population Region** It has a population of 250-500 persons living per sq km.

(iii) **Low Density Population Region** It has a population density lesser than 250 persons per sq km. It consists of the states Arunachal Pradesh, Mizoram, etc.

4. How does density of population depend upon topography and climatic conditions?

Ans. Density of population depends upon topography and climatic conditions in the following ways

- Rugged topography and unfavourable climatic conditions are primarily responsible for sparse (not dense) population. For example, Arunachal Pradesh has very little population due to hilly areas.
- Moderate to low rainfall, rocky terrain and less fertile soils have led to moderate population densities. e.g. Assam and Peninsular states of India.
- Flat plains, fertile soil and abundant rainfall lead to high population densities, e.g. Northern Plains and Kerala.

5. How is growth in population expressed? Explain.

Ans. The growth of population is the change in the number of inhabitants of a country during a specific period (mostly during 10 years).

The growth in population can be expressed in two ways

(i) **Absolute Numbers** It is the magnitude of increase of population in a year or decade. It is obtained by subtracting the earlier population from the current population.

(ii) **Annual Growth Rate** It is the rate of increase of population in one year. It is measured in per cent per annum.

6. Explain the term annual growth rate of population. How is it affected by the birth rate?

Ans. The rate at which the number of individuals in a population increase in an year as compared to the population of previous year (base year) is called annual growth rate of population.

The annual growth rate is affected by the birth rate in the following ways

- If the birth rate increases, the annual growth rate generally increases and vice-versa.
- If the birth rate is greater than death rate, annual growth rate is higher.
- If birth rate is lower than death rate, annual growth rate declines.

7. "Resources, calamities and disasters all are meaningful only in relation to human beings." Explain the statement with suitable arguments. Competency Based

Ans. Resources, calamities and disasters are all meaningful only in relation to human beings. The statement highlights the importance of the human resource as

- It is the people who develop the economy and society.
- It is the people who make and use resources.
- Resources have no meaning without the people. e.g. coal is just a piece of rock until people were able to make it usable through technology.
- Natural events, like a flood or a Tsunami, becomes a disaster, only when they affect a crowded village or a town.

8. Discuss how does the gradual decline in birth rates contribute to the changing trend in the rate of population growth. Competency Based

Build answer around these points

- **Population until 1980**
- **Rapid population growth**
- **Population since 1981**

Ans. The gradual decline in the birth rate has contributed to the changing trend in the rate of population growth in the following phases

- **Prior to 1980** India experienced a explosive population growth due to high fertility rates and declining mortality rates.
- **Rapid Population Growth** India faced a demographic challenge characterised by rapid population growth. It effected resources like education, healthcare and jobs. It presented both challenges and opportunities
- **Population Since 1981** India started witnessing shift in its demographic trends as various initiatives were implemented to address the challenges posed by rapid population growth. These initiatives included family planning programme, awareness campaigns and improved healthcare services.

9. Read the statements given below.

Statement 1 (S1) Birth rate is the number of live births per thousand persons in a year. It is a major component of growth because in India.

Statement 2 (S2) Death rate is the number of deaths per five thousand persons in a year. The main cause of the rate of growth of the Indian population has been the rapid decline in death rates.

Explain, which statement is incorrect, why? **Competency Based**

Ans. Statement 2 is incorrect. The death rate is not measured per five thousand persons. It is measured as the number of deaths per thousand persons in a year. The death rate is an important component in demographic analysis. The decline in death rate has also contributed significantly to the population growth in India.

Statement 1 is correct because the birth rate is the number of live births per thousand of the population every year. Birth rate is a crude measure of fertility of a population and a important determinant of population growth.

10. Population density provides a better picture of the uneven distribution. Population density is calculated as the number of persons per unit area. India is one of the most densely populated countries of the world.

(i) Why is population density a better indicator in studying population?

(ii) Which two countries have higher average population densities than India? **Competency Based**

Ans. (i) Population density is a better indicator because it offers a clear view of how people are distributed in a given area. This measurement allows a deeper understanding of settlement pattern and favourable conditions available at a place.

(ii) Bangladesh and Japan have higher average population densities than India. Bangladesh, with its smaller land area and substantial population, surpasses India in population density. Japan, despite being geographically smaller than India, has a higher population density due to its dense urbanisation and limited habitable space.

Long Answer Type Questions

1. What is migration? Which are the two types of migration? Describe the trends of migration in India.

Ans. Migration is the movement of people across regions and territories. This movement can occur within a country or between countries. People can migrate due to various reasons such as economic opportunities, better living conditions, educational pursuits and environmental factors. Migration play an important role in shaping cultures and societies.

Types of Migration The two types of migration are internal (within the country from one area to another) and international (between two or more than two countries). Internal migration does not change the size of the population, but influences the distribution of population within the country.

Trends of Migration in India In India, most of the migrations occur from the rural to urban areas. This is due to poverty and unemployment in rural areas and better employment opportunities and better living conditions in the urban areas.

Rural-urban migration has resulted in a continuous increase in the percentage of population in the cities and towns. The urban population has increased from 17.29% of total population in 1951 to 31.8% in 2011.

2. Why do people migrate from rural to urban areas?

Ans. People migrate from one place to another due to variety of reasons. The push and pull factors are responsible. The 'push factors' of migration are those factors which force people to leave a place e.g. poverty, drought. People leave rural places due to

- non-availability of job opportunities
- shortage of land
- political unrest
- difficult economic conditions
- disasters/catastrophe (drought, floods, etc.)
- decline of traditional industries (cottage, small-scale industries).

The 'pull factors' of migration are those factors which attract people towards itself. e.g. employment opportunity, quality lifestyle, etc.

People are attracted towards the urban areas for

- change of a job
- education
- improved living conditions
- security
- adequate basic amenities
- better housing facility
- medical care
- better way of life

3. Explain any five significant characteristics of the adolescent population of India.

Ans. Five significant characteristics of the adolescent population of India are as follows

(i) Adolescent population constitutes one-fifth of the total population of India.

(ii) They are generally grouped in the age group of 10 to 19 years.

(iii) Nutritional requirements of adolescents are higher than those of normal child or adult.

(iv) In India, a large number of adolescent girls suffer from anaemia.

(v) The adolescent girls have to be sensitised about the problems faced by them.

4. Read the information about migration and answer the question that follows.

In India, most migrations have been from rural to urban areas because of the "push" factor in rural areas. These are adverse conditions of poverty and unemployment in the rural areas and the "pull" of the city in terms of increased employment opportunities and better living conditions.

What was the factors that drive rural-to-urban migration in India considering both 'push' and 'Pull' factors. Competency Based

Ans. India's rural-to-urban migration is primarily driven by a combination of 'push' and 'pull' factors. These are discussed below

- **Push factors** Rural areas often struggle with limited economic possibilities. It leads to low income and unemployment. This pushes persons to seek better job opportunities in urban areas. Rural areas also may not have adequate access to education, healthcare, sanitation, etc which encourage persons to migrate for better living conditions.
- **Pull factors** Cities generally have a wider range of employment options in various sectors, attracting persons looking for better job opportunities and higher wages. Urban areas also provide better education, healthcare, sanitation and infrastructure that can be important pull factor for persons.

5 The NPP 2000, which set the national socio-demographic goals for the year 2010, said if its strategies were implemented, India's population, which was projected to be 116 crore by 2010, could be capped at 110 crore.

Source (edited): Times of India

Explain an overview of the National Population Policy (NPP) 2000 and its significance in the context of family planning in India. Competency Based

Ans. The National Population Policy (NPP) 2000 is a strategic framework introduced by the Government of India to address population-related challenges. It emphasises voluntary family planning, recognising individual choices.

The policy promotes education by advocating free and compulsory schooling up to 14 years. It aims to enhance healthcare outcomes by reducing infant mortality rates and achieving universal immunisation.

The National Population Policy (NPP) 2000 holds important significance in India's family planning efforts. It prioritises voluntary family planning, respecting individual choices. The policy integrates education, healthcare and delayed marriage to influence family planning decisions.

By fostering a people-centered approach, the NPP 2000 emphasises community participation and calculated decision-making, contributing to the overall effectiveness of family planning initiatives in India.

6. Mr. X conducted a research on population of India and learned that India's growth in birth rate is getting higher year by year and the population is increasing really fast. He wanted to take a step for development regarding population of India. He decided to give education regarding increasing in population and their causes. So he opened a education center in Y city, where 15+ people can come to learn about the population of India.

What changes will occurs when people will get education regarding population and how does it will help in all over in India? Competency Based

Ans. Mr. X's initiative to provide education in Y city can lead to transformative changes. Firstly, increased awareness about population growth and its causes may inspire responsible family planning decisions among the villagers.

As individuals gain knowledge, there is potential for improved health outcomes, including maternal and child health. Empowering women through education can enhance their role in family planning and contribute to socio-economic development.

At a community level, the education center fosters a culture of informed decision-making, impacting not only Y city but also neighboring cities.

Scaling this approach nationwide could create a decrease in birth rate and promote a national shift towards sustainable population growth and socio-economic development in India.

Case Based Question

1 Read the sources given below and answer the questions that follow.

Source A Adolescent Population

The most significant feature of the Indian population is the size of its adolescent population. It constitutes one-fifth of the total population of India. Adolescents are, generally, grouped in the age group of 10 to 19 years. They are the most important resource for the future.

(i) Evaluate the importance of adolescent population in India.

Source B Requirements of Adolescent

Nutrition requirements of adolescents are higher than those of a normal child or adult. Poor nutrition can lead to deficiency and stunted growth. But in India, the diet available to adolescents is inadequate in all nutrients. A large number of adolescent girls suffer from anaemia. Their problems have so far not received adequate attention in the process of development.

(ii) To what extent is the adolescent population vulnerable to diseases in India?

Source C Spreading Awareness

The adolescent girls have to be sensitised to the problems they confront. Awareness among them can be improved through the spread of literacy and education.

(iii) Examine the role of education in solving the problems of adolescent girls.

Ans. (i) The adolescent comprises of the persons in age group 10-19 years. They are important for India as they constitute the maximum percentage of population in India and they are the most important resource for the future.

(ii) The adolescent population is vulnerable to diseases in India mainly due to insufficient nutrition. The adolescent population has higher requirements of nutrition than an adult or a child. In India, adolescents do not get proper diet. No proper policy have been formulated for the development of adolescents. Thus, they are suffering from a number of diseases like anaemia in adolescent girls and so on.

(iii) Education and literacy can improve awareness among the adolescent girls. This would make them better understand the problems faced by them. If they are made aware of their problems, they would be able to handle them appropriately.

Map Based Question

1 On the political map of India, locate and label the following with appropriate symbols.

(i) The state having highest density of population.

(ii) The state having lowest density of population.

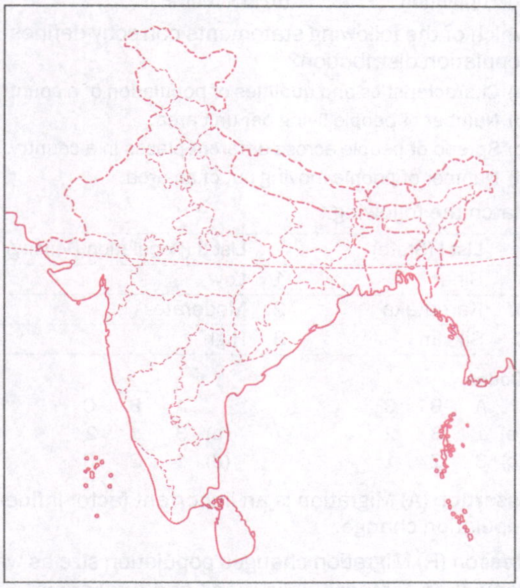

Ans.

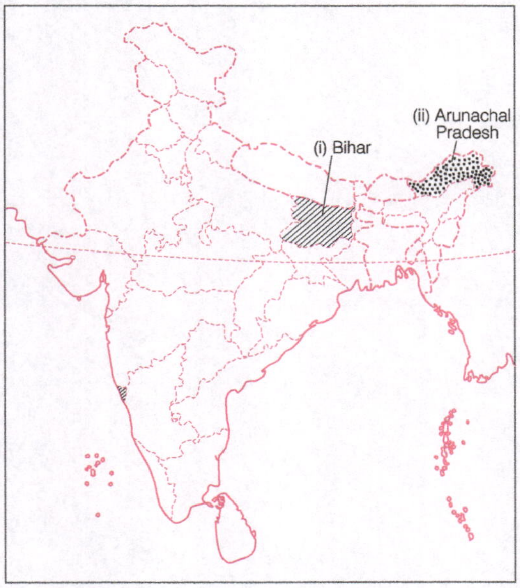

ASSESSMENT EXERCISE

Multiple Choice Questions (MCQs)

1. The central element in the study of social studies is

(a) Resources (b) Disasters

(c) Population (d) Environment

2. Which of the following statements correctly defines population distribution?

(a) Characteristics and qualities of population of a country.

(b) Number of people living per unit area.

(c) Spread of people across different places in a country.

(d) Number of people moving out of an area.

3. Match the following.

	List I (State)		**List II** (Population Density)
A.	Bihar	1.	Low
B.	Karnataka	2.	Moderate
C.	Sikkim	3.	High

Codes

	A	B	C		A	B	C
(a)	1	3	2	(b)	3	1	2
(c)	3	2	1	(d)	1	2	3

4. **Assertion** (A) Migration is an important factor influencing population change.

Reason (R) Migration changes population size as well as population composition in urban and rural areas.

Codes

(a) Both A and R are true and R is the correct explanation of A

(b) Both A and R are true, but R is not the correct explanation of A

(c) Both A is true, but R is false

(d) Both A is false, but R is true

Subjective Questions (VSA, SA & LA)

1. What was India's approximate population as per Census 2011?

2. What is the reason for a large proportion of children in the population of a country?

3. Enumerate the reasons for sparse population in states like Arunachal Pradesh, Mizoram and Jammu and Kashmir.

4. How adolescent population of India is boon for the economy?

5. India's sex ratio is considered as unfavourable for women. What can be the long-term problems in a state in which this ratio remains unfavourable for many years?

6. Give reasons for the shift in the occupational structure from primary to secondary and tertiary sectors. What are its consequences?

CHAPTER 1

What is Democracy? Why Democracy?

Democracy is the most prevalent form of government in the world today. The word 'Democracy' comes from a Greek word 'Demokratia'. In Greek 'Demo' means 'People' and 'Kratio' means 'Power'. So, democracy is the rule by the people. In this chapter, we will discuss the features of democratic form of government. It also discusses about the difference between democratic government and non-democratic government.

1.1 Meaning of Democracy

Democracy is a form of government in which the rulers are elected by the people.

According to Abraham Lincoln–"Democracy is government of the people, by the people and for the people".

In a democratic country, people choose their government by elections. In this way, it is different from other forms of government.

1.2 Features of Democracy

- Rulers are elected by the people to take all the major decisions.
- Elections offer a choice and fair opportunity to the people to change their current rulers.
- This choice and opportunity is available to all the people on an equal basis.
- It is a form of government where the elected leaders have to perform some functions and respect rights of the citizen.

Examples of Non-Democratic Nations in the World

Some examples of non-democratic government in the world are as follows

- In Myanmar there is army rule. The rulers are not elected by the people.
- Dictators like **Pinochet of Chile** are not elected by the people.
- In monarchies such as Saudi Arabia, the king is the ruler not because the people have chosen, but because they are born in a royal family.

Major Decisions by Elected Leaders

In democracy the final decision making power must rest with those people who are elected.

This feature can be analysed through the example of **General Musharraf's rule of Pakistan** from 1999.

In Pakistan, General Pervez Musharraf led a military regime in October, 1999. He overthrew a democratically elected government and declared himself the Chief Executive of the country. Later, he changed his designation to President.

In 2002, he organised a **referendum**[1] in the country that granted him a five years extension. According to Pakistani media and human rights organisations, the referendum was based on malpractices and fraud.

In August, 2002, Musharraf issued a **Legal Framework Order** that amended the Constitution of Pakistan. According to this order, the President can dismiss the national or provincial assemblies.

The work of the civilian **Cabinet**[2] was supervised by a National Security Council dominated by military officers. Elected representative had some power, but the final power was in the hands of military officers and General Musharraf himself. This condition cannot be termed as people's rule.

This happens in many dictatorships and monarchies. They formally have an elected parliament and government but the real power is with those who are not elected.

1 **Referendum** It is a direct and universal vote in which an entire electorate is invited to vote on a particular proposal.

2 **Cabinet** The committee of senior ministers responsible for controlling government policy.

Free and Fair Electoral Competition

Democracy must be based on a free and fair election, where those currently in power have a fair chance of losing.

This feature of democracy can be understood from the cases of **China** and **Mexico**.

Case of China

The members of China's Parliament called **Quanguo Renmin Daibiao Dahui (National People's Congress)**, are elected by the people after every five years.

The National People's Congress has the power to appoint the President of the country. The National People's Congress has nearly 3,000 members elected from all over China. Some members are elected by the army.

Before contesting elections, a candidate needs the approval of the **Chinese Communist Party**. Only its members or members of eight smaller parties associated with the Communist Party were allowed to contest elections held in 2002-03. The government is always formed by the Communist Party.

Case of Mexico

Mexico became independent in 1930. It holds elections after every six years to elect its President. It has never been under military or dictator's rule.

However till 2000, all the Presidential elections were won by the **PRI (Institutional Revolutionary Party)**. Opposition parties contested but never managed to win.

PRI used dirty tricks to win the elections, such as

- All employed in government offices had to attend its party meetings.
- Teachers of government schools used to force parents to vote for the PRI.
- Media largely ignored the activities of opposition political parties except to criticise them.
- Polling booths were shifted from one place to another in the last minute, which made it to difficult for people to caste their votes.
- The PRI spent a large amount of money in the campaign for its candidates.

In both the cases of China and Mexico, elections does not offer the people any serious choice. These are not fair elections. Holding elections of any kind is not sufficient.

One Person, One Vote, One Value

Democracy is based on a fundamental principle of political equality. In a democracy, each adult citizen must have one vote and each vote must have one value.

The Principle of Universal Adult Franchise is accepted all over the world. However, there are many examples which denies the equal Right to Vote.

For example,

- In **Saudi Arabia**, till 2015 women did not have the Right to Vote.
- **Estonia** has made its citizenship rules in such a way that people belonging to Russian minority find it difficult to get the **Right to Vote**.
- In **Fiji**, the electoral system is such that, the vote of an indigenous Fijian has more value than that of an Indian-Fijian.

Rule of Law and Respect for Rights

A democratic government rules within limits set by constitutional law and citizen's rights. This can be analysed through the example of **Zimbabwe**.

Zimbabwe attained independence from White minority rule in 1980. From then onwards, the country has been ruled by a party **ZANU-PF** which led the freedom struggle.

The party leader, **Robert Mugabe**, has been the President of the country since independence. President Mugabe was popular but he also used unfair practices in elections.

Over the years his government changed the constitution several times to increase the powers of the President and make him less accountable.

Opposition party workers were harassed and their meeting disrupted. Public protests and demonstrations against the government were declared illegal.

Television and radio were controlled by the government and gave only the ruling party's version. There were independent newspapers but the government harassed those journalists who went against it.

The government ignored some court judgements that went against it and pressurised judges.

President Mugabe was removed from office in 2017.

The example of Zimbabwe shows the following

Popular governments can be undemocratic and popular leaders can be autocratic.

- If we wish to assess a democracy, it is important to look at the elections. But it is equally important to look before and after the elections.
- There should be sufficient room for normal political activity, including political opposition, in the period before elections.

- The state should respect the basic rights of citizens, like freedom of expression, freedom to protest and freedom to take political action. Further, these rights should be protected by an independent judiciary whose orders should be obeyed by all.

There are some conditions that apply to the way a government is run after the elections, which are as follows

- A democratic government cannot do whatever it likes, simply because it has won an election.
- It has to respect some basic rules and guarantees to the minorities. Every major decision has to go through many debates.
- Every office bearer has certain rights and responsibilities assigned by the constitution and the law. Each of them are accountable not only to the people, but also to other independent officials.

Try These

1. How often are elections held in China?
2. Which political party dominates elections in China?
3. In which year did women in Saudi Arabia gain voting rights?
4. Who led Zimbabwe after independence?

1.3 Need or Arguments for Democracy?

- Democracy is better than any other form of government in responding to the needs of the people. Democracy requires that the rulers have to attend to the needs of the people.
- Democratic government is more accountable form of government.
- Democracy is based on consultation and discussion which reduces the possibility of taking hasty and irresponsible decisions. Thus, democracy improves the quality of decision-making.
- Democracy provides a method to deal with differences and conflicts. Only in a democracy, different groups can live with one another peacefully. In a diverse country like India where people are from different religion and language, democracy keeps our country together.
- Democracy enhances the dignity of citizens. In democracy, the poorest and the least educated have the same status as the rich and the educated, because democracy is based on the principle of political equality.
- Democracy allows us to correct our own mistakes.
- In democracy, either the rulers have to change their decisions or the rulers can be changed. From the above arguments in favour of democracy, we can conclude that democracy cannot give us everything, but it is clearly better than any other form of government.

Comparative Study of Democracies : India and China

- The worst recorded famine in the world was the 1958-1961 China's famine. In this, around 3 crore people died. During the same period, the economic condition of India was similar to that of China, but India did not have any kind of famine. According to economists, this was due to different government policies in India and China.
- As India is a democratic country, its government responded differently to food scarcity. Due to this, no large-scale famine has ever affected independent India. If China too had free press, opposition party, etc like India to criticise the government, so many people would not have died in the famine. This example tells why democracy is considered as the best form of government.

Arguments against Democracy

- Leaders keep changing in a democracy. This leads to instability.
- Democracy is all about political competition and power play. There is no scope for **morality**[3].
- Many people have to be consulted in a democracy which leads to unnecessary delays.
- Elected leaders do not always know the best interests of the people which leads to bad decisions.
- Democracy leads to corruption, as it is based on electoral competition.
- Ordinary people do not know what is good for them so they may not be able to decide anything properly.
- Democracy leads to frequent changes in leadership. Sometimes this can set back big decisions and affect the government's efficiency.
- Democracy ensures that people can take their decisions. But this does not guarantee that their decisions will be good. People can make mistakes.

3 **Morality** means Principles concerning the distinction between right and wrong.

1.4 Broader Meanings of Democracy

The most common form of democracy is **representative democracy**. In this, the majority of people rule through their elected representatives.

This become necessary because

- Modern democracies involve such a large number of people that it is physically impossible for them to sit together and take collective decisions.
- The citizen does not have the time, the desire or the skills to take part in all the decisions, therefore representatives are needed.

Democratic Decision-Making

A democratic decision involves consultation with and consent of all those people who are affected by that decision.

Powerful and non-powerful people should have the same role in taking the decisions. This can apply to a government or a family or any other organisation.

Thus, democracy is a principle that can be applied to any sphere of life and can take many forms.

The most common form of democracy in today's world is being ruled by people's elected representatives. However, for a small community, there can be other ways of making democratic decisions.

Every democracy has to try to realise the ideals of democratic decision-making. Every democracy requires a constant effort to save and strengthen democratic forms of decision-making. The future of a country depends not only on its leaders but also on the actions of its citizens.

Other forms of government like monarchy, dictatorship or one-party rule do not require all citizens to take part in politics. However, democracy depends on active political participation by all the citizens.

Try These

1. **What principle is democracy based on?**
2. **What do critics claim ordinary people lack in a democracy?**
3. **Why does the frequent change of leaders in a democracy lead to instability?**
4. **Which form of government requires consultation and consent of all the people?**

Mind Map

WHAT IS DEMOCRACY? WHY DEMOCRACY?

Meaning of Democracy

- Democracy is a form of government in which the rulers are elected by the people.
- In a democratic country, people choose their government by elections.

Features of Democracy

- Rulers are elected by the people who takes all the major decisions.
- Elections offer a choice and fair opportunity to the people to change their current rulers.
- Choice and opportunity is available to all the people on an equal basis.
- Democracy is a form of government where the elected leaders have to do some functions and respect some rights of the citizen.

Broader Meanings of Democracy

- The most common form a democracy takes is of a representative democracy.
- In representative democracy, the majority of people rule through their elected representatives.

Need for Democracy

- Democratic government is more accountable form of government.
- It improves the quality of decision making.
- It provides a method to deal with differences and conflicts.

Arguments for Democracy

- Leaders keep changing democracy which leads to instability.
- Democracy leads to corruption.
- There is no scope for morality as democracy is all about political competition and power play.

Democratic Decision Making

- Democracy is a principle that can be applied to any sphere of life and can take many forms.
- The most common form of democracy in today's world is being ruled by people's elected representatives.

NCERT FOLDER

Covering Intext Questions and Exercises of NCERT

INTEXT QUESTIONS

Q.1 I have heard a different version. Democracy is off the people, far (from) the people and (where they) buy the people. Why don't we accept that?

Ans. In some cases, the democracy is off the people, far (from) the people and (where they) buy the people i.e. where the democracy does not belong to the people, it is not for them but far away from them; the democracy is not by the people but the candidates win the votes with money. It means that true democracy does not exist.

However, these cases are exceptions and not the rule, which will gradually go away with the passage of time.

Q.2 Ribiang went back home and collected some most famous quotations on democracy. This time she did not mention the names of the people who said or wrote these. She wants you to read these and comment on how good or useful these thoughts are

(a) Democracy gives every man the right to be his own oppressor.

(b) Democracy consists of choosing your dictators after they have told you what you think it is you want to hear.

(c) Man's capacity for justice makes democracy possible, but man's inclination to injustice makes democracy necessary.

(d) Democracy is a device that insures we shall be governed no better than we deserve.

(e) All the ills of democracy can be cured by more democracy.

Ans. (a) and (b) The first and second thoughts are about those forms of government in which the people have the right to elect their ruler without having options. It means they have to elect the candidate only from the ruling party.

(c) In the third thought, it suggests that if man accepts justice, then democracy is possible. But when the man follows injustice, democracy is necessary in this condition to give justice to others.

(d) In the fourth thought, it suggests that there must be a balance between the form of government and our need.

The strongest argument for democracy is about what it does to the citizens. Democracy recognises our needs and enhances our dignity.

(e) In the last thought, there is scope for changing the features and activities of democracy as per our need. There is no guarantee that mistakes cannot be made in democracy. The advantage is that there is a scope for correction.

Either the rulers have to change their decisions or the rulers can be changed. In this way, the ills of democracy can be cured.

Q.3 This cartoon was drawn in the context of Latin America.

Do you think it applies to the Pakistani situation as well? Think of other countries where this could apply. Does this happen sometimes in our country as well?

Ans. The cartoon suggests booth capturing in elections by using arms. This can be applied to Pakistan. In Pakistan, General Musharraf with the help of army officials controlled the elected representatives. This could be applied to Iraq.

Q.4 Read these five examples of working or denial of democracy. Match each of these with the relevant feature of democracy discussed above.

Example	Feature
King of Bhutan has declared that in future he will be guided by the advice given to him by elected representatives.	Rule of law
Many Tamil workers who migrated from India were not given a Right to Vote in Sri Lanka.	Respect for Rights
The king of Nepal imposed a ban on political gatherings, demonstrations and rallies.	One person, one vote, one value
The Indian Supreme Court held that the dissolution of Bihar Assembly was unconstitutional.	Free and fair electoral competition
Political parties in Bangladesh have agreed that a neutral government should rule the country at the time of elections.	Major decision by elected leaders

Ans.

Example	Feature
King of Bhutan ..... representatives.	Major decisions by elected leaders (working)
Many Tamil workers ..... Sri Lanka.	One person, one vote, one value (denial)
The King of Nepal …. rallies.	Respect for Rights (denial)
The Indian Supreme Court …. unconstitutional.	Rule of Law (working)
Political parties ….. time of elections.	Free and fair electoral competition (working)

Q.5 What would have happened if India was not a democracy? Could we have stayed together as a single nation?

Ans. If India was not a democracy then we would have not stayed together as a single nation. India has a multi-religious, multi-cultural and multi-linguistic population.

If there was no democracy, then all the people could not have followed their religion and customs with freedom and there would have been conflicts between different religious and linguistic groups during which the other minorities would have lived in fear and insecurity. But democracy provides peaceful solutions to every problem. It provides the best method of dealing with differences and conflicts.

Q.6 Rajesh and Muzaffar read an article. It showed that no democracy has ever gone to war with another democracy. Wars take place only when one of the two governments is non-democratic. The article said that this was great merit of democracy.

After reading the essay, Rajesh and Muzaffar had different reactions. Rajesh said that this was not a good argument for democracy. It was just a matter of chance.

It is possible that in future democracies may have wars. Muzaffar said that it could not be a matter of chance. Democracies take decisions in such a way that it reduces the chances of war.

Which of the two positions do you agree with and why?

Ans. I agree with Muzaffar's argument. In democracy, the decision is taken after discussion and keeping in view the welfare of the people. So, the chances of war are minimised in democracy, but we cannot say that it is not possible. Some wars were fought between two democracies like India and Pakistan, e.g. 'Kargil War', when both countries were democratic countries.

Q.7 In my village, the Gram Sabha never meets. Is that democratic?

Ans. The Gram Sabha should meet regularly to carry out its functions for the welfare of the village people, but if the Gram Sabha does not meet, then it is not democratic.

EXERCISE

Q.1 Here is some information about four countries. Based on this information, how would you classify each of these countries? Write 'democratic', 'undemocratic' or 'not sure' against each of these.

(a) **Country A** People who do not accept the country's official religion i.e. do not have a right to vote.

(b) **Country B** The same party has been winning elections for the last twenty years.

(c) **Country C** Ruling party has lost in the last three elections.

(d) **Country D** There is no independent Election Commission.

Ans. (a) Undemocratic (b) Not sure
(c) Democratic (d) Undemocratic

Q.2 Here is some information about four countries. Based on this information, how would you classify each of these countries? Write 'democratic', 'undemocratic' or 'not sure' against each of these.

(a) **Country P** The Parliament cannot pass a law about the Army without the consent of the Chief of Army.

(b) **Country Q** The Parliament cannot pass a law reducing the powers of the Judiciary.

(c) **Country R** The country's leaders cannot sign any treaty with another country without taking permission from its neighbouring country.

(d) **Country S** All the major economic decisions about the country are taken by officials of the Central Bank which the Ministers cannot change.

Ans. (a) Undemocratic (b) Democratic

(c) Undemocratic (d) Undemocratic

Q.3 Which of these is not a good argument in favour of democracy? Why?

(a) People feel free and equal in a democracy.

(b) Democracies resolve conflict in a better way than others.

(c) Democratic government is more accountable to the people.

(d) Democracies are more prosperous than others.

Ans. (d) Democracies are more prosperous than others is not a good argument in favour of democracy because countries of the Middle East like UAE and Saudi Arabia are economically strong, but they have non-democratic governments, whereas India is a developing country, but is a democracy.

The poor countries can be democratic while the rich ones may not be. A good monarch can make his country more prosperous than some democracies.

Q.4 Each of these statements contains a democratic and an undemocratic element. Write out the two separately for each statement.

(a) A Minister said that some laws have to be passed by the Parliament in order to conform the regulations decided by the World Trade Organisation.

(b) The Election Commission ordered re-polling in a constituency where large scale rigging was reported.

(c) Women's representation in the Parliament has barely reached 10%. This led women's organisations to demand one-third seats for women.

Ans. (a) Passing of laws by the Parliament is democratic, whereas passing in conformity to the regulations decided by World Trade Organisation (WTO) is undemocratic.

(b) To order repoll in a constituency by the Election Commission is democratic, whereas large scale rigging is undemocratic.

(c) Women's representation in the Parliament never reaching 10% is undemocratic, whereas demand by women's organisations to reserve one-third seats for women is democratic.

Q.5 Which of these is not a valid reason for arguing that there is a lesser possibility of famine in a democratic country?

(a) Opposition parties can draw attention to hunger and starvation.

(b) A free press can report suffering from famine in different parts of the country.

(c) Government fears its defeat in the next elections.

(d) People are free to believe in and practise any religion.

Ans. (d) It is not a valid reason for arguing that there is a lesser possibility of famine in a democratic country, because practising a religion is not related to preventing famines in any way.

Q.6 There are 40 villages in a district where the government has made no provision for drinking water. These villagers met and considered many methods of forcing the government to respond to their need. Which of these is not a democratic method?

(a) Filing a case in the courts claiming that water is part of right to life.

(b) Boycotting the next elections to give a message to all parties.

(c) Organising public meetings against government's policies.

(d) Paying money to government officials to get water.

Ans. (d) It is not a democratic method.

Q.7 Write a response to the following arguments against democracy.

(a) Army is the most disciplined and corruption- free organisation in the country. Therefore, Army should rule the country.

(b) Rule of the majority means the rule of ignorant people. What we need is the rule of the wise, even if they are in small numbers.

(c) If we want religious leaders to guide us in spiritual matters, why not invite them to guide us in politics as well. The country should be ruled by religious leaders.

Ans. (a) This statement is wrong. The Army is for the defence of the country. Its primary duty is defence and not governance. Also, army officers are not elected by people.

(b) This statement is wrong. Rule of majority is democratic, as it represents the views of all sections of people. Illiterate and poor people cannot be called ignorant. At least, they can realise which representative is good for them. Democracy means equal opportunity to all without any discrimination.

(c) This statement is wrong. We should not mix religion and politics, especially in a multi-racial, multi-religious and multi-linguistic country like India. Besides, many religious leaders do not have any experience of administration.

Q.8 Are the following statements in keeping with democracy as a value? Why?

(a) **Father to daughter** I don't want to hear your opinion about your marriage. In our family, children marry where the parents tell them to.

(b) **Teacher to student** Don't disturb my concentration by asking me questions in the classroom.

(c) **Employee to the officer** Our working hours must be reduced according to the law.

Ans. (a) The first statement is undemocratic because a girl is not allowed to give her opinion relating to her own marriage. Just as the people have the right to choose their representatives, the girl should also be allowed to have a role in the selection or choice of her husband.

(b) The second statement is undemocratic because the student is not being allowed to ask questions.

(c) The third statement is democratic because it calls for the reduction of working hours according to the law.

Q.9 Consider the following facts about a country and decide if you would call it a democracy. Give reasons to support your decision.

(a) All the citizens of the country have right to vote. Elections are held regularly.

(b) The country took loan from international agencies. One of the conditions for giving loan was that the government would reduce its expenses on education and health.

(c) People speak more than seven languages but education is available only in one language, the language spoken by 52% people of that country.

(d) Several organisations have given a call for peaceful demonstrations and nationwide strikes in the country to oppose these policies. Government has arrested these leaders.

(e) The government owns the radio and television in the country. All the newspapers have to get permission from the government to publish any news about government's policies and protests.

Ans. (a) A country where all the citizens have a right to vote and elections are held regularly can certainly be called democratic, because the basic conditions are being fulfilled.

(b) Democratic countries are generally welfare states. If a country reduces expenses on education and health, it will definitely harm the people. Thus, the country is undemocratic, as it could only get the loan by reducing its expenses on education and health.

(c) In a multi-lingual country, making any one language as the official language or national language is a complicated situation. In democracy, people should enjoy the freedom to have education in their own language. Thus, the country is undemocratic.

(d) The country is not democratic because the people are not allowed to hold peaceful demonstrations or oppose government policies.

(e) A country which imposes censorship of both print and electronic media is undemocratic because freedom of speech and expression is a fundamental right of the people in a democracy.

REVIEW EXERCISE

Including Competency Based Questions

Part I

Multiple Choice Questions (MCQs)

1. **Democracy is a form of government in which the rulers are elected by**
   (a) rich people (b) royal families
   (c) the king (d) the people

2. **In a democracy, the final decision-making power is in hands of those who are**
   (a) nominated by the government
   (b) elected by the people
   (c) authorised by the President to do so
   (d) authorised by the Prime Minister to do so

3. **Which of the following features of democracy is/are responsible to improve the quality of decision-making?**
   (a) Democracy is based on consultation and discussion
   (b) Democratic decisions always involve many persons
   (c) Decisions are taken after discussions and meetings
   (d) All of the above

4. When did General Pervez Musharraf led a military coup in Pakistan?

(a) October, 1999
(b) July, 1997
(c) August, 2000
(d) April, 2000

5. In which year, General Pervez Musharraf held a referendum which granted him five years extension as a President?

(a) 2004 (b) 2003
(c) 2000 (d) 2002

6. How many members (approx) are elected to the National People's Congress from all over China?

(a) 3000 (b) 3100
(c) 3200 (d) 4000

7. After which regular intervals, elections are held in China for electing the country's Parliament?

(a) 6 years (b) 4 years
(c) 5 years (d) 7 years

8. Since its independence in ...., Mexico holds elections after every six years to elect its President.

(a) 1930 (b) 1928
(c) 1935 (d) 1947

9. Which party always won elections in Mexico since its independence in 1930 until 2000?

(a) Mexican Revolutionary Party
(b) Institutional Revolutionary Party
(c) Socialist Revolutionary Party
(d) Institutional Party

10. One person, One vote means

(a) All person must vote for one person.
(b) Each person has one vote and each vote has one value.
(c) Each person can vote only once in his life.
(d) None of the above

11. When did Zimbabwe attained independence from White minority rule?

(a) 1970 (b) 1980
(c) 1985 (d) 1987

12. Which one of the following is considered as an accountable form of government?

(a) Autocratic government
(b) Dictator government
(c) Democratic government
(d) Military government

13. Which one of the following is not followed in a democratic form of government?

(a) Dignity of citizens
(b) Assurance of political rights to the citizens
(c) Restriction on freedom of speech and expression
(d) Consultation in decision-making

14. What do we mean by a democratic decision?

(a) Decision taken by a Parliament
(b) Decision taken by an executive
(c) Decision taken by the head of a state
(d) Decision taken by discussions and consultations

15. In context of an ideal democracy, "True democracy will come to this country only when no one goes ......"

(a) unemployed (b) landless
(c) hungry to bed (d) None of these

16. Which form of government requires all citizens to take part in politics?

(a) Monarchy (b) Dictatorship
(c) One-party government (d) Democracy

17. Find the incorrect option.

(a) Democracy is based on a fundamental principle of political equality.
(b) Democracy enhances the dignity of citizens.
(c) Democracy leads to corruption, as it is based on electoral competition.
(d) A democratic government is not accountable form of government.

18. Mira, a civic activist in a metropolitan city, noticed an increasing trend in urban planning decisions favouring commercial spaces over green spaces, leading to significant environmental concerns. She decided to understand the impact of such decisions on the city's overall well-being.

Which of the following is least likely to be an outcome of urban planning decisions favouring commercial spaces over green spaces? **Competency Based**

(a) Increased air pollution due to reduced green cover
(b) Enhanced biodiversity within the city
(c) Rising temperatures and urban heat island effect
(d) Degradation of mental health due to lack of natural areas

19. Juan, a 35-years-old man from a country with a history of autocratic rule, has experienced limited access to basic education due to economic hardships. He's concerned about the governance system in his country.

According to the features outlined, which aspect of democracy would potentially address Juan's concerns most effectively? **Competency Based**

(a) Ensuring that elected leaders are accountable to the people
(b) Providing a method to deal with conflicts and differences in society
(c) Guaranteeing the rule of law and respecting citizens' rights
(d) Making sure every citizen has equal information and resources for decision-making

20. **It is unthinkable that there will be no elections. If there are no elections, there will be no democracy.**
Source : The Indian Express
What fundamental principle about democracy does the headline emphasise? **Competency Based**
(a) The necessity of electoral competition for effective governance
(b) The significance of consistent leadership in a democratic system
(c) The direct correlation between elections and the existence of democracy
(d) The importance of avoiding electoral delays for a functional democracy.

21. **Considering the principles and features of democracy, which of the following statements aligns most closely with the fundamental characteristics of democratic decision-making?** **Competency Based**
(a) "Democracy solely relies on the majority opinion without considering the concerns of the minority groups."
(b) "In a democracy, the government's decisions should not be restricted by constitutional laws and citizens' rights."
(c) "Equal participation of citizens in decision-making is crucial for democracy, necessitating equitable access to information, education, resources and commitment."
(d) "Democracy thrives on decisions made by a selected elite group to ensure efficiency and progress, excluding broader public involvement."

22. **Why is the principle of one person, one vote, one value considered crucial in a democracy?**
(a) It ensures that every citizen's vote carries equal weight regardless of their background or status, promoting political equality within a society. This upholds the fundamental principle of democracy where each individual has an equal say in decision-making.
(b) It emphasises the value of wealth and social standing in determining the significance of one's vote, creating an imbalance in political representation and decision-making.
(c) It allows certain sections of society, such as the elite or educated individuals, to wield greater influence in the electoral process, thereby restricting the fair distribution of power among citizens.
(d) It discourages certain groups, particularly marginalised communities, from participating in the democratic process, thereby undermining the core principle of inclusive governance.

23. **Arrange the following in correct sequence.**
I. Military coup in Pakistan
II. Legal Framework Order in Pakistan
III. Mexico got its independence
IV. Zimbabwe attained independence

Codes
(a) IV, II, III, I (b) III, IV, I, II
(c) I, II, III, IV (d) II, I, IV, III

24. **Identify the distinguishing characteristics of a democratic government based on the provided information. Choose the appropriate options from the following statements** **Competency Based**
I. Rulers in a democracy are appointed through hereditary succession.
II. The final decision-making power in a democracy lies with military officers.
III. Free and fair elections constitute a fundamental aspect of democracy.
IV. Democracy primarily relies on one person's absolute authority in decision-making.

Options
(a) Statements I and III are appropriate.
(b) Statements II and IV are appropriate.
(c) Statement III is appropriate.
(d) Statements I and IV are appropriate.

25. **Consider the statements given below and choose the correct answer.** **Competency Based**
Statement I General Pervez Musharraf assumed power in Pakistan through a military coup in 1999 and extended his rule via a controversial referendum granting himself an additional five years.
Statement II The Institutional Revolutionary Party (PRI) consistently won elections in Mexico until 2000, employing alleged unfair tactics that hindered genuine opposition success.

Codes
(a) Statement I is correct, but statement II is incorrect.
(b) Statement I is incorrect, but statement II is correct.
(c) Both statements I and II are incorrect.
(d) Both statements I and II are correct.

Answers

1. (d)	**2.** (b)	**3.** (d)	**4.** (a)	**5.** (d)
6. (a)	**7.** (c)	**8.** (a)	**9.** (b)	**10.** (b)
11. (b)	**12.** (c)	**13.** (c)	**14.** (d)	**15.** (c)
16. (d)	**17.** (d)	**18.** (b)	**19.** (c)	**20.** (c)
21. (c)	**22.** (a)	**23.** (b)	**24.** (c)	**25.** (d)

Match the Following

1.

List I	List II
A. Legal Framework Order	1. Ruling party in China
B. National People's Congress	2. Issued by Musharraf
C. Institutional Revolutionary Party	3. Leader Robert Mugabe
D. ZANU-PF	4. Formed in 1930 in Mexico

Codes

	A	B	C	D		A	B	C	D
(a)	2	1	4	3	(b)	1	2	3	4
(c)	4	1	2	3	(d)	3	4	1	2

Ans. (a)

Assertion-Reason

1. Assertion (A) A democratic government can do whatever it likes, simply because it has won an election.

Reason (R) A democratic government rules within limits set by constitutional law and citizen's rights.

Codes

(a) Both A and R are correct and R is the correct explanation of A
(b) Both A and R are correct, but R is not the correct explanation of A
(c) A is true, but R is false
(d) A is false, but R is true

2. Assertion (A) Democracy is a form of government where rulers are chosen through free and fair elections.

Reason (R) In a democracy, decision-making power rests with those who are elected by the people.

Codes

(a) Both A and R are correct and R is the correct explanation of A
(b) Both A and R are correct, but R is not the correct explanation of A
(c) A is true, but R is false
(d) A is false, but R is true

3. Assertion (A) Democracy requires a constant effort to weaken democratic forms of decision-making.

Reason (R) Every citizen in a democracy must have equal information, basic education, resources and commitment to play an equal role in decision-making.

Codes

(a) Both A and R are correct and R is the correct explanation of A
(b) Both A and R are correct, but R is not the correct explanation of A
(c) A is true, but R is false
(d) A is false, but R is true

4. Assertion (A) Democracy improves the quality of decision-making by involving consultation and discussion.

Reason (R) Democratic governments are less accountable to the people.

Codes

(a) Both A and R are correct and R is the correct explanation of A
(b) Both A and R are correct, but R is not the correct explanation of A
(c) A is true, but R is false
(d) A is false, but R is true

Ans. 1. (d) A is false, but R is true
2. (a) Both A and R are correct and R is the correct explanation of A
3. (d) A is false, but R is true
4. (c) A is true, but R is false

Picture Based Questions

1. What is the message given by the people in this image?

(a) Equality of right to vote and equal value of each man's vote.
(b) Elections must offer a real choice between political parties.
(c) Political equality is a right of each individual.
(d) None of the above

2. What does the crown of leaves on democracy in the picture represent?

(a) Sign of victory (b) Sign of wisdom
(c) Sign of loss (d) None of these

3. What event does the given picture represent?

(a) Massacre in Tiananmen square in 1989.
(b) Restriction by Chinese Government on Internet
(c) Chinese Government declaring war.
(d) None of the above

4. What does the hidden side of the dictator in the picture depicts?

(a) Government or social situation
(b) Courage of the dictator
(c) Brutal side of the dictator
(d) None of the above

5. What does this cartoon imply about the politician's attitude towards poverty alleviation?

(a) The politician is proud of the progress made in poverty alleviation and wants to celebrate it.
(b) The politician is indifferent to the problem of poverty and does not care about the people's needs.
(c) The politician is aware of the problem of poverty but does not have the will or the means to solve it.
(d) The politician is optimistic about the future and believes that poverty will be eradicated soon.

Ans. 1. (a) Equality of right to vote and equal value of each man's vote.
2. (a) Sign of victory
3. (b) Restriction by Chinese Government on Internet
4. (c) Brutal side of the dictator
5. (b) The politician is indifferent to the problem of poverty and does not care about the people's needs.

Case Based Question

1. Read the source given below and answer the questions that follow.

Party called PRI (Institutional Revolutionary Party). Opposition parties did contest elections, but never managed to win. The PRI was known to use many dirty tricks to win elections. All those who were employed in government offices had to attend its party meetings. Teachers of government schools used to force parents to vote for the PRI. Media largely ignored the activities of opposition political parties except to criticize them. Sometimes the polling booths were shifted from one place to another in the last minute, which made it difficult for people to cast their votes. The PRI spent a large sum of money in the campaign for its candidates. Should we consider the elections described above as examples of people electing their rulers?

(i) Which one problem highlighted regarding elections in China?
(a) Lack of eligible candidates
(b) Limited choice for voters
(c) Excessive interference by the ruling party
(d) Unfair voting procedures

(ii) What is the main issue with elections in Mexico?
(a) Lack of voter turnout
(b) Manipulation of election results
(c) Absence of political alternatives
(d) Unreliable polling stations

(iii) Which one of the following features is not suggested for understanding democracy?
(a) Transparency in government proceedings
(b) Open access to political information
(c) Freedom of speech
(d) Leader keep changing in a democracy

(iv) Democracy ensures which key aspects regarding elections
(a) No elections
(b) Limited voter participation
(c) Both (a) and (b)
(d) Universal Adult Suffrage

Ans. (i) (b) Limited choice for voters
(ii) (b) Manipulation of election results
(iii) (d) Leader keep changing in a democracy
(iv) (d) Universal Adult Suffrage

Part II

Very Short Answer Type Questions

1. Which country out of France, USA, Myanmar and India is not a true democratic country?

Ans. Myanmar is not a true democratic country because it is ruled by military rulers.

2. What was the designation taken by Pervez Musharraf for himself when he overthrew the democratic government of Pakistan in 1999?

Ans. General Pervez Musharraf declared himself the Chief Executive of Pakistan when he overthrew the democratic government of Pakistan, in 1999.

3. With what motive did General Pervez Musharraf issue a 'Legal Framework Order' in August, 2002?

Ans. The motive was to ensure that he had the ultimate power to decide how he wanted Pakistan to be ruled.

4. Suggest one of the important features of democracy.

Ans. One important feature of democracy is that the final decision-making power rests with those elected by the people.

5. Which party always forms the government in China?

Ans. The Communist Party of China always forms the Government in China.

6. What is the name of the Chinese Parliament?

Ans. The name of the Chinese Parliament is National People's Congress ('Quanguo Renmin Daibiao Dahui' in Chinese Mandarin language).

7. From 1930, which country holds elections after every six years and which has never been under a military or dictator's rule?

Ans. The country is Mexico.

8. Do the women of Saudi Arabia have the right to vote?

Ans. Till 2015, the women of Saudi Arabia did not have the right to vote. But now, they have been given this right.

9. Everyone understands that the basic principle of parliamentary democracy is the accountability of the Council of Ministers to Parliament. Its time has been wasted, the history of parliamentary democracy has been besmirched in our country.

Competency Based

Source: Economic Times

(I) In a parliamentary democracy, the accountability of the Council of Ministers to Parliament is fundamental. How does this principle align with the key features of democracy?

Ans. (i) The principle of collective responsibility of the Council of Ministers to Parliament ensures that the executive is accountable to the legislature for its policies and actions, and that the legislature can scrutinise and criticise the executive through various means. It prevents the concentration of power in one person or party and promotes a system of checks and balances among different organs of the state.

10. A group of students is discussing various forms of government. Sarah argues that democracy is the most accountable form of government. Tom disagrees, stating that democracy can lead to instability due to frequent changes in leadership. Using the provided information, discuss Sarah's viewpoints regarding the accountability and stability of a democratic government, providing examples to support your explanation.

Competency Based

Ans. Sarah's view emphasises democracy's accountability through citizen involvement and decision making quality. For instance, Zimbabwe's case reflects how lack of accountability led to rights violation.

Short Answer Type Questions

1. Mention three essential features of democracy.

Or What is democracy? What are its two features?

Ans. Democracy is a form of government in which the rulers are elected by the people.

Some features of democracy are

(i) A democracy must be based on a free and fair election, where those currently in power have a fair chance of losing.

(ii) In a democracy, each adult citizen must have one vote and each vote must have one value.

(iii) In a democracy, government rules within limits set by constitutional law and citizens' rights.

2. Why are China, Estonia and Saudi Arabia not truly democratic countries? State one reason for each one of them.

Or Why are China and Saudi Arabia non-democratic countries though they declare themselves as democracies? State one reason for each of the countries.

Ans. China, Estonia and Saudi Arabia are not truly democratic countries because

(i) In China, before contesting the election, the candidate needs the approval of the Chinese Communist Party.

(ii) Estonia made its citizenship rules in such a manner that people belonging to Russian minority find it difficult to get the right to vote.

(iii) In Saudi Arabia, women did not have the right to vote, until 2015.

Although these countries declare themselves as democracies, the fundamental principle of 'political equality ' is denied in all the cases. Thus, these are not truly democratic countries.

3. State the freedoms which are usually taken away when democracy is overthrown by a military regime.

Ans. The freedoms usually taken away by a military regime are

- There will be no freedom of expression and speech.
- In a non-democratic government, the rulers do not have to act according to the wishes of the people. The needs of the people can be ignored by the military ruler.
- In democracy, no one is a permanent loser or winner. But in a military regime, the same ruler or ruling party can rule the country for a very long time.
- In a military regime, there is no freedom to form political associations or organise protests and political action. Political freedom of the citizen is completely denied in a military regime.

4. Is China a democratic country? Give two arguments in favour of your answer.

Or **China is a communist country where elections are held after every five years but still it cannot be called a democratic country. Explain the reason.**

Ans. China is not a democratic country because

(i) For contesting election to the Chinese Parliament, the candidates need the approval of the Chinese Communist Party. The people contesting the elections, should be the member of any of the eight parties only. No other party is allowed to contest in the elections.

(ii) There is one party rule, i.e. Communist Party of China, which is not the indication of a true democracy.

5. 'Till 2000, Mexican people seem to have a choice to elect their leader, but practically they had no choice.' Support this statement with three suitable reasons.

Ans. In Mexico, people seemed to have a choice as elections were held regularly. But in practice, they had no choice because there was no way the ruling party could be defeated even if most of the people were against it.

Until the elections held in the year 2000, every election in Mexico was won by a party called PRI (Institutional Revolutionary Party). Opposition parties did contest elections, but never managed to win due to illegal means used by PRI to win elections such as

- Government employees were forced to attend party meetings.
- Teachers in government schools forced students' parents to vote for the PRI.
- Media mostly ignored the activities of opposition political parties except criticising them.
- Sometimes polling booths were shifted from one place to another at the last minute, making it difficult for people to cast their votes.
- The PRI spent a large sum of money in the campaign for its candidates.

6. 'Democracy is all about political competition and power play. There is no scope for morality'. Justify the statement by giving arguments against democracy.

Ans. It is a fact that in a democracy, the majority decides what is to be done, whether it is right or wrong. Thus it is a play of power, whether it is morally right or wrong.

The arguments against democracy are

(i) Democracy leads to corruption, as it is based on electoral competition. Elections can be won by money power, muscle power or both.

(ii) Many elected leaders do not work for the best interest of the people as their interest lies in political competition and winning the elections only.

(iii) Bad, unwise and faulty decisions are sometimes taken, as there is power play in democracy.

7. "Democracy is considered the best form of government and is clearly better than any other alternative." Mention three relevant points that show what it offers.

Ans. The three relevant points that show what democracy offers are

(i) A democratic government is a more accountable form of government. A democracy requires that the rulers have to attend to the needs of the people.

(ii) Democracy is based on negotiation and deliberation, which improves the quality of decision-making.

(iii) It allows us to correct our own mistakes. In democracy, there is always a scope that the rulers can change their wrong decisions or the rulers themselves can be changed.

8. How does democracy improve the quality of decision-making?

Ans. Democracy improve the equality of decision making in the following ways

- Democracy is based on consultation and discussion.
- A democratic decision always involves many persons, discussions and meetings. Those who are not powerful have the same say in taking the decisions as those who are powerful.
- The elected representatives come from different backgrounds. They all are given equal say to tell their views on a particular issue.

9. Explain the meaning of representative democracy. How is it significant in the contemporary world?

Ans Representative democracy is a form of government founded on the principle of elected individuals representing the people, as opposed to autocracy and direct democracy.

Representative democracy is significant in the contemporary world due to the following reasons

(i) The representatives form an independent ruling body charged with the responsibility of acting in the people's interest.

(ii) Today representative democracies are much more common than direct democracies.

(iii) Representative democracy usually has a Parliament. The members of Parliament are elected through universal adult franchise.

(iv) This practice enhances the dignity of citizens.

10. "A democratic government is more accountable to the people and involves various features that distinguish it from other forms of governance." Competency Based

(i) Explain how the concept of accountability manifests within a democratic government.

(ii) Explain three distinct features of democracy that set it apart from other forms of governance.

Ans. (i) Accountability in a democratic government refers to the obligation of elected representatives to answer to the citizens for their actions and decisions. In democracies, leaders are held responsible for their conduct through various mechanisms such as regular elections, transparency in decision-making and responsiveness to public concerns.

(ii) Features distinguishing democracy from other forms of governance are

(i) **Free and Fair Elections** The main feature of democracy is to conduct free and fair elections.

(ii) **Rule of Law and Citizen Rights** Democracies operate under the rule of law, ensuring that leaders are bound by constitutional limitations and citizen rights are protected.

(iii) **Accountability to Citizens** In democracies, leaders are accountable to the citizens.

11. Evaluate the impact on governance if a country were to operate without any democratic principles. Elaborate on the consequences based on the following factors. Competency Based

- **Decision-making quality and efficiency**
- **Handling conflicts and differences within the society**

Ans. If a country were to operate without any democratic principles, it would have a very negative impact on governance. Some of the consequences are

- Without democracy, the government would not have to consult with various stakeholders or experts before making decisions. The government would not have to consider the interests and preferences of different groups or sectors in society or balance competing values and goals.
- Without democracy, the government would not have to respect the diversity and pluralism of society. The government would not have to accommodate different opinions or perspectives or foster dialogue and cooperation among different groups or individuals.

12. Read the statements given below regarding the features and facets of democracy. Competency Based

Statement 1 (S1) Democracy enhances the dignity of citizens by providing equality in decision-making.

Statement 2 (S2) The involvement of electoral competition in a democracy gives rise to corruption.

Explain how these statements - S1 and S2 - reflect the dual nature of democracy in its advantages and challenges. Use relevant examples or arguments to support your explanation.

Ans. Statement 1 highlights democracy's core aspect of providing equal dignity through participation. However, Statement 2 acknowledges the challenge of corruption linked to electoral competition.

Democracy treats everyone equally but faces issues like corruption due to fierce competition during elections. This shows that while democracy respects people, it needs strong solutions to fight corruption caused by competitive politics, displaying both its benefits and challenges for citizens.

This dual nature signifies that while democracy uplifts citizenry, it demands strong measures to tackle corruption arising from competitive politics. This shows how democracy express essential features of both empowerment and challenges for citizens.

13. Mr. Z, a local activist in a developing country, notices a community struggling with corrupt practices affecting local elections. Several candidates use unethical means to influence voters, compromising the fairness of the electoral process.

How can Mr. Z address this issue to uphold the integrity of democracy in the community and ensure fair representation in governance? Competency Based

Ans. Mr. Z, the local activist, could combat corrupt electoral practices by initiating voter education campaigns. He can organise workshops, seminars and public discussions to raise awareness about ethical voting and the impact of corrupt practices on democracy.

Collaborating with authorities and NGOs, he can establish anonymous reporting channels for electoral misconduct. Mr. Z may also engage community leaders to advocate for fair elections, encouraging citizens to prioritise candidates with transparent agendas.

These actions can encourage the community's commitment to uphold democratic values and ensuring just representation in governance.

Long Answer Type Questions

1. Why Pakistan under General Musharraf can not be called a democracy? State any five reasons.

Ans. Pakistan under General Musharraf cannot be called a democracy due to following reasons

(i) General Musharraf conducted a military regime in October 1999, overthrowing a democratically elected government.

(ii) In 2002, Musharraf organised a referendum which, was based on malpractices and fraud.

(iii) In August 2002, Musharraf issued a 'Legal Framework Order' to give him the power to dismiss the national and provincial assemblies, which is undemocratic.

(iv) The work of the civilian cabinet was supervised by a National Security Council dominated by military officers, none of whom were elected. This is also undemocratic.

(v) In a democracy, elections were held and the elected representatives have some powers. However, in this case the final power rested with military officers and General Musharraf himself, which is against democracy.

2. How did Robert Mugabe's party ZANU PF violate the features of a democratically elected government?

Ans. Robert Mugabe's party ZANU PF violated the features of a democratically elected government by adopting the following methods

- The Constitution was changed several times to increase the powers of the President and make him less accountable. A law had been made for limiting the right to criticise the President.
- Opposition party workers were harassed and their meetings were disrupted.
- Public protests and demonstrations against the government were declared illegal.
- Television and radio were controlled by the government and gave only the ruling party's version.
- The government harassed those journalists who went against it.
- The government ignored some court judgements that went against it and had pressurised judges.

3. What are the difficulties people face in non-democratic countries?

Ans. People face the following difficulties in non-democratic countries

- People have no security of life. For example, in Chile, thousands of people were killed by military rulers.
- People are not free to express their opinions. Criticising the government or rulers in a non-democratic country would lead to severe punishments.
- There is no freedom for the people either to elect their government or to be elected. Even if they find any government or rulers not benefiting them or looking after their well-being, they cannot change them.
- No opposition parties or opposition leader is tolerated.
- In the absence of a democratic government, there is no socio-economic equality. Societies in such countries remain divided among privileged and non-privileged classes, which results in corruption in every department of the government.
- Ordinary people cannot aspire for any good post. People are always at the mercy of the autocratic ruler or the dictator.

4. A local council is interested in implementing democratic principles in its decision-making processes.

Outline the key steps this council should take to ensure effective democratic decision-making. Discuss why these steps are fundamental in fostering a democratic environment within a local governing body. **Competency Based**

Ans. The local council should take following steps to make sure its decisions are democratic.

- Make its work clear and open to the public. It should have meetings, forums and ways for people to share their opinions and needs.
- Teach the people about democracy and how they can take part in it. It should give them the information and skills they need to join in the decision-making.
- Have rules and limits to stop some people or groups from having too much power and becoming dictators.
- Make decisions together with all the people who are affected by them. It should make them feel responsible for the decisions.

These steps are important because they make the council more honest, fair, respectful, and responsive to the people, which are the main qualities of a good democracy at the local level.

5. A famous Politician criticised the Indian government over the suspension of over 140 MPs, calling it a "travesty of parliamentary democracy." He claimed that no country had ever suspended or expelled 150 lawmakers in the history of parliamentary democracy. He argued that the government's refusal to discuss a security breach in Parliament led to the opposition's protest, and the reaction to the protest was disproportionate.

Source: Economic Times

Analyse the event which formed the principles of democracy, accountability and fair representation. Discuss these principles. **Competency Based**

Ans. The principles of democracy, accountability and fair representation is the event of the suspension of over 140 MPs from the Indian Parliament.

These principles are discussed below

- **Democracy** is a system where the people chose their leaders and have a say in how they are governed. One of the features of democracy is participation, which means that all citizens have the right to take part in the political process, mainly through voting. By suspending the MPs, the government may be seen as undermining the voice and choice of the people who elected them and reducing their representation in the Parliament.
- **Accountability** is another feature of democracy, which means that the elected representatives are answerable to the people who elected them, and can be removed from office if they fail to perform their duties. The government may argue that the suspension of the MPs was a way of holding them accountable for their disorderly conduct and disruption of the House proceedings. However, the opposition may contend that the suspension was arbitrary and undemocratic, and violated their right to dissent and demand explanations from the government on the security breach issue.
- **Fair representation** is a principle that ensures that all groups and sectors in society have equal access to the free enjoyment of their rights and opportunities, and that their interests and preferences are considered and balanced in decision-making. The suspension of the MPs may affect the fair representation of the opposition parties and their constituencies in the Parliament and may create an imbalance of power and influence in favour of the ruling party.

Case Based Questions

1. Read the sources given below and answer the questions that follow.

Source A Free and fair electoral competition

In the Mexican example, people seemed to really have a choice but in practice they had no choice. There was no way the ruling party could be defeated, even if people were against it. These are not fair elections.

(i) To what extent do you think that Mexico is not a democratic country?

Source B What is Democracy?

The army rulers of Myanmar were not elected by the people. Those who happened to be in control of the army became the rulers of the country. People had no say in this decision. Dictators like Pinochet (Chile) are not elected by the people. This also applies to monarchies. The kings of Saudi Arabia rule not because the people have chosen them to do so but because they happen to be born into the royal family.

(ii) What similarity can be seen in the political structures of different countries mentioned here.

Source C One person, One Vote, One Value

In Fiji, the electoral system is such that the vote of an indigenous Fiji has more value than that of an Indian-Fijian. Democracy is based on a fundamental principle of political equality.

That gives us the third feature of democracy: in a democracy, each adult citizen must have one vote and each vote must have one value.

(iii) In your opinion can Fiji be called a democracy?

Ans. (i) Mexico cannot be considered a democratic country. To a certain extent, it is a democracy as elections are held. However, people have no choice as the ruling party cannot be defeated.This means elections are not held in a fair and clean way, so it cannot be considered as a democracy.

(ii) The political structures of the countries mentioned in the paragraph are Myanmar, Chile and Saudi Arabia. The political structures show that these countries are monarchies and there is no democracy. Military rule in Myanmar, Dictatorship in Chile and rule by Royal family in Saudi Arabia shows the absence of democracy.

(iii) To a certain extent, Fiji is a democratic country because government is chosen by the system of elections. However, the electoral system points to a loophole. Indian-Fijian's vote has less value than indigenous Fijian. Therefore, the country does not practice true democracy.

2. Read the source given below and answer the questions that follow.

China's famine of 1958-1961 was the worst recorded famine in world history. Nearly three crore people died in this famine. During those day, India's economic condition was not much better than China. Yet India did not have a famine of the kind China had. Economists think that this was a result of different government policies in the two countries. The existence of democracy in India made the Indian government respond to food scarcity in a way that the Chinese government did not.

They point out that no large-scale famine has ever taken place in an independent and democratic country. If China too had multiparty elections, an opposition party and a press full to criticise the government, then so many people may not have died in the famine.

This example brings out one of the reasons why democracy is considered the best form of government Democracy is better than any other form of government in responding to the needs of the people. A non-democratic government may and can respond to the people's needs, but it all depends on the wishes of the people who rule.

(i) Policies adopted by a democratic government can change the condition of people in the country. Comment.

(ii) Explain with example, that democratic government is more responsive.

(iii) What did the Economists think on comparing the situation of India and China?

Ans. (i) The policies adopted by a democratic government are directed towards the welfare of the people. The Indian government's policy to reduce food scarcity resulted in avoidance of any large scale famines in the country. But China, inspite of being better economically developed than India, suffered from famine. This shows that policies of a democratic government can change the condition of the people.

(ii) Democracy is better and more responsive than any other form of government because it responds to the needs of the people. For instance, if China too had multiparty elections, an opposition party and a press which is free to criticise the government, then alot of people may not have died in the famine. Democratic government is always more responsible towards the needs of the people.

(iii) The Economists think that this was the result of different government policies in the two countries. The existence of democracy in India made the Indian government respond to food scarcity in a way that Chinese government did not. They point out that no large-scale famine has ever taken place in an independent and democratic country.

ASSESSMENT EXERCISE

Multiple Choice Questions (MCQs)

1. A democracy must be based on which type of elections?
(a) Proportional election (b) Free and fair election
(c) Both (a) and (b) (d) None of these

2. In which one of the following countries women did not have the right to vote until 2025?
(a) Pakistan (b) Nepal
(c) Afghanistan (d) Saudi Arabia

3. Which form of government requires all citizens to take part in politics?
(a) Monarchy (b) Dictatorship
(c) One-party government (d) Democracy

4. Find the incorrect option.
(a) A democratic government can do whatever it likes because it has won an election.
(b) Democratic government has to respect some basic rules.
(c) Every office bearer has certain rights and responsibilities assigned by the Constitution.
(d) None of the above

Subjective Questions (VSA, SA & LA)

1. What is democracy in simple term?

2. When did General Musharraf bring back army rule in Pakistan?

3. How is the President of China elected?

4. What are the various forms of government? Describe them in brief.

5. Compare the democratic system in China with that of Mexico.

6. How does democracy enhance the dignity of citizens?

7. Assess any three conditions that apply to the way a democratic government is run after the elections.

8. Political parties in Bangladesh have agreed that a neutral government should rule the country at the time of elections. How will this ensure free and fair electoral competition?

9. 'It is said that democracy is not an ideal form of government'. How should democracy be improved to make it an ideal form of government?

10. Is India a democratic country? Write any three arguments in favour of your answer.

11. According to you, what is the strongest argument for democracy? How does it make the people the rulers?

12. 'Democracy is based on consultation and discussion'. Explain this statement.

Constitutional Design

CHAPTER 2

In a democracy, there are specific rules that both citizens and the government must follow. These rules collectively form the Constitution, which is the supreme law of the country. The Constitution outlines the rights of citizens, defines the powers of the government, and guides how the government should function.

2.1 Democratic Constitution in South Africa

South Africa became independent and got its democratic Constitution[1] after a long struggle for freedom. **Nelson Mandela** fought for its freedom and for rights and equality among black and white people.

Alongwith seven other leaders, Nelson Mandela was sentenced to life imprisonment in 1964 for opposing the apartheid[2] regime. He spent 27 years in South Africa's most dreaded (fearful) prison, Robben Island.

Struggle against Apartheid

Apartheid was the name of a system of racial discrimination unique to South Africa. It was imposed by the white Europeans on South Africa.

In the 17th and 18th centuries, European trading companies took control of South Africa by force.

Unlike India, many **whites** settled there and became the rulers. Due to this settlement of whites, the system of apartheid divided the people on the basis of their skin colour.

The native people of South Africa made up about three-fourth of the population and were called **blacks.** Besides these two classes, there were people of mixed classes who were called **coloured** and **migrated Indians.**

The white rulers treated all non-whites as inferiors. The apartheid system particularly oppressed the blacks in the following ways

- The non-whites did not have voting rights and they were forbidden from living in white areas.
- The non-whites could work in white areas only if they had a permit.
- Trains, buses and all the public places like hotels, cinema halls, theatres, beaches, swimming pools, public toilets, etc were separate for the whites and blacks. This was known as **segregation.**
- Blacks could not enter a church where the whites worshipped. They did not even have the right to form associations or protest against the whites.

Since 1950, the blacks, coloured and Indians fought against the apartheid system. They launched protest marches and strikes. **The African National Congress** (ANC) led the movement.

Many workers' unions, the Communist Party and sensitive whites joined the ANC to oppose apartheid. Apartheid was declared unjust and racist by several countries.

However, the white racist government continued to rule by detaining, torturing and killing thousands of black and coloured people.

Towards a New Constitution

As protest and struggles against apartheid had increased, the government changed its policies by repealing discriminatory laws. Ban on political parties and restrictions on the media were removed.

After spending 28 years in jail, Nelson Mandela was released. Finally at the midnight of 26th April, 1994, the new democratic state of the Republic[3] of South Africa emerged. The apartheid government came to an end, paving the way for the formation of a multi-racial government.

---

1 Constitution It is the supreme law of a country, containing fundamental rules governing the politics and society in a country.

2 Apartheid It was the official policy of racial separation and ill-treatment of blacks followed by the government of South Africa between 1948 and 1989.

3 Republic It refers to a country in which the Head of State is elected and is not hereditary.

Equality of Races in South Africa

After the emergence of the democratic South Africa, black leaders appealed to fellow blacks to forgive the whites for the atrocities they had committed while in power.

They wanted to build up a new South Africa based on equality of all races and men and women on democratic values, social justice and human rights.

The party that ruled through oppression and the party that led the freedom struggle compromised together to draw up a common Constitution.

They made a Constitution after two years of discussion which gave to its citizens the most extensive rights available in any country.

The **Preamble**[4] to the South African Constitution outlines that everybody should become part of the solution to every problem, irrespective of whatever they might have done or represented in the past.

The South African Constitution inspires democrats all over the world. Thus, South Africa became a model of **democracy**[5].

Try These

1. In which year was Nelson Mandela sentenced to life imprisonment?
2. Where did Mandela spend 28 years for opposing apartheid?
3. Name the organisation that led the struggle against apartheid in South Africa.
4. The New Democratic State of the Republic of South Africa emerged on which date?

2.2 Need for the Constitution

The South African example helps us understand why a Constitution is needed. In their new democracy, both the black majority and white minority had to live together as equals despite their mistrust and fears. The black majority wanted majority rule and social rights, while the white minority wanted to protect their privileges and property.

After tough negotiations, they reached a compromise. The whites accepted majority rule and basic rights for the poor, while the blacks agreed that majority rule wouldn't take away the property of the minority. To ensure trust, they wrote down rules that everyone had to follow. These rules decided how rulers would be chosen, their powers, and citizens' rights. These rules, which no government could easily change, became their Constitution.

This need for a Constitution is not unique to South Africa. Every country and group with diverse people needs basic rules to resolve differences. Whether it's a government, club, or society, a Constitution sets the rules for working together.

Constitution is required to safeguard the interests of common people; whether they belong to major community or minor community. Thus, the Constitution of a country is a set of written rules that are accepted by all people living together in a country.

The Constitution is the supreme law that determines the relationship among people living in a territory (called citizens) and also the relationship between the people and government.

A Constitution is needed for the following reasons

- It generates a degree of trust and coordination among people that is necessary for the different kinds of people living together.
- It specifies how the government will be constituted and who will have the power to take decisions.
- It lays down limits to the powers of the government and also specifies the rights of the citizens.
- It also expresses the aspirations of the people about creating a good society.

Not every nation with a Constitution is a democratic nation. However, Constitutions are a feature of all democratic nations.

2.3 Making of the Indian Constitution

India's Constitution was drawn up under very difficult circumstances. The making of the Constitution for a huge and diverse country like India was not an easy affair. The country was born through a partition on the basis of religious differences. Atleast 10 lakh people were killed on both sides of the border.

The British left the decision to the rulers of princely states i.e. to merge with India or Pakistan, or remain independent. The Constitution-makers were anxious about the present and future of the nation.

The Path to Constitution

The **consensus**[6] of creating the Indian Constitution had evolved during the freedom struggle.

4 **Preamble** It refers to an introductory statement in a Constitution which states the reasons and guiding values of the Constitution.

5 **Democracy** It is a form of government which is chosen by the people to work for their welfare.

6 **Consensus** It refers to a general agreement among a group of people.

There were different views regarding what path India should take after Independence, but some basic ideas were accepted by everyone.

In 1928, **Motilal Nehru** and eight other Congress leaders drafted a Constitution for India. At the **Karachi Session** of the **Indian National Congress** in 1931, the leaders decided how the Indian Constitution should look like.

Some important principles like Universal Adult Franchise, Right to Freedom and Equality, Rights of Minorities, etc were included in the Constitutions. Some basic values were accepted by all leaders, much before the Constituent Assembly met to deliberate on the Constitution.

Colonial rule influenced the design of political institutions. Under British rule, only a few people had voting rights, and the British created weak legislatures based on this limited voting system. In 1937, elections for **Provincial Legislatures**[7] and **Ministries** were held all over British India. These were not fully democratic **governments**. The Indian Constitution adopted many institutional details and procedures from colonial laws like the **Government of India Act, 1935.**

Many of our leaders were inspired by the ideals of the French Revolution, the Socialist Revolution of Russia, the practice of Parliamentary democracy in Britain and the Bill of Rights in the US.

The **Socialist Revolution in Russia** had inspired many Indians to think of shaping a system based on social and economic equality.

They didn't just copy what others did. At every step, they asked if these ideas were right for our country. All of this helped in making our Constitution.

The Constituent Assembly

The drafting of the Constitution was done by an assembly of elected representatives called the Constituent Assembly.

Elections to the Constituent Assembly were held in July 1946. Its **first meeting** was held in December 1946. After partition of India and Pakistan, the Constituent Assembly was divided into Constituent Assemblies of India and Pakistan. The Constituent Assembly that wrote the Indian Constitution constituted 299 members.

The Assembly adopted the Constitution on 26th November, 1949 but it came into effect on 26th January, 1950. To mark this day, 26th January is celebrated as **Republic Day** every year.

The Assembly was dominated by the Indian National Congress, which included a variety of political and regional groups of people.

It also represented members from different language groups, castes, classes, religions and occupations.

Finally, the Constituent Assembly worked in a systematic, open and consensual (with mutual consent) manner, which gave sacred quality to the Constitution.

First some basic principles were decided and agreed upon. Then, **Drafting Committee** under the Chairmanship of **Dr BR Ambedkar** prepared a **draft**[8] Constitution for discussion.

The discussion on the drafting the Constitution took place **clause**[9] by clause. More than two thousands amendments were considered. The members of the Drafting Committee completed the work in 114 days spread over three years.

More than two thousand **Constitutional amendments**[10] were made. Every document presented and every word spoken in the Constituent Assembly has been recorded and preserved. These are called **Constituent Assembly**[11] **Debates** and have been printed in 12 bulky volumes.

These debates provide the reason behind every provision of the Constitution and are used to interpret the meaning of the Constitution.

Important Members of Constituent Assembly

- **Sardar Vallabhbhai Patel (1875-1950)** He was a lawyer and leader of Bardoli Peasant Satyagraha. He was **Deputy Prime Minister** and Minister of Home, Information and Broadcasting in the Interim Government. He played a decisive role in the integration of the Indian princely states.

7 **Provincial Legislature** It is a governing body that makes laws and can also amend and repeal them.
8 **Draft** A preliminary version of a legal document.
9 **Clause** A distinct section of a document.
10 **Constitutional Amendment** A change in the Constitution made by the Supreme legislative body in a country.
11 **Constituent Assembly** It is a body assembled for the purpose of drafting the Constitution.

- **Sarojini Naidu (1879-1949)** She was a poet, writer and political activist. She was among the foremost women leaders in the Congress. Later on she was appointed as **Governor** of Uttar Pradesh.
- **Dr Rajendra Prasad (1884-1963)** He was the President of the Constituent Assembly. He was lawyer and known for his role in the Champaran Satyagraha. He was the **President of Congress** three times. Later on he became the **First President** of India.
- **H C Mookherjee (1887-1956)** He was **Vice-Chairman** of the Constituent Assembly, reputed author, educationist, Congress leader, member of All India Christian Council and a member of the Bengal Legislative Assembly.
- **Kanhaiyalal Maniklal Munshi (1887-1971)** He was an Advocate, Historian and Linguist. He was also a Congress leader and Gandhian. Later, he became the minister in the Union Cabinet and founder of the Swatantra Party.
- **Abul Kalam Azad (1888-1958)** He was an educationist, author, theologian, scholar of Arabic, Congress leader and active in the national movement. He opposed Muslim separatist politics. He was the first Education Minister in first Union Cabinet.
- **Pt Jawaharlal Nehru (1889-1964)** He was the first Prime Minister of the Interim Government. He was a lawyer and Congress leader and was an advocate of socialism, democracy and anti-imperialism. He was the first Prime Minister of India.

  'Tryst[12] with Destiny' was a speech delivered by Jawaharlal Nehru to the Indian Constituent Assembly in the Parliament on the eve of India's Independence on 14th August, 1947.
- **Dr Bhimrao Ramji Ambedkar (1891-1956)** He was Chairman of the Drafting Committee, social revolutionary thinker and agitator against caste divisions and caste based inequalities. He was the law minister in the first cabinet of post-independence India. He was the founder of Republic Party of India.
- **TT Krishnamachari (1899-1974)** He was a **member** of Drafting Committee, Entrepreneur and Congress leader. Later, he was the **Finance Minister** in the Union Cabinet.
- **Baldev Singh (1901-1961)** He was a successful Entrepreneur and leader of the Panthic Akali Party in the Punjab Assembly and was a nominee of the Congress in the Constituent Assembly. He was the Defence Minister of the Union Cabinet.
- **Shyama Prasad Mukherjee (1901-1953)** He was **Minister for Industry and Supply** in the Interim Government. Besides being an educationist and lawyer, he was active in Hindu Mahasabha. He was the Founder President of the Bharatiya Jansangh.
- **Somnath Lahiri (1901-1984)** He was a writer, editor and leader of the Communist Party of India. Later, he became the Member of West Bengal Legislative Assembly.
- **Jaipal Singh (1903-1970)** He was a sportsman and an educationist. He was also the Captain of the First National Hockey Team. Later, he was the Founder President of Adivasi Maha Sabha and founder of Jharkhand Party.
- **G Durgabai Deshmukh (1909-1981)** She was an advocate and public activist for women's emancipation. She founded the **Andhra Mahila Sabha** and was a Congress leader. She was the founder Chairperson of Central Social Welfare Board.

Legitimacy of the Indian Constitution Today

The Constitution does not reflect the view of its members alone, but expresses a broad consensus of the time it originated.

Many countries of the world had to rewrite their Constitution afresh because the basic rules were not acceptable to all major social groups or political parties.

Over the years, several groups have questioned some provisions of the Constitution but no large social group or political party has ever questioned its legitimacy.

Another reason for accepting the Constitution is that the Constituent Assembly represented the people of India. It could not be chosen directly by all the people, as there was no Universal Adult Franchise at that time.

The Constituent Assembly was elected by the members of the existing Provincial Legislatures. This ensured a fair geographical share of members from all regions of the country.

12 Tryst A meeting or a meeting place that has been agreed upon.

2.4 Guiding Values of the Indian Constitution

To understand the Indian Constitution properly we need to understand its overall philosophy. The **philosophy**[13] of the Constitution can be understood by knowing the views of some prominent leaders about our Constitution, as well as the Preamble to our Constitution.

The views of Mahatma Gandhi, BR Ambedkar and Jawaharlal Nehru about Constitution are given below

Mahatma Gandhi

He was not a member of the Constituent Assembly, but many members of it followed his vision. In **1931**, he had expressed himself in his magazine **Young India**. He wanted to frame a Constitution that provides an effective voice to the poor and underprivileged.

He wanted the Constitution to promote harmonious living of all communities in the country. It prohibits untouchability, use of intoxicating drinks and drugs in the country. It should give equality to women with men.

Dr BR Ambedkar

BR Ambedkar played a key role in the making of the Constitution. His vision of removing inequalities from India was different. He is known as the **Father of the Indian Constitution**. He often bitterly criticised Gandhi and his vision. He wanted political, social and economic equality for all.

He feared that if we deny equality in social and economic life for long, democracy will be in great danger.

Jawaharlal Nehru

He wanted equality of opportunity to all, end of poverty and ignorance and control of diseases. He wanted all responsible persons to dedicate themselves to the service of society.

2.5 Philosophy of the Constitution

The values that inspired and guided the freedom struggle formed the foundation for India's democracy. The Constitution begins with a short statement of its basic values. This is called the Prleamble to the Constitution. It guide all the Articles of the Indian Constitution.

It is inspired by the American model of the Constitution which begins with a Preamble.

The Preamble provides a standard to examine and evaluate any law and action of government, to find out whether it is good or bad. It is the **soul of the Indian Constitution**.

The Preamble contains the Philosophy on which the entire Constitution has been built.

The preamble to the Indian Constitution is given below

> **WE, THE PEOPLE OF INDIA,** having solemnly resolved to constitute India into a **SOVEREIGN, SOCIALIST, SECULAR, DEMOCRATIC REPUBLIC,**
> and to secure to all its citizens:
> **JUSTICE,** Social, Economic and Political;
> **LIBERTY** of thought, expression, belief, faith and worship;
> **EQUALITY** of status and of opportunity;
> and to promote among them all
> **FRATERNITY** assuring the dignity of the individualand the unity and integrity of the Nation;
> **IN OUR CONSTITUENT ASSEMBLY** this twenty-sixth day of November, 1949, do **HEREBY ADOPT, ENACT AND GIVE TO OURSELVES THIS CONSTITUTION.**

Important Terms used in Preamble

- **We, the People of India** The Constitution has been drawn up and enacted by the people of India through their representatives.
- **Sovereign** India is a free country and no external power can dictate the Government of India.
- **Socialist** Wealth is generated socially and should be shared equally by society.
- **Secular** There is no official religion and all religions are treated with equal respect by the government.
- **Democratic** We have adopted a form of government in which people elect their rulers and hold them accountable.

13 **Philosophy** The most fundamental principles underlying one's thoughts and actions.

- **Republic** The head of state is an elected person and it is not a hereditary position.
- **Justice** The laws should not discriminate between citizens on the basis of caste, religion and gender. The government should work for the welfare of the poor and oppressed so that social inequalities are reduced.
- **Liberty** Citizens are free to express their opinions and there are no unreasonable restrictions on their liberty.
- **Equality** All citizens are equal before the law, irrespective of differences in socio-economic conditions.
- **Fraternity** Each citizen should respect the feeling of brother-hood and no one should treat a fellow citizen as inferior.
- The terms 'socialist' and 'secular' were added in preamble through the 42nd constitutional amendment in 1976.

Institutional Design

A Constitution is mainly about putting the values and philosophy into institutional arrangements. Indian Constitution detail these arrangements. The Constitution describes the institutional arrangements in legal language.

The makers of the Constitution made a provision for making amendments to the Constitution from time-to-time. These changes are called **Constitutional Amendments.** This ensures consitution is updated regularly reflect changing to needs of society. There are three major aspects

(i) It lays down the procedure for choosing persons to govern the country.

(ii) It defines who will have how much power to take the decision.

(iii) It puts limits to what the government can do by providing some rights to the citizen that cannot be violated.

Try These

1. **The Karachi Session of Indian National Congress was held in which year?**
2. **In which year, the first meeting of Constituent Assembly was held?**
3. **The Constituent Assembly that wrote the Indian Constitution constituted how many members?**
4. **Who was the head of the Drafting Committee?**

Mind Map

CONSTITUTIONAL DESIGN

Need for the Constitution
- Generates a degree of trust and coordination among people that is necessary for the different kinds of people living together.
- Specifies how the government will be constituted and who will have the power to make decision.
- Lays down limits to the powers of the government and also specifies the rights of the citizens.

Guiding Values of the Indian Constitution

Dr BR Ambedkar
- He was the father of the Indian Constitution.
- He criticised Gandhi and his vision.
- He wanted political, social and economic equality for all.

Mahatma Gandhi
- He wanted to frame a Constitution that provides an effective voice to the poor and underprivileged.
- He wanted the Constitution to promote harmonious living of all communities in the country.

Making of the Indian Constitution

The Path to Constitution
- In 1928, Motilal Nehru and eight other Congress leaders drafted a Constitution for India.
- Important topics like Universal Adult Franchise, Right to Freedom and Equality, Rights of Minorities, etc were discussed at the Karachi session of the Indian National Congress in 1931.

Important Members of Constituent Assembly
- Sardar Vallabhbhai Patel
- Sarojini Naidu
- Dr. Rajendra Prasad
- HC Mookherjee
- Kanhaiyalal Maniklal Munshi
- Abul Kalam Azad
- Pt. Jawaharlal Nehru
- Baldev Singh
- Somnath Lahiri
- G Durgabai Deshmukh

The Constituent Assembly
- The drafting of the Indian Constitution was done by the Constituent Assembly.
- Elections to the Constituent Assembly were held in July 1946.
- The Constituent Assembly that wrote the Indian Constitution consisted 299 members.
- The Assembly adopted the Constitution on 26th November, 1949 but it came into effect on 26th January, 1950.

Democratic Constitution in South Africa
- South Africa became independent and got its democratic Constitution after a long struggle for freedom.
- Nelson Mandela fought for freedom rights and equality for black and white people.

Struggle Against Apartheid
- Apartheid was the name of a system of racial discrimination unique to South Africa.
- It was imposed by the White Europeans on South Africa.
- Since 1950, blacks, coloured and Indians fought against the Apartheid system.
- The African National Congress led the movement.

Equality of Races in South Africa
- The Preamble to the South African Constitution outlines that everybody should become part of the solution to every problem, irrespective of whatever they might have done or represented in the past.
- The South African Constitution inspires democrats all over the world.
- South Africa became a model of democracy.

Towards a New Constitution
- The ban on political parties and restrictions on the media were removed.
- Nelson Mandela was released after he spent 28 years in jail.
- At the midnight of 26th April, 1994, the new democratic state of the Republic of South Africa emerged.
- The apartheid government came to an end, paving the way for the formation of a multi-racial government.

Philosophy of the Constitution
- The Constitution begins with a short statement of its basic values, which is called the Preamble to the Constitution.
- The Preamble contains the philosophy on which the entire Constitution has been built.
- The Preamble provides a standard to examine and evaluate any law and action of government.

Institutional Design
- The makers of the Constitution made a provision for making amendments to the Constitution which are called as Constitutional Amendments.
- The Constitution lays down the procedure for choosing persons to govern the country.
- It defines who will have how much power to take the decision
- It puts limits to what the government can do, by providing some rights to the citizen that cannot be violated.

NCERT FOLDER

Covering Intext Questions and Exercises of NCERT

INTEXT QUESTIONS

Q.1 Does the story of South African struggle for freedom remind you of the Indian National Movement? Make a list of similarities and dissimilarities between the two on the following points

(a) Nature of colonialism
(b) Relationship between different communities
(c) Leadership: Gandhi/ Mandela
(d) Party that led the struggle: African National Congress/ Indian National Congress
(e) Method of struggle

Ans. Yes, the story of South African struggle for freedom reminds us of the Indian National Movement.

(a) Nature of colonialism

Similarities During the 17th and 18th centuries, the trading companies from Europe occupied South Africa forcibly in the same way that they had occupied India.

Dissimilarities Unlike India, a large number of whites had settled in South Africa and became the local rulers.

(b) Relationship between different communities

Similarities The white rulers treated all non-whites as inferiors in both the countries. The whites regarded Indians and Africans inferior and uncivilised people.

Dissimilarities The relationship between different religions and regional communities in India was cordial. They all believed themselves to be Indians. But in South Africa, different communities like the whites, blacks, coloured people and Indians did not have cordial relations or respect for each other.

(c) Leadership : Gandhi/ Mandela

Similarities Both were apostles of truth and non-violence.

Dissimilarities Nelson Mandela was sentenced to life imprisonment; though Gandhiji was also put behind the bars several times, he was not sentenced to life imprisonment.

(d) Party that led the struggle : ANC/ INC

Similarities Both the African National Congress (ANC) and the Indian National Congress (INC) were umbrella organisations working at national level.

Dissimilarities The purpose of both the parties was different. ANC was fighting against apartheid and the segregation policies of the racial African Government, whereas the INC was fighting against the British rule in India.

(e) Method of struggle

Similarities Both the South African struggle and Indian National Movement followed the same policy, i.e. the policy of non-violence.

Dissimilarities In South Africa, there was only one group, that of the moderates, who adopted peaceful means against the government, whereas in India besides the moderates, there were also the extremists, who used violent methods to attain their goal of freedom.

Q.2 This is not fair! What was the point in having a Constituent Assembly in India if all the basics were already decided?

Ans. We cannot say that there was no point in having a Constituent Assembly to discuss and frame a Constitution if the basics had already been decided. The basics were related to Right to Freedom, Universal Adult Franchise and Rights of Minorities, which are the basis of any democratic society.

These basics were the guiding principles which were further developed and expanded to establish a welfare state.

In a democracy, it is the Constituent Assembly which makes the Constitution with the help of the basics.

Q.3 Read the information about the makers of the Indian Constitution given in the side columns in the NCERT. You don't need to memorise this information. Just give examples from these to support the following statements.

(a) The Assembly had many members who were not with the Congress.
(b) The Assembly represented members from different social groups.
(c) Members of the Assembly believed in different ideologies.

Ans. (a) Sarat Chandra Bose (1889-1950), Jaipal Singh (1903-70), Bhimrao Ramji Ambedkar (1891-1956), Shyama Prasad Mukherjee (1901-53) were not with the Congress.

(b) Some members who represented different social groups were
   (i) Vallabhbhai Patel – Landlords
   (ii) Abul Kalam Azad – Muslims
   (iii) Jaipal Singh – Tribals
   (iv) Bhimrao Ramji Ambedkar – Depressed classes

(c) The following members believed in different ideologies were
   (i) Socialists and Communists – Pt Jawaharlal Nehru
   (ii) Gandhian ideals – K M Munshi
   (iii) Rightists – Sardar Vallabhbhai Patel

Q.4 Read the three quotations carefully.

(i) I shall strive for a Constitution which will release India from all thralldom and patronage. I shall work for an India in which the poorest shall feel that it is their country in whose making they have an effective voice; an India in which there shall be no high class and low class of people; an India in which all communities shall live in perfect harmony. There can be no room in such an India for the curse of untouchability or the curse of the intoxicating drinks and drugs. Women will enjoy the same rights as men. I shall be satisfied with nothing else.

(ii) On the 26th January, 1950, we are going to enter a life of contradictions. In politics we will have equality and in social and economic life we will have inequality. In politics we will be recognising the principle of one man one vote and one vote one value. In our social and economic life, we shall, by reason of our social and economic structure, continue to deny the principle of one man one value. How long shall we continue to live this life of contradictions?

How long shall we continue to deny equality in our social and economic life? If we continue to deny it for long, we will do so only by putting our political democracy in peril.

(iii) Long years ago we made a tryst with destiny and now the time comes when we shall redeem our pledge, not wholly or in full measure, but very substantially. At the stroke of the midnight hour, when the world sleeps, India will awake to life and freedom. A moment comes, which comes but rarely in history, when we step out from the old to the new, when an age ends, and when the soul of a nation, long suppressed, finds utterance. It is fitting that at this solemn moment we take the pledge of dedication to the service of India and her people and to the still larger cause of humanity..

Freedom and power bring responsibility. The responsibility rests upon this Assembly, a sovereign body representing the sovereign people of India. Before the birth of freedom we have endured all the pains of labour and our hearts are heavy with the memory of this sorrow. Some of those pains continue even now. Nevertheless, the past is over and it is the future that beckons to us now.

That future is not one of ease or resting but of incessant striving so that we may fulfil the pledges we have so often taken and the one we shall take today. The service of India means the service of the millions who suffer. It means the ending of poverty and ignorance and disease and inequality of opportunity. The ambition of the greatest man of our generation has been to wipe every tear from every eye. That may be beyond us, but as long as there are tears and suffering, so long our work will not be over.

(a) Can you identify central idea that is common to all these three quotations?

Ans. The central idea that is common to all these three quotations is the ending of inequality in Indian society.

(b) What are the differences in their ways of expressing that common idea?

Ans. The differences in expressing their common ideas is given below

- **Gandhiji** strived for an India in which there should be no higher or lower class of people and all communities should live in perfect harmony.
- **Dr BR Ambedkar** felt that, in terms of politics people would have equality but in social and economic life people would face inequality.
- **Jawaharlal Nehru** believed that the service of India meant the service of the millions who suffered. It meant ending of poverty, ignorance, disease and inequality of opportunity among the people. It was the duty of the leader to remove the sufferings of common men.

Q.5 Compare the Preambles to the Constitutions of the United States of America, India and South Africa.

(a) Make a list of ideas that are common to all these three.

Ans. The ideas that are common to all these three are

- Each of these Preambles starts with,"We, the people." It means, the source of all authority to govern these countries are the people of these countries.
- In all these three, the idea of justice is embodied.

(b) Note down at least one of the major differences among them.

Ans. In the Preamble to the Constitution of the United States, there is a statement for the formation of a more perfect union, which is not there in the Preambles to the Indian and South African Constitutions.

(c) Which of the three makes a reference to the past?

Ans. The Preamble to the Constitution of South Africa makes a reference to the past.

(d) Which of these does not invoke God?

Ans. The Preambles to the Constitutions of the United States and India do not invoke God.

Both the Preambles suggest that citizens have complete freedom to follow any religion. There is no official religion.

EXERCISE

Q.1 Here are some false statements. Identify the mistake in each case and rewrite these correctly based on what you have read in this chapter.

(a) Leaders of the freedom movement had an open mind about whether the country should be democratic or not after independence.

(b) Members of the Constituent Assembly of India held the same views on all provisions of the Constitution.

(c) A country that has a Constitution must be a democracy.

(d) Constitution cannot be amended because it is the Supreme Law of a country.

Ans. (a) Leaders of the freedom movement had a consensus that the country should be democratic after independence.

(b) The members of the Constituent Assembly of India held same views on the principles of the Constitution.

(c) A country that is democratic must have a Constitution.

(d) The Constitution needs to be amended because it has to be in accordance with people's aspirations and changes in society.

Q.2 Which of these was the most salient underlying conflict in the making of a democratic Constitution in South Africa?

(a) Between South Africa and its neighbours.

(b) Between men and women.

(c) Between the white majority and the black minority.

(d) Between the coloured minority and the black majority.

Ans. (d) Between the coloured minority and the black majority.

Q.3 Which of these is a provision that a democratic Constitution does not have?

(a) Powers of the head of the state

(b) Name of the head of the state

(c) Powers of the Legislature

(d) Name of the country

Ans. (b) Name of the head of the state

Q.4 Match the following leaders with their roles in the making of the Constitution

List I	List II
(a) Motilal Nehru	(i) President of the Constituent Assembly
(b) B R Ambedkar	(ii) Member of the Constituent Assembly
(c) Rajendra Prasad	(iii) Chairman of the Drafting Committee
(d) Sarojini Naidu	(iv) Prepared a Constitution for India in 1928

Ans. (a)-(iv), (b)-(iii), (c)-(i), (d)-(ii).

Q.5 Read again the extracts from Nehru's speech "Tryst with Destiny" and answer the following

(a) Why did Nehru use the expression "not wholly or in full measure" in the first sentence?

(b) What pledge did he want the makers of the Indian Constitution to take?

(c) "The ambition of the greatest man of our generation has been to wipe every tear from every eye". Who was he referring to?

Ans. (a) Pt Jawaharlal Nehru used the expression 'not wholly or in full measure' because the task of building a large nation like India was a gigantic one which cannot even be completed in one's lifetime.

(b) Pt Jawaharlal Nehru wanted the makers of the Constitution to take a pledge of dedication to the service of the nation and her people and to the still larger cause of humanity.

(c) Pt Jawaharlal Nehru was referring to Mahatma Gandhi.

Q.6 Here are some of the guiding values of the Constitution and their meanings. Rewrite them by matching them correctly.

(a) Sovereign	(i) Government will not favour any religion.
(b) Republic	(ii) People have the supreme right to make decisions.
(c) Fraternity	(iii) Head of the state is an elected person.
(d) Secular	(iv) People should live like brothers and sisters.

Ans. (a)-(ii), (b)-(iii), (c)-(iv), (d)-(i).

Q.7 Here are different opinions about what made India a democracy. How much importance would you give to each of these factors?

(a) Democracy in India is a gift of the British rulers. We received training to work with representative legislative institutions under the British rule.

(b) Freedom struggle challenged the colonial exploitation and denial of different freedoms to Indians. Free India could not be anything but democratic.

(c) We were lucky to have leaders who had democratic convictions. The denial of democracy in several other newly independent countries shows the important role of these leaders.

Ans. (a) Democracy in India was not a gift of the British rulers. It was decided by our Constituent Assembly that India will have a democratic form of government. At the same time we cannot ignore the fact that India received some training to work with representative legislative institutions under the Acts of 1919 and 1935.

(b) Freedom struggle against colonial exploitation contributed a lot to make India a democracy because it spread the idea of nationalism and inculcated the practice of making decisions by consensus.

(c) India had leaders like Mahatma Gandhi, Jawaharlal Nehru, Dr BR Ambedkar, etc who were in favour of democracy. They drafted a democratic constitution. Whereas leaders like Kwame Nkrumah of Ghana, General Musharraf of Pakistan and the military leaders of Myanmmar left democratic convictions and denied democracy.

Thus, we are lucky to have the above mentioned leaders who propagated the idea of democracy.

Q.8 Read the following extract from a conduct book for 'Married Women', published in 1912. 'God has made the female species delicate and fragile both physically and emotionally, pitiably incapable of self-defence. They are destined thus by God to remain in male protection - of father, husband and son - all their lives. Women should, therefore, not despair, but feel obliged that they can dedicate themselves to the service of men'.

Do you think the values expressed in this para reflected the values underlying our Constitution? Or does this go against the constitutional values?

Ans. No, the values expressed in the above paragraph do not reflect the values underlying our Constitution.

It goes against the constitutional values because in this paragraph, women are shown as unequal, weak and fragile who should serve men, whereas the Constitution provides equality for both men and women. The governmental policies also favour women to bring them in mainstream.

Q.9 Read the following statements about a Constitution. Give reasons why each of these is true or not true.

(a) The authority of the rules of the Constitution is the same as that of any other law.

(b) Constitution lays down how different organs of the government will be formed.

(c) Rights of citizens and limits on the power of the government are laid down in the Constitution.

(d) A Constitution is about institutions, not about values.

Ans. (a) **Not true** Constitution is the Supreme Law. It describes how government elects and their powers, rights of the citizens and their protection. This is totally different than any other law.

(b) **True** Constitution defines the role of the Legislature, the Executive and the Judiciary and how they should be formed and by whom.

(c) **True** Constitution set up limits the power of government through different institutions and also talks about the right of citizens.

(d) **Not true** The Constitution contains all the values and which the institutions have to promote. The preamble to the Constitution is a good example of this and states clearly that justice, liberty, equality and fraternity have to be promoted.

REVIEW EXERCISE

Including Competency Based Questions

Part I

Multiple Choice Questions (MCQs)

1. In which year Nelson Mandela was sentenced to life imprisonment?

(a) 1960 (b) 1982
(c) 1964 (d) 1952

2. The native people of South Africa are .... in colour.

(a) black (b) white
(c) blonde (d) red

3. Which organisation led the struggle against the policies of segregation in South Africa?

(a) The African National Congress
(b) Agang South Africa
(c) United Democratic Movement
(d) National Freedom Party

4. Who gave this statement–"I have cherished the ideal of a democratic and free society in which all persons live together in harmony and with equal opportunities"?

(a) BR Ambedkar (b) Nelson Mandela
(c) Aung San Suu Kyi (d) Nkrumah

5. The title of autobiography written by Nelson Mandela is

(a) Long Walk to Freedom
(b) The Story of My Life
(c) Running with Scissors
(d) A Walk in the Woods

6. Which national leader first tried to draft a Constitution for India?

(a) Jawaharlal Nehru (b) Motilal Nehru
(c) Mahatma Gandhi (d) BR Ambedkar

7. The Indian Constitution adopted many institutional details and procedures from which colonial laws of the Government of India?

(a) Government of India Act, 1858
(b) Indian Councils Act, 1892
(c) Charter Act, 1853
(d) Government of India Act, 1935

8. How many members were there in the Constituent Assembly, of the Indian Constitution?

(a) 199 (b) 273
(c) 299 (d) 229

9. The 'Bill of Rights' which inspired the Indian leaders is associated with which country?

(a) Ireland (b) France
(c) Canada (d) USA

10. India became a Republic on which of the following dates?

(a) 26th November, 1949 (b) 22nd July, 1949
(c) 26th January, 1950 (d) 15th August, 1947

11. What was Mahatma Gandhi's vision for the Constitution as expressed in his 1931 article in Young India?

(a) The Constitution should enforce strict laws
(b) The Constitution should eliminate inequality
(c) The Constitution should promote political power over moral values
(d) The Constitution should protect the British Raj

12. Who among the following considered that the truth and non-violence are key ingredients of their philosophy?

(a) Mahatma Gandhi
(b) Nelson Mandela
(c) Subhash Chandra Bose
(d) Both (a) and (b)

13. The Constitution begins with a short statement of its basic values called the

(a) Resolution (b) Preamble
(c) Preface (d) Schedule

14. Who gave a historical speech 'Tryst with Destiny' on 15th August, 1947?

(a) Mahatma Gandhi
(b) Jawaharlal Nehru
(c) Shyama Prasad Mukherjee
(d) Dr BR Ambedkar

15. Consider the following statement regarding the Indian Constitution. Which one of the following is/are correct?

(a) It is a detailed document which is rigid in nature.
(b) It puts limits to what the government can do for providing rights to its citizens.
(c) The Constitution was enforced on 26th January, 1950.
(d) Both (b) and (c)

16. Find the incorrect option.

(a) Dr BR Ambedkar was the Chairman of Drafting Committee.

(b) Shyama Prasad Mukherjee was the founder President of the Bharatiya Jana Sangh.

(c) Mahatma Gandhi was a member of Constituent Assembly.

(d) HC Mukherjee was the Vice-Chairman of the Constituent Assembly.

17. Identify the person with the help of following information. **Competency Based**

- He was Minister for Industry and Supply in the Interim Government.
- He was active in Hindu Mahasabha.
- He was an educationist and lawyer.
- He was the founder President of the Bharatiya Jana Sangh.

Options

(a) Mahatma Gandhi (b) Jaipal Singh

(c) Shyama Prasad Mukherjee (d) TT Krishnamachari

18. Arrange the following incorrect sequence.

I. The Constituent Assembly adopted the Constitution.

II. Elections for provincial Legislatures and Ministries were held all over British India.

III. Motilal Nehru and eight other Congress leaders drafted a Constitution for India.

IV. Karachi Session of Indian National Congress was held.

Codes

(a) III, IV, II, I (b) I, III, II, IV

(c) IV, III, I, II (d) II, I, IV, III

Answers

1. (c)	**2.** (a)	**3.** (a)	**4.** (b)	**5.** (a)
6. (b)	**7.** (d)	**8.** (c)	**9.** (d)	**10.** (c)
11. (b)	**12.** (d)	**13.** (b)	**14.** (b)	**15.** (d)
16. (c)	**17.** (c)	**18.** (a)		

Match the Following

1.

List I	List II
A. TT Krishnamachari	1. Vice-Chairman of Constituent Assembly
B. HC Mookheerje	2. Member of Drafting Committee
C. Sardar Vallabh Bhai Patel	3. Chairman of Constituent Assembly
D. Dr Rajendra Prasad	4. Deputy Prime Minister

Codes

	A	B	C	D		A	B	C	D
(a)	2	1	4	3	(b)	1	3	4	2
(c)	4	1	2	3	(b)	3	1	2	4

Ans. (a)

Assertion-Reason

1. Assertion (A) The Constitution of a country is a set of written rules that are accepted by all people living in a country.

Reason (R) It generates a degree of trust and coordination among people that is necessary for different kinds of people living together.

Codes

(a) Both A and R are true and R is the correct explanation of A

(b) Both A and R are true, but R is not the correct explanation of A

(c) A is true, but R is false

(d) A is false, but R is true

2. Assertion (A) The white rulers treated all non-whites as inferiors.

Reason (R) The white rulers divided the people and labelled them on the basis of their skin colour.

Codes

(a) Both A and R are true and R is the correct explanation of A

(b) Both A and R are true, but R is not the correct explanation of A

(c) A is true, but R is false

(d) A is false, but R is true

3. Assertion (A) The South African Constitution inspires democrats all over the world.

Reason (R) The Constitution is based on social equality and justice.

Codes

(a) Both A and R are true and R is the correct explanation of A

(b) Both A and R are true, but R is not the correct explanation of A

(c) A is true, but R is false

(d) A is false, but R is true

4. Assertion (A) The protests and struggles against apartheid had increased.

Reason (R) Government realised that they could no longer keep the black under their rule of repression.

Codes

(a) Both A and R are true and R is the correct explanation of A

(b) Both A and R are true, but R is not the correct explanation of A

(c) A is true, but R is false

(d) A is false, but R is true

Ans. 1. (a) Both A and R are true and R is the correct explanation of A
2. (b) Both A and R are true, but R is not the correct explanation of A
3. (a) Both A and R are true and R is the correct explanation of A
4. (b) Both A and R are true, but R is not the correct explanation of A

Picture Based Question

1. The image captures the spirit of South Africa. Why it is known as a 'Rainbow nation'?

(a) The people are unified together like colours of rainbow despite of their different colour complexions.
(b) The spirit of South Africa inspired democrats all over the world.
(c) The determination of people helps them to unite and that leads to formation of a Rainbow nation.
(d) None of the above

Ans. (c) The determination of people helps them to unite and that leads to formation of a Rainbow nation.

Very Short Answer Type Questions

1. For which offence was Nelson Mandela tried by the white South African government?

Ans. Nelson Mandela was tried for treason by the white South African government.

2. "I have fought against the white domination and I have fought against the black domination." Who said this sentence?

Ans. Nelson Mandela made this statement.

Case Based Question

1 Read the source given below and answer the questions that follow.

After long negotiations both parties agreed to a compromise. The whites agreed to the principle of majority rule and that of one person one vote. They also agreed to accept some basic rights for the poor and the workers. The blacks agreed that majority rule would not be absolute. They agreed that the majority would not take away the property of the white minority. This compromise was not easy. How was this compromise going to be implemented? Even if they managed to trust each other, what was the guarantee that this trust will not be broken in future?

(i) The whites agreed to the principle of .... rule and that of one person one vote.

(a) Majority (b) Dictatorial
(c) Minority (d) All of these

(ii) What compromises did the white makes?

(a) They agreed that majority would not be absolute.
(b) They agreed to accept some basic rights for the poor and the workers.
(c) They agreed that the majority would not take away the property of the white minority.
(d) None of the above

(iii) On which compromises did the blacks agreed upon?

(a) The majority rule would not be absolute.
(b) Agreed that majority would not take away the property of the white minority.
(c) Absolute majority rule.
(d) Both (a) and (b)

Ans. (i) (a) Majority
(ii) (b) They agreed to accept some basic rights for the poor and the workers.
(iii) (d) Both (a) and (b)

Part II

3. Prior to 1992, South Africa practiced a form of racial discrimination. What is it termed as?

Ans. The racial discrimination practiced in South Africa prior to 1992 was called apartheid.

4. In which country did a large number of 'whites' settle and become the local rulers?

Ans. The country is South Africa.

5. On what basis the system of apartheid divided the people and labelled?

Ans. On the basis of skin colour, the system of apartheid divided people.

6. On which day did South Africa gain independence from the rule of the white minority?

Ans. South Africa gained independence from the rule of the white minority on 26th April, 1994.

7. Which Constitution has inspired democrats all over the world?

Ans. The Constitution of South Africa has inspired democrats all over the world.

8. What did the white minority in South Africa wanted to protect through their new Constitution?

Ans. The white minority in South Africa wanted to protect their privileges and property through their new Constitution.

9. Which national leader tried to draft a Constitution for India as far back in 1928?

Ans. Pandit Motilal Nehru tried to draft a Constitution for India in 1928.

10. When were the elections to the Constituent Assembly held in India?

Ans. The elections to the Constituent Assembly were held in July 1946.

11. After the partition of India and Pakistan, the Constituent Assembly was divided into how many Assemblies?

Ans. It was divided into two assemblies. The Constituent Assemblies of India and Pakistan were separated.

12. When did the Constituent Assembly adopt the Constitution of India?

Ans. The Constituent Assembly adopted the Constitution on 26th November, 1949.

13. Name some important members of the Constituent Assembly.

Ans. Some important members of the Constituent Assembly were Dr Rajendra Prasad, Dr B R Ambedkar, Pandit Jawaharlal Nehru, Dr S Radhakrishnan, K M Munshi, etc.

14. Which part of the Indian Constitution is called soul of the Constitution?

Ans. The Preamble of the Indian Constitution is called soul of the Constitution.

Short Answer Type Questions

1. What do you mean by the 'Policy of Apartheid'? How did this policy come to an end?

Ans. The 'Policy of Apartheid' was a system of racial discrimination unique to South Africa. It was imposed on the blacks by the white Europeans. In this system, the blacks were forbidden from living in white areas. They could work in white areas only if they had a permit. Trains, buses, and other public places like, hotels, hospitals, schools, colleges, etc were separate for the whites and the blacks.

This policy came to an end on 26th April, 1994, when the Republic of South Africa was born with a multi-racial government.

2. How did the blacks of South Africa fight against the practice of apartheid?

or **Describe any three efforts made by the people of South Africa to struggle against the apartheid system.**

Ans. The following three efforts were made by the people of South Africa to struggle against the apartheid system

(i) From 1950 onwards, the blacks, coloured and Indians fought against the apartheid system. They launched protest marches and strikes.

(ii) The African National Congress led the struggle against this policy of segregation. Many workers' unions and the Communist Party joined this movement.

(iii) Many whites joined the ANC and played a leading role in this movement.

3. "The system of apartheid followed in South Africa was unjust and racist." Support the statement with three points.

Or **"The apartheid system in South Africa was particularly oppressive for the blacks." Justify the statement with arguments.**

Ans. The system of apartheid followed in South Africa was unjust and racist because

(i) The blacks were forbidden from living in white areas. They could work in white areas only if they had a permit.

(ii) Trains, buses and public places like hotels, hospitals, schools and colleges, etc were separate for the whites and blacks.

(iii) Blacks could not form associations or protest against the terrible treatment.

Thus, the apartheid system was particularly oppressive for the blacks.

4. Throw some light on the composition of the Constituent Assembly.

Ans. The Constituent Assembly of India was made to draft the Constitution of India. It was constituted in 1946 under the provisions of the Cabinet Mission Plan. This Assembly originally had 389 members but due to the partition of the country, its membership was reduced to 299.

The Constituent Assembly was composed of eminent persons like Pt Jawaharlal Nehru, Sardar Vallabhbhai Patel, Maulana Abdul Kalam Azad, Dr BR Ambedkar, etc. The women members like Sarojini Naidu and G Durgabai Deshmukh played an important role.

5. What was the procedure adopted for making the Indian Constitution?

Ans. The following procedure was adopted for making the Indian Constitution :

- The 'Drafting Committee' chaired by Dr BR Ambedkar prepared a draft of the Indian Constitution for discussion.
- Several rounds of discussion took place on the Draft Constitution, clause by clause. The members worked for 114 days spread over three years.
- More than two thousand amendments were considered. Every document presented and every word spoken in the Constituent Assembly has been recorded and preserved.

6. Why do we accept even today the Constitution made by the Constituent Assembly more than 60 years ago? Explain any three reasons.

Ans. We accept even today the Constitution made by the Constituent Assembly more than 60 years ago, due to following reasons :

(i) India is a land of diversity which is visible in the matters of caste, religion, region, language, economic status etc. In such a huge diversity conflicts are inevitable. But, the Constitution of India protects the interests of every section of society and lays the foundation for a harmonious society.

(ii) India has an experience of long colonial past and it remained a victim of colonial exploitations for centuries. But, after the implementation of the Constitution, we are sovereign which means no external powers can regulate us in any matters.

(iii) The Constitution of India has a flexible nature which opens enough scope for amendments, if required for the welfare of its citizens. To maintain law and order, the dignity and rights of the citizens, the Constitution made some provisions for amendment from time to time.

7. Mention any three characteristics of the Indian Constitution.

or **Highlight the salient features of the Constitution of India.**

Ans. The Indian Constitution is very long and detailed document. The features of Constitution are

(i) Values that inspired and guided the freedom struggle are incorporated in the Constitution.

(ii) It generates trust and coordination that is necessary for different kinds of people to live together in our country.

(iii) The Indian Constitution lays down a procedure for choosing persons to govern the country. It specifies how the government will be constituted and who will have power to take which decisions.

8. What is the significance of the 'Preamble' to the Indian Constitution?

Ans. Indian Constitution begins with a short statement of its basic values. This is called the Preamble to the Constitution. The significance of the Preamble is as follows

(i) The Preamble to the Indian Constitution contains the philosophy on which the entire Constitution has been built.

(ii) It is regarded as the soul of the Indian Constitution. It provides a standard to examine and evaluate any law and action of government to find out whether it is good or bad.

(iii) It guides all the Articles of the Indian Constitution.

Long Answer Type Questions

1. Explain with five facts the transition from apartheid to democracy and multi-racial government in South Africa.

Ans. Following are the five facts that describe the transition from apartheid to democracy and multi-racial government in South Africa

(i) After two years of discussion and debate leaders of South Africa came out with one of the finest Constitutions in the world.

(ii) The new Constitution gave to its citizens the most extensive rights available in any country.

(iii) They decided that in the search for a solution to the problems, everybody was included and given equal rights and respect in the Constitution.

(iv) The leaders of South Africa agreed that everybody should become part of the solution, whatever they might have done or represented in the past.

(v) The apartheid government came to an end in South Africa paving way for the formation of a multi-racial government or a democratic government here.

2. Evaluate how the white minority and the black majority agreed to draw up a common Constitution for South Africa.

or **How was the new Constitution of South Africa formed?**

Ans. The white minority and the black majority agreed to draw up a common Constitution for South Africa in the following ways :

(i) The white regime changed its repressive policies and repealed its discriminatory laws. Ban on Political Parties and restrictions on media were lifted.

(ii) The black leaders appealed to fellow blacks to forgive the whites for the atrocities committed by them.

(iii) There were long sessions of debates and discussions and they searched a solution to the existing problems.
(iv) It was agreed that everyone should be a part of the country irrespective of the differences and whatever they had done in the past.
(v) The Constitution tried to build a new South Africa based on equality of all races and men and women, on democratic values, social justice and human rights.

3. What is a Constitution? Why do we need a Constitution? Give any five reasons.

or **Why do we need a Constitution in a democracy? Explain any three reasons.**

or **Why do we need a Constitution? Describe any three main functions of a Constitution.**

Ans. The Constitution of a country is a set of written rules that are accepted by all people living together in a country. Constitution is the Supreme law that determines the relationship among people living in a territory (called citizens) and also the relationship between the people and government.

We need a Constitution because

(i) It generates a degree of trust and coordination that is necessary for different kinds of people to live together.
(ii) It specifies how the government will be constituted and who will have power to take which decisions.
(iii) It lays down limits to the powers of the government and tells us what are the rights of the citizens.
(iv) It expresses the aspirations of the people about creating a good society.
(v) The Indian Constitution safeguards the interests of minorities, the backward classes, poor and weaker sections of our society. It gives Universal Adult Franchise to all and establishes equality for all.

Thus, it has become a practice in all democracies to have a written Constitution.

4. What were some of the key influences on the making of the Indian Constitution? How did Indian leaders adapt them to suit country's needs?

Ans. The making of the Constitution for a huge and diverse country like India was not an easy affair.

The major factors which contributed to the making of our Constitution were

(i) People of India at that time were emerging from the status of subjects to that of citizens. They became conscious of their rights and privileges.
(ii) Our leaders gained confidence to learn from other countries, but on our own terms. Many of them were inspired by the ideals of the French Revolution.
(iii) Our leaders were also influenced by the practices of Parliamentary democracy in Britain and the Bill of Rights in the US.
(iv) Social Revolution in Russia inspired many Indians to think of shaping a system based on social and economic equality.
(v) The makers of the Constitution were not simply imitating the Constitution of other countries. At each step, they were questioning whether the values and ideals they accepted suited our country or not.

5. Describe any five difficulties faced by the framers of the Indian Constitution.

Ans. The difficulties faced by the framers of the Indian Constitution were

(i) The first difficulty was that the Constitution had to ensure that the people were given certain fundamental rights, which had not been available earlier.
(ii) The second difficulty was partition of the country. This was a shocking experience for the people as well as the lawmakers. They had to continue their deliberations in this background.
(iii) The third difficulty was the decision that British had left to the princely states to decide whether to join either country or remain independent. This problem had to be kept in mind while framing the Constitution.
(iv) The fourth difficulty in framing the constitution was preserving the interest of all the people as India was a vast and varied country with diverse regions, languages, cultures, customs and beliefs.
(v) The fifth difficulty was that the framers of the Indian Constitution had to ensure that the country remained united after the Constitution came into force.

6. Assess the contribution made by the Constituent Assembly to form the Indian Constitution.

Ans. The following were the contributions made by the Constituent Assembly to form the Indian Constitution are

- It reflected the broad consensus of its time, i.e., its provisions were accepted by all major social groups and political parties.
- It's formation ensured a fair geographical share of the members from all regions of the country.

- It accomodated the opposition in a fair way and gave opportunities to raise their concerns before arriving at a conclusion.
- It worked in a systematic and open way. First basic principles were decided and agreed upon and then the draft was prepared.
- Several rounds of long debates and discussions were held. Every document presented and words spoken were carefully recorded and preserved. This was done to keep a record for further reference.

7. Explain the key words used in the Preamble of the Constitution of India.

or Explain any five major ideals enshrined in the Preamble to the Indian Constitution.

Ans. The key words used in the Preamble of the Indian Constitution are as follows

- **Sovereign** People have supreme right to make decisions on internal as well as external matters.
- **Socialist** Wealth is generated socially and should be shared equally by society.
- **Secular** Citizens have complete freedom to follow any religion. But there is no official religion.
- **Democratic** A form of government where people enjoy equal political rights, elect their rulers and hold them accountable.
- **Republic** The head of the state is an elected person and not a hereditary position.
- **Justice** Citizens cannot be discriminated on the grounds of caste, religion and gender
- **Liberty** There are no unreasonable restrictions on the citizens in what they think, how they wish to express their thoughts and the way they wish to follow up their thoughts in action.
- **Equality** All are equal before the law.
- **Fraternity** All of us should behave as if we are members of the same family. No one should treat a fellow citizen as inferior.

8. How has the Indian Constitution embodied the basic values into its institutional arrangements? Explain.

Ans. The Indian Constitution embodied the basic values into its institutional arrangements in the following ways

(i) Values that inspired and guided Indian freedom struggle and later developed by it formed the foundation of Indian democracy. These values were included in the Preamble of Indian Constitution.

(ii) The Indian Constitution begins with a short statement of its basic values. This is called the Preamble to the Constitution. Inspired by the American Constitution, Indian Constitution also begins with the Preamble.

(iii) The Preamble guide all the articles of the Indian Constitution. It contains the philosophy on which the entire Constitution in dependent.

(iv) The Preamble provides a standard to examine and evaluate any law and action of the government. It also determines whether it is good or bad.

(v) Indian Constitution embodies these values into institutional arrangement. But the laws of the constitution are not static and unalterable. These can be changed with people's aspirations and changes in society.

Case Based Questions

1 Read the sources given below and answer the following questions.

Source A Towards a New Constitution

The South African constitution inspires democrats all over the world. A state denounced by the entire world till 1994 as the most undemocratic one is now seen as a model of democracy. What made this change possible was the determination of the people of South Africa to work together, to transform bitter experiences into the binding glue of a Rainbow nation.

(i) On what basis South Africa wanted to build a new nation? Justify

Source B Path to Constitution

Despite all the difficulties, there was a big advantage for the makers of the Indian Constitution. Unlike South Africa, they did not have to create a consensus about what a democratic India should look like. Much of this consensus had evolved during the freedom struggle. Our national movement was not merely a struggle against a foreign rule. It was also a struggle to rejuvenate our country and to transform our society and politics. There were sharp differences of opinion within the freedom struggle about the path, India should take after Independence.

(ii) To what extent it was difficult for India to frame a Constitution after Independence for a unified India? Illustrate.

Source C Institutional Design

Those who crafted the Indian Constitution felt that it has to be in accordance with people's aspirations and changes in society. They did not see it as a sacred, static and unalterable law. So, they made provisions to incorporate changes from time to time. These changes are called constitutional amendments.

The Constitution describes the institutional arrangements in a very legal language.
It defines who will have how much power to take which decisions. And it puts limits to what the government can do by providing some rights to the citizen that cannot be violated.

(iii) Why do you think Constitution framers make provisions for amendments in the Indian Constitution? Illustrate two reasons.

Ans. (i) South Africa wanted to build a new nation based on equality of all races, on democratic values, social justice and human rights.

(ii) It was really difficult for India to frame a Constitution after independence for a unified India because

- The country was born through a partition on the basis of religious differences and it was a traumatic experience for all.
- At that time people emerged from the status of subjects to that of citizen.
- The political status of princely states were not certain and the country did not look secure.

(iii) The Constitution framers make provisions for amendments in the Indian Constitution because of the following reasons

- Indian Constitution had to be in accordance with people's aspirations and changes in the society.
- They were aware of the coming future needs of the fast changing Indian Society.

2. Read the source given below and answer the questions that follow.

The white rulers treated all non-whites as inferiors slowly, the apartheid system started oppressing blacks. In this system, the non-whites did not have voting rights and they were forbidden from living in white areas.

The non-whites could work in white areas only if they had a permit. Trains, buses, taxis, hospitals, schools, colleges, etc were all separate for the whites and blacks. This was known as segregation. Blacks could not enter a church where the whites worshipped and even they did not have the right to form associations or protest against the whites. But, after the emergence of democratic South Africa, black leaders appealed to fellow blacks to forgive the whites for the atrocities they had committed while in power. They wanted to build up a new South Africa based on equality of all races.

(i) Which type of tactics did the white racist government of South Africa used to continue their rule?

(ii) "The apartheid system was particularly oppressive for blacks." Justify by giving two reasons.

(iii) What would have happened in South Africa if the black majority had decided to take revenge on the whites for all their oppression and exploitation?

Ans. (i) The white racist government continued to rule by detaining, torturing and killing thousands of black and coloured people.

(ii) The apartheid system was particularly oppressive for blacks because of the following reasons :

(a) They were forbidden from living in white areas. They could work in white areas only if they had a permit to do so.

(b) They could not even visit the churches where the whites worshipped. Blacks could not form associations or protest against the terrible treatment.

(iii) If the blacks had not forgiven the whites for all their oppression and exploitation and decided to take revenge upon them, there would have been bloodshed every where.

It could have led to a division of the country and they would not be seen as a united and peaceful South Africa.

ASSESSMENT EXERCISE

Multiple Choice Questions (MCQs)

1. How did the apartheid regime categorise the South African population, and what was the impact of this classification on the people of mixed races and those of Indian origin?
(a) They were all considered equal citizens with equal voting rights
(b) They were all categorised as 'blacks' and treated the same way
(c) Mixed races were labeled 'coloured' and people of Indian origin faced specific restrictions
(d) People of Indian origin were given the same rights as white people

2. Who was the Chairman of the Drafting Committee that drafted the Indian Constitution?
(a) Dr Rajendra Prasad (b) Jaipal Singh
(c) Dr BR Ambedkar (d) Baldev Singh

3. What helped South Africa transition peacefully from apartheid to democracy?
(a) International support
(b) Goodwill and mutual trust between historical enemies
(c) Repression by the government
(d) Punishment of the white minority

4. What was the name of the jail in which Nelson Mandela spent his imprisonment?
(a) Ribbon Island
(b) Robben Island
(c) Rincon Island
(d) None of these

Subjective Questions (VSA, SA & LA)

1. What do you mean by 'Constitutional Amendments'?

2. Why is the term fraternity added in the Preamble?

3. Describe three weaknesses of democracy observed in India.

4. How was the Constituent Assembly formed?

5. Why do you think the Indian Constitution is still considered legitimate even after more than seven decades?

6. What efforts were made to form a new Constitution after Independence in South Africa?

7. Give the historical development of the Constitution of our country.

CHAPTER 3

Electoral Politics

In a democracy, people are governed through the elected representatives. This chapter discusses about how these representatives are elected. So, it begins by analysing why election are necessary in democracy. The basic idea here is to distinguish democratic elections from non-democratic elections. It also discusses about an assessment of whether an election in India are free and fair. It also examines the role of the Election Commission in ensuring free and fair elections.

3.1 Election

The mechanism or procedure by which people choose their representatives at regular intervals is called election.

Need of Election

Elections take place regularly in any democracy. They also take place in many countries that are not democratic. Elections are necessary due to the following reasons

- Elections solve the problems of assessing people on the basis of education, knowledge or experience.
- Elections help in analysing whether the people like their representatives or not.
- Elections ensure that the representatives rule as per the wishes of the people and make sure that those who are not working for the people, do not remain their representatives.

In an election, the voters make many choices like

- They can choose who will make laws for them.
- They can choose who will form the government and take major decisions.
- They can choose the party whose policies will guide the government and law-making.

Conditions for Elections to be Democratic

The list of the minimum conditions of a democratic election are

- Everyone should have the right to choose representative. It means everyone has one vote and every vote has equal value.
- Political parties and candidates should be **free to contest elections** and offer some real choices to the voters.
- The choices should be offered at regular intervals by conducting elections after a certain period.
- The candidates preferred by the people should get elected.
- Elections should be conducted in a free and fair manner where people can choose representatives according to their wish.

Our Constitution entitles every citizen to elect her/his representative and to be elected as a representative. Thus, the Constitution makers made provision of reserved constituencies to ensure representation of every section of society, especially the weaker sections.

Political Competition

Political competition takes place when different political parties compete to gain the confidence and the vote of the voters. They make promises and give incentives to motivate the voters to vote them.

This electoral competition has many demerits like

- It creates a sense of **disunity** and **factionalism**[1] (groupism) and party-politics in every locality.
- Different political parties and candidates often use dirty tricks like **booth capturincg**[2] to win **elections.**
- The pressure to win electoral fights does not allow to form useful long-term policies.
- Some good people who may wish to serve the country, do not enter in electoral competition.

1 Factionalism It refers to splitting up of a group in small factions. In this political concept, a group of persons form a minority in a larger group.
2 Booth Capturing It means supporters or hired people of party or a candidate gain physical control of a polling booth and caste false votes by threatening everyone or by preventing genuine voters from reaching the polling booth.

The electoral competition also has some merits like

- Regular electoral competition provides incentives to political parties and leaders. If they can satisfy the voters with their work, they will be able to win again.
- Important issues are raised by the political parties and leaders due to the competition.
- It helps to force political parties and leaders to serve the people.

Assembly Electrons in Haryana–A Case Study

- **Formation of a New Party** Haryana had been ruled by Congress Party since 1982. At that time, Chaudhary Devi Lal was an opposition leader. He led a movement called **Nyaya Yudh** (struggle for justice) and formed a new party called **Lok Dal.**
- **Election Campaign** In election campaign of 1987 Assembly Election, Devi Lal promised voters that if his party win, he would waive loans of farmers and small businessmen. He promised that this would be the first action of his government.
- **Voting** As people were unhappy with existing government, they were attracted by Devi Lal's promise. They voted in favour of Lok Dal and its allies which won 76 out of 90 seats in the State Assembly.
- **Announcement of Results** Lok Dal won 60 seats alone and thus, had a clear majority in the Assembly. Congress got only 5 seats. As the election result was announced, the existing Chief Minister of Congress resigned.
- **Appointment of Chief Minister** The newly elected Members of Legislative Assembly (MLAs) of Lok Dal chose Devi Lal as their leader. The Governor invited Devi Lal to be the new Chief Minister. After three days of election result, he became the Chief Minister.
He instantly issued a government order waiving the outstanding loans of small farmers, agricultural labourers and small businessmen.
- **New Election** Lok Dal ruled the state for 4 years. In 1991 election, Lok Dal did not win people's support. This time Congress won the election and formed the new government.

3.2 System of Elections in India

In India, **Lok Sabha** and **Vidhan Sabha** (Assembly) elections are held regularly after every **five years**. After five years, the term of all the elected representatives comes to an end. The Lok Sabha or Vidhan Sabha stands 'dissolved'.

Elections are held in all constituencies at the same time, either on the same day or within a few days. This is known as **General Election.**

Sometimes election is held only for one constituency[3] to fill the vacancy caused by death or resignation of a member. This is known as By-election[4].

Electoral Constituencies

In India, an area based system of representation is followed, where the country is divided into different areas for purpose of elections. These are called **Electoral Constituencies**. Every voter who lives in an area, votes for one representative.

For Lok Sabha election, India is divided into 543 constituencies. The representative elected from each constituency is called **Member of Parliament** or an **MP.**

Our Constitution requires that each constituency should have an equal population living within it.

For Vidhan Sabha election, each state is divided into a specific number of assembly constituencies and the elected representative of each assembly constituency is called the **Member of Legislative Assembly** or an **MLA.**

Each parliamentary constituency has several assembly constituencies within it. The same principle applies for **Panchayat** and **Municipal elections.** Each village or town is divided into different wards that are like constituencies.

Each ward elects one member of the village or the urban local body. Sometimes these constituencies are counted as **seats**, as each constituency represents one seat in the assembly.

Reserved Constituencies

Our Constitution allows everyone to vote and be elected. However, the makers were concerned that weaker sections might not have enough resources or support to win elections. This could result in their voices being missing from Parliament and Assemblies, making democracy less fair. To solve this, they created reserved constituencies for these sections.

Some constituencies are reserved for people who belong to the **Scheduled Castes** (SC) and **Scheduled Tribes** (ST). In a SC reserved constituency, only someone who belongs to the SCs can contest for election.

3 Constituency It means voters in a geographical area who elect a representative to the legislative bodies.

4 By-election It refers to the election that are held in particular constituencies due to death or resignation of the Member of Assembly (MLA) or the Member of Parliament (MP).

Similarly, in a ST constituency, only some one who belongs to the STs can contest for election.

This system of reservation was extended later to other weaker sections at the district and local level.

In many states, seats in rural (panchayat) and urban (municipalities and corporations) local bodies are reserved for **Other Backward Classes** (OBC).

The proportion of seats reserved varies from state to state. **One-third of the seats are reserved** in rural and urban local bodies for **women candidates.**

> **KNOWLEDGE PLUS** At present, in the Lok Sabha, 84 seats are reserved for the Scheduled Castes (SC) and 47 for the Scheduled Tribes (ST) (as on 26th January, 2019). This number is in proportion to their share in the total population.

Voters' List

In a democratic election, the list of those who are eligible to vote is officially called the **Electoral Roll**[5] and is commonly known as the Voters' List.

It is the responsibility of the government to get the names of all the eligible voters put on the voters' list.

The right to vote falls under **Universal Adult Franchise**[6]. It means all the citizens who are aged 18 years and above can vote in an election regardless of his or her caste, religion or gender. Some criminals and persons with unsound mind can be denied the right to vote in rare situations.

As new persons attain voting age, names are added to the voters' list and names of those who move out of a place or those who died are deleted.

A complete revision of the list takes place every five years. This is done to ensure that it remains up to date.

In the last few years, a new system of **Election Photo Identity Card** (EPIC) has been introduced. However, this card has not been made compulsory for voting and voters can show any other proofs of identity like the ration card, driving licence or Aadhaar Card to cast a vote.

Nomination of Candidates

Anyone who is a voter can also become a candidate in elections. However, to be a candidate in election, the minimum age is 25 years.

Political parties nominate their candidates who get the party support and symbol. Party's nomination is often called **Party Ticket.**

The candidate has to fill a **nomination form** and give some money as a **security deposit.**

Recently, a new system of declaration has been introduced on direction from the Supreme Court. Every candidate has to make a legal declaration giving full details of

- Educational qualifications of the candidate.
- Details of the assets and liabilities of the candidate and his/her family.
- Serious criminal cases pending against the candidate.

This information provided by the candidates has to be made public so that the voters can make their decision on the basis of the information.

Educational Qualifications for Candidates

There is no educational qualification for candidates for being an MP or an MLA. However, the relevant qualification for candidates is the ability to understand people's concerns, problems and to represent people's interests.

Putting an educational qualification would go against the spirit of democracy because it would deprive a majority of the citizens right to contest elections.

Election Campaign

Election campaign means the promotion (or propaganda) of the policies, offers and promises that the candidates make to voters to fulfill, if they are elected.

In this way, voters can decide the candidate to vote for. They vote for the candidate whose policies they like.

In India, election campaigning takes place for a two-week period between the announcement of the final list of candidates and the date of polling.

During this period, the candidates contact their voters, political leaders, address election meetings and political parties mobilise their supporters. This is also the period when television news and newspapers are covered with election-related stories and debates.

Political parties start preparing for elections in advance before they actually take place. In election campaigns, political parties try to focus public attention on some big issues. They want to attract the public to that issue and get their votes on that basis.

Code of Conduct and Laws

There are some election laws to regulate election campaign, so that every political party and candidate gets

5 **Electoral Roll** It is the voters' list prepared by a door to door survey to include only bonafide voters and minimise role of bogus voters.

6 **Universal Adult Franchise** Every Indian citizen of 18 years and above has the right to vote irrespective of caste, creed and sex.

equal chance to campaign. According to these laws, no party or candidate can

- bribe or threaten voters.
- appeal to them in the name of caste or religion.
- use government resources for election campaign.
- spend more than ₹ 25 lakh in a constituency for a Lok Sabha election or ₹ 10 lakh in a constituency in an Assembly Election.

If any party or candidate is found violating any of the above law, their candidature can be rejected by the court even after they have won the election.

In addition to the laws, all the political parties in our country have agreed to a model Code of Conduct[7] for election campaign. According to this,

- no party or candidate can use any place of worship for election propaganda.
- no candidate can use government vehicles, aircrafts and officials for elections.
- once elections are announced, ministers shall not lay foundation stones of any project, take any big policy decision or make any promise of providing public facilities.

Some Slogans Given by Different Political Parties During Elections

- The Congress party led by **Indira Gandhi** gave the slogan of **Garibi Hatao (Remove poverty)** in the Lok Sabha elections of 1971. The party promised to recreate all the policies of the government to remove poverty from the country.
- Janata Party gave the slogan **Save Democracy** in the Lok Sabha election held in 1977.
- The Left Front gave the slogan **Land to the Tiller** in the West Bengal Assembly elections held in 1977.
- NT Rama Rao, the leader of the Telugu Desam Party gave the slogan **Protect the Self-Respect of the Telugus** in Andhra Pradesh Assembly elections in 1983.

Polling and Counting of Votes

The final stage of an election is the day, when the voters cast or 'poll' their vote. It is called an **Election day.**

Every person whose name is on the voters' list can go to a nearby **polling booth**[8] and cast his/her vote.

Once the voter goes inside the booth, the election official identify him/ her, put a mark on the voter's finger and allow him/ her to cast his/ her vote.

An agent of each candidate is allowed to sit inside the polling booth and ensure that the voting takes place in a fair way.

Earlier voting was done by putting a stamp on the ballot paper. A **ballot paper** is a sheet of paper on which the names of the contesting candidates alongwith party name and symbols are listed.

Now, **Electronic Voting Machines** (EVMs) are used to record votes where voter presses button against name of the candidate (party symbols) for whom, he/she wants to cast his/her vote.

Independent candidates too have their own symbols, alloted by Election Commission.

Once the polling is over, all the EVMs are sealed and taken to a secure place. A few days later, on a fixed date, all the EVMs are opened and the votes secured by each candidate are counted.

The candidate who secures the highest number of votes from a constituency is declared elected.

In a general election, usually the counting of votes in all the constituencies takes place at the same time, on the same day. Television channels, radio and newspapers report this event.

Within a few hours of counting, all the results are declared and it becomes clear as to who will form the next government.

Try These

1. **In which case the by-elections are held?**
2. **India has how many Lok Sabha constituencies?**
3. **How many seats are reserved for women in local bodies?**
4. **What is EPIC? Is it mandatory?**
5. **'Land to the Tiller' was the slogan given by whom?**

3.3 Democratic Elections in India

There are many factors which ensure that elections held in India are democratic. These are discussed below

Independent Election Commission

In our country, elections are conducted by an independent and very powerful Election Commission (EC). It enjoys the same kind of independence as the judiciary enjoys.

The **Chief Election Commissioner** (CEC) is appointed by the President of India. After appointed, CEC is not answerable to the President or the government.

Powers enjoyed by the Election Commission are

- It takes decisions on every aspect of conduct and control of elections from the announcement of elections to the declaration of results.

7 Code of Conduct It is a set of norms and guidelines to be followed by political parties and contesting candidates during election time
8 Polling Booth It is a make shift place where people go to caste their votes on the election day.

- It implements the code of conduct and punishes any candidate or party that violates it.
- During the election period, the Election Commission can order the government to follow some guidelines. These guidelines prevent use and misuse of governmental power to enhance its chances to win elections or to transfer some government officials.
- Government officers on election duty, work under the control of the Election Commission and not the government.
- If election officials come to the opinion that polling was not fair in some booths or even an entire constituency, they order a repoll.
- The ruling parties often do not like what the EC does. But they have to obey.

Popular Participation

If the election process is not free or fair, people will not continue to participate in the exercise.

People's participation in election is usually measured by **voter turnout** figures. Turnout indicates the per cent of eligible voters who actually cast their vote.

Over the last 50 years, the turnout in Europe and North America has declined. In India this voters turn out has either remained stable or actually gone up.

In India, the poor, illiterate and underprivileged people vote in larger proportion as compared to the rich and privileged sections. This is in contrast to Western democracies.

In India, people care about elections because they believe their vote can help change policies and improve the country.

Acceptance of Election Outcome

If elections are not free or fair, the outcome always favours the powerful. In such a situation, the ruling parties do not lose elections. But this is not the case in **rigged election**[9]. Usually the losing party does not accept the outcome.

The outcome of India's election is given below

- The ruling parties routinely lose elections in India both at the National and State Level.
- In the US, an **incumbent**[10] or sitting elected representative rarely loses an election. But in India, about half of the sitting MPs or MLAs lose elections.
- Candidates who are known to have spent a lot of money on buying votes and those with known criminal connection often lose elections.
- Except some disputed elections, the electoral outcomes are usually accepted by the defeated party as 'people's verdict'.

Challenges to Free and Fair Elections

Elections in India are mostly free and fair. The winning party forms the government because people choose it. Some candidates may win unfairly using money power. However, the overall result reflects the people's choice. This makes Indian elections democratic.

Many unfair practices are used in elections such as

- Inclusion of false names and exclusion of genuine names in the voters list.
- Misuse of government facilities and officials by the ruling party.
- Excessive use of money by rich candidates and big parties.
- Manipulation of voters and fraud practices during the polling period.
- Candidates and parties with a lot of money may not be sure of their victory, but they do enjoy a big and unfair advantage over smaller parties and independent candidates.
- Some candidates with criminal records are able to secure party tickets from major parties.
- Some families tend to dominate political parties; tickets are distributed to relatives from these families.
- Elections offer only little choice to ordinary citizens as both the major parties are quite similar to each other in policies and practice.
- Smaller parties and independent candidates suffer a huge disadvantage compared to bigger parties in terms of money power and organisational support.

These challenges exist not only in India, but also in many established democracies.

Try These

1. **The Chief Election Commissioner is appointed by whom?**
2. **What do common people in India believe they can influence through election?**
3. **This method is used to measure people's participation in an election. Identify this method.**
4. **In which country an incumbent representative rarely loses an election?**

9 **Rigged Election Means** It refers to cheating in an election by controlling the votes or the result.
10 **Incumbent Means** It refers to a person who is currently in an official position.

Mind Map

ELECTORAL POLITICS

Need of Election
- Elections solve the problems of accessing people on the basis of education, knowledge or experience.
- They help in analysing that people like their representatives or not.

Conditions for Elections to be Democratic
- Everyone should have the right to choose representative.
- Political parties and candidates are free to contest elections.
- Elections should be conducted in a free and fair manner.
- Candidates preferred by the people should get elected.

Demerits
- Creates a sense of disunity and factionalism and party politics in every locality.
- Use of dirty tricks like booth capturing to win elections by political parties and leaders.
- Pressure to win electoral fights does not allow to form useful long term policies.

Election
The mechanism or procedure by which people chose their representatives at regular intervals

Political Competition

Merits
- Regular electoral competition provides incentives to political parties and leaders.
- Important issues are raised due to the competition by political parties and leaders.
- Helps to force political parties and leaders to serve the people.

System of Elections in India
- Lok Sabha and Rajya Sabha elections are held regularly after every five years.
- Elections are held in all constituencies at the same time, either on the same day or within few days called as General Election
- The elections involve the following processes
  - Electoral Constituencies
  - Reserved Constituencies
  - Voter's List
  - Nomination of Candidates
  - Election Campaign
  - Code of Conduct and Laws
  - Polling and Counting of Votes

Democratic Elections in India

Challenges to Free and Fair Elections
- Inclusion of false names and exclusion of genuine names in the voters list.
- Misuse of government facilities and officials by the ruling party.
- Manipulation of voters and fraud practices during the polling period.
- Some candidates are able to secure party tickets from major parties.

Acceptance of Election Outcome
- Ruling parties routinely lose elections in India .
- In the US, an incumbent or sitting elected representative rarely loses an election.
- Candidates with known criminal connection often lose elections.
- Electoral outcomes are usually accepted by the defeated party as people's verdict.

Independent Election Commission
- Takes decisions on every aspect of conduct and control of elections.
- Implements the code of conduct and punishes any candidate or party who violates it.
- The Chief Election Commissioner is appointed by the President of India.

Popular Participation
- If the election process is not free or fair, people will not continue to participate in the exercise.
- People's participation in election is usually measured by voter turnout figures.

NCERT FOLDER

Covering Intext Questions and Exercises of NCERT

INTEXT QUESTIONS

Q.1 Do most leaders fulfil their election promises?

Ans. During an elections, most of the leaders make many big promises to the people (voters) to win their support and vote. However, after the elections, the political leaders forget their promises and most of them do not fulfil their election promises.

Q.2 The time is after midnight. An expectant crowd sitting for the past five hours in a chowk of the town is waiting for its leader to come. The organisers assure and reassure the crowd that he would be here any moment. The crowd stands up whenever a passing vehicle comes that way. It arouses hopes that he has come.

The leader is Mr Devi Lal, Chief of the Haryana Sangharsh Samiti, who was to address a meeting in Karnal on Thursday night. The 76-year-old leader, is a very busy man these days.

His day starts at 8 am and ends after 11 pm, he had already addressed nine election meetings since morning been constantly addressing public meetings for the past 23 months and preparing for this election.

Jagdeep and Navpreet read this story and drew the following conclusions. Can you say which of these are right or wrong (or if the information given in the story is inadequate to call them right or wrong).

(a) Elections can lead to changes in the policy of the government.

(b) The Governor invited Devi Lal to become the Chief Minister because he was impressed with his speeches.

(c) People are unhappy with every ruling party and vote against it in the next election.

(d) The party that wins the election forms the government.

(e) The election led to a lot of economic development in Haryana.

(f) The Congress Chief Minister need not have resigned after his party lost elections.

Ans. (a) Right (b) Wrong

(c) Wrong (d) Inadequate information

(e) Wrong

(f) Inadequate information

Q.3 We have seen why democracies need to have elections. But why do rulers in non-democratic countries need to hold elections?

Ans. Rulers in non-democratic countries need to hold elections because they want to show the world that they are not unpopular and they have the support of the people of the country which will improve their image in the eyes of the world.

Secondly, they want to show that their government and position has been achieved legally and according to the constitutional provisions.

Q.4 Ah! So, elections are like exams where politicians and parties know if they have passed or failed. But who are the examiners?

Ans. The examiners in this case are the voters, who give them marks in the form of votes.

Q.5 Like in Panchayats should we not have at least one-third seats in the Parliament and Assemblies reserved for women?

Ans. One-third of the seats are reserved for women in the Panchayats, but unfortunately even today representation of women in the State Assemblies and Parliament is very low. The women constitute 50% of our society.

So, we need to reserve at least one-third seats in the Assemblies and the Parliament for women. This will help them to uplift their status in society.

Q.6 See the map below and answer the following questions.

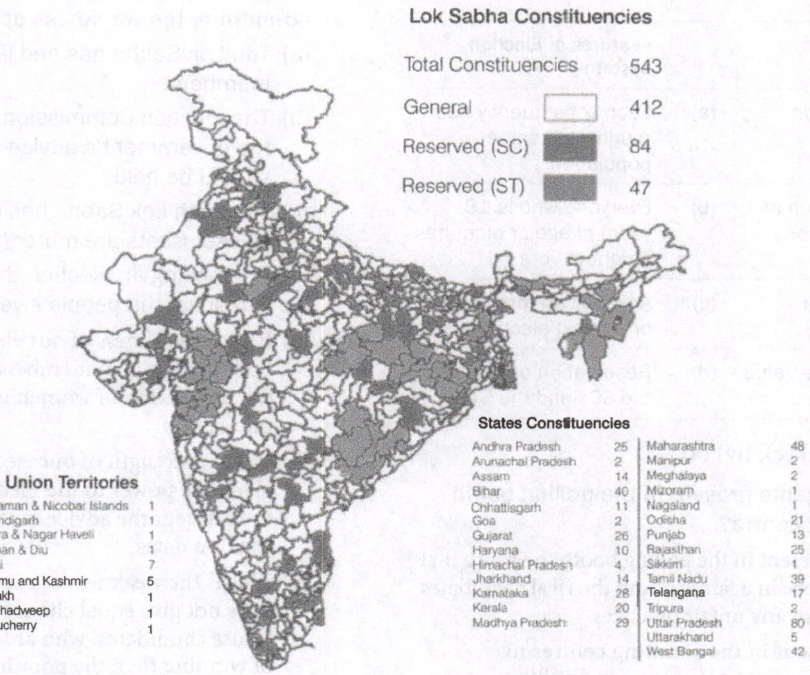

(a) What is the number of Lok Sabha constituencies in your state and the neighbouring two states?

(b) Which states have more than 30 Lok Sabha constituencies?

(c) Why do some states have such a large number of constituencies?

(d) Why are some constituencies small in area while others are very big?

(e) Are the constituencies reserved for the SCs and STs evenly spread all over the entire country or are there more in some areas?

Ans. (a) Do it yourself.

(b) The states which have more than 30 Lok Sabha constituencies are Bihar, Maharashtra, Tamil Nadu, Uttar Pradesh and West Bengal.

(c) Some states have large number of constituencies because of their population.

(d) Some constituencies are small in area while others are very big because each constituency is fixed on the basis of number of the voters. The area does not matter. If a smaller area has equal number of voters as a big area, both will be treated as constituencies.

(e) The constituencies reserved for the SCs and STs are not evenly spread all over the entire country, but are more in some areas.

Q.7 Why are the candidates required to give a detailed statement of their property ?

Ans. Candidates are required to give a detailed statement of their property at the time of election because the Election Commission is trying to control the misuse of money power in elections.

The candidate has to give information about his assets movable and immovable, debts to financial institution, tax status, income and wealth.

With this information, the voters will be able to know more about the candidates and make their own choices.

Q.8 Match the following features of our electoral system with the principles they reflect.

	Principles		Features of Election System
(i)	Universal Adult Franchise	(a)	Each constituency has roughly the same population.
(ii)	Representation of Weaker Sections	(b)	Everyone who is 18 years of age or older has a right to vote.
(iii)	Open Political Competition	(c)	Anyone can form a party or contest elections.
(iv)	One Vote-One Value	(d)	Reservation of seats for the SCs and the STs.

Ans. (i) (b), (ii) (d), (iii) (c), (iv) (a)

Q.9 Why are party agents present in the polling booth and the counting centre?

Ans. Party agents are present in the polling booth to ensure that the voting takes place in a fair way and the rival candidates are not able to adopt any unfair practices.

They are also present in the counting centres to ensure that the counting is done properly without any unfair means.

Q.10 Identify the fair and the unfair electoral practices among the following.

(a) A minister flags off a new train in his constituency a week before polling day.

(b) A candidate promises that she will get a new train for her constituency if she is elected.

(c) Supporters of a candidate take the voters to a temple and make them take an oath that they will vote for him.

(d) The supporters of a candidate distribute blankets in slums in return for a promise for vote.

Ans. (a) Unfair electoral practice

(b) Fair electoral practice

(c) Unfair electoral practice

(d) Unfair electoral practice

Q.11 Why does the Election Commission have so much power? Is this good for democracy?

Ans. The Election Commission in India is very powerful so that it is able to perform its functions efficiently in a proper manner.

This is good for democracy because only a powerful and independent Election Commission can ensure free and fair elections by preventing malpractices and unfair means in the elections.

Q.12 Here are some facts on Indian elections. Comment on each of these to say whether they reflect the strength or the weakness of our electoral system.

(a) The Lok Sabha has had less than 12% women members.

(b) The Election Commission often refuses to accept the government's advice about when the elections should be held.

(c) The 16th Lok Sabha has more than 440 members whose assets are more than ₹ 1 crore.

(d) After losing an election the Chief Minister said, "I respect the people's verdict".

Ans. (a) It is the weakness of our electoral system which sends only 12% women members to the Lok Sabha while the population of women is nearly 50% of the total population.

(b) It is the strength of our electoral system which has given the power to the Election Commission to refuse or to accept the advice of the ruling party about the election dates.

(c) This is the weakness of our electoral system, which does not give equal chance to both poor and rich. Those candidates, who are rich, have a better chance of winning than the poor in our country.

(d) This is the strength of our electoral system which enjoys the faith of both the defeated and winning candidates. Barring very few disputed elections, the electoral outcomes are usually accepted as 'people's verdict' by the defeated party.

EXERCISE

Q.1 Which of the following statements about the reasons for conducting elections are false?

(a) Elections enable people to judge the performance of the government.

(b) People select the representative of their choice in an election.

(c) Elections enable people to evaluate the performance of the judiciary.

(d) People can indicate which policies they prefer.

Ans. (c) Elections enable people to evaluate the performance of the judiciary.

Q.2 Which of these is not a good reason to say that Indian elections are democratic?

(a) India has the largest number of voters in the world.

(b) India's Election Commission is very powerful.

(c) In India, everyone above the age of 18 has a right to vote.

(d) In India, the losing parties accept the electoral verdict.

Ans. (a) India has the largest number of voters in the world.

Q.3 Match the following.

(a)	It is necessary to keep the voters list up to date because.	(i)	There is a fair representation of all sections of our society.
(b)	Some constituencies are reserved for SCs and STs so that	(ii)	Everyone has equal opportunity to elect their representative
(c)	Everyone has one and only one vote so that	(iii)	All candidates must have a fair chance of competing in elections
(d)	Party in power is not allowed to use government vehicles because	(iv)	Some people may have moved away from the area where they voted last

Ans. (a) (iv), (b) (i), (c) (ii), (d) (iii)

Q.4 List all the different election related activities mentioned in the chapter and arrange them in a time sequence, beginning with the first activity and ending with the last.

Some of these activities are given below releasing election manifestos; counting of votes; making of voters' list; election campaign; declaration of election results; casting of votes; ordering of re-poll; announcing election schedule; filing nomination.

Ans. The following list contains the different election related activities of the electoral process, beginning with the first activity and ending with the last

(i) Making of voters list
(ii) Announcing election schedule
(iii) Filing of nomination
(iv) Releasing election manifestos
(v) Election campaign
(vi) Casting of votes
(vii) Ordering of re-poll
(viii) Counting of votes
(ix) Declaration of election results

Q.5 Surekha is an officer incharge of ensuring free and fair elections in an Assembly constituency in a state. Describe what should she focus on for each of the following stages of election.

(a) Election campaign
(b) Polling day
(c) Counting day

Ans. (a) **Election Campaign** During an election, Surekha should ensure that candidates or their supporters do not

- use muscle power to threaten the voters.
- use money power to influence the voters.
- use government machinery and resources.
- spend more money than the limit fixed by the Election Commission.
- distribute money or other things (saris, sewing machines, umbrellas) among voters during or election campaign.
- ask for votes in the name of caste or religion.

(b) **Polling Day** On polling day, Surekha has to ensure that

- booth capturing does not take place.
- fake votes are not cast.
- poor and weaker sections of society are able to cast their vote freely and without fear.
- no unauthorised person should be allowed to enter polling booth.

(c) **Counting Day** On the counting day, Surekha will have to ensure that

- the voting machines are intact.
- the counting should begin in the presence of the candidates and their agents.
- counting should be done carefully and accurately.
- no unauthorised person should be allowed into the counting centre.
- after the counting, results are declared by the authorised official.

Q.6 The table below gives the proportion of different communities among the candidates who won elections to the US Congress. Compare these to the proportion of these communities in the population of the US. Based on this, would you suggest a system of reservations in the US Congress? If yes, why and for which communities? If no, why not?

	Proportion of the Community (in per cent) in the	
	House of representatives	Population of US
Blacks	8	13
Hispanics	5	13
Whites	86	70

Ans. Based on the figures, given in the table, it is clear that Blacks and Hispanics have much less representation than their population in the US Congress. Therefore, to give them proper representation, reservation should be provided to them.

Q.7 Can we draw the following conclusions from the information given in this chapter? Give two facts to support your position for each of these.

(a) Election Commission of India does not have enough powers to conduct free and fair elections in the country.
(b) There is a high level of popular participation in the elections in our country.

(c) It is very easy for the party in power to win an election.

(d) Many reforms are needed to make our elections completely free and fair.

Ans. (a) No, this conclusion is wrong because the Election Commission is indeed powerful enough to ensure free and fair elections. The Election Commission has complete control over all the functionaries connected with the conduct of fair elections. It can order repoll if there is report of rigging.

(b) This conclusion is right. Nowadays, people are more aware and more and more people have started to cast their vote and the voting percentage has gone up. Ruling parties often lose elections due to change in voting preference by the people.

(c) This is a wrong conclusion, because the party in power often loses elections. In India mostly the sitting MPs or the ruling party loses the elections.

(d) This conclusion is right. Though the role of money and muscle power has been reduced, there is still need to control it further. Because some politicians and political parties are still able to take advantage of money power in elections.

Many candidates with criminal records use muscle power to threaten and terrorise other candidates and voters which needs to be checked.

Q.8 Chinappa was convicted for torturing his wife for dowry. Satbir was held guilty of practising untouchability. The court did not allow either of them to contest elections. Does this decision go against the principles of democratic elections?

Ans. This decision of the court preventing Chinappa and Satbir from contesting elections does not go against the principles of democratic elections because both have been found guilty of breaking the law by the court.

Criminals should not be allowed to hold position of power because they are not good citizens and could harm interests of the people.

Q.9 Here are some reports of electoral malpractices from different parts of the world. Is there anything that these countries can learn from India to improve their elections? What would you suggest in each case?

(a) During an election in Nigeria, the officer incharge of counting votes deliberately increased the votes of one candidate and declared him elected. The court later found out that more than 5 lakh votes cast for one candidate were counted in favour of another.

(b) Just before elections in Fiji, a pamphlet was distributed warning voters that a vote for former Prime Minister, Mahendra Chaudhary will lead to bloodshed. This was a threat to voters of Indian origin.

(c) In the US, each state has its own method of voting, its own procedure of counting and its own authority for conducting elections. Authorities in the state of Florida took many controversial decisions that favoured Mr Bush in the Presidential elections in 2000. But no one could change those decisions.

Ans. (a) If the malpractice has been proved in a court, the elections should be declared null and void and re-election should be held in that constituency. The officer incharge of the counting should be given strict punishment for committing such irregularity. The system of counting should be such that the counting officer shall not be able to do this.

In India, this is not possible as counting agents of all the candidates are present in the counting centre and counting of votes takes place in their presence. In this case, representatives of each candidate should be present to make sure that the votes are counted in a fair way.

(b) To issue such a pamphlet is definitely an election malpractice. The circulation of such a pamphlet should be checked immediately. The source of the pamphlet, a person, candidate or political party should be found out and punished, as it violates the principle of democratic elections. In India, this type of election campaign is not possible as the Election Commission of India always makes vigil on the procedures of election campaign. If any party violates the code of conduct, the Election Commission will punish it.

(c) Since each state in the USA has it own method of voting, its own procedure of counting and its own authority for conducting elections, the decisions taken by the state of Florida must be according to the election laws passed by that state.

No one could challenge those decisions as those must have been taken in accordance with the laws made by that state.

In India, since states are not authorised to make their own laws for election, such a situation can not arise. Election Commission as an independent body is solely responsible for conducting elections throughout the country.

Q.10 Here are some reports of malpractices in Indian elections. Identify what is the problem in each case. What should be done to correct the situation?

(a) Following the announcement of elections, the minister promised to provide financial aid to reopen the closed sugar mill.

(b) Opposition parties alleged that their statements and campaign was not given due attention in Doordarshan and All India Radio.

(c) An inquiry by the Election Commission showed that electoral rolls of a state contain name of 20 lakh fake voters.

(d) The hoodlums of a political party were moving with guns, physically preventing supporters of other political parties to meet the voters and attacking meetings of other parties.

Ans. (a) The problem here is that, after announcement of elections it is not legal to announce policy decisions according to the code of conduct.

According to the election law, no minister or member of the legislature can take decisions regarding projects which could influence the elections. Thus, the minister should not be allowed to contest the election.

(b) The problem in this situation is identified as the misuse of Government resources by the ruling party.

The solution to this problem is that, the Election Commission must ensure that all political parties are given equal opportunity to appear on Doordarshan and All India Radio. Election Commission must take action against misuse of this media.

(c) Problem in this situation is electoral rolls have not been revised. The presence of fake voters means that the elections were rigged by the authorities who prepared the electoral rolls.

(d) Problem identified in this situation is that by using hoodlums, the political party is terrorising its rivals. The elections were not free and fair.

Solution to this problem is that, the Election Commission should order the arrest of the hoodlums and ban the party from the elections.

Q.11 Ramesh was not in class when this chapter was being taught. He came the next day and repeated what he had heard from his father. Can you tell Ramesh what is wrong with these statements?

(a) Women always vote the way men tell them to. So, what is the point of giving them the right to vote?

(b) Party politics creates tension in society. Elections should be decided by consensus not by competition.

(c) Only graduates should be allowed to stand as candidates for elections.

Ans. (a) The statement is wrong because the policy of secret ballot ensures that an individual can vote for whoever he/she wants. Women are fully capable of taking decisions on their own and selecting the candidate they like.

(b) Party politics and competition in election certainly creates tension in society. But elections should not be decided by consensus. This is because in modern states, where population is very large, it is not possible to have consensus on election. Competition works as both deterrent and motivator for the political candidates. A fear of losing the election and a motivation for winning the elections work in favour of people.

(c) Only allowing graduates to stand as candidates for elections is wrong. It is not necessary that a graduate person will be more sensitive to the needs of the people or that he will turn out to be an honest and sincere person.

To prescribe educational qualifications (graduate level) would go against the spirit of democracy. In India, it will deprive a large section of the country's citizens the right to contest elections. However, it is better to have educated politicians, but being graduate should not be a compulsion.

REVIEW EXERCISE

Including Competency Based Questions

Part I

Multiple Choice Questions (MCQs)

1. Since 1982 to 1987, Haryana was ruled by which political party?

(a) Haryana Sangharsh Samiti
(b) Bhartiya Janata Party
(c) Congress Party
(d) Communist Party of India

2. Which one of the following is not a factor that makes an election democratic?

(a) There should be something to choose from.
(b) Parties and candidates should be free to contest elections.
(c) The choice should not be offered at regular intervals.
(d) The candidate preferred by the people should get elected.

3. Which of the following terms is used when election is held only for one constituency to fill the vacancy caused by death or resignation of a member?

(a) Constituency election (b) General election

(c) By-election (d) Assembly election

4. Which of the following terms is used for the areas when our country is divided into different areas for purposes of elections?

(a) Panchayats (b) Wards

(c) Blocks (d) Constituencies

5. What do we mean when we say that a constituency is reserved for the Scheduled Castes (SC)?

(a) Any candidate can contest the election but only the SC candidate will be declared winner.

(b) Any candidate can contest the election but only SC women candidate will be declared winner.

(c) Only SC candidate can contest the election.

(d) None of the above

6. What proportion of seats are reserved in rural and urban local bodies for women candidates?

(a) One-third of the total seats

(b) Two-third of the total seats

(c) Half of the total seats

(d) One-fourth of the total seats

7. Each state is divided into a specific number of

(a) Block Constituencies

(b) District Constituencies

(c) Assembly Constituencies

(d) Ward Constituencies

8. The list of those people who are eligible to vote is officially called

(a) Voter's List (b) Electoral Roll

(c) Elector's List (d) Constituency List

9. Which of the following state has the largest number of Lok Sabha seats?

(a) Maharashtra (b) Andhra Pradesh

(c) Bihar (d) Uttar Pradesh

10. Which of the following Union Territories has the largest number of Lok Sabha seats?

(a) Chandigarh (b) Delhi

(c) Lakshadweep (d) Puducherry

11. What does EVM stand for?

(a) Electronic Vending Machine

(b) Electronic Voting Machine

(c) Electoral Voting Machine

(d) Electoral Volunteer Mechanism

12. The power and independence of Election Commission (EC) of India is equivalent to which one of the following?

(a) Governor (b) Assistant Commissioner of Police

(c) Judiciary (d) National Human Rights Commission

13. The Chief Election Commissioner is appointed by whom among the following?

(a) Lok Sabha Speaker

(b) The Chief Justice of India

(c) The President of India

(d) The Vice-President of India

14. In India, which of the following sections vote(s) in larger proportion as compared to the rich and privileged sections?

(a) Poor (b) Illiterate

(c) Underprivileged (d) All of these

15. People's participation in an election is usually measured by voter .... figures.

(a) physical (b) education

(c) turnout (d) economic

16. Find the incorrect option.

(a) Elections should be conducted in free and fair manner.

(b) Everyone should have the right to choose their representative.

(c) Elections are necessary and mandatory in all forms of government.

(d) Elections are held in all constituencies at the same time, either on the same day or within a few days.

17. Consider the statements given below and choose the correct answer. **Competency Based**

Statement I In our country, elections are conducted by the independent and very powerful election commission.

Statement II CEC is appointed by the President as well removed by the Attorney General of India.

Options

(a) Statement I is correct and II is incorrect.

(b) Statement I is incorrect and II is correct.

(c) Both I and II are correct.

(d) Both I and II are correct.

18. "Debates often arise over educational qualifications of politicians". Why do you think Constitution makers did not make education a criteria for candidates?

I. They believed that educational qualifications are irrelevant for political representation.

II. Putting an educational qualification would go against the spirit of democracy because it would deprive the majority of the people.

III. They prioritised the ability to understand and represent people's concerns over formal education.

Options

(a) Statements I and II are appropriate.

(b) All the statements are appropriate

(c) Only statement II is appropriate

(d) Statements II and III are appropriate

19. **Arrange the following in the correct sequence.**

I. 'Save Democracy' was the slogan given by Janata Party.

II. Indira Gandhi gave the slogan of 'Garibi Hatao'.

III. 'Protect the Self-Respect of the Telugus' was the slogan in the Andhra Pradesh Assembly elections.

Codes

(a) I, II, III (b) II, I, III

(c) II, III, I (d) III, II, I

20. **As the election day nears, rumors spread about misleading social media campaigns targeting candidates named Sheena and Rakesh. Accusation arises between the campaigns with Sheena blaming Rakesh for spreading wrong information about the scam in education and Rakesh accusing Sheena for doing corruption. The atmosphere becomes tense and the voters are struggling to vote for which candidate.**

Accordingly, which resolutional initiative would be the most crucial for improving the transparency of the election ? **Competency Based**

I. To address the growing concern, the election commission has to launch an emergency investigation team to unfold the truth.

II. Election commission has to demolish the tickets of both the candidates as they both are guilty without an investigation.

III. No action needs to be taken let the voters decide who is right or wrong by themselves

Options

(a) I and III (b) I and II

(c) Only I (d) I and III

21. **In a democratic country named okra land, elections are governed by the comprehensive code of conduct to ensure fair,transparent and ethical electoral processes. The code prohibits actions that could undermine the integrity of the electoral system or manipulative public opinions.**

Which of the following candidates did not follow the code of conduct ? **Competency Based**

Candidate (A) Made promises during their campaign that were later found to be unrealistic.

Candidate (B) Exceeded the prescribed limits for campaign spending and accepting donations, etc.

Candidate (C) Reports emerged that individuals are hampering the voters' vote on the day of elections.

Codes

(a) Candidates A and B (b) Candidates B and C

(c) Candidates A,B,C (d) Candidates C and A

Answers

1. (c)	**2.** (c)	**3.** (c)	**4.** (d)	**5.** (c)
6. (a)	**7.** (c)	**8.** (b)	**9.** (d)	**10.** (b)
11. (b)	**12.** (c)	**13.** (c)	**14.** (d)	**15.** (c)
16. (c)	**17.** (a)	**18.** (b)	**19.** (b)	**20.** (c)
21. (c)				

Match the Following

1.

	List I (Slogans)	List II (Political Parties)
A.	Land to the Tiller	1. Congress Party
B.	Garibi Hatao	2. Telugu Desan Party
C.	Save Democracy	3. Left Front
D.	Protect the Self-respect of the Telugus	4. Janata Party

Codes

	A	B	C	D		A	B	C	D
(a)	2	4	1	3	(b)	1	2	3	4
(c)	4	1	2	3	(d)	3	1	4	2

Ans. (d)

Assertion-Reason

1. **Assertion** (A) There is no educational qualification for candidates for being an MP or an MLA.

Reason (R) The ralevant qualification for candidates is the ability to understand people's concerns, problems and to represent people's interests.

Codes

(a) Both A and R are true and R is the correct explanation of A

(b) Both A and R are true, but R is not the correct explanation of A

(c) A is true, but R is false

(d) A is false, but R is true

2. **Assertion** (A) Political competition takes place when different political parties compete to gain the confidence and the vote of voters.

Reason (R) Regular electoral competition provides incentives to political parties and leaders. If they can satisfy the voters with their work. They will be able to win again.

Codes

(a) Both A and R are true and R is the correct explanation of A

(b) Both A and R are true, but R is not the correct explanation of A

(c) A is true, but R is false

(d) A is false, but R is true

3. **Assertion** (A) Different political parties and candidates often use dirty tricks like booth capturing to win elections.

Reason (R) Elections give choices to voters to chose among the best and reveals the real motive of political parties.

Codes

(a) Both A and R are true and R is the correct explanation of A

(b) Both A and R are true, but R is not the correct explanation of A

(c) A is true, but R is false

(d) A is false, but R is true

4. **Assertion** (A) Sometimes elections are held only for one constituency to fill the vacancy is called By- election.

Reason (R) Elections are held in all constituencies at the same time or same day or within few days is called general elections.

Codes

(a) Both A and R are true and R is the correct explanation of A

(b) Both A and R are true, but R is not the correct explanation of A

(c) A is true, but R is false

(d) A is false, but R is true

Ans. 1. (a) Both A and R are true, but R is the correct explanation of A

2. (b) Both A and R are true, but R is not the correct explanation of A

3. (b) Both A and R are true, but R is not the correct explanation of A

4. (b) Both A and R are true, but R is not the correct explanation of A

Picture Based Questions

1. **What does the given picture depict ?**

(a) Most of the leaders make many big promises to the voters.

(b) After the elections, political leaders forget their promises.

(c) People select their representative as per their choice in an election.

(d) Both (a) and (b)

2. **What are the characteristics and implications of family or dynastic politics in India as given in the picture below?**

(a) Ordinary members of the party cannot rise to the top of the party.

(b) More or less found in each any every state.

(c) Most of the sons and daughters of politicians who have entered politics has no political experience

(d) All of the above

Ans. 1. (d) Both (a) and (b)   2. (d) All of the above

Case Based Question

1. **Read the source given below and answer the questions that follow.**

Our Constitution makers were aware of these problems. Yet they opted for free competition in elections as the way to select our future leaders. They did so because this system works better in the long run. In an ideal world all political leaders know what is good for the people and are motivated only by a desire to serve them. Political competition is not necessary in such an ideal world. But that is not what happens in real life. Political leaders all over the world, like all other professionals, are motivated by a desire to advance their political careers. They want to remain in power or get power and positions for themselves.They may wish to serve the people as well, but it is risky to depend entirely on their sense of duty. Besides even when they wish to serve the people, they may not know what is required to do so, or their ideas may not match what the people really want.

(i) Our Constitution makers were concerned about which problems ?

(a) Unhealthy competition

(b) party politics

(c) disunity and factionalism

(d) All of the above

(ii) What creates a sense of disunity and factionalism ?

(a) Democracy

(b) Political competition

(c) Non-democracy

(d) Extreme political competition

(iii) How does electoral competition work ?

(a) By giving speeches and campaigns.

(b) By newspaper and periodicals.

(c) It gives the political contestants incentives.

(d) If they fail to satisfy the voters with their work they will not be able to win again.

(iv) What is the merit of regular electoral competition?

(a) Different political parties and leaders often level allegations against each other.

(b) Parties know that if they raise the issue of what people want their chances of winning increases.

(c) Regular electoral competitions provide incentives to political parties and leaders.

(d) Both (b) and (c) are correct

Ans. (i) (d) All of the above

(ii) (b) Political competition

(iii) (a) By giving speeches and campaigns.

(iv) (d) Both (b) and (c) are correct

Part II

Very Short Answer Type Questions

1. What is election symbol?

Ans. At the time of election, certain symbols are alloted by Election Commission to political parties. They are called election symbols.

2. Write one merit of an electoral competition.

Ans. One merit of an electoral competition is that it gives choice to voters to choose best among the contesting candidates.

3. What is the meaning of free and fair elections?

Ans. When the voters are allowed to cast vote according to their wishes without any pressure and interference, it is called free and fair elections.

4. When does the by-election occur?

Ans. When any vacancy occurs due to death or resignation of a candidate, election becomes necessary and it is known as by-election.

5. What is the tenure for which a member of Parliament is elected?

Ans. The Member of Parliament is elected for a term of five years.

6. What is the number of Lok Sabha constituencies at present?

Ans. The number of Lok Sabha constituencies at present is 543.

7. What is the motive behind reserved constituencies?

Ans. The motive behind reserved constituencies is to ensure proper representation of the weaker sections like Scheduled Castes and Scheduled Tribes.

8. What is official name of voters' list?

Ans. Voters' list is officially known as electoral roll.

9. What is the minimum age for voting in India?

Ans. The minimum age for voting in India is 18 years.

10. How many seats are reserved for Scheduled Castes (SCs) and Scheduled Tribes (STs) in the Lok Sabha?

Ans. At present, 84 seats are reserved for the Scheduled Castes (SCs) and 47 for the Scheduled Tribes (STs) in the Lok Sabha.

11. Who appoints Chief Electoral Officer?

Ans. Chief Election Commissioner in consultation with State Government appoints Chief Electoral Officer.

12. Do you think communal electorate is a feature of election system in India?

Ans. No, communal electorate is not a feature of election system in India.

13. Two high profile celebrities with opposing political views decide to run against each other for a prominent political office. The campaign becomes a media presentation, raising questions about the role of fame in politics. Which committee or commission will play a crucial role in conducting free and fair elections? **Competency Based**

Ans. The Election Commission of India (ECI) is an independent constitutional authority that plays a crucial role. It is responsible for administering election processes at the national and state levels.

14. Our nation experiences a notable mass movement, during which a dynamic and inspiring young leader emerges, rallying the youth with pledges of progressive agenda. This signifies a change in political landscape as younger demographics advocate for a more inclusive future. What is the eligibility criteria for youth to become a member of parliament? **Competency Based**

Ans. The criteria by which a young youth can be eligible to become a member of Parliament is that a person must be a citizen of India and not less than 30 years of age in the case of Rajya Sabha and not less than 25 years of age in the case of Lok Sabha.

Short Answer Type Questions

1. What makes an election democratic?

Ans. Following conditions make an election democratic

(i) Election must be held regularly in every five years.

(ii) Every eligible voter must have one vote with equal value.

(iii) There should be more than one party so that voters can get some real choice.

(iv) Elections should be conducted in a free and fair manner and people should have full freedom to vote for any candidate they like.

2. Write any five demerits of electoral competition.

or **Write any three demerits of electoral competition.**

Ans. Following are the demerits of electoral competition

(i) An electoral competition creates a sense of 'disunity' and 'factionalism' in every locality.

(ii) The pressure of winning electoral competition does not allow sensible long-term policies to be formulated.

(iii) Some good people do not enter electoral competition they do not like the unfair competition in politics.

(iv) Candidates in electoral competition who ask for vote on communal and caste lines destroy the basic idea of democracy.

(v) Different political parties and candidates often use dirty tricks (like distributing money, liquor among the poor section of voters) in electoral competition to win elections.

3. Differentiate between the General Election and By-election.

Ans. Differences between the general election and by-election are as follows

General election	By-election
Elections are held in all constituencies at the same time either on the same day or within a few days. This is called a general election.	Election is held only for one constituency to fill the vacancy caused by death or resignation of a member. This is called a by-election.
Elections are held regularly after every five years.	Election is held before the expiry of 6 months from the date the seat falls vacant.
The representative elected in general election is elected for a full term of five years not for the remaining period of the house.	The representative elected in by-election is elected for the remaining period of the house not for five years.

4. What is the model code of conduct for election campaign?

or **What is the model code of conduct for election campaign which is accepted by all the political parties in our country?**

Ans. A set of norms and guidelines to be followed by political and contesting candidates during election time is known as model code of conduct.

According to this, no party or candidate can

(i) use any place of worship for election propaganda.

(ii) use government vehicles, aircrafts and officials for elections.

(iii) lay foundation stones of any project, after the date of elections are announced.

5. Describe any three functions of the Election Commission of India.

Ans. The three major functions of Election Commission of India are

(i) Election Commission takes decisions on every aspect of conduct and control of elections.

(ii) It implements the code of conduct and can punish any candidate or party that violates it.

(iii) It controls the government officers who are posted on the election duty.

6. Mention any two provisions which ensure the independency of the Election Commission.

Ans. Two provisions which ensure the independency of the Election Commission are as follows

(i) The members of the Election Commission are appointed by the President of India, but the members are not answerable to the President of India.

(ii) It is virtually impossible for the government to remove the members even if their work is not liked by the government.

7. Mention any three allegations about unfair practices in elections, reported in newspapers and television.

Ans. Newspapers and television generally report the following three allegations about unfair practices in elections

(i) Inclusion of false names and exclusion of genuine names in the voters' list.

(ii) Misuse of government facilities and officials by the ruling party.

(iii) Excessive use of money by rich candidates and big parties.

8. Highlight some issues which bring many limitations and challenges of Indian elections to our attention.

***or* Explain the challenges and limitation to free and fair elections in India.**

Ans. Important issues which bring many limitations and challenges of Indian elections to our attention are as follows

- Candidates and parties with lot of money enjoy a big and unfair advantage over smaller parties or independent candidates.
- Candidates with criminal records have been able to push others out of electoral race and secure a ticket from major parties.
- Some families tend to dominate political parties and secure tickets for their own family members.
- Smaller parties and independents suffer a huge disadvantage compared to bigger parties.

9. "One final test of the free and fairness of election lies in the outcome itself." Justify the statement with the help of the outcomes of India's elections.

***or* Describe the importance of outcome of election in India.**

Ans. The following points state outcomes of elections in India

- The ruling parties routinely lose elections in India both at the national and state levels.

  In fact, the ruling party lose every two out of the three elections held in the last fifteen years.
- Candidates who are known to have spent a lot of money on 'buying votes' and those with known criminal connections often lose elections.
- Except in very few disputed elections, the electoral outcomes are usually accepted as 'people's verdict' by defeated party.

  So, considering the above points, it is truly said that one final test of the free and fairness of election lies in the outcome itself.

10. In what way does the concept of electoral constituencies contribute to upholding democratic principles?

Ans. The concept of electoral constituencies contributes to upholding democratic principle are as follows

(a) **Representation** Constituencies ensure that each geographical area or community is represented in the legislative body.

(b) **Accountability** Constituencies establish a direct link between elected representatives and their constituents. Representatives are accountable to the people within their constituencies for their actions and decisions.

(c) **Fairness and Equal Representation** Constituencies are often designed to ensure equal representation by balancing population sizes. This principle, known as "one person, one vote," helps to prevent the dominance of specific regions or groups over others.

(d) **Local Issues and Responsiveness** Electoral constituencies allow elected representatives to focus on local issues that are important to their constituents. This responsiveness to local needs enhances the democratic process by ensuring that governance is adopted to the diverse needs of different communities.

(e) **Encouragement of Political Participation** Constituencies provide a framework for political participation at the grassroots level. By engaging with their local representatives and participating in constituency-based activities, citizens becomes more actively involved in the political process.

Long Answer Type Questions

1. What is Universal Adult Franchise? Why has it been adopted in India?

Ans. When the right to vote or franchise is given to every adult in a state, it is known as the Universal Adult Franchise.

Reasons for adopting Universal Adult Franchise in India are

- It makes democracy broad based. It enhances self-respect and prestige of the common people.
- It establishes political equality among all the people of the society.
- It enables minorities to protect and safeguard their interests so that they have an equal say in decisions that affect them.

2. How does our election law regulate campaigns?

Ans. Our election law regulate to uphold the principles of fairness, transparency and accountability throughout the electoral journey. According to our election law

- no one can bribe or threaten voters.
- use any place of worship or appeal to the voters in the name of religion or caste.
- use government resources, government vehicles, air crafts for elections.
- spend more than ₹ 25 lakh in a constituency for a Lok Sabha election and ₹ 10 lakh in a constituency for an Assembly election.
- Once elections are announced, no minister can lay foundation stones of any project or take any policy decision.

3. Do you think education qualification should be necessary for the candidate aspiring to fight elections? Give your views in favour or against it.

Ans. No, educational qualification should not be necessary for the candidate aspiring to fight elections.

Following are the reasons against the statement

- Educational qualification are not relevant to all kinds of job.
- Relevant qualification for being an MLA or an MP is the ability to understand and people's concerns, problems and the ways to solve them.
- Whether they can do so or it is examined by voters after five years.
- Putting an educational qualification would go against the spirit of democracy. It would deprive large number of people to get elected.

4. What is a reserved constituency ? Why there is a need for a reserved constituency ?

Ans. Reserved constituencies are the constituencies which are reserved for the people who belong to the Scheduled Castes (SC) and Scheduled Tribes (ST).

In a SC reserved constituency only someone who belongs to the Scheduled Castes can contest elections. Similarly only those belonging to the Scheduled Tribes can contest an election from a constituency reserved for ST.

There is a need of reserved constituency due to the following reasons

- **Political Equality for Weaker Sections** Our Constitution entitles every citizen to elect his/her representative and to be elected as a representative. The Constitution makers, however, were worried that in an open electoral competition, certain weaker sections may not stand a good chance to get elected to the Lok Sabha and the State Legislative Assemblies. Those who are influential and resourceful may prevent them from winning elections.
  If that happens, that would make our democracy less representative and less democratic. So, the makers of our constitution thought of a special system of reserved constituencies for weaker sections.
- **Gender Equality** It provide equal representation to women candidates as one-third of the seats are reserved in rural and urban local bodies.

5. Why slogans are used by political parties? Mention any four successful slogans given by different political parties in various elections.

Ans. In election campaign, political parties use slogans to attract the public and get them to vote for their party on that basis.

Four successful slogans given by different political parties in various elections are

(i) The Congress Party led by Indira Gandhi gave the slogan of 'Garibi Hatao' (Remove Poverty) in the Lok Sabha election of 1971.

(ii) Janata Party gave the slogan 'Save Democracy' in the Lok Sabha election of 1977.

(iii) The Left Front gave the slogan 'Land to the Tiller' in the West Bengal Assembly election of 1977.

(iv) NT Rama Rao, the leader of The Telugu Desam Party gave the slogan 'Protect the Self-Respect of the Telugus' in Andhra Pradesh election in 1983.

Case Based Questions

1. Read the source given below and answer the questions that follow.

Election and all about Competition

Political competition takes place when different political parties compete to gain the confidence and the vote of the voters. They make promises and give incentives to motivate the voters to vote them. This electoral competition has many demerits like it creates a sense of disunity and factionalism as well as party politics in every locality. Different political parties and candidates often use dirty tricks like booth capturing to win elections. The competition leads to the idea of being dragged into unhealthy competition. That is why good people do not enter and participate in the political competition but regular electoral competition provides incentives to political parties and leaders. If they can satisfy the voters with their work, they will be able to win again.

(i) Define the term political competition.

(ii) To what extent do you agree that electoral competition leads to electoral fights. Give reasons.

(iii) How is electoral competition helpful to political parties and leaders to win an election? Justify.

Ans. (i) Political competition takes place when different political parties compete to gain the confidence and the vote of the voters.

(ii) Yes, we agree that electoral competition leads to electoral fights among the political parties and leaders as different political parties and leaders often make allegations against one another. Parties and candidates often use dirty tricks to win elections. Political parties try to get the support of the people on the basis of religion, caste, etc. All this creates disunity in the society and also leads to communal riots.

(iii) Electoral competition is helpful to political parties as it provides incentives to political parties and leaders. If they can satisfy the voters with their work, they will be able to win again. In a democratic set up, it is necessary to have electoral competition as it generates confidence and motivate the voters to vote for a suitable political party.

2. Read the sources given below and answer the following questions that follow.

Source A Election Campaign in India

The main purpose of election is to give people a chance to chose the representatives, the government and the policies they prefer. In our country, campaigns take place for a two-week period between the announcement of the final list of candidates and the date of polling. During this period the candidates address election meetings and try to mobilise their supporters.

Source B A Democratic Election

All democratic countries hold elections regularly. In democracy everyone should be able to chose the representative. This means that everyone should have one vote and every vote should have equal value. In India, parties and candidates should be free to contest elections and should offer some real choice to the voters. Elections are held here regularly after every five years. Elections are held in a free and fair manner where people can chose as they really wish.

The final stage of an election is the day, when the voters cast or 'pole' their vote is called an Election Day.

Source C Polling the Vote

Every person whose name is on the voter's list can go to a nearby polling booth and cast his/her vote through a secret ballot. An agent of each candidate is allowed to sit inside the polling booth to ensure that the voting takes place in a fair way. Earlier voting was done by putting a stamp on the ballot paper. A ballot paper is a sheet of paper on which names of the constesting candidates alongwith party names and symbols are listed. Now, Electronic Voting Machines (EVM's) are used to record votes. Where voter presses button against the name of his candidate, he/she wants to cast his/her vote.

(i) Define the term Election Day.

(ii) To what extent elections in India democratic? Give one reason.

(iii) Is it easy for the political party to win an election in India ? Justify.

Ans. (i) The final stage of an election is the day, when the voters cast or pole their vote. This is called an Election Day.

(ii) Like any other democratic countries, elections are held in India regularly. One of the reasons that makes elections in India democratic is that here elections are held regularly after every five years in a free and fair way.

(iii) No, it is not easy for the party in power to win an election in India.

ASSESSMENT EXERCISE

Multiple Choice Questions (MCQs)

1. The Chief Election Commissioner (CEC) of India is appointed by the ....
(a) Parliament
(b) President of India
(c) Prime Minister of India
(d) Cabinet of Ministers

2. A ballot paper is a sheet of paper which contains the names of the ....
(a) Presidents of the registered parties
(b) registered parties
(c) contesting candidates
(d) All of the above

3. **Assertion** (A) Elections are essential for any representative democracy.
Reason (R) Elections allow people to choose their representatives and change them if they are not satisfied.
Codes
(a) Both A and R are true and R is the correct explanation of A
(b) Both A and R are true, but R is not the correct explanation of A
(c) A is true, but R is false
(d) A is false, but R is true

4. Find the incorrect option.
(a) No party or candidate can bribe or threaten voters.
(b) Parties or candidate are allowed to spend more than ₹ 25 lakh in a constituency for a Lok Sabha elections.
(c) No party can use government resources for election campaign.
(d) No political party can appeal to the voters in the name of caste or religion.

5. Match the following.

List I	List II
A. Rigged Elections	1. Election is held for one constituency to fill the vacancy caused by death or resignation.
B. By-Elections	2. Elections are held in all constituencies at the same time.
C. General Elections	3. Elections held on the basis of fraud or malpractices.

Codes

	A	B	C
(a)	3	1	2
(b)	3	2	1
(c)	1	2	3
(d)	1	3	2

Subjective Questions (VSA, SA & LA)

1. Explain the process of maintaining an updated voters' list in India. Why is this process important for ensuring fair elections?

2. What are the eligibility criteria for becoming a candidate in Indian elections?

3. Highlight the differences between the requirements for voters and candidates.

4. Explain the difference between By-election and Mid-term election.

5. Are the constituencies reserved for the SCs and STs evenly spread all over the entire country or are there more in some areas?

6. What is Secret Ballot System?

7. Explain the difference between the Ballot paper and EVM.

8. Enumerate any three challenges of free and fair elections.

9. Discuss the importance of election manifesto.

10. Suggest five reforms in the electoral system of India.

CHAPTER 4

Working of Institutions

In a democracy, the rulers have to work with and within institutions. In this process, they come across three institutions i.e. Legislature, Executive and Judiciary that play a key role in making decisions. This chapter is about the working of such institutions in a democracy. It tries to understand this by looking at the manner in which major decisions are taken and implemented in our country. It also looks at how disputes regarding these decisions are resolved.

4.1 Process of taking a Major Policy Decision

A major policy decision is taken through a government[1] order. To know the process of taking a major policy decision, it is important to know about government order and its issuing.

A Government Order

- **Issuing of Government Order** A government order is a written direction on an issue signed by a government authority (office). It is called an Office Memorandum[2].

  For example, one such order was issued by the Government of India on 13th August, 1990 regarding a major policy decision. It allows 27% reservation[3] of Socially and Educationally Backward Classes (SEBC) in civil posts and services under the Government of India.
- **Controversy Over the Order** The issuing of order sometimes led to the countrywide protest. Some of the protests are violent. As a result, the issue becomes the most debated in the media with different views and opinions.
- **Different views Regarding Reservation** People reacted strongly because this decision impacted thousands of jobs. Some believed caste inequalities in India made job reservations necessary. They felt it would give fair chances to communities that had been underrepresented in government jobs. Others felt this was unfair as it would limit job opportunities for more qualified people from non-backward communities. Some worried it would increase caste divisions and harm national unity.
- **Appeal to Stop Implementation of Order** Some persons and associations filed a number of cases in courts against the order. They appealed to declare the order invalid and stop its implementation.
- **Indira Sawhney case : Court's Intervention and Modification in Order** Some people and groups opposed this order and filed many cases in court, asking to declare it invalid and stop its implementation. The Supreme Court combined all these cases into one called the 'Indira Sawhney and others vs Union of India' case.

  Eleven judges heard both sides, and in 1992, the court ruled by majority that the government's order was valid. However, it asked the government to change the order so that wealthy people in backward classes would not get reservation benefits.

1 Government It is a set of institutions that have the power to make, implement and interpret laws, so as to ensure an orderly life.
2 Office Memorandum It is a communication issued by an appropriate authority stating the policy or decision of the government.
3 Reservation It is a policy that declare some positions in government employment and educational institutions 'reserved' for people and communities, who have been discriminated against, are disadvantaged and backward.

On 8th September, 1993 the government issued a new order, and the dispute was resolved. This policy has been followed since then.

The Decision Makers

The major decision makers involved in a government order are

- **President** He is the head of the state and is the highest formal authority in the country.
- **Prime Minister** He is the head of the government and actually exercises all governmental powers. He takes most of the decisions in the Cabinet meetings.
- **Parliament** It consists of the President and two houses i.e. **Lok Sabha** and **Rajya Sabha**.

Mandal Commission Report

In 1979, the Government of India had appointed the **Second Backward Classes Commission**. It was popularly known as **Mandal Commission**, headed by **BP Mandal**.

The commission gave its report in 1980 and made recommendation of 27% of reservation in government jobs for the socially and educationally backward classes. The report and recommendation were discussed in the Parliament but were not implemented.

On 6th August, 1990, a formal decision for implementation of the Mandal Commission report was taken by the cabinet of the then **Janata Dal Government** under the leadership of **VP Singh**.

The Prime Minister informed both the houses of the Parliament about the decision. The decision over reservations was widely **protested** by the people as it affected thousands of job opportunities.

Need for Political Institutions

Governing a country involves many important tasks. The government formulates and implements several welfare schemes. It ensures security, provides education and health services, collects taxes, and uses funds for administration, defence, and welfare. To carry out these activities, some people make decisions while others implement them. If disputes arise, there should be someone to resolve them. These tasks are managed by various arrangements known as **political institutions**[4]. There are several such institutions at work in our democracy. These are

- The **Prime Minister** and the **cabinet** are institutions that take all important policy decisions.
- The **civil servants,** working together are responsible for taking steps to implement the minister's decisions.
- The **Supreme Court** is an institution where disputes between citizens and the government are finally settled.

Institutions involve rules and regulations, which limits the authority of the leaders. Without the functions of the tasks assigned to political institution, the democracy cannot work.

Institutions make it difficult to have a good decision taken very quickly. But they also make it equally difficult to rush through (take quickly) a bad decision. Thus, the democratic governments favour institutions.

4.2 Parliament

In all democracies, an assembly of elected representatives exercises **Supreme Political Authority** on behalf of the people. In India such a national assembly of elected representatives is called Parliament. At the **state** level, it is called **Legislature or Legislative Assembly**[5].

All the decisions taken by the government, before implementation are discussed in the Parliament. Decisions can be implemented only after the approval by the Parliament.

Need of Parliament

- Parliament is the final authority for making new laws. The task of making laws is so important that these assemblies are called legislatures. Parliaments can create, change or abolish laws.
- Parliaments all over the world exercise some control over those who run the Government. In some countries like India this control is direct and full. Those who run the Government can take decisions only as long as they enjoy support of Parliament.
- Parliament controls all the money of the government. In most countries, the public money can be spent only when the Parliament sanctions it.
- Parliament is the highest forum of discussion and debate on public issues and national policy in any country. Parliament can seek information about any matter.

4 **Political Institution** It is a set of governing bodies for regulating the conduct of government and political life in the country.

5 **Legislature or Legislative Assembly** It is an assembly of people's representatives with the power to enact laws for a country. In addion to enacting laws, legislatures have authority to raise taxes, and adopt the budget and other money bills.

Two Houses of Parliament

The Parliament plays a central role in modern democracies. Large countries have divided the role and powers of Parliament into two parts. They are called **Chambers or Houses.**

Indian Parliament consists of two houses or chambers which are

(i) **Lok Sabha** (House of the People) or **Lower Chamber** It is usually directly elected by the people and exercises the real power on behalf of the people. The Lok Sabha or the Lower House is composed of the elected representatives of the people. The Prime Minister must have the support of a majority of Lok Sabha members.

(ii) **Rajya Sabha** (Council of States) or **Upper Chamber** It is indirectly elected and performs special functions such as interest of various states, regions or federal units. The Rajya Sabha or Upper House represents the interests of the States and Union Territories.

The **President of India** is a part of the **Parliament,** although he/she is not a member of either house. Due to this reason, all laws made in the houses come into force only after they receive the assent of the President.

Special Powers of Lok Sabha over Rajya Sabha

- Our Constitution does give the Rajya Sabha some special powers over the states. But on most matters, the Lok Sabha exercises supreme power.
- Any ordinary law needs to be passed by both the houses. However, if there is a difference between the two houses, the final decision is taken in a joint session. Due to larger number of members, the view of Lok Sabha will prevail in such a session.
- Lok Sabha exercises more powers in money matters. Once the Lok Sabha passes the budget of the government or any other money-related law or **Money Bill**[6], the Rajya Sabha cannot reject it.
- The Rajya Sabha can only delay money bill by **14 days** or suggest to change it. However, the Lok Sabha may or may not accept these suggestions.
- The Lok Sabha controls the **Council of Ministers.** Only a person who enjoys the support of the majority of the members in the Lok Sabha is appointed as the Prime Minister.
- If the majority of the Lok Sabha members say that they have **no confidence** in the Council of Ministers, all ministers including the Prime Minister have to quit. However, the Rajya Sabha does not have this power.

Try These

1. **Who is considered as the head of the state and the highest formal authority in the country?**
2. **Who is the final authority for making new laws and changing existing laws in our country?**
3. **Which house of parliament consists of indirectly elected members?**
4. **How many days the Rajya Sabha can delay Money Bill?**

4.3 Political Executive

The functionaries who take day-to-day decisions but do not exercise supreme power on behalf of the people are known as **executive**[7]. They are called executive because they are in charge of the execution of the policies of the government.

In a democratic country, two categories make up the executive. They are

(i) Political Executive

- They are elected by the people for a specific period. They take major decisions. Political leaders fall in this categories.
- They have more power than the permanent executive. This is because the political executive is elected by the people and in a democracy, will of people is supreme.
- They are answerable to the people for all consequences of their decisions.
- They can take advice of the permanent executive and then decide the overall framework and objectives of the policy to be implemented.

(ii) Permanent Executive

- They are appointed on a long-term basis. Persons working as permanent executive in civil services are known as **civil servants.**
- They remain in office even when the ruling party changes.
- They work under political executive and assist them for carrying out daily administration.
- They are more educated and have expertise on the subject of ministry. For example, advisor of the finance ministry know more about economics than the finance minister. But still decision of the finance minister will be the final.

6 **Money Bill** Bill dealing with money matters like taxes, income, expenditure and grants.

7 **Executive** A body of persons having authority to initiate major policies, make decisions and implement them on the basis of constitution and laws of the country.

Prime Minister

The Prime Minister is the head of the government and actually exercises all the government powers. It is the most important **political institution** in the country.

The President appoints the leader of the majority party or the coalition of parties that commands a majority in the Lok Sabha as a Prime Minister.

In case, no single party gets a majority, the President appoints the person who could secure a majority support.

The Prime Minister does not have a fixed tenure. He continues in power as long as he remains the leader of the majority party or coalition party.

Powers of the Prime Minister

- The Prime Minister is free to choose ministers, as long as they are Members of Parliament.
- He chairs and takes most of the decisions in the Cabinet meetings.
- He coordinates the work of different departments and his decisions are final in case disagreements arise between departments.
- He exercises general supervision of different ministries and all ministers work under his leadership.
- He distributes and redistributes work to the ministers.
- He also has the power to dismiss ministers. When the Prime Minister quits, the entire ministry quits.
- The Prime Minister is the most powerful institution in India's Cabinet. In recent years, Prime Ministers have gained more power, often leading to a Prime Ministerial form of government. However, in coalition governments, the Prime Minister's power is limited by the need to work with different groups and partners to keep the government running.

Council of Ministers

It is the official name for the body that includes all the ministers. It usually has 60 to 80 ministers of different ranks. The Council of Ministers comprise

(i) **Cabinet Ministers** They are usually top level leaders of the ruling party or parties who are incharge of the major ministries. Cabinet is the inner ring of the Council of Ministers. It comprises about 25 ministers. Cabinet ministers meet to take decisions in the name of the council of ministers.

(ii) **Ministers of State with Independent Charge** They are usually incharge of smaller ministries. They participate in the Cabinet meetings only when specially invited.

(iii) **Ministers of State** They are attached to and required to assist Cabinet Ministers.

Appointment of Council of Ministers

After the appointment of the Prime Minister, the President appoints the Council of Ministers on the advice of Prime Minister.

Council of Ministers are usually from the party or coalition that has majority in Lok Sabha.

Sometimes, a person who is not a member of Parliament can also become a minister. However, such a person has to get elected to one of the Houses of Parliament within 6 months of his appointment.

Cabinet Form of Government

In most of the countries, the **parliamentary democracy** is often known as Cabinet form of government. This is because, it is not possible for all ministers to meet regularly and discuss everything, so the decisions are taken in Cabinet meetings.

In this form, no minister can openly criticise any decision of the government even if it is about another ministry or department.

Every Ministry has secretaries, who are civil servants. The **secretaries** provide the necessary background information to the ministers to take decisions.

The Cabinet as a team is assisted by the **Cabinet Secretariat**. This includes many senior civil servants who try to coordinate the working of different ministeries.

The President

The President is the **head of the state.** In our political system, the head of the state exercises only nominal powers.

The President supervises the overall functioning of all the political institutions in the country so that they operate in harmony to achieve the objectives of the state.

The President is not directly elected by the people. The elected Members of Parliament (MPs) and the elected Members of the Legislative Assemblies (MLAs) elect the President.

A candidate standing for President's post has to get their majority of votes to win the election. This ensures that the President can be seen to represent the entire nation, but not direct popular mandate as the Prime Minister. This ensures President remainly only a nominal executive.

Powers of the President

- All governmental activities take place in the name of the President. All laws and major policy decisions of the government are issued in President's name.
- All major appointments are made in the name of the President. These include the appointment of the **Chief Justice of India**, the **Judges of the Supreme Court** and the **High Courts** of the states, the **Governors** of the states, the **Election Commissioners, Ambassadors** to other countries, etc.
- All international treaties and agreements are made in the name of the President.
- The President is the **supreme commander of the defence forces** of India.
- The President has emergency powers i.e. powers to deal with an unexpected and critical situation. For example, power to declare emergency or **President's rule**[8] and issuing an **ordinance**[9].

> **KNOWLEDGE PLUS** The President of India administers the oath to the Chief Justice of the Supreme Court and the Prime Minister of India.

Limitation on the Powers of the President

- The President exercises all the powers only on the advice of the **Council of Ministers.**
- The President can ask the Council of Ministers to reconsider its advice. However, if the same advice is given again, he/she is bound to act according to it.
- A bill passed by the Parliament becomes a law only after the President gives approval to it. If the President wants, he/she can delay this for sometime and send the bill back to the Parliament for reconsideration. However, if the Parliament passes the bill again, he/she has to sign it.

> **The Presidential System**
>
> In many countries of the world, the President is both the head of the state and the head of the government. The President of **United** States of America (USA) is the well known example of this kind of President.
>
> The US President is directly elected by the people. He personally chooses and appoints all ministers. The law making is still done by the Legislature (called the Congress), but the President can veto any law.
>
> The President does not need the support of the majority of members in the Congress and neither he is answerable to them.
>
> He has a fixed tenure of four years and completes it even if his party does not have a majority in the Congress.
>
> This model is followed in most of the countires of **Latin America**, and many other ex-Soviet Union countries. This system of government is called the **Presidential form of government**.

4.4 The Judiciary

Judiciary refers to an institution empowered to administer justice and provide a mechanism for the resolution of legal disputes.

The Indian judiciary consists of a **Supreme Court** for the entire nation, **High Courts** and **Subordinate Courts**[10] in the states and **District Courts** and the courts at local level.

India has an **integrated judiciary**[11]. It means that the Supreme Court controls the judicial administration in the country. Its decisions are binding on all other courts of the country.

The Supreme Court can take up any dispute between
- citizens of the country
- citizens and government
- two or more State Governments
- governments at the Union and State level

Independence of Judiciary

It means that the judiciary is not under the control of the legislature or the executive. The judges do not act on the direction of the government or according to the wishes of the political party in power.

---

8 **President's Rule** If the President gets a report from the Governor or any other source that the government of the state cannot be carried on in accordance with the Constitution, he can impose President's rule.

9 **Ordinance** It is a direction issued by the President, when Parliament is not in session. It has the force of law for 6 months.

10 **Subordinate Courts** The courts which function under the supervision and orders of the High Court.

11 **Judiciary** India has a single judicial system for the entire country connected by a number of courts with the Supreme Court at the apex of the entire judicial system.

Appointment and Removal of Judges

- The judges of the Supreme Court and the High Courts are appointed by the **President** on the advice of the **Prime Minister** and in consultation with the **Chief Justice** of the **Supreme Court**.
- The senior judges of the Supreme Court select the new judges of the Supreme Court and the High Courts. The seniormost judge of the Supreme Court is usually appointed as the Chief Justice.

A judge can be removed only by an **impeachment**[12] motion passed separately by two-third members of the two houses of the Parliament. It has never happened in the history of Indian democracy.

Powers of Judiciary

- The Supreme Court and the High Courts have the power to interpret the Constitution of the country.
- They can declare any law of the legislature or the actions of the executive invalid, whether at the **Union level or State level**, if they find such a law or action is against the Constitution.
- They can determine the constitutional validity of any legislation or action of the executive in the country, when it is challenged before them. This is known as the **judicial review**. The Supreme Court of India has also ruled that the core or basic principles of the Constitution cannot be changed by the Parliament.

Judiciary as a Highest Authority

The powers and the independence of the Indian judiciary allow it to act as the guardian of the Fundamental Rights.

Any one, can approach the courts if public interest is hurt by the actions of government. This is called **Public Interest Litigation** (PIL).

The courts intervene to prevent the misuse of the government's power to make decisions. They check malpractices on the part of public officials. That is why, the judiciary enjoys a high level of confidence among the people.

Try These

1. **What are the primary responsibilities of top-level ministeries within government?**
2. **What is Public Interest litigation?**
3. **How many members of the Parliament should pass impeachment motion to remove a judge?**
4. **Who act as the guardian of the Fundamental Rights?**

12 Impeachment A procedure through which the President, Vice-President or the Chief Justice of India can be removed.

Mind Map

WORKING OF INSTITUTIONS

A Government Order
- On 13th August, 1990, the Government of India issued an order known as Office Memorandum.
- It declared 27% of the vacancies in Civil posts and services under the Government of India are reserved for Socially and Educationally Backward Classes.

The Decision Makers
- President
- Prime Minister
- Parliament

Process of Taking a Major Policy Decision

Need for Political Institutions
- The Prime Minister and the Cabinet
- Civil Servants
- Supreme Court

Need of Parliament
- Parliament is the final authority for making new laws and changing existing laws in any country.
- It controls all the money of the government.
- It is the highest forum of discussion and debate on public issues and National Policy.

Lok Sabha
- It is directly elected by the people and exercises the real power on behalf of the people.
- It is composed of elected representatives of the people.

Two Houses of Parliament

Parliament

Rajya Sabha
- It is indirectly elected and performs special functions such as interests of various states, regions or federal units.
- It represents the interests of the States and Union Territories.

Political Executive

Prime Minister
- The Prime Minister is the head of the government.
- He chairs and takes most of the decisions in the cabinet meetings.

Permanent Executive
Persons working as permanent executive in civil services are known as civil servants

Council of Ministers
It includes all the ministers of different ranks as
- Cabinet Ministers
- Ministers of State with Independent charge
- Ministers of State

President
- The President is the head of the State
- He appoints the Chief Justice of India, the judges of the Supreme Court and the High Courts of the state, the Governors of the State, the Election Commissioners, Ambassadors to other Countries, etc

Appointment and Removal of Judges
- The judges of the Supreme Court and High Court are appointed by the President on the advice of the Prime Minister in consultation with the Chief Justice of the Supreme Court.
- Senior Judges of the Supreme Court select the new judges of Supreme Court and High Court.

The Judiciary

Powers of Judiciary
Supreme Court and High Court have the power to interpret the Constitution of the country

Judiciary as the Highest Authority
Anyone can approach the courts if public interest is hurt by the actions of government which is called Public Interest Litigation.

Independence of Judiciary
- Judiciary is not under the control of the Legislature or Executive.
- Judges do not act on the direction of the government or according to the political party in power.

NCERT FOLDER

Covering Intext Questions and Exercises of NCERT

INTEXT QUESTIONS

Q.1 Is every Office Memorandum a major political decision? If not, what made the memorandum - O.M. No. 36012/31/90-EST (SCT) dated 13th August, 1990 different?

Ans. Every Office Memorandum is not a major political decision, most of them are routine in nature. This Office Memorandum O.M. No. 36012/31/90-EST (SCT), dated 13th August, 1990, relating to reservation for the Socially and Educationally Backward Classes (SEBCs) in government services was different because it affected all the sections of society.

The benefit of job reservation was till then available only to Scheduled Castes and Scheduled Tribes. Now a third category, SEBCs was introduced. Moreover, this reservation issue was a major source of controversy for several years and led to many agitations and court cases.

Q.2 Who did what in this case of reservations for backward classes?

Supreme Court	Made formal announcement about this decision
Cabinet	Implemented the decision by issuing an order
President	Took the decision to give 27% job reservations
Government officials	Upheld reservations as valid

Ans. The columns are matched as given below

Who	**Did What**
Supreme Court	Upheld reservations as valid
Cabinet	Took the decision to give 27% job reservations
President	Made formal announcement about this decision
Government officials	Implemented the decision by issuing an order

Q.3 Which institutions are at work in the running of your school? Would it be better if one person alone took all the decisions regarding management of your school?

Ans. The institutions of the school which perform different functions are the Principal's office, the school's administrative office, the different departments like sports, medical room, library and teachers.

No, it would not be good if one person takes all the decisions regarding the management of our school. Because a large number of activities are going on all the time. It is not possible for one person to take proper decisions on all issues. Even if one person does take these decisions, he or she might not be able to take these properly as it might be taken in haste or without understanding its implications.

Q.4 What is the point in having so much debate and discussion in the Parliament when we know that the view of the ruling party is going to prevail?

Ans. The view of the ruling party prevails in Parliament, but we should have debates and discussions because this helps to bring out the positive and negative points of the issue under consideration.

The positive aspects might be adopted by the ruling party and similarly, negative aspects could be omitted even if the entire bill is not changed.

To give the information to the public regarding the topic for a particular decision which is going to be taken by the ruling party, debate and discussion are necessary in the Parliament.

Also, it is not certain that the ruling party is open to ideas and discussions which might influence the ruling party to adopt new ideas. Thus, open debate and discussion are essential for democracy.

Q.5 When the Parliament is in session, there is a special programme everyday on Doordarshan about the proceedings in Lok Sabha and Rajya Sabha. Watch the proceedings or read about them in the newspapers and note the following

(a) Powers of the two Houses of Parliament

(b) Role of the Speaker

(c) Role of the Opposition

Ans. (a) **Powers of the two Houses of Parliament** The Lok Sabha members are directly elected by the voters and are the final voice in the passing of any laws. The Rajya Sabha members are indirectly elected or nominated and they function mostly in an advisory capacity. But the consent of both Houses is required for passing any bill, making a law or making amendments to the Constitution.

(b) **Role of the Speaker** (Lok Sabha)

The Speaker's main functions are

- Regulate the proceedings of the Houses.

- Maintain discipline in the House and to interpret its rules of procedure.
- Supervise parliamentary committees.
- Permit the moving of various kinds of motions and resolutions like the motion of no confidence, motion of adjournment, motion of censure, etc.

(c) **Role of the Opposition** The major function of the opposition is to act as a check on the ruling party, so that any faults of theirs are exposed and any mistake made by the ruling party can be corrected. They can even bring a no-confidence motion against the government if it is seen to be not functioning properly.

Q.6 Why does the textbook refer to the President as 'she'? Have we ever had a woman President in our country?

Ans. The book refers to the President as she shows that the highest office in India can also be occupied by a woman. Yes, we have had a woman President in our country. Pratibha Devi Singh Patil has been the first woman President of our country. She served as the 12th President (July 2007–July 2012) in our country. She was supported by United Progressive Alliance (UPA) and left parties.

Q.7 What is better for a democracy : a Prime Minister who can do whatever he wishes or a Prime Minister who needs to consult other leaders and parties?

Ans. Both these cases are not better for a democracy. If a Prime Minister is free to do as he wishes, there is a possibility that he might develop authoritarian or dictatorial tendencies.

On the other hand, if all the time he has to consult other leaders and parties, it would hamper his working. Therefore, he should have freedom of taking decisions, but he should also consult with other leaders of parties on important issues.

Q.8 Why are people allowed to go to courts against the government's decisions?

Ans. People are allowed to go to courts against the government's decision because sometimes the actions of the government or a law passed by the government might hurt the public interest or might be against the spirit of the Constitution.

In such cases, citizens have the right to go to court to get justice. Such cases are called Public Interest Litigations (PILs).

In case of violation of Fundamental Rights by the government, the citizen can go to the courts for justice. Then the courts intervene to prevent the misuse of power by the government.

Q.9 Give one reason each to argue that Indian judiciary is independent with respect to

(a) Appointment of Judges

(b) Removal of Judges

(c) Powers of the Judiciary

Ans. (a) **Appointment of Judges** The Judges of the Supreme Court and the High Courts are appointed by the President on the recommendation of the Prime Minister and in consultation with the Chief Justice of India.

In actual practice, the Senior Judges of the Supreme Court select new Judges for the Supreme Court as well as for the High Courts. Here, seniority and merit are the main considerations with hardly any scope for manipulation by anybody.

(b) **Removal of Judges** The procedure of removal of Judges of the Supreme Court and High Courts is very difficult to actually carry out.

They can be removed only on the basis of an impeachment motion passed by two-thirds majority in both Houses of Parliament separately. So, removal of judges cannot be done arbitrarily.

(c) **Powers of the Judiciary** The powers are clearly spelt out in the Constitution and they cannot be diluted by Parliament or by any presidential order. So, no politician can reduce or increase their powers.

The Supreme Court has the power to declare any law as illegal made by Parliament if it goes against the Constitution. This ensures the independence of judiciary in a modern democracy.

EXERCISE

Q.1 If you are elected as the President of India, which of the following decisions can you take on your own?

(a) Select the person you take on your own.

(b) Dismiss a Prime Minister who has a majority in Lok Sabha.

(c) Ask for reconsideration of a bill passed by both the houses.

(d) Nominate the leaders of your choice to the Council of Ministers.

Ans. (c) Ask for reconsideration of a bill passed by both the houses.

Q.2 Who among the following is a part of the political executive?

(a) District Collector

(b) Secretary of the Ministry of Home Affairs

(c) Home Minister

(d) Director General of Police

Ans. (c) Home Minister

Q.3 Which of the following statements about the judiciary is false?

(a) Every law passed by the Parliament needs approval of the Supreme Court.

(b) Judiciary can strike down a law if it goes against the spirit of the Constitution.

(c) Judiciary is independent of the executive.

(d) Any citizen can approach the courts if her rights are violated.

Ans. (a) Every law passed by the Parliament needs approval of the Supreme Court.

Q.4 Which of the following institutions can make changes to an existing law of the country?

(a) The Supreme Court (b) The President

(c) The Prime Minister (d) The Parliament

Ans. (d) The Parliament

Q.5 Match the ministry with the news that the ministry may have released.

	Column A		Column B
A.	A new policy is being made to increase the jute exports from the country	(i)	Ministry of Defence
B.	Telephone services will be made more accessible to rural areas	(ii)	Ministry of Agriculture, Food and Public Distribution
C.	The price of rice and wheat sold under the Public Distribution System will go down	(iii)	Ministry of Health
D.	A Pulse Polio campaign will be launched	(iv)	Ministry of Commerce and Industry
E.	The allowances of the soldiers posted on high altitudes will be increased	(v)	Ministry of Communications and Information Technology

Ans. (A)–(iv), (B)–(v), (C)–(ii), (D)–(iii), (E)–(i)

Q.6 Of all the institutions that we have studied in this chapter, name the one that exercises the powers on each of the following matters.

(a) Decision on allocation of money for developing infrastructure like roads, irrigation, etc., and different welfare activities for the citizens.

(b) Considers the recommendation of a committee on a law to regulate the stock exchange.

(c) Decides on a legal dispute between two State Governments.

(d) Implements the decision to provide relief for the victims of an earthquake.

Ans. (a) Parliament (Lok Sabha Money Bill)

(b) Parliament

(c) The Supreme Court

(d) The Executive

Q.7 Why is the Prime Minister in India not directly elected by the people?

(a) In a parliamentary democracy, only the leader of the majority party in the Lok Sabha can become the Prime Minister.

(b) Lok Sabha can remove the Prime Minister and the Council of Ministers even before the expiry of their term.

(c) Since, the Prime Minister is appointed by the President there is no need for it.

(d) Direct election of the Prime Minister will involve lot of expenditure on election.

Ans. The most appropriate answer is option '(a)'. Because, the Prime Minister should be a person who has the support of the majority of the members, so that he has no difficulty in implementing his policies and passing of laws in Parliament.

Since he is the leader of the majority party, he cannot act and take decisions all by himself or become a dictator.

Q.8 Three friends went to watch a film that showed the hero becoming Chief Minister for a day and making big changes in the state. Imran said this is what the country needs. Rizwan said this kind of a personal rule without institutions is dangerous. Shankar said all this is a fantasy. No minister can do anything in one day. What would be your reaction to such a film?

Ans. My reaction would be in favour of Rizwan who said that rule without institutions is dangerous. Institutions channelise the functioning of administration. Moreover, such films are unrealistic and cater only to the entertainment of the people.

The actions and decisions shown in the films are not practical.

Before taking big decisions or making changes, there is a need to first consider its positive and negative factors, its advantages and disadvantages, which needs time and planning. So, such films should not be taken seriously.

Q.9 A teacher was making preparations for a mock Parliament. She called two students to act as leaders of two political parties. She gave them an option : Each one could choose to have a majority either in the mock Lok Sabha or in the mock Rajya Sabha. If this choice was given to you, which one would you choose and why?

Ans. I would choose to have a majority in the mock Lok Sabha because the Lok Sabha is more powerful than the Rajya Sabha in the following ways

(i) Money Bills can originate only in the Lok Sabha.

(ii) In case of a joint session, the Lok Sabha prevails in the voting because it has more members.

(iii) The Council of Ministers are responsible and answerable to the Lok Sabha.

(iv) The Lok Sabha is directly elected by the voters of the country and represents the will of the people.

Q.10 After reading the example of the reservation order, three students had different reactions about the role of the judiciary. Which view, according to you, is a correct reading of the role of judiciary?

(a) Srinivas argues that since the Supreme Court agreed with the government, it is not independent.

(b) Anjaiah says that judiciary is independent because it could have given a verdict against the government order. The Supreme Court did direct the government to modify it.

(c) Vijaya thinks that the judiciary is neither independent nor conformist, but acts as a mediator between opposing parties. The court struck a good balance between those who supported and those who opposed the order.

Ans. (b) The view of Anjaiah is correct regarding the role of the judiciary. It has to act independently and will not mediate between parties.

It can give verdict against the government order. It can also direct the government to modify the decision in the interest of the nation. For example, the Supreme Court's role in the case of Mandal Commission.

REVIEW EXERCISE

Including Competency Based Questions

Part I

Multiple Choice Questions (MCQs)

1. The Parliament consists of how many houses?

(a) Two (b) Three
(c) Four (d) One

2. The Prime Minister must have support of a majority of

(a) Rajya Sabha (b) States
(c) Lok Sabha (d) Cabinet Ministers

3. Which of the following is called as 'Upper Chamber' of Parliament?

(a) Lok Sabha (b) President's Office
(c) Prime Minister's Office (d) Rajya Sabha

4. No confidence motion can be passed in ....

(a) Rajya Sabha (b) Lok Sabha
(c) The Council of Ministers (d) All of these

5. For how many days the Rajya Sabha can delay a Money Bill?

(a) 10 days (b) 12 days
(c) 14 days (d) 11 days

6. If there is a difference between Lok Sabha and Rajya Sabha, in what way the final decision is taken?

(a) Under the guidance of the President
(b) Under the guidance of the Prime Minister
(c) In a joint session of both the houses
(d) Under the guidance of the speaker of Lok Sabha

7. Who among the following is the head of the government?

(a) The President
(b) The Vice-President
(c) The Speaker of Lok Sabha
(d) The Prime Minister

8. Consider the following statement which defines the powers of the Prime Minister.

(a) The Prime Minister coordinates the work of different departments and his decisions are final.
(b) He chairs and takes most of the decisions in the Cabinet meetings.
(c) All laws and major policy decisions of the government are issued on his name.
(d) Both (a) and (b)

9. Who among the following is the highest formal authority in the country?

(a) The Chief Justice of India
(b) The Prime Minister of India
(c) The President of India
(d) The Vice-President of India

10. **Which one of the following is not a part of Indian Judiciary System?**

(a) High Courts in the States (b) The Supreme Court
(c) Village Panchayat (d) District Courts

11 **The decisions of which one of the following courts is binding to all other courts of the country?**

(a) District Courts
(b) The High Courts of the States
(c) The Supreme Court
(d) None of the above

12 **Which of the following disputes is/are taken up by the Supreme Court?**

(a) Between citizens and government
(b) Between two or more State Governments
(c) Between governments at the Union and State level
(d) All of the above

13 **Which one of the following is incorrect about the Supreme Court of India?**

(a) It is the highest court of appeal in civil and criminal cases.
(b) It cannot take up any dispute between citizens of the country.
(c) It can hear appeals against the decisions of the High Courts.
(d) None of the above

14 **Consider the following statement regarding the limitations on the powers of President.**

(a) The President exercises all the powers only on the advice of the Council of Ministers.
(b) The President can ask the Council of Ministers to reconsider its advice. But if the same advice is given again, he/she is bound to act according to it.
(c) All major appointments are made in the name of the President.
(d) Both (a) and (b)

15 **Find the incorrect option.**

(a) A major policy decision is taken through a government order.
(b) A government order is a written direction on an issue signed by a government authority.
(c) One of the debatable government order was issued on 13th August, 1990.
(d) None of the above

16 **Find the incorrect option**

(a) Judiciary is empowered to administer justice and provide a mechanism for the resolution of legal disputes.
(b) India has an integrated or unified judiciary.
(c) The High Court controls the judicial administration in the country.
(d) The Judiciary is not under the control of Legislature or the Executive.

17 **Identify the executive with the help of following information.**

- He is the head of the government.
- It does not have a fixed tenure.
- He chairs and takes most of the decision in the cabinet meetings.
- He also has the power to dismiss ministers.

Options

(a) The President
(b) The Prime Minister
(c) The Speaker of Lok Sabha
(d) Council of Ministers

18 **The Council of Ministers consisted of key holders of institutions like Finance, Home Affairs, Health, Education and Environment, each headed by a minister with a unique background and expertise. One day, a critical situation arose: a public health crisis emerged due to the outbreak of a new infectious disease.**

Which ministry will call for the emergency meeting and it will be headed by whome ? **Competency Based**

(a) Ministry of Home Affairs headed by the head of state.
(b) Ministry of Health and Family Welfare headed by the Health Minister.
(c) Ministry of Environment, Forest and Climate Change headed by the head of government.
(d) None of the above

19 **Arrange the following in a correct sequence.**

I. A formal decision for implementation of Mandal Commission.
II. Appointment of Second Backward Classes Commission by Government of India.
III. Mandal Commission gave its report and recommendations.
IV. Lok Sabha elections won by Janata Dal.

Codes

(a) II, III, IV, I (b) I, IV, II, III
(c) III, IV, I, II (d) IV, I, III, II

20 **Vansh Arora and Rajeev Saxena are best friends who study in St. George school. Vansh's father is a politician whereas, Rajeev's father is Civil servant. In some simultaneous conversation they started talking about their parents' tenure and role of their parents.**

Which among the following reflects their fathers crucial role and tenure in government ? **Competency Based**

I. Rajeev's father always remain in the service until he gets retire or resign though he is a permanent executive.
II. Vansh's father elected by the people for a specific period though he is political executive.

III. Rajeev's father elected by the people for a specific period though he is political executive.

IV. Vansh's father always remain in the service until he gets retire or resign though he is a permanent executive.

Codes

(a) I and IV statements are appropriate

(b) II and III statements are appropriate

(c) I and II statements are appropriate

(d) III and IV statements are appropriate

Answers

1. (a)	**2.** (c)	**3.** (d)	**4.** (b)	**5.** (c)
6. (c)	**7.** (d)	**8.** (d)	**9.** (c)	**10.** (c)
11. (c)	**12.** (d)	**13.** (b)	**14.** (d)	**15.** (d)
16. (c)	**17.** (b)	**18.** (b)	**19.** (a)	**20.** (c)

Match the Following

1

List I	List II
A. Lower Chamber	1. Political Leaders
B. Upper Chamber	2. Civil Servants
C. Permanent Executive	3. Lok Sabha
D. Political Executive	4. Rajya Sabha

Codes

	A	B	C	D		A	B	C	D
(a)	3	4	2	1	(b)	2	1	4	3
(c)	4	1	2	3	(b)	4	1	3	2

2

List I	List II
A. Prime Minister	1. Head of the State
B. President	2. Head of the Government
C. Member of Parliament	3. Elected members of State Legislatures
D. Member of Legislative Assemblies	4. Elected members of both the houses of Parliament

Codes

	A	B	C	D		A	B	C	D
(a)	3	4	2	1	(b)	2	1	4	3
(c)	4	1	2	3	(b)	4	1	3	2

Ans. 1. (a) 2. (b)

Assertion-Reason

1 Assertion (A) The President can never claim the kind of direct popular mandate that the Prime Minister can.

Reason (R) The President of India is elected indirectly by an electoral college with the system of proportional representation.

Codes

(a) Both A and R are true and R is the correct explanation of A

(b) Both A and R are true, but R is not the correct explanation of A

(c) A is true, but R is false

(d) A is false, but R is true

2 Assertion (A) The Political Executive has more powers than the Permanent Executive.

Reason (R) The Political Executive is elected by the people and in a democracy will of the people is supreme.

Codes

(a) Both A and R are true and R is the correct explanation of A

(b) Both A and R are true, but R is not the correct explanation of A

(c) A is true, but R is false

(d) A is false, but R is true

3. Assertion (A) The Supreme Court controls the judicial administration in the country.

Reason (R) The Supreme Court and the High Courts have the power to interpret the Constitution of the country.

Codes

(a) Both A and R are true and R is the correct explanation of A

(b) Both A and R are true, but R is not the correct explanation of A

(c) A is true, but R is false

(d) A is false, but R is true

4. Assertion (A) The President of India is like the Queen of Britain whose functions are to a large extent formed.

Reason (R) In our political system the head of the State exercises only nominal powers.

Codes

(a) Both A and R are true and R is the correct explanation of A

(b) Both A and R are true, but R is not the correct explanation of A

(c) A is true, but R is false

(d) A is false, but R is true

Ans. 1. (a) Both A and R are true and R is the correct explanation of A

2. (a) Both A and R are true and R is the correct explanation of A

3. (b) Both A and R are true, but R is not the correct explanation of A

4. (a) Both A and R are true and R is the correct explanation of A

Picture Based Question

1. What does the given picture depict?

(a) It refers to riots which took place when reservation quota was made into a law.
(b) Reservation of State constituencies.
(c) Reservation of women candidates in Lok Sabha.
(d) None of the above

Ans. (a) It refers to riots which took place when reservation quota was made into a law.

Case Based Question

1. Read the source given below and answer the questions that follow.

But we should remember that the President exercises all these powers only on the advice of the Council of Ministers. The President can ask the Council of Ministers to reconsider its advice. But if the same advice is given again, she is bound to act according to it. Similarly, a bill passed by the Parliament becomes a law only after the President gives assent to it. If the President wants, she can delay this for some time and send the bill back to Parliament for reconsideration.

But if Parliament passes the bill again, she has to sign it. So you may wonder what does the President really do? Can she do anything on her own at all? There is one very important thing she should do on her own: appoint the Prime Minister. When a party or coalition of parties secures a clear majority in the elections, the President has to appoint the leader of the majority party or the coalition that enjoys majority support in the Lok Sabha.

(i) In a Parliamentary system, what role does the President typically play in the formation of the government?
(a) Appoints the Prime Minister
(b) Approves bills
(c) Acts as the Head of State
(d) Chairs the legislature

(ii) In whose name are all international treaties and agreement made?
(a) Head of the Government
(b) Head of the state
(c) Head of embassy
(d) None of the above

(iii) Which of the following powers are not exercised by the President ?
(a) All laws and major policy decisions of the government are executed after the assent of the President.
(b) All the major appointments are done by the president like Chief Justice of India, the Judges of the Supreme Court Etc.
(c) The President distributes and redistributes work to the ministers.
(d) The President is the supreme commander of the defense forces of India.

(iv) When will the power of discretion be exercised by the President ?
(a) When there is no majority party in the Lok Sabha and he has to choose a Prime Minister
(b) When the ruling party loses its majority in the Lok Sabha.
(c) When he decides to refer the advice of the union cabinet back for reconsideration
(d) All of the above

Ans. (i) (a) Appoints the Prime Minister
(ii) (b) Head of the state
(iii) (c) The President distributes and redistributes work to the ministers.
(iv) (d) All of the above

Part II

Very Short Answer Type Questions

1 What does SEBC stand for?

Ans. SEBC stands for Socially and Educationally Backward Classes.

2 Which political institutions take all important policy decisions?

Ans. The Prime Minister and the Cabinet are institutions that take all important policy decisions.

3 Who is the final authority for making laws in any country?

Ans. The Parliament is the final authority for making laws in any country.

4 What is Lok Sabha?

Ans. Lok Sabha is the Lower House of the Indian Parliament, which is directly elected by the people and exercises the real power on behalf of the people.

5 In which House of the Parliament a Money Bill can be introduced?

Ans. A Money Bill can be introduced only in Lok Sabha.

6 In what ways Lok Sabha exercises supreme power over Rajya Sabha?

Ans. Lok Sabha exercises more powers on money matter and during the joint session, final decision is taken by Lok Sabha because of its large number of members.

7 Can the Houses of the Parliament be dissolved?

Ans. Rajya Sabha is a permanent House, so it cannot be dissolved whereas Lok Sabha can be dissolved.

8 When does a bill become a law?

Ans. A bill becomes a law after it is passed by both houses of Parliament and assent given by the President.

9 How are members of Council of Ministers appointed?

Ans. The members of Council of Ministers are appointed by the President on the advice of the Prime Ministers.

10 Who is the highest executive authority of India?

Ans. The President is the highest executive authority of India.

Short Answer Type Questions

1. Explain the "Indira Sawhney and others vs Union of India case" along with its major reforms.

Ans. The "Indira Sawhney and others vs Union of India case" was filed by some persons and associations regarding the governmental decision on 27% reservation for the SEBC.

The major reform was that Supreme Court modified the original order and declared that well-to-do persons among the backward classes should be excluded from getting benefit of the reservation.

Hence, the Department of Personnel and Training issued another Office Memorandum on 8th September, 1993.

2. 'Lok Sabha is more powerful than Rajya Sabha'. Analyse the statement.'

***or* How does Lok Sabha exercise supreme power?**

Ans. Lok Sabha exercises supreme power or it is more powerful than Rajya Sabha in the following ways

- Any ordinary law needs to be passed by both the houses but in case of conflict, view of Lok Sabha prevails because it has large number of members.
- Once the Lok Sabha passes the budget or any other money related law, Rajya Sabha cannot reject it. The Rajya Sabha can delay it for a maximum of 14 days or suggest changes in it which may or may not be accepted by the Lok Sabha.
- Most importantly, the Lok Sabha controls the Council of Ministers. If the majority of the Lok Sabha members say that they have no confidence in the Council of Ministers, then all the ministers including the Prime Minister have to resign.

Thus, it can be concluded that Lok Sabha is more powerful than Rajya Sabha.

3. Distinguish between Political executives and Permanent executives.

Ans. The points given below distinguish Political and Permanent executive :

Political Executive	Permanent Executive
Elected by the people (voters) for specific period.	Appointed on a long-term basis.
Political leaders are political executives.	Civil servants are the permanent executives.
Answerable to the people.	Answerable to the government.

4 Write any three constraints on the powers of the Prime Minister of a coalition government.

Ans. The three constraints or limitations on the powers of Prime Minister of coalition government are

(i) The Prime Minister has to accommodate different groups and factions in his party as well as his alliance partners.

(ii) The Prime Minister has to pay attention to the views and positions of his coalition partners for the survival of his government.

(iii) The agenda and policies of the government are usually decided as a common minimum programme which includes all the views and demands of coalition partners.

5. Mention any three legislative powers of the President of India.

Ans. Three legislative powers of the President of India are

(i) The President is not a member of either house of the Parliament. But she is an integral part of the legislative process. She plays an important role in making of laws. Bill becomes a law only after President's assent.

(ii) The President has the power to dissolve the Lok Sabha. She can summon joint sitting of both houses of Parliament.

(iii) The President has the power to send messages to either house of the Parliament either regarding any pending bill or any other matter.

6. Explain the limitations of the powers of the President.

Ans. The limitations of the powers of the President are

- The President exercises all the powers on the advice of the Council of Ministers.
- The President can ask the Council of Ministers to reconsider his advice. But if the same advice is given again, he/she is bound to act according to it.
- Similarly, a bill passed by the Parliament becomes a law only after the President gives assent to it. If the President wants, he/she can delay this for sometime and send the bill back to the Parliament for reconsideration. But, if the Parliament passes the bill again, he/she has to sign it.

7. Difference between the powers of the President of USA and the President of India.

Ans. Differences between the powers of the President of USA and the President of India are

President of USA	President of India
He is directly elected by the people for this position for the tenure of four years.	The President of India is the head of the state. He is indirectly elected by the MP's and MLA's
He personally chooses and appoints his ministers. This is called the Presidential form of Government.	President appoints other ministers on the advice of the PM. He exercises only the nominal powers. This is a feature of parliamentary form of government.

8. "Indian judiciary is considered one of the most powerful in the world." Give any three reasons.

Ans. Indian judiciary is considered one of the most powerful in the world because

(i) The Mode of appointment and removal of Judges of Supreme Court and High Courts makes Indian judiciary powerful.

A Judge can be removed only by an impeachment motion.

(ii) The Supreme Court and the High Court have the power to interpret the Constitution of the country.

(iii) Our judiciary is independent of legislative and executive control. It can take decisions independently.

9. MR. X lives in a country where there are no executives, only legislative and judiciary functions. What do you think, is the government balanced? If not, then analyse how does it cause imbalance in the government ? **Competency Based**

Ans. No, I don't think the government is balanced. A government structure that lacks an executive branch may face challenges in terms of balance and efficiency that leads to an imbalanced form of government.

Typically, a balanced government consists of three main branches i.e. Legislative, Executive and Judiciary. Each branch has distinct roles and responsibilities to provide checks and balances on the others, promoting accountability and preventing the abuse of power. Without an executive branch, several key functions traditionally handled by executives may be compromised like execution of laws, administrative functions and policy implementation.

Long Answer Type Questions

1. Briefly write about Mandal Commission. Why was the Mandal Commission set-up? What did it recommend to the government?

Ans. The Mandal Commission was the Second Backward Classes Commission appointed by the Government of India in the year 1979. B P Mandal was the head of Mandal Commission.

The Mandal Commission was appointed in order to :

(i) determine the criteria to identify the Socially and Educationally Backward Classes (SEBCs) in India.

(ii) recommend steps to be taken for their advancement.

The commission gave its report in 1980 and made recommendations that 27% of the government jobs to be reserved for the Socially and Educationally Backward Classes.

The report and recommendations were discussed in the Parliament. On 6th August, 1990, the Government of India under the leadership of VP Singh took a formal decision to implement the recommendations.

2. Why is there a need for political institutions?

Ans. A democracy works well when the political institutions, like the Prime Minister and the Cabinet, the Civil Servants, the Supreme Court, etc perform functions assigned to them.

The need for these political institutions are

- **To take decisions** Countries need political institutions to take decisions regarding the welfare of the people. Institutions formulate various policies and welfare schemes.
- **To implement the decisions** The decisions which have been taken care of are to be implemented. So, countries need institutions to implement the decisions.
- **To solve the disputes** Institutions are needed to solve the disputes between various institutions.
- **To take right decisions** Institutions are also needed to help the government to take the right decisions. They determine what is wrong and what is right.

3. Explain the major powers and functions of the Parliament.

Ans. In India, a national assembly of elected representatives is called Parliament. The major powers and functions of the Parliament are

- The Parliament is the final authority for making laws in any country. In India, it makes laws on the subjects of Union List, Concurrent List and in certain cases on State List.
- The Parliament can pass a resolution of no-confidence against the ministry and ask it to resign. Those who run the government can take decisions only so long as they enjoy support of the Parliament.
- The Parliament controls all the money that government has. The governmental budget is passed in the Parliament.
- The Parliament is the highest forum of discussion and debate on public issues and national policies.
- The Parliament can seek information from and ask questions to the government and its ministers on any matter.
- The Parliament elects President, Vice-President, Speaker, Deputy Speaker, Vice-Chairman of Rajya Sabha, etc. It can also remove President, Vice-President, Judges of the Supreme Court and High Courts by passing a resolution of impeachment against them.

4. Give three differences between the Lok Sabha and the Rajya Sabha.

Ans. In our country, the Parliament consists of the President and two houses, i.e. the Council of States (Rajya Sabha) and the House of the People (Lok Sabha).

The differences between these two are

Lok Sabha	Rajya Sabha
The members of the Lok Sabha are directly elected by the people.	The members of the Rajya Sabha are indirectly elected by the members of the Legislative Assemblies.
The Lok Sabha exercises more power in money matters. Over the Lok Sabha passed the bill, the Rajya Sabha cannot reject it.	Rajya Sabha can delay in Money Bill for 14 days or suggest changes in it.
The House can be dissolved before the expiry of the tenure.	It cannot be dissolved, it is a permanent house.

5. Describe the powers and functions of the Prime Minister of India.

***Or* "The Prime Minister is the head of the government." Justify the statement.**

Ans. The Prime Minister of India has wide ranging powers and functions as follows

- The Prime Minister is free to choose ministers. He distributes and redistributes work to the ministers. All ministers work under his leadership.
- Being the Chairman of the Cabinet, the Prime Minister presides over the meetings of the Cabinet. He coordinates the work of different departments. His decisions are final in case disagreement arises between different departments.
- The Prime Minister communicates to the President all decisions of the Council of Ministers relating to the administration of union and proposals of legislation.

Thus, it can be concluded that Prime Minister is the head of the government.

6. Who appoints the Council of Ministers and who can be included in it?

Ans. The President appoints the Ministers of the Council of Ministers on the advice of the Prime Minister. The Ministers are usually from the party or the coalition that has the majority in the Lok Sabha.

The Council of Ministers is the official name for the body that includes all the ministers. It usually has 60 to 80 ministers of different ranks.

The Council of Ministers have collective responsibility to the Lok Sabha. It includes three types of ministers which as follows

(i) **Cabinet Ministers** They are usually top leaders of the ruling party or parties who are incharge of the major ministries.

They meet to take decisions in the name of the Council of Ministers. Cabinet is the inner ring of the Council of Ministers.

(ii) **Ministers of State with Independent Charge** They are usually incharge of smaller ministries. They participate in the Cabinet meetings only when specially invited.

(iii) **Ministers of State** They are attached to and required to assist Cabinet members.

7. Describe the powers of the Supreme Court.

Ans. Powers of the Supreme Court are

- The Supreme Court can take up any dispute
  - between citizens of the country.
  - between citizens and government.
  - between two or more State Governments.
  - between governments at the union and state level.
- It is the highest court of appeal in criminal and civil cases. The Supreme Court can hear appeals both in criminal and civil cases against decisions of the High Courts.
- The Supreme Court gives legal advice to the President of India on any legal or constitutional matter referred to it.

- The Supreme Court has the power to interpret the Constitution of the country.
- The powers and independence of judiciary allows Supreme Court to act as the guardian of Fundamental Rights.

8. Read the information given below and answer the following questions.

The Indian judicial system has a pendency problem. This is known—a primary problem of every governance reform and economic growth debate. That makes the news that lower courts in Kerala, Punjab, Himachal Pradesh, Haryana, and Chandigarh have disposed of almost all cases that had been pending for a decade or more as welcome as it is surprising. Today, there are only a total of 11,000 cases pending for over 10 years in these four states and the Union territory of Chandigarh.

Why an independent and powerful judiciary is considered essential for democracies?

Competency Based

Ans. The independent and powerful judiciary is considered essential for democracies because independence of the judiciary means that it is not under the control of the legislature or the executive. The judges do not act on the direction of the government or according to the wishes of the party in power. This ensures fair judgement. That is why all modern democracies have courts that are independent of the legislatures and the executive.

The judges of the Supreme Court and the High Courts are appointed by the President on the advice of the Prime Minister and in consulation with the Chief Justice of the Supreme Court. There is very little scope for interference by the political executive. Once a person is appointed as judge of the Supreme Court or the High Court it is nearly impossible to remove him or her from that position.

Case Based Questions

1 Read the sources given below and answer the questions that follow.

Source A The President of India

Presidents all over the world are not always nominal executive like the President of India. In many countries of the world, the President is both the head of the state and head of the government.

(i) The President of India is referred as a nominal head of the state. Illustrate

Source B The President of USA

The President of the United States of America is the most well known example of this kind of President. The US President is directly elected by the people. He personally chooses and appoints all ministers.

(ii) The President of USA has the power of the 'Veto'. Justify the statement

Source C Power of the President

The Law making is still done by the Legislature (called the Congress in the US), but the President can veto any law. Most importantly, the President does not need the support of the majority of members in the Congress and neither is he answerable to them. He has a fixed tenure of four years and completes it even if his Party does not have a majority in the Congress. This model is followed in most of the countries of Latin America and many of the ex-Soviet Union countries.

(iii) Do you think US President is more powerful than India's President? Give reasons.

Ans. (i) The President of India is referred to as the nominal head of the state because India follows a parliamentary system of government. He is not the real head of the executive, as the real power is exercised by the Prime Minister and Council of Ministers.

(ii) The President of USA has the power of the veto, which means he can stop legislation from becoming any law.

The President does not need the support of the majority of members in Congress and neither he is answerable to them.

(iii) Yes, we agree that US President is more powerful because he is both the head of the State and head of the Government whereas the Indian President is only the head of the State. So, we can say that the President of US is the real executive.

2 Read the source given below and answer the questions that follow.

India has an integrated or unified judiciary. The Judiciary is not under the control of the Legislature or the Executive. The Judges do not act on the direction of the government or according to the wishes of the political party in power. The Judge of the Supreme Court and the High Courts are appointed by the President on the advice of the Prime Minister and in consultation with the Chief Justice of the Supreme Court. The Supreme Court and the High Courts have the power to interpret the Constitution of the country. They can determine the constitutional validity of any legislation or action of the executive in the country, when it is challenged before them.

This is known as the judicial review. The powers and the independence of Indian Judiciary allow it to act as a guardian of the Fundamental Rights.

(i) How has the Indian Constitution ensured the Independence of Judiciary? Give reason.

(ii) India has an integrated Judiciary. Explain this statement.

(iii) Indian Judiciary enjoys a high level of confidence among the people. Give reasons.

Ans. (i) The Indian Constitution ensured the independence of Judiciary as the judiciary is not under the influence or control of any individual or authority.

(ii) India has an integrated Judiciary. The Supreme Court controls the judicial administration in the country. Its decisions are binding on all the courts of the country. It is the highest court of appeal in civil and criminal cases. It can hear appeals against the decisions of the high courts.

(iii) Indian Judiciary enjoys a high level of confidence among the people due to the following reasons

(a) Indian Judiciary act as the guardian of the Fundamental Rights. Citizens have the right to approach the courts to seek remedy in case of any violation of their rights.

(b) The courts also intervene to prevent the misuse of the government's power to make decisions for the people.

ASSESSMENT EXERCISE

Multiple Choice Questions (MCQs)

1. PIL is the abbreviation for ....

(a) Public Interest Legislature
(b) Public Interest Litigation
(c) Public Information Litigation
(d) None of the above

2. What is the meaning of the term 'Office Memorandum'?

(a) Order issued by the Government of India
(b) An important office record
(c) Memory of working in an office
(d) An important defence document

3. Why does the minister take the final decisions, even on technical matters?

(a) Because the minister is an expert in all areas
(b) Because the minister is an elected representative and answerable to the people
(c) Because civil servants are not knowledgeable
(d) Because ministers are always educated in all subjects

4. Which of the following is true about the political executive?

(a) They are appointed for a long term
(b) They are elected by the people for a specific period
(c) They work under the guidance of the civil services
(d) They are permanent members of the government

Subjective Questions (VSA, SA & LA)

1. How many judges are there in the Supreme Court of India?

2. How do institutions ensure democratic decision-making, and why is involving a wider set of people important?

3. Why do democratic governments insist on institutions?

4. Mention any two functions of Council of Ministers.

5. Why does the Lok Sabha have more power in money-related matters compared to the Rajya Sabha, and what is the significance of this?

6. What features of judiciary make it most powerful in the world?

7. Why does judiciary enjoy high level of confidence among people with reference to Public Interest Litigation (PIL)? Give your view point.

8. Why does political executive have more power than the permanent executive? Explain?

9. Describe the role of the President of India in appointment of the Prime Minister.

Democratic Rights

CHAPTER 5

Democratic rights are the socially recognised rights which are written into law in a democracy. The importance of rights can be judged by the one whose life has absence of rights. This chapter explores how these rights can be used by an ordinary citizen. This chapter also discuss who will protect and enforce them.

5.1 Meaning of Rights

Rights are reasonable claims of persons recognised in society and sanctioned by law.

A right is possible when a person makes a claim that is equally possible for others.

Rights should be made available to others in an equal measure. Thus, a right comes with an obligation to respect other rights.

A right becomes meaningful only when it is accepted by society. Society decides what is right and wrong, and these ideas can change over time. Long ago, women did not have the right to vote, but now it is considered unfair if they are denied this right.

When rights are written into laws, they become strong and enforceable.

When fellow citizens or the government do not respect their rights, it is called **violation of rights**. In such situations, citizen can approach courts to protect their rights.

5.2 Life Without Rights

The following three examples viz, prison in Guantanamo Bay, citizens' rights in Saudi Arabia and ethnic massacre in Kosovo describe how the life would be without rights.

Prison in Guantanamo Bay

About 600 people were secretly picked up by the US forces from all over the world and put in a prison in Guantanamo Bay, an area near Cuba controlled by American Navy.

According to the American Government, they were enemies of the US and linked to the attack on New York on 11th September, 2001.

There was no trial before any magistrate in the US and these prisoners could not even approach courts in their own country.

Amnesty International[1] reported that the prisoners were being tortured in ways that violated the US laws.

Despite the provisions of international treaties, prisoners were being denied the treatment they must get. They were not freed even after being found not guilty.

Citizens' Rights in Saudi Arabia

The position of the citizens in Saudi Arabia with regard to their government is as follows

- Saudi Arabia is ruled over by a hereditary king and the people have no role in electing or changing their rulers.
- The king selects the Legislature as well as the Executive. He appoints the judges and can change any of their decisions.
- Citizens cannot form political parties or any political organisations.
- Media cannot report anything that the monarch does not like.
- There is no freedom of religion. Every citizen is required to be Muslim. Non-Muslim residents can follow their religion in private, but not in public.

1 Amnesty International It is an international organisation of volunteers, who campaign for human rights. The organisation brings out independent reports on the violation of the human rights all over the world.

- Women are subjected to many public restrictions. The **testimony**[2] of one man is considered equal to that of two women.

Note *There are many countries in the world where conditions like Saudi Arabia exist.*

Ethnic Massacre in Kosovo

Kosovo was a province of Yugoslavia before its split. In this province, Albanians were in majority.

But in the entire country, Serbs were in majority and Albanians were in minority. Many Serbs leaders thought that the **ethnic minorities** like Albanians should either leave the country or accept the dominance of Serbs.

A brutal massacre took place in Kosovo in which thousands of Albanians were killed. This massacre was carried out by the army of their own country, working under the direction of a leader who came to power through democratic elections. Finally, several other countries **intervened** to stop this massacre. Milosevic lost power and was tried by the International Court of Justice for crimes against humanity.

5.3 Rights in a Democracy

Everyone wants a system where atleast a minimum assurance is guaranteed to all, whether he/she is powerful or weak, rich or poor, majority or minority. No one should be arrested without proper reason and information.

If it happens then he/she should have a fair chance to defend themselves. This assurance should not only be on paper. There should be someone to enforce them and to punish those who violate them. This is real spirit behind the rights.

In other words, it is a system where at least a minimum assurance is guaranteed to everyone–powerful or weak, rich or poor, majority or minority. This is the spirit behind thinking about rights. For example, the prisoners in Guantanamo Bay, women in Saudi Arabia and Albanians in Kosovo cases, were denied security, dignity and fair play (justice).

Need of Rights in a Democracy

- Rights are necessary for the survival of a democracy. In a democracy, every citizen has the **Right to Vote** and the **Right to be Elected** to government.
- Rights protect minorities from the oppression of majority. They ensure that majority cannot do whatever it wishes to do.
- Rights are guarantees which can be used when things go wrong. Specially, when some citizens may wish to take away the rights of others.
- Some rights need to be placed higher than the government, so that the government cannot violate them. In most democracies, the basic rights of the citizen are written down in the Constitution.

Try These

1. **Which International organisation reported that the prisoners in Guantanamo Bay were tortured?**
2. **In Saudi Arabia, who appoint the judges and selects the legislature as well as executive?**
3. **Who was elected as the leader of Yugoslavia?**
4. **This Ethnic group was in majority in Kosovo. They were expected to leave the country. Identify this group.**

5.4 Rights in the Indian Constitution

Some rights which are fundamental to our life are given a special status in Indian Constitution. They are called **Fundamental Rights.** They are an important basic feature of India's constitution.

The six Fundamental Rights recognised by the Constitution are as follows

1. Right to Equality

The Constitution says that the government shall not deny the equality before the law or the equal protection of the laws to any person in India.

It means that the laws apply in the same manner to all, regardless of a person's status. This is called the **rule of law.**

Rule of Law is the foundation of any democracy. It means that no person is above the law. The government shall not discriminate against any citizen on grounds only of religion, race, caste, sex or place of birth.

Every citizen shall have access to public places like shops, restaurants, hotels and cinema halls.

Reservations

The Government of India has provided reservation for **Scheduled Castes** (SCs), **Scheduled Tribes** (STs) and **Other Backward Classes** (OBCs).

Reservation is not against the Right to Equality because, equality does not mean giving everyone the same treatment, but it means giving everyone an equal opportunity to achieve, according to the capability of a particular person. Thus, according to the Constitution the reservations of this kind are not a violation of the Right to Equality.

2 **Testimony** It refers to a formal statement given in a court of law.

Untouchability

Untouchability is the extreme form of **social discrimination**. The Constitution directs the government to put an end to the practice of untouchability.

Untouchability does not mean refusal to touch people belonging to certain castes. Rather, it refers to any belief or social practice which looks down upon people on account of their birth with certain caste labels.

Such social practice denies people to interact with others or access to public places as equal citizens. So, the Constitution made untouchability a punishable influence.

Various Forms of Untouchability

In 1999, **P Sainath** wrote a series of news reports in the newspaper, **The Hindu**, describing untouchability and caste discrimination that was still being practised against Dalits or persons belonging to Scheduled Castes.

P. Sainath travelled many places of the country and found various forms of untouchability. These were

- Tea stalls kept two kinds of cups, one for Dalits and one for others.
- Barbers refused to serve Dalit clients.
- Dalit students were made to sit separately in the classroom and drink water from separate pitcher.
- Dalit grooms were not allowed to ride a horse in the wedding procession.
- Dalits were not allowed to use common handpump or if they did, the handpump was washed to purify it.

2. Right to Freedom

Freedom means absence of constraint (restrictions). In practical life, it means absence of interference in our affairs by others, whether individual or the government.

Under the Indian Constitution, all citizens have the right to

- Freedom of speech and expression
- Assembly in a peaceful manner
- Form associations and unions
- Move freely throughout the country
- Reside in any part of the country
- Practice any profession or to carry on any occupation, trade or business

Nobody can exercise freedom in such a manner that violates other's rights to freedom.

The government can impose certain reasonable restrictions on our freedom in the larger interests of the society.

Freedom of Speech and Expression

The freedom of speech and expression is one of the essential features of any democracy. Our ideas and personality develop only when we are able to freely communicate with others.

Our views are expressed through pamphlets, magazines, newspapers, paintings, poetry or songs. However, this freedom cannot be used to initiate violence against others and excite people to rebel against government.

It also cannot be used to defame others by saying false and mean things that cause damage to a person's reputation.

Assembly in a Peaceful Manner/Form Associations

Citizens have the freedom to hold meetings, processions, rallies and demonstrations on any issue. But such meetings should be peaceful and people participating in these should not carry weapons. Citizens also can form associations to promote their interests.

Freedom to Travel/Choice of Occupations

The citizen have the freedom to travel to any part of the country and are free to reside or settle in any part of the territory of India.

The same freedom extends to choice of occupations. No one can force a person to do or not to do a certain job.

Personal Liberty

The Constitution says that no person can be deprived of his life or personal liberty except according to procedure established by law. It means that no person can be killed unless the court has ordered a death sentence.

It also means that a government or police officer cannot arrest or detain any citizen unless he has proper legal justification.

When police arrests someone, they have to follow some procedures like

- A person who is arrested and detained in custody will have to be informed of the reasons for such arrest and detention.
- Such a person shall be produced before the nearest magistrate within a period of 24 hours of arrest.
- Such a person has the right to consult a lawyer or engage a lawyer for his own defence.

3. Right Against Exploitation

Constitution makers thought it is necessary to write down certain clear provisions to prevent exploitation of the weaker sections of the society.

The Constitution mentions following three conditions and declares them illegal

(i) The Constitution prohibits **traffic**[3] in human beings. Traffic here means selling and buying of human beings, usually, women or children, for immoral purposes.

(ii) The Constitution also prohibits forced labour or **Begar**[4] in any form. Begar is a practice where the worker is forced to render service to the master free of charge or at a nominal remuneration. When this practice takes place on a life long basis, it is called the practice of **bonded labour.**

(iii) The Constitution prohibits **child labour.** No one can employ a child below the age of 14 to work in any factory or mine or any other hazardous work, such as railways and ports.

4. Right to Freedom of Religion

Every person has a **right to profess, practice and propagate the religion,** in which he or she believes. Every religious group or sect is free to manage its religious affairs.

Freedom to propagate one's religion does not mean that a person has right to force another person to convert into his religion by means of force, fraud, inducement or allurement.

A secular state is one that does not establish any one religion as official religion. India is a secular state. In India, no privilege or favour is provided to any particular religion.

The government cannot force any person to pay any tax for the promotion or maintenance of any particular religion or religious institution. There shall be no religious instruction in the government educational institutions.

5.Cultural and Educational Rights

Since democracy gives power to the majority, minorities need special protection. Their language, culture and religion may be ignored. Thus, our Constitution provides the following cultural and educational rights to the minorities

- Any section of citizens with a distinct language or culture have a right to conserve it.
- Admission to any educational institution maintained by government or receiving government aid cannot be denied to any citizen on the grounds of religion or language.
- All minorities have the right to establish and administer educational institutions of their choice.

6. Right to Constitutional Remedies

The Fundamental Rights in the Constitution are important because they are enforceable. There is a right to seek the enforcement of these mentioned rights which is called the **Right to Constitutional Remedies.** This right makes other rights effective.

When any of the Fundamental Rights are violated, then citizens can directly approach the Supreme Court or the High Court.

Both courts have the power to issue **Writ**[5] (Habeas Corpus, Mandamus, Prohibition, Quo Warranto and Certiorari) for the enforcement of the rights.

Dr Ambedkar called the Right to Constitutional Remedies *'the heart and soul'* of our Constitution.

5.5 Securing the Fundamental Rights

If any act of the Legislature or the Executive takes away or limits any of the Fundamental Rights, it will be invalid.

Courts also enforce the fundamental rights against private individuals and bodies.

In case of any violation of Fundamental Right the aggrieved person can go to a court for remedy. But now, any person can go to court against the violation of the Fundamental right, if it is of social or public interest. It is called **Public interest Litigation** (PIL).

Under the PIL, any citizen or group of citizens can approach the Supreme Court or High Court for the protection of public interest against a particular law or action of the government.

National Human Rights Commission (NHRC)

It is an independent commission established in 1993. The Commission is appointed by the President.

The Commission focuses on helping the victims to secure their human rights. These include all the rights granted to the citizens by the Constitution.

The Commission also considers the Human Rights mentioned in the UN sponsored international treaties that India has signed.

The NHRC makes independent and credible inquiry into any case of violation of human rights. It presents its findings and recommendations to the government.

3 **Traffic** It refers to selling and buying of men, women or children for immoral purposes.

4 **Begar** It is a practice where the worker is forced to render service to the 'master' free of charge or at a nominal remuneration.

5 **Writ** It is a formal document containing an order of the court to the government issued only by High Court or the Supreme Court.

5.6 Expanding Scope of Rights

Our Constitution and law offers a wider range of rights apart from the Fundamental Rights. Fundamental rights are the source of all rights. The scope of rights has expanded over the years. Recently the Supreme Court has expanded the meaning of the right to life to include the right to food. From time to time, the court gave judgements to expand the scope of rights.

Also, rights are not limited only to fundamental rights as enumerated in the constitution. Constitution provides many more rights, which may not be fundamental rights.

Certain rights like Right to Freedom of Press, Right to Education and Right to Information are derived from Fundamental Rights.

Parliament has enacted a law giving the right to information to the citizens. This act was made under the Fundamental Right to freedom of thought and expression. According to Right to Information, anybody can demand information regarding the functions of a government department or official.

Some rights that Constitution provides apart from Fundamental Rights are the Right to Property and Right to Vote in Election. These are not Fundamental Rights, but these are **Constitutional Rights**.

Sometimes, the expansion of rights takes place in the form of human rights. Human rights are universal moral claims[6] that may or may not have been recognised by law. In that sense, these claims are not rights that are defined earlier.

With the expansion of democracy all over the world, there is greater pressure on governments to accept these claims. Some international covenants[7] have contributed to the expansion of rights.

International Covenant on Economic, Social and Cultural Rights

The international covenant recognises many rights that are not directly a part of the Fundamental Rights in the Indian Constitution. This covenant is regarded as a standard of human rights by human right activists all over the world.

The rights in this covenant include

- Right to work i.e. opportunity to everyone to earn livelihood by working.
- Right to safe and healthy working conditions, fair wages that can provide decent standard of living for the workers and their families.
- Right to adequate standard of living including adequate food, clothing and housing.
- Right to social security and insurance.
- Right to health i.e. medical care during illness, special care for women during child birth and prevention of epidemics.
- Right to education i.e. free and compulsory primary education, equal access to higher education.

Conclusion

Thus, the scope of rights has been expanding and new rights are evolving over time. They are result of the struggle of people.

New rights emerge, as societies develop or as new constitutions are made. For example, the Constitution of South Africa guarantees its citizens several kinds of new rights. These are

- Right to Privacy which guarantees that citizens or their home cannot be searched, their phones cannot be tapped and their communication cannot be opened.
- Right to an Environment that is not harmful to their health or well being.
- Right to have adequate housing.
- Right to have access to health care services, sufficient food and water and no one may be refused emergency medical treatment.

Try These

1. **Who has the authority to issue writs?**
2. **What is the extreme form of social discrimination?**
3. **Which right is called the Heart and Soul of the Indian Constitution?**
4. **Which right gives opportunity to earn livelihood by working?**

6 Claim It refers to the demand for legal or moral entitlements, a person makes on fellow citizens, society or the government.

7 Covenant It is a promise made by individuals, groups or countries to uphold a rule or principle. It is legally binding on the signatories to the agreement or the statement.

Mind Map

DEMOCRATIC RIGHTS

Life Without Rights

Prison in Guantanamo Bay
- About 600 people were secretly picked up by the US forces from all over the world.
- There was no trial before any magistrate in the US and the prisoners could not even approach courts in their own country.

Citizen's Rights in Saudi Arabia
- In Saudi Arabia, the king selects the Legislature as well as Executive.
- Citizens cannot form political parties or any political organisation.
- There is no freedom of religion. Every citizens is required to be Muslim.
- Women are subjected to many restrictions.

Ethnic Massacre in Kosovo
- In Kosovo, Albanians were in majority, but in the entire country Serbs were in majority and Albanians were in minority.
- A brutal massacre took place in Kosovo, in which many Albanians were killed.
- Finally, several other countries intervened to stop this massacre.

Rights in a Democracy
- Rights are necessary for the survival of democracy.
- Rights protect minorities from the oppression of majority.
- Rights are guarantees which can be used when things go wrong.

Meaning of Rights
- Rights are reasonable claims of persons recognised in society and sanctioned by law.
- When fellow citizens or the government do not respect their rights, it is called violation of rights.

Securing Fundamental Rights
Any person can go to court against the violation of the Fundamental Right, if it is of social or public interest. It is called Public Interest Litigation (PIL).

Expanding Scope of Rights
- Constitution provides certain rights apart from fundamental rights such as right to property and right to vote in election which are called as constitutional rights.
- Human Rights are moral claims that may or may not have been recognised by law.

Rights in the Indian Constitution

Right Against Exploitation
- The Constitution prohibits selling and buying of human beings, for immoral purposes.
- The Constitution prohibits forced labour or begar.
- The Constitution prohibits child labour.

Right to Freedom
- Right to freedom of speech and expression
- Right to assembly in a peaceful manner
- Right to form associations and unions
- Right to move freely throughout the country
- Right to reside in any part of the country
- Right to practice any profession or to carry on any occupation, trade or business.

Right to Constitutional Remedies
The right to seek the enforcement of the Fundamental Rights is called the Right to Constitutional Remedies.

Right to Freedom of Religion
- Every person has a right to profess, practice and propagate the religion, in which he or she believes.
- The government cannot force any person to pay any tax for the promotion or maintenance of any particular religion or religious institution.

Right to Equality
- The government says that it shall not deny the equality before the law or the equal protection of the laws to any person in India.
- The government shall not discriminate against any citizen on grounds of religion, race, caste, sex or place of birth.
- Every citizen shall have access to public places like shops, restaurants, hotels and cinema halls.

Cultural and Educational Rights
- Any section of citizens with a distnict language or culture have a right to conserve it.
- All minorities have the right to establish and administer educational institutions of their choice.
- Admission to any educational institution maintained by government or receiving government aid cannot be denied to any citizen on the grounds of religion or language.

NCERT FOLDER

Covering Intext Questions and Exercises of NCERT

INTEXT QUESTIONS

Q.1 If you were a Serb, would you support what Milosevic did in Kosovo? Do you think this project of establishing Serb dominance was good for the Serbs?

Ans. If I were a Serb, I would not support what Milosevic did in Kosovo because what he did was very unjust and discriminatory towards the Albanians.

This method of establishing Serb dominance was not good for the Serbs because this action of Milosevic led to conflict and hostility between the Serbs and the Albanians.

Q.2 What are the examples of elected governments not protecting or even attacking the rights of their own citizens? Why do they do that?

Ans. Examples of elected governments not protecting or even attacking the rights of their own citizens are

- Ethnic massacre of Albanians in Kosovo.
- Policy of apartheid in South Africa.
- Rule of Augusto Pinochet in Chile.
- Rule of Robert Mugabe in Zimbabwe.

These elected rulers wanted to hold their own power and keep the people under their control so that they would not oppose them and they could rule without problems.

Q.3 Everyone knows that the rich can have better lawyers in the courts. What is the point in talking about equality before law?

Ans. It is true that the rich can have better lawyers in the courts, but the law is the same for everyone. Being rich or having good lawyers does not mean that equality of law also changes.

Whether a person is rich or poor, the law remains the same for all citizens. The judiciary follows the rule of law for all without discriminating.

Q.4 'Go to the playground of the school or any stadium and watch a 400 metre race on any track. Why are the competitors in the outer lane placed ahead of those in the inner lane at the starting point of the race'? What would happen if all the competitors start the race from the same line? Which of these would be an equal and fair race? Apply this example to a competition for jobs.

Ans. Since, the outer lane has a bigger circumference than the inner lane, more than 400 metre distance will be covered in one round of the track.

Thus competitors in the outer lane are placed ahead, so that they are given an equal opportunity compared to the person in the inner lane.

If all the competitors start at the same line, the outer track competitors will have to run a longer distance, which will not be fair. So, in the first case, it will be a fair race.

Similarly, in a competition for jobs, if the Scheduled Castes are given reservations, they can compete on an equal basis, because they are educationally and culturally backward, although they may be fit for the job for which they have applied.

Q.5 Observe any big public building. Is there a ramp for physically handicapped? Are there any other facilities that make it possible for physically handicapped to use the building in the same way as any one else?

Should these special facilities be provided, if it leads to extra expenditure on the building? Do these special provisions go against the principle of equality?

Ans. In many public buildings like hospitals and big offices, there are such ramps. Some airports have special toilets for the physically handicapped.

These special provisions do not go against the Right to Equality, as handicapped persons also have the same rights as normal citizens and the government must provide for them accordingly.

Yes, there are several facilities that makes it possible for physically handicapped to use the building in the same way as anyone else.

Some of these facilities are

- Widening Doorways to allow a wheelchair to pass through easily.
- Installation of Handrail to support the bodyweight at the critical places like Staircase, Ramp, Toilet, passage with a change of level, etc.
- Relocating light switches and door handles to a level that consider people who have difficulty in reaching.
- Provision of atleast one lift shall be made for the wheelchair user in the building.

Yes, these facilities should be provided, even if it leads to extra expenditure on the building.

Q.6 Should the freedom of expression be extended to those who are spreading wrong and narrow minded ideas? Should they be allowed to confuse the public?

Ans. No, the freedom of expression should not be extended to those who are spreading wrong and narrow minded ideas, since it is harmful for the society and democracy. No, they should not be allowed to confuse the public because it would be wrong to do so. Spreading wrong information for personal gains is wrong.

Their views can instigate violence, which is dangerous for our society. Nobody can use freedom of speech and expression to incite people or rebel against government.

Q.7 Are these cases instances of violation of the Right to Freedom? If yes, which constitutional provision does each violate?

(a) The Government of India banned Salman Rushdie's book 'the Satanic Verses' on the ground that it was disrespectful to Prophet Muhammed and was likely to hurt the feelings of the Muslim community.

(b) Every film has to be approved by the Censor Board of the Government before it can be shown to the public. But, there is no such restriction if the same story is published in a book or a magazine.

(c) The government is considering a proposal that there will be industrial zones or sectors of the economy, where workers will not be allowed to form unions or go on strike.

(d) City administration has imposed a ban on use of public microphones after 10 pm. in view of the approaching secondary school examinations.

Ans. (a) Yes, this violates the Right to Freedom of Thought and Expression.

(b) Yes, this violates the Right to Freedom of Thought and Expression.

(c) Yes, this violates the Right to Freedom to form associations and unions.

(d) No, this is not a violation of the Right to Freedom because the Constitution restricts freedom to a group of people (who are likely to use public microphones after 10 pm.) as long as that freedom does not affect or hamper freedom of anyone else. Also the ban is imposed in the larger interests of the people.

Q.8 The Constitution does not give people their religion. Then, how can it give people the Right to Practise their Religion?

Ans. It is true that the Constitution does not give the people their religion. However, it does not prevent the people from the Right to Practice their Religion, because the Constitution provides every person with a right to profess, practice and propagate the religion he or she believes.

Every religious group or sect is free to manage its religious affairs. In this way, our Constitution gives people the Right to practice their religion.

Q.9 Read the following news reports and identify the right that is being debated in each of these cases.

(a) An emergency session of the Shiromani Gurdwara Prabandhak Committee (SGPC) rejected the proposal to form a separate body to manage the affairs of Sikh shrines in Haryana. It warned the government that the Sikh community would not tolerate any interference in their religious affairs (June 2005).

(b) The Allahabad High Court quashed the Central Law, which gave Aligarh Muslim University its minority status and held illegal reservation of seats for Muslims in its post- graduate medical courses (January 2006).

(c) The Rajasthan Government has decided to enact an anti-conversion law. Christian leaders have said that the Bill would aggravate the sense of insecurity and fear in the minds of minorities (March 2005).

Ans. (a) Here, it is the Right to Freedom of Religion.

(b) Here, it is the Right to Equality.

(c) Here, it is the Right to Freedom of Religion.

Q.10 Can the President of India stop you from approaching the Supreme Court to secure your Fundamental Rights?

Ans. No, the President of India even cannot stop me from approaching the Supreme Court to secure my Fundamental Rights because the Fundamental Rights have been enshrined in our Constitution.

This means that our Constitution provides and protects these rights and they can not be taken away or violated by any person or government action or law, which also includes the President of India.

The Right to Constitutional Remedies is a Fundamental Right, according to which we have the right to approach the Supreme Court in case of violation of rights by any person or government or law. So, nobody can stop us from going to court to secure our Fundamental Rights.

Q.11 Read about the National Human Rights Commission and answer the given question.

Do you notice references to the National Human Rights Commission (NHRC) in the news collage on this page? These references reflect the growing awareness of human rights and struggles for human dignity.

Many cases of human rights violations in diverse fields, for instance, Gujarat riots, are being brought to the public notice from across India. Human rights organisations and the media often criticise government agencies for not seriously pursuing these cases or catching the culprits. Someone had to intervene on behalf of the victims.

This is where the National Human Rights Commission stepped in. This is an independent commission set up by law in 1993. Like judiciary, the Commission is independent of the government. The Commission is appointed by the President and includes retired judges, officers and eminent citizens.

Yet it does not have the burden of deciding court cases. So, it can focus on helping the victims secure their human rights. These include all the rights granted to the citizens by the Constitution. For NHRC, human rights also include the rights mentioned in the UN sponsored international treaties that India has signed. The NHRC cannot by itself punish the guilty. That is the responsibility of courts. The NHRC is there to make independent and credible inquiry into any case of violation of human rights.

It also inquiries into any case of abetment of such violation or negligence in controlling it by any government officer and takes other general steps to promote human rights in the country. The Commission presents its findings and recommendations to the government or intervene in the court on behalf of the victims. It has wide ranging powers to carry out its inquiry.

Like any court, it can summon witnesses, question any government official, demand any official paper, visit any prison for inspection or send its own team for on the spot inquiry.

Citizen of India can write a letter to this address to complain against the violation of Human Rights: National Human Rights Commission, Faridkot House, Copernicus Marg, New Delhi 110001. There is no fee or any formal procedure to approach the NHRC. Like NHRC, there are State Human Rights Commissions in 26 states of the country.

Are the rights only for adults? Which of these rights are available to children?

Ans. No, Fundamental Rights, are not only for the adults, they are available to all the citizens of the country without any discrimination. Right against exploitation is specially devoted to children because it protects the children from exploitation.

These rights prohibit child labour. No one can employ a child below the age of 14 to work in any factory or mine or in any other hazardous work such as railways and ports.

Using this right as a basis, many laws have been made to prohibit children from working in industries such as beedi making, fire crackers, matches, printing and dyeing.

EXERCISE

Q.1 Which of the following is not an instance of an exercise of a Fundamental Right?

(a) Workers from Bihar go to the Punjab to work on the farms
(b) Christian missions set up a chain of missionary schools
(c) Men and women government employees get the same salary
(d) Parents' property is inherited by their children

Ans. (d) Parents' property is inherited by their children is not a Fundamental Right.

Q.2 Which of the following freedoms is not available to an Indian citizen?

(a) Freedom to criticise the government
(b) Freedom to participate in armed revolution
(c) Freedom to start a movement to change the government
(d) Freedom to oppose the central values of the Constitution

Ans. (b) Freedom to participate in armed revolution

Q.3 Which of the following rights is available under the Indian Constitution?

(a) Right to Work
(b) Right to Adequate Livelihood
(c) Right to Protect One's Culture
(d) Right to Privacy

Ans. (c) Right to protect one's culture. It comes under the Cultural and Educational Rights.

Q.4 Name the Fundamental Right under which each of the following rights falls.

(a) Freedom to propagate one's religion
(b) Right to life
(c) Abolition of untouchability
(d) Ban on bonded labour

Ans. (a) Right to Freedom of Religion
(b) Right to Personal Liberty
(c) Right to Equality
(d) Right against Exploitation

Q.5 Which of these statements about the relationship between democracy and rights is more valid? Give reasons for your preference.

(a) Every country that is a democracy gives rights to its citizens.
(b) Every country that gives rights to its citizens is a democracy.
(c) Giving rights is good, but it is not necessary for a democracy.

Ans. Statement (a) is the most valid statement, Every country that is a democracy gives rights to its citizens. Every country which provides rights to its citizens might not be a democracy but, it is essential for a democracy to provide rights to its citizens.

Q.6 Are these restrictions on the right to freedom justified? Give reasons for your answer.

(a) Indian citizens need permission to visit some border areas of the country for reasons of security.

(b) Outsiders are not allowed to buy property in some areas to protect the interest of the local population.

(c) The government bans the publication of a book that can go against the ruling party in the next elections.

Ans. (a) This is justified. Right to Freedom is for all the citizens which grants them to move freely anywhere in the country but due to security reasons some areas are restricted as the freedom of movement by every citizen can prove dangerous for the security of India.

(b) In certain cases, this can be justified to maintain the cultural or ethnic identity of the local population.

(c) Statement (c) is not justified because it violates the Right to Freedom of Speech and Expression of citizens. They have the right to express their views about the working of the government.

Q.7 Manoj went to a college to apply for admission into an MBA course. The clerk refused to take his application and said "You, the son of a sweeper, wish to be a manager! has anyone done this job in your community? Go to the municipality office and apply for a sweeper's position". Which of Manoj's fundamental rights are being violated in this instance? Spell these out in a letter from Manoj to the District Collector.

Ans. Right to Equality and Right to Freedom are violated in Manoj's case.

To,

The District Collector,

XYZ District

Sub: Redressal required of violation of my Right to Equality for admission in a College

Dear Sir,

I wish to inform you that my admission for pursuing a course leading to the MBA degree in ABC college in your district has been refused because the clerk of the college said, "You are the son of a sweeper. Nobody from your community has done such a course," This is totally unjust and a violation of my Right to Equality.

I am fully qualified to apply for the course, having already completed my graduation.

You are requested to look into this problem and talk to the authorities of the concerned college to accept my application.

Thank you

Sincerely yours

(Manoj)

Q.8 When Madhurima went to the property registration office, the Registrar told her 'You can't write your name as Madhurima Bannerjee d/o AK Bannerjee'. You are married, so, you must give your husband's name.

Your husband's surname is Rao. So, your name should be changed to Madhurima Rao. She did not agree. She said If my husband's name has not changed after marriage, why should mine?' In your opinion, who is right in this dispute? and why?

Ans. In this dispute, Madhurima is right. The registrar by questioning and interfering in her personal affairs, is violating her right to freedom. Also, the social question of adopting the husband's surname has roots in a religious practice which treats women as weaker and inferior. In lieu of this, forcing Madhurima to change her name is to control her right to equality and right to freedom of religion.

Q.9 Thousands of tribals and other forest dwellers gathered at Piparia in Hoshangabad district in Madhya Pradesh to protest against their proposed displacement from the Satpura National Park and Bori Wildlife Sanctuary.

They argue that such a displacement is an attack on their livelihood and beliefs. Government claims that their displacement is essential for the development of the area and for protection of wildlife. Write a petition on behalf of the forest dwellers to the NHRC, a response from the government and a report of the NHRC on this matter.

Ans. (i) The Petition should be as follows

We, the tribal and the forest people have been living in and near the forests for hundreds of years and have earned our livelihood from the forests. The forests are our home and place of work.

It is wrong to displace us from our traditional homes. By doing so, you are taking away our livelihood and traditions because we know no other work. We request the NHRC (National Human Rights Commission) to take up our cause and prevent our displacement from the forest due to the setting up of the wildlife sanctuaries.

(ii) **The Response of the Government** The government, in order to protect the wildlife which is near extinction, has decided to set up wildlife parks and wildlife sanctuaries and provide natural habitats to the endangered species and other animals. For doing this, human interference has to be stopped and so the tribals and forest dwellers are to be displaced from these areas. However, keeping in mind the welfare of the tribals and ensuring a future for them, tribals will be rehabilitated in some other suitable place.

(iii) **NHRC Report** The National Human Rights Commission gave its report on the proposed displacement of the tribals and the forest dwellers from the wildlife parks and sanctuaries like the Satpura National Park, Bori Wildlife Sanctuary and Panchmarhi Wildlife Sanctuary. NHRC said that the tribals and the forest dwellers have since ages lived in the forests and also earned their livelihood from the forests. However, realising the importance of the forests in their lives they have taken care not to harm it or damage it in any manner. They have co-existed in the forests with all the flora and fauna and they have many beliefs and traditions, which infact protect the forests and the animals. Finally, they are not a threat to the flora and the fauna and they can help to protect, preserve and conserve the forest flora and fauna, so they should be allowed to live in the forests as a part of the forest.

REVIEW EXERCISE

Including Competency Based Questions

Part I

Multiple Choice Questions (MCQs)

1. Which of the following countries became victim of a major terror attack on 11th September, 2001?

(a) India (b) USA
(c) Russia (d) France

2. The prison in Guantanamo Bay is under which of the following Navies?

(a) French Navy (b) Indian Navy
(c) American Navy (d) Russian Navy

3. Which of the following countries is ruled by a hereditary king?

(a) Afghanistan
(b) Iran
(c) Bangladesh
(d) Saudi Arabia

4. Which one of the following is not correct about the political conditions in Saudi Arabia?

(a) Citizens can form political parties or political organisations.
(b) Media cannot report anything that the monarch does not like.
(c) Non-Muslim residents can follow their religion in private, but not in public.
(c) Women are subjected to many public restrictions.

5. Kosovo was a province of which of the following countries before its split?

(a) Albania (b) Afghanistan
(c) Yugoslavia (d) Egypt

6. Which of the following is/are true meaning of the rule of law?

(a) The government shall not deny to any person in India equality before the law.
(b) The laws apply in the same manner to all, regardless of a person's status.
(c) No person is above the law.
(d) All of the above

7. Which one of the following is not a Fundamental Right in India?

(a) Right to Constitutional Remedies
(b) Right against Exploitation
(c) Right of Property
(d) Right to Freedom of Religion

8. Which one of following is incorrect about an arrested person in India?

(a) He has to be informed of the reasons for his arrest and detention.
(b) He has to be produced before the nearest magistrate within a period of 24 hours of arrest.
(c) He has to be produced before a court within 24 hours of arrest if a judge asks to the police to do so.
(d) He has the right to consult a lawyer for his defence.

9. Fundamental Rights are guaranteed against the actions of which of the following?

(a) Legislature
(b) Executive
(c) Any authorities instituted by the government
(d) All of the above

10. **In which year, National Human Rights Commission was set-up?**

(a) 1990 (b) 1993 (c) 1989 (d) 1982

11. **Which one of the following is not a Fundamental Right under Right to Freedom of Religion?**

(a) Right to establish and maintain institutions for religious and charitable purposes.

(b) Declaration of one's religious beliefs and faiths openly and freely.

(c) Right to sacrifice animals

(d) None of the above

12. **Who among the following is responsible to appoint National Human Rights Commission?**

(a) The President of India

(b) The Chief Justice of India

(c) The Prime Minister of India

(d) The Vice-President of India

13. **Find the incorrect option regarding a secular state like India:**

(a) It does not establish any one religion as official religion.

(b) No privilege or favour is provided to any particular religion.

(c) The government can't compel any person to pay any tax for maintenance of religious institution.

(d) There shall be religious instruction in the government educational institutions.

14. **Identify the reason as to why NHRC is an important institution when it comes to ensuring the human rights of the public?** **Competency Based**

I. It focuses on helping the victims to secure their human rights granted to the citizens by the Constitution.

II. NHRCs often engage themselves in raising awareness about human rights issues.

III. The NHRC is there to make independent and credible inquiries into any case of violation of human rights.

IV. They can't inquire into any case of promoting such violation or negligence in controlling by any government officer.

Options

(a) Statements I and II are appropriate

(b) Statements I, II and III are appropriate

(c) All the Statements are appropriate

(d) Only Statement IV is appropriate

Answers

1. (b)	**2.** (c)	**3.** (d)	**4.** (a)	**5.** (c)
6. (d)	**7.** (c)	**8.** (c)	**9.** (d)	**10.** (b)
11. (c)	**12.** (a)	**13.** (d)	**14.** (b)	

Match the Following

1.

List I	List II
A. Right to Freedom of Religion	1. Freedom to propagate one's own religion
B. Right against Exploitation	2. Abolition of Untouchability
C. Right to Equality	3. Ban on Bonded Labour

Codes

	A	B	C		A	B	C
(a)	1	2	3	(b)	3	1	2
(c)	1	3	2	(d)	1	3	2

2.

List I	List II
A. Right to Work	1. Medical care during illness
B. Right to Privacy	2. Opportunity to everyone to earn livelihood
C. Right to Health	3. Communication cannot be opened

Codes

	A	B	C		A	B	C
(a)	2	3	1	(b)	3	2	1
(c)	1	3	2	(d)	1	3	2

Ans. 1. (d) 2. (a)

Assertion-Reason

1. **Assertion** (A) The NHRC can make independent and credible inquiry into any case of violation of human rights.

Reason (R) The National Human Rights Commission (NHRC) is an independent Commission.

Codes

(a) Both A and R are true and R is the correct explanation of A

(b) Both A and R are true, but R is not the correct explanation of A

(c) A is true, but R is false

(d) A is false, but R is true

2. **Assertion** (A) The Government of India has provided reservation for SC's, ST's and OBC's.

Reason (R) These reservations are against the Right to Equality.

Codes

(a) Both A and R are true and R is the correct explanation of A

(b) Both A and R are true, but R is not the correct explanation of A

(c) A is true, but R is false

(d) A is false, but R is true

3. Assertion (A) The Constitution says that no person can be deprived of his life or personal liberty.

Reason (R) Every person has a right to profess, practice and propagate the religion.

Codes

(a) Both A and R are true and R is the correct explanation of A.

(b) Both A and R are true, but R is not the correct explanation of A

(c) A is true, but R is false

(d) A is false, but R is true

4. Assertion (A) Fundamental rights are the source of all rights including legal rights.

Reason (R) Certain rights like right to freedom of press, right to information, right to education are derived from fundamental rights.

Codes

(a) Both A and R are true and R is the correct explanation of A

(b) Both A and R are true, but R is not the correct explanation of A

(c) A is true, but R is false

(d) A is false, but R is true

Ans. 1. (a) Both A and R are true and R is the correct explanation of A

2. (c) A is true, but R is false

3. (b) Both A and R are true, but R is not the correct explanation of A

4. (a) Both A and R are true and R is the correct explanation of A

Case Based Question

1. Read the source given below and answer the questions that follow.

Rights are necessary for the very sustenance of a democracy. In a democracy every citizen has to have the right to vote and the right to be elected to government. For democratic elections to take place, it is necessary that citizens should have the right to express their opinion, form political parties and take part in political activities. Rights also perform a very special role in a democracy. Rights protect minorities from the oppression of the majority. They ensure that the majority cannot do whatever it likes. Rights are guarantees which can be used when things go wrong. Things may go wrong when some citizens may wish to take away the rights of others.

This usually happens when those in majority want to dominate those in minority. The government should protect the citizens' rights in such a situation. But sometimes elected governments may not protect or may even attack the rights of their own citizens. That is why some rights need to be placed higher than the government, so that the government cannot violate them. In most democracies the basic rights of the citizens are written down in the constitution.

(i) The principle of majority rule means that

(a) The majority always makes correct decisions.

(b) The majority has the right to make decisions, but with respect to minority rights.

(c) The minority has the sole right to make decisions.

(d) Decision-making is solely in the hands of the government.

(ii) The protection of minority rights contributes to

(a) a stable and inclusive democracy.

(b) excessive concentration of power in the majority.

(c) suppression of majority voices.

(d) None of the above

(iii) The purpose of protecting minority rights is to

(a) promote discrimination.

(b) ensure equal treatment and representation.

(c) suppress minority voices.

(d) concentrate power in the majority.

(iv) Which document often serves as a safeguard for minority rights in democratic countries?

(a) Constitution

(b) Executive orders

(c) Political party manifestos

(d) Public referendums

Ans. (i) (b) The majority has the right to make decisions, but with respect to minority rights.

(ii) (a) a stable and inclusive democracy.

(iii) (b) ensure equal treatment and representation.

(iv) (a) Constitution

Part II

Very Short Answer Type Questions

1. What was the reason given by America for imprisoning people at Guantanamo Bay?

Ans. The reason given by America for imprisoning people at Guantanamo Bay was that it considered the people as their enemies and linked them to the attack on New York on 11th September, 2001.

2. Which body exposed to the world that prisoners at Guantanamo Bay were being tortured in ways that violated the US laws?

Ans. Amnesty International, an international human rights organisation reported that prisoners at Guantanamo Bay were being tortured in ways that violated the US laws.

3. What was Slobodan Milosevic's attitude towards the Albanians?

Ans. Slobodan Milosevic was a narrow-minded Serb nationalist, who wanted Serbs to dominate the Albanians, as his government was hostile to the Kosovo Albanians.

4. How did the Massacre of Albanians finally ended?

Ans. The Massacre of Albanians finally ended when several other countries intervened. Milosevic was tried by the International Court of Justice.

5. What are rights?

Ans. Rights are reasonable claims of person recognised by society and sanctioned by law.

6. How many Fundamental Rights does the Indian Constitution provide?

Ans. Indian Constitution provides six Fundamental Rights.

7. What is a secular state?

Ans. In a secular state, no religion can get any privilege or favour and there is no official religion.

8. Which Fundamental Right ensures the ban on bonded labour?

Ans. The Fundamental Right, which ensures the ban on bonded labour is 'right against exploitation'.

9. What is the minimum age below which no one can employ a child?

Ans. No one can employ a child below the age of 14 to work in any factory.

10. Which Fundamental Right says that no person can be deprived of his life or personal liberty except according to procedure established by law?

Ans. Right to Freedom 'Protection of life and personal liberty' ensures all citizens the right to life and personal liberty.

11. Name any two political rights.

Ans. Two political rights are Right to Vote and Right to Contest Election.

12. What makes any political system democratic?

Ans. Elections and institutions need to be combined with enjoyment of rights which makes any political system democratic.

13. Give any two features of Fundamental Rights.

Ans. Two important features of Fundamental Rights are that these are limited and enforceable.

14. According to which Fundamental Right, the public places should be accessible to all the persons?

Ans. Under Right to Equality, the public places should be accessible to all the persons.

15. If our Fundamental Rights are violated, where can we seek the remedy?

Ans. If our Fundamental Rights are violated, we seek remedy from the Supreme Court or High Court.

16. Name the writs issued by courts in India.

Ans. Writs issued by courts in India are Habeaus Corpus, Mandamus, Prohibition, Quo Warranto and Certiorari.

17. Anaya is from Kannuroo village her father migrated to mumbai along with her mother and Anaya from where she continued the education. In her summer vacation she came to visit her village and heard about this cultural practice where the tradition is to restrict the education of girls beyond elementary school. Anaya's parents were forced by the villagers to follow the tradition. **Competency Based**

(i) Which right is getting exploited?

(ii) Which institution has the authority to address this issue?

Ans. (i) The right that is being exploited in this scenario is the right to education, specifically for girls.

(ii) The institutions that have the authority to address this issue are NHRC, Government Education Department and NGO's.

Short Answer Type Questions

1. Describe the ethnic massacre in Kosovo.

Ans. The ethnic massacre in Kosovo is developed in the following ways

- Kosovo was a province of Yugoslavia before its split. In this province, the Serbs were in minority and Albanians were in majority. But in the entire country, Serbs were in majority.

- A narrow-minded Serb nationalist Milosevic had won the elections. His government was hostile to the Kosovo Albanians.
- Milosevic wanted the Serbs to dominate the country. Many other serb leaders also thought that ethnic minorities, Albanians should either leave the country or accept the dominance of the serbs.
- There were several instances of killings based on ethnic prejudices during Milosevic's rule. The ethnic massacre in Kosovo was carried out by the army of their own country.

2. Why do we need rights in a democracy?

Ans. We need rights in a democracy because of the following reasons

- Rights protect minorities from the oppression of majority. They ensure that the majority cannot do whetever it likes.
- Rights are necessary in a democracy so that citizens can express their opinion, form political parties and take part in political activities.
- The government is expected to protect citizens rights. But, sometimes the elected governments may not protect or even attack the rights of their own citizens. That is why, some rights need to be placed higher than the government, so that the government can not violate them.

3. 'Rights are reasonable claims of persons recognised by society and sanctioned by law.' Why should these claims be reasonable? Explain.

Ans. Rights are reasonable claims because

- Rights are those conditions which allow for the fullest development of individuals' personality.
- They are the claims that we make on society and on government.
- They are made available to others and one's right becomes one's duty to respect the rights of others.
- Rights are sanctioned by the law, they need to have legal backing. They are justiciable and enforceable. In case, rights are violated, we can approach courts.

4. Why Fundamental Rights are given a special status in the Indian Constitution? Give Reason.

Ans. Fundamental Rights are given a special status in the Indian Constitution because of the following reasons

- These rights are essential for all round development of the citizens.
- Fundamental Rights have been given to all citizens by the Constitution and no government can abolish them.
- These rights protect minorities from the oppression of majority.
- These are enforceable in the court of law.

5. Mention the Fundamental Rights which have been provided to the citizens by the Constitution.

Ans. The Indian Constitution provides the following Fundamental Rights

(i) Right to Equality
(ii) Right to Freedom
(iii) Right against Exploitation
(iv) Right to Freedom of Religion
(v) Cultural and Educational Rights
(vi) Right to Constitutional Remedies

Fundamental Rights are necessary for the very sustenance of our democracy. These Fundamental Rights are given a special status in our Constitution.

6. Why has the Constitution of India made untouchability a punishable offence? Give reasons.

Ans. Untouchability has been made a punishable offence by the Constitution of India because of the following reasons

- The Constitution mentions untouchability as an extreme form of social discrimination and clearly directs the government to put an end to it.
- It does not only means refusal to touch a person belonging to certain castes. It is a belief or social practice which looks down upon certain castes on account of their birth with certain caste labels.
- Untouchability denies interaction of people of certain castes with others or access to public places as equal citizens. That is why, the Constitution has declared untouchability as a punishable offence.

7. State any three provisions made in the Constitution to prevent exploitation of the weaker sections.

Ans. The three provisions made in Constitution to prevent exploitation of the weaker sections are

(i) The Constitution prohibits traffic in human beings because traffic is selling and buying of human beings especially the weaker sections.
(ii) The Constitution prohibits forced labour or begar in any forms because begar is a practice where the worker is forced to render service to the master free of charge or at a nominal remuneration.
(iii) The Constitution also prohibits child labour. No one can employ a child below the age of 14 to work in any factory or mine or any hazardous work.

8. What legal procedures have to be followed by a police officer if he arrest or detain any citizen?

Ans. The legal procedures are discussed below

- A person who is arrested and detained will have to be informed the reasons for such arrest and detention.

- A person who is detained and arrested shall be produced before the nearest magistrate within a period of 24 hours of arrest.
- Such person have the right to engage a lawyer for his/her defence.

9. "It is the language, culture and religion of minorities that need special protection". What provisions have been made by the Indian Constitution for the protection of the minorities?

Ans. The provisions made by the Indian Constitution for the protection of minorities are

- Any section of citizens with a distinct language or culture have a right to conserve it.
- Admission to any educational institution maintained by government or receiving government aid cannot be denied to any citizen on the grounds of religion or language.
- All minorities have the right to establish and administer educational institutions of their choice.

Thus, it can be concluded that language, culture and religion of minorities need special protection.

10. Mention any three constitutional provisions that make India a secular state.

Ans. Indian Constitution makers provided provisions for India to be a secular country so that people of different religions can exist peacefully.

The Constitutional provisions that make India secular are

(i) The Constitution provides to all its citizens the freedom to profess, practice and propagate any religion of their choice.

(ii) There is no official religion for India.

(iii) There shall be no religious instruction in the government educational institutions. Every religious group or sect is free to manage its religious affairs.

11. "The Right to Constitutional Remedy is the 'heart and soul' of the Indian Constitution". Justify the statement.

***or* Who said that the Right to Constitutional Remedies is the 'heart and soul of our Constitution? What does this statement mean?**

***or* Why is the Right to Constitutional Remedies considered the 'heart and soul of our Constitution'? Explain any three reason.**

Ans. Dr. BR Ambedkar said that the Right to Constitutional Remedies is the heart and soul of the Indian Constitution due to the following reasons

(i) When any of our rights is violated, we can seek remedy through courts. If it is a Fundamental Right, we can directly approach the Supreme Court or the High Court of the state.

(ii) If any act of Legislature or Executive takes away or limits any of the Fundamental Rights, it will be invalid. We can challenge such laws of the Central or the State Government in the court of law through the Right to Constitutional Remedies.

(iii) Right to Constitutional Remedies makes other rights effective. This right is the guardian of other rights.

12. (a) When was National Human Rights Commission established?

(b) What are the main objectives of Commission?

Ans. (a) National Human Rights Commission was established in 1993.

(b) The main objective of the Commission are

- The Commission focuses on helping the victims to secure their human rights. These include all the rights granted to the citizens by the Constitution.
- The Commission also considers the Human Rights mentioned in the UN sponsored international treaties that India has signed.
- The Commission makes independent and credible inquiry into any case of violation of human rights. The Commission presents its findings and recommendations to the government.

13 Describe rights that the Constitution of South Africa guarantees to its citizens.

Ans. The Constitution of South Africa guarantees its citizens serveral kinds of new rights. These are

- Right to privacy so that citizens or their home can not be searched, their phone cannot be tapped, their communication cannot be opened.
- Right to an environment that is not harmful to their health or well-being.
- Right to have access to adequate housing.
- Right to have access to health care services, sufficient food and water. No one may be refused emergency medical treatment.

14. Reyansh, started working in manufacturing enterprises ltd. as a supervisor. Where he has to supervise the work of labourers. He hired some labourers who are below 14 years who are not even adults with more than 14 hours of working without paying them much. Recently the safety audit report came which certainly states zero safety measures in the industry and identifies the chances of potential hazards. **Competency Based**

(i) Which specific evil of the Constitution is applicable here?

(ii) What does the government strictly prohibit in such cases?

Ans. (i) The specific evil of the Constitution applicable here is the exploitation of child labour and the lack of safety measures, which goes against the right against exploitation and the right to life with dignity.

The Constitution prohibits child labour. No one can employ a child below the age of fourteen to work in a factory or mine or in any other hazardous work, such as railways or ports. The Amendment Act completely prohibits the employment of children below 14 years.

(ii) The government strictly prohibits long working hours, and lack of safety measures in industries in such cases. Many laws have been made to prohibit children from working in industries such as beedi making, firecrackers and matches, printing and dyeing. The constitution mentions specific evils and declares them illegal. Our Constitution prohibits forced labour in any form. The government secretly prohibits towards long working hours and lack of safety measures in industries in such cases.

Long Answer Type Questions

1. What was the Amensty International's report regarding the prisoners in Guantanamo Bay? Explain in detail.

Ans. Amnesty International which is an international human rights organisation, collected information in Guantanamo Bay and reported

- Families of prisoners, media or even UN representatives were not allowed to meet these prisoners. The US army arrested them, interrogated them and decided whether to keep them there or not.
- There was no trial before any magistrate in the US nor could these prisoners approach courts in their own country.
- The prisoners were being tortured in ways that violated United States law.
- They were being denied the treatment that even prisoners of war must get as per international treaties.
- Prisoners were not released ever after they were not officially declared guilty.

2. Explain the type of government Saudi Arabia have. What are its main features?

Ans. Saudi Arabia is a monarchy, ruled by a hereditary king and the people have no role in electing or changing the rulers.

The main features of this type of government are

- The king selects the legislature, the executive and also appoints the judges and can change any of their decisions.
- Citizens cannot form political parties or any political organisation.
- Media cannot report anything that the Monarch does not like. There is no freedom of religion. Every citizen is required to be a Muslim. Non-Muslim residents can follow their religion in private but not in public
- Women are subjected to many public restrictions. The testimony of one man is considered equal to that of two women.

3. List out any four characteristics of Fundamental Rights.

Ans. Some rights which are fundamental to our life are given a special status in our Constitution, these are called Fundamental Rights.

Some features of Fundamental Rights are as follows

(i) **Universal** These rights are universal which means they are for all the citizens of India without any discrimination.

(ii) **Restrictions** Our rights are not absolute but there are certain restrictions imposed on each of them.

(iii) **Justiciable** Fundamental Rights are justiciable means citizens can move to the courts if any individual or government is violating his/her rights.

(iv) **Comprehensive** These rights have comprehensive approach. They tend to safeguard our social, economic, cultural and religious interests.

4. Freedom of Speech and Expression is one of the essential features of democracy. Explain the statement with suitable reasons.

Ans. Freedom of Speech and Expression is one of the essential features of democracy due to the following reasons

- It allows an individual to take part in public activities.
- It includes freedom to hold opinions without interference and to seek, receive and import information and ideas through any media.
- Mass media is an instrument for exercising the Freedom of Speech and Expression which is important for a democratic society.
- Freedom of Speech is not the freedom to hurt or harm others in the political arena or in the society.
- The betterment of society depends on the right exercise of freedom which should not be taken away from the common people.

5. Write any four features of the Right to Equality as a Fundamental Right.

or **Explain the main provisions of the Right to Equality.**

Ans. Right to Equality is an important right provided in the Indian Constitution. It guarantees the following

(i) **Equality before law** the Constitution guarantees that all citizens shall be equally protected by the laws of the country. It means that the state cannot discriminate any of the Indian citizen on the basis of their caste, creed, colour, sex, gender, religion or place of birth.

(ii) **Social equality and equal access to public areas** states that every person shall have equal access to public places like public parks, museums, wells, bathing ghats, temples, etc.

(iii) **Equality in matters of public employment** states that all citizens can apply for government jobs. But, this right shall not be conferred to overseas citizens of India.

(iv) **Abolition of Untouchability** the Constitution abolishes the practice of untouchability and anyone found doing so is punishable by law.

6. Describe any five freedoms granted to the citizens of India under the Right to Freedom.

or **Right to Freedom is the 'cluster of freedoms'. Justify.**

or **"Right to Freedom is not only a right but also a group of many rights".**

or **Describe any five freedoms granted to the citizens of india under the Right to Freedom.**

Ans. The Right to Freedom is considered as the 'cluster of six freedom'. Article 19 of Indian Constitution guarantees the following freedoms to all the citizens

(i) Freedom of Speech and Expression is one of the essential features of any democracy. Our ideas and personality develop only when we are able to freely communicate with others.
Although, this freedom cannot be used to instigate violence against others.

(ii) Citizens have the freedom to hold meetings, processions, rallies and demonstrations on any issue. But such meetings, have to be peaceful. They should not lead to public disorder.

(iii) Citizens have the freedom to form associations, unions to promote their interests.

(iv) Citizens have the freedom to travel to any part of the country.

(v) Citizens are free to reside and settle in any part of the territory of India.

(vi) Citizens have the freedom to practice any profession or to carry any occupation, trade or business.

Thus, it is justified that Right to Freedom is cluster of freedom.

7. What is the role of International Covenant in the expansion of rights?

Ans. International Covenant has contributed to the expansion of rights. It binds the signatory countries to provide some rights to the citizens.
International Covenant on economic, social and cultural rights recognises many rights that are not directly a part of the fundamental rights in the Indian Constitution. This includes

(i) Rights to work, opportunity to everyone to earn livelihood by working.

(ii) Right to safe and healthy working conditions with fair wages that can provide a decent standard of living for workers and their families.

(iii) Right to adequate standard of living including adequate food, clothing and housing.

(iv) Right to social security and insurance.

(v) Right to health, medial care during illness, special care for women during childcare and prevention of epidemics.

(vi) Right to education, free and compulsory primary education, equal access to higher education.

8. A person X is poor and from a minority. He was arrested by the police without even a proper statement for the arrest and not even given the right to hire a lawyer. This news got leaked in the media. According to you, What stance has to be taken by the government? "Critically examine the role of a specific institution who ensures the right of a person". Competency Based

Ans. In this situation, the role of the judiciary, particularly the judicial system and its commitment to upholding the rule of law, becomes crucial. The judiciary should play a critical role in ensuring that the rights of the individual, regardless of their economic status or minority status, are protected.

The person has the right to a fair trial, legal representation, and due process. If these rights are violated, the judiciary should intervene to rectify the situation, ensuring justice and upholding the principles of a democratic and just society.

The government must develop a system that respects and protects the fundamental rights of every individual, and the judiciary acts as a check and balance in this regard. Sometimes the NHRC also plays a critical role representing human rights in front of the courts.

Case Based Questions

1. Read the sources given below and answer the questions that follows.

Source A Ethnic Massacre in Kosovo

This is what happened to an Albanian family in a town in Kosovo. 74 year old Batisha Hoxha was sitting in her kitchen with her 77 year old husband, Izet, staying warm by the stove.

They had heard explosions but did not realise that Serbian troops had already entered the town. The next thing she knew, five or six soldiers had burst through the front door and were demanding "where are your children?" They shot Izet three times in the chest recalled Batisha. With her husband dying before her, the soldiers pulled the wedding ring off her finger and told her to get out.

She was standing on the street in the rain with no house, no husband, no possessions but the clothes she was wearing.

(i) What do you think can be done in a democratic country to avoid the situation like Kosovo?

Source B Cultural and Educational Rights

The Constitution specifies the cultural and educational rights of the minorities. It held that any section of citizens with a distinct language of culture have a right to conserve it. It also emphasize Admission to any educational institution maintained by the government or receiving government aid cannot be denied to any citizen on the ground of religion or language. All minorities have the right to establish and administer educational institutions of their choice. Here minority does not mean only religious minority at the national level. In some places people speaking a particular language are in majority. People speaking a different language are in a minority.

(ii) Why do you think that the cultural and educational rights of the minorities need special attention? Justify

Source C Freedom to Travel

As citizens we have the freedom to travel to any part of the country. We are free to reside and settle in any part of the territory of India. Let us say, a person who belongs to the state of Assam wants to start a business in Hyderabad.

He may not have any connection with that city, he may not have seen it ever. Yet as a citizen of India he has the right to set up base there. The same freedom extends to choice of occupations. No one can force you to do or not to do a certain job.

(iii) Evaluate the statement, citizens of India exercise freedom to travel to any part of the country.

Ans. (i) In a democratic country, there must be a system where minimum freedom is granted to its citizens and this freedom can be enforced also.

(ii) The cultural and educational rights of the minorities need special attention because these rights of minorities may get neglected or undermined under the impact of the languages, culture or religion of the majority.

(iii) The citizens of India are free to reside and settle in any part of the territory of India. This allows lakhs of citizens to migrate from villages to towns and poorer regions to more prosperous regions.

2. Read the source given below and answer the questions that follow.

The Constitution says that the government shall not deny to any person in India equality before the law or the equal protection of the laws. It means that the laws apply in the same manner to all regardless of person's status. This is called the rule of law. Rule of law is the foundation of any democracy. It means that no person is above the law.

There cannot be any distinction between the political leader, government official and an ordinary citizen. Every citizen, from the Prime Minister to small farmer in a remote village is subjected to the same laws. No person can legally claim any special treatment or privilege just because he or she happens to be an important person. For example. a few years ago a former PM of the country faced a court case on charges of cheating.

The court finally declared that he was not guilty. But, as long as the case continued, he had to go to the court, give evidence and fill papers, just like any other citizen. Equality means giving everyone an equal opportunity to achieve whatever one is capable of. Sometimes, it is necessary to give special treatment to someone in order to ensure equal opportunity.

(i) Do you think the Rule of Law prevails in India.

(ii) How is the Right to Equality exercised in a democratic country like India?

(iii) Mention the two exceptions related to the Right to Equality as a Fundamental Right. Given reasons

Ans. (i) Yes, the Rule of Law prevails in India because in our country, all are equal in the eyes of law, regardless of a person's status.

(ii) The Right to Equality is exercised in the following manner

(a) By prohibiting discrimination against any citizen on the grounds of religion, caste, ethnicity, gender or place of birth.

(b) Every citizen shall have access to public places like shops, hotels, etc.

(c) Giving equal opportunity to all citizens.

(d) Provide reservations for SC's, ST's, OBC's women, physically handicapped in some kinds of jobs to ensure equal opportunity.

(iii) Exceptions related to the Right to Equality are

(a) The state may make any special provision for women and children.

(b) The state may reserve some posts for members of backward class.

ASSESSMENT EXERCISE

Multiple Choice Questions (MCQs)

1. The freedom .... is not included in the Right to Freedom given in the Constitution of India..

(a) of speech and expression
(b) to practice any profession
(c) to assemble with arms
(d) to form associations

2. Which one of the following is a violation of the Right to Life or personal liberty?

(a) An arrested person is informed of the reason for arrest.
(b) He is produced in a court within 24 hours of being arrested.
(c) He is not allowed to consult a lawyer.
(d) He was shown the warrant for his arrest in advance.

3. Match the following.

List I	List II
A. Right to Freedom	1. Freedom to propagate one's own religion
B. Right against Exploitation	2. Right to Life
C. Right to Equality	3. Abolition of Untouchability
D. Right to Freedom of Religion	4. Ban on Bonded Labour
E. Right to Constitutional Remedies	5. Make the Fundamental Rights more effective

Codes

	A	B	C	D	E		A	B	C	D	E
(a)	2	4	3	1	5	(b)	3	2	1	5	4
(c)	1	2	5	4	3	(d)	3	2	4	5	1

4. Assertion (A) Freedom means absence of constraints.

Reason (R) Practically, it means absence of interference in our affairs by others.

Codes

(a) Both A and R are true and R is the correct explanation of A
(b) Both A and R are true, but R is not the correct explanation of A
(c) A is true, but R is false
(d) A is false, but R is true

Subjective Questions (VSA, SA & LA)

1. Which Fundamental Right bans untouchability?

2. Mention any two Constitutional provisions for the protection of women and children in India.

3. What is the position of women in Saudi Arabia?

4. Why cannot the government compel any person to pay any tax for the promotion or maintenance of any particular religion ?

5. Do the women of Saudi Arabia have voting power?

6. What is the importance of National Human Rights Commission in securing the Human Rights?

7. "The Right to Freedom of Speech and Expression does not come without qualifications". Explain.

8. How is the scope of rights always expanding?

The Story of Village Palampur

CHAPTER 1

The story of village Palampur is a narrative based on a research study by Gilbert Etienna of a village in Bulandshahr district in Western Uttar Pradesh. The purpose of the story is to introduce some basic concepts relating to production.

1.1 Overview of Palampur Village

Farming is the main **production activity** in Palampur. Other production activities like dairy farming, manufacturing, transportation and shopkeeping are practiced on a limited scale.

These production activities need various types of resources like natural resources, man-made items, human effort, money, etc.

Palampur is well-connected with neighbouring villages and towns. Raiganj, a big village is 3 kms from Palampur. An all weather road connects the village to Raiganj and further on the nearest small town of Shahpur.

Out of the 450 families living in Palampur, about 80 upper caste families own the majority of land in the village.

Their houses are made of brick with cement plastering. The SCs (*dalits*) in the village comprise about one-third of the population and live in one corner of the village in smaller houses, some of which are constructed with mud and straw.

Many houses in Palampur have electric connections. Electricity powers all the tubewells and is used in various types of small business.

Palampur has two primary schools and one high school. It also has a government primary health centre and a private dispensary.

1.2 Organisation of Production

The aim of production is to produce the goods and services. There are four factors required for production. These are follows.

- **Land** It is the first requirement. Other natural resources like water, minerals, forests, etc are also needed.
- **Labour** It includes people who are used for carrying out the production activities. They may be manual workers or highly skilled or educated persons. Each worker provides the labour, necessary for production.
- **Physical Capital** It includes two sub-components
  - (i) **Fixed Capital** It includes assets or capital investments that are needed to start production of goods or services are called fixed capital, e.g. buildings, machines, tools, ranging from plough to generators, turbines, computers, etc.
  - (ii) **Working Capital** It includes raw materials and money in hand are called working capital. These are used at the time of production activities i.e. to purchase raw materials and services required and to sell finished goods.
- **Human Capital** It is the knowledge and enterprise. It is required to put together all the above inputs to produce the output, either to be used by the producer himself or to sell in the market.

1.3 Farming in Palampur

Fixed Land

Farming is the main production activity in Palampur. 75 per cent of the working people living in Palampur are dependent on farming for their livelihood. They are either farmers or farm labourers.

In Palampur, the land area under cultivation is fixed due to which the farm production cannot be raised. Since 1960, there has been no expansion in the land area under cultivation.

Some of the wastelands in the village had been converted into cultivable land. There is no further scope to increase farm production by bringing new land under cultivation.

Land Measurement

- The standard unit of measuring land is hectare. One hectare is 100 m^2.
- In villages it might be measured in local units like bigha, guintha etc.

Ways to Grow More from the Same Land

Multiple Cropping

To increase production from the same piece of land, farmers do multiple cropping, *i.e.,* they grow at least two main crops on a piece of land during the year.

Multiple cropping in Palampur is practiced in the following ways

- During the rainy season (**Kharif**[1]), farmers grow *jowar* and *bajra*, which are used as cattle feed. It is followed by potato cultivation in the months of October to December as the third crop.
- During the winter season (**Rabi**[2]), farmers sow wheat. From the produced wheat, farmers keep enough wheat for their family's consumption and sell the rest of the wheat in the market at Raiganj.
- A part of the land is also alloted to sugarcane production which is harvested once every year. Sugarcane in its raw form or as jaggery is sold to traders in Shahpur.

Better Irrigation Facilities

The village of Palampur has a **well-developed system of irrigation**. Availability of electricity impacted the development of irrigation.

Persian wheels that irrigated small fields through wells are replaced by tubewells. Due to this, by mid-1970s, the entire cultivated area of 200 hectares in the village was brought under irrigation.

KNOWLEDGE PLUS Only the riverine plains and coastal regions are well irrigated in India. On other hand Deccan plateau have low level of irrigation. Only 40% of total cultivated area is irrigated while other is dependent on rainfall.

Modern Farming Methods

Production can also be increased using modern farming methods for higher **yield**[3]. Till the mid-1960s, farmers used traditional seeds, which needed less irrigation, but gave relatively low yields. They also used readily available cow dung and other natural manure as fertilisers.

The **Green Revolution**[4] in the late 1960s introduced **High Yielding Varieties (HYVs)** of seeds to the Indian farmers which increased their production of wheat and rice.

HYV seeds require irrigation (plenty of water) along with **chemical fertilisers**[5], pesticides, etc to give higher yield.

In India, farmers of Punjab, Haryana and Western Uttar Pradesh were the first to use modern methods of farming.

Some farmers also bought farm machinery like tractors and threshers. This made ploughing and harvesting faster and were rewarded with higher yields of wheat.

In Palampur, with the HYV seeds, the yield of wheat went up to 3200 kg per hectare as compared to 1300 kg per hectare with the traditional seeds.

Sustenance of Land

Land is a natural resource and thus it should be carefully used. Due to large amounts of water required in modern farming methods, the water level below the ground has reduced. This further impact the fertility of the soil.

Modern farming methods have over used the natural resources. In many areas, Green Revolution has resulted in loss of soil fertility due to increased use of chemical fertilisers.

Effects of Chemical Fertilisers

Chemical fertilisers provide minerals which dissolve in water and are immediately available to plants. But these minerals may not be retained in the soil for long. They may escape from the soil and pollute groundwater, rivers and lakes.

Continuous use of chemical fertilisers has led to degradation of soil health.

The chemical fertilisers kill the bacteria and micro-organisms in the soil and reduce its natural fertility.

The consumption of chemical fertilisers in Punjab is highest in the country.

1 **Kharif** It refers to the season in which the crop sown at the beginning of summer rains and harvested in autumn.
2 **Rabi** It refers to the season in which the crop sown in winter and harvested in spring.
3 **Yield** It refers to the amount of crop produced in a given piece of land during a single season.
4 **Green Revolution** It was an agricultural revolution in 1960s that increased agricultural production of food grains (especially wheat and rice).
5 **Chemical fertilisers** It was is a substance applied to soils or directly onto plants to provide nutrients, optimal for their growth and development.

Distribution of Land in Palampur

- In Palampur, all the people are engaged in agriculture, so they do not have sufficient land for cultivation. Out of 450 families in Palampur, 150 families are landless and most of them are *dalits*.
- 240 families out of those which own land, cultivate small plots of land less than 2 hectares, which does not bring adequate income to the farmer family.
- Remaining 60 families of medium and large farmers cultivate more than 2 hectares of land. A few of them have land extending over 10 hectares or more.

Farm Labour

Farming requires a lot of hard work. Small farmers with their families cultivate their own fields. Thus, they provide the labour required for farming themselves.

Farm labourers come either from landless families or families cultivating small plots of land. These labourers are paid in cash or crops and sometimes they get meals also.

The labourers may not be hired for the full year. They may be hired on a daily basis or for particular activities like sowing and harvesting.

There is a heavy competition for work among the farm labourers in Palampur. So, they agree to work for lower wages although the minium wage for a farm labourer set by the government was higher.

Some labourers have also entered in the non-farm sector in the village and some live on the mercy of moneylenders.

Capital Needed in Farming

As modern farming methods require a great deal of capital, the farmer needs more money for it.

Small farmers have to borrow money to arrange the capital. They borrow from large farmers, village moneylenders or traders who supply various inputs for cultivation. The rate of interest on such loans is very high. They are put to great distress to repay the loan.

On the other hand, the large and medium farmers have their own savings from farming. Thus, they are able to arrange for the capital needed.

Sale of Surplus Farm Products

The large and medium farmers of Palampur retain a part of the produced grain for their own use and sell the **surplus**[6] in the market. Traders in the market buy these grains for selling them to the shopkeepers in cities and towns.

These farmers earn a good amount of money through this sale. Later, they use this money to purchase inputs for the next farming season, purchase capital equipment or even give loans to small farmers.

Some farmers also use this money to start activities in the non-farm sector. Thus, this surplus money increases their working capital as well as fixed capital.

1.4 Non-Farm Activities of Palampur

Only about 25 per cent of the working population in Palampur has acquired non-agricultural or non-farm activities. These are

- **Dairy** It is a common activity in Palampur. People feed their buffaloes on various kinds of grass, *jowar* and *bajra* grown in the rainy season.

  The milk produced is sold in the nearby large village, Raiganj. The milk is transported to far away towns and cities from collection cum chilling centres at Raiganj. These centres has been set-up by two traders of Shahpur town.
- **Small-Scale Manufacturing** In Palampur less than fifty people are engaged in the manufacturing sector. It is done on a small-scale.

  This manufacturing is carried out mostly at home or in the fields with the help of family labour. Labourers are not hired for manufacturing.
- **Trade** A very few people in Palampur are involved in trading (exchange of goods). The traders of Palampur are shopkeepers who buy various goods from wholesale markets in the cities and sell them in the village.
- **Transport** A number of vehicles run on the road that connects Palampur to Raiganj. Many people are in the transport services i.e. *rickshawallahs*, *tongawallahs*, jeep, tractor, truck drivers and people driving the traditional bogey and bullock cart.

The number of people involved in transport has grown over the last several years.

Try These

1. **What per cent of the working population is dependant on farming in Palampur?**
2. **What types of crops are grown in Palampur?**
3. **What was the third crop grown by the farmers in Palampur?**
4. **Mention the seeds introduced to the Indian farmers to increases their production of crops.**
5. **Which type of non-farm activities are done by the people of Palampur?**

6 **Surplus** An amount excess of something needed.

Mind Map

THE STORY OF VILLAGE PALAMPUR

Overview of Palampur Village

- Farming is the main production activity.
- Houses are made of brick with cement plastering.
- It has well-developed system of roads, transport, electricity, irrigation, schools and health facilities.

Organisation of Production

- Its aim is to produce the goods and services.
- Land is the first requirement along with other natural resources such as water, forests and minerals.
- Human capital is also required to put together knowledge and enterprise to produce the output.
- Labour is used for carrying out the production activities.
- Physical capital is the third requirement. Assets or capital investments that are needed to start production of goods is called fixed capital.
- Raw materials and money in hand that are used at the time of production activities is called working capital.

Non-Farm Activities of Palampur

- Dairy
- Small-Scale Manufacturing
- Trade
- Transport

Farming in Palampur

- Land area under cultivation in Palampur is practically fixed.
- Ways to grow more from the same land in Palampur.
  - Multiple cropping
  - Better irrigation facilities
  - Use of HYV seeds
- It is necessary to use land carefully for sustenance of land
- In Palampur, about one-third of 450 families are landless. Of the remaining families who own land, 248 families cultivate small plots of land less than 2 hectares in size.
- Labour is a necessary factor for production.
- Farmer needs more money as modern farming methods require more capital.
- They are able to arrange for the capital for farming from their own savings.

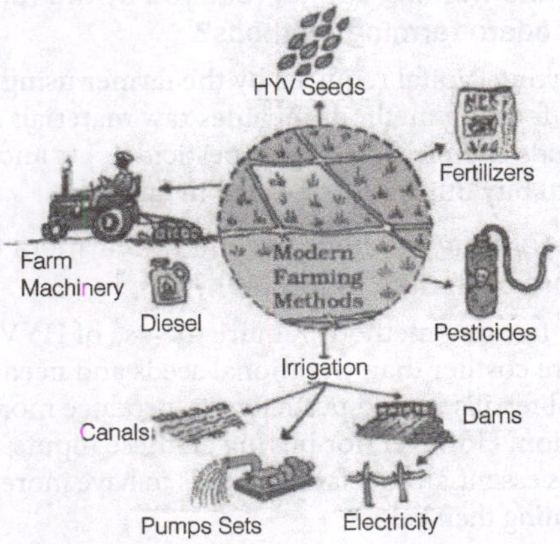

NCERT FOLDER

Covering Intext Questions and Exercises of NCERT

INTEXT QUESTIONS

Q.1 You have read about the crops grown in Palampur. Fill the following table based on the information of the crops grown in your region.

Name of Crop	Month Sown	Month Harvested	Sources of Irrigation *(rain, tanks, tubewells, canals, etc)*

Ans. Information about crops grown in our region is given below

Name of Crop	Month Sown	Month Harvested	Source of Irrigation (rain, tanks, tubewells, canals, etc)
Wheat	October, December	April, June	Tubewells and canals
Rice	June, July	September, October	Rain, canals and tubewells
Jowar and Bajra	June, July	September, October	Rainfall, canals and tubewells

Q.2 What is the difference between multiple cropping and modern farming method?

Ans. Multiple cropping means to grow more than one crop on a piece of land during the year. It is the most common way of increasing production on a given piece of land. (It does not need modern farming methods.)

On the other hand, modern farming method means the use of HYV seeds, tubewells for irrigation, chemical fertilisers and pesticides, as well as machinery like tractors and threshers to increase the production.

Q.3 What is the working capital required by the farmer using modern farming methods?

Ans. The working capital required by the farmer using modern farming methods includes raw materials like HYV seeds chemical fertilisers, pesticides, etc and money to buy other items needed in farms.

Q.4 Modern farming methods require the farmers to start with more cash than before. Why?

Ans. Modern farming methods require the use of HYV seeds, which are costlier than traditional seeds and need chemical fertilisers and pesticides to produce more production. However, for buying all these inputs, a lot of money is essential, so a farmer needs to have more cash to start farming than before.

Q.5 Identify the work being done on the field in the pictures (i) to (vi) and arrange them in a proper sequence.

(i) (ii) (iii) (iv) (v) (vi)

Ans. The work being done on the field in each picture is given below

(i) Cutting of crops
(ii) Ploughing by bullocks
(iii) Spraying of insecticides
(iv) Sowing
(v) Cultivation by traditional methods
(vi) Cultivation by modern methods

The proper sequence from sowing to harvesting is given below

(i) (ii) (iii) (iv) (v) (vi)

Q.6 Why are farm labourers like Dala and Ramkali poor?

Ans. The farm labourers like Dala and Ramkali were poor because

- They are landless farm labourers who work on daily wages in Palampur.
- The minimum wage for farm labourer set by the government is ₹ 300 per day, but they get only ₹ 160 per day.

- There is a heavy competition for work among the farm labourers in Palampur, so they agree to work for lower wages.
- They remain out of work for most days of the year and have to take loan from the moneylenders to fulfil their basic needs. Due to this seasonal unemployment, they are unable to repay the loan and fall into a debt trap.

Q.7 Gosaipur and Majauli are two villages in North Bihar. Out of a total of 850 households in the two villages, there are more than 250 men who are employed in rural Punjab and Haryana or in Delhi, Mumbai, Surat, Hyderabad or Nagpur. Such migration is common in most villages across India.

Why do people migrate? Can you describe (based on your imagination) the work that the migrants of Gosaipur and Majauli might do at the place of destination?

Ans. Mostly people migrate in search of employment or better job opportunities to the cities like Mumbai, Delhi, etc, or to prosperous agricultural regions like Punjab and Haryana to work as a farm labourers.

This migration usually takes place when a person is unemployed or in seasonal unemployment, which may be due to lack of land, displacement, negative impact of natural disasters like drought, floods, etc.

The migrants from Gosaipur and Majauli who went to cities will probably find work as casual labourers, industrial workers, street hawkers, rickshaw pullers, headload workers or as domestic aid in homes, hotels, etc.

Those who went to rural areas of Punjab and Haryana will probably work as farm labourers, as agriculture is the main occupation of the rural people in these states.

Q.8 (a) What capital did Mishrilal need to set up his jaggery manufacturing unit?

(b) Who provides the labour in this case?

(c) Can you guess why Mishrilal is unable to increase his profit?

(d) Could you think of any reasons when he might face a loss?

(e) Why does Mishrilal sell his jaggery to traders in Shahpur and not in his village?

Ans. (a) To set up his manufacturing unit, Mishrilal needed the following capital

- Fixed capital in the form of a sugarcane crushing machine.
- Working capital in the form of money for buying sugarcane from other farmers for crushing and for paying the electricity bill of running the crushing machine.

(b) The labour is provided by him and his family. Otherwise, he will employ landless labourers.

(c) Mishrilal is unable to increase his profit because

- Most of the land holdings in the village are very small in size and production of sugarcane is low as more area is under wheat. So, raw material is also in less amount.
- He has to pay for electricity to run the machine.
- As his industry is small-scale, production is less.

(d) Conditions under which he might face a loss can be any of the following

- If his crushing machine breaks down, his production will reduce or totally stop.
- If drought or other calamity occurs, the production of sugarcane in nearby areas will reduce; his jaggery production will come down, leading to a loss.
- If the demand for jaggery decreases, he will not be able to sell enough jaggery in the market.
- If any other costs like electricity, labour or transportation increases, then he may face losses.

(e) Mishrilal sells his jaggery to traders in Shahpur and not in his village because

- Palampur is a small village with 450 families and there is not a large demand for jaggery.
- Shahpur is a town where people come from different surrounding villages to buy things and hence, there is more demand for jaggery.

Q.9 In what way is Kareem's capital and labour different from Mishrilal's?

Ans. Both Kareem and Mishrilal have fixed capital in the form of machines, but Kareem has a larger fixed capital. Kareem has such kind of capital that can be used to educate and provide employment skills to many persons with minimum labour involvement.

While Mishrilal's capital is used by only one person at a time and requires more physical labour. Kareem has also employed educated and qualified computer teachers, whereas Mishrilal's labour is mainly unskilled labour.

Q.10 Why didn't someone start a computer centre earlier? Discuss the possible reasons.

Ans. Nobody started a computer centre earlier due to the following reasons

- As very few educated people were there in the village, there was not demand for computer courses.
- The villagers were not aware of the employment potential of computer courses and hence, nobody thought that such a business could be successful.
- Teaching faculty for computer courses was not available in the village earlier.

Q.11 **(a) What is Kishora's fixed capital?**

(b) What do you think would be his working capital?

(c) In how many production activities is Kishora involved?

(d) Would you say that Kishora has benefitted from better roads in Palampur?

Ans. (a) Kishora's fixed capital is the buffalo and wooden cart which he has purchased with the bank loan.

(b) The money that he earns from selling the milk and transporting goods on his bullock cart excluding his living expenses will be his working capital.

(c) Kishora is involved in the following production activities

(i) Selling of buffalo's milk.

(ii) Transportation of various items.

(iii) Bringing clay from the river Ganga for the potter.

(iv) Transporting jaggery, etc to Shahpur.

(d) Kishora has certainly benefitted from better roads in Palampur because of his involvement in transport business. Better roads enable him to easily transport goods from one place to another, run his business successfully and earn profits. This would have been more difficult in the absence of proper roads.

EXERCISE

Q.1 **Every village in India is surveyed once in ten years during the Census and some of the details are presented in the following format. Fill up the following based on information on Palampur.**

(a) Location (b) Total Area of the Village

(c) Land Use (in hectares)

Cultivated Land		Land not available for cultivation (Area covering dwellings, roads, ponds, grazing ground)
Irrigated	Unirrigated	
		26 hectares

(d) Facilities

Educational	–
Medical	–
Market	–
Electricity supply	–
Communication	–
Nearest town	–

Ans. (a) **Location** Palampur is located 3 km from Raiganj which is a big village. The nearest town is Shahpur. It is well connected with neighbouring villages and towns. An all weather road connects the village to Raiganj and further to the nearest small town of Shahpur.

(b) The total area of Palampur village is 246 hectares.

(c) **Land Use** (in hectares)

Cultivated Land		Land not available for cultivation *(Area covering dwellings, roads, ponds, grazing ground)*
Irrigated	Unirrigated	
200 hectares	20 hectares	26 hectares

(d) **Facilities**

Educational	Palampur has two primary schools and one high school.
Medical	There is a primary health centre run by the government and one private dispensary.
Market	Market has some general stores and shops selling eatables.
Electricity supply	Most of the houses have electric connections. Electricity powers the tubewells and is used in running various small businesses.
Communication	A well developed system of roads exist connecting it to nearby areas.
Nearest town	Shahpur

Q.2 **Modern farming methods require more inputs which are manufactured in industry. Do you agree?**

Ans. Yes, it is true that modern farming methods require more inputs which are manufactured in industry, e.g.

(i) Insecticides, pesticides and chemical fertilisers, required for increasing the yield per hectare, are all manufactured in industries.

(ii) Farmers use farm machinery like tractors, threshers and harvesters, which are also manufactured in industries.

(iii) Tubewell equipment and water pumps used for irrigation are also manufactured in industries.

Q.3 **How did the spread of electricity help farmers in Palampur?**

Ans. The spread of electricity helped the farmers in the following ways

- Irrigation is now done through electric-run tubewells, that reduces the farmers' dependence on rainfall which also enables larger areas of land to be irrigated.
- Irrigation improvement allowed farmers to grow three different crops in a year. It helped to increase farm production in the village.

Q.4 **Is it important to increase the area under irrigation. Why?**

Ans. Yes, it is very important to increase the area under irrigation because

- Irrigation is basic input for growing crops.
- The modern HYV seeds need assured irrigation.

- The other modern inputs like chemical fertilisers and pesticides also become ineffective if irrigation is not available.
- Through irrigation crops can be grown in dry region.
- Arrival of monsoon is also uncertain, so we need irrigation facilities.

Q.5 Construct a table on the distribution of land among the 450 families of Palampur.

Ans. Distribution of land among the 450 families of Palampur is

Families with no land (mainly dalits)	150 families
Families with less than two hectares	240 families
Families with two or more than two hectares	60 families

Q.6 Why are the wages for farm labourers in Palampur less than minimum wages?

Ans. The wages for farm labourers in Palampur is less than minimum wages because there is a heavy competition for work among the farm labourers in Palampur and people agree to work for lower wages. The minimum wages for a farm labourer set by the government is ₹ 300 per day, but wages of farm labourers in Palampur are less than minimum wages i.e. ₹ 160.

Q.7 What are the different ways of increasing production on the same piece of land? Use examples to explain?

Ans. The different ways of increasing production on the same piece of land are

(i) **Multiple cropping** When more than one crop is grown on a piece of land during the year, it is known as multiple cropping. It is the most common way to increase production on a given piece of land. All farmers in Palampur grow at least two main crops and many are growing potato as the third crop for the past 15 to 20 years.

(ii) **Use of modern farming methods** Modern farming methods also help to increase the yield per hectare. Farmers of Punjab, Haryana and Western Uttar Pradesh were the first to try modern farming methods in India. They have used farm machinery like tractors and threshers, which made ploughing and harvesting faster. They were rewarded with high yield of wheat, increasing from 1300 kg per hectare to 3200 kg per hectare with HYV seeds. The farmers have installed tubewells for irrigation and made use of HYV seeds, chemical fertilisers and pesticides in farming.

Q.8 Describe the work of a farmer with 1 hectare of land.

Ans. A farmer having 1 hectare of land for farming can be described as a subsistence farmer because 1 hectare of land is too small even for the sustenance of a small family.

Since, land area is too small, the farmer will have to work hard to produce more. But due to lack of capital he will not be able to buy HYV seeds or chemical fertiliser. He will use ordinary seeds bullocks to plough, manual irrigation and will need help of his family members to produce more from that land.

Q.9 How do the medium and large farmers obtain capital for farming? How is it different from the small farmers?

Ans. The medium and large farmers have their own savings from farming due to a good surplus crop from their large landholdings. They sell this surplus crop in the market and earn profits.

Then they deposit this amount in bank account for next season crop and lend some money to small farmers at a very high interest rates. So they are able to arrange for the capital needed.

In contrast, small farmers have to borrow money to arrange the capital. They borrow from large farmers, village moneylenders or the traders who supply various inputs for cultivation. They do not have surplus crop as their land is too small. Whatever is produced, gets consumed by their family so they do not earn profits neither save money.

Q.10 On what terms did Savita get a loan from Tejpal Singh? Would Savita's condition be different if she could get a loan from the bank at a low rate of interest?

Ans. Savita, a small farmer, in order to cultivate wheat on her one hectare of land, decides to borrow money from Tejpal Singh, a large farmer.

The terms on which Savita gets loan from Tejpal Singh are

- Savita has to agree to give an interest rate of 24% for 4 months, which is a very high interest rate.
- Savita also has to promise to work on his field as farm labourer during the harvest season at ₹ 100 per day.
- The rate of interest charged by Tejpal Singh was much higher than that of banks.

If Savita had taken a loan from the bank, interest would have been much lower, she could have easily repaid the loan and her condition would have been far better.

Q.11 Talk to some old residents in your region and write a short report on the changes in irrigation and changes in production methods during the last 30 years.

Ans. On talking to two old residents Ramlal and Dharam Singh, I came to know about the following methods

- **The Irrigation Method** They used traditional irrigation methods in our area. They told me that earlier they were dependent on rainfall and later on, they started to use the Persian wheel to draw water from the wells. With development of technology, tubewells were used for better and more effective irrigation.

- **Farming Production Method** In the farming methods, traditionally they ploughed the field with ploughs drawn by bullocks, which was a very difficult and time consuming process. They used ordinary seeds and cow dung as manure.

However, with changes in technology, the farmers started using HYV seeds, chemical fertilisers, insecticides, pesticides and modern machinery like tractors and threshers, which has led to an increase in yield per hectare and improved the lives of the farmers. Thus, there is a vast change in the irrigation and production methods during the last 30 years.

Q.12 What can be done so that more non-farm production activities can be started in villages?

Ans. To start more non-farm production activities, the following steps can be taken.

(i) Banks should provide loans at low interest rate, so that the poor villagers can start some business, which could help them earn a living.

(ii) Government should be more active and initiate effective employment generating schemes.

(iii) Government should provide training to the villagers in different skills.

(iv) Government should provide facilities for transportation and selling of locally manufactured goods of the villagers in the cities.

(v) Small-scale industries should be started by entrepreneurs in rural areas to employ the villagers trained in various skills.

REVIEW EXERCISE

Including Competency Based Questions

Part I

Multiple Choice Questions (MCQs)

1. Main economic activity in village Palampur is

(a) fishing (b) agriculture
(c) horticulture (d) manufacturing

2. Primary sector does not include

(a) forestry (b) mining
(c) fishing (d) transport

3. When more than one crop is grown on the same piece of land in a year, it is called

(a) crop rotation (b) multiple cropping
(c) kharif crop (d) rabi crop

4. Green Revolution took place in India in

(a) late 1960s (b) mid 1960s (c) late 1970s (d) early 1960s

5. What is the effect of Green Revolution on soil?

(a) It enhances soil fertility
(b) It increased crop yield
(c) It decreases production
(d) None of the above

6. Consider the following statements associated with Palampur village and choose the correct option.

(a) In Palampur, about one-third of the 450 families are landless.
(b) Fising is the main production activity in Palampur.
(c) Palampur is not well-connected with neighbouring villages and towns.
(d) In Palampur, there is no medical facilities.

7. Which of the following is a factor of production?

(a) Land (b) Labour
(c) Physical capital (d) All of these

8. Fixed capital of a dairy farmer is

(a) buffaloes and cows (b) milk chilling machine
(c) tempo to transport milk (d) All of these

9. Find the incorrect option.

(a) Palampur is having well developed road.
(b) Many houses in Palampur have electric connection.
(c) Palampur has a government primary health centre and a private dispensary.
(d) In Palampur, people are dependent on fishing for their livelihood.

10. In Palampur, where farming is the primary production activity and 75% of the population depends on farming for their livelihood. They could be farmers or farm labourers.

Accordingly, which development measure would be most crucial for enhancing the well-being of the community?

(a) Establishing a university for higher education.
(b) Establishing a local school to provide education for the farmers' children.
(c) Introducing modern technology for efficient farming practices.
(d) Promoting tourism to create additional sources of income for the community.

11. **Ghanshyam, a large farmer in Palampur has just bought a harvester. Seeing this, some farm labourers who work in his farm are unhappy. One of them said that now they will have even less work. Last year they worked for five months but this year they are not likely to work at all.** **Competency Based**
Select the option that best signifies this situation.
(a) Small farmers take loans from big farmers.
(b) Small farmers produce less crops than big farmers.
(c) Harvester is much more productive then human.
(d) Small farmers are dependant on big farmers for work.

12. **Dala is a landless farm labourer who works on daily wages in Palampur. This means he must regularly look for work. The minimum wages for a farm labourer set by the government is ₹ 300 per day (March 2019), but Dala gets only ₹ 160.**
Why Dala gets only ₹ 160 per day, when government set the minimum wages for farm labourer, ₹ 300 per day ? **Competency Based**
(a) Dala is illitrate
(b) Dala belongs to SCs
(c) Heavy competition for work among form labourers
(d) Dala has no land to cultivates.

13. **Consider the statements given below and choose the correct answer.**
Statement I Labour being the most abundant factor of production, it would be ideal if new ways of farming used much more labour.
Statement II The labour, looking for opportunities is thus migrating to neighbouring villages, towns and cities.
Codes
(a) Statement I is correct and Statement II is incorrect
(b) Statement I is incorrect and Statement II is correct
(c) Both Statements I and II are incorrect
(d) Both Statements I and II are correct

Answers

1. (b) **2.** (d) **3.** (b) **4.** (a) **5.** (b)
6. (a) **7.** (d) **8.** (a) **9.** (d) **10.** (c)
11. (d) **12.** (c) **13.** (d)

Match the Following

1.

List I (Factors of Production)	List II (Examples)
A. Land	1. Natural Resources
B. Fixed Capital	2. Assets
C. Working Capital	3. Raw Materials and Money
D. Human Capital	4. Knowledge and Enterprises

Codes

	A	B	C	D		A	B	C	D
(a)	1	2	3	4	(b)	4	3	2	1
(c)	2	3	4	1	(d)	4	2	1	3

2.

List I	List II
A. HYV seeds, tractor, fertilisers	1. Non-farm activities
B. Dairy, rice mill, shops	2. Big farmers
C. Borrowing of money	3. Modern farming method
D. Sale of surplus crops	4. Small farmers

Codes

	A	B	C	D		A	B	C	D
(a)	1	4	2	3	(b)	2	3	1	4
(c)	4	1	2	3	(d)	3	1	4	2

Ans. 1. (a) 2. (d)

Assertion-Reason

1. **Assertion** (A) Though there are a variety of non-farm activities in Palampur, only a few people are involved in it.
Reason (R) Loan facilities and markets to sell non-farm products are not well developed in Palampur.
Codes
(a) Both A and R are true and R is the correct explanation of A
(b) Both A and R are true, but R is not the correct explanation of A
(c) A is true, but R is false
(d) A is false, but R is true

2. **Assertion** (A) All the village in India do not have a high level of irrigation as in Palampur.
Reason (R) To increase production from the same piece of land, farmers do multiple cropping.
Codes
(a) Both A and R are true and R is the correct explanation of A
(b) Both A and R are true, but R is not the correct explanation of A
(c) A is true, but R is false
(d) A is false, but R is true

3. **Assertion** (A) The Indian Government has set ₹ 200 per day (March 2019) as the minimum wage.
Reason (R) There is a heavy competition for work among the farm labourers in Palampur, so people agree to work for lower wage.
Codes
(a) Both A and R are true and R is the correct explanation of A
(b) Both A and R are true, but R is not the correct explanation of A
(c) A is true, but R is false
(d) A is false, but R is true

4. **Assertion** (A) At present, the non-farm sector in the village is not very large.
Reason (R) Out of every 100 workers in the rural areas in India, only 24 are engaged in non-farm activities.

Codes
(a) Both A and R are true and R is the correct explanation of A
(b) Both A and R are true, but R is not the correct explanation of A
(c) A is true, but R is false
(d) A is false, but R is true

5. **Assertion** (A) Modern farming depletes soil fertility and groundwater.
Reason (R) Chemical fertilisers and continuous groundwater extraction harm these resources, emphasising the need for sustainable practices in agriculture.
Codes
(a) Both A and R are true and R is the correct explanation of A
(b) Both A and R are true, but R is not the correct explanation of A
(c) A is true, but R is false
(d) A is false, but R is true

Ans. 1. (a) Both A and R are true, and R is the correct explanation of A
2. (b) Both A and R are true, but R is not the correct explanation of A
3. (d) A is false, but R is true
4. (b) Both A and R are true, but R is not the correct explanation of A
5. (a) Both A and R are true and R is the correct explanation of A

Picture Based Questions

1. **In the given picture, identify the Kharif crop.**

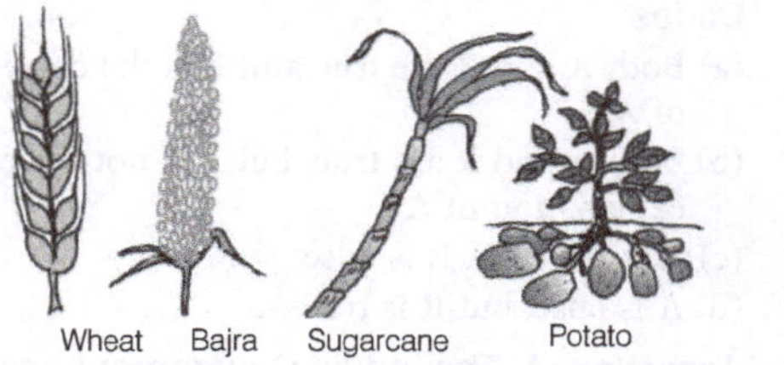

(a) Wheat (b) Bajra (c) Sugarcane (d) Potato

2. **This is the picture of agricultural farms in Palampur. Select the title that best describes the picture.**

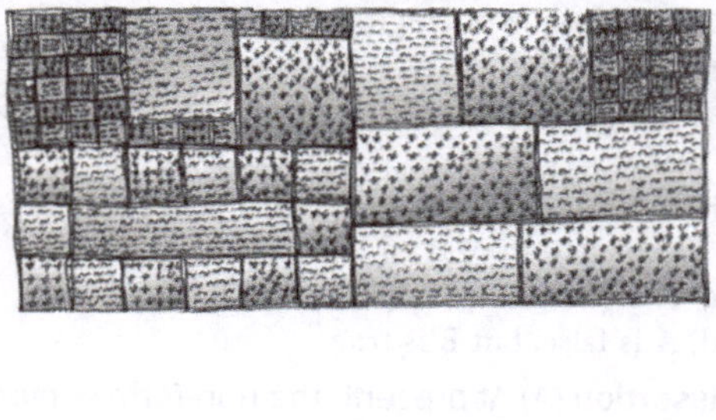

(a) Land of big and middle farmers.
(b) Unequal distribution of land in Palampur.
(c) Land distribution of small farmers.
(d) Equal distribution of land in Palampur.

Ans. 1. (b) Bajra
2. (b) Unequal distribution of land in Palampur.

Case Based Question

1. **Read the source given below and answer the questions that follow.**
Like Tejpal Singh, other large and medium farmers sell the surplus farm products. A part of the earnings is saved and kept for buying capital for the next season. Thus, they are able to arrange for the capital for farming from their own savings. Some farmers might also use the savings to buy cattle, trucks, or to set up shops. As we shall see, these constitute the capital for non-farm activities.

(i) What does Tejpal Singh do with the surplus wheat from his lands?
(a) Consumes it all
(b) Donates it to the community
(c) Sells it at the market
(d) Stores it for future use

(ii) What did Tejpal Singh do with most of his earnings from selling wheat last year?
(a) Invested in real estate
(b) Saved for capital
(c) Spent it on luxury items
(d) Donated it to charity

(iii) How did Tejpal Singh utilise his savings from last year?
(a) Purchased new lands
(b) Invested in the stock market
(c) Buy capital for next season
(d) Went on a vacation

(iv) What was the purpose of Tejpal Singh arranging working capital for farming with his savings?
(a) To purchase luxury items
(b) To increase fixed capital
(c) To support local charities
(d) To fund farming activities in the next season

Ans. (i) (c) Sells it at the market
(ii) (b) Saved for capital
(iii) (c) Buy capital for next season
(iv) (d) To fund farming activities in the next season

Part II

Very Short Answer Type Questions

1. Why farmers in Palampur are able to grow three crops in a year?

Ans. The farmers in Palampur are able to grow three crops in year due to proper irrigation facilities and electricities that make irrigation possible.

2. In which season wheat is grown in Palampur village?

Ans. During *rabi* season (winter), wheat is grown in Palampur village.

3. Before electric run tubewells what was the main source of irrigation in Palampur?

Ans. The persian wheel was used as the main source of irrigation in Palampur before electric run tubewells.

4. What was the major advantage of using HYV seeds in agriculture?

Ans. The major advantage of using HYV seeds in agriculture was more production of crops in the same amount of land in one cropping season.

5. What is the disadvantage of using chemical fertilisers in modern farming methods?

Ans. The disadvantage of using chemicals is that they kill bacteria and microbes, which are essential for soil fertility.

6. Which farmers, out of landless farmers, small farmers or medium and large farmers, hire labour to work in the fields?

Ans. Small farmers do not need additional labour, as they work with their family members in the fields. Only the medium and large farmers have extensive work, which requires them to hire additional labour, for which landless farmers or labourers are hired.

7. What are the non-farming activities being carried out in Palampur?

Ans. Some of the non-farming activities being carried out in Palampur are manufacturing, transport, shopkeeping and computer education.

8. During which season do farmers of Palampur grow jowar and bajra?

Ans. During the rainy season (*kharif*) the farmers of Palampur grow *jowar* and *bajra*.

9. Name the various forms of transport visible on the road from Palampur to Shahpur.

Ans. Forms of transport seen are bullock carts, tongas, bogeys, motorcycles, jeeps, tractors and trucks.

10. Is it true that foodgrains output in India has increased significantly in last few years because larger areas of land have been brought under cultivation?

Ans. This is not true. The foodgrains output has increased due to use of modern methods of agriculture with technological help.

11. Kishora is a farm labourer. Like other such labourers, Kishora found it difficult to meet his family's needs from the wages that he received. A few years back Kishora took a loan from the bank. This was under a government programme. Competency Based

(i) Under what government programme did Kishora receive a loan?

(ii) What was the purpose of this programme?

Ans. (i) Kishora received a loan under a government programme that provided cheap loans to poor landless households.

(ii) The purpose of this programme was to support individuals like Kishora in improving their economic conditions by offering financial assistance for specific activities, such as acquiring assets like livestock, which could generate income and enhance livelihoods.

12. Tejpal Singh agrees to give Savita the loan at an interest rate of 24 per cent for four months,which is a very high interest rate. Savita also has to promise to work on his field as a farm labourer during the harvest season at ₹ 35 per day. Competency Based

Why does Savita agree to these tough conditions, despite the challenges she anticipates?

Ans. Savita agrees to these tough conditions, despite the anticipated challenges, because she recognises the pressing need for financial assistance and understands the difficulty of securing loans elsewhere. The urgency of fulfilling household responsibilities makes her accept the terms set by Tejpal Singh.

Short Answer Type Questions

1. Which capital can be considered as the best: land, labour, physical capital or human capital and why?

Ans. Human capital is considered the best because it is the major asset for any economic activity's success. Investment in human capital will provide higher income and production because it can coordinate all the resources together to achieve the optimum amount of production.

It includes labour for processing the inputs as well as knowledge and enterprise required to produce the output.

2. Explain the term physical capital. Mention its different types with examples.

Ans. Physical capital is the variety of inputs which is required at every stage during production such as tools, equipments, machines and raw materials.

The two different types of physical capital are

(i) **Fixed Capital** It can be used in production over many years. e.g., tools and machines.

(ii) **Working Capital** Raw materials and money in hand are called working capital. Working capital is used up during the production activity, resulting in finished goods and services required. Production requires various raw materials like seeds used by farmers.

Some money is always required during production to make payments and buy other necessary items.

3. Highlight the basic constraint in raising production from a farm.

Ans. The basic constraints in raising production from a farm are

(i) The land area under cultivation, is fixed.

(ii) There has been no expansion in land area under cultivation after 1960. By then, some of the wastelands in the village had been converted to cultivable land.

(iii) There exists no further scope to increase farm production by bringing new land under cultivation, as there is no further land available in the village.

4. How was multiple cropping practiced in Palampur? Explain.

Ans. Multiple cropping was practiced in Palampur by growing a number of crops which are as follows

- Farmers grow *jowar* and *bajra* during the rainy season (*kharif*).
- They grow potatoes and other vegetables in between the *kharif* and *rabi* crops.
- Wheat is grown in winter (*rabi*) season.
- Sugarcane is also grown in some parts of land. This is harvested once a year.

5. State the importance of growing more than one crop on a piece of land.

Ans. The importance of growing more than one crop on a piece of land is as follow

- It retains the fertility of the soil.
- It uses the same area for more crop production.
- It benefits the farmer economically.
- The farmer's increased earning makes arranging for the working capital easier.
- It generates employment for many people throughout the year.

6. Why is it important to develop irrigation facilities? Explain.

Ans. It is important to develop irrigation facilities for the following reasons

- Having irrigation facilities makes the farmer independent of the irregularities of monsoon as he can compensate for any rainfall shortage by using irrigation.
- Irrigation allows the cultivation of more than one crop in a year, as water is available throughout the year.
- With irrigation, it is possible to provide the necessary water as use of modern farming methods, HYV seeds, chemical fertilisers, insecticides and pesticides requires more water than traditional agriculture.

7. Mention any three negative effects of the Green Revolution.

Ans. The negative effects of the Green Revolution are

- Modern farming methods used in the Green Revolution have overused the natural resource base. All the nutrients in the soil are finished.
- Soil fertility is lost due to increased use of chemical fertilisers. The chemicals have killed the bacteria which used to keep the soil fertile earlier.
- Continuous use of groundwater for irrigation through tubewells has reduced the water table which was built up over a number of years.

8. How is land distributed amongst the farmers of Palampur? Explain.

or **Describe the land distribution of the farmers of Palampur.**

or **Explain the distribution of land among farmers in Palampur.**

Ans. The distribution of land in Palampur is as follows

- In Palampur, about one-third of the total 450 families are landless *i.e.,* 150 families are landless.
- 240 families cultivate small plots of less than 2 hectares.
- There are 60 families of medium and large farmers who cultivate more than 2 hectares of land.
- Few large farmers have landholdings extending to 10 hectares or more. Half of the area of the village is covered with plots quite large in size.

Thus, land in Palampur is unevenly distributed.

9. Rama is a farm labourer in a village who works all the year round to meet his expenses. Being a farm labourer Rama and many others face a number of problems in terms of employment. State any three such problems. **Competency Based**

Ans. The problems faced by Rama and many other farm labourers in term of employment are as follows

(i) Rama and most of the farm labourers are landless labourers. They have no right over the crops of the land on which they work.

(ii) Wages provided by the landowners vary from place to place. Sometimes they are lower than the minimum wages fixed by the government.

(iii) There is also a wide variation in the duration of employment. It may be on a daily basis or for one farm activity like harvesting or for the whole year.

10. From where do the small farmers get capital for farming? How does it affect the farmers?

Ans. The small farmers have to borrow money to get capital for farming, either from large farmers, the village moneylenders, or the traders who supply various inputs for cultivation.

It affects these farmers adversely, because the rate of interest on such loans is very high. The small farmers repay these loans and the interest with great difficulty, or in case of a bad harvest, fall into a debt trap.

11. Write any three differences between land and capital.

Ans. Differences between land and capital are

Land	Capital
It is a passive factor of production.	It is an active factor of production.
It requires human effort to make it a productive resource.	It comprises man-made inputs which help actively in increasing production.
No activity can take place in absence of land. It is the basis of all human activities.	Capital is essential for better growth. But, it also needs land for existence or to act upon.

12. Highlight five differences between traditional and modern methods of farming. Competency Based

Ans. Five differences between traditional and modern methods of farming are as follows

Traditional Methods	Modern Methods
Seeds used are simple and traditional	HYV seeds are used.
Irrigation is done through wells and tanks	Irrigation is done through dams, tubewells and canals.
Fertiliser used is manure from cow dung.	Chemical fertilisers are used.
Farmers use bullocks for ploughing the field.	Tractors are used.
Manual labour is used for all activities.	Modern machinery is used for all activities.

13. Farmers in Western Uttar Pradesh were pioneers in adopting modern farming methods. They utilised tubewells for irrigation, employed High-Yielding Variety (HYV) seeds, chemical fertilisers, and pesticides. Additionally, some farmers invested in farm machinery such as tractors and threshers.

(i) What were some key components of the modern farming methods adopted by farmers in Western Uttar Pradesh? Competency Based

Ans. Farmers in Western Uttar Pradesh embraced modern farming by utilising tubewells for irrigation, employing High Yielding Variety (HYV) seeds, chemical fertilisers, and pesticides. Additionally, some invested in farm machinery such as tractors and threshers, facilitating faster ploughing and harvesting.

(ii) How were farmers in Western Uttar Pradesh rewarded for adopting modern farming methods?

Ans. Farmers in the region were rewarded with high yields of wheat as a result of implementing modern farming practices, including the use of technology, improved seeds and efficient machinery.

Long Answer Type Questions

1. State any five reasons to show that Palampur is a developed village.

Ans. Palampur is a developed village due to the following reasons

(i) Palampur is well-connected with neighbouring villages and towns. Raiganj is a big village 3 kms from Palampur. An all weather road connects the village to Raiganj and further to the nearest town of Shahpur.

(ii) Many kinds of vehicles use this road to transport milk, jaggery and other commodities to markets and wholesalers.

(iii) Palampur houses 450 families. The 80 upper caste families have their houses made of bricks and cement plastering.

(iv) Most of the houses have electric connection. Electricity powers all the tubewells in the fields and is used in various types of small business. Palampur has two primary schools and one high school.

(v) There is a primary health centre run by government and one private dispensary where the sick are treated.

2. What is the aim of production? State four requirements needed for production of goods and services.

Ans. The aim of production is to produce the goods and services we want. Production of goods requires four inputs, which are called factors of production. These are

(i) **Land** It is the first requirement. Other natural resources like water, minerals, forests, etc are also used.

(ii) **Labour** It is used for carrying out the production activities. Some work may be done through manual labour and other work may require highly skilled or educated persons.

(iii) **Physical Capital** Items like machinery, building, tools, etc are called fixed capital. They can be used repeatedly for a long time, while raw material and money in hand are called working capital. Working capital is used up during the production activity, resulting in finished goods and services whereas fixed capital is used again and again.

(iv) **Human Capital** It is the knowledge and enterprise required to put together all the above inputs to produce the output, which can either be sold in market or consumed by the person producing the output.

3. How are the farmers in village Palampur able to grow more crops from the same land? Explain.

Or **How can one grow more than one crop on the same piece of land? Explain.**

Ans. Palampur's farmers follow multiple cropping. They grow atleast two main crops. Many of them also grow vegetables as a third crop.

The following points state how the farmers in Palampur are able to grow more crops from the same land

(i) There is a well-developed system of irrigation in Palampur that enables the farmers to grow three different crops in a year.

(ii) Electricity came early to Palampur. It has played a pivotal role in transformation of the irrigation system in the village. The existing Persian wheels were replaced by electric run tubewells which could irrigate much larger areas of land.

(iii) The Green Revolution introduced HYV seeds and modern farming methods.

(iv) Effective use of HYVs, chemical fertilisers and modern agricultural technologies resulted in better agricultural yield from the same land.

4. What are the features of Green Revolution? How it differs from traditional farming?

Ans. Major features of Green Revolution in India were

- Use of High Yielding Varieties (HYV) of seeds. HYV seeds helped to produce much greater amounts of grain on a single plant.
- Use of advanced technology, chemical fertilisers, pesticides and a well-developed system of irrigation.
- This revolution solved the food crisis in India and made India self-sufficient in foodgrains.
- This led to higher income growth and reduced poverty.
- In many areas, Green Revolution is associated with loss of soil fertility due to increased use of chemical fertilisers. Also, continuous use of groundwater for tubewell irrigation has reduced the water table below the ground.

The Green Revolution is different from traditional farming in terms of using new methods, technology, mechanised equipment, HYV seeds, tubewell irrigation and chemicals. While the traditional method uses primitive methods of cultivation manure and wells or tanks for irrigation.

5. What is land? Suggest any three ways to sustain land.

Ans. Land is the basic natural resource that is required as a factor or an input in many production activities. Land is a fixed asset, it cannot be expanded or produced. Many of human activities depend on land. It is necessary to be careful in its use.

Three ways to sustain land are

(i) Soil is the vital part of land. Chemical fertilisers and pesticides reduce its fertility and pollute soil in many ways. So, there should be emphasis on use of bio-compost and eco-friendly methods to keep the soil fertile.

(ii) Some farming practices help in making land sustainable. These practices include intensity of cropping, rotation of crops, multiple cropping, etc.

(iii) The modern farming methods should be used carefully and rationally according to scientific standards, so that soil profile is saved from further damage.

6. Name any four non-farm production activities practiced in Palampur. Give brief descriptions of any three.

Or **Explain any four non-farm production activities of village Palampur.**

Ans. Non-farm activities practiced in Palampur are

(i) **Dairy Farming** Many families are involved in dairying. They keep buffaloes for supplying the milk to the collection-cum-chilling centre at Raiganj, the milk being processed further for supply in towns and cities.

(ii) **Small-Scale Manufacturing** This involves simple production methods and are done on small-scale. Jaggery is manufactured by crushing the sugarcane grown and processing it. For this, an electric powered sugarcane crushing machine has been installed by the farmer Mishrilal. He sells the jaggery produced to traders at Shahpur, the nearby town.

(iii) **Shopkeeping** It is a useful service provided to the villagers, as they do not have to go far away to buy goods of daily use. Palampur's shopkeepers buy various goods from wholesalers in the cities to sell in the village. Some of them have also opened shops selling eatables near the village bus stand.

(iv) **Transport** There are different means of transport in Palampur like rikshaws, tangas, trucks, jeeps and tractors. These means of transport are used to transport goods and people from village to cities and the people get paid for this.

7. Distinguish between the condition of a farmer who is working in his own farm and a landless labourer.

Ans. Difference between farmers and landless labourers are as follows

Landless Labourers	Farmers with Land
They do not have even a small plot of land.	On the other hand, they occupy medium or large farmlands.
They are hired by medium or large farmers.	They hire landless labourers for work on their field.
They have no right over the crops grown by them on the farmers field.	They have the right to use their crops grown on their farms.
They work for daily wages, so, they have no savings with them.	After selling their surplus crop, they have a good amount to deposit in bank account.
They are exploited by large farmers most of the time, as they hire them on less than the minimum wages fixed by the government.	They exploit the small farmers or landless labourers by paying them lower wages as there is heavy competition for work among farm labourers.

8. A small-scale farmer in a rural village took a loan from a local money lender at a high rate of interest. Unable to repay the interest, he sought another loan from a landlord to settle the initial interest debt.

Discuss the potential consequences the farmer might encounter in this situation, considering economic factors and the impact on his livelihood. **Competency Based**

Ans. The small-scale farmer in this situation may face severe economic consequences

- If the farmer fails to repay the loans, he might be forced to sell his land, livestock, or other assets to cover the debt.
- The farmer's livelihood may be compromised as a significant portion of his income may go towards servicing debts rather than investing in agricultural inputs or improving farm productivity.
- The burden of debt can cause immense stress and anxiety, affecting the farmer's mental and physical health.
- The farmer might have to take on additional work to generate income, leading to longer working hours and less time for essential activities like caring for his family or improving his farm.
- As income gets diverted towards debt repayment, the farmer might have less money to purchase food or invest in his farm.

Case Based Questions

1. Read the sources given below and answer the questions that follow.

Source A Story of Mishrilal

Mishrilal has purchased a mechanical sugarcane crushing machine run on electricity and has set it up on his field. Sugarcane crushing was earlier done with the help of bullocks, but people prefer to do it by machines these days. Mishrilal also buys sugarcane from other farmers and processes it into jaggery. The jaggery is then sold to traders at Shahpur. In the process, Mishrilal makes a small profit.

(i) Sugarcane crushing under taken in the village is what type of activity?

Source B Will the Land Sustain?

In many areas, Green Revolution is associated with the loss of soil fertility due to increased use of chemical fertilisers. Also, continuous use of groundwater for tubewell irrigation has led to the depletion of the water-table. Environmental resources, like soil fertility and groundwater, are built up over the years. Once destroyed it is very difficult to restore them. We must take care of the environment to ensure future development of agriculture.

(ii) Why there is loss of soil fertility as an effect of Green Revolution?

Source C How is land distributed between the farmers of Palampur?

Of the remaining families who own land, 240 families cultivate small plots of land less than 2 hectares in size. Cultivation of such plots doesn't bring adequate income to the farmer family.

(iii) Why do so many families of farmers cultivate such small plots of land?

Ans. (i) Sugarcane crushing under takens in the village is the first steps in manufacture of jaggery from raw sugarcane. Thus, it is a manufacturing activity.

(ii) The Green Revolution resulted in more production of crops which in turn utilised the soil nutrients at a faster rate. This leads to loss of soil fertility.

(iii) Land in Palampur is fixeds and 75% of the people who are working are dependent on farming for their livelihood. Since, land is fixed and maximum people are dependent on land. So, they are forced to cultivate small plots of land.

2. Read the source given below and answer the questions that follow.

The Green Revolution in the late 1960s introduced the Indian farmer to cultivation of wheat and rice using High Yielding Varieties (HYVs) of seeds. Compared to the traditional seeds, the HYV seeds promised to produce much greater amounts of grain on a single plant. As a result, the same piece of land would now produce far larger quantities of foodgrains than was possible earlier. HYV seeds, however, needed plenty of water and also chemical fertilisers and pesticides to produce best results.

Higher yields were possible only from a combination of HYV seeds, irrigation, chemical fertilisers, pesticides, etc. Farmers of Punjab, Haryana and Western Uttar Pradesh were the first to try out the modern farming method in India.

The farmers in these regions set up tubewells for irrigation and made use of HYV seeds, chemical fertilisers and pesticides in farming. Some of them bought farm machinery, like tractors and threshers, which made ploughing and harvesting faster. They were rewarded with high yields of wheat.

(i) What method adopted by Indian farmers enabled them to grow more from same piece of land?

(ii) Green revolution is beneficial for the Indian farmers. Explain.

(iii) Which modern implements and items were used by Indian farmers?

Ans. (i) The method of green revolution enabled the farmers to grow more from same piece of land.

(ii) The Green Revolution enabled the Indian farmers to cultivate wheat and rice using High Yielding Varieties (HYV) of seeds, irrigation chemical fertilisers, insecticides and pesticides, etc. This increased their income from agriculture.

(iii) The modern implements used by the Indian farmers were tubewells, tractors, threshers and harvesters, which made ploughing and harvesting faster. The farmers also used fertilisers and pesticides to increase their farm yield.

ASSESSMENT EXERCISE

Multiple Choice Questions (MCQs)

1. Which of the following is a Kharif crop?

(a) Sugarcane (b) Wheat
(c) Bajra (d) All of these

2. To grow more than one crop on the same piece of land is called

(a) multiple cropping
(b) mixed farming
(c) plantation farming
(d) None of the above

3. Consider the following statements associated with farm labourers and select the correct option.

(a) Farm labourers come either from landless families or families cultivating small plots of land.
(b) Farmer labourers have a right over the crops grown on the land.
(c) There is no competition for work among the farm labourer in Palampur.
(d) Farm labourers hired for the full year.

Subjective Questions (VSA, SA & LA)

1. What refers to a rapid and sustained increase in the output of agriculture over a long period of time?

2. What are the requirements of multiple cropping?

3. How do medium and large farmers fulfil their requirements?

4. What is the meaning of working capital? What is its effect on day-to-day farming activities?

5. Explain why modern farming methods require more investment from the farmer's side as compared to the traditional farming methods followed earlier.

6. What could be the scope for landless labourers and small farmers to make their vulnerable life well in villages? Suggest some ways in this direction.

7. Explain why modern farming methods increase production cost, at the same time harming the physical environment.

8. Irrigation is necessary in modern methods of agriculture. Analyse its importance.

People as Resource

CHAPTER 2

Human capital develops when a country invests in its people through activities like education, training and healthcare. Human capital represents the accumulated skills and useful knowledge that individual possess. In this chapter, we will understand how a nation can benefit from its population turning it into an asset rather than a burden.

2.1 Overview

Population is an asset for the economy rather than a liability. Like other resources population is also known as **Human Resource**. It becomes human capital when investments are made in the form of healthcare, training and education.

Human capital is the collection of skills and useful knowledge that people have. **Land** and **capital** are made useful by **human capital**. That is why human capital is superior to other forms of capital.

People as a resource refers to a country's working people in terms of their existing productive skills and abilities. This productive nature of population helps to develop the Gross National Product[1] (GNP) of a country through its abilities.

When the existing human resource is further developed by becoming more educated and healthy, it is called **human capital formation** which adds to the productive power of the country like physical capital formation.

Investment in Human Capital

Investment in human capital through education, training and medical care yields a return just like investment in physical capital.

For example, more educated or better trained persons earn higher income because they give higher productivity to their employers. In the same way, a healthier person can also give higher productivity and earn a good income.

Population can be turned into a productive asset by

- spending resources on education and health for all.
- giving training to industrial and agricultural workers for using modern technology.
- providing useful scientific researches and so on.

Investment in Education and Health

Investment in human resources through education and medical care can give high rates of return in future. This investment on people is the same as investment in land and capital.

Educated parents are found to invest more heavily on the education of their children. They are also more aware of their children's needs of nutrition and hygiene. A virtuous cycle[2] is created in this case.

In contrast, a **vicious cycle** is created for those parents who are themselves not educated and lacking in hygiene and keep their children in a similarly disadvantaged state.

Countries like Japan have invested heavily in human resources because they did not have any natural resources. They import the natural resources needed by the country.

They have invested on people especially in the field of education and health. These people have made efficient use of other resources like land and capital. Efficiency and technology evolved by people have made these countries developed.

1 Gross National Product It is a measure to value what the country's citizens produce in a financial year. It also measure the value of produce which is produced outside the country by the citizens of the country.

2 Virtuous cycle It is a condition in which a favourable circumstance or result gives rise to another that subsequently supports the first condition.

2.2 Economic Activities

Activities which add value to the National Income are called **economic activities.**

Economic activities has two parts

(i) **Market Activities** These activities involve payment to the person who performs an activity. For example, production of the goods or services including government services.

(ii) **Non-market Activities** These activities are not paid as **production** of these activities is for **self-consumption.** These can be the consumption and processing of primary products and production of fixed assets for own use. For example, a mother, looking after children. Men works in the fields, and earn money, which they spend on rearing of their families are market activities.

Women are not paid for the household work done by them in the family and also not recognised in the National Income. This division of labour between men and women in families is due to historical and cultural reasons.

Economic activities can be classified into three sectors based on the activities done. These are as follows :

(i) **Primary Sector** All activities which use natural resources are included in this sector.

Primary sector comprises of agriculture, forestry, dairy farming, animal husbandry, fisheries, poultry farming, mining and quarrying.

(ii) **Secondary Sector** All activities which use products produced in the primary sector for manufacturing of goods are included in this sector.

All manufacturing processes and construction activities are included in the Secondary sector.

(iii) **Tertiary Sector** All activities which support the primary and secondary sectors are included in this sector.

These include trade, transportation, communication, sales and services, education, health, tourism, banking, insurance, legal services, government etc.

Employment Structure in Three Sectors

The employment structure is characterised by self-employment in the primary sector.

Agriculture is the most labour absorbing sector of the economy, but there is problem of disguised umemployment in this sector. This results in a decline in the dependence of the population on agriculture partly. Most of the primary sector activities are self employment i.e. where the whole family contributes in the work.

The secondary sector absorbs labour force in its small scale manufacturing units. Tertiary sector also absorbs labour. Some of the surplus labour in agriculture moves to these two sectors. In tertiary sector, new services like biotechnology and information technology are appearing.

Education and Skill: Determinants of Earning

Education and skill are the major determinants of earning of any individual in the market. A majority of women have low education and low skill formation compared to men.

Most women work in sectors where there is no job security, lack of legal protection and provides irregular and low income.

There is also absence of basic facilities like maternity leave, childcare leave and other social security systems. On the other hand, women with high education and skill are paid equally as men.

Among the organised sector teaching and medicine attract women the most. Some women also work in administrative and other services including jobs, that need high levels of scientific and technological competence.

Try These

1. **Mention the country that has invested heavily in its human resources.**
2. **What is the term for the sector that manufactures goods?**
3. **Govinda works as Human Resource Manager in a bank. Which sector of the economy does he work in?**
4. **Mention the activities that are not paid for, as their production is for self-consumption.**

2.3 Quality of Population

The quality of population depends upon the literacy rate, health of a person indicated by life expectancy and skill formation which is acquired by the people of the country.

The quality of the population ultimately decides the growth rate of the country. Literate and healthy population are an assest for a country.

Education

Education is an important input for the growth of human resource. Education opens new opportunities for people, provides new aspirations and develops values of life.

Education increases the National Income as well as the **cultural richness** and efficiency of governance.

Vocational education[3] has been developed to equip a large number of high school students with occupations related to knowledge and skills.

Literacy is not only a right, it is also needed if the citizens are to perform their duties and enjoy their rights properly.

In 2010-11, the literacy rates have increased from 18% in 1951 to 85% in 2018.

Female literacy remains much lower than male literacy all over India. Literacy among males is nearly 16.1% higher than females and it is also about 14.2% higher in urban areas as compared to rural areas.

There is also wide variation in literacy rates from one region of the country to another. For example, there is about 94% literacy in Kerala, but 62% in Bihar.

The expenditure on education as a percentage of GDP has declined to 2.8% in 2020-21.

The **Gross Enrolment Ratio** (GER) in Higher Education in age group 18-23 years is 27% in 2019-20.

Government Steps to Provide Education to All

Government has taken many steps towards providing elementary education to all. Government's strategy focuses on

- increasing access, quality, adoption of states- specific curriculum modification, vocationalisation and networking on the use of information technology.
- providing distance education as well as merging of formal, non-formal, distance and IT education institutions.

Some important steps are

- The primary school system has expanded to over 7,78,842 lakh in 2019-20 in India.
- Government's initiative of Sarva Shiksha Abhiyan[4] aims at providing elementary education to all children in the age group of 6 to 14 years.
- **Mid-day Meal Scheme** has been implemented to encourage attendance and retention of school children and improve their nutritional status.
- There is provision for providing universal access, retention and quality in elementary education with a special emphasis on girls.
- Special schools called as **Navodaya Vidyalaya** have been established in each district in India.

Health

Proper health helps a person to realise his potential and ability to fight illness. Good health is crucial for overall well-being. Therefore, the country has prioritised improving the health of its population. The Government's National Policy on Health aims at improving the access to healthcare, family welfare and nutritional services, with a special focus on underprivileged sections of the population.

During the last 50 years, India has built up a vast healthcare, manpower and infrastructure required at primary, secondary and tertiary sectors in government as well as the private sector. Its results are

- Life expectancy[5] has increased to over 67.2 years in 2021 which is a very good sign, as an increase in life expectancy and improvement in childcare are useful in assessing the future progress of the country. An increase in lifespan is an indicator of a good quality of life marked by self-confidence.
- Infant Mortality Rate[6] (IMR) has come down from 147 in the year 1951 to 28 in the year 2020. IMR involves the protection of children from infection, ensuring the nutrition of both the mother and the child, and childcare.
- Crude Birth Rate[7] (CBR) has dropped to 20 (2020) and Crude Death Rate[8] (CDR) to 6 (2020) within the same duration of time.

2.4 Unemployment

Unemployment is the situation when people who are willing to work at the existing wages cannot find jobs. The workforce includes all people from the age of 15 years to 59 years.

Children and elderly people (60 years and over) are not included in workforce, so they are not to be considered as unemployed.

In the case of India, there is unemployment in both rural and urban areas. In rural areas, there is seasonal and disguised

3 Vocational education It refers to an education that prepares people for specific trades, crafts and careers at various levels from a tradesman or craftsman to a professional position in engineering, accountancy, nursing, medicine, architecture, pharmacy, law, etc.

4 Sarva Shiksha Abhiyan It is a Government of India programme aimed at the universalisation of elementary education in a time-bound manner making education free to children of ages 6-14.

5 Life Expectancy It is a statistical measure of the average time an individual is expected to live.

6 Infant Mortality Rate (IMR) It is the death of a child under one year of age.

7 Birth Rate It is the number of babies born for every 1000 people during a particular period of time.

8 Death Rate It is the number of people per 1000 who die during a period of time.

unemployment whereas urban areas have mostly educated unemployment. These are discussed below :

- **Seasonal Unemployment** happens when people are not able to find jobs during some months of the year. People dependent upon agriculture usually face this kind of unemployment.
  Sometimes, farmers have a lot to do during busy seasons like planting and harvesting. But there are other times, like certain months, when there isn't as much work for people who rely on farming.
- **Disguised Unemployment** In this kind of unemployment, people appear to be employed.
  For example, an agriculture field requires the service of five people but eight people are working in the same field then, these three extra people come under the category of disguised unemployed. Production will not decrease when three people are removed.
- **Educated Unemployment** In urban areas, many young people with matriculation, graduation and post-graduation degrees are not able to find jobs. This situation leads to educated unemployment.
  A paradoxical manpower situation (contradictory situation) is observed when there is surplus manpower in some category and shortage of manpower in others.
  On one side, there are technically qualified individuals facing unemployment, and on the other side, there is a shortage of the technical skills needed for economic growth.
  In India, the official unemployment rate seems low in statistics. However, many people, despite being considered employed, earn low incomes and have low productivity.
  Although they appear to work all year, their work may not provide sufficient income or match their potential. It often feels like they're compelled to do the work.
  These individuals might prefer other types of work, but due to economic constraints, they engage in any available activity, even if it doesn't pay well. Their earnings barely cover basic needs, keeping them at a subsistence level.

Effects of Unemployment

Increase in unemployment is an indicator of a depressed economy. It also wastes the human resource.

Unemployment effects the economy in the following ways

- Unemployment leads to the wastage of manpower resource. People who can be an asset for the economy into a liability.
- Feeling of hopelessness and despair occurs among the youth. People do not have enough money to support their family.
- Unemployment tends to increase economic overload[9].
- The dependence of the unemployed on the working population increases.
- The quality of life of an individual as well as of society is adversely affected.
- There is a general decline in health status and rising withdrawal from the school system.

Try These

1. **Which scheme is implemented to encourage attendance and improve the nutritional status of children?**
2. **What is the term for the number of babies born per 1000 people during a year?**
3. **Name the special schools that are established in each district of India.**
4. **In which sector most of the work force is indulged in Indian economy?**

9 Economic overload A situation when less number of employed people are supporting more number of unemployed people.

Mind Map

Human Resource

- Land and Capital are made useful by human capital.
- When the existing human resource is further developed by becoming more educated and healthy it is called human capital formation.

Education

- Increases the National Income as well as the cultural richness and efficiency of governance.
- Sarva Siksha Abhiyan aims at providing elementary education to all children of age 6 to 14 years of age.
- Mid-day Meal scheme has been implemented.
- Special schools known as Navodaya Vidyalaya have been established.

Health

- The Government's National Policy on health aims at improving the health of its population.
- Life Expectancy has increased.
- Infant Mortality Rate has decreased.
- Crude Birth Rate and Crude Death rate have decreased.

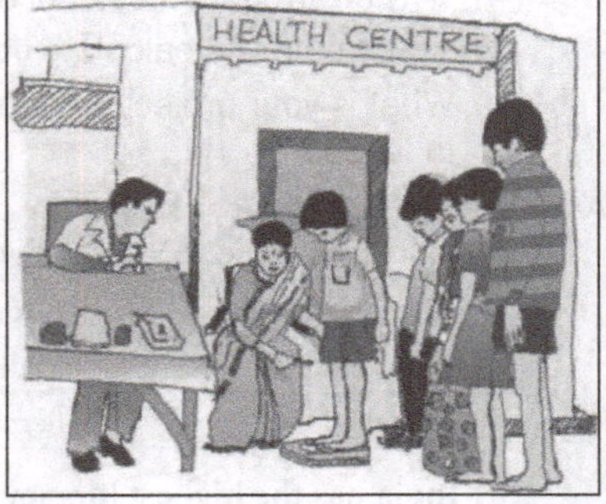

Investment in Human Capital

- Spending resources on education and health for all.
- Giving training to industrial and agricultural workers.
- Providing useful scientific researches.

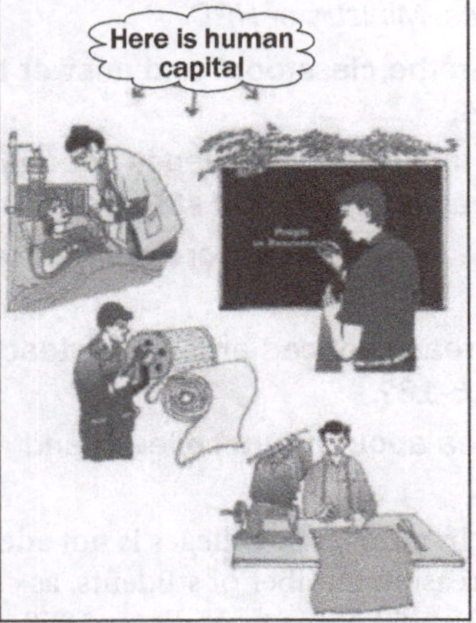

Quality of Population

The quality of education depends upon the literacy rate.

PEOPLE AS A RESOURCE

Unemployment

Seasonal Unemployment

It happens when people are not able to find jobs during some months of the year.

Disguised Unemployment

In this kind of unemployment people appear to be employed.

Educated Unemployment

In urban areas, many young people with matriculation, graduation and post graduation degrees are not able to find jobs which leads to educated unemployment.

Economic Activities by Men and Women

- Economic activities add value to the National Income.
- Economic activities have two parts
  - (i) **Market Activities** These activities involve payment to the person who performs an activity.
  - (ii) **Non- Market Activities** These activities are not paid as production of these activities are for self-consumption.

Investment in Education and Health

- Investment in human resources through education and medical care can give high return in future.
- Educated parents invest more heavily on the education, and are more aware of the nutrition and hygiene of their children.

Sectors

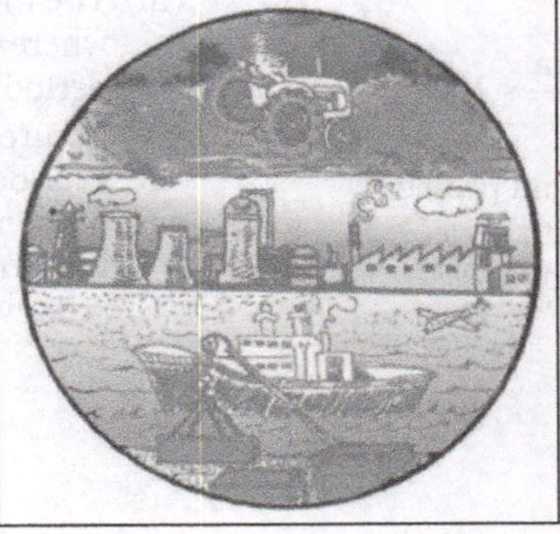

Primary

All activities which use natural resources, e.g. agriculture forestry, mining, etc

Secondary

All activities which use products produced in primary sector, e.g. construction and manufacturing processes, etc.

Tertiary

All activities which support the primary and secondary sectors, e.g. transportation communication, etc

NCERT FOLDER

Covering Intext Questions and Exercises of NCERT

INTEXT QUESTIONS

Q.1 Study the graph and answer the following questions.

(i) Have the literacy rates of the population increased since 1951?

(ii) In which year has India the highest literacy rate?

(iii) Why is literacy rate high among the males of India?

(iv) Why are women less educated than men?

(v) How would you calculate literacy rate in India?

(vi) What is your projection about India's literacy rate in 2025?

Ans. (i) Yes, the literacy rates of the population have increased since 1951 as shown below

Literacy in 1951	Literacy in 2017
Male-28%	Male-83%
Female-11%	Female-70%

(ii) India has the highest literacy rate in 2017.

(iii) India traditionally has a patriarchal society where more importance is given to males. Culturally, due to division of labour, the males are expected to go out of their homes for work so they have better access to education. Poor families, due to monetary constraints, prefer to send only their sons to school and not their daughters.

Therefore, literacy rate is higher among the males.

(iv) Women are less educated than men because preference is given to the boys or sons in the family for education because they are considered as the future of the family.

Traditionally, the girls are expected to stay at home and look after domestic chores. So, education among girls is not encouraged. Because of the above reasons, women are less educated than men.

(v) The literacy rate can be calculated on the basis of the number of literate people divided by the population and multiplied by 100.

Literacy Rate

$$= \frac{\text{Number of literate People in India}}{\text{Population of India}} \times 100$$

(vi) Based on the last ten years' trends, I would project India's literacy rate to be 78% in 2025, with male literacy being 89% and female literacy being 78%.

Q.2 Number of Institutions of Higher Education, Enrollment and Faculty.

Year	*Number of Colleges*	*Number of Universities*	*Students*	*Teachers*
1950-51	750	30	2,63,000	24,000
1990-91	7,346	177	49,25,000	2,72,000
1998-99	11,089	238	74,17,000	3,42,000
2010-11	33,023	523	186,70,050	8,16,966
2012-13	37,204	628	223,02,938	9,25,396
2014-15	40,760	711	265,85,437	12,61,350
2015-16	41,435	753	284,84,741	14,38,000
2016-17	42,338	795	294,27,158*	14,70,190*
2017-18	41,012	851	366,42,378	12,84,957
2018-19	39,931	993	37,399,388	14,16,299
2019-20	44,374	1,236	38,275,207	12,07,204
2020-21	46,007	1074	3,94,34,256	14,82,890

***Source** UGC Annual Report 2019-20 and Selected Educational Statistics, Ministry of HRD*

Discuss this table in the classroom and answer the following questions.

(i) Is the increase in number of colleges adequate to admit the increasing number of students?

(ii) Do you think we should have more number of universities?

(iii) What is the increase noticed among the teachers in the year 2015-16?

(iv) What is your idea about future colleges and universities?

Ans. (i) No, the increase in number of colleges is not adequate to admit the increasing number of students, as can be seen in column 2 and 3 of the table. From 1950 onwards, the colleges have increased about 50 times, while the students have increased by about 110 times.

(ii) We need not have more universities, although each university will need to affiliate more colleges to cater to the increase in the number of colleges.

(iii) The increase of teachers in 2015-16 is about 12.284%, whereas the number of students during the same period have gone up by 6.667%.

(iv) Future colleges and universities must impart skill-based education so that the students passing out of them are able to find productive jobs. There is no further requirement for academic degrees which do not give jobs to the students.

EXERCISE

Q.1 What do you understand by 'people as a resource'?

Ans. People as Resource refers to a country's working population in terms of their existing production skills and abilities.

Q.2 How is human resource different from other resources like land and physical capital?

Ans. Human resource is different from other resources due to the following reasons

Land and Other Resources	Human Resources
Land and other resources are fixed, limited and specified.	Human resources can be nurtured through education and health.
Other resources can't change or affect human resources.	Human resources can bring changes in other resources.
Land and physical capital can't become useful on its own.	Human resources can make use of land and physical capital.

Q. 3. What is the role of education in human capital formation?

Ans. Education plays a significant and very vital role in human capital formation in the following ways

- Education helps humans to achieve and realise their full potential.
- It helps to make people successful in their life in the form of higher incomes earned through better jobs and higher productivity.
- Education helps the people by broadening their knowledge and providing them training.
- It opens new scopes for earning like doing business, job, etc.
- It contribute towards the growth of society.
- It enhances the national income, cultural richness and the efficiency of the governance.

Q.4 What is the role of health in human capital formation?

Ans. Health plays an important role in human capital formation in the following ways

- A person with good health can work efficiently.
- Healthy people can realise their full potential and contribute better to the society and to the country.
- By increasing their working capacity, healthy people can improve their standard of living.

Q.5 What part does health play in the individual's working life?

Ans. Health plays an important role in the individual's working life as

- An unhealthy person cannot work efficiently.
- If the body is healthy, only then the mind can perform well.
- A healthy person is able to work harder and better, thus earning more and living a better life.

Q.6 What are the various activities undertaken in the primary sector, secondary sector and tertiary sector?

Ans. The various activities undertaken in these sectors are

- **Primary sector** Primary occupations have a direct link with nature of physical environment. For example agriculture, forestry, animal husbandry, fishing, poultry farming and mining.
- **Secondary sector** In the secondary sector manufacturing and construction work take place.
- **Tertiary sector** This sector mainly provides services to the primary and secondary activities. For example, trade, transport, communication, banking, education, health, tourism, services and insurance.

Q.7 What is the difference between economic activities and non-economic activities?

Ans. The differences between economic and non-economic activities are

Economic Activities	Non-Economic Activities
Activities which contribute to the National Income are called economic activities.	These activities do not contribute to the National Income.
These are done for pay or profit.	These activities are not paid.
Examples are manufacturing, teaching, banking, etc.	Examples are housewives working at home (take care of children, house chores etc), social service etc. including all non-profit services.

Q.8 Why are women employed in low paid work?

Ans. Women are employed in low paid work due to the following reasons

- As a majority of the women in India have lesser education and lesser skill than men due to traditional reasons, they are paid less than men or are mostly employed in low paid work.
- Another reason is that jobs involving physical labour are entrusted to men only due to their physique; here women cannot do as much physical work as men.
- Women also generally have an additional responsibility of looking after their family and children, so they cannot be as regular as men in their duties. Thus, they are often given non-critical and low paid work.

Q.9 How will you explain the term unemployment?

Ans. Unemployment is a situation where someone of working age is not able to get a job. It is expressed as a percentage of the total available workforce. The level of unemployment varies with economic conditions and other circumstances.

Q.10 What is the difference between disguised unemployment and seasonal unemployment?

Ans. Difference between disguised unemployment and seasonal unemployment are as follows

Disguised Unemployment	Seasonal Unemployment
In case of disguised unemployment, people appear to be employed, but are actually not employed.	Seasonal unemployment happens when people are not able to find jobs during some months of the year.
It is mostly found in agriculture.	It is mostly found in agro based industries.
It is mainly found in rural areas.	It is found both in rural as well as urban areas.

Q.11 Why is educated unemployed, a peculiar problem of India ?

Ans. Educated unemployment is a peculiar problem of India due to the following reasons

- It is mainly found in urban areas as education level is high there.
- People with educational degrees like Matriculation, Graduation and Post Graduation are not able to find jobs.
- There exists a paradoxical manpower situation which means surplus manpower in some areas and shortages in the other.
- In India, there is surplus manpower of technically qualified people due to which there is unemployment among them. But at the same time, there is shortage of technical skills also needed for economic growth.
- Secondary and tertiary sectors have failed to provide employment so people are still dependent on primary sector.

Q.12 In which field do you think India can build the maximum employment opportunity?

Ans. The field in which India can build the maximum employment is the service sector.

Only the tertiary or service sector can generate the maximum employment opportunity, for which the unemployed will have to be trained.

In primary sector there is no further scope because there is already disguised unemployment.

In secondary sector, small scale manufacturing is the most labour absorbing sector.

Q.13 Can you suggest some measures in the education system to mitigate the problem of the educated unemployed?

Ans. Some measures can be adopted in education system to solve the problem of educated unemployed people are

- System of education should be changed so as to provide skill based education so that students find appropriate jobs.
- Education about new services like biotechnology, information technology should be introduced to prepare students for employment in advanced technical skills.
- More opportunities should be made available in the Tertiary sector, where more educated unemployed people can find jobs.

Q.14 Can you imagine some village which initially had no job opportunities but later came up with many?

Ans. Rampur was a small village which initially depended on agriculture and on rainfall. Then electricity reached the village and people could irrigate their fields and could grow 2 to 3 crops in a year to get more work. Some people started small-scale industries which could be run by electricity and provide employment to people.

A school was established so that the population can become educated and as a result, they could seek employment in and outside the village. The village became prosperous and soon had better health, education, transport and job facilities.

Q.15 Which capital would you consider the best-land, labour, physical capital and human capital? Why?

Ans. Human capital is the most important capital, because all other types of capital can be utilised only by humans.

If humans do not develop and process other capital or resources and make them usable, they would remain undeveloped and unutilised, because on their own, they are useless and of no use to anybody.

If we develop human capital, then all other resources will automatically develop and lead to progress.

Human capital is the stock of skill and knowledge with proper education, training and medical care, this resource can be turned into an asset for the country.

If human capital is of high quality than it can greatly help in the progress of a country. Therefore, Japan has invested in its human capital.

REVIEW EXERCISE

Including Competency Based Questions

Part I

Multiple Choice Questions (MCQs)

1. Large population can be turned into a productive asset by
(a) increasing employment level
(b) stopping migration
(c) investing in human capital
(d) improving medical facilities

2. In which of the following conditions, virtuous cycle is created?
(a) Parents invest more heavily on the education of their children.
(b) Parents are more aware of their children's needs of nutrition and hygiene.
(c) Both (a) and (b)
(d) None of the above

3. Sprinkling crops with insecticide is an activity of which sector?
(a) Primary sector (b) Secondary sector
(c) Tertiary sector (d) Manufacturing sector

4. Which of the following is the primary activity?
(a) Fishing (b) Transport
(c) Education (d) None of these

5. Which of the following is an activity performed by tertiary sector?
(a) Working in farms (b) Transporting goods
(c) Manufacturing clothes (d) Studying in a college

6. Which of the following is a non-economic activity?
(a) Teacher teaching in school
(b) Farmer working in his own farm
(c) Tailor stitching his own clothes
(d) Restaurant owner cooking for customers

7. Seasonal unemployment is related to which regions?
(a) Urban regions (b) Rural regions
(c) Both (a) and (b) (d) None of these

8. The work force population includes people from
(a) 15 to 59 years (b) 14 to 50 years
(c) 21 to 50 years (d) 22 to 60 years

9. Market activities involve remuneration to anyone who performs. These include production of goods or services, including government service Competency Based

Which of the following statements accurately reflects the concept of market activities, as described in the above lines?
(a) Market activities are solely performed for pay or profit.
(b) Remuneration is not a factor in determining market activities.
(c) Any activity performed for charity is considered a market activity.
(d) Remuneration is essential only for certain types of market activities.

10. Geeta, mother of Vilas, earned an income by selling fish. Thus, women are paid for their work when they enter the labour market. Their earning like that of their male counterpart is determined on the basis of education and skill. A majority of women have meagre education and low skill information. Women are paid low compared to men. Most women work where job security is not there. Employment in this sector is characterised by irregular and low income.

Why are rural women employed in low paid jobs?
(a) They do not need to work in high-paid jobs.
(b) They lack in education or the necessary skill.
(c) They are not allowed by their families to do high paid jobs.
(d) They are not aware of the wage structure.

11. Sakal goes to a village school and learns the technique of kite making. His family gives him nutritious food. Vilas works with his mother in a shop to earn a living. He wants to go to school but never had the opportunity to do so.

Who has better prospects of earning when they grow up ?
(a) Vilas (b) Sakal
(c) Both (a) and (b) (d) Cannot be determined

12. Read the following data and select the appropriate option from the following.

Trends in Literacy Rates in-Post Independent India

Year	Male	Female
Literacy Rate of 2017	78%	70%
Literacy Rate of 2011	72%	64%

(**Source :** Census of India, Office Register General, India 2021)

How much percentage of boys is not literate in 2017?
(a) 22% (b) 31%
(c) 17% (d) 37%

13. Identify the type of unemployment with the help of following information.

- In this kind of unemployment people who are visibly employed are not actually employed.
- Such employment does not contribute to the output of an economy.
- It is usually associated with family employment or self-employed labour and not wage labour.

Options

(a) Educated unemployment (b) Seasonal unemployment
(c) Disguised unemployment (d) None of these

14. Arrange in sequence.

I. Formation of quality human capital
II. Providing computer technology skill
III. Investment in primary school
IV. Getting medical care during birth

Codes

(a) IV, III, II, I (b) III, I, IV, II
(c) III, IV, I, II (d) I, III, IV, III

15. In the context of unemployment in rural and urban areas, which of the following statements accurately describes the characteristics of seasonal unemployment?

I. Seasonal unemployment primarily affects people dependent on agriculture due to fluctuations in demand for labor during different months of the year.
II. Seasonal unemployment occurs when individuals with education find it challenging to secure employment in urban areas.
III. Seasonal unemployment is a widespread issue in urban areas, particularly during certain months of the year.
IV. Seasonal unemployment is more prevalent in rural areas during winter seasons.

Codes

(a) Only I (b) Only II (c) Only III (d) Only IV

16. Population is an asset for the economy rather than a liability. Population can be turned into a productive asset by **Competency Based**

I. Investment in healthcare and well-being.
II. Education and skill development.
III. Economic opportunities and entrepreneurship.
IV. Social and political participation.

Codes

(a) Only I (b) III and IV (c) I and II (d) All of these

Answers

1. (c)	2. (c)	3. (a)	4. (a)	5. (b)
6. (c)	7. (b)	8. (a)	9. (a)	10. (b)
11. (b)	12. (a)	13. (c)	14. (a)	15. (a)
16. (d)				

Match the Following

1.

	List I	List II
A.	Non-economic Activity	1. Construction of a building
B.	Primary Activity	2. Doctor treating patients
C.	Secondary Activity	3. Cooking for family
D.	Tertiary Activity	4. Fisherman catching fish

Codes

	A	B	C	D		A	B	C	D
(a)	4	2	1	3	(b)	3	4	1	2
(c)	2	3	4	1	(d)	1	4	3	2

Ans. (b)

Assertion-Reason

1. **Assertion** (A) Unemployment leads to wastage of manpower resources.

Reason (R) Increase in unemployment is an indicator of depressed economy.

Codes

(a) Both A and R are true and R is the correct explanation of A
(b) Both A and R are true, but R is not the correct explanation of A
(c) A is true, but R is false
(d) A is false, but R is true

2. Assertion (A) For many decades in India, a large population has been considered a liability rather than an asset.

Reason (R) Population becomes human capital when there is investment made in the form of education, training and medical care.

Codes

(a) Both A and R are true and R is the correct explanation of A
(b) Both A and R are true, but R is not the correct explanation of A
(c) A is true, but R is false
(d) A is false, but R is true

3. Assertion (A) Investment in human capital (through education, training, medical care) yields a return.

Reason (R) Due to historical and cultural reasons there is a division of labour between men and women in the family.

Codes

(a) Both A and R are true and R is the correct explanation of A
(b) Both A and R are true, but R is not the correct explanation of A
(c) A is true, but R is false
(d) A is false, but R is true

4. Assertion (A) Trade, transport, communication, banking, education, health, tourism, services, insurance, etc. are included in the tertiary sector.

Reason (R) The activities in this sector result in the production of goods and services.

Codes

(a) Both A and R are true and R is the correct explanation of A
(b) Both A and R are true, but R is not the correct explanation of A
(c) A is true, but R is false
(d) A is false, but R is true

5. Assertion (A) Seasonal unemployment happens when people are not able to find jobs during some months of the year.

Reason (R) People dependant upon manufacturing usually face seasonal unemployment.

Codes

(a) Both A and R are true and R is the correct explanation of A
(b) Both A and R are true, but R is not the correct explanation of A
(c) A is true, but R is false
(d) A is false, but R is true

Ans. 1. (a) Both A and R are true and R is the correct explanation of A

2. (b) Both A and R are true, but R is not the correct explanation of A

3. (b) Both A and R are true, but R is not the correct explanation of A

4. (c) A is true, but R is false

5. (c) A is true, but R is false

Case Based Question

1. Read the source given below and answer the questions that follow

A majority of women have meagre education and low skill formation. Women are paid low compared to men. Most women work where job security is not there. Various activities relating to legal protection is meagre. Employment in this sector is characterised by irregular and low income. In this sector there is an absence of basic facilities like maternity leave, childcare and other social security systems. However, women with high education and skill formation are paid at par with the men.

(i) What determines the pay equality between men and women, according to the passage?

(a) Educational background and skill formation
(b) Organised sector employment
(c) Administrative services
(d) Job preferences in teaching and medicine

(ii) According to the passage, what is a significant issue related to women's income in the workforce?

(a) Equal pay for equal work
(b) High income for all women
(c) Irregular and low income for many women
(d) Job security for all women

(iii) Which sector attracts women with high education and skill formation the most?

(a) Teaching and medicine
(b) Administrative services
(c) Scientific and technological jobs
(d) Organised sector jobs

(iv) What is highlighted as a trend among some women in terms of career choices?

(a) Preference for lower-paying jobs
(b) Avoidance of high levels of scientific and technological competence
(c) Pursuing jobs in the organised sector
(d) Entering administrative and other services requiring high competence

Ans (i) (a) Educational background and skill formation

(ii) (c) Irregular and low income for many women

(iii) (a) Teaching and medicine

(iv) (d) Entering administrative and other services requiring high competence

Part II

Very Short Answer Type Questions

1. What is human capital?

Ans. Investment made in the form of education and medical care to improve, the quality of population so that it becomes a great asset is called as human capital.

2. Why education has an important role in human capital formation?

Ans. Education broadens the knowledge of people and provides them training, thus in having an important role in human capital formation.

3. Which Asian country invested its major part of resources on people, especially in the field of education and health?

Ans. Japan is the Asian country which has invested heavily in human resources, especially in the field of education and health.

4. Navodaya Vidyalayas have been started for which kind of school children?

Ans. Navodaya Vidyalayas have been started for talented school children residing in rural areas.

5. *Sarva Shiksha Abhiyan* is meant to provide what kind of education? What was its impact?

Ans. *Sarva Shiksha Abhiyan* is meant to provide Elementary education (upto class VIII) to children in the age group of 6 to 14 years. It impacted on increased enrollment of girls reflects a shift, promoting gender equality and recognising education's importance for all.

6. What is the meaning of vocational education? State its one characteristic.

Ans. Vocational education means training for a specific vocation i.e. training for being employed in a particular job.

Characteristic It improves the competency level of the students.

7. What is Infant Mortality Rate?

Ans. Infant Mortality Rate (IMR) is the number of deaths of infants under one year of age per 1000 live births.

8. In terms of health, what do you mean by SC, PHC and CHC.

Ans. In terms of health SC means Sub Centre, PHC means Primary Health Centre and CHC means Community Health Centre.

9. Economists say unemployment figures are inadequate to capture the distress in India's labour market, which includes issues like underemployment, low participation of women in the labour force and youth unemployment.
Source : Economic Times

. (i) "Low participation of women in the labour force" refer to which type of situation? Competency Based

Ans. "Low participation of women in the labor force" refers to a situation where a relatively small percentage of women are actively engaged in the workforce, indicating challenges or barriers that limit women's involvement in economic activities and employment opportunities.

Short Answer Type Questions

1 Why is human resource superior to any other resource? Explain with the help of three arguments.

Ans. Human resource is considered to be the best resource because

- It is a way of referring to country's working people in terms of their existing productive skills and abilities.
- Population of a country helps to increase its country's Gross National Product by producing goods and services and even searching for new ones.
- When existing human resource is developed by becoming more educated and healthy, we call it human capital formation that adds to the productive power of country just like physical capital formation.

2. Describe the role of human capital in the production process. Name two investment that can improve the quality of human capital.

Ans. Role of human capital in the production process are as follows

- Human capital is the most important capital, because all other types of capital can be utilised only by humans.
- Humans are the ones who develop and process resources and use them to produce another goods and commodities. Without human capital these resources are of no use and even not consider as resources.
- If we develop human capital the production process and all other will automatically develop and lead to progress.

Investment on health and education can improve the quality of human capital, as these two help to raise the standard and quality of living of people, thus, activate the entire production process.

3. Distinguish between physical and human capital.

Ans. Differences between physical and human capital are as follows

Physical Capital	Human Capital
Physical capital includes the variety of inputs required at all stages of a production activity.	Human capital is the stock of competencies, knowledge, social and personality attributes, including creativity, embodied in the ability to perform labour so as to produce economic value.
This includes fixed capital in the form of machinery, land and building and working capital in the form of raw materials, cash in hand, etc.	It refers to the persons performing the economic activity like labourers, knowledgeable persons and others involved in the activity.

4. What does a 'virtuous cycle' created by the educated parents mean? Explain.

Ans. A 'virtuous cycle' is created by the educated parents when they invest heavily on the education and skill training of their children because these children realise the importance of education.

As a result, the child gets good employment opportunities in future because of his/her good education. It is the outcome of a good investment spend on his/her by his/her parents. These children are also aware about the value of proper nutrition and hygiene. Thus, this is how a virtuous cycle is created.

5. How have the various activities been classified into sectors? Give one example from each sector.

Ans. Various activities classified into three sectors that are

(i) **Primary sector** These activities harvest or extract natural products from the Earth; it involves production of raw materials and food products. e.g. agriculture, dairy farming, mining, etc.

(ii) **Secondary sector** These activities involve manufacturing of finished goods. e.g. construction.

(iii) **Tertiary sector** All activities which support the Primary and Secondary sectors with services belong to this sector. e.g. transportation, banking, trade etc.

6. How are children of educated parents different from those of uneducated parents? Give three points of difference.

Ans. The children of educated parents are different from those of uneducated parents in the following ways

Children of educated parents	Children of uneducated parents
These parents realise the importance of education. So, they invest more heavily on education of their children.	Uneducated parents often do not realise the importance of education. They do not spend heavily on the education of their children.
These children are conscious of proper nutrition and hygiene. So, children of educated parents tend to be in proper health.	Health status of these children is not so good because uneducated parents do not take care of their health properly.
These children are better educated and healthy. So, they are highly productive and yield a higher return in future.	These children lack in better education and health, so they are not expected to yield a high return in future.

7. Satpal is a farmer who owns a land. He is also an educated person. He sent his both children (a daughter and a son) to a city college for higher studies. For this purpose, he invests more heavily on his children's education.

Why do educated parents like Satpal invest more heavily on their children's education? Give three reasons. Competency Based

Ans. Educated parents invest more heavily on their children's education because

(i) A child too with investment made on his/her education can yield a higher return in future in the form of higher earning and greater contribution to society.

(ii) Educated parents realise the importance of education.

(iii) With proper education a child can become an assest rather than a liability for a country's economy.

8. Distinguish between market and non-market activities with three points of distinction.

or **Explain market and non-market activities. Under which activity would you classify government services?**

Ans. Two types of economic activities and differences between them are as follows

Market activities	Non-market activities
Market activities involve remuneration to the person who performs an activity for pay or profit.	These economic activities involve production for self-consumption.
These are socially useful activities which includes the production and consumption of goods.	They are not done for pay or profit.
For example, teacher teaches in a school, man works in bank, workers in industries or factories, etc.	For example, subsistence farming, processing of primary products, etc.

Government services will be classified under market activities.

9. Why are rural women employed on very low wages?

Ans. It is true that rural women are employed on very low wages because

- In the patriarchal society, especially in rural areas, parents do not invest much on their daughters. They do not get enough opportunity to do jobs.
- In rural areas, girls are not given proper education or skill training for doing jobs.
- Girls are involved more in household duties and their is a traditional belief that they should not go out of home to work.

10. On what factors does the quality of population depend?

or **How does education enhance the quality of population? Explain.**

or **Analyse the role of education in the formation of human capital.**

Ans. The quality of population depends upon the literacy rate, health of a person, life expectancy and skill formation acquired by the people of the country.

Education is the most important factor that ultimately decides the quality of population because of following reasons

(i) Better educated people earn higher incomes because of higher productivity of the more educated or the better trained persons. This contributes to growth of society.

(ii) The quality of the population ultimately decides the growth rate of the country, leading to the growth of society.

(iii) Education enhances the National Income, cultural richness and increases the efficiency of governance, thus contributing to growth of society.

11. What is the purpose of *Sarva Shiksha Abhiyan*? What are its goals?

Ans. The basic aim of Sarva Shiksha Abhiyan is providing elementary education to all children of age group 6 to 14 years. Additionally, it is an effort to universalise elementary education by community ownership of the school system. It was started in response to the demand for quality basic education all over the country.

The SSA programme is also an attempt to provide an opportunity for improving human capabilities of all children through provision of community owned quality education in a mission mode. The Mid-day Meal scheme is a part of it to reduce the dropout rate of children from schools.

12. Why does unemployment have a detrimental effect on the overall growth of an economy?

Ans. Unemployment has a detrimental effect on the overall growth of an economy due to the following reasons

- Unemployment tends to increase economic overload, i.e. the dependence of the unemployed persons on the people who are working goes up.
- Unemployment adversely affects the quality of life of people, as they have to live at subsistence level, which leads to poor health and even increase in school dropouts.
- If unemployment continues, it wastes resources which can be gainfully employed.
- Unemployment hampers overall economic growth by reducing the productive capacity of the economy. Idle human resources mean a lower output of goods and services.

13. 'Employment structure is characterised by self-employment in the primary sector'. Explain this statement.

Ans. Employment structure is characterised by self-employment in the primary sector. This statement refers to the agricultural sector, where most of the people are small farmers with land holdings of less than two hectares.

They are self-employed because the whole family works on the land, though not all are really needed. The entire family shares what has been produced. This concept of sharing of work in the field and sharing the produce raised reduces the hardship of unemployment in rural areas.

14. Discuss the most likely impact of unemployment. Build the answer around these points.

- **Social consequences**
- **Income inequality**
- **Economic slowdown**

Ans The most likely impacts of unemployment are

- Unemployment can have severe social consequences, including increased crime rates, mental health issues, and social unrest. It can erode the social fabric of a community.
- Unemployment contributes to income inequality as those without jobs face financial difficulties, while those employed may enjoy higher incomes. This division can lead to social unrest and tensions.

Long Answer Type Questions

1. How can large population be turned into a productive asset? Explain.

Ans. People are the important resource of a country. If a country invests more on its peoples' welfare they can be turned into a productive asset.

The following points explain this

- If a nation provides better education and training then this investment will develop more skilled and innovative workforce. Thus, this can contribute in the growth of the economy.
- Investment in the form of education will ensure good employment opportunities to the people who can not only raise their standard of living through earnings but also will contribute to the National Income of the country.
- Investment on healthcare facilities of the population will allow people to avail these facilities and can lead to healthy environment for them to flourish and develop.
- The government should create jobs in different sectors of economy so that, unemployment ratio may go down.
- The government should invest in the rural and backward regions and in modernisation of agriculture, so as to bridge urban-rural divide.

Through this investment, the population of rural and backward areas can be transformed into an asset.

2. Describe five unfavourable effects of population growth in a country like India.

Ans. Five unfavourable effects of population growth in a country like India are

(i) **Illiteracy** Excessive population growth leads to less education opportunities available for students due to the limited educational resources available.

(ii) **Poverty** As family size becomes larger, poorer families go deeper into poverty, as the family income remains the same.

(iii) **Unemployment** Increase in population causes increase in unemployment, as more people need to be employed compared to the jobs available.

(iv) **Strain on Natural Resources** Population growth leads to excessive strain on the natural resources available like fuel, vegetation, water, minerals etc.

(v) **Food Shortage** High population causes higher pressure on agriculture to produce more, besides people not being able to get adequate supply of food.

3. Explain the initiatives taken by the government to improve elementary education in India.

Ans. The initiatives taken by the government to improve elementary education in India are

- Sarva Shiksha Abhiyan aims at the universalisation of elementary education in a time-bound manner, making it free to children between the ages of 6 and 14 years, with a special emphasis on girls' education. It has been embodied as a right under the Right to Education Act.
- Mid-day Meal scheme has been implemented to encourage attendance and retention of children and improve their nutritional status.
- Navodaya Vidyalayas (i.e. model schools) have been opened in each district as ideal schools, whose facilities and methods can be replicated by other schools.
- Vocational streams have been developed to enable a larger number of high school students to find jobs in occupations related to knowledge and skills.
- Bridge courses and back-to-school camps have been initiated to increase the enrollment in elementary education.

4. "Human resource is an indispensable factor of production." Elucidate.

Ans. Human resource is the term used for people who constitute the workforce for an organisation or country through their existing productive skill and abilities.

Human resource is an indispensable factor of every economic activity due to the following reasons

- Every productive activity needs land, labour, physical capital and human capital as its factors of production.
- No production activity is possible without human factors. It is humans that turn other resources useful by their wisdom and endeavours.
- Human resource is not only the essential factor of production, but it also activates other factors of production.
- It is the human resource that operates every sector of economy whether it is primary sector like agriculture, secondary sector like automobile manufacturing or tertiary sector like financial services. No resource on the Earth can be useful or activated without human endeavour.

5. What is unemployment? Name two types of unemployment prevailing in India. What are the disadvantages of unemployment?

Ans. Unemployment is the situation when people who are willing to work at the existing wages cannot find jobs.

Two types of unemployment found in India are

(i) **Seasonal Unemployment** It happens when people are not able to find jobs during some months of the year. People dependent upon agriculture usually face this kind of unemployment.

(ii) **Disguised Unemployment** In this kind of unemployment people who are visibly employed are not actually employed. This occurs when all the members of a family of a small farmer are working in the fields, but all may not be required.

Similar is the case of family-owned shops, where all family members may be working at the shop, but all are not required. Actually they are working at less than full productivity.

Disadvantages of unemployment are

- It is a wastage of manpower resource.
- It increases the economic overload.
- It tends to increase the number of dependent population.
- Increase in unemployment is an indicator of a depressed economy.

6. Explain any five effects of unemployment in India.

Ans. Five effects of unemployment in India are

(i) **Loss of Human Resources** The problem of unemployment causes loss of human resources. Labourers spend their maximum time in search of employment.

(ii) **Increase in Poverty** Unemployment deprives a man of all sources of income. As a result, he grows poor. Therefore, unemployment generates poverty.

(iii) **Social Problems** Unemployment breeds many social problems including dishonesty, gambling, bribery, theft etc. As a result of unemployment, social security is jeopardised.

(iv) **Political Instability** Unemployment gives birth to political instability in the country. Unemployed persons lose all faith in democratic values and peaceful means.

(v) **Exploitation of Labour** In the state of unemployment, labourers are exploited to the maximum possible extent. Those labourers who get work have to work under adverse conditions and low wages.

7. 'Illiterate and unhealthy population are a liability for the economy'. Justify the statement with suitable examples.

Ans. The illiterate and unhealthy population are a liability for economy due to the following reasons

- Illiterate and unhealthy people are unable to use land and capital efficiently, thus leading to less earnings.
- Illiterate people are generally unsuccessful in life because they are dependent on literate people for many activities. Their employment potential is low, as they can only be used for menial jobs, thus earning much less than literate people.

- An unhealthy person has less productivity than a normal person, thus earning less and becoming a liability for the economy. More has to be spent on his medical care, thus utilising more scarce resources.
- Such people become a liability by making the country poorer and retard the development of the nation.

8. The employment structure is characterised by self-employment in the primary sector. The whole family contributes in the field even though not everybody is really needed. So there is disguised unemployment in the agriculture sector. Justify the statements with relevant points. Competency Based

Ans The employment structure in primary sector is characterised by self-employment and disguised unemployment. The statement can be justified with the following relevant points

- Families work for themselves in the primary sector in many agricultural situations, especially when it comes to subsistence farming. This involves working on their own land or family-owned farms.
- Disguised unemployment often occurs when there are limited opportunities for alternative employment in non-agricultural sectors. As a result, surplus labor remains in the agricultural sector, even when not fully utilised.
- Disguised unemployment in agriculture may indicate a lack of diversification in the rural economy.
- The involvement of more labor than required in agriculture can lead to low productivity and efficiency.
- The entire family engages in farming, even when not everyone is needed, leading to inefficiencies as some contribute labor to agricultural tasks beyond what is strictly required.

Case Based Questions

1. Read the sources given below and answer the questions that follow

Source A Sarva Shiksha Abhiyan

Sarva Shiksha Abhiyan is a significant step towards providing elementary education to all children in the age group of 6-14 years by 2010. It is a time-bound initiative of the Central government, in partnership with the states, the local government and the community for achieving the goal of universalisation of elementary education. Along with it, bridge courses and back to school camps have been initiated to increase the enrolment in elementary education. Mid-day Meal scheme has been implemented to encourage attendance and retention of children and improve their nutritional status.

(i) What is the main aim of Sarva Shiksha Abhiyan?

Source B Education

Education enhances the national income, cultural richness and increases the efficiency of governance. There is a provision made for providing universal access, retention of quality in elementary education with a special emphasis on girls. There is also an establishement of pace setting of schools like Navodaya Vidhyalya in each district. Vocational streams have been developed to equip large number of high school students with occupations related to knowledge and skills.

The plan outlay an education has increased from ₹ 151 crore in the first plan to ₹ 3766.90 crore in the eleventh plan.

(ii) Why have vocational streams been developed?

Source C Health

The health of a person helps him to realise his/her potential and the ability to fight illness. He/she will not be able to maximise his/her output to the overall growth of the organisation. Health is an indispensable basis for realising one's well being.

Henceforth, improvement in the health status of the population has been the priority of the country. Our national policy, too, aims at improving the accessibility of healthcare, family welfare and nutritional service with a special focus on the underprivileged segment of the population.

(iii) Why health status of the population has been the priority of a country?

Ans. (i) The main aim of Sarva Shiksha Abhiyan is to achieve the goals of universalisation of elementary education.

(ii) Vocational streams have been developed to equip large number of high school students with occupations related to knowledge and skills.

(iii) Health status of the population has been the priority of a country because healthy citizens are the basic factors of production. The good health, also increases the efficiency of the worker. Hence, it is required for overall development of people.

2. Read the source given below and answer the questions that follow

In case of India we have unemployment in rural and urban areas. However, the nature of unemployment differs in rural and urban areas. In case of rural areas, there is seasonal and disguised unemployment. Urban areas have mostly educated unemployment. Unemployment leads to wastage of manpower resource. People who are an asset for the economy turn into a liability. There is a feeling of hopelessness and despair among the youth. People do not have enough money to support their family. Inability of educated people who are willing to work to find gainful employment implies a great social waste. It tends to increase economic overload. Increase in unemployment is an indicator of a depressed economy. It also wastes the resource, which could have been gainfully employed.

(i) How does unemployment problem differ in rural areas?

(ii) What are the major factors responsible for unemployment in India?

(iii) In what extent do you think that people can become liability? How can this condition be improved?

Ans. (i) In rural areas, there is seasonal and disguised unemployment, whereas urban areas have educated unemployment.

(ii) The major factors responsible for unemployment in India are as follows

- There is rapid growth of population.
- People are more dependent on agriculture.
- There is slow pace of infrastructure growth.
- Due to short age of capital, industrialisation process is very slow.

(iii) People can become liability for an economy/ company when

- There is not enough job opportunities for people.
- People do not have enough money to support their family.
- More people are dependent on a person who is working.

This type of condition can be improved by

- providing enough job opportunities to people.
- providing good wages to poeple to support their family.
- making people an asset for the economy by using their skills in a proper way.

ASSESSMENT EXERCISE

Multiple Choice Questions (MCQs)

1. Which of the following investments in human resources should be done for better economic growth?

(a) Modern technology (b) Healthcare and education
(c) Food and drink (d) Education and transportation

2. Sarva Shiksha Abhiyan is meant to provide .... education.

(a) primary (b) secondary (c) elementary (d) nursery

3. Primary sector activities will include which of the following?

(a) Distribution of milk to urban consumers
(b) Producing cars in a factory
(c) A lawyer fighting a case in a court
(d) Sprinkling insecticides over crops

4. Which of the following statements is/are associated with unemployment?

(a) It has a detrimental impact on the overall growth of an economy.
(b) It does not lead to wastage of manpower resources.
(c) It tends to increase economic overload.
(d) Both (a) and (c)

Subjective Questions (VSA, SA & LA)

1. In which category will you classify the activity of 'bribe-taking'?

2. Services rendered by housewives can be included in which of the categories of income?

3. What is the literacy rate of India as per the Census of 2011?

4. Which state of India has the highest literacy rate?

5. Explain the investments required in human beings to make them useful resources.

6. Human resource is superior to cash in hand. Give three reasons to justify this statement.

7. Explain any three ways of investment in human resource that can give high returns in future.

8. 'Health is the priority of the country'. Justify the statement giving three arguments.

9. People are the greatest resource that a country has. Explain.

10. What do you understand by human capital formation? Explain the initiatives of the Indian Government to enhance health and education facilities, two in each area.

Poverty as a Challenge

CHAPTER 3

Poverty is a condition in which a person lacks the financial resources and essential things to enjoy minimum standards of life. It is the most difficult challenge faced by independent India.

In 2011-12, roughly 270 million (or 27 crore) people in India live in poverty. This means India has the largest single concentration of the poor in the world.

1.1 Two Cases of Poverty

The two cases given below show the many dimensions of poverty, including lack of proper food, shelter, healthcare, education as well as clean water and sanitation. They also show lack of a regular means of livelihood.

(i) **Urban Case** Ram Saran is a daily wage labourer in a flour mill near Ranchi in Jharkhand. He earns around ₹ 1,500 per month when he finds employment. He supports his family of 6 persons, besides sending some money to his old parents.

His wife Santa Devi works as a part time maid and earn₹ 800. His elder son also works in a tea shop and earns ₹ 300. None of his 4 children (aged between 12 years to 6 months) go to school.

The family lives in a one-room rented house on the outer areas of the city. The younger children of house are undernourished. They have two pairs of clothes and footwear and no access to healthcare.

(ii) **Rural Case** Lakha Singh belongs to a small village near Meerut in Uttar Pradesh. His family does not own any land, so they do odd jobs for big farmers, and earns ₹ 50 per day. Often, they get some foodgrain or other item instead of cash.

Lakha Singh is not literate and his family of 8 people lives in a *kuchha* hut near the edge of the village. They have no access to healthcare, cannot afford new clothes or even soap or oil.

These two typical cases illustrate many dimensions of poverty as follows

- Poverty means hunger and lack of shelter.
- It is a situation in which parents are not able to send their children to school or where sick people cannot afford treatment.
- Poverty also means lack of clean water and sanitation facilities.
- It also means lack of a regular job at a minimum decent level.
- It means to living with a sense of helplessness.

Poor people are in a situation in which they are ill-treated at almost every place in farms, factories, government offices, hospitals, railway stations etc.

Mahatma Gandhi always insisted that India would be truly independent only when the poorest of the country become free of human suffering.

Poverty According to Social Scientists

Social scientists analyse poverty from many indicators besides levels of income and consumption. These indicators are

- Illiteracy level
- Lack of general resistance due to malnutrition
- Lack of access to healthcare
- Lack of job opportunities
- Lack of access to sanitation and safe drinking water, etc.

Social Exclusion

According to this concept, poverty must be seen as situation where the poor, who are living in a poor surrounding should live with other poor people. They are excluded from enjoying social equality in better surroundings.

Social exclusion can be both a cause as well as a result of poverty. In simple terms, it's a process through which certain individuals or groups are excluded from the benefits and opportunities that others, often considered more privileged, get to enjoy.

In India, caste system is based on social exclusion. People belonging to certain caste were prevented from enjoying equal facilities, benefits and opportunities. This caused more damage than the lower income.

Vulnerability

It is a measure, which describes the greater probability of certain communities or individuals of becoming or remaining poor in the coming time.

For example, members of a backward caste or individuals like widow or physically handicapped person.

It is determined by various options available to different communities for finding an alternative living in terms of assets, education, job, health, etc.

It is also analysed by the ability of these communities to face various risks like natural disasters (Earthquakes, Tsunami), terrorism, etc.

Poverty Line

Poverty line is a method used to measure poverty in a country. It is based on the income or consumption levels.

A person will be considered poor if his income or consumption level is below 'a minimum level' which is needed to fulfill his basic needs.

Poverty line may vary with time and place as what is necessary to satisfy the basic needs is different at different times and in different countries.

In India, a minimum level of food requirement (as determined by its calorific value), clothing, footwear, fuel, lighting, educational and medical requirements, etc are determined for estimating the poverty line.

The present formula for food requirement while estimating the poverty line is based on the desired calorie requirement[1]. Food items, such as cereals, pulses, vegetables, milk, oil, sugar, etc together form calorie needs. The calorie needs are different for every person depending on age, sex and the type of work he does.

In India, the calorie requirement is **2400 calories** per person per day in **rural areas** and **2100 calories** per person per day in **urban areas.**

Due to the increased physical activity undertaken by individuals in rural areas, the calories required by the people living in rural areas are higher than those in urban areas.

The money required for buying these calorie requirements in terms of food grains and other items is revised periodically based on rise in prices of these goods.

In the year 2011-12, the poverty line for a person was fixed at ₹ 816 per month for rural areas and ₹ 1000 for urban areas.

Despite less calorie requirement,the higher amount for urban areas has been fixed because of high prices of many essential products.

In this way, in 2011-12, a family of five members earning **less than ₹4,080** per month in **rural areas** and **₹ 5000 per month** in **urban areas** will be considered as lying below poverty line.

- Sample Surveys for determining poverty line in India are carried out by the **National Sample Survey Organisation** (NSSO).
- For making comparison between developing countries many international organisations like the **World Bank** use a uniform standard method. As per this method, the poverty line is level of minimum availability of the equivalent of $1.90 per person per day.

Try These

1. **Identify the condition in which a person lacks the financial resources.**
2. **Surveys for determining the poverty line in India are carried out by which organisation?**
3. **Name any two states which have seen a significant decline in poverty.**
4. **Name any one indicator of poverty.**
5. **What is the calorie requirement per person per day in urban areas?**

1.2 Poverty Estimation in India

There is decline in poverty ratios in India from about 45% in 1993-94 to 37.2% in 2004-05.

The proportion of people below poverty line further came down to about 22% in 2011-12. If the trend continues, people below poverty line may come down to less than 20% in the next few years.

The percentage of people living under poverty, declined in the earlier two decades (1973-1993).

The number of poor declined from 407 million in 2004-05 to 270 million in 2011-12.

An average annual decline of 2.2 percentage was recorded during 2004-05 to 2011-12.

Vulnerable Groups

The proportion of people below poverty line among social groups and economic categories varies widely in India.

1 **Calorie Requirement** It is the quantity of food that is capable of producing the required amount of energy needed by a normal person.

Social groups which are more vulnerable to poverty are **Scheduled Castes** (SCs) and **Scheduled Tribes** (STs).

Economic groups which are more vulnerable to poverty are **rural agricultural labour households** and the **urban casual labour households.**

However, some recent studies have shown that all these groups except the Scheduled Tribes group, have witnessed a decline in poverty in the 1990s.

The average for people having income below poverty line for all groups in India is 22 out of 100. However, 43 out of 100 people belonging to Scheduled Tribes are not able to meet their basic needs.

Similarly, 34% of casual workers in urban areas are below poverty line. About 34% of casual labour farm (in rural areas) and 29% of Scheduled Castes are also poor.

There is a great difference in incomes among the members within the poor families. It is observed that female infants, women and elderly members in the poor families are not given equal access to resources available to the family.

Inter-State Disparities

The proportion of poor people is not the same in every state.

While overall poverty has been decreasing at the state level since the early seventies, the success in reducing poverty differs from one state to another.

In 2011-12 estimates, all India HCR (**Head Count Ratio**[2]) was 21.9%. The states like Madhya Pradesh, Assam, Uttar Pradesh, Bihar and Odisha had above all India poverty level.

Bihar and Odisha continue to be the two poorest states with poverty ratios of 33.7% and 32.6%, respectively. Both rural and urban poverty are high in Odisha, Madhya Pradesh, Bihar and Uttar Pradesh.

In states like Kerala, Maharashtra, Andhra Pradesh, Tamil Nadu, Gujarat and West Bengal, there is a significant decline in poverty.

The states which are successful in reducing poverty have adopted different methods.

Some examples are

- Punjab and Haryana have traditionally succeeded in reducing poverty with the help of high agricultural growth rates.
- Kerala has focused more on human resource development.
- In West Bengal, land reform measures have helped in reducing poverty.
- In Andhra Pradesh and Tamil Nadu, **'Public Distribution System**[3] of food grains could have been responsible for reducing poverty.

Global Poverty Scenario

The proportion of people living under poverty in different countries is defined by the World Bank as living on less than $ 2.15 per day. Extreme economic poverty has reduced in the world from 16.27% in 2010 to 9.05% in 2019 (as per the **World Bank**[4]) but still there are vast regional differences. These are stated below

- In South-East Asian countries and China, there is decline in poverty due to rapid **economic growth**[5] and massive investments in human resource development.
- In China, the number of poors has come down from 2.1% in 2014 to 1.2% in 2015 to 0.1% in 2020.
- In the South Asian countries like (India, Pakistan, Sri Lanka, Nepal, Bangladesh and Bhutan), the decline has also been rapid from 12.8% in 2017 to 10.9% in 2021. With decline in the percentage of the poor, the number of poor has also declined significantly from 233 million in 2017 to 207 million in 2021.
- In Sub-Saharan Africa, poverty has declined from 36.6% in 2017 to 35.4% in 2019.
- In Latin America, the ratio of poverty has increased from 4.4% in 2017 to 4.6% in 2021.
- Poverty has also resurfaced at 3% in 2000 in some of former socialist countries like Russia.
- It is seen that poverty has also resurfaced (appear again) in some of the former socialist countries like Russia, where officially it was non-existent earlier.
- The new **Sustainable Development goals**[6] of the United Nations, proposes ending all types of poverty by 2030.

---

2 **Head Count Ratio** It is the proportion of a population that lives below the poverty line.

3 **Public Distribution System** It means distribution of essential commodities like wheat, rice, sugar and kerosene to larger section of the society, mostly vulnerable people, through a network of Fair Price Shops on a recurring basis.

4 **World Bank** It is an international organisation dedicated to providing financing, advice and research to developing nations to aid their economic advancement.

5 **Economic Growth** It is a term which defines an increase in real output of a country.

6 **Sustainable Development Goals** The sustainable development goals are set of 17 global objectives established by United Nations in 2015..

Causes of Poverty

There were various causes for widespread of poverty in India. Some of them are as follows

- During the British Colonial period, there was a low level of economic development. Their policies ruined traditional handicrafts and discouraged industrial development, reducing job opportunities and income growth.
- The low level of economic development persisted until 1980s and was accompanied by population increase. These two factors made the growth rate of per capita income very low.
- The failure to both promote economic growth and implement population control contributed to the ongoing cycle of poverty.
- The Green Revolution improved opportunities in agriculture but only in certain areas of the country.
- The growth in population increased the number of job seekers which further led to poverty.
- Socio-cultural (i.e. traditions) and economic factors lead to extra expenditure, which ultimately increases poverty. As to fulfil social obligations on ceremonies, even many poor people spends a lots of money.
- There is unequal distribution of land and other resources, that is why there are large income inequalities.
- Land reforms have not been properly implemented and lack of adequate land resources is also a reason for many people to be poor.
- Small farmers borrow money for seeds, fertilisers and pesticides, etc and later on fail to pay which results in **debt trap**. This high level of indebtedness is both the cause and effect of poverty.

Anti-Poverty Measures

Removal of poverty has been one of the major objectives of Indian developmental strategy. The current anti-poverty strategy of the government is based on following two objectives

(i) Promotion of Economic Growth

Over a period of 30 years during early eighties, there were little per capita income growth and not much reduction in poverty.

The higher growth rates have helped significantly in the reduction of poverty.

There is strong linkage between economic growth and poverty reduction. Economic growth widens (increase in scope/area) opportunities and provides the resources needed to invest in human development.

High economic growth also encourages people to send their children (including the girl child) to school with hope of better economic returns from investing in education.

However, the poor may not take direct advantage of economic growth. Due to lack of growth in agricultural sector, large number of people remain poor in rural areas.

(ii) Targeted Anti-Poverty Programmes

Government has introduced following anti-poverty programmes

Prime Minister Rozgar Yojana (PMRY) It was launched in 1993. The aim of the programme is to create self-employment opportunities for educated unemployed youth in rural areas and small towns. They are helped in setting up small business and industries.

Rural Employment Generation Programme (REGP) It was launched in 1995. The aim of the programme is to create self-employment opportunities in rural areas and small towns. A target for creating 25 lakh new jobs has been set for the programme under the Tenth Five Year plan.

Swarnajayanti Gram Swarozgar Yojana (SGSY) It was launched in 1999. The programme aims at bringing the assisted poor families above the poverty line by organising them into Self Help Groups, through a mix of bank credit and government subsidy.

Pradhan Mantri Gramodaya Yojana (PMGY) It was launched in 2000. Under this scheme, additional central assistance is given to states for basic services such as primary health, primary education, rural shelter, rural drinking water and rural electrification.

Mahatma Gandhi National Rural Employment Guarantee Act (MGNREGA) It was launched in 2005. It aims to provide 100 days of wage employment to every household to ensure livelihood security in rural areas.

It also aimed at sustainable development to address the cause of drought, deforestation and soil erosion. One-third of the proposed jobs under MGNREGA have been reserved for women. In this scheme, the share of SC, ST and Women are 23%, 17% and 53%, respectively.

The results of these programmes have been mixed due to lack of proper implementation and improper targeting. Also, some schemes overlap others.

Thus, the benefits of these schemes are not fully reaching the deserving poor. So, now the government is emphasising more on proper monitoring of all these programmes.

The Challenges Ahead

Poverty reduction is still a major challenge in India, due to the wide differences between rural and urban areas and among different states.

The official definition of poverty only captures a limited aspect of what poverty really means to people. It focuses on a 'minimum' subsistence level of living rather than a 'reasonable' standard of living.

Further, poverty should include not only the matter of adequate amount of food, but other factors like education, healthcare, shelter, job security, gender equality, dignity and so on. They give us the concept of human poverty. Poverty reduction is expected to be lower in next decade. In addition to anti-poverty measures government require to focus on the following to reduce poverty.

- To provide healthcare, education and job security for all.
- To achieve gender equality and dignity for the poor.

Try These

1. **Rural agricultural labour household comes under which vulnerable group?**
2. **Name any one social group which is vulnerable to poverty.**
3. **What does PMRY stand for?**
4. **When was MGNREGA launched?**
5. **In which five year plan a target of creating 25 lakhs new jobs was set under REGP?**

Mind Map

POVERTY AS A CHALLENGE

Poverty According to Social Scientists

Social Indicators of Poverty
- Illiteracy level
- Lack of general resistance due to malnutrition
- Lack of access to healthcare
- Lack of job opportunities
- Lack of access to sanitation and safe drinking water

Social Exclusion
- Poverty must be seen in terms of the poor who are living in a poor surrounding with poor people.
- They are excluded from enjoying social equality of wealthy people in better surroundings.

Vulnerability
- It describes the greater probability of certain communities or individuals of becoming or remaining poor in the coming time.
- It is determined by the options available to different communities for finding an alternative living in terms of assets, education, health and job opportunities.

Poverty Line
- A method used to measure poverty in a country based on the income or consumption levels but now, it is based on calorie requirement.
- In India, the calorie requirement is 2400 calories per person per day in rural areas and 2100 calories per person per day in urban areas.

Vulnerable Groups
- The group which faces greater risk at the time of natural calamity are called vulnerable groups.
- Social Groups which are more vulnerable to poverty are SCs and STs.
- Economic groups which are more vulnerable to poverty are Rural Agricultural Labour Households and Urban Casual Labour Households.
- The average for people below Poverty line for all groups in India is 22 out of 100.

Anti-Poverty Measures
- Prime Minister Rozgar Yojana (1993)
- Rural Employment Generation Programme (1995)
- Pradhan Mantri Gramodaya Yojana (2000)
- Mahatma Gandhi National Rural Employment Guarantee Act (2005)

Poverty Estimation in India
- There is decline in poverty ratios in India from about 45% in 1993-94 to 37.2% in 2004-05.
- An average annual decline of 2.2% was recorded during 2004-05 to 2011-12.

Global Poverty Scenario
- In China, the number of poor has come down from 2.1% in 2014 to 1.2% in 2015 to 0.1% in 2020.
- In Sub-Saharan Africa, poverty has declined from 36.6% in 2017 to 35.4% in 2019.
- In Latin America, the ratio of poverty has increased from 4.4% in 2017 to 4.6% in 2021.

Inter-State Disparities
- The states like Madhya Pradesh, Assam, Uttar Pradesh, Bihar and Odisha have above all India poverty level.
- Bihar and Odisha continue to be the two poorest states with poverty ratios of 33.7% and 32.6% respectively (2011).

Causes of Poverty
- The growth in population increased the number of job seekers which led to poverty.
- There are large income inequalities due to unequal distribution of land and other resources.
- Land reforms have not been properly implemented and lack of adequate land resource is a reason for many people to be poor.
- Small farmers borrow money for seeds, fertilisers, etc, and later on fail to pay, which results in debt trap.

NCERT FOLDER

Covering Intext Questions and Exercises of NCERT

INTEXT QUESTIONS

Q.1 Study the given cases of poverty and discuss the following issues related to poverty.

Urban Case

Thirty-three years old Ram Saran works as a daily-wage labourer in a wheat flour mill near Ranchi in Jharkhand. He manages to earn around ₹ 1,500 a month when he finds employment, which is not often. The money is not enough to sustain his family of six– that includes his wife and 4 children aged between 12 years to 6 months.

He has to send money home to his old parents who live in a village near Ramgarh. His father a landless labourer, depends on Ram Saran and his brother who lives in Hazaribagh, for sustenance.

Ram Saran lives in a one-room rented house in a crowded basti in the outskirts of the city.

It's a temporary shack built of bricks and clay tiles. His wife Santa Devi, works as a part time maid in a few houses and manages to earn another ₹ 800. They manage a meagre meal of dal and rice twice a day, but there's never enough for all of them.

His elder son works as a helper in a tea shop to supplement the family income and earns another ₹ 300, while his 10-year-old daughter takes care of the younger siblings.

None of the children go to school. They have only two pairs of hand-me-down clothes each. New ones are bought only when the old clothes become unwearable. Shoes are a luxury. The younger kids are undernourished. They have no access to healthcare when they fall ill.

Rural Case

Lakha Singh belongs to a small village near Meerut in Uttar Pradesh. His family doesn't own any land, so they do odd jobs for the big farmers. Work is erratic and so is income.

At times, they get paid ₹ 50 for a hard day's work. But often it's in kind like a few kilograms of wheat or dal or even vegetables for toiling in the farm through the day.

The family of eight cannot always manage two square meals a day. Lakha lives in a kuchha hut on the outskirts of the village. The women of the family spend the day chopping fodder and collecting firewood in the fields.

His father a TB patient, passed away 2 years ago due to lack of medication. His mother now suffers from the same disease and life is slowly ebbing away. Although, the village has a primary school.

Lakha never went there. He had to start earning when he was 10 years old. New clothes happen once in a few years. Even soap and oil are a luxury for the family.

Issues related to poverty

(a) Landlessness (b) Unemployment
(c) Size of families (d) Illiteracy
(e) Poor health/malnutrition (f) Child labour
(g) Helplessness

Ans. (a) **Landlessness** Landless labourers in the villages are generally poor. They earn very low wages. They are also subject to seasonal unemployment, when they have to do odd jobs at very low income.

(b) **Unemployment** In agriculture sector a person couldn't get permanent employment for the entire year. During lean season (lacking season), they become unemployed. Thus, couldn't earn any income, which may lead to poverty.

(c) **Size of families** When the number of persons in a family increases, the incomes of the family becomes insufficient to provide them with the essentials for proper living. This ultimately leads to poverty.

(d) **Illiteracy** Due to poverty, the parents are not able to send their children to school. When these children become adults and enter the job market, they are unable to find well-paying jobs, resulting again in poverty. Thus, illiteracy and poverty depend on each other.

(e) **Poor health/malnutrition** Poverty causes malnutrition and poor health, as the poor people cannot afford adequate amounts of nutritious food or proper medical services.

(f) **Child labour** Poverty forces the parents to make their children work, although there is a law against child labour. This makes the children drop out from school, resulting in their not getting well-paying jobs when they grow up.

(g) **Helplessness** Due to poverty, the poor people become helpless and are willing to do any work for a low income. This leads them further into poverty.

Q.2 Why do different countries use different poverty lines?

Ans. The different countries use different poverty lines because

- The calorie requirement of different human races is different depending on their physical condition and dietary habits. Those races which have greater height and built require higher calories.
- The per capita income in different countries is also different i.e. per capita income is higher in developed countries as compared to developing countries.
- The standard of living of Western countries is higher than that of developing countries.
- The cost of essential items used in calculating poverty line is higher in the developed countries.

Q.3 Study the table given below and answer the following questions.

Estimates of Poverty in India

	Poverty ratio (%)			Number of poor (in millions)		
Year	Rural	Urban	Total	Rural	Urban	Total
1993-94	50.7	32	45	329	75	404
2004-05	42	26	37.2	326	81.8	407
2009-10	34	21	30	278	76	355
2011-12	26	14	22	217	53	270

Source India in figures, 2018, Government of India Central Statistics Office.

(a) Even if poverty ratio declined between 1993-94 and 2004-05, why did the number of poor remain at about 407 million?

(b) Are the dynamics of poverty reduction the same in rural and urban India?

Ans. (a) The poverty ratio declined between 1993-94 and 2004-05, but the number of poor remained at about 407 million because the total population of the country is increased during the same period.

Out of this increased population, more people got employment due to the Green Revolution, establishment of more industries and growth of the tertiary sector. As a result, the poverty ratio declined.

(b) The dynamics of poverty reduction are not the same in rural and urban areas because the conditions in both the areas are completely different.

In urban areas, poverty has decreased due to expansion of the service sector, increased industrialisation and consequent increase of jobs. This has resulted in migration to cities and towns from rural areas.

In rural areas, poverty has reduced due to improved agricultural practices resulting in higher incomes. Some contribution to this improvement is due to the migration to urban areas.

Q.4 Study the following graph

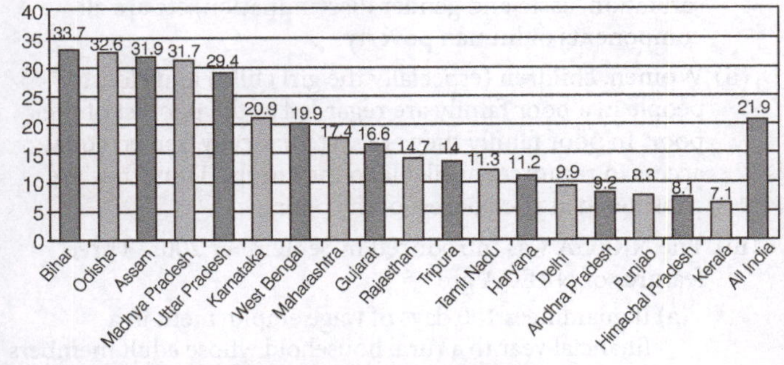

Now answer the following on its basis.

(a) Identify the three states where poverty ratio is the highest.

(b) Identify the three states where poverty ratio is the lowest.

Ans. (a) The three states with highest poverty ratio are Bihar (33.7%), Odisha (32.6%) and Assam (31.9%).

(b) The three states with lowest poverty ratio are Kerala (7.1%), Himachal Pradesh (8.1%) and Punjab (8.3%).

EXERCISE

Q.1 Describe how the poverty line is estimated in India.

Ans. Poverty line is estimated by the National Sample Survey Organisation (NSSO) by conducting sample surveys. A person is considered below the poverty line if his/her income or consumption level falls below a 'minimum level' necessary to fulfil basic needs. While determining the poverty line, a minimum level of food requirement, clothing, footwear, fuel, light, educational and medical requirements, etc are determined for subsistence.

Estimating the poverty line is also based on the desired calories requirement. It is 2400 calories per person per day in the rural areas and 2100 calories in the urban areas.

In terms of income, the poverty line is fixed at ₹ 816/ month for rural areas and 1000 for urban areas for the year 2010-11. If any family has less than this fixed income, it is considered as below the poverty line.

Q.2 Do you think that present methodology of poverty estimation is appropriate?

Ans. No, the present methodology of poverty estimation is not appropriate because it takes into account only the basic needs of food, clothing, fuel, etc. The quality of these basic necessities is the lowest quality available.

The amount which is fixed as the poverty line does not include the margin for the constant price fluctuations and price rise which is constantly occurring.

Q.3 Describe the poverty trends in India since 1973.

Ans. The trends in poverty since 1973 are

- There is substantial decline in poverty ratio from 55% in 1973 to 45.3% in 1993 and 21.9% in 2011-12.
- Rural poverty has declined sharply from 56% in 1973 to 25.7% in 2011-12 and the numbers from 261 million to 216.5 million.
- The latest estimates indicate a significant reduction in the total urban and rural number of poor to be about 270.3 million, down from 321 million in 1973.

Q.4 Discuss the major reasons for poverty in India.

Ans. The major reasons of poverty in India are

- **Low level of economic development under the British colonial administration** The policies of the colonial government ruined traditional handicrafts and discouraged development of industries like textiles.

- **Low rate of India's economic growth after independence** This resulted in less job opportunities and low growth rates of incomes, accompanied by a high growth rate of population hence increasing poverty.
- **Lack of land resources** Land reforms aimed at redistribution of assets in rural areas have not been implemented effectively.
- **Backwardness in agriculture** People mostly use old, traditional and subsistence methods of farming. This requires much labour and time. Effects of irrigation and the Green Revolution were limited to only some parts of India.

Q.5 Identify the social and economic groups which are most vulnerable to poverty in India.

Ans. The social groups which are most vulnerable to poverty are the Scheduled Castes and Scheduled Tribes households. The Scheduled Castes are not allowed to avail the facilities given to others due to the prevailing caste system, leading to poverty.

The economic groups vulnerable to poverty are the rural agricultural labour and the urban casual labour households. The rural agricultural labour have no land of their own and are thus, not able to earn enough to meet their daily needs, leading to poverty.

Q.6 Give an account of inter-state disparities of poverty in India.

Ans. There is huge disparities among states regarding incidence of poverty. The following facts disclose about the inter-state disparity of poverty in India

- The success rate of poverty reduction varies from state to state. Poverty is still a serious problem in some of the states such as Odisha, Bihar, Uttar Pradesh, etc.
- In 20 states and Union Territories, the poverty ratio is less than the national average. There is a significant decline of poverty in Kerala.
- Bihar and Odisha continue to be the two poorest states with poverty ratio of 33.7% and 32.6%, respectively. Illiteracy, social backwardness, etc are the causes.
- States like Punjab, Haryana and Himachal Pradesh have very low percentage of population living below the poverty line.

Q.7 Describe global poverty trends.

Ans. As per data, there has been substantial reduction in global poverty. It has fallen from 16.27% in 2010 to 9.05% in 2019.

Poverty declined in China and South-East Asian countries as a result of rapid economic growth and huge investments in the development of human resources.

In Latin America and the Caribbean, the ratio of poverty has slightly increased.

In Sub-Saharan Africa, poverty saw an upward trend due to successive droughts. It rose from 36.6% in 2017 to 35.4% in 2019.

Poverty has again resurfaced in some of the former socialist countries like Russia, where formerly it was non-existent.

Q.8 Describe current government strategy of poverty alleviation.

Ans. The current anti-poverty strategy of the government has two approaches i.e. promotion of economic growth and targeted anti-poverty programmes.

Economic growth widens opportunities and provide resources needed to invest in human development.

To enable the poor to take advantage of this economic growth, the government has formulated several anti-poverty schemes to affect poverty directly or indirectly. Such schemes are Prime Minister Rozgar Yojana (PMRY), Rural Employment Generation Programme (REGP), Swarnajayanti Gram Swarozgar Yojana (SGSY), Pradhan Mantri Gramodaya Yojana (PMGY), Antyodaya Anna Yojana (AAY), National Food for Work Programme (NFWP) and National Rural Employment Guarantee Act (NREGA).

There is also a proposal for establishing National and State Employment Guarantee Funds. However, despite the good intentions of these schemes, the benefits have not fully reached the deserving poor.

Hence, the major emphasis in recent years has been on proper implementation and monitoring of all the poverty alleviation programmes.

Q.9 Answer the following questions briefly.
(i) What do you understand by human poverty?
(ii) Who are the poorest of the poor?
(iii) What are the main features of the National Rural Employment Guarantee Act (NREGA) 2005?

Ans. (i) Human poverty refers to the denial of political, social and economic opportunities to an individual to maintain a 'reasonable' standard of living. Illiteracy, lack of job opportunities, lack of access to proper healthcare and sanitation, caste and gender discrimination, etc are all components of human poverty.

(ii) Women, children (especially the girl child) and elderly people in a poor family are regarded as the poorest of the poor. In poor family they are systematically denied equal access to resources available to the family. Thus, they are considered as the poorest of the poor.

(iii) The NREGA was introduced in September 2005. Three features of NREGA are

(a) It guarantees 100 days of wage employment in a financial year to a rural household whose adult members volunteer to do unskilled manual work. One-third of the proposed jobs would be reserved for women.

(b) The scheme will initially be started in 200 districts. Later on, the scheme will be extended to 600 districts.

REVIEW EXERCISE

Including Competency Based Questions

Part I

Multiple Choice Questions (MCQs)

1. What causes social exclusion in society?

(a) Income (b) Education
(c) Family (d) Caste system

2. In rural areas, average calories required per person per day is

(a) 2400 calories (b) 1400 calories
(c) 3000 calories (d) 3500 calories

3. Choose the correct statement.

(a) Every fifth person in India lives in poverty.
(b) Every third person in India lives in poverty.
(c) Every second person in India lives in poverty.
(d) Every fourth person in India lives in poverty.

4. Poverty in Kerala declined significantly because of

(a) large industries
(b) availability of natural resources
(c) development of human resources
(d) All of the above

5. Percentage of poverty in Sub-Saharan Africa in 2017 was

(a) 50 (b) 57 (c) 41 (d) 36.6%

6. Which value determines international poverty line?

(a) $ 4 a day (b) $ 2 a day
(c) $ 2.15 a day (d) $ 8 a day

7. Find the incorrect option.

(a) Poverty line is an imaginary line used by any country to determine its poverty.
(b) Nation Sample Survey Organisation was established in 1970.
(c) Poverty among social groups and economic categories varies widely in India.
(d) In 2011-12 estimates, all India HCR (Head Count Ratio) was 21.9%.

8. Ram has a 25-year -old unmarried sister and four children aged between 1 year to 16 years. Three of them are girls, the youngest is a son.

None of the girls go to school. Buying books and other things for school-going girls is a luxury he cannot afford

Accordingly, what development objective would be the most crucial for improving Ram's and his family's well-being? Competency Based

(a) Increasing access to clean water in their community
(b) Reducing the impact of deforestation in village
(c) Creating more job opportunities for them and other villagers
(d) Ensuring equal rights and opportunities for education, irrespective of gender, in their community

9. Poverty is a complex and insidious determinant of health caused by systemic factors that can persist for generations in a family. Beginning before birth and continuing throughout an individual's life, poverty can significantly impact health and health outcomes.

Source : AAFP

Which of the following statements aligns with the article's description of poverty's impact on health? Competency Based

(a) Poverty primarily affects health directly through poor dietary choices.
(b) While poverty negatively impacts health, its effects can be transmitted across generations.
(c) Addressing health issues in individuals living in poverty can effectively break the cycle of disadvantage.
(d) Poverty's influence on health outcomes begins and ends with access to medical care.

10. In the process of determining the poverty line in India, what factors are considered to establish the minimum level of subsistence, and how are these factors quantified for calculation?

(a) Only clothing and footwear are considered, and their prices are multiplied by their quantities in rupees.
(b) Food requirement is the sole consideration, and it is based on a fixed quantity of calories needed for subsistence.
(c) A combination of factors such as food, clothing, footwear, fuel, light, education, and medical requirements are considered, and their physical quantities are multiplied by their prices in rupees.
(d) Only the desired calorie requirement is considered, and its price in rupees is multiplied by the quantity needed for subsistence.

11. When discussing vulnerability to poverty, what factors contribute to the greater probability of certain communities or individuals becoming or remaining poor in the coming years? Choose the appropriate statements among the following options.

I. Limited availability of alternative living options in terms of assets, education, health and job opportunities.

II. Presence of skilled professionals who can understand technical aspects of poverty alleviation.
III. Utilisation of the cheapest manufacturing location.
IV. Proximity to markets in affluent regions like the US and Europe.

Options

(a) Statements I is appropriate.
(b) Statements I, II, and III are appropriate.
(c) All the Statements are appropriate.
(d) Only Statement IV is appropriate.

12. Consider the statements given below and choose the correct answer. Competency Based

Statement I In poor families all suffer, but some suffer more than others.

Statement II In some cases women, elderly people and female infants are denied equal access to resources available to the family.

Options

(a) Statement I is correct and Statement II is incorrect.
(b) Statement I is incorrect and Statement II is correct.
(c) Both statements I and II are incorrect.
(d) Both statements I and II are correct.

13. Particularly in surplus states, to divert land from production of coarse grains, which is the staple food of the poor, to the production of rice and wheat. The intensive utilisation of water in the cultivation of rice has also led to environmental degradation and fall in the water level, threatening the sustainability of the agricultural development in these states.

Some economists have opposed the idea of providing MSP to farmers; which among the following is appropriate reason? Competency Based

(a) Division of land from coarse grains to rice and wheat
(b) MSP promotes multiple cropping
(c) It promotes management of crops
(d) Makes agriculture more sustainable

14. Sivaraman lives in a small village near Karur town in Tamil Nadu. Karur is famous for its handloom and powerloom fabrics. There are 100 families in the village. Sivaraman an *Aryunthathiyar* (cobbler) by caste now works as an agricultural labourer for ₹ 160 per day. But that's only for five to six months in a year. At other times, he does odd jobs in the town.

Why did Sivaraman need to do odd jobs in the town apart from agriculture? Competency Based

(a) Agriculture only provides seasonal work
(b) Physical weakness
(c) Lack of skills to work in agriculture
(d) Aryunthathiyar caste is not allowed to work in agriculture for entire year.

15. Read the following data and select the appropriate option from the following

Estimate Poverty in India (Tendulkar Methodology)	Poverty Ratio (%)	
	Rural	Urban
Poverty in 2004-05	42	26
Poverty in 2009-10	34	21
Poverty in 2011-12	26	14

Source : India in figures; 2018, Government of India Central Statistics office.

As compared to 2004-05, what is the poverty ratio of urban areas in 2011-12?

(a) 10% (b) 15% (c) 12% (d) 18%

16. Arrange the following in correct sequence.

I. Prime Minister Rozgar Yojana
II. Rural Employment Generation Programme
III. Pradhan Mantri Gramodaya Yojana
IV. Antyodaya Anna Yojana

Codes

(a) I, IV, II, III (b) III, II, I, IV (c) I, II, III, IV (d) IV, III, II, I

17. Prime Minister Rozgar Yojana (PMRY) was started in 1993. The aim of the programme is

I. to create self-employment opportunities
II. to help educated unemployed youth in rural areas and small towns.
III. to help in setting up small business and industries.
IV. to promote higher education

Codes

(a) Only I (b) III and IV (c) I , II and III (d) Only II

Answers

1. (d)	2. (a)	3. (a)	4. (c)	5. (d)
6. (c)	7. (b)	8. (d)	9. (b)	10. (c)
11. (a)	12. (d)	13. (a)	14. (a)	15. (c)
16. (c)	17. (c)			

Match the Following

1.

List I (Launched Year)	List II (Programme)
A. 1950	1. NSSO
B. 1993	2. PM Rozgar Yojana
C. 1995	3. Rural Employment Generation Programme
D. 1999	4. Swarnajayanti Gram Swarozgar Yojana

Codes

	A	B	C	D		A	B	C	D
(a)	1	2	3	4	(b)	4	3	2	1
(c)	1	3	4	2	(d)	3	4	1	2

Ans. (a)

Assertion-Reason

1. **Assertion** (A) Poverty line is an imaginary line used by any country to determine its poverty.
   Reason (R) It varies time to time, place to place and country to country.
   Codes
   (a) Both A and R are true and R is the correct explanation of A
   (b) Both A and R are true, but R is not the correct explanation of A
   (c) A is true, but R is false
   (d) A is false, but R is true
2. **Assertion** (A) The proportion of poor people is not the same in every state.
   Reason (R) In 2011-12 estimates all India HCR (Head Count Ratio) was 21.9%.
   Codes
   (a) Both A and R are true and R is the correct explanation of A
   (b) Both A and R are true, but R is not the correct explanation of A
   (c) A is true, but R is false
   (d) A is false, but R is true
3. **Assertion** (A) Mahatma Gandhi National Rural Employment Guarantee Act, 2005 aims to provide 100 days of wage employment to every household to ensure livelihood security in rural areas.
   Reason (R) It also aimed at sustainable development to address the cause of drought, deforestation and soil erosion.
   Codes
   (a) Both A and R are true and R is the correct explanation of A
   (b) Both A and R are true, but R is not the correct explanation of A
   (c) A is true but, R is false
   (d) A is false, but R is true
4. **Assertion** (A) Mahatama Gandhi always insisted that India would be truly independent only when the poorest of its people become free of human suffering.
   Reason (R) The present formula for food requirement while estimating the poverty line is based on the desired calorie requirement.
   Codes
   (a) Both A and R are true and R is the correct explanation of A
   (b) Both A and R are true, but R is not the correct explanation of A
   (c) A is true, but R is false
   (d) A is false, but R is true

Ans. 1. (b) Both A and R are true, but R is not the correct explanation of A
2. (b) Both A and R are true, but R is not the correct explanation of A
3. (b) Both A and R are true, but R is not the correct explanation of A
4. (b) Both A and R are true, but R is not the correct explanation of A

Case Based Question

1. **Read the source given below and answer the questions that follow.**
   Unable to find proper jobs in cities, many people started working as rickshaw pullers, vendors, construction workers, domestic servants etc. With irregular small incomes, these people could not afford expensive housing. They started living in slums on the outskirts of the cities and the problems of poverty, largely a rural phenomenon, also became the feature of the urban sector. Another feature of high poverty rates has been the huge income inequalities. One of the major reasons for this is the unequal distribution of land and other resources.
   (i) What did the combination of high population growth and low per capita income growth result in?
   (a) Economic prosperity
   (b) Poverty cycle
   (c) Population decline
   (d) Technological advancement
   (ii) Which major policy initiative aimed at addressing income inequalities by redistributing assets in rural areas?
   (a) Education reforms
   (b) Industrial development
   (c) Land reforms
   (d) Healthcare reforms
   (iii) What limited the effects of job creation in the agriculture sector to some parts of India?
   (a) Lack of government policies
   (b) Limited technological advancements
   (c) Green revolution
   (d) Regional disparities
   (iv) What is highlighted as a challenge in addressing income inequalities despite various policies?
   (a) Lack of awareness
   (b) Inefficient implementation of policies
   (c) Overemphasis on urban development
   (d) Technological advancements

Ans. (i) (b) Poverty cycle
(ii) (c) Land reforms
(iii) (b) Limited technological advancements
(iv) (b) Inefficient implementation of policies

Part II

Very Short Answer Type Questions

1. Write two main dimensions of poverty.

Ans. Hunger and lack of shelter are two main dimensions of poverty.

2. What do we mean by the term 'vulnerability to poverty'?

Ans. 'Vulnerability to poverty' means the chances of some communities or persons to become poor or remain poor in the future.

3. What does the term 'poverty line' refers to?

Ans. Poverty line is an imaginary line which is used to estimate poverty in a country. It varies from one country to another country.

4. How a person is considered as poor?

Ans. A person is considered poor if the income or consumption level of a person falls below a given 'minimum level' necessary to fulfil the basic needs.

5. On what factors do calorie needs vary for a person?

Ans. The calorie needs vary depending on sex, age and type of work that a person does.

6. What is the average number of calories required per person per day in urban areas of India?

Ans. The average number of calories required per person per day in rural areas of India is 2100.

7. Which agency conducts the periodical sample surveys for estimating the poverty line in India?

or **How is poverty line estimated periodically?**

Ans. Poverty line is estimated periodically by the National Sample Survey Organisation (NSSO) by conducting sample surveys.

8. Give the definition of poverty line as defined by the World Bank?

Ans. World Bank defines poverty line in terms of minimum availability of the equivalent of $1.90 per person per day.

9. 'Poverty line may vary with time and place'. Support the statement with an example.

or **Why does the poverty line vary with time and place?**

Ans. Poverty line may vary with time and place as the basic needs of people are different at different countries and different time.

10. Name four categories of people who are vulnerable to poverty.

Ans. Scheduled Castes, Scheduled Tribes, rural agricultural labour households and urban casual labour households are vulnerable to poverty.

11. By what method has the state of West Bengal reduced rural poverty?

Ans. Proper implementation of land reforms have helped to reduce rural poverty in West Bengal.

12. Name any two causes of poverty.

Ans. Two causes of poverty are

(i) Low level of economic development during British rule.

(ii) Failure in agriculture.

13. What are anti-poverty measures?

Ans. Anti-poverty measures include

(i) Promotion of economic growth.

(ii) Targeted anti-poverty programmes.

14. Who implements the National Food for Work Programme?

Ans. The Central Government implements the National Food for Work Programme.

15. Since poverty has many facets, social scientists look at it through a variety of indicators. Usually the indicators used are related to the levels of income and consumption. Competency Based

(i) How do social scientists typically approach the examination of poverty, considering its multifaceted nature, and what is a common indicator they use?

(ii) In the context of poverty analysis, what specific aspects are often captured by indicators related to levels of income and consumption?

Ans. (i) Social scientists typically approach the examination of poverty by considering its multifaceted nature through various indicators. A common indicator they frequently use is the level of income.

(ii) In the context of poverty analysis, indicators related to levels of income and consumption often capture aspects such as economic well-being, standard of living, and the ability to meet basic needs.

16. Lakha Singh belongs to a small village near Meerut in Uttar Pradesh. His family doesn't own any land, so they do odd jobs for the big farmers. Work is erratic and so is income. At times they get paid ₹ 50 for a hard day's work.

Discuss the socio-economic challenges faced by Lakha Singh and his family in the context of their livelihood and income. Explain with an example. Competency Based

Ans. The socio-economic challenges faced by Lakha Singh and his family include absence of land ownership which leads them to rely on unpredictable jobs for large landowners. The irregular nature of work contributes to fluctuating incomes, such as they receive only ₹ 50 for a hard day's work. This lack of stable employment and meager earnings shows the vulnerability and economic instability faced by Lakha Singh's family.

Short Answer Type Questions

1. Explain three impacts of poverty in India.

Ans. The various impact of poverty in India are as follows

(i) **Impact on health** One of the most devastating impacts that poverty has on the overall health of the nation. The problem of malnutrition is widespread in all age groups, especially in children. Children from poor backgrounds are twice as susceptible to suffer from anemia, nutrient deficiencies, impaired vision and even cardiac problems.

(ii) **Child Labour** It is the result of poverty. Large families fail to meet the monetary needs of the members. Thus, children as young as 6-7 years are made to start earning in order to contribute to the family income.

(iii) **Homelessness** Due to poverty the condition of homelessness arises. Homelessness affects children's health, women safety and overall increase in criminal activities.

2. How far is it correct to say that social exclusion can be both a cause as well as a consequence of poverty? Explain.

Ans. Social exclusion can be a cause as well as a consequence of poverty in the usual sense.

Social exclusion as a cause

We can say that social exclusion is a cause. It is because social exclusion is a process through which individuals or groups are excluded from facilities, benefits and opportunities that the people enjoy.

A typical example is the working of the caste system in India, in which people belonging to certain castes are excluded from equal opportunities.

Social Exclusion as a consequence

Due to social exclusion, people in some sections of our society become poor. They do not have the opportunities like other people. As a consequence of this they are facing poverty.

3. (a) What are the different methods to estimate poverty?

(b) Who conducts the sample surveys to estimate poverty lines?

Ans. (a) The methods used to estimate poverty line are

(i) **Consumption method** In this method, the average calorie requirement of a person is multiplied to the current prices. In India the accepted average calorie requirement is 2400 calories per person per day in rural areas and 2100 calories per person per day in urban areas. Calorie requirement in rural areas are considered to be higher than in urban areas because people living in rural areas engage themselves in more physical work.

(ii) **Income method** In this method, the poverty line is estimated with the help of minimum income required. In the year 2011-12, the poverty line for a person was fixed at ₹ 816 per month for the rural areas and ₹ 1,000 per month for the urban areas. The higher amount for urban areas is because of high prices of essential products in urban areas.

(b) National Sample Survey Organisation (NSSO) conducts sample surveys to estimate poverty lines.

4. Explain the principle measures taken in Punjab, Kerala and West Bengal to reduce poverty.

Ans. Following are the factors that helped Punjab, Kerala and West Bengal in reducing poverty

(i) **Punjab** It has succeeded in reducing poverty by agricultural growth.

(ii) **Kerala** It has succeeded in reducing poverty by investing on human resource development. Kerala is the highest literate state of the country.

(iii) **West Bengal** In West Bengal, land reform measures have helped in reducing poverty.

5. How colonial rule and income inequalities causes of poverty in India?

Ans. In following ways colonial rule and income inequalities causes poverty in India

Colonial Rule One of the historical reasons for poverty is the low level of economic development under the British colonial administration. The policies of the colonial government ruined traditional handicrafts and discouraged development of industries like textiles.

Income Inequalities These have resulted from non-availability of land to rural landless labourers. Thus, they are forced to work for low wages for the large farmers, causing poverty to them, as they are not able to meet their daily needs with their meagre earnings.

6. Describe the contribution of Green Revolution to eradicate the poverty in India.

Ans. The contribution of green revolution in eradicating the poverty in India are as follows

- Green revolution has increased the production and productivity of agriculture, mostly in West and North-West.
- It enhanced food security and also created many job opportunities in agriculture.
- It has helped to reduce poverty in certain part of India. But as the effects are limited to some parts so, in these regions, there is still significant number of poor people.

7. How is socio-cultural and economic factor responsible for poverty in India?

Ans. Socio-economic and cultural factors are responsible for poverty in India in the following ways

- **Socio-cultural Cause of Poverty** In order to fulfil social obligations and observe religious ceremonies, most people in India including the poor used to spent lot of money. This takes them back to poverty.
- **Economic Cause of Poverty** Small farmers used to take loans to buy seeds, fertilisers, pesticides etc. When there is crop failure they become indebted. This takes them under debt trap and lead to poverty.

8. Describe the status of poverty during the early independence period?

Ans. The status of poverty during the early independence period was

- During early independence period, the poverty rate was very high in India.
- The economic growth during this period was also very low.
- There was about 45% poverty in the early 1950s which remained the same till the early eighties.

9. Which circumstances compelled the government to start targeted anti-poverty programmes? Mention the names of any two such programmes.

Ans. Following circumstances compelled the government to start targeted anti-poverty programmes

(i) Since the poor are not able to take advantage from the opportunities created for them, the growth in the agriculture sector is much below expectations. This led to the need of anti-poverty programmes.

(ii) In agriculture sector, large number of poor people are unemployed, therefore, the need for targeted anti-poverty programmes was felt.

Such programmes are as follows

- National Rural Employment Guarantee Act, 2005
- National Employment Guarantee Funds
- National Food for Work Programme
- Prime Minister Rozgar Yojana (PMRY), Swarnajayanti Gram Swarozgar Yojana (SGSY) Pradhan Mantri Gramodaya Yojana (PMGY) and Antyodaya Anna Yojana (AAY).

10. Why were the poverty alleviation programmes not successful in most parts of India?

Ans. The poverty alleviation programmes were not successful in most parts of India because

- Lack of proper implementation and right targeting.
- There has been a lot of overlapping of schemes.
- Every year a huge number is added to the population pool of the country. This renders the scheme ineffective.
- Despite good intentions, the benefits of these schemes do not fully reach to the deserving poor.

11. "In poor families all suffer, but some suffer more than others." Validate the statement. Competency Based

Ans. Poor people are the ones who suffer from poverty the most. Landlessness, hunger, lack of shelter, unemployment, large family size, illiteracy, poor health, malnutrition, child labour, helplessness, etc. are features of poor people. In the poor families some people like women, elderly people and female infants suffer more as they are systematically denied equal access to resources available to the family. As these are dependent group, thus, they receive very less care and resources to consume. Thus, it can be concluded that in poor families all suffer, but some suffer more than others.

12. Differentiate between 'minimum subsistence level of living' and a 'reasonable level of living'. Competency Based

Ans. Differences between minimum subsistence level of living and reasonable level of living are

Minimum subsistence level of living	Reasonable level of living
It is a much narrower concept and captures only a limited part of what poverty really means to people.	It is a much broader concept and include all forms of human poverty.
All current anti-poverty measures are targeted to remove this type of poverty.	For better success of anti-poverty measures, Government should include this concept to define poverty.
It includes basic minimum needs like food, cloth and shelter.	Beside basic minimum needs, it includes education, healthcare, employment, etc.

13. The proportion of people below the poverty line is also not the same for all social groups and economic categories in India. Social groups, which are most vulnerable to poverty are Scheduled Caste and Scheduled Tribe households.

Why do Scheduled Caste and Scheduled Tribe households in India face higher vulnerability to poverty compared to other social groups? Substantiate your answer by giving any three reasons. Competency Based

Ans. Scheduled Caste and Scheduled Tribe households in India face higher vulnerability to poverty compared to other social groups because

(i) Scheduled Castes (SC) and Scheduled Tribes (ST) have historically faced social discrimination and marginalisation. The deeply rooted caste system in India has continued inequalities, limiting access to resources, opportunities, and social mobility for these groups.

(ii) SC and ST communities often face barriers to accessing quality education and employment opportunities. Limited education results in fewer skills and qualifications, restricting their ability to secure well-paying jobs.

(iii) Many SC and ST households in rural areas often face landlessness or have limited access to agricultural land. Agriculture is a primary source of livelihood in rural India, and the lack of land ownership or secure rights hinders their ability to generate sustainable income.

Long Answer Type Questions

1. Describe how the poverty is seen by social scientists.

Or **How is poverty interpreted by the social scientists? Explain.**

Ans. The indicators which are used by social scientists to interpret the poverty are as follows

- **Illiteracy level** It is a situation where parents are unable to send their children to school.
- **Lack of access to healthcare** It is a situation in which sick people cannot afford treatment.
- **Lack of access to drinking water** It means lack of safe and clean drinking water facilities.
- **Lack of job opportunity** It means no availability of regular job opportunity.
- **Lack of general resistance** It means lack of general resistance due to malnutrition.
- **Lack of sanitation** It means lack of cleaning of our surroundings.

Social scientists defines poverty as a multi-dimensional problem, including not just income but also social exclusion and vulnerability.

2. What is poverty line? What are the calories and rupees fixed for rural and urban areas for measuring the poverty line?

Or **Define the term poor and what is accepted average calories requirement in India for rural and urban areas.**

Ans. Poverty Line It is an imaginary line used by any country to determine its poverty. It may vary with time and place as what is necessary to satisfy the basic needs is different at different times and in different countries.

A person will be considered poor if his income or consumption level is below 'a minimum level' which is needed to fulfil his basic needs.

The accepted average of calories requirement in India is 2400 calories per person per day in rural areas and 2100 calories in urban areas. It is high in the rural areas because of more physical work done by the rural people.

The poverty line fixed for the rural and urban areas in India according to the year 2012 was ₹ 816 and ₹ 1000 per person per month, respectively. It is higher in urban areas because of high prices of many essential commodities in urban areas.

3. Discuss the condition of social groups which are most vulnerable to poverty in India.

Ans. Social groups which are most vulnerable to poverty are Scheduled Caste and Scheduled Tribe households. The condition of social groups in India is discussed through the points given below

- Although, the average for people below poverty line for all groups in India is 22, 43 out of 100 people belonging to Scheduled Tribes are not able to meet their basic needs.
- Similarly, 29% of Scheduled Castes in India are living under poverty line.
- The double disadvantage of being a landless casual wage labour household in the socially disadvantage social groups of the Scheduled Caste or the Scheduled Tribe population highlights the seriousness of the problem.
- Some studies have shown that except for the Scheduled Tribe households, all the other three groups (i.e. SCs, rural agricultural labourers and the urban casual labours household) have seen a decline in poverty in the 1990s.
- Remarkably, in the poor families, women, children especially the girl child and old people suffer more than others due to unequal access to the resources.

4. "There is a strong link between economic growth and poverty reduction." Explain the statement.

Or **Do you think economic growth is linked with the reduction of poverty? Give any three arguments in support of your answer.**

Ans. It is true that there is a strong link between economic growth and poverty reduction.

This can be justified through the following arguments

(i) The higher growth rates have helped significantly in the reduction of poverty. For e.g. in the 1980s. India's economic growth was one of the fastest in the world. The growth rate rose from the average of about 3.5% a year in the 1970s to about 6 % during the 1980s and 1990s.

(ii) Economic growth widens opportunities and provides the resources needed to invest in human development.

(iii) This also encourages people to send their children (including girls), to schools in the hope of getting better economic returns from investing in education. Thus, it can be concluded that there is a strong link between economic growth and poverty reduction.

5. Write a note on any five programmes that have been developed for eradication of poverty in India.

Ans. Some programmes that have been developed for eradication of poverty in India are

(i) **Pradhan Mantri Rozgar Yojana (PMRY)** This programme was launched in 1993. It is aimed at providing self-employment opportunity to educated unemployed youth in the rural and urban areas. Under this programme, scheduled banks provide loans at a lower interest rate to start small business and set up industries.

(ii) **Rural Employment Generation Programme (REGP)** This programme was launched in 1995. The aim of the programme is to create self-employment opportunity in rural areas and small towns. A target for creating 25 lakh new jobs has been set for this programme under the Tenth Five Year Plan.

(iii) **Swarnajayanti Gram Swarozgar Yojana (SGSY)** This scheme was launched in 1999. This programme aims at bringing the rural poor families above the poverty line. To achieve this goal, it organises them into Self Help Groups (SHGs) through a mix of bank credit and government subsidy.

(iv) **Pradhan Mantri Gramodaya Yojana (PMGY)** This programme was launched in 2000. Under this programme, the Central Government provides additional assistance to the State Government for improving basic services in the village. The major basic services covered under this programme are primary health, primary education, rural shelter, rural drinking water and rural electrification.

(v) **National Food for Work Programme** (NFWP) This programme was launched in 2004. This programme is open to all rural poor who are in need of wage employment and desire to do manual unskilled work. It is implemented as a 100% centrally sponsored scheme. Under this scheme, foodgrains are provided free of cost to the states. Later this scheme was merged with NREGA.

6. Read the information about industry growth and answer the question that follows.

While determining the poverty line in India, a minimum level of food requirement, clothing, footwear, fuel and light, educational and medical requirement, etc., are determined for subsistence. These physical quantities are multiplied by their prices in rupees.

What is the basis of the present formula for food requirement in estimating the poverty line? Why is the formula revised periodically? **Competency Based**

Ans. The present formula for determining the poverty line in India relies on establishing a minimum calorie requirement for subsistence.

It considers factors such as age, sex, and the type of work a person engages in. Cereals, pulses, vegetables, milk, oil, and sugar collectively contribute to fulfilling these calorie needs. The accepted average calorie requirement is 2400 calories per person per day in rural areas and 2100 calories in urban areas.

The monetary expenditure for food requirements, used in determining the poverty line in India, is revised periodically to adjust the rise in prices of essential items such as food grains. The aim is to ensure that the poverty line reflects the current economic conditions and cost of living.

Case Based Questions

1. Read the sources given below and answer the questions that follow.

Source A Poverty as seen by social scientists

Since poverty has many facets, social scientists look at it through a variety of indicators. Usually the indicators used are related to the levels of income and consumption. But now poverty is looked through other social indicators like illiteracy level, lack of general resistance due to malnutrition, lack of access to healthcare, lack of job opportunities, lack of access to safe drinking water, sanitation etc. Analysis of poverty based on social exclusion and vulnerability is now becoming very common.

(i) How do the social scientists analyse poverty?

Source B Social exclusion

According to this concept, poverty must be seen in terms of the poor having to live only in a poor surrounding with other poor people, excluded from enjoying social equality of better-off people in better surroundings. Social exclusion can be both a cause as well as a consequence of poverty in the usual sense. Broadly, it is a process through which individuals or groups are excluded from facilities, benefits and opportunities that others (their "betters") enjoy.

(ii) Can social exclusions cause poverty in rural areas?

Source C Vulnerability

Vulnerability to poverty is a measure, which describes the greater probability of certain communities (say, members of a backward caste) or individuals (such as a widow or a physically handicapped person) of becoming, or remaining, poor in the coming years. Vulnerability is determined by the options available to different communities for finding an alternative living in terms of assets, education, health and job opportunities.

(iii) What is the vulnerability of poverty?

Ans. (i) Social scientists analyse poverty through various indicators related to the levels of income and consumption.

(ii) Yes, social exclusion of the Scheduled Castes in rural areas is a major cause of poverty.

(iii) Vulnerability of poverty is a measure, which describes the greater probability of certain communities or individuals of becoming or remaining poor in the coming years.

2. Read the source given below and answer the questions that follow.

While determining the poverty line in India, a minimum level of food requirement, clothing, footwear, fuel and light, educational and medical requirement, etc., are determined for subsistence.

These physical quantities are multiplied by their prices in rupees. The present formula for food requirement while estimating the poverty line is based on the desired calorie requirement.

Food items, such as cereals, pulses, vegetable, milk, oil, sugar, etc together provide these needed calories. The calorie needs vary depending on age, sex and the type of work that a person does. The accepted average calorie requirement in India is 2400 calories per person per day in rural areas and 2100 calories per person per day in urban areas.

Since people living in rural areas engage themselves in more physical work, calorie requirements in rural areas are considered to be higher than in urban areas. The poverty line is estimated periodically (normally every five years) by conducting sample surveys. These surveys are carried out by the National Sample Survey Organisation (NSSO).

(i) If a person wants to determine poverty line in India then which factors should be used to determine for subsistence?

(ii) How is the food requirement estimated in poverty line?

(iii) Why is the calorie requirement of rural areas more than that in urban areas?

Ans. (i) If a person wants to determine poverty line in India, then a minimum level of food requirement, clothing, footwear, fuel and light, educational and medical requirement etc. are determined for subsistence.

(ii) Food requirement is estimated in poverty line through the desired calorie requirement, from food items, such as cereals, pulses, vegetables, milk, oil, sugar, etc. These together provide the needed calories.

(iii) Since people living in rural areas engage themselves in more physical work, calorie requirements in rural areas is considered to be higher than in urban areas.

ASSESSMENT EXERCISE

Multiple Choice Questions (MCQs)

1. Which of the following states of India has the highest poverty ratio?

(a) Bihar (b) Odisha
(c) Jharkhand (d) Madhya Pradesh

2. Which among the following is the method to estimate the poverty line in India?

(a) Invested method
(b) Capital method
(c) Human method
(d) Income method

3. Consider the following statements associated with MGNREGA and choose the correct option.

(a) MGNREGA provide 100 days of wage employment in a financial year.
(b) The scheme provided employment to 220 crore persons.
(c) MGNREGA was introduced in 2008.
(d) The average wage has increased to 182 in 2013-14 from 60 in 2006-07.

4. Arrange the following in sequence.

I. NSSO
II. MGNREGA
III. PM Gramodaya Yojana
IV. Antyodaya Anna Yojana

Codes

(a) I, II, III, IV (b) I, III, IV, II
(c) II, IV, I, III (d) IV, I, II, III

Subjective Questions (VSA, SA & LA)

1. How is social exclusion linked to poverty?

2. Which international organisation uses $ 2.15 per day as a poverty line standard?

3. In a poor family, women are paid significantly less for the same work as men. They are often denied access to healthcare and proper nutrition compared to male members of the family.
How does gender inequality increases the poverty?

4. The Pradhan Mantri Gramodaya Yojana (PMGY) launched in 2000, additional central assistance is given to states for basic services such as primary health, primary education, rural shelter, rural drinking water and rural electrification.
How did PMGY prove to be beneficial for people?

5. Which body is responsible for conducting sample surveys for estimation of the poverty line?

6. What are the reasons for limited success of the poverty alleviation programme in India?

7. Mention four main causes of poverty in India?

8. Describe any two poverty alleviation programmes, currently being implemented in India.

9. How is economic growth and poverty reduction linked with each other? Substantiate.

CHAPTER 4

Food Security in India

Food is essential for living as air is for breathing. The assurance of food security relies on the effectiveness of the Public Distribution System (PDS) and the governments proactive measures to address potential threats to this security. In this chapter, we will learn about the food security scenario in India.

4.1 Meaning of Food Security

Food security refers to **availability**, **accessibility** and **affordability** of food to all people at all times. Food security depends on the **Public Distribution System**[1] and government's initiative, and action when security is threatened.

Food security has following three dimensions

(i) **Availability of Food** It means food production within the country, food imports and the previous years stock stored in government granaries[2].

(ii) **Accessibility of Food** It means food is within reach of every person.

(iii) **Affordability of Food** It means that an individual has enough money to buy sufficient, safe and nutritious food to meet one's dietary needs.

Thus, food security is ensured in a country only if

- Enough food is available for all the persons.
- All persons have the capacity to buy food of acceptable quality.
- There is no barrier on access to food.

The **1995 World Food Summit** declared that 'Food security at the individual, household, regional, national and global levels exists when all people, at all times, have physical and economic access to sufficient, safe and nutritious food to meet their dietary needs and food preferences for an active and healthy life.' The declaration further recognises that 'poverty eradication is essential to improve access to food.'

A New Dimension to Food Security

In the 1970s, food security was understood as the availability of adequate supply of basic food stuff at all times.

Amartya Sen added a new dimension to this traditional meaning of food security. He emphasised that people should have 'access' to food through 'entitlements'. These entitlements are combination of what one can produce, exchange in the market along with state or other supplies provided by society.

4.2 Need of Food Security

Generally, the poor section of the society face the problem of food security. However, persons above the poverty line might also face the problem of food security when the country faces a national disaster **calamity**[3] like earthquake, **drought**[4], flood, tsunami, widespread failure of crops causing **famine**[5], etc.

If such calamity happens in a very widespread area or is stretched over a longer time period, it may cause a situation of **starvation**[6].

A massive starvation might become a famine. A famine is characterised by widespread deaths due to starvation and epidemics.

It is caused by forced use of impure water or decaying food, and loss of body resistance due to weakening from starvation.

1 **Public Distribution System** A system in which the food procured by the Food Corporation of India (FCI) is distributed through government regulated ration shops among the poorer section of society.

2 **Granaries** It refers to a storehouse or stock of grains.

3 **Calamity** It is an event causing great and often sudden damage or suffering. For e.g. flood, drought, famine, etc.

4 **Drought** It is a prolonged period of abnormally low rainfall, leading to a shortage of water.

5 **Famine** It is a situation in which large number of people have little or no food and many of them die.

6 **Starvation** It is a situation where intense suffering or even death caused by lack of food.

The most devastating famine in India was the **famine of Bengal** in 1943. This famine killed 30 lakh people in the province of Bengal.

People who were affected the most in Bengal famine of 1943 were agricultural labourers, fisherman, transport workers and other casual labourers. They were affected due to the dramatically increasing price of rice.

Today, famine like conditions exist in many parts of the country, leading to starvation deaths at times.

Natural calamities and pandemic may also lead to food shortage. For example, COVID-19 pandemics had an adverse impact upon the food security. Restriction on the movement of people and goods and services impacted economic activity.

4.3 Food Insecure People

Food and nutrition insecurity has affected a large section of people in India. The most affected people are **landless people, traditional artisans, self-employed workers** and beggars.

In urban areas, the food insecure families are those whose working members are generally employed in underpaid occupations and casual labour market. These workers are largely engaged in seasonal activities and are paid very low wages.

The social composition along with the inability to buy food also plays a role in food insecurity. For example, the **SCs, STs** and some sections of the **OBCs** who have either poor land- base or very low land productivity are prone to food insecurity.

Migrants who left their hometown because of natural disaster in search of work are also among the most food insecure people.

Further, many pregnant and nursing mothers and also children under the age of 5 years are food insecure people.

Economically backward states with high level of poverty, tribal and remote areas and regions more prone to natural disasters consist the largest number of food insecure people.

These regions are Eastern and South-Eastern parts of Uttar Pradesh, Bihar, Odisha, Jharkhand, West Bengal, Chhattisgarh, Maharashtra and parts of Madhya Pradesh.

KNOWLEDGE PLUS The National Health and Family Survey[7] (NHFS) conducted during 1998-99 estimated that approximately 11 crore women and children in India are food insecure.

Hunger

It is another aspect, which indicates food insecurity. Hunger is not just a sign of poverty but it also causes poverty. To achieve food security, current hunger should be removed and the risk of future hunger should be reduced.

Hunger has two dimensions i.e. chronic and seasonal. These are as follows

- **Chronic Hunger** It is a consequence of a diet which is regularly inadequate in quantity and quality. This is caused due to lack of income to buy food for survival.

  Chronic hunger has reduced in rural areas from 2.3% of households in 1983 to 0.7% in 1999 - 2000. In urban areas, it has reduced from 0.8% to 0.3% during the same period.

- **Seasonal Hunger** It is related to seasonal cycles of food growing and harvesting. It is prevalent in rural areas because of the seasonal nature of agricultural activities. In urban areas, casual construction workers suffer from seasonal hunger when they do not get work, e.g. during rainy season. This type of hunger exists when a person is unable to get work for the entire year.

  The proportion of households experiencing seasonal hunger in rural areas has reduced significantly from 16.2% in 1983 to 2.6% in 1999-2000. In urban areas, it has reduced from 5.6% to only 0.6% during the same period.

Measures for Self-Sufficiency in Foodgrains

India is aiming at self-sufficiency in foodgrains since independence and has adopted all measures to achieve self-sufficiency in foodgrains.

The **Green Revolution** during the late 1960s and early 1970s helped significantly in increasing production of food grains, although the success varied from region to region.

Indira Gandhi, the then Prime Minister of India, officially recorded the progress of the Green Revolution in agriculture by releasing a special stamp entitled **Wheat Revolution** in July 1968. The success of wheat was later repeated in rice.

The highest growth rate of foodgrains was achieved in Uttar Pradesh and Madhya Pradesh, which was 55 and 33 million tonnes in 2020-21.

The total foodgrain production was 310 million tonnes in 2020-21 and it has changed to 315 million tonnes in 2021-22. Uttar Pradesh and Madhya Pradesh recorded a significant production in wheat which was 36 and 18 million tonnes in 2020-21, respectively.

7 **National Health and Family Survey (NHFS)** It is a large-scale, multi-round survey conducted by the Ministry of Health and Family Welfare.

West Bengal and Uttar Pradesh recorded significant production of rice which was 17 and 16 million tonnes in 2020-21, respectively.

Try These

1. **When was the National Health and Family Survey conducted?**
2. **In which year the most devastating famine of India known as the Bengal famine occurred?**
3. **Name two dimensions of Hunger.**
4. **What was the special stamp entitled, taken out in July 1968 to mark the progress of the Green Revolution?**

4.4 Food Security in India

The Green Revolution started in early 70s helped avoiding famines even during adverse weather conditions. India has become self-sufficient during last 30 years in foodgrains due to the variety of crops grown.

Foodgrains availability even in adverse conditions has been ensured by the government through a food security system. This system consists of a **Buffer Stock** and **Public Distribution System** (PDS).

Buffer Stock

It is the stock of foodgrains (wheat and rice) procured by the government through the **Food Corporation of India**[8] (FCI). FCI purchases wheat and rice from farmers of those states which have surplus production.

The farmers are paid a **Minimum Support Price**[9] (MSP) for their crops. The MSP is announced before the sowing season to give an incentive to the farmers to grow more crops.

The purchased foodgrains are stored in granaries as a **buffer stock**. This stock is maintained to distribute foodgrains in the deficit areas and among the poorer strata of the society at a price lower than the market price, known as **issue price**.

The buffer stock also helps to resolve the problem of food shortage during adverse weather conditions or during the period of calamity.

Public Distribution System

The food procured by the FCI is distributed by the government among the poorer sections of the society. This system of food distribution is called the Public Distribution System (PDS).

The PDS operates through rationing. The rationing system was introduced in India in 1940s after the Bengal famine. It was revived in 1960s prior to **Green Revolution** when the country was facing acute food shortage.

Ration shops are now present in most localities, villages, towns and cities. Ration shops are also known as **fair price shops**. They keep stock of foodgrains, sugar and kerosene oil for cooking.

PDS was strengthened in mid 1970s after the report of NSSO for high poverty levels. Three food intervention programmes were initiated PDS; ICDS (Integrated Child Development Services) in 1975 and Food For Work Programme (FFW) in 1977-78.

The FFW programme now comes under **The National Food Security Act, 2013.** This act provides for food and nutritional security and enables people to live a life with dignity. 75% of rural population and 50% of urban population are categorised as eligible households for food security.

Poverty Alleviation Programmes (PAPs) are initiated mostly in rural areas and are aimed to provide food security to the poor people. Employment generation programmes are also initiated under PAPs that ensures food security by raising the income of the poor.

KNOWLEDGE PLUS There are three kinds of Ration cards
(i) Antyodaya card for the poorest of the poor.
(ii) BPL card for families below the poverty line.
(iii) APL card for all others.

Current Status of Public Distribution System

The Public Distribution System (PDS) is an important step taken by the Government of India towards ensuring food security.

In the beginning, the PDS coverage was universal with no discrimination between the poor and non-poor.

In 1992, a **Revamped Public Distribution System** (RPDS) was started in 1,700 blocks of the country to provide the benefit of PDS in remote and backward areas.

In 1997, a **Targeted Public Distribution System** (TPDS) was introduced to target the 'poor in all areas', with a lower issue price for foodgrains for them compared to the price paid by non-poor people.

Further in year 2000, two special schemes **Antyodaya Anna** Yojana (AAY) and **Annapurna Scheme** (APS) were launched.

8 Food Corporation of India (FCI) It was set-up under the Food Corporation's Act,1964, to support operations for safeguarding the farmers, distribution of foodgrains throughout the country for PDS.

9 Minimum Support Price (MSP) It is the pre-announced price that the farmers are paid for their crops by the Food Corporation of India.

Antyodaya Anna Yojana (AAY)

Antyodaya Anna Yojana (AAY) was launched in December, 2000. It is for the poorest of the poor.

Under this scheme, 2 crore of the poorest among the BPL families covered under the Targeted Public Distribution System (TPDS) were identified as of 2003.

Poor families were identified by the respective state rural development departments through a Below Poverty Line (BPL) survey.

25 kg of foodgrains were made available to each eligible family at a highly **subsidised rate**[10] of ₹ 2 per kg for wheat and ₹ 3 per kg for rice. This quantity was increased from 25 kg to 35 kg from April 2002.

The PDS (Public Distribution System) has contributed in the following ways

- It has effectively helped the government control and stabilise food prices.
- It has helped in avoiding widespread hunger and famine by supplying food from surplus regions to deficit ones.
- The MSP and procurement has led to an increase in foodgrain production and provided income security to farmers in certain regions.

Problems with PDS

- Inspite of overflowing granaries and accumulation of food grains in FCI, poor people face hunger. Food grains either decay or eaten away by rats. This adds to wastage and deterioration in grain quality.
- The storage of massive food stocks is responsible for high carrying costs and maintenance cost. With the introduction of TPDS, three levels of prices are fixed for three different income groups.
- The food prices in ration shops for APL groups is quite closer to market price. Due to this, they do not have incentive to buy from ration shops.
- PDS has become ineffective in many regions of the country because dealers running the ration shops are indulged in malpractices. These malpractices include
  (i) Diverting the grains to open market to get better margin.
  (ii) Selling poor quality grains at ration shops.
  (iii) Irregular opening of the shops.

All this leads to greater piling of food grains in FCI and unsold stocks in ration shops.

Problems with MSP

Some states producing surplus wheat and rice, like Punjab, Haryana, Uttar Pradesh (Western), Andhra Pradesh, West Bengal (to some extent) put pressure on the government to raise the MSP.

This increase the cost of procuring food grains by the government. For this, freezing of MSP is suggested as a measure.

Increase in MSP of wheat and rice have induced farmers to divert their production to these two grains only. This ignores the production of coarse grains which is staple food of the poor.

The intensive utilisation of water in rice cultivation has led to problems of environmental degradation and fall in the water table, thus threatening the agricultural development in the states producing surplus foodgrains.

4.5 Role of Cooperatives in Food Security

The role played by cooperatives in food security of India is important especially in the Southern and Western parts of the country.

The cooperative societies set-up shops to sell low priced goods to poor people. For example, out of all fair price shops running in Tamil Nadu, around 94% are being run by the cooperatives.

The examples shown below are success stories of cooperatives in order to contribute in food security of India

(i) In Delhi, Mother Dairy is making progress in providing milk and vegetables to the consumers at controlled rate decided by Government of Delhi.

(ii) Amul is another success story of cooperatives in milk and milk products from Gujarat. It has brought about the **White Revolution** in the country.

(iii) In Maharashtra, Academy of Development Science (ADS) has facilitated a network of NGOs for setting up grain banks in different regions. ADS organises training and capacity building programmes on food security for NGOs. The ADS Grain Bank programme is acknowledged as a successful and innovative food security intervention.

Try These

1. **When was the Targeted Public Distribution System introduced?**
2. **Through which organisation does the government procure food grains for the buffer stock?**
3. **Which scheme was introduced to target the foodgrain distribution to 'Poor in all areas'?**
4. **In which state, more than 90% of fair price shops are run by the cooperatives?**
5. **Which era of revolution was brought by Amul in India?**

10 Subsidised Rate It is the price of goods and services at which they are sold by the government, after buying them from the producers.

Mind Map

FOOD SECURITY IN INDIA

Role of Cooperatives in Food Security

- Mother Dairy provides milk and vegetables to consumer in Delhi.
- Amul brought White Revolution in the country.
- Academy of Developmental Science in Maharashtra, a innovative food security intervention.

Public Distribution System

- The system in which the food procured by the FCI is distributed by the Government among the poorer sections of the society.
- Ration shops are present in villages, towns and cities, also known as Fair Price Shops.
- There are three kinds of ration cards-Antyodaya cards for the poorest of the poor, BPL cards for those below poverty line and APL cards for all others.

Current Status

- Revamped Public Distribution System was introduced in 1992.
- Targeted Public Distribution System was introduced in 1997.
- Antyodaya Anna Yojana (AAY) was launched in 2000.
- Annapurna Scheme (APS) was launched in 2000.

Buffer Stock

- Stock of foodgrains procured by the government through the Food Corporation of India (FCI).
- The farmers are paid a Minimum Support Price for their crops.

Meaning of Food Security

- Availability of food
- Accessibility of food
- Affordability of food

Hunger

To achieve food security, current hunger should be removed and the risk of future hunger should be reduced.

Food Insecure People

The most affected people are landless people, traditional artisans, self-employed workers and beggars.

Need of Food Security

- The most devastating famine was the famine of Bengal in 1943.
- Natural calamities and Pandemic like COVID-19 also lead to food shortage.
- Food Security is needed in a country to ensure food at all times.

Chronic Hunger

It is a consequence of a diet which is regularly inadequate in quantity and quality.

Seasonal Hunger

This type of hunger exists when a person is unable to get work for the entire year.

Measures for Self-Sufficiency in Food Grains

- The Green Revolution during the late 1960s and early 1970s helped significantly in increasing the production of food grains.
- Indira Gandhi recorded the progress of the Green Revolution in agriculture by releasing a special stamp entitled Wheat Revolution in July 1968.

NCERT FOLDER

Covering Intext Questions and Exercises of NCERT

INTEXT QUESTIONS

Q.1 Consider the following table

Production of Rice in the Province of Bengal

Year	Production (Lakh tonnes)	Imports (Lakh tonnes)	Exports (Lakh tonnes)	Total Availability (Lakh tonnes)
1938	85	–	–	85
1939	79	04	–	83
1940	82	03	–	85
1941	68	02	–	70
1942	93	–	01	92
1943	76	03	–	79

(a) Some people say that the Bengal famine happened because there was a shortage of rice. Study the table and find out whether you agree with the statement.

(b) Which year shows a drastic decline in food availability?

Ans. (a) No, I do not agree that the Bengal famine happened due to a shortage of rice. From the table, the availability was much higher than in 1941, although lower than in 1942. However, there can be a number of other causes like improper distribution, malnutrition or disease, etc.

(b) The year showing a drastic decline in food availability is 1941.

Q.2 Story of Ramu

Ramu works as a casual labourer in agriculture in Raipur village. His eldest son Somu who is 10 years old also works as a *pali* to look after the cattle of the Sarpanch of the village Satpal Singh. Somu is employed for the whole year by the Sarpanch and is paid a sum of ₹ 1,000 for this work. Ramu has three more sons and two daughters, but they are too young to work on the field. His wife Sunhari is also (part time) working as house cleaner for the livestock, removing and managing cow dung. She gets ½ litre milk and some cooked food along with vegetables for her daily work.

Besides she also works in the field along with her husband in the busy season and supplements his earnings. Agriculture being a seasonal activity employs Ramu only during times of sowing, transplanting and harvesting. He remains unemployed for about 4 months during the period of plant consolidation and maturing in a year. He looks for work in other activities. Sometimes, he gets employment in brick laying or in construction activities in the village.

By all his efforts, Ramu is able to earn enough either in cash or kind for him to buy essentials for two square meals for his family. However, during the days when he is unable to get some work, he and his family really face difficulties and sometimes his small kids have to sleep without food. Milk and vegetables are not a regular part of meals in the family. Ramu is food insecure during 4 months when he remains unemployed because of the seasonal nature of agriculture work.

On the basis of above story, answer the following questions.

(a) Why is agriculture a seasonal activity?

(b) Why is Ramu unemployed for about 4 months in a year?

(c) What does Ramu do when he is unemployed?

(d) Who are supplementing income in Ramu's family?

(e) Why does Ramu face difficulty when he is unable to have work?

(f) When is Ramu food insecure?

Ans. (a) Agriculture is a seasonal activity because it has a sowing season and a harvesting season. That time is a very busy period for farmers. Most of the work is done during these periods. When the plants are growing and maturing, no significant amount of work is there.

(b) Ramu is unemployed for 4 months in a year as he works as a casual labourer in farms. He get work only during sowing and harvesting season, rest of the time he has no work.

(c) When Ramu is unemployed then he looks for work in other activities. Sometimes he gets employment in brick laying or in construction activities.

(d) Ramu's wife Sunhari and his son Somu are supplementing income in Ramu's family. Somu works for the Sarpanch by looking after the cattle and is paid ₹ 1,000 for this work. Sunhari also works as house cleaner and a casual labourer during the busy season. She gets $\frac{1}{2}$ litre milk and some cooked food along with vegetables for her daily work.

(e) When Ramu is unable to get any work then he faces difficulty in getting two meals a day for his family.

(f) Ramu is food insecure during 4 months when he remains unemployed because of the seasonal nature of agricultural work.

Q.4 Story of Ahmad

Ahmad is a rickshaw puller in Bengaluru. He has shifted from Jhumri Taliah along with his 3 brothers, 2 sisters and old parents. He stays in a *jhuggi*. The survival of all members of his family depends on his daily earnings from pulling rickshaw.

However, he does not have a secured employment and his earnings fluctuate everyday. During some days, he gets enough earning for him to save some amount after buying all his day-to-day necessities. On other days, he barely earns enough to buy his daily necessities.

However, fortunately, Ahmad has a yellow card, which is PDS Card for below poverty line people. With this card, Ahmad gets sufficient quantity of wheat, rice, sugar and kerosene oil for his daily use. He gets these essentials at half of the market price.

He purchases his monthly stock during a particular day when the ration shop is opened for below poverty people. In this way, Ahmad is able to eke out his survival with less than sufficient earnings for his big family where he is the only earning member.

On the basis of above story, answer the following questions.

(a) Does Ahmad have a regular income from rickshaw pulling?

(b) How does the yellow card help Ahmad to run his family even with small earnings from rickshaw pulling?

Ans. (a) Ahmad, a rickshaw puller does not have a regular income from rickshaw pulling, his earnings fluctuate everyday. Sometimes, he gets enough earning to save some amount after buying his day to day necessities. On other days, he is barely able to earn enough to survive.

(b) Ahmad has a Yellow card which is a PDS card for below poverty line people. With this card, Ahmad gets sufficient quantity of wheat, rice, sugar and kerosene oil for his daily use at rates below the market rates. In this way, Ahmad is able to survive even with less income from rickshaw pulling.

Q.5 Study the graph below and answer the following questions.

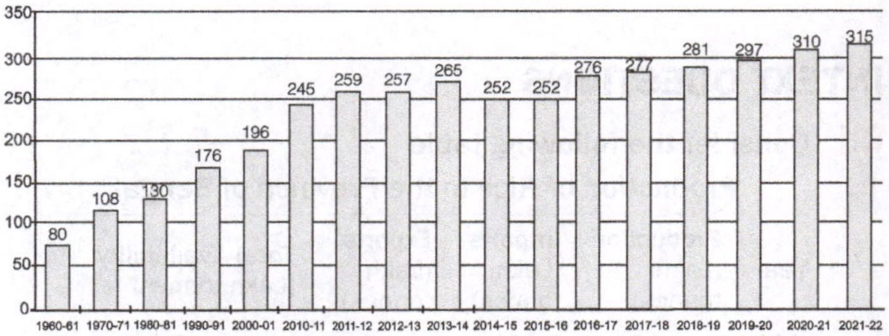

• Production of Foodgrains in India (million tonnes)

(*a*) In which year did our country cross the 200 million tonnes per year mark in foodgrain production?

(*b*) In which decade did India experience the highest decadal increase in foodgrain production?

(*c*) Is production increase consistent in India since 2000-01?

Ans. (a) In the years 2010-11, 2011-12, 2012-13, 2013-14, 2014-15, 2015-16 and 2016-17, India crossed the 200 million tonnes per year mark in foodgrain production.

(b) India experienced the highest decadal increase in 2013-14 in food grain.

(c) No, the increase in foodgrain production were not consistent after 2000-01.

Q.6 Study the graph given below.

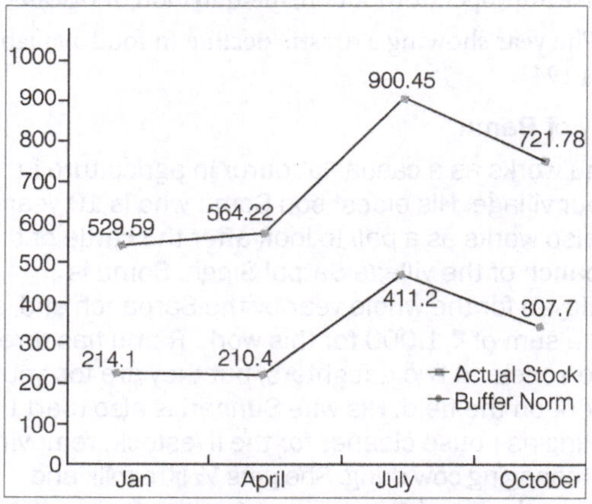

(*a*) In which recent year foodgrain stock with the government was maximum?

(*b*) What is the minimum buffer stock norm for the FCI?

(*c*) Why were the FCI granaries overflowing with foodgrains?

Ans. (a) The foodgrain stock with the Government of India was maximum (65.3 tonnes) in July 2020.

(b) 210.4 million tonnes is the minimum buffer stock norm for the FCI.

(c) The FCI granaries were overflowing with foodgrains because of increased foodgrain procurement by FCI, compared to the actual requirement.

EXERCISE

Q.1 How is food security ensured in India?

Ans. Food security is ensured in India on the basis of the two components i.e. Buffer stock and Public Distribution System (PDS). These are discussed below

(i) **Buffer Stock** It is the stock of foodgrains, namely wheat and rice procured by the government through Food Cooperation of India (FCI). The FCI purchases wheat and rice from the farmers in states where there is surplus production.

The purchased foodgrains are stored in granaries. This is done to distribute food grains in the deficit areas and among the poor strata of society at a price lower than market price, also known as issue price. This helps in resolving the problem of shortage of food.

(ii) **Public Distribution System (PDS)** The stored food is distributed to the poor people through ration shops, also known as fair price shops. The items are sold to the poor people at a price lower than the market price.

Q.2 Which people are more prone to food insecurity?

Ans. The following people are more prone to food insecurity

- The SCs, STs and some sections of the OBCs who have either very little land or very low land productivity.
- The people affected by natural disasters, who have to migrate to other areas in search of work, are also among the most food insecure people.
- Women is at a high risk of malnutrition. This is a matter of serious concern as it puts even the unborn baby at the risk.

Q.3 Which states are more food insecure in India?

Ans. The economically backward states in India with high incidence of poverty are more food insecure.

The states of Uttar Pradesh (Eastern and South-Eastern parts), Bihar, Jharkhand, Odisha, West Bengal, Chhattisgarh, parts of Madhya Pradesh and Maharashtra account for the large number of food insecure people in India.

Q.4 Do you believe that Green Revolution has made India self-sufficient in foodgrains? How?

Ans. Yes, Green Revolution has made India self sufficient in foodgrains in the following ways

(a) **Increase in Production** As a result of Green Revolution production of food grains has increased. The total foodgrain production was 310 million tonnes in 2020-21 and it has changed to 315 million tonnes in 2021-22.

(b) **Over Flowing Buffer Stocks** Due to the success of Green Revolution the stock is much more than the minimum norms.

(c) **Control over Imports** Before the success of Green Revolution, India was dependent on other countries for its foodgrain requirement but now India imports of foodgrains are negligible.

Q.5 "A section of people in India are still without food." Why?

Ans. Despite achieving food self-sufficiency through the Green Revolution, a significant portion of India's population still faces food insecurity due to poverty because

In rural areas, landless individuals, traditional artisans, self-employed workers, poor, and beggars are particularly vulnerable. Similarly, in urban areas, casual labourers, low-wage workers, and those engaged in seasonal work struggle to access an adequate food supply throughout the year.

Despite government efforts such as creating buffer stocks, implementing the Public Distribution System (PDS), and initiating poverty alleviation programs, many individuals still do not receive timely assistance, often due to government inefficiencies and corruption.

Additionally, poor observation of these schemes leads to food wastage in storage facilities and weakens their effectiveness. Corruption within the PDS and prevalent poverty increases the problem, leaving a large portion of the population without access to food.

Q.6 What happens to the supply of food when there is a disaster or a calamity?

Ans. When there is a disaster or a calamity, the production of foodgrains decrease in the affected areas.

The reasons are

- Due to any calamity or disaster like drought, earthquake, flood, Tsunami, etc there is widespread failure of crops. This adversly affects food production.
- Due to shortage of food, price rise up.
- Black marketing and hoarding is also one of the major factors responsible for high price rise during any calamity.
- Due to high price of food, some people cannot afford it.
- If the calamity happens in a very widespread area or is stretched over a longer time period, it may cause a situation of starvation.

Q.7 Differentiate between seasonal hunger and chronic hunger.

Ans. The differences between seasonal hunger and chronic hunger can be summarised as follows

Seasonal Hunger	Chronic Hunger
Seasonal hunger is related to cycles of food growing and harvesting.	Chronic hunger is a consequence of diets persistently inadequate in terms of quantity and/or quality.
This is prevalent in rural areas because of seasonal nature of agricultural activities and in the urban areas because of the casual labour.	Poor people suffer from chronic hunger because of their very low income and inability to buy food even for survival. This is mostly seen in the rural areas.
It occurs in a community or society at only certain times of the year.	It occurs when people lack the opportunity to earn enough money to be educated and gain skills to meet their basic needs.
This hunger causes malnutrition but not death.	If this hunger continues for long time then it leads to death.

Q.8 What has our government done to provide food security to the poor? Discuss any two schemes launched by the government.

Ans. The government has designed the food security system carefully to ensure availability of food to all sections of the society. This system is composed of two components, i.e. Buffer Stock and PDS.

The government has opened more than 4.6 lakh ration shops (fair price shops) to distribute food to the poor people at reasonable price.

Two schemes launched by government are

(i) **Antyodaya Anna Yojana** (AAY) It was launched in December 2000. Under this scheme, one crore of the poorest among the BPL families covered under the targeted PDS were identified. Poor families were identified by the respective state rural developments through a Below Poverty Line (BPL) survey. 25 kg of foodgrains were made available to each eligible family at a highly subsidised rate of ₹ 2 per kg for wheat and ₹ 3 per kg for rice. This quantity has been enhanced from 25 to 35 kg from April 2002.

(ii) **Annapurna Scheme** (APS) It was launched in 2000, for poor senior citizens. The function of scheme was linked with existing network of the PDS. Under this scheme, 10 kg of foodgrains were made available to them free of cost.

Q.9 Why is buffer stock created by the government?

Ans. Due to the following reasons, buffer stock is created by the government

- A buffer stock of foodgrains is created by the government, so that it can be distributed in food deficit areas and among the poorer strata of society at a price much lower than the market price.
- A buffer stock also helps to resolve the problem of food shortage during adverse weather conditions, a disaster or a calamity.
- Maintaining buffer stock is a step taken by the government in order to ensure food security.

Q.10 Write notes on

(*a*) Minimum Support Price (*b*) Buffer Stock
(*c*) Issue Price (*d*) Fair Price Shops

Ans. (a) **Minimum Support Price** (MSP) It is the pre-announced price at which the government purchases foodgrains (rice and wheat) from the farmers in order to create a buffer stock.

The Minimum Support Price is declared by the government every year before the growing season. This provides incentives to the farmers for raising the production of the crops.

The rising Minimum Support Prices of rice and wheat have induced farmers to divert land from the production of coarse grains, the staple food of the poor, to the production of these crops. This have raised the maintenance cost of procuring foodgrains.

(b) **Buffer Stock** It is the stock of foodgrains (usually wheat and rice) procured by the government through the Food Corporation of India. The foodgrains purchased from the farmers are stored in granaries. This stock of grains is known as buffer stock.

(c) **Issue Price** It is the price at which government sells foodgrains to the poorer strata of the society through PDS.

This price is lower than the market price. This also helps to resolve the problem of shortage of food during adverse weather conditions or during the periods of calamity.

(d) **Fair Price Shops** The food procured by the Food Corporation of India is distributed through government-regulated ration shops which are also known as fair price shops. The prices at which food materials are sold at these shops are lower than the market prices. The low pricing is to benefit the poorer strata of society.

That is why, these shops are called fair price shops. Fair price shops keep stocks of foodgrains, sugar and kerosene oil. Any family with a ration card can buy a stipulated amount of these items every month from the nearby ration shop.

Q.11 What are the problems in the functioning of ration shops?

Ans. The problems in the functioning of the ration shops are

- Some of the ration shop dealers adopt malpractices. They illegally divert the grains to the open market for better gains.
- Some of the ration shop dealers sell only poor quality of grains.
- Some dealers do not open their shops regularly and the poor people cannot draw their ration quota timely.
- Due to poor quality of food grains, many people do not buy from the ration shops. This leads accumulation of the stock and more deterioration in the quality of food grains in these shops.

Q.12 Write a note on the role of cooperatives in providing food and related items.

Ans. The cooperatives play an important role in food security in India, especially in the Southern and Western parts of the country in the following ways

- The cooperatives societies setup shops to sell low priced goods to poor people. e.g. in Tamil Nadu, around 94% shops are run by the cooperatives.
- Mother Dairy in Delhi, sells milk and vegetables to the people at reasonable rate which is decided by Delhi Government.
- Amul is another success story of cooperatives in milk and milk products from Gujarat. It has brought about White Revolution in India.
- In Maharashtra, Academy of Development Science (ADS) has facilitated a network of NGOs for setting up Grain Banks in different regions.

REVIEW EXERCISE

Including Competency Based Questions

Part I

Multiple Choice Questions (MCQs)

1. What is meant by food security?

(a) Availability of food to rich people.
(b) Availability of food to urban people.
(c) Availability of food to poor people.
(d) Availability of food to all sections of people.

2. When did the famine in Bengal occur?

(a) 1955 (b) 1943
(c) 1922 (d) 1914

3. Which group(s) of people is/are generally considered food insecure?

(a) Landless agricultural labourers
(b) People of ill-paid occupations
(c) Backward people
(d) All of the above

4. Yellow card is issued to which group of people?

(a) Unemployed people (b) People below poverty line
(c) Rural people (d) All of these

5. What does FCI stand for?

(a) Food Company of India
(b) Food Corporation of India
(c) Food Corporate in India
(d) Food Commission of India

6. Buffer Stock is created to

(a) distribute foodgrains in the deficit areas.
(b) avoid wastage of food.
(c) maintain Minimum Support Price.
(d) All of the above

7. Foodgrains in buffer stock is procured by government through

(a) Food Corporation of India
(b) State government
(c) Ministry of Home Affairs
(d) None of the above

8. Identify the term associated with following information.

- It is consequence of a diet which is regularly inadequate in quantity and quality.
- This is caused due to lack of income to buy food for survival.
- This is mainly seen in rural areas where people cannot afford quality food due to low income.
- It pattern continues for a long time which can also lead to death.

Options

(a) Chronic Hunger (b) Seasonal Hunger
(c) Nutrient Hunger (d) Physical Hunger

9. Consider the following statements associated with poverty line and select the correct option.

(a) A common method used to measure poverty is based on the income or consumption levels.
(b) Poverty line may not vary with time and place.
(c) A person not having car in India may be considered poor.
(d) In 2011-12 poverty line for a person was fixed at ₹ 916 per month for rural areas.

10 Hariya works as a casual labourer in the farms owned by the village Sarpanch. He is employed from July to September in Sarpanch's rice fields and from October to January in cattle farms. When is Hariya food insecure?

(a) July - January (b) September - October
(c) June - February (d) February - June

11. A 35-years-old farmer in a rural village, struggles to feed his family due to the unpredictable weather patterns affecting crop yields. Despite his hard work, he faces challenges in providing consistent meals.

Accordingly, what development intervention would be most beneficial for a farmer and his community's food security?

(a) Implementing advanced irrigation systems to mitigate the impact of erratic weather on crop production.
(b) Establishing a local farmers' cooperative to enhance collective bargaining power for fair prices.
(c) Introducing genetically modified crops that are more resistant to extreme weather conditions.
(d) Improving transportation infrastructure to facilitate easier access to markets for selling agricultural produce.

12. Non-implementation of MSP and below-MSP-procurement of a large number of crops, has been one of the major hurdles in 'crop diversification' which is so vital for Indian agriculture and in saving the environment. Ineffective implementation of MSP and 'non-procurement' of all the crops at the MSP is also one of the main concerns of farmers.

SOURCE- The Hindi Article

In light of the challenges posed by the non-implementation of MSP and below-MSP procurement affecting crop diversification in Indian agriculture, what approach should be prioritised to address these issues? Competency Based

(a) Exploring alternative methods of crop procurement and pricing to encourage crop diversification and support farmers.
(b) The emphasis should be solely on effective implementation of MSP to ensure fair prices for all crops, promoting agricultural diversity.
(c) Maintaining the current system and focusing on other agricultural reforms is a more practical approach.
(d) The government should intervene to fix the pricing issues, and other aspects will naturally fall into place.

13. PDS dealers are sometimes found resorting to malpractices like diverting the grains to the open market to get better margin, selling poor quality grains at ration shops, irregular opening of the shops, etc. It is common to find that ration shops regularly have unsold stocks of poor quality grains left.

Amidst reports of malpractices in the Public Distribution System (PDS), which measure would be most effective in addressing these issues and ensuring fair distribution of grains? Competency Based

(a) Imposing stricter penalties on PDS dealers engaging in malpractices to discourage such behavior.
(b) Increasing government surveillance on ration shops to monitor their operations regularly.
(c) Privatising the PDS to introduce competition and market forces, promoting efficiency and accountability.
(d) Conducting awareness campaigns to educate citizens on their rights and responsibilities in the PDS, encouraging community participation in monitoring.

14. Why is the Public Distribution System (PDS) considered crucial in stabilising prices, making food available at affordable rates and averting widespread hunger in India?

(a) Because it ensures a direct link between surplus and deficit regions, allowing for the efficient transfer of food resources.
(b) Because it promotes a competitive market by allowing private enterprises to participate in food distribution.
(c) Because it directly controls and regulates food prices to ensure affordability for consumers.
(d) Because it facilitates income security for farmers through a fixed minimum support price and procurement policies.

15. Arrange the following in sequence on the basis of the year in which they were launched starting from the earliest.

I. Antyodaya Anna Yojana (AAY)
II. Integrated Child Development Services (ICDS)
III. Food-For Work (FFW)
IV. National Food Security Act

Codes

(a) II, III, I, IV
(b) I, II, III, IV
(c) IV, III, II, I
(d) III, IV, II, I

16. Which of the following statements accurately describes the impact of increased food grain procurement at enhanced MSP in certain Indian states?

I. The procurement is evenly distributed among all states, ensuring a fair representation.
II. Farmers in surplus states, such as Punjab and Haryana, are diversifying crops to prioritise coarse grains, benefiting the poor.

III. Environmental degradation and a decline in water levels are occurring due to the intensive cultivation of rice in certain prosperous regions.

IV. The increase in MSP has primarily affected rice production, leading to a decrease in wheat cultivation.

Codes

(a) Only I (b) Only II
(c) Only III (d) Only IV

17. Consider the statements given below and choose the correct answer. Competency Based

Statement I The cooperatives are also playing an important role in food security in India especially in the Southern and Western parts of the country.

Statement II In Maharashtra, Academy of Development Science (ADS) has facilitated a network of NGOs for setting up grain banks in different regions.

Options

(a) Statement I is correct and Statement II is incorrect.
(b) Statement I is incorrect and Statement II is correct
(c) Both Statements I and II are incorrect
(d) Both Statements I and II are correct

18. Read the data and find out the year in which maximum rice is produced in the province of Bengal.

Year	Production (Lakh tonnes)	Imports (Lakh tonnes)	Exports (Lakh tonnes)	Total Availability (Lakh tonnes)
1941	68	02	–	70
1942	93	–	01	92
1943	76	03	–	79

Sources : AK 1981

(a) 1941 (b) 1942
(c) 1943 (d) Both (b) and (c)

Answers

1. (d)	**2.** (b)	**3.** (d)	**4.** (b)	**5.** (b)
6. (a)	**7.** (a)	**8.** (a)	**9.** (a)	**10.** (d)
11. (a)	**12.** (a)	**13.** (b)	**14.** (a)	**15.** (a)
16. (c)	**17.** (d)	**18.** (b)		

Match the Following

1.

List I (Year of Introduced)	List II (Programme)
A. 1992	1. PDS (Public Distribution System)
B. 1997	2. TPDS (Targeted Public Distribution System)
C. 2000	3. AAY (Antyodaya Anna Yojana)
D. 2013	4. NFSA (National Food Security Act)

Codes

	A	B	C	D		A	B	C	D
(a)	1	2	3	4	(b)	4	3	2	1
(c)	3	4	2	1	(d)	2	1	4	3

Ans. (a)

Assertion-Reason

1. Assertion (A) The most devastating famine that occurred in India was the Famine of Bengal in 1943.

Reason (R) Shortage of rice in 1943 led to this famine in Bengal.

Codes

(a) Both A and R are true and R is the correct explanation of A
(b) Both A and R are true, but R is not the correct explanation of A
(c) A is true, but R is false
(d) A is false, but R is true

2. Assertion (A) A large section of people suffer from food and nutrition insecurity in India.

Reason (R) Due to social composition of the society and peoples inability to buy food.

Codes

(a) Both A and R are true and R is the correct explanation of A
(b) Both A and R are true, but R is not the correct explanation of A
(c) A is true, but R is false
(d) A is false, but R is true

3. Assertion (A) Food imports and previous years stocks may ensure food availability but cannot ensure food affordability.

Reason (R) Government can make the food available but for the affordability an individual should have enough money to buy sufficient quantity and nutritious food.

Codes

(a) Both A and R are true and R is the correct explanation of A
(b) Both A and R are true, but R is not the correct explanation of A
(c) A is true, but R is false
(d) A is false, but R is true

4. Assertion (A) Poor people suffer from chronic hunger because of their very low income and in turn inability to buy food even for survival.

Reason (R) Seasonal hunger is related to cycles of food growing and harvesting.

Codes

(a) Both A and R are true and R is the correct explanation of A

(b) Both A and R are true, but R is not the correct explanation of A

(c) A is true, but R is false

(d) A is false, but R is true

5. Assertion (A) Buffer stock is the stock of food grains, namely wheat and rice.

Reason (R) The MSP is declared by the government every year before the sowing season to provide incentives to farmers for raising the production of these crops.

Codes

(a) Both A and R are true and R is the correct explanation of A

(b) Both A and R are true, but R is not the correct explanation of A

(c) A is true, but R is false

(d) A is false, but R is true

Ans. 1. (c) A is true, but R is false

2. (a) Both A and R are true and R is the correct explanation of A

3. (a) Both A and R are true and R is the correct explanation of A

4. (b) Both A and R are true, but R is not the correct explanation of A

5. (b) Both A and R are true, but R is not the correct explanation of A

Picture Based Questions

1. Study the picture and select the condition which is shown in the given picture.

(a) Self-sufficiency in food grains

(b) Fair Price Shops

(c) Massive starvation and food insecurity

(d) Types of hunger

2. Study the picture carefully and choose the title that closely relates to the given picture.

(a) Buffer Stock

(b) Food Corporation of India

(c) Minimum Support Price

(d) Public Distribution System

Ans. 1. (c) Massive starvation and food insecurity

2. (d) Public Distribution System

Case Based Question

1. Read the source given below and answer the questions that follow.

Public Distribution System (PDS) is the most important step taken by the Government of India (GoI) towards ensuring food security. In the beginning, the coverage of PDS was universal with no discrimination between the poor and the non-poor. Over the years, the policy related to PDS has been revised to make it more efficient and targeted. While some of the programmes such as PDS, mid-day meals, etc. are exclusively food security programmes, most of the PAPs also enhance food security. Employment programmes greatly contribute to food security by increasing the income of the poor.

(i) What is the primary objective of the Public Distribution System (PDS)?

(a) Economic growth

(b) Stabilising prices and making food available

(c) Infrastructure development

(d) Social welfare programmes

(ii) How does the PDS contribute to averting widespread hunger and famine?

(a) By increasing taxes

(b) By supplying food from surplus to deficit regions

(c) By promoting exports
(d) By reducing government spending

(iii) What role does the PDS play in favour of poor households?
(a) Increasing prices
(b) Implementing austerity measures
(c) Prices revision in favour of poor households
(d) Privatising food distribution

(iv) Which regions benefit from the PDS in terms of foodgrain production and distribution?
(a) Only surplus regions
(b) Only deficit regions
(c) Both surplus and deficit regions
(d) None of the above

Ans. (i) (b) Stabilising prices and making food available
(ii) (b) By supplying food from surplus to deficit regions
(iii) (c) Prices revision in favour of poor households
(iv) (c) Both surplus and deficit regions

Part II

Very Short Answer Type Questions

1. What do you mean by availability of food?

Ans. Availability of food means the food currently available in the country including countrys food production and food imports.

2. What do you mean by accessibility of food?

Ans. Accessibility of food means that food is within reach of everybody.

3. What do you mean by affordability of food?

Ans. Affordability of food means that people can buy enough quantity of nutritious food to fulfill their requirement.

4. Which was the most devastating famine that occurred in India during the 20th century?

Ans. The most devastating famine was the Famine of Bengal in 1943, in which 30 lakh people died.

5. What do you mean by hunger?

Ans. Hunger refers to lack of food. In economics, the term hunger can be associated with food insecurity caused due to poverty.

6. Define chronic hunger.

Ans. Chronic hunger is a consequence of persistently inadequate diets in terms of quality and/or quantity of food.

7. Which groups of people suffer from food insecurity the most?

Ans. Beggars, casual labourers, etc suffer from food insecurity the most due to their uncertain income.

8. What do you mean by Buffer Stock?

Ans. Buffer Stock is the stock of foodgrains (mainly rice and wheat) procured by the government. The Food Corporation of India maintains and manages the Buffer stocks.

9. What do you mean by Public Distribution System?

Ans. Public Distribution System is a food intervention programme that aims to provide foodgrains and other essential items to poor people. The PDS is operational through ration shops spread throughout the country.

10. What is a subsidy?

Ans. Subsidy is a payment given by the government to the producers so that there cost of production decreases. In this way, the producers can produce at cheaper prices and earn good income by the sale of that commodity in the market.

11. What are cooperative societies?

Ans. Cooperative societies are organisations that set up shops to sell essential items at low prices. These are managed by local people or the government. Mother Dairy and Amul are examples of successful cooperative societies.

12. "Climate change is rapidly intensifying, increasing pressure on food systems, rural livelihoods, and ecosystems more broadly. While some places may benefit from a longer growing season amid rising temperatures, changing weather patterns and advancing desertification have reduced the average growth in agricultural productivity."

Source : Economic Times Competency Based

(i) What challenges are posed to food systems, rural livelihoods, and ecosystems due to the rapidly intensifying climate change, as mentioned in the passage?

(ii) Why has the average growth in agricultural productivity reduced, as mentioned in the passage?

Ans. (i) The challenges include increased pressure on food systems, rural livelihoods, and ecosystems, with changing weather patterns and advancing desertification have reduced the average growth in agricultural productivity.

(ii) The reduction in the average growth in agricultural productivity is due to changing weather patterns and advancing desertification resulting from rapid climate change.

13. The SCs, STs and some sections of the OBCs (lower castes among them) who have either poor land-base or very low land productivity are prone to food insecurity.

Mention the factors contributing to the vulnerability of SCs, STs, and certain sections of the OBCs (particularly lower castes) to food insecurity due to poor land-base or very low land productivity.

Competency Based

Ans. SCs, STs and some OBCs are particularly vulnerable to food insecurity due to their low land productivity or poor land base. Their problems are made worse by restricting access to fertile land, which reduces agricultural productivity and food self-sufficiency. Because of socioeconomic inequality, this group is more vulnerable because they have less access to opportunities and resources.

Short Answer Type Questions

1. What do you understand by the different dimensions of food security?

or **What are the three dimensions of food security?**

or **Define the term 'food security' and explain its three dimensions.**

Ans. Food security can be defined as the availability, accessibility (including entitlements) and affordability of food to all people at all times. The dimensions of food security are

(i) **Availability of food** It means food production within the country, food imports and the previous years stock in government granaries.

(ii) **Accessibility** It means food is within reach of every person.

(iii) **Affordability** It means an individual has enough money to buy sufficient, safe and nutritious food to meet his dietary need.

2. Describe the impact of famine.

or **What is a famine? How are people affected by a famine?**

Ans. A famine is characterised by widespread deaths due to starvation and epidemics caused by forced use of contaminated water or decaying food and loss of body resistance due to weakening from starvation.

This occurs due to a severe shortage of food resulting from crop failure or other calamity. Famine increases the price of food drastically, making it unaffordable for the weaker sections of the population.

3. What is common in a casual labourer, cobbler, petty shopkeeper, auto-rickshaw driver, beggar, gardener, cycle mechanic and a roadside barber? Explain the relationship between their nature of work, income earned and poverty faced.

Ans. The common thing in a casual labourer, cobbler, petty shopkeeper, auto-rickshaw driver, beggar, gardener, cycle mechnanic and a roadside barber is that all these people face chronic and/or seasonal hunger because of the nature of their activities.
This is explained in the table below

Nature of Work	Income Earned	Poverty Faced
Casual labourer	Irregular and low	Both chronic and seasonal hunger
Cobbler	Irregular	Chronic hunger
Petty shopkeeper	Irregular	Chronic hunger
Auto-rickshaw driver	Irregular	Chronic hunger
Beggar	Irregular and low	Chronic hunger
Gardener	Irregular	Both chronic and seasonal hunger
Cycle mechanic	Irregular	Chronic hunger
Roadside barber	Irregular	Chronic hunger

4. "Hunger is an important aspect indicating food insecurity." Give an argument in favour of this statement alongwith its dimensions.

Ans. Hunger is an important aspect indicating food insecurity. Hunger is not just an indicator of poverty, it causes poverty. Achieving food security therefore involves eliminating current hunger and reducing the risks of future hunger.

Hunger has chronic and seasonal dimensions. Chronic hunger is a result of constantly inadequate diets in terms of quantity and/or quality. Poor people suffer from chronic hunger because of their very low income and thus are unable to buy food even for survival.

Seasonal hunger is related to cycles of food growing and harvesting. This is prevalent in rural areas because of the seasonal nature of agricultural activities and in urban areas because of casual labourers, e.g. there is less work for casual construction labourers during the rainy season. This type of hunger also exists when a person is unable to get work for the entire year.

5. Read the two case studies given below and answer the questions that follow **Competency Based**

I. Fareed runs a small tea stall besides a bank. He is able to provide two meals a day to his family of four. However, the meals lack in nutritional value like green leafy vegetables, dals, curd, etc.

II. Arjun is a worker in the woollen factory and is able to provide two square meals a day to his family of four during the winter months. However, during the summer months, when he is unemployed and has to take up casual jobs, he can't afford this.

(a) Which of the given families faces chronic hunger and why?

(b) Which of the given families faces seasonal hunger and why?

(c) Where in India would you find a greater proportion of people suffering from seasonal hunger and why?

Ans. (a) Fareed's family faces chronic hunger because its diet is regularly deficient in quantity and quality as Fareed is not having enough income to buy an adequate standard of food.

(b) Arjun's family faces seasonal hunger, because during summer he is out of work and so not able to provide his family even two proper meals on a regular basis.

(c) In rural areas, we find a greater proportion of people suffering from seasonal hunger because the agricultural labourers are only employed for a few months in year. Apart from agriculture, other sources of earning are not developed so workers remain without work.

7. How do fair price shops help food distribution in India?

Ans. Fair price shops provide foodgrains like wheat, rice, sugar and kerosene oil on a monthly basis to ration card holders at lower than the market prices. This enables the poorer sections of society to have food security. There are more than 5.5 lakh Fair Price Shops to help food distribution in India.

The fair price shops sells food items to people at different prices depending on the type of ration card they hold. There are three types of ration cards i.e. for APL, BPL and Antayodaya families.

8. Discuss the most likely impact if India operated without a Minimum Support Price (MSP) system. Build the answer around these points Competency Based

- **Agricultural income and farmer livelihoods**
- **Food security at the national level**
- **Farmer distress and rural unrest**

Ans. The most likely impacts if India operated without a Minimum Support Price (MSP) system are as follows

- Agricultural income and farmer livelihoods may suffer, as the assured floor price acts as a safety net, ensuring economic stability for farmers.
- Lack of MSP might put national food security at risk because the program encourages farmers to grow staple crops that are necessary for the nation's survival.
- Farmer distress and rural unrest are likely to escalate without MSP, as it shields farmers from market fluctuations, providing stability crucial for their well-being and preventing social upheaval.

Long Answer Type Questions

1. Where did the Great Famine of 1943 take place? How many people were killed in this famine? Are we prepared to handle such situation in present. If yes, how?

Ans. The Great Famine of 1943 took place in West Bengal. It was the most devastating famine that occurred in India. This famine killed 30 lakh people in Bengal. The incidence like this has not happened in India again.

Yes, India is prepared to handle such situation in present India's preparedness to fight 1943 like situation are

- Enough food is available for all the persons as India is aiming at self-sufficiency of food grains.
- All persons have the capacity to buy food of acceptable quality.
- There is no barrier on access to food.
- Through Buffer Stock and PDS government has ensured availability of food to all sections of the society.
- With the use of technology in agriculture, production of foodgrains have increased.

2. Explain the measures adopted by the government of India to achieve self-sufficiency in foodgrains.

or **How has India achieved self-sufficiency in foodgrains since independence? Describe.**

Ans. After independence, Indian policy makers adopted all measures to achieve self-sufficiency in foodgrains.

Following measures were adopted by government of India to achieve self-sufficiency in foodgrains

- India adopted a new strategy in agriculture, which resulted in 'Green Revolution' especially in the production of wheat and rice.
- The government has made the provision of Buffer Stock meant to distribute foodgrains in the deficit areas and among the poorer strata of society at a price lower than the market price.

  This also helps to resolve the problem of shortage of food during adverse weather conditions or during the periods of calamity.
- The government has made provision of Public Distribution System (PDS). This is meant for distribution of foodgrains through government regulated shops among the poorer sections of the society.
- The government has also initiated several programmes like Poverty Alleviation Programmes (PAPs) and Food for Work Programme to ensure affordability of food by providing employment.

3. What are the major functions of the Food Corporation of India?

Ans. The Food Corporation of India was set up to fulfil the following objectives of the National Food Policy. These are

- Supporting and encouraging crop production by declaring MSP so that farmers can sell their crops to FCI.
- Distribution of foodgrains throughout the country through the Public Distribution System.
- Maintaining a satisfactory level of buffer stocks of foodgrains to ensure National Food Security.
- Intervention in the foodgrains market whenever required for regularising the prices.

FCI has played a significant role in India's success in providing food security by maintaining buffer stocks.

4. Highlight the journey of the rationing system in India.

Ans. The rationing system is a system of distribution of scarce resources in a controlled way. This system began in India in 1940s against the back drop of Bengal famine.

The following points highlight the journey of rationing system in India

- The rationing system was introduced in India during British rule.
- It was revived after independence due to an acute shortage of foodgrains, prior to the Green Revolution.
- Due to a high incidence of poverty in the mid-1970s, Public Distribution System (PDS) for foodgrains was strengthened.
- Under PDS, ration shops were established throughout the country that provides wheat, rice, sugar, kerosene at prices much lower than the market price.
- At present, the ration shops sell food grains at low prices to three categories of ration card holders i.e APL, BPL and AAY.

5. Seasonal hunger is related to cycles of food growing and harvesting. This is prevalent in rural areas because of the seasonal nature of agricultural activities and in urban areas because of casual labourers. Justify the statements with relevant points. **Competency Based**

Ans. Seasonal hunger happens when people face food shortages at certain times of the year.It is related to cycles of food growing and harvesting.

This happens in the following cases

- In rural areas, this often occurs because farming activities have seasons. For example, there may be less food available between planting and harvesting times.
- In urban areas, casual laborers, like construction workers, struggle to find work during certain seasons. This means they have less money to buy food.

So, both in rural and urban areas, people experience hunger because of these seasonal changes in work and food production. This makes it difficult for them to get enough food to eat regularly.

As a result, seasonal hunger highlights the challenges people face in getting food during specific times of the year, whether they're farmers waiting for crops or city workers waiting for jobs.

Case Based Questions

1. Read the sources given below and answer the questions that follow.

Source A Why Food Security?

Due to a natural calamity, say drought, total production of food grains decreases. It creates a shortage of food in the affected areas. Due to shortage of food, the prices goes up. At the high prices, some people cannot afford to buy food. If such calamity happens in a very wide spread area or is stretched over a longer time period, it may cause a situation of starvation. A massive starvation might take a turn of famine.

(i) How does the situation of starvation arise?

Source B Food Security Means

Food security means availability, accessibility and affordability of food to all people at all times. The poor households are more vulnerable to food insecurity whenever there is a problem of production or distribution of food crops.

Food security depends on the Public Distribution System (PDS) and government vigilance and action at times, when this security is threatened.

(ii) To what extent do you think that food security depends on government?

Source C What is Buffer Stock?

Do you know why this Buffer Stock is created by the government? This is done to distribute foodgrains in the deficit areas and among the poorer strata of the society at a price lower than the market price also known as Issue Price. This also helps resolve the problem of shortage of food during adverse weather conditions or during the periods of calamity.

(iii) How is food secured ensured in a country?

Ans. (i) Situation of starvation arise when any calamity happens in a very widespread area or is stretched over a large time period.

(ii) Food security depends on government to a large extent as it is a major role of the PDS to see that food is properly distributed in the country. Since PDS is a government department therefore it is for the government to ensure food security.

(iii) Food security is ensured in a country only if enough food is available for all persons. Moreover, people should have the capacity to buy food of acceptable quality and there is no barrier on access to food.

2. Read the source given below and answer the questions that follow.

The increased food grains procurement at enhanced MSP is the result of the pressure exerted by leading foodgrain producing states, such as Punjab, Haryana and Andhra Pradesh. Moreover, as the procurement is concentrated in a few prosperous regions (Punjab, Haryana, Western Uttar Pradesh, Andhra Pradesh and to a lesser extent in West Bengal) and mainly of two crops wheat and rice increase in MSP has induced farmers, particularly in surplus states, to divert land from production of coarse grains, which is the staple food of the poor, to the production of rice and wheat. The intensive utilisation of water in the cultivation of rice has also led to environmental degradation and fall in the water level, threatening the sustainability of the agricultural development in these states.

(i) Which states achieved the highest rate of growth in foodgrain production?

(ii) What is the impact of intensive utilisation of water in the cultivation of rice on the environment?

(iii) How has Minimum Support Price (MSP) supported the farmers?

Ans. (i) Punjab and Haryana, achieved the highest rate of growth in foodgrain production.

(ii) The intensive utilisation of water in the cultivation of rice has also led to

- Environmental degradation and fall in the water level,
- This has threatened the sustainability of the agricultural development in the states of Punjab and Haryana.

(iii) Minimum Support Price supported farmers in the following ways

- The farmers are encouraged to raise their agricultural production.
- MSP raises the income of the farmers by which they can buy more agricultural inputs for better yields.

ASSESSMENT EXERCISE

Multiple Choice Questions (MCQs)

1. At what price does the government purchase the foodgrains for having a buffer stock?

(a) Controlled price (b) Issue price
(c) Minimum support price (d) Maximum support price

2. In which year was ICDS introduced?

(a) 1965 (b) 1975
(c) 1985 (d) 1995

3. Consider the following statements related to chronic hunger and select the correct option.

(a) It is a consequence of a diet regularly deficient in quantity and quality.
(b) It has reduced in urban areas 4.3% of households in 1983.
(c) It has reduced 0.8% in rural areas in 1983.
(d) All of the above

4. Arrange the following in sequence of the years in which they were launched starting with the earliest.

I. TPDS II. AAY
III. ICDS IV. FFW

Codes

(a) I, III, IV, II (b) I, II, III, IV
(c) IV, I, II, III (d) III, IV, I, II

Subjective Questions (VSA, SA & LA)

1. What are the types of ration card currently issued?

2. Why is it necessary to provide food security in India?

3. Distinguish between Issue Price and MSP.

4. Why is a ration shop called 'Fair Price Shop'? Why does government have a system of different ration cards?

5. Why does every government need to maintain a buffer stock and how does it help?

6. What are the consequences of the excessive reserves of foodgrains in India?

7. How many types of ration cards are there ? What are the problems in the functioning of ration shops?

Getting Acquainted with Disaster Management

CHAPTER 1

India has been grappling with the challenge of managing disasters, both natural and man-made, which occur on a massive scale and can cause widespread disruption. These disasters, ranging from earthquakes to floods to droughts, have brought the issue of disaster management to the forefront of public discourse in the country.

It can be classified into the following categories Water and Climate Disaster, Geological Disaster, Biological Disaster, Industrial Disaster, Nuclear Disasters and Man-made Disasters.

1.1 What is Hazard?

A hazard is a dangerous event that could cause injury, loss of life or damage to property, livelihood or the environment. Hazards can be natural or human induced. Some hazards are also considered as socio-natural, i.e. they are caused due to a combination of human negligence and natural factors.

Examples of **natural hazards**[1] are **tsunami**[2], earthquakes, volcanic eruptions, cyclones, etc.

Human induced hazards[3] include rail, road and air accidents, terrorist attacks, wars, riots, etc. **Socio-natural hazards**[4] may include floods, landslides and droughts caused by multiple factors.

What is a Disaster?

A disaster is an event which results in widespread human loss, accompanied by loss of livelihood and property and causing suffering and loss in a particular area.

Some of the common features that are generally seen in areas affected by disasters are

- Disruption in the normal functioning of society affecting a large number of people.
- It affects the community by a significant loss of lives, property and livelihood, besides giving a blow to the economy. Society needs outside assistance to deal with these losses.
- A big blow to the country's economy.
- Cyclone 'Sidr' is an example of a hazard turning into a disaster.

Cyclone Sidr

Cyclone Sidr hit Bangladesh on the evening of 15th November, 2007. The cyclone originated from a depression over the Bay of Bengal on 11th November and hit the offshore islands on the 15th. It made landfall across the Southern coast from Cox's Bazaar towards the Satkhira district. According to the Bangladesh Meteorological Department, it had a radius of 500 km with the eye of the storm 74 km wide. With wind speeds reaching between 220 to 240 km per hour, it killed more than 3000 people and affected more than 27 districts of Bangladesh.

UN Agencies, Government of India and many NGOs have come forward to support the affected areas and bring life back to normalcy.

1 **Natural hazards** These are possibilities of natural events that may cause loss of life or injury, property damage, social and economic disruption or environmental degradation.

2 **Tsunami** A very large ocean wave caused by an underwater earthquake or volcanic eruption.

3 **Human induced hazards** It is an event that is caused by human activities and can have negative impacts on people, property and the environment.

4 **Socio-natural hazards** It is hazard that results from a combination of natural and human caused factors.

Types of Disaster

Disasters can be categorised into various types based on speed and cause or origin

(a) Based on the speed, a disaster can be termed as slow or rapid.

(i) **Slow onset disasters** are those that may take many months to form and may even last upto years. Examples of these are drought, famine, pest infestation, environmental degradation etc.

(ii) **Rapid onset disasters** are those that are triggered by a sudden shock. The impact of such a disaster can be short-lived or long-term. Examples are volcanic eruptions, flash floods, cyclones, earthquakes and tsunamis.

(b) Based on the cause, a disaster can be natural or human induced.

(i) **Natural Disaster** A natural disaster is an event that is caused by a natural hazard and leads to human, material, economic and environmental losses which exceed the ability of those affected to cope with.

Examples of natural disasters are

- 2004 — Indian Ocean Tsunami
- 2007 — Cyclone in Myanmar
- 2008 — Earthquake in China

(ii) **Human Induced Disaster** A serious disruption of normal life triggered by humans, this hazard causes human, material, economic and environmental losses which exceeds the ability of those affected to cope with.

Examples of human induced disasters are

- 1984 — Bhopal Gas tragedy
- 1997 — Uphaar Cinema fire (Delhi)
- 2002 — Rajdhani Train derailment
- 2003 — Kumbakonam School Fire tragedy
- 2008 — Jaipur Serial blasts

When Does a Hazard Lead to a Disaster?

A hazard becomes a disaster when its impact on the community is so severe that people cannot handle the situation, resulting in widespread deaths, injuries, property damage and destruction.

The Bhuj earthquake on 26th January, 2001 is such an example; it killed more than 10000 people and became a disaster owing to its immediate impact on society.

Contrary to this, if an earthquake strikes a desert which is uninhabited, it would not cause direct and immediate damage to society, and thus would not be termed as a disaster.

1.2 What is Vulnerability?

Vulnerability is the condition, determined by physical, social, economic and environmental factors or processes, which increases the susceptibility of a community to the impact of hazards.

(Source: Living with Risk, UN ISDR 2002)

For instance, during the Gujarat Earthquake (2001), people living in the old city of Bhuj with narrow roads, newly constructed unsafe high rise buildings and a high density of population faced more injuries and loss of life during the earthquake than those living in the suburbs of Bhuj.

Usually people who are socially and economically underprivileged are the ones who are most vulnerable to disasters.

Among people, the younger children, the elderly and the physically challenged persons are more likely to be affected by disasters.

1.3 What is Risk?

Risk is the probability of harmful consequences or expected losses, such as deaths, injuries, loss of property and livelihood, disruption in economic activity and environmental degradation resulting from interactions between hazards and vulnerable conditions.

(Source: Reducing Disaster Risk, UNDP 2004)

The village of Samiyarpettai in Tamil Nadu reported fewer deaths in comparison with the other neighbouring village after the 2004 tsunami. This was because the community members were better trained in search and rescue, evacuation and first aid. Thus, risks often exist within the social system.

For instance, during the recurrent urban floods in Mumbai, the poor living in slums face greater adverse effects of floods (both immediate and long-term) than the others living in the city.

These effects also include loss of daily wages, damage to workspace in homes, electrocution, water-borne diseases, etc. Moreover, the poor people do not have insurance and they are not always adequately compensated by the government and aid agencies for their losses.

1.4 Disaster Management

Disaster Management covers the range of activities designed to maintain control over disasters/ emergency situations and to provide a framework for helping people to avoid, reduce the effects of or recover from the impact of disasters. These activities may be related to preparedness, mitigation, emergency response, relief and recovery and may be conducted before, during or after a disaster.

(Source: Living with Risk, UN ISDR 2004)

Phases of Disaster Management

The different phases of Disaster Management are

1. Disaster Strikes 2. Emergency Response and Relief
3. Rehabilitation and Reconstruction
4. Mitigation
5. Preparedness

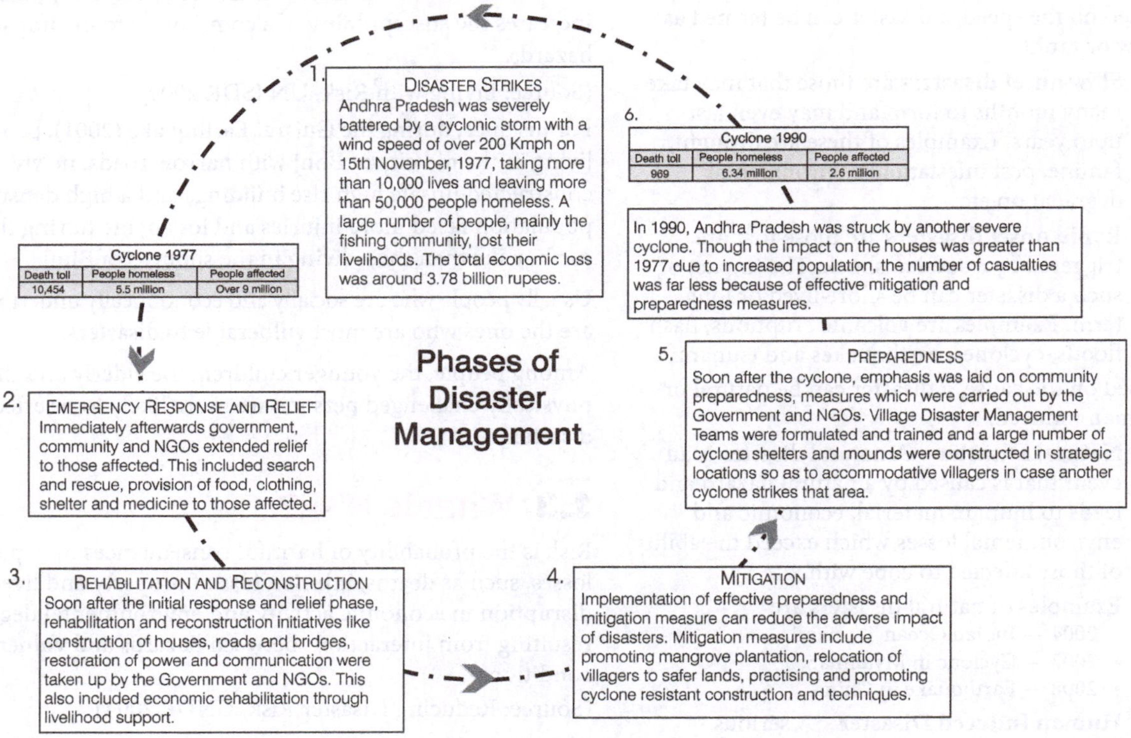

These phases of Disaster Management are often carried out simultaneously after a disaster.

As soon as a disaster strikes a community, a locality or an area, immediate **response and relief**[5] activities are carried out by various arms of the government, Non-Governmental Organisations (NGOs) and other agencies and individuals.

The operations involved include search and rescue of affected persons, first aid, provision of food, clothing, shelter and medicine to the affected and so on.

After this initial response and relief phase, **rehabilitation and reconstruction**[6] activities are taken up. Communication links, roads, housing and electric power are restored by the arms of the government and other agencies. This phase includes economic rehabilitation for those people who have lost their livelihoods.

Long-term mitigation for reducing the impact of further disasters is then taken up. This includes both structural and non-structural measures.

Structural measures can include construction of earthquake-resistant buildings, raising river embankments to prevent floods etc. These measures are termed as **mitigation**[7] measures. Non-structural measures can include raising awareness in the community for better **preparedness**[8] in case of future disasters, mapping flood plains, etc.

5 **Response and relief** Response refers to the actions taken immediately after a disaster occurs to manage and address its effect. Relief refers to the aid and assistance provided to those affected by the disaster.

6 **Rehabilitation and reconstruction** Rehabilitation and reconstruction are activities that help restore a community's livelihoods, assets and production level after a disaster.

7 **Mitigation** Mitigation is the lessening or minimising of the adverse impacts of a hazardous event.

8 **Preparedness** Activities and measures taken before a hazardous event to ensure effective response to the impact of hazards.

REVIEW EXERCISE

Covering Textbook Questions

ACTIVITIES

ACTIVITY 1 QUIZ

Q.1 Can a disaster be prevented? Enumerate some of the ways through which impact of a disaster can be reduced.

Ans. No, a disaster cannot be prevented, but its effect can be reduced through proper Disaster Management.

Some of the ways through which impact of a disaster can be reduced are

(i) Emergency response and relief
(ii) Rehabilitation and reconstruction
(iii) Mitigation
(iv) Preparedness

Q.2 List at least 10 risk inducing factors in home, school or office.

Ans. **Home** Gas stove, gas cylinder, room heater, water heating rod, electrical appliances, etc.

School Swings, chemicals in lab, swimming pool.

Office Lifts, fire in building, etc.

Q.3 List the hazards in the mountainous areas, coastal regions and plateau areas of India.

Ans. **Mountains** Landslides, deforestation, forest fires, land subsidence, avalanches, volcanic eruption, earthquakes, flash floods, hailstorms, etc.

Plateau Drought, landslides, deforestation, etc.

Coastal regions Tsunami, cyclones or floods, etc.

Q.4 What do you understand by mitigation? Why is it important? Give three examples of non-structural mitigation.

Ans. **Mitigation** Any action taken to minimise the extent and effect of a disaster or potential disaster is known as mitigation. Mitigation can take place before, during or after a disaster, but the term is most often used to refer to the action against potential disasters.

Mitigation is important because

- It helps to reduce the impact of disasters and reduces loss of life and property.
- By adopting mitigation strategies, the communities are able to recover and resume normal lives rapidly.

Examples of non-structural mitigation are

- Training in Disaster Management
- Regulating land use
- Educating the public
- Raising awareness
- Hazard mapping

Q.5 List the people and structures that were vulnerable and at risk during the tsunami that hit the Southern coast of the country on 26th December, 2004.

Ans. People vulnerable and at risk during a tsunami will be

(i) Fishermen when they are near the coast or if they are removing the fish after reaching the shore.
(ii) Sailors if they are near the coast or if they are on the ship which is berthed in the port.
(iii) People living on the coast or even near the coast, especially around estuaries of rivers.
(iv) Anybody who is near the sea either for work or for sport when the tsunami strikes.

Structures vulnerable and at risk during a tsunami will be

(i) homes, offices and other buildings on the seacoast or near it.
(ii) communication towers, electricity poles or other man made structures on the coast or near it.
(iii) trees on or near the coast.

Q.6 Given below are pictures based on the various phases of Disaster Management. Identify the various steps that are shown in the pictures and arrange them in the order of occurrence.

Ans. The various steps in order of occurrence are

Pictures no.	Phase of Disaster Management
1.	Response and relief
2.	Rehabilitation and reconstruction
3.	Mitigation
4.	Preparedness

ACTIVITY 2 POWERPOINT PRESENTATION/ FIELD SURVEY/ACTIVITY

Topic

Develop a PowerPoint presentation with the following parameters from one of the recent occurrences in India

(i) Content of the subject matter
(ii) Location of the disaster
(iii) Vulnerabilities
(iv) Impact
(v) Rehabilitation Plan
(vi) Critical analysis of the pre-disaster preparedness plans

or

Field Survey based on a preset questionnaire.
If you are in one of the areas which has been affected by a disaster, study the impact of that disaster on children and teachers (psycho-social impact, loss of instructional time, economic loss to the school etc)

or

Prepare a list of activities that need to be taken care of by the administrators for camp management of a camp set-up temporarily for people affected by the disaster (pre, during and post disaster).

Learning Objectives

After the task the students shall be able to

- understand the concept of Disaster Management in totality.
- comprehend the purpose of each of the terms used in the presentation/ survey/ activity.
- distinguish between the phases of Disaster Management in terms of the activities involved.
- understand the logical order of presentation (only in case of the Power Point presentation).

Procedure

(i) Teacher may divide the students into groups to carry out the above three types of work. Some groups may prepare the presentation, some groups may carry out the survey and the rest may do the camp management activity.
(ii) Teacher will assess all activities based on content, presentation and involvement of the group members.
(iii) A short discussion will be held on each activity immediately after it is presented.

ACTIVITY 3 GROUP DISCUSSION

Topic

On a newspaper clipping about a disaster.
e.g. Hurricane Sandy slams the East Coast of USA.
"Sandy, a massive storm described by forecasters as one of the largest to ever hit the United States, thrashed the East Coast, flooding towns and leaving millions without power."

Learning Objectives

The students will be able to

- comprehend the nature of the disaster.
- analyse the impact of the disaster on the persons affected, their livelihoods, the economy and society of the concerned area.
- develop oratory skills and self-confidence.

Procedure

The teacher will give the topic to the students one week in advance to collect additional information on various related aspects.

Discussion should be conducted keeping the following points in mind

(i) The background - what is a hurricane, forecast and advance preparation etc.
(ii) Nature of the actual hurricane - details of when and where it struck, some details of devastation caused etc.
(iii) Impact on persons affected, their livelihoods, the economy and society of the concerned area.
(iv) Mitigation measures proposed to be adopted.

Feedback

If from peer assessment or from the teacher's observation, some shortcomings are found in understanding the concepts, then the teacher should arrange for some remedial measures.
If the students fail to understand the proper meaning of a hurricane, the teacher can give some facts of other well-known hurricanes to make comprehension easier.

ACTIVITY 4

Project

The Uttarakhand flood and cyclone Phailin were the two worst natural disasters that happened in the year 2013.

The Uttarakhand flood caused massive destruction and claimed thousands of lives while cyclone Phailin passed with very minimal damage of lives and properties than its predecessor that caused ten thousand people dead in 1999.

Compare these two disasters on the following points

- Origin
- Death and Damage
- Mitigation methods/measures before, during and after disaster.
- Preparedness for disaster
- Effective use of Disaster Management techniques.
- Response and relief.

Learning Outcomes

The students will be able to

- comprehend the nature of disaster.
- analyse the impact of preparedness and mitigation measures.
- understand the importance of effective use of Disaster Management.

Procedure

(i) Collect information from Internet, newspapers, magazines and other information sources about these incidents.

(ii) Prepare a tabular form of presentation and write about both incidents on the above mentioned points.

(iii) Critical analysis of Disaster Management in both cases with rating of its success in points out of 10.

(iv) Give a presentation in the class.

Time

One week

Assessment Criteria

- Effectiveness of Presentation
- Creativity
- Analytical ability
- Interpretation of facts

Follow-Up

Teacher can discuss some other incidents that show effective use or failure in use of Disaster Management techniques.

ACTIVITY 5 DEBATE

Topic

Structural and non-structural mitigation measures in India are very effective.

Learning Outcomes

The students will be able to

- describe details of mitigation measures of both categories.
- analyse the impact of the mitigation measures.
- develop the skill of organising one's thoughts.
- develop oratory skill and self-confidence.

Procedure

(i) The class would be divided into two teams, one for the motion and one against it.

(ii) Two speakers will represent each team with one member of each team speaking on structural mitigation and the other member on non-structural mitigation measures. Team members will choose their speakers.

(iii) All members of each team will collect points or arguments with evidence in support of their stand.

(iv) Two members from each team will be selected for the rebuttal.

(v) Teacher will chair the debate.

Assessment Criteria

Assessment will be made by the teacher for

- relevance of content
- clarity of the argument
- logical approach
- quality of rebuttal

ACTIVITY 6 MOCK DRILL

Topic

Use of fire extinguisher

Procedure

This activity will be done outdoors in or near the playground of the school.

The teacher may demonstrate herself/himself using one of the fire extinguishers installed in the school or may ask a qualified firefighter to do the same.

Afterwards, some of the students may be asked to put out small mock fires.

Then a general feedback session may take place.

ACTIVITY 7 PROJECT

Topic

Make a Disaster Management Project on Flooding.

Learning Outcomes

After doing the project the student will be able to

- comprehend the nature of disasters like floods.
- understand its major types.
- understand the present scenario in India.

Procedure

- Teacher will give the topic to the students three days before the project date.
- Teacher will give appropriate instructions to the students to collect useful information from various sources like Internet, newspaper, magazines, news channels and other information sources about the project topic.
- Prepare some key points based on the topic and explain them further.

Answer/Hints

Flooding A situation in which an area of land becomes covered with water because of heavy rain or when a river overflows its banks.

Two types of flooding can be distinguished

(a) **Coastal flooding** Storm surges are an abnormal rise in sea water level associated with hurricanes and other storms at sea. Surges result from on-shore winds and/or intense low pressure formations and ocean storms. Water level is controlled by wind, atmospheric pressure, existing astronomical tides, waves and swell, local coastal topography and bathymetry and the storm's proximity to the coast.

Most often, destruction by storm surge is attributable to

- Wave impact and the physical shock on objects associated with the passing of the wave front.
- Hydrostatic/dynamic forces and the effects of water lifting and carrying objects.

The most significant damage often results from the direct impact of waves on fixed structures. Indirect impacts include flooding and undermining of major infrastructure such as coastal highways and railway lines.

Flooding of deltas and other low-lying coastal areas is exacerbated by the influence of tidal action, storm waves and frequent river channel shifts.

(b) **River flooding** Land-borne floods occur when the capacity of stream channels to conduct water is exceeded and water overflows the river's banks. Floods are natural phenomena and may be expected to occur at irregular intervals on all streams and rivers. Settlement of flood plain areas is a major cause of flood damage.

India is the worst flood-affected country in the world after Bangladesh and accounts for one-fifth of the global death count due to floods. About 40 million hectares or nearly 1/8th of India's geographical area is flood-prone. An estimated 8 million hectares of land are affected annually. The cropped area affected annually ranges from 3.5 million hectares during normal floods to 10 million hectares during the worst floods.

Assessment Criteria

- Effectiveness of presentation
- Creativity
- Analytical ability
- Interpretation of facts
- Originality of thought and presentation

Follow-Up

After finishing the project, teacher can ask the students to take effective participation in a presentation in the class/or can organise a quiz competition in the class based on the project.

Specific Hazards and Mitigation

CHAPTER 2

The Indian sub-continent is plike floods, cyclones, earthquakes, landslides, drought etc, which cause loss of lives and livelihoods as well as destruction of property and infrastructure. For better preparedness to minimise the adverse effects of disasters due to these hazards, many measures can be taken by government, NGOs and the community at large.

2.1 Mitigation

Mitigation refers to any measure taken to minimise the impact of a disaster or potential disaster. Mitigation can take place before, during or after a disaster, but the term is most often used to refer to actions taken against potential disasters.

Significance of Mitigation

Mitigation measures include activities like

- construction of river embankments, strengthening existing buildings, enforcing building codes strictly, following seismic design standards and wind-bracing requirements for new construction or repairing existing buildings.
- construction of houses away from hazardous areas.
- retrofitting public buildings to withstand strong winds or ground shaking.
- building community shelters to protect people living in areas prone to various hazards.

Mitigation's Value to Society

(i) Mitigation creates safer communities by reducing losses of life and property.

(ii) Mitigation enables individuals and communities to recover more rapidly from disasters.

(iii) Mitigation lessens the financial impact of disasters on government and communities.

Types of Mitigation

They are classified under two types

(i) **Structural mitigation**[1] It includes activities such as construction of river embankments or strengthening existing buildings, etc.

(ii) **Non-structural mitigation**[2] It includes activities such as training in disaster management, regulating land use, public education, etc.

2.2 Floods

Floods are temporary situations where large areas of land get covered with water. This can happen because of heavy rainfall, strong storms, rising water levels in rivers or reservoirs, a dam breaking or the melting of snow and ice. Floods are a recurring problem in India with about 12% of its total land area prone to floods. Floods can happen gradually due to heavy rain, taking many hours, or suddenly (called 'flash flood') due to breach of water control structures like a dam or **retaining wall**[3].

Warning

Except for flash floods, there is usually a reasonable warning period. The Central Water Commission, Irrigation and Flood Control Department and Water Resources Department of Government of India are responsible for flood detection, tracking, receiving warning and disseminating information.

1 **Structural mitigation** Any measure taken to minimise the effect of a disaster or potential disaster which involves construction or maintenance of buildings and other structures

2 **Non-structural mitigation** Any measure taken to minimise the effect of a disaster or potential disaster which does not involve construction or maintenance of buildings and other structures. Examples are forecasting and warning systems, land use control, hazardous area mapping etc.

3 **Retaining wall** This structure is designed to restrain soil to unnatural slopes. Such walls are used to bound soils between two different elevations, often in areas of terrain possessing undesirable slopes. Examples are roads built on hillsides, which require a retaining wall on their side to prevent landslides.

Flood warning information is disseminated by the following means

- Government channels
- High priority telegrams (not used now)
- Doordarshan and the local cable channels
- All India Radio
- Bulletins in the press
- Satellite-based disaster warning system
- Fax
- Telephones

Flood Mitigation Strategies

There are a large number of structural and non-structural mitigation measures that can be taken up to reduce the impact of floods in areas that are frequently battered by floods.

Some of the mitigation strategies include

Structural Mitigation

(a) **Watershed management** Timely cleaning, desilting and deepening of natural water reservoirs and drainage channels must be taken up.

(b) **Reservoirs** The entire natural water storage place should be cleaned on a regular basis, especially before the monsoon season. Encroachments on tanks and ponds or natural drainage channels should be removed well before the onset of monsoon.

(c) **Buildings on elevated area** The buildings in flood prone areas should be constructed on an elevated area and, if necessary, on stilts and platforms.

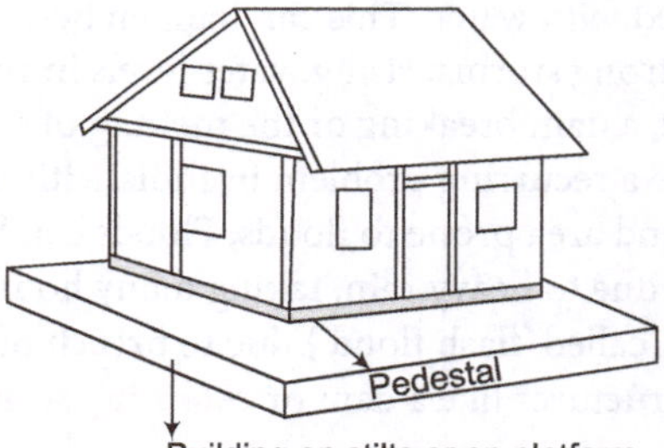

Building on stilts or on platform

Khash Dhalai Flood Shelter

Flood shelters like this are just one example of how communities can protect themselves from the worst of the floods. Banks of Earth are raised by upto 5 m and cover an area of several kilometres. The people dig a huge pond in the middle and use this earth to raise the ground.
Whenever the floods come, people can take their livestock, possessions, Even their homes - to safety. The pond in the middle becomes an important source of food, as it is used to farm fish.

(d) **Natural water retention basins** Construction of flood protection embankments, ring bunds and other bunds. Dams and levees can also be constructed and used as temporary water storage space, which will reduce the chances of lower plains getting flooded.

(e) **Flood control measures** Measures can be taken to reduce the run-off by reforestation, protection of vegetation, cleaning of debris from streams, etc.

Non-Structural Mitigation

(a) **Mapping of flood plains** It is the first step involved in reducing risk of floods.

(b) **Land use control** It will reduce the danger to life and property when water inundates the flood plains and coastal areas.

(c) **Flood forecasting and warning** Better facilities would help in reducing the impact of floods.

Note Buildings should not be constructed in areas near where rivers turn, flood plains or mudflows.

- No major development should be permitted in areas which are subjected to flooding.
- Important facilities like hospitals should be located in safer and elevated areas.

2.3 Cyclones

Cyclones are violent storms, often of vast extent, characterised by high winds rotating around a calm centre of low atmospheric pressure. This centre moves onward, often with a velocity of 50 km per hour.

Super Cyclones

On 29th October,1999, a super cyclone with wind speed 260-300 km/hr hit the coast of Odisha that was created in the Bay of Bengal, with water levels more than 10 m higher than normal. The super storm travelled more than 250 km inland and within a period of 36 hours ravaged more than 200 lakh hectares of land, felling trees and vegetation. The violent cyclone was merciless and killed thousands.

Warning

- Cyclones have been recurrent phenomena in the coastal parts of India. Cyclones strike suddenly, although it takes time for a cyclone to build up.
- Satellite tracking can track the movement, the build up and likely path of a cyclone.
- Warning is given and evacuations are done all along the projected path.

- However, landfall predictions can give only a few hours notice to the threatened population, as it is difficult to predict its landfall with total accuracy.
- The Indian Meteorological Department issues warnings against severe weather phenomena like tropical cyclones, heavy rains and snow, cold and heat waves, etc.
- On 14th November, 2007, a cyclone warning was issued to the people living in the coastal areas of Odisha and West Bengal as there was a possibility of cyclone 'Sidr' making a landfall in these states.
- Cyclone warning is disseminated by several means such as satellite based disaster warning systems, radio, telephone, television, fax, public announcements and bulletins in the press.
- District administration took adequate steps to relocate the people to safe cyclone shelters that were constructed after the state faced a severe super cyclone in 1999.

Cyclone Mitigation Strategies

Cyclone mitigation strategies can be categorised as

Structural Mitigation

(a) **Multi-purpose cyclone shelters** Shelters with suitable designs need to be constructed in appropriate locations in coastal areas. Cyclone shelters can be used as schools or community centres at normal times.

(b) **Engineered structures** Structures that can withstand wind forces need to be built with locally available materials.

It is advised to construct houses on stilts or on Earth mounds.

Buildings should be wind and water resistant.

All elements holding the structures need to be properly anchored to resist uplift or flying off of objects. For instance, overhangs of roofs should be avoided and projections should be tied down.

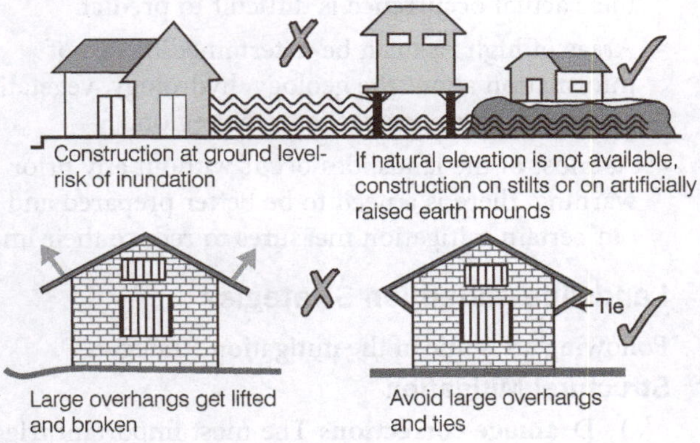

(c) **Protection against wind** Construction of houses should not be done right on the coast, but either behind a mound or hillock. This will act as a protection against strong cyclonic winds. Fishermen are normally affected, as they stay very close to the coastline.

(d) **Coastal belt plantation** Planting a shelter belt along the coastline will mitigate the impact of strong winds. It will also check soil erosion and inward sand drift, thereby protecting cultivation fields and houses which are located in coastal areas.

(e) **Construction of roads** Roads constructed in coastal areas should be elevated. The East coast road from West Bengal to Kanyakumari is one such example.

Non-Structural Mitigation

(a) **Hazard mapping** This map will illustrate the areas vulnerable to cyclones in any given year. It is an effective mitigation tool.

(b) **Land use control** It should be designed so that only the least critical activities are conducted in vulnerable areas. Location of settlements in the flood plains is of utmost risk. Vulnerable areas should be used for parks, grazing or playgrounds.

(c) **Cyclone forecasting and warning** Better forecasting of cyclones, as well as early and timely warning to the people who are likely to be affected, leads to better preparedness and reduced impact to life, property, livelihoods and infrastructure.

2.4 Earthquakes

An earthquake is a sudden shaking of the ground that occurs when energy is released in the Earth's crust.

It can cause ground shaking, soil liquefaction, landslides, fires and tsunamis.

Warning

- Earthquake is a sudden onset hazard and can happen at any time of the year, day or night with sudden impact without any warning.
- There is no accepted method of earthquakes prediction.
- To reduce the impact of earthquakes (regular phenomena in countries like Japan and Indonesia), various mitigation strategies have been taken up by the governments and people of these countries.

Earthquake Mitigation Strategies

Some of the mitigation strategies are

Structural Mitigation

(a) **Engineered structures** Structures should be designed and built to withstand ground shaking.

(b) **Architectural and engineering inputs** Both these inputs need to be put together to improve building design and construction practice.

(c) **Soil type** It must be analysed before construction and structures must not be built on soft soil.

Note Buildings built on soft soils are more likely to get damaged even if the earthquake is not particularly strong in magnitude. A similar problem occurs in the alluvial plains and on the river banks. Heavy damages are sustained when ground is soft.

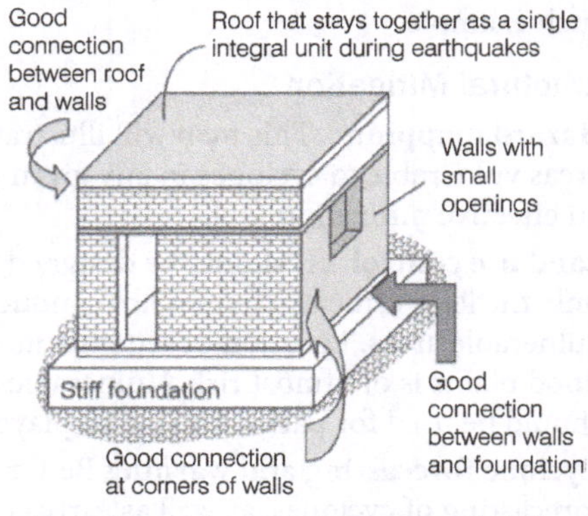

• Essential requirements in a masonry building

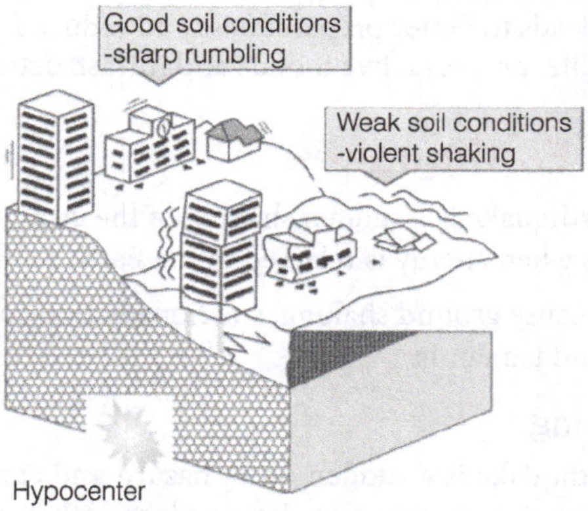

• Effect of soil type on ground shaking

Non-Structural Mitigation

(a) **Enforcing Building Codes**

- The Bureau of Indian Standards has published building codes and guidelines for safe construction to reduce the impact of earthquakes.
- Before the buildings are constructed, the building plan has to be checked by the municipality to verify if the structure conforms to the building guidelines set by the government. Many existing buildings like hospitals, important government offices, schools, fire stations, etc need to be retrofitted with safety devices based on these guidelines, as they play a very crucial role in case an earthquake strikes.

(b) **Public Awareness**

- Sensitisation and training programmes for architects, builders, contractors, designers, engineers, financiers, government functionaries, house owners, masons, etc.
- Reduce possible damages from secondary effects like fire, floods, landslides, etc by identifying potential landslide sites and restricting construction in those areas.

2.5 Landslides

Landslides are slippery masses of rock, Earth or debris which move by the force of their own weight down slopes or river banks. Landslides are primarily associated with mountainous terrain; these can also occur in areas such as surface excavations for highways, buildings and open pit mines.

Landslides are a major natural disaster in hilly terrains like the Himalayas, Western Ghats and in the North-Eastern parts of the country. They destroy life and property almost perennially and cause devastating damage to the transportation and communication network.

Warning

- Normally landslides occur gradually; however, at times sudden failure (sliding) can occur without warning.
- They may take place in combination with earthquakes, floods and volcanic eruptions.
- There are no clearly established warning systems in place indicating occurrence of landslides, and hence, their actual occurrence is difficult to predict.
- Areas of high risk can be determined by use of information about the geology, hydrology, vegetation cover and past occurrence in the region.
- As most of the landslides occur without any prior warning, there is a need to be better prepared and carry out certain mitigation measures to reduce their impact.

Landslide Mitigation Strategies

Following are some of the mitigation strategies

Structural Mitigation

(a) **Drainage corrections** The most important triggering mechanism for mass movement of soil is water infiltration into the land area during heavy rains.

Hence, the natural way of preventing this situation is by reducing water infiltration and allowing excess water to move down without hindrance.

In such a situation, the first and foremost mitigation measure is drainage correction. This involves maintenance of natural drainage channels, both micro and macro, in vulnerable slopes.

(b) **Engineered structures** Structures with strong foundations can withstand ground movement forces. Underground installations (pipes, cables etc) should be made flexible to move in order to withstand forces caused by landslides.

(c) **Retaining walls** These walls can be built to stop land from slipping (these walls are seen along roads in hill stations).

(d) **Increasing vegetation** Increase in vegetation cover is the cheapest and most effective way of arresting (stopping) landslides. This helps to bind the top layer of the soil with layers below, while preventing excessive water run-off and soil erosion.

Non-Structural Mitigation

(a) **Hazard mapping** This will locate areas prone to slope failures. This will identify avoidance of areas for building settlements.

(b) **Land use practices** Practices such as preserving existing natural vegetation (forest and natural grassland) in good condition should be adopted.

- Denuded upper slopes must be reforested with suitable tree species.
- In construction of roads, irrigation canals etc, proper care is to be taken to avoid blockage of natural drainage.

(c) **Awareness generation** The public should be educated about signs that a landslide is imminent, so that personal safety measures may be taken. They should also gather information on indigenous methods used to reduce the impact of landslides.

2.6 Drought

A drought is a prolonged period of dry weather that occurs when there is a lack of precipitation, resulting in a water shortage. Droughts can last for days, months or years and can occur anywhere in the world.

Warning

According to the Indian Meteorological Department, a region is said to be drought affected if the overall rainfall deficiency in the region is over 10% of the long period average; and more than 20% of the area of the region is affected by such drought conditions.

In general, drought means different things to different people. To a meteorologist, drought may mean absence of rain, whereas to a farmer or agriculturist, it means deficiency of soil moisture in the crop root zone, as this zone supports crop growth and productivity. To a hydrologist, drought means depleting water levels in lakes and reservoirs, while for a Municipal Corporation, it may mean the shortage of availability of drinking water.

Drought Prompts First Ever Emergency Food Operation in Nepal (23rd May, 2006)

Ten of Nepal's 75 districts are affected by the drought, which is following the driest winter on record in the region, among the poorest parts of this badly impoverished country. Earlier this month, World Food Programme (WFP) revealed that 47% of Nepalis do not have enough food to live active and healthy lives.

About half of all children are malnourished. But while the national poverty rate is about 31% in the Karnali region and affected adjoining districts, it is 45%, said De Margerie.

In normal years, there is a 'hunger gap' in Karnali, the period between harvests when food stocks run out and people survive by buying food with what little money they earn as day labourers, or with cash repatriated by relatives who have migrated for jobs.

The above story shows that drought impacts rainfed crops to start with and subsequently irrigated crops.

Drought Mitigation Strategies

Reducing risks or impacts of drought in the future involves mostly preparedness and, if carried out appropriately, can, in many cases, eliminate much of the impact. Some of the mitigation strategies are

Structural Mitigation

It includes revival of traditional water harvesting structures (canals, tanks etc) like 'Baolis' in Rajasthan or 'Jhalara' in Gujarat, as well as construction of new water harvesting structures in houses and farm areas.

This is carried out by allowing the run-off water from all areas to collect at a common point in houses and allowing the run-off water to infiltrate into the soil (thus, increasing groundwater level) in farms.

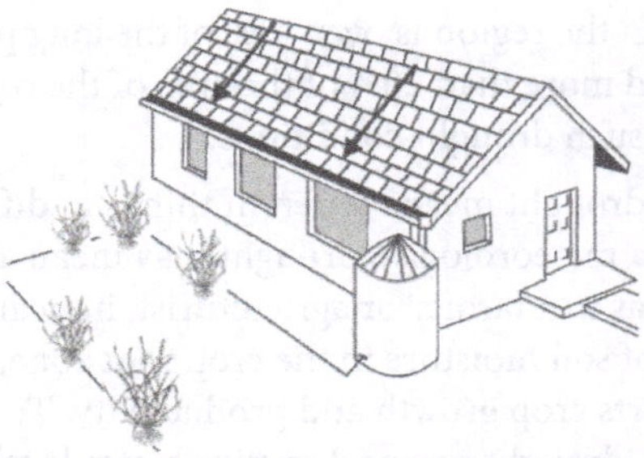

Source : US Rooftop rainwater harvesting: Roof acts as catchments, draining the water to a cistern.

Crop Insurance Scheme

Comprehensive Crop Insurance Scheme was introduced from 1985 kharif season with the objective of providing financial support to the farmers in the event of crop failure due to natural vagaries like droughts and floods. It is offered by the General Insurance Corporation of India and its subsidiaries.
This scheme covers foodgrains and oilseeds.

Non-Structural Mitigation

(a) **Drought monitoring** As it is a slow onset disaster, all components of the hydrological system must be monitored to assess the potential for a drought and timely decisions should be taken accordingly. In areas often affected by drought, awareness programmes for the community by the government and NGOs must be held to educate them on water conservation strategies, land use planning and livelihood planning.

(b) **Land use planning** Land use based on its capability helps in optimum use of land and water, preventing undue demand due to its misuse.

(c) **Livelihood planning** It involves identification of livelihoods which are least likely to be affected by drought like collection of non-timber forest products, community forestry, carpentry, raising goats etc.

(d) **Crop insurance** This is an insurance given to the farmers, who have lost their crops because of lack of water supply.

Ralegaon Siddhi

A success story of drought mitigation is Ralegaon Siddhi village in Ahmednagar district of Maharashtra. During the 1980s, the village had few trees and the topsoil had blown off, reducing agriculture and thus, reducing people to poverty and unemployment. Social activist Anna Hazare started a movement for water harvesting by building check dams and tanks to trap whatever rain was falling.

The villagers planted trees to conserve the soil, and now after 25 years, the area under irrigation has increased from about 32 hectares then to 525 hectares today. Migration to the towns has stopped and income per capita has increased 10 times, all without any funding or grant, but only with people's enterprise.

REVIEW EXERCISE

Covering Textbook Questions

ACTIVITIES

ACTIVITY 1 PICTURE COMPREHENSION

1. A seismometer is an instrument which is used for measuring earthquakes. Collect information and pictures on various ancient ways of measuring earthquakes of various countries of the world.

Ans. Do it yourself.

A Chinese method is mentioned below

Nearly 2000 years ago, the ancient Chinese made a special vase that had several sculpted dragons mounted all around the sides of the vase. Each dragon held in its mouth a metal ball. When the ground shook, some of the balls would fall from the mouths of the dragons into the waiting mouths of the sculpted frogs to show how the ground had moved.

2. Prepare a brochure for an NGO to create an awareness about use of traditional water harvesting systems.

Ans. Do it yourself.

3. Read and review any book related to drought, e.g. P Sainath's 'Everybody Loves a Good Drought' and Anupam Mishra's 'Rajasthan Ki Rajat Boonde'.

Ans. Do it yourself.

ACTIVITY 2 REPORT SKILL

1. Interview a Bank Manager on how crop insurance is given and report to class.

Ans. Some details of the history of crop insurance in India are given below as a background

Crop insurance is undertaken by agricultural producers, including farmers and others to protect themselves against either the loss of their crops due to natural disasters such as hail, drought and floods or the loss of revenue due to decline in the prices of agricultural commodities. In a country like India, where crop production has been subjected to vagaries of weather and large-scale damages due to attack of pests and diseases, crop insurance assumes a vital role in the stable growth of this sector.

An All Risk Comprehensive Crop Insurance Scheme (CCIS) for major crops was introduced in 1985, coinciding with the introduction of the 7th Five Year Plan and subsequently, replaced by National Agricultural Insurance Scheme (NAIS) *w.e.f.* 1999-2000. These schemes have been preceded by years of preparation, studies, planning, experiments and trials on a pilot basis. Agriculture Insurance Company of India Limited (AIC) has been formed by the Government of India consequent to the announcement of budget of 2003 to serve the needs of farmers better. To move towards a sustainable actuarial regime, it was proposed to establish a new corporation for agriculture insurance.

AIC has taken over the implementation of National Agricultural Insurance Scheme (NAIS), which until 2003 was implemented by General Insurance Corporation of India. In future, AIC would also be transacting other insurance businesses directly or indirectly concerning agriculture and its allied activities.

2. Discuss various methods of recycling water in your school and at home. List how recycled water can be used.

Ans. Do it yourself.

Hints

After suitable filtration through charcoal, gravel and sand, waste water from toilets can be used for the following purposes

(i) Irrigating agricultural fields, garden plants, etc.

(ii) Flushing of toilets.

(iii) Use in industrial processes.

(iv) Recharging of groundwater.

(v) Construction activities like concrete mixing.

ACTIVITY 3 QUIZ ON FLOODS

1. What are floods that happen suddenly called?

Ans. Flash floods.

2. What is the difference between flood and flash flood?

Ans. Flash flood is a flood which happens suddenly due to breach of water control structures, spillover or a heavy downpour in nearby areas.

Normal floods occur gradually over many hours due to increase in water levels in rivers and water reservoirs, causing inundation.

3. Identify three causes of floods in rural and urban areas.

Ans. Causes of floods in rural areas

(i) Heavy rain over a flat or low lying area.

(ii) A river breaching its embankments due to high water flow or heavy rain in the river's catchment area.

(iii) Any drainage obstructions like landslides, land subsidence etc after heavy rains.

Causes of floods in urban areas

(i) Lack of proper drainage or poor sewerage system.

(ii) High intensity rainfall for a long time.

(iii) A river passing through an urban area breaching its embankments due to high water flow or heavy rain in the river's catchment area.

4. What is reducing disaster risk called?

Ans. Reducing disaster risk is known as mitigation.

5. What percentage of our land areas is prone to floods?

Ans. More than 12% of land areas in India is prone to floods.

6. Name the government department at the district level responsible for flood warning in remote areas.

Ans. Irrigation and Flood Control Department.

7. What food would you store in a flood prone area?

Ans. Non-perishable food like biscuits, dry fruits and sufficient potable water should be stored in a cool, dry area off the flood or even higher in flood prone areas. Do not store them above the stove, under the sink, in a damp garage or basement or any place exposed to high or low temperature extremes.

8. Name three rivers in India which are frequently affected by floods.

Ans. Ganga, Kosi and Brahmaputra are three major rivers prone to flooding.

ACTIVITY 4 CASE STUDY

1. Identify the areas that are normally affected by drought in India and write a short narrative on the impact of the drought on the community along with a case study.

Ans. **The major drought prone regions** of India are Vidarbha region of Maharashtra, North Karnataka, Telangana, Odisha, Jharkhand, Gujarat and Western Rajasthan.

Impact of drought Drought affects all communities, but in different ways. Among landless, marginal and small families, male members start to migrate early. Females and the aged are often left behind to take care of themselves. In Jharkhand in 2004, many of the starvation deaths reported have been of women and the aged.

Landless, marginal and small farmers reduce their consumption of cereals, pulses and other items. The consumption of irregular foods like khuddi (broken rice), wild roots, gethi, chakora sag and other forest produce increases (in some areas people eat these even in normal times). People add more water to dilute foodgrains.

ACTIVITY 5 ASSIGNMENT

1. Answer the questions based on the given pictures.

(a) What kind of flood control measure has been adopted in the picture on top?

(b) What are the purposes of such a measure?

(c) Give one disadvantage of the measure shown in the picture on top and an advantage of the measure shown in the picture at bottom.

(d) Which are the ideal areas you would use to construct these kinds of roofing?

Ans. (a) The flood control measure adopted in the first picture is construction of houses on stilts.

(b) The purpose is to raise the height of the houses above the expected flood level, so that the flood waters do not enter the houses.

(c) One disadvantage of the flood control measure shown in the first picture is that even though the homes are protected, but the sources of food are not protected in case the flood lasts for sometime. The advantage of the measure shown in the second picture is that, in case of a flood, the pond in the middle will fill-up with water and so it becomes an important source of food, as it is used to farm fish.

(d) The ideal areas that we should construct these kinds of sloping roofs is an area where there is excessive rainfall and water should not be allowed to collect on rooftops, otherwise it may lead to seepage.

2. **(a) Name two states which are highly prone to earthquakes.**

(b) Suggest any one mitigation measure for earthquakes.

Ans. (a) Two states highly prone to earthquakes are Gujarat and Uttarakhand.

(b) There can be many mitigation measures, structural as well as non-structural. A structural measure is not to build any building on soft soil like sandy soil or alluvial plains on river banks.

Also, the buildings require to be constructed with material specified for better resistance to earthquakes (e.g. better cement to sand ratio for the mortar). Non-structural mitigation measures can include building public awareness, retrofitting public buildings with safety devices, enforcing building codes, restricting construction in landslide prone areas etc.

3. **How can desilting help in flood control?**

Ans. Desilting helps in flood control by deepening the natural drainage channel, thus reducing the flood level.

4. **How can 'ring bunds' help in controlling floods on hill slopes?**

Ans. On hill slopes, the soil is removed by weathering and erosion by flowing water. Any location below a hill slope will be flooded when heavy rain or water flow is there. A ring bund binds the soil so that the erosion is minimised and it also prevents flood water from entering the area at the bottom of the hill slope.

5. **Which are the two most effective methods of warning of a tropical cyclone?**

Ans. The most effective methods of warning of a tropical cyclone are

(i) **Satellite tracking** Satellites can track the movement, build-up and likely path of the cyclone and it enables estimation of the likely time when it will hit a particular area.

(ii) **Weather radars** These use Doppler technology and can provide rainfall estimates, wind estimates and the centre location of a tropical cyclone.

6. **What are human activities leading to landslides?**

Ans. Landslides are slippery masses of rock, earth and other debris which move down slopes by the force of their own weight. Human activities causing landslides include unplanned cutting/excavation of a hillside for making a road, building construction or in open pit mining.

7. **What are appropriate water harvesting methods to control drought?**

Ans. To control drought, traditional water harvesting structures like 'Baolis' in Rajasthan or 'Jhalara' in Gujarat should be revived. Further, construction of canals and tanks for river water and rain water conservation respectively, should be taken up in drought prone areas.

8. **The following questions may be asked on correlation of geomorphology and land use planning**

(a) How can the denuded upper slopes of hills be protected from landslides?

(b) What are the geographical factors that help in determining high risk zones for a disaster?

(c) What do you understand by watershed management?

Ans. (a) The best method for protecting the denuded upper slopes of hills from landslides is to reforest these slopes with suitable tree species, so that the soil is not further eroded.

(b) Each disaster has different high risk zones peculiar to it. For instance, locations which lie on or near geological faults in the Earth's crust are in the high risk zone of earthquakes.

Similarly, locations with high percentage of arable lands (i.e. heavy population density) and with high physical vulnerability, especially in coastal areas, are in the high risk zone of tropical cyclones. Low lying areas near rivers are at high risk during floods. A high risk zone for landslides will be hill slopes. High risk areas for droughts are low rainfall areas with sandy soil.

(c) Watershed management is a term used to describe the process of implementing land use practices and water management practices to protect and improve the quality of the water and other natural resources within a watershed by managing the use of those land and water resources in a comprehensive manner. This will include cleaning, desilting and deepening of natural water reservoirs and drainage channels.

9. **Some questions on mitigation measures may be asked.**

(a) How does hazard mapping help in preparedness?

(b) How can building codes and guidelines help in reducing architectural disasters?

(c) Suggest mitigation measures to protect the highways connecting hill stations.

Ans. (a) A hazard map is a map that highlights areas that are affected or vulnerable to a particular hazard. They are typically created for natural hazards such as earthquakes, volcano eruptions, landslides, floods and tsunamis.

Hazard maps help prevent serious damage and deaths by preparing people in advance through adequate awareness and publicity measures in those areas, so that they can take mitigation measures.

(b) Building codes and guidelines have been published by Bureau of Indian Standards for safe construction in hazard prone areas. If they are adhered to, they will help in reducing architectural disasters e.g. the building codes for earthquake prone areas specify the soil on which the buildings can be constructed and the materials which should be used. Similarly, there are building codes and guidelines for cyclone prone areas.

(c) Highways connecting hill stations are usually subject to damage from landslides.

(i) One structural mitigation measure is to construct retaining walls by the sides of the road to prevent the land from slipping.

(ii) Increasing the vegetation cover by planting trees and preserving existing natural vegetation helps to bind the top layer of the soil with the layers below and also prevents excessive water run-off and soil erosion.

(iii) Also, we should construct roads so that the natural drainage channels are not blocked.

ACTIVITY 6 QUIZ

1. What do you understand by structural and non-structural mitigation efforts? Suggest any two for each of the hazards discussed in the chapter.

Ans. Mitigation means to reduce the impact of disasters. Mitigation is of two types

(i) **Structural mitigation** It involves activities like construction of river embankments, strengthening existing buildings, etc.

(ii) **Non-structural mitigation** It involves activities like training in disaster management, regulating land use, public education, etc.

Hazards	Structural Mitigation Efforts	Non-Structural Mitigation Efforts
Flood	(a) Watershed management	(a) Mapping of flood plains
	(b) Construction of reservoirs	(b) Land use control
Earthquake	(a) Engineered structures	(a) Enforcing building codes
	(b) Soil type	(b) Public awareness
Cyclone	(a) Multipurpose cyclone shelters	(a) Hazard mapping
	(b) Engineered structures	(b) Land use control
Landslide	(a) Drainage corrections	(a) Hazard mapping
	(b) Retaining walls	(b) Awareness generation
Drought	(a) Revival of traditional water harvesting structures	(a) Land use planning
	(b) Construction of water harvesting structures	(b) Drought monitoring

2. What is hazard mapping? How is it an effective mitigation tool for cyclones?

Ans. Hazard mapping means to prepare a map which shows or reflects areas which are prone to hazards.

A cyclone hazard map will illustrate the areas vulnerable to cyclones in any given year and a Disaster Management Plan can be prepared accordingly to face the disaster effectively. Thus, it will prove to be an effective mitigation tool.

3. What is water harvesting? How is it a good measure for overcoming shortage of water?

Ans. Rainwater harvesting is a technique of collecting rainwater and storing it in tanks or channeling it into the water table through handpumps. Other methods are building check dams and channeling water into lakes and ponds.

Following are the reasons for overcoming shortage of water

(i) Rainwater harvesting is especially popular in Rajasthan, where there is storage of water which is collected from the rooftop and sent through pipes into underground tanks called 'tankas', to be used when there is shortage of water.

(ii) By channeling the surface run-off water into the ground, the water table level can be increased and the water can be used when needed.

4. Explain why it is women and children who are the most affected in drought prone areas.

Ans. Women and children are the most affected in drought prone areas because they are physically weaker and so have less capability to face drought.

5. Explain any two structural mitigation strategies for floods.

Ans. Two structural mitigation strategies are

(i) **Watershed management** Timely cleaning, desilting and deepening of natural water reservoirs and drainage channels (both urban and rural) must be taken up.

(ii) **Buildings on elevated area** The buildings in flood prone areas should be constructed on an elevated area and, if necessary, on stilts or platforms.

6. List the agencies that play a major role in the issuing of cyclone warning.

Ans. The agencies that play a major role in the issuing of cyclone warning are

- Satellite-based disaster warning systems
- Radio
- Television
- Public announcements and bulletins in press

ACTIVITY 7 TEST BASED ON NEWS REPORT

Read the following report and answer the questions.

Report

From 1975, Ralegaon Siddhi a village in Ahmednagar district of Maharashtra was affected by severe drought. Agriculture failed, leaving people jobless. The per capita income was unbelievably low at ₹ 271 per annum. A revolution led by Anna Hazare helped the villagers to combat the recurrent drought that the community faced. Community effort and cooperation helped Ralegoan Siddhi to overcome its recurring problem. The villagers carried out mitigation activities like plantation of trees on the hill side, making terraces on the hills to check erosion, digging canals to retain water and stopping open grazing areas. Work began with the percolation tank construction in the village. In 1975, the water tank of the village would not hold water. The embankment wall leaked. Hazare got people to voluntarily repair the embankment. The seven wells below it swelled with water for the first time in the living memory of the people.

The above example of Ralegaon Siddhi village shows that community efforts and cooperation from the local government and non-governmental organisations helped the people of Ralegaon Siddhi to prevent the recurring problem from becoming a disaster.

1. The above paragraph shows which hazardous activity?

Ans. The above paragraph shows recurrent drought situation.

2. Who led the revolution in Ralegaon Siddhi to overcome the recurrent drought situation?

Ans. Anna Hazare, a well-known social activist, started a revolution in Ralegaon Siddhi to overcome the recurrent drought situation.

3. Write about the vulnerable situation faced by people of Ralegaon Siddhi during the period of severe drought.

Ans. The people of Ralegaon Siddhi were suffering from abject poverty during the period of severe drought about thirty years ago. The village had no trees, the top soil had blown-off, there was no agriculture and people were jobless. The per capita income was unbelievably low at ₹ 271 per annum.

4. What mitigation activities were adopted by the people of Ralegaon Siddhi to overcome the recurring drought situation?

Ans. After starting the movement in Ralegaon Siddhi by Anna Hazare, the villagers carried out mitigation activities like plantation of trees on the hill side, making terraces on the hills to check soil erosion, digging canals to retain water and stopping open grazing.

Work began with the percolation tank constructed in the village. People repaired the embankment wall of the tank in the village which leaked.

The seven wells below it swelled with water for the first time in the living memory of the people. The village now has a massive area of about 1300 acres under irrigation.

The migration for jobs has stopped and the per captia income has increased ten times from ₹ 225 to 2250 in this span of time. It became possible because of the hardship of the villagers.

5. Give a suitable title to the given paragraph.

Ans. Title

(i) Ralegaon Siddhi — From Severity to Happiness

(ii) Ralegaon Siddhi — A Voluntary Effort

ACTIVITY 8 REPORT WRITING

Topic

Bhuj Earthquake

Objective

Develop awareness and knowledge about the Bhuj earthquake.

Skill Developed

Develop social awareness and knowledge about the consequences of the devastating disaster.

Assessment Criteria

- Creative writing skill
- Accuracy
- Correctness of information
- Legibility

Hint

Description of Bhuj Earthquake

On the morning of 26th January, 2001, the nations 52nd Republic Day, a devastating earthquake occurred in the Kutch district of the state of Gujarat. The earthquake was felt as far away as Delhi in the North, West Bengal in the East and Chennai in the South.

Bhuj town and village Bhachau, 60 km East of Bhuj, were the worst affected, and many other areas of Gujarat including its state capital Ahmedabad were badly affected. The earthquake devastated Bhuj and nearby regions of Gujarat, causing extensive loss of life and property. The total loss of life due to the earthquake is 13805 and 1205198 houses have been damaged.

Follow-Up

Teachers can also give information about the further natural and man-made hazards and disasters along with their mitigation measures.

Preventing Common Human-induced Disasters

CHAPTER 3

Human-induced disasters is a man-made disaster that has an element of human intent, negligence, or error involving a failure of a man-made system, as opposed to natural disasters resulting from natural hazards. Such man-made disasters are crime, arson, civil disorder, terrorism, war, biological/chemical threat, cyber-attacks,etc.

3.1 Weapons of Mass Destruction (WMD)

As the name implies, Weapons of Mass Destruction (WMD) bring huge loss of life, property and environment. These cover Nuclear, Biological, Chemical (NBC) and increasingly, radiological weapons. All these terms fall in the larger category of human-induced hazards. There is controversy regarding first use of the term, either in 1937 (Guernica air bombardment, Spain) or in 1945 (with reference to nuclear weapons). Following the atomic bombings of Hiroshima and Nagasaki and progressing through Cold War, the term came to refer more to non-conventional weapons. Current phase of widespread usage begun with the US-led invasion of Iraq (2003).

Nuclear Accidents

A **nuclear weapon** is an explosive weapon. It derives its destructive force from the energy released by nuclear reactions of fission or a combination of fusion and fission. A small nuclear weapon is more powerful than the largest conventional explosives. A single weapon can destroy an entire city. Basically, there are two types of nuclear weapons

(i) **Atomic bombs** They produce their explosive energy through nuclear fission reactions. They are also known as A-bombs or fission bombs.

(ii) **Hydrogen bombs** They produce a large amount of its energy through nuclear fusion reactions. They can be thousand times more powerful than fission bombs because energy released by them is much more. They are also known as H-bombs, thermonuclear or fusion bombs.

With the developing scientific research in the world, several countries have acquired the technology to produce Nuclear Arms. Terrorists or criminals might steal nuclear materials to make dirty bombs. These bombs can be used to harm people and cause trouble. Risk of accidental exposure to harmful radiation is also possible for people working with nuclear reactors generating electric power or by people coming into contact with radioactive material, which has not been disposed off properly by the authorities or research institutions.

Common Indicators of Radioactivity

A nuclear explosion is followed by a blast like the mushroom cloud. It has the following common indicators

- Nausea
- Dizziness
- Vomiting
- Disorientation
- No odour
- A wave of heat

Protection Measures

We can protect ourselves from nuclear radiation and attacks by taking the following precautions

- Do not panic in the event of such an accident or attack.
- Do not look at the blast, as it can cause instant blindness.
- Close doors and windows, stay indoors until instructions are received from the authorities. If you have to move outdoors, await their instructions.
- Cover all food and water. Do not consume food, water or milk obtained after a nuclear explosion.

Hiroshima and Nagasaki Atomic Explosions

Enola Gay and Little Boy

On 6th August, 1945, an American B-29 bomber, the 'Enola Gay' dropped an 8,900 pound atomic weapon over the city of Hiroshima. 2000 feet above the ground, the bomb dubbed **'Little Boy'**[1] detonated, instantly levelling almost 90% of the city. The destruction was incredible. More than 10 square miles of the city were instantly devastated. A city centre was literally vapourised and other parts of the city were on fire. In this, around 66,000 people were killed and 69,000 get injured.

Fat Man

On 9th August, another plane dropped a larger bomb, code named 'Fat Man' over Nagasaki. Due to local geography, it was spared from total devastation but one-third of the city was destroyed and it killed more than 39,000 people and injured 25,000.

3.2 Chemical and Industrial Accidents

With the development of science and technology, chemicals usage has increased everywhere, but some chemicals helpful to mankind and on the other, they can be hazardous to human beings and the environment. Manufacturing of these chemicals is also a source of contamination, as it uses hazardous materials as ingredients.

Some of these chemicals are found in every household like in hair spray and deodorant, nail polish and remover, toilet bowl cleaner, wall paint and furniture polish. Sites where such hazardous chemicals may be present include automobile service stations, hospitals and hazardous waste disposal areas.

Chemical accidents occur in chemical plants, in transportation accidents due to lack of proper storage, use or disposal.

Bhopal Gas Tragedy

Chemical WMDs[2] are simple to manufacture by anti-social elements and they are difficult to detect as most of them are colourless and odourless. Usually, a technique of dispersion of the WMD is used as it is simple and effective.

A prominent example of a chemical industrial accident was the Bhopal Gas Tragedy of 1984, which killed more than 3,000 people. Here, a highly toxic gas was released into the air at Union Carbide India Limited (UCIL) a, pesticide plant.

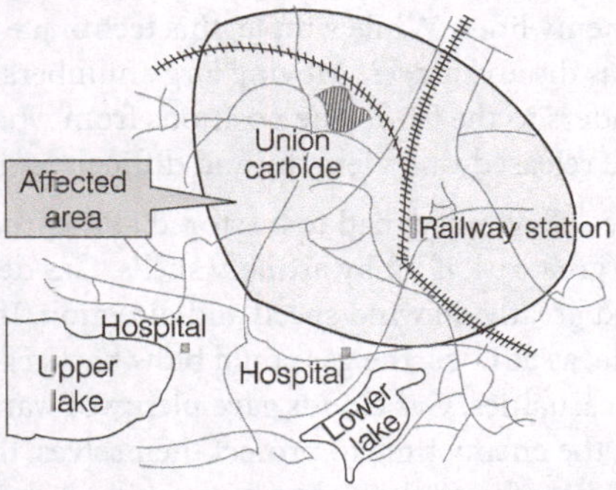

• Bhopal, showing the area affected by the leakage of toxic gas

Warning

The onset of an industrial/chemical accident can be rapid (in a few minutes or hours) or sudden. It may be without any warning depending upon the nature of occurrence. Release of chemicals may be due to human error or technological failure. It can also be released because of natural activities such as earthquake, natural fire, floods, etc.

Bhopal Chemical Gas leak disaster occured on 2nd-3rd December 1984 and was one of the worst industrial disasters of all time in India. The tragedy was a technological accident in which 45 tonnes of highly poisonous methyl isocyanate (MIC) gas alongwith hydrogen cyanide and other reaction products leaked out of the pesticide factory of union carbide into the night air of Bhopal at around 12.30 am.

Thousands died in the immediate aftermath. The official death toll reached, 3,598 in 1989. Thousands, who survived, however, faced a fate worse than death.

1 Little Boy It was the first nuclear weapon used in warfare. This bomb was the result of the Manhattan project, which began in June 1942. Manhattan project was a research programme during World War II, by United States.

2 Chemical WMD Chemical weapons are a type of Weapon of Mass Destruction (WMD) that can be used to harm or kill people, animals or plants.

Dispersion

Dispersion is the simplest technique of delivering an agent to its target. It consists of placing the chemical agent upon or adjacent to a target immediately before dissemination, so that the material is most efficiently used.

World War I saw the earliest implementation of this technique, when German forces at Ypres simply opened cylinders of chlorine and allowed the wind to carry the gas across enemy lines. While simple, this technique had numerous disadvantages. Moving large numbers of heavy gas cylinders to the front-line positions from where the gas would be released was a lengthy and difficult logistical task.

Stockpiles of cylinders had to be stored at the front-line, posing a great risk if hit by artillery shells. Gas delivery depended greatly on wind speed and direction. If the wind was fickle, as at Loos, the gas could blow back, causing friendly casualties. Gas clouds gave plenty of warning, allowing the enemy time to protect themselves, though many soldiers found the sight of a creeping gas cloud unnerving. Also gas clouds had limited penetration, capable only of affecting the front-line trenches before dissipating. Although, it produced limited results in World War I, this technique shows how simple chemical weapon dissemination can be.

3.3 Impact and Elements at Risk

Loss due to a chemical or industrial accident can be high, as usually there is no or little warning. Hazardous chemicals can cause death, serious injury, long-lasting health effects (including genetic deformities in future generations) and damage to buildings, homes and other property. Usually, people residing in the areas close to industrial establishments or working in the plant itself are under greater threat.

In many cases, farmers face loss of crops because of the toxic gases released by industries into the atmosphere or release of untreated toxic effluents into the groundwater, thus polluting it. The initial symptoms of chemical leakage are burning sensation and redness in the nostrils and eyes, irritation followed by dizziness and disorientation. Other symptoms are a pungent or bitter-sweet smell of a gas in the air.

Gas Well Blowout, China

A gas well in China burst on 23rd, December releasing poisonous gases. This happened because of a mistake during drilling. Atleast 191 people died, and approx 40,000 people had to leave their homes in Gaoqiao city.

3.4 Mitigation Strategies

Knowing the method to mitigate chemical accidents, reduces the risk of injury in an emergency.

These risk reduction measures include the following

Hazard Mapping

Hazard mapping is the process of establishing geographically where and to what extent particular hazards are likely to pose a threat to people, property and the environment. Inventories and maps of storage locations of chemicals alongwith their characteristics should be known to all and displayed prominently in the area.

The map should indicate the area most likely to be affected in case an accident occurs. The nature of the accident can be different. It can be fire, explosion, spillage, gas cloud, etc. Safe routes of evacuation in case of emergency should be marked on this map and people should be trained to use them.

Land Use Planning

Industrial areas should be located away from densely populated residential areas. Preferably, a green belt like a buffer zone (green belt) should separate these areas.

Safe methods of waste disposal should be part of the plan to set-up any industry, keeping the local needs in mind. Waste disposal sites should be identified by the people setting up the industry.

Community Preparedness

The community should improve its fire fighting and pollution dispersion capabilities. They should be fully aware of the measures to be taken in case of an accident.

They must be trained in the action to be taken in case of an accident or disaster. Community members should monitor the pollution levels of the industry and participate in mock drills for evacuation.

Other Possible Measures

- Improve fire resistance and warning systems.
- Improve fire fighting and pollution dispersion capabilities.
- Develop emergency relief and evacuation planning for employees and nearby settlements.
- Incident response training should be provided to the employees of the industry.
- Maintain a wind flow diagram of the region.
- Limit storage capacity of the toxic substances.
- Insurance for industries and safety legislations.

Anthrax 'Likely' in US Postal Deaths

Time : Monday, 22nd October, 2001, 20:57 GMT 21:57 UK

Suspiciously, two postal workers in the US died. About them following news was broadcast by the BBC News Service.

Two postal workers in Washington DC who died from unexplained causes were 'likely' to be infected with anthrax, US officials said. Their bodies are being tested for anthrax symptoms amid circumstances described by health officials as 'highly suspicious'.

The revelation came as US authorities confirmed that a second postal worker in the city had tested positive for anthrax infection, bringing the number of cases of infection nationwide to 10. The new victim had the more serious inhaled form of the disease. Of the cases of anthrax that have now been identified in the US, 6 are skin anthrax and 4 are inhaled anthrax. One man, an employee of a tabloid newspaper in Florida, died as a result of anthrax inhalation.

3.5 Biological Disasters

Biological weapons also known as 'poor man's nuclear bomb', are easy to manufacture and can be deployed without complicated delivery systems, besides having the ability to kill or injure a large number of people. Such a delivery system can be crop dusting aeroplanes or even perfume atomisers. Biological agents generally take a longer time (upto a few days) to take effect, compared to conventional, chemical or nuclear weapons. Thus, they are not recognised in their initial stages. Due to this, highly transmissible diseases like plague and small pox can result in widespread secondary exposure to others, including health care workers.

Do's and Don'ts for Biological Disasters

1. A biological attack is the release of germs or other biological substances. The germs must be inhaled, enter through a cut in the skin or be eaten to make the victim fall sick. Some biological agents cause contagious diseases, others do not.
2. A biological attack may or may not be immediately obvious. While it is possible that you will see signs of a biological attack, it is perhaps more likely that local health care workers will report a pattern of unusual illness.
3. You will probably learn of the danger through an emergency radio or TV broadcast. In rural areas, a loudspeaker or other methods are used for a cyclone warning, may be used to warn you.
4. If you become aware of an unusual or suspicious release of an unknown substance nearby, it doesn't hurt to protect yourself and others.
5. Get away from the substance as quickly as possible.
6. Cover your mouth and nose with layers of fabric that can filter the air but still allow breathing.

Important to Know

The first symptoms of a possible chemical leakage are irritation, burning and redness in the nostrils and eyes, followed by nausea, dizziness and disorientation. Pungent or bitter-sweet smells indicate the presence of a gas in the air.

Panic induced fleeing during a gas leakage is harmful. Stay calm, in the same place, put a wet cloth on your face and breath through it. Most gases will dissolve in water.

Lying down close to the ground may help, since most hazardous gases are lighter than air and will tend to rise upwards.

Do you know that 100 gm of anthrax released over a major city may cause upto 3 million casualties.

REVIEW EXERCISE

Covering Textbook Questions

ACTIVITIES

ACTIVITY 1 DEBATE

Topic

Should India Go Ahead with Nuclear Tests?

Learning Outcomes

By working on this activity, students will be able to

- understand the concept of nuclear tests and their impact on our neighbouring countries.
- evaluate the financial and political implications of conducting a nuclear test on our relationships with financially powerful countries like the USA.

Procedure

(i) Students may be divided into two groups, for and against the motion.
(ii) Each speaker is given 2-3 minutes time.
(iii) Some students are reserved for interjection.
(iv) Too many counter arguments will not be allowed.

Assessment Criteria

Best speaker gets maximum points on the basis of strong and relevant points

- Delivery
- Reasoning with evidences
- Good relevant questions of interjection will fetch points

Follow Up

The teacher may dwell on the concepts where ideas are not clear.

ACTIVITY 2 PROJECT

Topic

Chemical Disaster at Jaipur in 2009

Find out details of the chemical disaster that occurred in Jaipur during 2009 and explain the following

(a) Causes of the disaster.
(b) Consequences of the disaster on the affected people and the environment.

Learning Outcome

To understand the causes and the consequences of chemical disasters and preventive measures required to prevent such disasters in future.

Procedure

(i) This is an individual project.
(ii) Give details of the disaster, i.e. what happened and where, what was the damage, how many lives were lost and the resultant damage, i.e. consequences.
(iii) Find out whether there was a report on an enquiry about the disaster and what were probably the causes for the disaster.
(vi) Suggest contingency plans for the rehabilitation of the disaster affected people.

Assessment Criteria

- Correctness of information
- Neatness
- Analysis
- Practical nature of rehabilitation measures

Follow Up

The teacher may point out errors and inform the correct answers.

Hint

Some details of the disaster are given below for reference. Other information should be obtained from newspaper reports of that period and the internet.

Chemical Disaster at Jaipur

This occurred on 29th October, 2009 at 7:36 pm. A fire broke out at the Jaipur fuel storage and distribution terminal owned by the Indian Oil Company (IOC) at Sitapura industrial area on the outskirts of Jaipur. The oil depot at Sitapura industrial area is about 16 km away from the city of Jaipur.

The Meteorological Department recorded a tremor measuring 2.3 on the Richter scale around the time of the first explosion at 7:36 pm which resulted in shattering of glass windows nearly 3 km from the accident site (probably due to an explosion).

This occurred when petrol was being transferred from the Indian Oil Corporation's oil depot to a pipeline. There were at least 40 Indian Oil Corporation employees at the terminal when it caught fire with an explosion.

Causes

All major chemical disasters and chemical accidents occur due to lack of safety measures, technical failures, human error or negligence or as a consequence of another disaster of natural origin like flooding, landslide, earthquake, etc.

The main reasons for chemical disasters are that most units do not make preventive safety arrangements or have a proper disaster management system.

Various investigations for the cause of the chemical disaster at Jaipur in 2009 reported a range of the following possibilities

- It occurred when petrol was being transferred from the oil depot to a pipeline. There was a leak in a valve in a pipeline which connected fuel tanks to distribution points. The pipeline was leaking after the daily routine of loading fuel into tankers.
- Experts say that the cause of the fire could be anything—from a leak in the tanks to a short circuit.
- There was an earthquake at 7:36 pm (it is not sure if there was an earthquake or if the explosions created a shock).

The Disaster Management Act, 2005 envisages that each revenue district must have a Disaster Management Plan. While 31 revenue districts of Rajasthan had placed the Disaster Management Plan on Rajasthan Government website, Jaipur district did not have any Disaster Management Plan.

A Disaster Management Plan for Jaipur district has now been put on the website on 17th November, 2009, i.e. 20 days after this disaster.

The main cause of this disaster was a poor safety and disaster management system. The chemical disaster at Jaipur is a stark instance of how safety aspects were reportedly, almost completely ignored by the public sector Indian Oil.

Consequensces

11 people lost their lives due to burns and asphyxia and more than 300 suffered injuries. IOC General Manager of Rajasthan Mr Gautam Bose and 8 other officers were arrested in connection with this disaster, as it was probably due to leakage of petrol during transfer from a storage tank.

- Jaipur fuel storage and distribution terminal of the Indian Oil Corporation can hold 1,00,000 kilolitres of petrol, diesel and kerosene in 11 storage tanks. In this case, all 11 tanks caught fire.
- Broken ceilings, shattered windowpanes and cracks in the walls of the nearby Infosys, Genpact and Genus Electronics offices occurred.
- Workshops of General Motors' new Chevrolet showroom, as well as workshops and offices of JWS Foods, Florence Foods, Sriram General Insurance, Morani Motors and Engineering College JECRC were damaged.
- Over 100 small/medium sized businesses in nearby areas may have been affected.
- Thick plumes of pollutant-laced smoke had spread to over dozens of villages and residential colonies nearby.
- Atmospheric pollution from the accident was a major health concern for residents in the area. People near to the accident area had some health problems like heaviness in the chest, sore throat, irritation in the eyes and skin.

Home Assignments

1. Collect 'news' from the internet on the Bhopal Disaster of 3rd December, 1984. Reflect your views on it.
2. The March 2010, incident of nuclear radiation at the scrap market at Mayapuri, New Delhi is an eye-opening event of nuclear exposure. Collect media reports on it and study the impact of nuclear radiation and what are the measures that need to be taken to prevent it. Prepare a list of do's and don'ts for your class with pictures.
3. Collect pictures and write short summary on the two different types of nuclear bombs.
4. Look for articles on the internet, magazines and books and find out incidents where improper usage of chemicals has affected the local community.
5. Organise a mock drill in your class for the various man-made disasters and see how you will prepare and respond to them.
6. How can we prevent and prepare for chemical disasters?
   - Find out what industries exist close to your city or village and whether any of the chemicals they use are hazardous.
   - Find out whether an emergency plan is in place to deal with industrial accidents and what antidotes can be used in case of poisoning of people, animals, water sources, etc.
   - Find out whether your local medical association is aware of how to treat patients suffering from exposure to these chemicals.
7. Make a report of your findings and take the help of your teacher to inform concerned authorities such as the District Magistrate, Block or Taluka Development Officer or Municipal Corporation as well as the closest PHC.
8. Make a chart of simple Do's and Don'ts in the event of a chemical disaster based upon information gathered from the industry.

Picture Based Questions

9. (a) Which disaster is associated with this picture? Mention its source.

(b) What were the toxic elements causing the disaster?

(c) Could this tragedy have been averted and if so, how?

Ans. (a) This is an atomic bomb explosion. Its source was the bomb named 'Enola Gay' dropped by the US Air Force on a Japanese city.

(b) The toxic elements were the products on nuclear fission.

(c) This tragedy could have been averted, if the USA had not decided to drop this bomb or if the Japanese had surrendered earlier.

10. (a) Identify the place of occurrence of this disaster.

(b) What is the shape of the clouds caused by atomic explosions?

Ans. (a) The Japanese city of Hiroshima.

(b) This shape is called 'mushroom' cloud.

Exercise

1. Why are nuclear bombs more hazardous than conventional bombs?

Ans. A nuclear bomb (weapon) is a type of explosion weapon that derives its destructive force from nuclear reactions of fission or a combination of fission and fusion. As a result, even a nuclear weapon (bomb) with a small yield is significantly more powerful than the largest conventional explosives and a single weapon is capable of destroying an entire city.

2. Find out at least two examples of common human-induced disasters in your environment. Suggest how they can be reduced or removed.

Ans. Two examples of human induced disasters are fires and road accidents.

(a) Fires can be prevented or reduced if

(i) people become more aware and responsible.

(ii) people do not keep inflammable materials near fire sources.

(iii) people do not leave lighted gas stoves unattended.

(iv) the wiring of electrical appliances should be maintained so that it does not cause a short circuit.

(v) we burst firecrackers in open spaces.

(vi) we improve fire fighting and pollution dispersion capability.

(b) Road accidents can be prevented or reduced if

(i) all road users follow traffic rules.

(ii) we drive vehicles only after having a valid driving licence.

(iii) fast or rash driving is avoided.

(iv) overtaking is done only when space permits.

3. What are the common human-induced hazards in your locality which according to you have the likelihood of becoming a disaster? What are the five different steps that you would take to reduce their impact?

Ans. The common human-induced hazards in our area are road accidents and fires.

The five different steps that can be taken to reduce the impact of these disasters are

(i) Creating public awareness.

(ii) Creating community preparedness.

(iii) Creating a resource map (both human and material).

(iv) Liaison with a government hospital.

(v) Coordination with NGOs.

4. Why do radiation disasters affect a larger area than chemical disaster?

Ans. A radiation disaster spreads gaseous radioactive particles in the atmosphere, which can travel far and wide due to wind. Even a few radioactive particles can cause severe radiation effects as they work by a chain reaction. In a chemical disaster, there is no chain reaction and it is limited only to the area where the chemical has spread. Due to this reason, a radiation disaster affects a larger area than a chemical disaster.

5. How will you use the dates 6th August and 9th August to create awareness about the ill-effects of nuclear disasters?

Ans. America dropped atomic bombs on the city of Hiroshima on 6th August, 1945 and on Nagasaki on 9th August, 1945 which largely destroyed both the cities. Both 6th and 9th August can be used to create awareness about the ill-effects of nuclear disasters through exhibitions in which the photos of the cities after the bombings could be displayed, showing the destruction to life and property.

Literature and information about the ill-effects on the subsequent generations could be made available. Seminars could be organised to create an opinion against the use of nuclear weapons on civilian population. These days can also be observed in schools by holding meetings in which the harmful effects of nuclear weapons are highlighted.[3]

6. What care must be taken for the disposal of biological wastes from pathological laboratories and hospitals?

Ans. Biological waste should be disposed because it may contain harmful germs or even viruses like HIV or HBV. If not disposed properly, it can infect normal human beings, with disastrous consequences.

Untreated medical waste (also called 'biological waste') can safely be disposed in sanitary landfills, provided procedures to prevent worker contact with this waste during disposal are employed.

Normally, this is done by wearing appropriate gloves and a nose and mouth mask which can allow breathing, while filtering the air being breathed.

7. List five measures to protect yourself from nuclear radiation and attacks.

Ans. Five measures to protect ourselves from nuclear radiation and attacks are

(i) Do not look at the fire blast, as it can cause instant blindness.

(ii) Close all doors and windows and stay indoors till further communication from the government comes. Radioactivity does not penetrate solid structures, though fire may cause damage to buildings.

(iii) Cover all food and water. Do not consume water, milk or food obtained following a nuclear blast.

(iv) Await government instructions/communications if you have to move out of your house.

(v) Do not panic and follow the above measures to protect yourselves properly.

8. Study figure and identify which natural disaster is most common and what parts of the Earth are most affected by it.

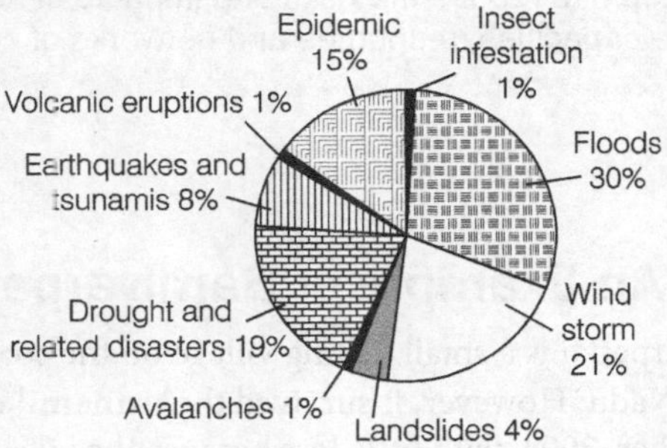

Ans. Floods are the most common natural disaster according to the given figure.

Floods are most common in those parts of the Earth which receive high rainfall and those areas which have large rivers flowing through them. Flooding can take place due to improper drainage facility which is because of human negligence. India, China and Bangladesh are some countries prone to floods. Other countries of the world also face floods from time to time, depending on the rainfall.

3

Community Planning for Disaster Management and Safety Tips for Schools and Homes

CHAPTER 4

Community planning for disaster management is a process of involving and empowering local people to reduce the risks and impacts of natural and human-made hazards. It aims to enhance the capacities, resources and networks of communities to cope with and recover from disaster.

4.1 An Example of Samiyarpettai

Samiyarpettai is a small fishing village on the coast of Tamil Nadu. However, it survived the **tsunami**[1] on 26th December, 2004, with little loss because the villagers had been trained on early warning, search and rescue, first aid, etc under the Disaster Risk Management Programme by the State Government supported by United Nations Development Programme (UNDP).

Other villages in nearby areas suffered extensive damage and loss of life due to the tsunami. The community of this village had been made self-sufficient and thus were able to respond effectively and quickly to save many lives. This highlights the role of the local community in cases of disaster preparedness, risk reduction, mitigation measures, etc.

Community Support During Disaster

During and after a disaster, most often the one who responds first are neighbours or people of community before any other authority or Non-Governmental Organisations (NGOs) support. These few hours during and after a disaster are critical and precious to save lives.

In a situation, when external help takes time to reach the affected site, these trained community members play a vital role and considered as **life saving assets.** They also play an important role in risk reduction, without whose a Disaster Management Plan could not be complete.

The Government of India strongly advocates the building of community capacities in various aspects of disaster response and urges communities to develop Disaster Management Plans to prevent, mitigate and prepare better to combat various hazards. Students and teachers as educated members of the society play a crucial role in guiding and facilitating the process of planning in communities to reduce disaster risks.

Community as a Heart of Disaster Management Initiative

Community acts like a heart of disaster management initiative because of the following reasons

- **First Responder** Since, the community is at the site of the disaster, it is the first one to respond to it. The first person to respond to the disaster usually a member of the local community.
- **Source of maximum information** People living in an area will have the best knowledge and 'up to date' information of the resources available in the area.
- **Local coping mechanisms** Most disasters in an area have happened before. Thus, there is a traditionally established coping mechanism handed down from one generation to the next. This should be the immediate response for the local environment, but it can be improved with better technical knowledge available now-a-days.
- **Self-help is in self interest** The community responds quickly in disasters because too much dependence on external help is usually time-consuming and often ineffective.

1 Tsunami It has been coined from the Japanese word 'Tsu meaning harbour and 'nami' meaning 'waves' thus, it literally means harbour waves. Tsunami is a series of waves generated by earthquakes, volcanic eruptions or underwater landslides and on reach 15 m or more in height devastating coastal communities.

4.2 The Story of a Learning Community (Sukhpar)

A 15 years old boy called Bharat lived in a village Sukhpar. Bharat's grandfather, Ramji was much respected man in Sukhpar and surrounding villages. One day, he told Bharat that the Block Development Officer (BDO) (head of an administrative unit at the sub-district level) had invited him for a meeting on **disaster management**. Out of curiosity, Bharat decided to accompany his grandfather, the Sarpanch and the Talati (Secretary of Village Panchayat) to the meeting.

What Happened in the Meeting at the Office of the Block Development Officer?

The Block Development Officer (BDO) had convened a meeting of village Sarpanches and other prominent citizens of nearby villages to ask them to prepare **Village Disaster Management Plans**[2] (VDMP) for each village. The BDO explained to them the steps to be followed in preparing the plan for each village.

Later, a **Village Disaster Management Committee**[3] (VDMC) was formed in the meeting to guide the residents in formulating the plan.

Role of Village Disaster Management Committee (VDMC)

The VDMC formed various Village Disaster Management Teams (VDMTs) to manage various aspects of the disaster.

These teams were

(i) Early Warning and Communication Team
(ii) Evacuation and Temporary Shelter Management Team
(iii) Search and Rescue Team
(iv) Health and First Aid Team
(v) Relief Coordination Team
(vi) Water and Sanitation Team

Based on the skills required in each team, the volunteers to be members of each team were decided.

It's Time to Act Now!

Subsequently, all the teams went into action to identify all the resources required in their area of operation. Simultaneously, hazard mapping of the area was done and the village map marked with appropriate symbols for ease of understanding of all residents.

Capacity Building

All the team members received training through the District Management Committee on various aspects of their duties and over a 6 months time period they were all trained, so that the village became a more confident community.

Tryout of the Plan

Once the training was complete, a mock drill for a cyclone disaster was carried out without the residents knowing that it was not an actually approaching cyclone. This was highly successful with all the members of the various teams carried out their duties successfully.

4.3 Safety Tips for Schools

The disaster management program in school include the following measures

- **Awareness among Teachers and School Management** It is required to make aware people of school like principal, management, teachers and main students, before making school disaster management programme.
- **Organisation of Disaster Management Committee** The head of this committee should be the principal. This committee includes teachers and members from local administration, health department, non-government organisation, Naitonal Cadet Core, National Social Service, Nehru Yuva Kendra Sangathan, etc.
- **Identification and Assessment of Danger** Danger can be structural or non-structural. Thus, it is important to identify the nature of danger.
- **List of Resources** Information about the resources in school that can be used at the time of danger, should be known. Human and physical resources in school are important to deal with human and natural disaster.
- **Map or Diagram** The map or diagram of the school should be provided to the students. Thus, it is easy for them to find a way out of the school at the time of danger. There are different maps or diagrams like social or physical map, resources map, vulnerability map and chart showing safe location of school and evacuating route.
- **Organisation of Disaster Management Teams** The disaster management teams like team for generating

2 Village Disaster Management Plan (VDMP) A plan prepared by the VDMC for disaster preparedness and response.

3 Village Disaster Management Committee (VDMC) A group of the village residents which creates awareness amongst the community members, so as to reduce the impact of any hazard and guide the community in the preparation of the VDMP. This committee is usually headed by the Sarpanch of the village.

awareness, warning and information dissemination team, first aid team and search and rescue team, should be organised.

- **Mock Practice** Mock drills should be done for handling the circumstances that might arise at the time of disaster.
- **Reassessment and Sanction of the Program** It is important to reassess the program to identify and remove defects from it. After the program is prepared, it should be sanctioned by disaster management committee.

4.5 Safety Tips for Homes

The measures used in the program of disaster management in school, can also be taken for the program of disaster management in homes. The family should be prepared for any future event. The students should discuss about the following with their families

- Disasters which can happen
- What kind of preparation should you have
- If you are asked to evacuate a place, then what will you do
- Where to meet after the house catches a fire
- If you got separated from your family during a disaster, then you should know about the place from where you can contact your family and relatives. You should also know the contact number of your family or relatives.

Family Disaster Kit

Every family should have a disaster kit in their homes. It might help you and your family at the time of disaster. It should include the following

- some warm clothes,
- dry food items and water,
- important documents,
- battery, charger, transistor,
- first aid box,
- medicines for sick person,
- blanket, pillow,
- photographs of family and pets, etc.

REVIEW EXERCISE

Covering Textbook Questions

EXERCISE

1. Identify the sequence of events that took place in Sukhpar and their significance in disaster risk management.

Ans. The following events took place in Sukhpur :

(i) There was a meeting on disaster management called by the BDO which was attended by Ramji, Bharat, the Sarpanch and the Talati (Secretary of the Village Panchayat).

(ii) They decided to prepare a Village Disaster Management Plan (VDMP).

(iii) The villagers of Sukhpar met in the primary school of the village, where the Block Development Officer (BDO) asked the villagers to run the Village Disaster Management Committee (VDMC) and Village Disaster Management Teams (VDMTs).

(iv) A map of the village was drawn on which more vulnerable areas were located and marked. The households, which had vulnerable people like the old, sick and ailing, small children, etc were also marked.

(v) The seaside was taken as a prominent natural feature of Sukhpar. Important locations such as the Public Health Centre (PHC), police station and the cooperative bank were marked on the map.

(vi) All those houses were identified which had aged members, infants, small children, expectant and lactating mothers and handicapped residents. These were marked with a 'V' for vulnerable as also the houses near the sea and next to the highway.

(vii) The masjid was marked to serve as an early warning system, as it had a public address system installed unit.

(viii) The school compound was identified as a safe haven (place) if the people needed to evacuate and stay there for a definite period.

(ix) After this exercise, the people of Sukhpar had become trained in disaster management and were ready to face any disaster efficiently. When they carried out the 'Tryout Plan,' it was a complete success.

2. How is the new Sukhpar different from the one before the communities met?

Ans. Earlier, before the communities had met to formulate a Village Disaster Plan, the people of Sukhpar were vulnerable to disaster. However, after the community meeting, they prepared a Village Disaster Management Plan and were now ready and better prepared to face any disaster efficiently and reduce the chances of destruction.

3. What qualities in Bharat made him different from others in the village? Is it possible to develop such qualities among your community? Explain.

Ans. Qualities like curiosity, leadership, responsibility and organising capacity in Bharat made him different from others. It is possible to develop some qualities like responsibility, helping attitude among the community, etc while others are in born.

4. What were the areas covered under the DMTs?

Ans. The areas that were covered under the DMTs are

(i) Early Warning and Communication
(ii) Evacuation and Temporary Shelter Management
(iii) Search and Rescue
(iv) Health and First Aid
(v) Relief Coordination
(vi) Water and Sanitation

5. What were the two construction-related mitigation techniques referred to in the story?

Ans. Two construction-related mitigation techniques were

(i) To build houses that are earthquake and cyclone resistant.
(ii) Retrofitting technique was adopted for dilapidated structures.

6. What were the contents of the Disaster Preparedness and Response Plan?

Ans. The contents of the Disaster Preparedness and Response Plan are

(i) **Disaster preparedness,** which includes

(a) Preparation of village vulnerability map which identified the safe places, low risk areas and the highly vulnerable areas and the estimated number of families residing in each of these zones.

This also identified the number and location of the vulnerable groups/populations such as the aged, handicapped, lactating mothers, pregnant women, seriously ill persons and small children in their village.

(b) Identification of key elements at risk such as life, health, property, livestock and livelihood.

(c) Listing the key activities that the community would do before, during and after a disaster like a cyclone or flood.

As an example, the key activities identified before the flood are flood warning, household readiness including documents (books, certificates, marksheets, etc of children) and family survival kit (dry food for 7 to 10 days alongwith other essential items like candles, matches, kerosene oil, etc) and safe keeping of valuables and other important documents.

(d) Formation of different task forces, training on health and first aid, water and sanitation, rescue and relief.

(e) Identification of key local resources such as bamboos, banana plants, etc for use in the preparation of machans (temporary shelters) and the local rafts, hand pumps which could be raised above the flood level to protect their source of water.

(f) Identification of specific places where the affected community would go alongwith their cattle to take shelter in event of a disaster.

(ii) **Disaster response,** which includes

(a) To rescue and evacuate trapped people.
(b) To provide first aid to the injured.
(c) To take care of children, women and disabled people.
(d) To transfer the seriously injured and people needing urgent medical attention to hospitals.
(e) To restore communicaton network and essential services.
(f) To clear debris blocking roads and communicaton networks.
(g) To provide shelter and relief to homeless people.
(h) To arrange for food and drinking water to the affected people.
(i) To take immediate measure for disposal of dead bodies and animal carcass to prevent to outbreak of epidemics.
(j) To take urgent measures for maintaining law and order.
(k) To take people to safer places in case of change of course of river due to floods.

PROJECT REPORT

A project report is a written document of what the *analyser* analyses in his/her project work. The project report needs to be prepared with great care and consideration.

ELEMENTS OF THE PROJECT

Try to ensure that your report contains the following elements

Title Page

This should include the project title, name of the company/product on which you are conducting your research and name of the student. You can also list the name of your school, class and subject teacher.

Acknowledgement

It is usual to thank those individuals, who have provided particularly useful assistance, technical or otherwise, during your project through acknowledgement.

Content Page

This should list the main sections and sub-sections of your report. Choose self-explanatory titles with their respective pages and use double spacing for clarity. Content should be impressive and explanatory, so that the reader would clearly understand the purpose of the project.

Introduction

This is one of the most important component of the project report. It should begin with a clear statement of what the project is about, so that the nature and scope of the project can be understood by the reader. It should summarise everything which you set out to achieve and provide a clear summary of the project's background, relevance and main contributions. The introduction should set the context for the project and should provide the reader with a summary of the key things to look out for, in the remainder of the report. It is useful in stating the main objectives of the project as part of the introduction.

Background

The background section of the report should set the project into action. It specifies the problem, what remedial actions are taken, what are its effects etc. It proposes the layout of the whole project.

Body of Report

The central part of the report usually consists of three or four sections detailing the technical work undertaken during the project. The structure of these sections is highly project dependent. They can reflect the chronological development of the project. It includes the detailed description regarding the matter of the project.

Evaluation

This might involve quantitative and qualitative evaluation such as expressibility, functionality, ease-of-use, etc of a product. At some point, you should also evaluate the strengths and weaknesses of what you have done. It includes certain questionnaires, sampling test, etc. which help in evaluating the result on the basis of truths and facts.

Conclusion

The conclusion should list the things, which have been learnt as a result of the work you have done. It shows the ultimate response of the project undertaken by a student. It should be expressive and impressive, so that a reader would clearly evaluate the result and rate you on the basis of your presentation.

CBSE Project on Disaster Management

A disaster is an event which results in widespread human loss, accompanied by loss of livelihood and property and causing suffering and loss in a particular area. It affects the community by a significant loss of lives, property and livelihood, besides giving a blow to the economy. Society requires external help to cope with these losses. The world is changing fast, more people are becoming vulnerable to disasters, often unable to tackle the situation. Here comes the necessity of disaster management. Disaster management covers the range of activities designed to maintain control over disasters/emergency situations and to provide a framework for helping people to avoid, reduce the effects of disaster or recover from the impact of disasters.

In CBSE syllabus, every student of class IX has to compulsorily undertake one project on Disaster Management. It is carefully designed to

(i) Create awareness in learners

(ii) Enable them to understand and corelate all aspects of disaster management

(iii) Relate theory with practice

(iv) Relation of different aspects with life

(v) Provide hands on experience

In order to realise the expected objectives completely, it would be required of the Principals/teachers to muster support from various local authorities and organisations like the Disaster Management Authorities, Relief, Rehabilitation and the Disaster Management Departments of the States, Office of the District Magistrate/Deputy Commissioners, Fire Service, Police, Civil Defense etc in the area where the schools are located. The teachers must ensure judicious selection by students of projects.

The topic of the project must be relevant to our country and society. Student should collect information from different newspapers, magazines, news channels and websites. It is to be noted here by all the teachers and students that the projects and models prepared should be made from eco-friendly products without incurring too much expenditure. The Project Report should be handwritten by the students themselves and comprise of not more than 15 foolscap pages. Student must paste lots of pictures related to the topic. He/she should represent the topic by covering all relevant aspects. The projects should be decorated properly.

Assessments of the Project

The distribution of marks over different aspects relating to project work is as follows:

S.No.	ASPECTS	MARKS
1.	Content accuracy, originality and analysis	2
2.	Presentation and creativity	2
3.	Viva Voce	1

The project carried out by the students subsequently be shared among themselves through interactive sessions such as exhibitions, panel discussions, etc. All documents pertaining to assessment of the project should be meticulously maintained by the concerned teacher of the school. A teacher should prepare a summary report by highlighting the following topics

- Objectives realised through individual or group interactions;
- Calendar of activities;
- Innovative ideas generated in this process;
- List of questions asked in viva voce.

PROJECT WORK

Title of the Project: Disaster Management

Topic of the Project : The Himalayan Tsunami, 2013

Objective : The case study will help to understand the reasons for the 2013 disaster and to find out ways to avoid such disasters in future.

Name : ....

School : ....

Year : ....

Class : ....

Submitted To : ....

PROJECT REPORT

ACKNOWLEDGEMENT

I would like to express my special thanks of gratitude to my teacher................ as well as our Principal .... who gave me the golden opportunity to do this wonderful project on the topic 'The Himalayan Tsunami, 2013'.

This project helped me a lot in gaining adequate knowledge about the topic. I have completed this project after proper analysis and research and I came to know about so many new things.

I am really thankful to all of my friends, co-partners and guide, who have devoted their precious time in completing my project. Secondly, I would also like to thank my parents or guardians who helped me a lot in finishing this project within the prescribed time.

I am making this project not only for marks but also to increase my knowledge and intellect development.

Thanks again to all who helped me.

CERTIFICATE

This is to Certify that the project work 'The Himalayan Tsunami, 2013' is the bonafide work of .... (Name of the student) who carried out the work under my supervision ....

Name and Signature of
Teacher/Supervisor

CONTENTS

Introduction

A disaster is an event that causes a lot of harm or damage. Disaster management is the organisation of resources and responsibilities for dealing with all humanitarian aspects of emergencies in order to lessen the impact of disasters. Uttarakhand is an Indian Himalayan state known for its rich spiritual and religious tourism, ecological richness and diversity, cultural ethos rooted in traditions. But this region is also known for its fragility of ecological and geological systems. Due to geo-climatic, ecological and socio-economic setting, the region is very vulnerable to natural disasters.

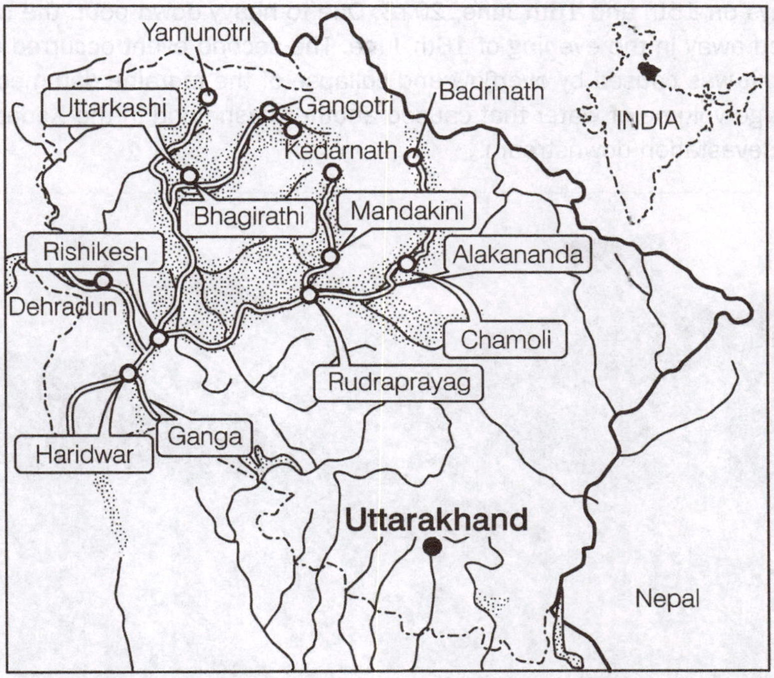

PROJECT REPORT

The Worst Disaster Happened

On June 2013, the state of Uttarakhand suffered its worst disaster in the living memory resulting in huge loss of lives and widespread destruction of infrastructure across the state. This disaster is popularly known as Himalayan Tsunami 2013. The disaster 2013 can be attributed to widespread exceptionally heavy rainfall across the state. The entire state was hit by 'heavy' to 'very heavy' rain fall resulting into flash floods and landslide in numerous areas. The districts of Bageshwar, Chamoli, Pithoragarh, Rudraprayag and Uttarkashi were the most affected areas.

The meteorological stations near Chorabari glacier recorded 325 mm rainfall at the base of the glaciers in two days on 15th and 16th June, 2013. Due to heavy down pour, the town of Rambara completely washed away in the evening of 16th June. The second event occurred on 17th June, 2013 at 6.45 am. It was caused by overflow and collapse of the moraine dammed Chorabari Lake which released large volume of water that caused another flash flood in the Kedarnath town leading to heavy devastation downstream.

- Kedarnath at the time of disaster

- Flash Floods at Rambara

PROJECT REPORT

• Houses Damaged

The torrential rains coupled with the collapse of the Chorabari lake led to flooding at the Kedarnath shrine and its adjacent areas of Rambara, Agastyamuni, Tilwara and Guptkashi. Other pilgrimage centres like Gangotri, Yamunotri and Badrinath, which are visited by thousands of devotees during the summer season were also severely affected. People were stranded for days to weeks at many isolated regions like Harshil, Roopkund and Hemkund Sahib. Over one lakh people were stuck in various parts of the state due to damaged roads, landslides, flash flood induced debris and absence of transport and communication.

• Roads Blocked and Damaged

The Causes behind the Disaster

From 14th to 17th June, 2013, Uttarakhand and adjoining areas received heavy rainfall which was about 37.5% more than the normal rainfall in monsoon. This caused the melting of Chorabari Glacier at the height of 3800 metres and eruption of the Mandakini river. Heavy rainfall for four consecutive days as well as melting snow aggravated the floods. Combined with the snowmelt, the June downpour caused heavy flooding in countless sites along the six tributaries of the Ganges that originate here.

An hour or two before the flash flood, scientific observers posted at the Chorabari lake, about a mile and half upstream from Kedarnath heard a loud bang. It may have been the noise of an avalanche or landslide that knocked loose the natural dam of ice and rock holding back the lake-draining it in minutes and sending the full force of waters down on to the town below.

There are about 20,000 glacial lakes in the whole Himalayan Range. More than 200 of these lakes have been classified as potentially dangerous. Scientists are monitoring all these lakes. Scientists explain that heavy snowfall in March, April and May is another cause for heavy rainfall. By June, the snow starts melting, thereby increasing the water levels in Himalayan rivers. Scientists of oceanography said that this disaster could have been caused by the paucity of low pressure systems (convective activity) in the Western pacific ocean.

The convective activity is associated with low pressure systems and these attract moisture bearing winds. This brought about a rapid advance of the monsoon across the sub-continent by winds originating in the Western Indian ocean. The intense rainfall in June actually helps in causing the snow to melt at a much faster rate.

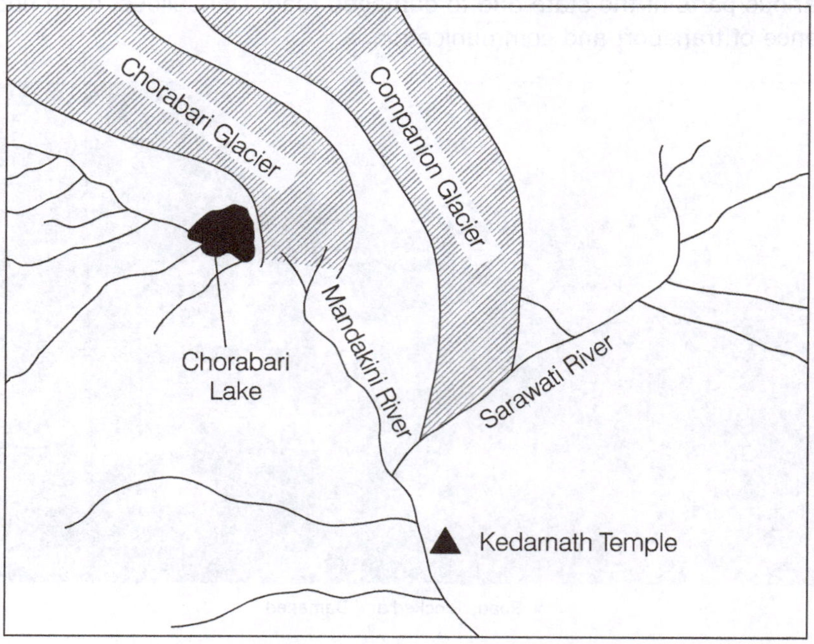

• The satellite view of Kedarnath Area

PROJECT REPORT

In Uttarakhand flash floods are very common hydro-meteorological hazards which occur due to excessive or high rainfall combined with rapid snowmelt, bursting of natural or constructed dams, cloud bursts etc. These floods are devastating because of the high velocity of water with huge energetic capacity to carry away everything on its way.

Every year Uttarakhand's Garhwal region receives pilgrims in thousands for Chhota Char Dham Yatra i.e. Gangotri, Yamunotri, Kedarnath and Badrinath. It also receives rains and suffers flood. But this time the loss is horrifying. According to Char Dham control room records, there were 26,000 people in Kedar valley on June 16th. This is where the temple is located. Records also show that 39,000 people had left the valley that day for Badrinath, Gangotri, Yamunotri and Hemkund Sahib. The government's figure of about 800 total deaths is too conservative.

The number clearly is in many thousands. The raging Bhagirathi, Alaknanda and Mandakini have swollen like never before and swept away whatever came in their way. According to Rakesh Sharma, state infrastructure development commissioner 2052 houses have been wiped out, 147 bridges have collapsed and 1307 roads have destroyed. The upper region of Uttarakhand was ruined beyond imagination.

Expansion of hydel projects, roads and tourism is making the Himalaya in Uttarakhand crumble. Experts said that unabated expansion of hydro-power projects and construction of roads to accommodate ever increasing tourism, especially religious tourism, are also major causes for the unprecedented scale of devastation. For the heavy traffic of tourists, government has to construct new roads and widen the existing ones. The Ganga in the upper reaches has been an engineer's play ground.

The Central Electricity Authority and the Uttarakhand Power Department have estimated the river's hydroelectric potential at some 9000 MW and have planned 70 odd projects on its tributaries. The rampant construction be it roads, hotels or dams has rendered the mountains unstable and destroyed the ecological balance of mountains. All these factors are responsible for this 'man-made disaster.'

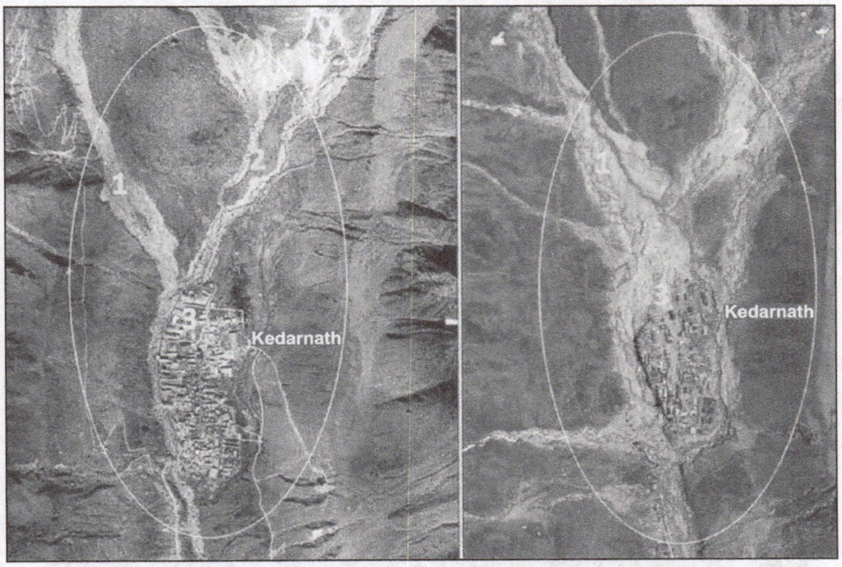

• Satellite image of Kedarnath-Before and After the Disaster

Impact of the Disaster

The disaster caused heavy loss of precious lives and extensive damage to private properties and public infrastructure. More than nine million people were affected by the flash floods. The five districts namely Bageshwar, Chamoli, Pithoragarh, Rudraprayag and Uttarkashi were the worst affected.

As far as casuality to human lives is concerned, State Government on 9th May, 2014 informed a total of 169 people died and over 4,021 people were reported missing (presumed to be dead) from different states of India. As per report, a total 4,200 villages were affected, 11091 livestock were lost and 2513 houses were fully damaged. More than 70,000 tourists and 1,00,000 local inhabitants were stranded in the difficult mountain terrain of the upper reaches of the Himalayas. The extent of damage as reported by State Government is depicted in Table below :

S NO	Item	Details
1.	Number of affected Districts	13
2.	Number of dead and missing persons (Presumed to be dead)	(169+4021)
3.	No of damaged Houses	
	(i) Fully damaged Pucca houses	2119
	(ii) Severely damaged pucca houses	3001
	(iii) Partially damaged pucca houses	11,759
	(iv) Fully damaged Kuchha houses	394
	(v) Severely damaged Kuchha houses	360
	(vi) Number of kuchha houses partially damaged	1,676
	(vii) Number of huts damaged	471
	(viii) Cowsheds damaged	361
4.	Animals Lost	
	(a) No. of big animals lost	3280
	(b) No of small animals lost	7811

*Indian Disaster Report 2013 (Uttarakhand Government)

• After flash flood in Kedarnath Valley

PROJECT REPORT

Emergency Rescue and Relief Operations by Different Agencies

Search, rescue and relief operations during Uttarakhand disaster were the most difficult operation carried out in the Indian history of disaster management.Various central and state government and non - government agencies played a significant role in making this operation successful, despite all the adverse conditions. All helped in the evacuation and relief operations. The Indian Air force, the Aviation Corps of the Indian Army and the Civil helicopters engaged by the Civil Aviation Department of the state government played a significant role in the rescue operations.

Without their dedicated service, the rescue operations would not have succeeded. All the relevant central ministries were mobilised as soon as the matter came to the notice.The National Disaster Response Force (NDRF) was asked to send their teams to Uttarakhand on 16th June itself. Government of India supported the state government in carrying out its evacuation and relief operations by providing support of armed forces and paramilitary forces, including NDRF. To restore the communication, 105 satellite phones were distributed by the government of India to various central and state agencies. Besides BSNL, restoration of communication were closely monitored by the National Crisis Management Committee.

Soon after the disaster struck, the state government initiated massive rescue and evacuation operations with the help of various central and state government agencies, like the Army, Air force and Central Paramilitary forces (ITBP, NDRF). Approximately 1,20,000 persons were stranded/ trapped in different locations including both pilgrims and local residents. They were safely evacuated and taken to the relief camps. The pilgrims were there after helped to board trains, buses or take their private transport/taxies etc to their home stations. The major part of the evacuation was accomplished in less than a fortnight making it one of the largest and swiftest rescue operation by the civil administration.

• Rescue Operations

PROJECT REPORT

Ministry of Home Affairs decided to depute NDRF to Kedarnath valley. The valley was completely cut-off from all land routes and the only mode of reaching the valley was through helicopters. The NDRF team was air dropped at Kedarnath. In extreme harsh weather conditions and with almost no support structure at Kedarnath, the NDRF personnel exhibited exceptional dedication to duty. The NDRF personnel carried out search and rescue operations in Kedarnath's jungle and remote areas. During operation NDRF personnel successfully rescued 9,044 people from different affected areas of Kedarnath (1053), Jungle chatti (907), Gaurikund (756), Guptkashi (1281), Sonprayag (2000), Sukhitop (120), and Badrinath (2,927). In addition, NDRF also rescued 14 foreigners of Singapore. The team provided medical aid to 881 pilgrims/tourists.

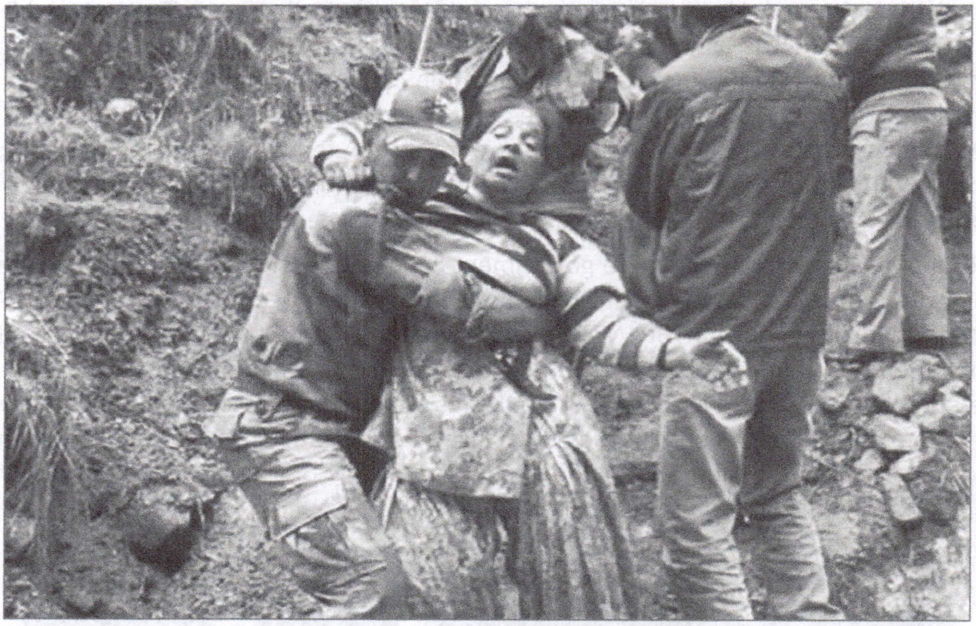

• Rescue Operations

Rescue and Relief Operations-An Overview

- NDRF deployed 14 teams for the operation and rescued more than 9,044 persons.
- ITBP (Indo-Tibetan Border Police) had deployed about 1600 personnel for the operation and rescued more than 33,000 persons.
- IAF (Indian Air force) had deployed about 45 helicopters for the operation and rescued more than 23,500 persons.
- Indian Army had deployed 8000 personnel including 150 special forces Troops and rescued more than 38,500 persons. 12 army helicopters were also deployed.
- Twenty civil air crafts were utilised by the State Government in the operations which evacuated approximately 12,000 persons.
- Nehru Institute of Mountaineering, Uttarkashi, formed five rescue teams of 20 instructors and local youth, and evacuted more than 6,500 stranded persons.

- More than 1,35,000 persons were evacuated from the affected areas in the shortest possible time, notwithstanding widespread destruction of roads, difficult terrain and extremely hostile weather.

• Rescue Operations

Conclusion

Lessons learnt from this disaster

The disaster revealed several infirmities in our preparedness, which need to be rectified at the earliest. Some of the important lessons learnt and key recommendations are listed below :

1. Flood Plain Zoning Act regulating construction within the flood plain of a river should be implemented strictly.
2. For clearance of all hydro-power and other mega projects in ecologically sensitive regions like Uttarakhand, the Disaster Impact Assessment (DIA) should also be made compulsory besides Environmental Impact Assessment (EIA).
3. Landslide risk zonation mapping be completed on priority basis.
4. Effective stabilisation of slopes in shear and weak zones be undertaken using scientific techniques available at national/ international levels.
5. Blasting for developmental activities be avoided as it may destabilise the weak rocks in mountaineous regions.
6. A special central programme be undertaken for construction of new roads and renovation of existing roads in a scientific manner.
7. Disaster management plans should be regularly reviewed and updated to enhance preparedness.
8. Emergency support organisations at state level *viz,* SDRF/Civil Defense and Home Guards be organised, trained and equipped to perform their role more effectively.
9. Tourism related development should not be allowed along the river banks.
10. Stockpiling of essential items like food grains, blankets, medicines etc must be ensured at block/panchayat levels in designated areas to be used during an emergency.

VIVA VOCE

1. The Himalayan Tsunami disaster happened in which state?

Ans. Uttarakhand

2. On which dates the Himalayan Tsunami disaster took place?

Ans. On 16th and 17th June.

3. Name two most affected districts by that disaster.

Ans. Chamoli and Pithoragarh.

4. Where exactly is Kedarnath temple located?

Ans. In Kedar valley along Mandakini river.

5. Which events caused the Himalayan Tsunami disaster?

Ans. Torrential rains at Chorabari glacier and collapse of Chorabari lake causing flash floods.

6. Name other holy places located near Kedarnath.

Ans. Badrinath, Hemkund Sahib, Gangotri.

7. Name of major river that flooded the adjoining areas of Kedarnath.

Ans. Mandakini river

8. Which town got completely washed away on 16th June?

Ans. The town of Rambara

9. Apart from natural causes, what are the manmade causes of such a disaster?

Ans. Unabated expansion of hydro power projects, over construction of roads, hotels and dams along the path of the three rivers i.e. Bhagirathi, Alaknanda and Mandakini.

10. Who carried the rescue operations?

Ans. Indian Air Force, Avaition Corps of the Indian Army, National Disaster Response Force, Civil Aviation Department of the State Government.

11. Why rescue measures were possible only through helicopters?

Ans. The roads got damaged due to landslides, flash flood induced debris and flooding of six tributaries of Ganga river.

12. Why this rescue operations is called swiftest operation?

Ans. Due to the fact that a major part of the rescue was completed in less than a fortnight.

13. What is the approximate number of people affected by this disaster?

Ans. Around 1,40,000 people.

14. Name the places visited in Chhote Char Dham Yatra.

Ans. Gangotri, Yamunotri, Kedarnath and Badrinath.

15. What type of tourism mostly takes place in Uttarakhand?

Ans. Religious tourism

INTER-DISCIPLINARY PROJECT

HISTORY

Forest Society and Colonialism

Report Making

Topic

The students will be asked to conduct research on people who are well-known for contributing towards protection of environment. They are

- Sunderlal Bahuguna
- Medha Patkar
- Rajendra Singh
- Chandi Prasad Bhatt

Procedure

The students can consult reference books and the internet. After the research is complete, the teacher would divide the class into three groups.

Group one to enact a scene based on environment movement and its significance. They have to make posters about the movement.

Group two has to make charts on the activities of the mentioned personalities.

Group three has to write paragraphs, poems for preservation of forests and ecological balance of the environment.

Hint

(i) **Sunderlal Bahuguna** (born 9th January, 1927) is a noted Garhwali environmentalist, Chipko Movement leader and a follower of Mahatma Gandhi's philosophy of non-violence and Satyagraha. For years, he has been fighting for the preservation of forests in the Himalayas, first as a member of the Chipko Movement in 1970s and later spearheaded the Anti-Tehri Dam Movement starting 1980s to early 2004.

He was one of the early environmentalists of India and later he and people associated with the Chipko Movement started taking up environmental issues, like against large dams, mining and deforestation, across the country. He was awarded the Padma Vibhushan, India's second highest civilian honour, on 26th January, 2009 and Padma Award on 14th April, 2009.

(ii) **Medha Patkar** (born 1st December, 1954) is an Indian social activist. She is known for her role in Narmada Bachao Andolan. She has also filed a public interest petition in the Bombay High Court against Lavasa project in Maharashtra alongwith other members of National Alliance of People's Movements (NAPM), including Anna Hazare.

She was raised by politically and socially active parents. She was often known for her extreme views on growth of country and liberalisation. She played a pivotal role in driving out the Tata Nano Plant from Singur, West Bengal.

(iii) **Rajendra Singh** (born 6th August, 1959) is a well-known water conservationist from Alwar district, Rajasthan. Also known as Waterman of India, he won the Ramon Magsaysay Award for Community Leadership in 2001 for his pioneering work in community-based efforts in water harvesting and water management.

He runs an NGO called 'Tarun Bharat Sangh' (TBS), which was founded in 1975. Starting from a single village in 1985, over the years TBS helped build over 8600 *johads* and other water conservation structures to collect rainwater for the dry seasons, has brought water back to over 1000 villages and revived five rivers in Rajasthan namely Arvari, Ruparel, Sarsa, Bhagani and Jahajwali.

(iv) **Chandi Prasad Bhatt** (born 1934) is a Gandhian environmentalist and social activist, who founded Dasholi Gram Swarajya Sangh (DGSS) in Gopeshwar in 1964, which later became a mother-organisation to the Chipko Movement, in which he was one of the pioneers.

For this, he has been awarded the Ramon Magsaysay Award for Community Leadership in 1982, followed by the Padma Bhushan in 2005.

Today he is known for his work on subaltern social ecology and considered one of India's first modern environmentalist. Inspired by the speech of Jayaprakash Narayan, Bhatt joined into Sarvodaya Movement and Gandhian campaigns of Bhoodan and Gramdan Movement.

He become the spokesperson of Chipko Movement and was appointed a member of the **National Forest Commission,** which reviewed all existing policies and legal frameworks relating to forest management and submitted its report to the government.

GEOGRAPHY

Natural Vegetation and Wildlife

Poster Making

Topic

Making a poster on a regional study of the relationship between Forests, Wildlife and Climate.

Learning Outcomes

By doing this activity, the student will be able to

- understand the relationship between climate and vegetation.
- understand how change in climate or environment is affecting natural existence of wildlife.

Procedure

Students are divided into groups of 5 students each.

- Each group is allotted a particular region of India–Kerala, Manipur, Assam, Jodhpur, Sunderban, Rann of Kuchchh, etc.
- Each group finds out the climate of the region, types of trees found there, characteristics of the vegetation, wildlife present and so on.
- If any animal of that area is endangered, find the reason for this.
- They can show the regions on a map.
- After assigning different regions of India to each group, the following questions may be given by the teacher for finding the information
  1. Which topography is found here–plain/plateau/mountain/desert, etc?
  2. How much is the rainfall?
  3. How are the summers and winters?
  4. What are the characteristics of the vegetation?
  5. Names of the different plant species and their use.
  6. Which animals are present and is any animal endangered? If so, why?
  7. Describe their habitat.

Hint

- In the group, the students who are probing in nature should find out information on climate, vegetation and wildlife.
- Those who have a flair for writing can do the writing on the poster.
- The ones good at drawing can do the map work or show the characteristics of the vegetation, draw the kinds of leaves, kind of roots (e.g., breathing roots in case of mangrove vegetation) and so on.
- The one who is a smart speaker assimilates the points and speaks about the poster display and on correlation of climate, vegetation and wildlife.
- Thus, all children with diverse talents will get an exposure and are judged for their talent.

Assessment Criteria

- Delineating correctly on the map.
- Identifying correct relation between climate and vegetation.
- Findings of plant and animal species.
- Setting correct correlation between human interference and animal extinction.

Follow Up

Correlate climate and vegetation of any other region and show the region on a map of India. Identify the vegetation around their home/school and later find the relationship with the climate of the region.

Skit

Topic

- Street Play/Story Telling on Wetland and Forest Preservation
- Importance of Tree Plantation

Learning Outcomes

The students will understand the importance of the natural habitat and the living organism and the harmful impact of human interference or on the importance of tree plantation.

Procedure

(i) Develop a street play to sensitise people on preserving wetlands and forests—these are often degraded as wasteland or on the importance of tree plantation.

(ii) Several groups may be formed and they can develop different roles of animals, birds, human beings and express their problems through their roles.

(iii) Finally, a positive message about environment conservation must come out of the play/story.

Assessment Criteria

Message conveyed, theme and expressive roles in the play

Follow Up

The message conveyed can be corrected or a good slogan added appropriately.

Project Work

Topic

Choose any one topic from the following

(i) Find some trees in your neighbourhood having medicinal values.

(ii) Find ten occupations getting raw material from forests and wildlife.

(iii) Write a poem or paragraph showing the importance of wildlife.

Learning Outcomes

After doing the project, the students will be able to do the followings

- Know about the medicinal value of various types of plants and trees available in their community.
- Know various kinds of occupations, getting raw material from forests and wildlife.
- Understand the importance of wildlife in the life of human beings.

Procedure

(i) The teacher will assign the projects to each student and asked them to choose anyone topic and write a project on it.

(ii) Students can collect relevant information based on the topic of the assignment from various sources like, internet, magazines, newspaper, etc.

- **Time Required : 1 day**

Hints

Assignment No. 1

(i) Some trees having medicinal values are (there are many others)

(a) **Amla Plant or Indian Gooseberry** This is one of the richest sources of Vitamin C. It is a medium size deciduous plant, which attains a height of 8 to 18 m. Amla is used to make herbal products, which helps get rid of health-related problems like hair fall, haemorrhage, leucorrhoea, skin diseases and discharge of blood from uterus.

(b) **Neem tree** It plays a significant role in Ayurvedic medicine. It helps to treat chickenpox, fever, skin diseases and headache.

(c) **Eucalyptus** It is a tall tree, with heights upto 100 m. Oil taken out of the eucalptus leaves has great medicinal value. It helps in purifying blood and lowering of blood sugar level. It cures problems of asthma, bronchitis, cardiac problems and fungal infections.

Assignment No. 2

(ii) Occupations getting following raw materials from forests and wildlife

(a) Carpentry

(b) Rubber industry

(c) Leather industry

(d) Ayurvedic medicine manufacturing

(e) Paper industry

(f) Glue industry

(g) Fruit and food production industry

(h) Hunting

(i) Resin extractor

(j) Perfume industry

Assignment No. 3

(iii) **Importance of Wildlife** Wildlife comprises of the innumerable varieties of wild plants, animals, fungi and microorganisms that exist on our planet Earth, rather than just cultivated plants and domesticated animals. We largely depend on this wildlife for every elementary requirement in our life.

The food we eat, the clothes we wear, the medicines we consume, a variety of building materials used for construction, numerous chemicals used for manufacturing our necessities, all are extracted from the wildlife existing around us. About 40,000 species of plants, animals, fungi and microscopic animals benefit us in some way or the other. The normal functioning or the biosphere depends on endless interactions amongst animals, plants and microorganisms.

Thus, in turn, maintains and improves human life further. These ecological processes are vital for agriculture, forestry, fisheries and other processes that support human life. Besides, there are several biological process wherein wildlife plays a key role, such as pollinisation, germination, seed dispersal, soil generation, nutrient cycling, habitat maintenance, waste breakdown and pest control.

Assessment Criteria

- Correctness of the information
- Punctuality
- Writing skill
- Presentation

PERIODIC ASSESSMENT

PEN PAPER TESTS

Test - 01

(i) Chapter covered in this test are History (Ch 5) and Economics (Ch 1).

(ii) Attempt any five questions.

01. ....are the pastoral communities of the mountains.

(a) Gujjars (b) Gaddis
(c) Sherpas (d) All of these

Ans (d) All of these

02. Who among the following is the main economic activity in Palampur?

(a) Mining (b) Fishing
(c) Agriculture (d) Animal husbandry

Ans (c) Agriculture

03. The Dhangars of Maharashtra are affected by which seasonal movements?

(a) Cold and snow
(b) Climatic disturbance
(c) Drought and flood
(d) Alternate monsoon and dry season

Ans (d) Alternate monsoon and dry season

04. Who is a person who puts together land, labour and capital?

(a) Moneylender (b) Entrepreneur
(c) Zamindar (d) Manager

Ans (b) Entrepreneur

05. Young men came to be recognised as the members of the .... in the Maasai society.

(a) younger's group (b) elder's group
(c) warrior class (d) royal group

Ans (c) warrior class

06. ...., a big village, is 3 kms from Palampur.

(a) Raiganj (b) Raniganj
(c) Raj nagar (d) Rampur

Ans (a) Raiganj

07. The pastoralist community who herded cattle in Karnataka and Andhra Pradesh were known as ....

(a) Kurumas (b) Gollas (c) Kurubas (d) Dhangars

Ans (c) Kurubas

08. Which of the following terms is used for measuring the crop produced on a given piece of land during a single year?

(a) Yield (b) Productivity (c) Cultivation (d) Output

Ans (a) Yield

09. There are two statements marked as Assertion (A) and Reason (R). Mark your answer as per the codes provided below:

Assertion (A) Land being a natural resource, it is necessary to be careful in its use.

Reason (R) Scientific reports indicate that the modern farming methods have overused the natural resource base.

Codes

(a) Both A and R are true and R is the correct explanation of A
(b) Both A and R are true, but R is not the correct explanation of A
(c) A is true, but R is false
(d) A is false, but R is true

Ans (b) Both A and R are true, but R is not the correct explanation of A

10. Match the following

	Community		Region
A.	Gaddis	1.	Himachal Pradesh
B.	Dhangars	2.	Maharashtra
C.	Banjaras	3.	Uttar Pradesh
D.	Raikas	4.	Rajasthan

Codes

	A	B	C	D		A	B	C	D
(a)	1	2	3	4	(b)	4	3	2	1
(c)	2	1	4	3	(d)	1	4	3	2

Ans (a)

Test - 02

Note See instructions in Test 1

01. Which of the following is fixed capital?

(a) Tools and machines (b) Fertilisers and pesticides
(c) Soil (d) Seeds

Ans (a) Tools and machines

02. **The .... of Maasai society wear traditional deep red 'shukas', brightly beaded jewellery and steel tipped spears.**

(a) warriors (b) elders (c) rulers (d) villagers

Ans (a) warriors

03. **What is done to surplus wheat in Palampur?**

(a) Sold in the market (b) Destroyed
(c) Stocked by self (d) Given in charity

Ans (a) Sold in the market

04. **............ per cent of the world's pastoral population is found in Africa.**

(a) 25 (b) 35 (c) 45 (d) 50

Ans (d) 50

05. **Marginal farmers are describes as**

(a) who use modern methods for farming.
(b) who practice crop rotation for farming.
(c) who did not have sufficient land for farming.
(d) who use modern methods of irrigation.

Ans (c) who did not have sufficient land for farming.

06. **The Samburu National Park is located in which among the following country?**

(a) Kenya (b) Tanzania (c) Congo (d) Jamaica

Ans (a) Kenya

07. **Identify the standard unit of measuring agricultural land .**

(a) Km^2 (b) Bigha (c) Guinea (d) Hectare

Ans (d) Hectare

08. **In which state of India do the 'Gaddi' shepherds live?**

(a) Jammu and Kashmir (b) Himachal Pradesh
(c) Maharashtra (d) Karnataka

Ans (b) Himachal Pradesh

09. There are two statements marked as Assertion (A) and Reason (R). Mark your answer as per the codes provided below.

Assertion (A) Under colonial rule, the life of pastoralists changed dramatically.

Reason (R) Their grazing grounds shrank, their movements were regulated and the revenue they had to pay increased.

Codes

(a) Both A and R are true and R is the correct explanation of A
(b) Both A and R are true, but R is not the correct explanation of A
(c) A is true, but R is false
(d) A is false, but R is true

Ans (a) Both A and R are true and R is the correct explanation of A

10. **Match the following**

List I	List II
A. Fixed capital	1. Assest
B. Working capital	2. Raw materials
C. Human capital	3. Knowledge and enterprises

Codes

	A	B	C		A	B	C
(a)	1	2	3	(b)	3	2	1
(c)	2	1	3	(d)	1	3	2

Ans. (a)

Test - 03

Note See instructions in Test 1

01. **Modern farming methods were tried in India for the first time in ....**

(a) Punjab (b) Western Uttar Pradesh
(c) Haryana (d) All of these

Ans (d) All of these

02. **Where is the Serengeti National Park in Africa situated?**

(a) Tanzania (b) Kenya
(c) Namibia (d) Zanzibar

Ans (a) Tanzania

03. **Where do most of the small farmers borrow money to arrange for the capital in Palampur?**

(a) Banks (b) Co-operative societies
(c) Village moneylenders (d) Friends and relatives

Ans (c) Village moneylenders

04. **.......... are people who do not live in one place but move from one area to another to earn their living.**

(a) Pastoralists (b) Nomads
(c) Peasants (d) Tribal people

Ans (b) Nomads

05. **Which one among the following is a non-farm activity?**

(a) Multiple cropping (b) Crop rotation
(c) Dairy farming (d) Modern farming

Ans (c) Dairy farming

06. **What are Bugyals?**

(a) Wastelands
(b) Pastures in the mountain's foot area
(c) Pastures above 12000 feet high mountains
(d) They are deserts

Ans (c) Pastures above 12000 feet high mountains

07. **The minimum wages for a farm labourer set by the government is ....**

(a) ₹ 300 per day (b) ₹ 200 per day
(c) ₹ 150 per day (d) ₹ 250 per day

Ans (a) ₹ 300 per day

08. **Nomadic tribes need to move from one place to another because ....**

(a) of seasonal changes
(b) in search of pastures
(c) to maintain ecological balance
(d) All of the above

Ans (b) in search of pastures

09. There are two statements marked as Assertion (A) and Reason (R). Mark your answer as per the codes provided below.

Assertion (A) Like pastoralists in India, the lives of African pastoralists have changed dramatically over the colonial and post-colonial periods.

Reason (R) The Maasai cattle herders live primarily in East Africa: 300, 000 in Southern Kenya and another 150,000 in Tanzania.

Codes

(a) Both A and R are true and R is the correct explanation of A
(b) Both A and R are true, but R is not the correct explanation of A
(c) A is true, but R is false
(d) A is false, but R is true

Ans (b) Both A and R are true but R is not the correct explanation of A

10. **Match the following.**

	List I (Community)		**List II** (Associated region)
A.	Kurubas	1.	Andhra Pradesh
B.	Maldharis	2.	Rann of Kutch
C.	Gujjar Bakarwals	3.	Jammu and Kashmir

Codes

	A	B	C		A	B	C
(a)	3	2	1	(b)	2	1	3
(c)	1	3	2	(d)	1	2	3

Ans. (d)

Test - 04

Note See instructions in Test 1

01. **In the year .... Tanganyika attained its independence.**

(a) 1961 (b) 1962
(c) 1963 (d) 1964

Ans (a) 1961

02. **Which one among the following is a non-farm activity?**

(a) Multiple cropping (b) Crop rotation
(c) Dairy farming (d) Modern farming

Ans (c) Dairy farming

03. **Which of the following statements best explains pastoral nomads?**

(a) The villagers who moved from one place to another.
(b) The people who do not have a permanent place to live in.
(c) The herdsman who moved from one place to another looking for pastures for their herd.
(d) Groups who moved from place to place for food.

Ans (c) The herdsman who moved from one place to another looking for pastures for their herd.

04. **The activities such as small manufacturing, transport, shopkeeping are referred to as .... .**

(a) non-economic activities
(b) non-farming activities
(c) non-traditional activities
(d) non-market activities

Ans (b) non-farming activities

05. **The pastoralists community who herded sheep and sold blankets in the states of Andhra Pradesh and Karnataka were known as ....**

(a) Kurumas (b) Kurubas
(c) Raikas (d) Both (a) and (b)

Ans (d) Both (a) and (b)

06. **In Palampur, there are 60 families of medium and large farmers who cultivate more than .... of land.**

(a) 2 hectares (b) 3 hectares
(c) 4 hectares (d) 6 hectares

Ans (a) 2 hectares

07. **Who was the Deputy Conservator of Forests at Darjeeling in the year 1913?**

(a) H S Gibson (b) Buchanan
(c) Francis Hamilton (d) De Brett

Ans (a) H S Gibson

08. **What is the source of capital for the large farmers?**

(a) Banks and own savings
(b) Moneylenders and relatives
(c) Banks and moneylenders
(d) Poor farmers

Ans (a) Banks and own savings

09. There are two statements marked as Assertion (A) and Reason (R). Mark your answer as per the codes provided below.

Assertion (A) In many areas, Green Revolution is associated with the loss of soil fertility due to increased use of chemical fertilisers.

Reason (R) Also, continuous use of groundwater for tubewell irrigation has led to the depletion of the water-table.

Codes

(a) Both A and R are true and R is the correct explanation of A
(b) Both A and R are true, but R is not the correct explanation of A
(c) A is true, but R is false
(d) A is false, but R is true

Ans (b) Both A and R are true, but R is not the correct explanation of A

10. Match the following.

	List I	List II
A.	1920s	1. Royal Commission on agriculture reported
B.	1933-34	2. Severe drought in Maasailand
C.	1961	3. Tanganyika attained independence

Codes

	A	B	C		A	B	C
(a)	1	2	3	(b)	3	2	1
(c)	2	1	3	(d)	1	3	2

Ans. (a)

Test - 05

Note See instructions in Test 1

01. When did Tanganyika come under British control?

(a) 1919 (b) 1916 (c) 1917 (d) 1918

Ans (a) 1919

02. Money in hand is an example of ....

(a) human capital (b) fixed capital
(c) working capital (d) physical capital

Ans (c) working capital

03. .... crop was sown in the Dhangars in the central plateau of Maharashtra.

(a) Bajra (b) Jowar
(c) Rice (d) Wheat

Ans (a) Bajra

04. Which one among the following is not fixed capital?

(a) Machines (b) Buildings
(c) Tools (d) Raw materials

Ans (d) Raw materials

05. The Nomadic cattle herders of Kaokoland belonged to which of the following countries?

(a) Namibia (b) Zambia
(c) Zimbabwe (d) South Africa

Ans (a) Namibia

06. High Yielding Variety seeds (HYVs) were introduced to Indian farmers as a result of ..... .

(a) White Revolution (b) Green Revolution
(c) IT Revolution (d) None of these

Ans (b) Green Revolution

07. Since when were the 'waste land' rules implemented in various parts of the country?

(a) 17th century
(b) Early 18th century
(c) Mid 19th century
(d) Late 19th century

Ans (c) Mid 19th century

08. Scope of farming activity is limited in Palampur due to ....

(a) fixed amount of land
(b) lack of irrigation
(c) lack of labour
(d) None of the above

Ans (a) fixed amount of land

09. There are two statements marked as Assertion (A) and Reason (R). Mark your answer as per the codes provided below.

Assertion (A) In Maasailand, as elsewhere in Africa, not all pastoralists were equally affected by the changes in the colonial period.

Reason (R) In pre-colonial times Maasai society was divided into two social categories-elders and warriors.

Codes

(a) Both A and R are true and R is the correct explanation of A
(b) Both A and R are true, but R is not the correct explanation of A
(c) A is true, but R is false
(d) A is false, but R is true

Ans (b) Both A and R are true, but R is not the correct explanation of A

10. Match the following.

	List I		List II
A.	Modern farming method	1.	HYV, tractor and fertilisers
B.	Non-farm activitites	2.	Dairy, shops, rice mill
C.	Big farmers	3.	Sale of surplus crops
D.	Small farmers	4.	Borrowing of money

Codes

	A	B	C	D		A	B	C	D
(a)	4	3	2	1	(b)	1	2	3	4
(c)	2	1	4	3	(d)	1	4	3	2

Ans (b)

Sample Question Paper 1 (Solved)

Social Science

Time : 3 hrs	M.M. : 80

General Instructions

1 Question paper comprises Six Sections – A, B, C, D, E and F. There are 37 questions in the question paper. All questions are compulsory.
2 Section A – From Question 1 to 20 are MCQs of 1 mark each.
3 Section B – Question no. 21 to 24 are Very Short Answer Type Questions, carrying 2 marks each. Answer to each question should not exceed 40 words.
4 Section C – Contains Questions 25 to 29 are Short Answer Type Questions, carrying 3 marks each. Answer to each question should not exceed 60 words
5 Section D – Question no. 30 to 33 are long answer type questions, carrying 5 marks each. Answer to each question should not exceed 120 words.
6 Section E – Questions no from 34 to 36 are case based questions with three sub questions and are of 4 marks each.
7 Section F – Question no. 37 is map based, carrying 5 marks with two parts, 37a from History (2 marks) and 37b from Geography (3 marks).

Section A (1×20 = 20)

1. Renu lives in Rajasthan, she wanted to visit Dudhwa national park with her family. Dudhwa National park located in which region? (1)

(a) Uttar Pradesh
(b) Andhra Pradesh
(c) Madhya Pradesh
(d) Gujarat

2. Manish gave his friend clues about Purvanchal hills. Which of the following clues are most useful in identifying the regions comprising the Purvanchal or Eastern hills and mountains? (1)

Clues

I. Composed of strong sandstones
II. Covered with dense forests
III. Includes the Patkai hills
IV. High deposits of minerals are found

(a) Clues I and II
(b) Clues I, II and III
(c) Clues II and IV
(d) Clues III and IV

3. Match the following. (1)

	List I		List II
A.	Rajasthan	1.	Tropic of Cancer passes through it
B.	Andhra Pradesh	2.	Located on West coast
C.	Kerala	3.	Located in East coast
D.	Mizoram	4.	North of the Tropic of Cancer

Codes

	A	B	C	D		A	B	C	D
(a)	4	3	2	1	(b)	1	2	3	4
(c)	4	1	2	3	(d)	3	4	1	2

4. Consider the following statements about the Kaveri Basin and select the correct option. (1)

I. Kaveri river originates in the Brahmagiri range of the Western Ghats.
II. If flows into the Bay of Bengal, South of the Cuddalore in Tamil Nadu.
III. The length of the river is about 760 km.

Codes

(a) Only I
(b) Only II
(c) Both I and III
(d) All of these

5. Interpret the following pie-diagram and choose the correct option for the following question. (1)

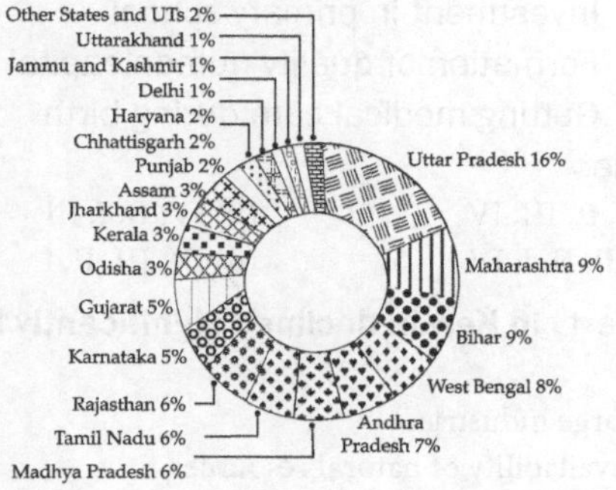

Why most of the peninsular states have moderate population densities?

(a) Highly developed agriculture
(b) Well-developed transportation networks
(c) Highly paid job opportunities
(d) Hilly, dissected and rocky nature of the terrain

6 The special feature(s) about this painting is/are that (1)

(a) it is one of the rare paintings by a woman artist.
(b) the painting is a female allegory of liberty.
(c) it symbolises the new Constitution of France.
(d) Both (a) and (b)

7. Consider the following statements and choose the correct option. (1)

I. In 1898, the Russian Social Democratic Workers Party was formed.

II. In 1915, Lenin returned to Russia from his exile.

III. All political parties in Russia were illegal before 1900.

IV. Collectivisation was first introduced by Lenin.

Codes

(a) Only I (b) Only II
(c) Both III and IV (d) All of these

8. Read the following statements about Hitler's rise to power and choose the correct option. (1)

I. Hitler was appointed Chancellor by President Clinton on 30th January, 1933.

II. The Fire Decree of 28th February, 1933 suspended civic rights guaranteed by the Weimar Constitution.

III. The Enabling Act passed on 3rd March, 1933 established Hitler's dictatorship in Germany.

IV. The Green Police uniform and the Gestapo were established to enforce Nazi rule.

Options

(a) I, II and III
(b) II, III and IV
(c) I, III and IV
(d) I, II and IV

9. Identify the place where the Imperial Forest Research Institute was set up in 1906. (1)

(a) New Delhi (b) Bombay
(c) Dehradun (d) Mussorie

10. What was the speciality of Nuremberg Rally? (1)

(a) It was held every year
(b) It demonstrated Nazi power
(c) It showed loyalty to Hitler
(d) All of the above

11. Match the following. (1)

List I (Thinker)	List II (Ideology)
A. Robert Owen	1. Proposed government support for cooperatives over capitalist enterprises.
B. Louis Blanc	2. Overthrow of capitalism and the establishment of a communist society.
C. Karl Marx	3. Contributed to Marxist theory and envisioned a future communist society.
D. Friedrich Engels	4. Advocate of cooperative communities

Codes

	A	B	C	D		A	B	C	D
(a)	1	3	2	4	(b)	4	1	2	3
(c)	2	3	1	4	(d)	3	1	4	2

12. Which among the following is considered as an accountable form of government? **(1)**

(a) Autocratic government
(b) Dictator government
(c) Democratic government
(d) Military government

13. Find the incorrect option. **(1)**

(a) Elections should be conducted in free and fair manner.
(b) Everyone should have the right to choose their representative.
(c) Elections are necessary and mandatory in all forms of government.
(d) Elections are held in all constituencies at the same time, either on the same day or within a few days.

14. Consider the statements given below and choose the correct answer. **(1)**

Statement I The Political Executive has more powers than the Permanent Executive.

Statement II The Political Executive is elected by the people and in a democracy, will of the people is supreme.

Codes

(a) Statement I is correct and statement II is incorrect
(b) Statement I is incorrect and II is correct
(c) Both statement I and statement II are incorrect
(d) Both statement I and statement II are correct

15. Fundamental Rights are guaranteed against the actions of which of the following? **(1)**

(a) Legislature
(b) Executive
(c) Any authorities instituted by the government
(d) All of the above

16. Consider the statements given below and choose the correct answer. **(1)**

Statement I Educated parents invest more heavily in their children's education and are conscious of proper nutrition and hygiene.

Statement II Disadvantaged parents, who are uneducated and lack hygiene, often keep their children in a similarly disadvantaged state.

Codes

(a) Statement I is correct and Statement II is incorrect
(b) Statement I is incorrect and Statement II is correct
(c) Both statement I and statement II are incorrect
(d) Both statement I and statement II are correct

17. Arrange the following in sequence. **(1)**

I. Providing computer technology skill
II. Investment in primary school
III. Formation of quality human capital
IV. Getting medical care during birth

Codes

(a) I, II, III, IV (b) IV, II, I, III
(c) III, II, I, IV (d) IV, III, II, I

18. Poverty in Kerala declined significantly because of **(1)**

(a) large industries
(b) availability of natural resources
(c) development of human resources
(d) All of the above

19. Read the following data and select the appropriate option from the following. **(1)**

Year	production (lakh tonnes)	Imports (lakh tonnes)	Exports (lakh tonnes)	Total Availability (lakh tonnes)
1938	85	–	–	85
1939	79	04	–	83
1940	82	03	–	85
1941	68	02	–	70

Source : *AK 1981 page 61*

In which year, the production and import of rice is maximum in province of Bengal?

(a) 1938 (b) 1939
(c) 1940 (d) 1941

20. Read the following data and select the appropriate option from the following. **(1)**

Estimates of Poverty in India		
Year	Poverty Ratio (%)	
	Rural	Urban
Poverty Ratio in India in 2011-12	26	14
Poverty Ratio in India in 2009-10	34	21
Poverty Ratio in India in 2004-05	42	26

In which year, the poverty ratio (%) in India is lowest in remote area?

(a) 2004-05 (b) 2009-10
(c) 2011-12 (d) Both (a) and (b)

Section B (2×4=8)

21. 'Russia's industrialisation in the early 20th century contributed to the increasing role of women in the urban workforce'. Justify the statement. **(2)**

22. Lakshadweep islands differ from the Andaman and Nicobar islands in terms of geographical location and composition. Justify the statement. **(2)**

23. Which country out of France, USA, Myanmar and India is not a true democratic country?

Or Li Wei, a young lawyer from Shanghai, found herself deeply interested in the workings of the Chinese Parliament. As a staunch advocate for legal reforms and civil rights, he followed the Parliament sessions and policies, seeking to understand its features and impact on Chinese society. **(2)**

What is the name of the Chinese Parliament? Mention its feature.

24. The growth rate of India's population started declining since 1981. Justify the statement. **(2)**

Section C (3 × 5 = 15)

25. Describe the procedure of the nomination of a candidate to contest in a particular election. **(3)**

Or What is the model code of conduct for election campaign?

26. When was the Enabling Act passed in Germany? How did this act establish dictatorship of Hitler in Germany? **(3)**

27. Read the statements given below regarding Physical Features of India.

Statement 1 (S1) One of the distinct features of the Peninsular plateau is the black soil area known as Deccan Trap.

Statement 2 (S2) The Aravali Hills lie on the western and northwestern margins of the Peninsular plateau.

Explain, which statement is correct and why? **(3)**

28. "In India majority of population lives below the poverty line. Government is taking measures to lessen poverty." You are the member of the commission appointed to suggest the areas/ issues concerned.

Which issues would you suggest regarding poverty alleviation? **(3)**

29. Rahul, a class 9th student, gave utmost importance to his health. He exercised daily and avoided junk food to maintain his health. He also used to inspire his friends and neighbours to take care of their health. Identify the reasons why health is considered crucial for both an individual and an organisation. **(3)**

Section D (5×4=20)

30. What is unemployment? Explain two types of unemployment found in rural areas. **(5)**

Or "Illiterate and unhealthy population are a liability for the economy." Justify the statement.

31. How did Hitler's regime influence German youth through education organisations and what were its long-term implications? **(5)**

Or How did Nazi Germany enforce gender roles and expectations among women and what were the consequences for those who deviated from these norms?

32. Marie, a tailor living in Paris during the French Revolution, found herself surrounded by the spirit of societal change. Born into the third estate, she was accustomed to the struggles of everyday life – long hours, meager wages, and the constant juggle of household responsibilities alongside her work.

Despite these challenges, Marie was determined to make her voice heard and advocate for the rights of women like herself. **(5)**

Or What changes were seen in the regime of Robespierre's government?

33. Describe the geological composition and distinctive features of the three main ranges of the Himalayas. **(5)**

Or How are the Himalayas divided regionally from West to East and what are the significant characteristics of the Purvanchal or Eastern hills and mountains?

Section E (4 × 3 = 12)

34. Read the source given below and answer the questions that follow.

Socialists were against private property, and saw it as the root of all social ills of the time. Why? Individuals owned the property that gave employment but the propertied were concerned only with personal gain and not with the welfare of those who made the property productive. So, if society as a whole rather than single individuals controlled property, more attention would be paid to collective social interests. Socialists wanted this change and campaigned for it.

Socialists had different visions of the future. Some believed in the idea of cooperatives. Robert Owen (1771-1858), a leading English manufacturer, sought to build a cooperative community called New Harmony in Indiana (USA). Other socialists felt that cooperatives could not be built on a wide scale only through individual initiative; they demanded that governments encourage cooperatives. In France, for instance, Louis Blanc (1813-1882) wanted the government to encourage cooperatives and replace capitalist enterprises. These cooperatives were to be associations of people who produced goods together and divided the profits according to the work done by members.

Karl Marx (1818-1883) and Friedrich Engels (1820-1895) added other ideas to this body of arguments. Marx argued that industrial society was 'capitalist'. Capitalists owned the capital invested in factories and the profit of capitalists was produced by workers. The conditions of workers could not improve as long as this profit was accumulated by private capitalists. Workers had to overthrow capitalism and the rule of private property. Marx believed that to free themselves from capitalist exploitation, workers had to construct a radically socialist society where all property was socially controlled. This would be a communist society.

(i) Who were socialists? (1)

(ii) According to Karl Marx, how workers could free themselves from capitalist exploitation? (1)

(iii) Mention any two features of socialists. (2)

35. Read the source given below and answer the questions that follow.

Besides the longitudinal divisions, the Himalayas have been divided on the basis of regions from West to East. These divisions have been demarcated by river valleys. For example, the part of Himalayas lying between Indus and Satluj has been traditionally known as Punjab Himalaya, but it is also known regionally as Kashmir and Himachal Himalaya from West to East respectively. The part of the Himalayas lying between Satluj and Kali rivers is known as Kumaon Himalayas. The Kali and Teesta rivers demarcate the Nepal Himalayas and the part lying between Teesta and Dihang rivers is known as Assam Himalayas. There are regional names also in these broad categories.

The Brahmaputra marks the Easternmost boundary of the Himalayas. Beyond the Dihang gorge, the Himalayas bend sharply to the South and spread along the Eastern boundary of India. They are known as the Purvanchal or the Eastern hills and mountains. These hills running through the North-Eastern states are mostly composed of strong sandstones, which are sedimentary rocks, covered with dense forests, they mostly run as parallel ranges and valleys. The Purvanchal comprises the Patkai Hills, the Naga Hills, the Manipur Hills and the Mizo Hills.

(i) Which part of the Himalayas lies between Indus and Satluj rivers? (1)

(ii) Name the rivers between which Kumaon and Assam Himalayas demarcated. (1)

(iii) How does the Purvanchal mountain composed? (2)

36. Read the source given below and answer the questions that follows.

The white rulers treated all non-whites as inferiors slowly, the apartheid system started oppressing blacks. In this system, the non-whites did not have voting rights and they were forbidden from living in white areas. The non-whites could work in white areas only if they had a permit. Trains, buses, taxis, hospitals, schools, colleges, etc were all separate for the whites and blacks. This was known as segregation. Blacks could not enter a Church where the whites worshipped and even they did not have the right to form associations or protest against the whites. But, after the emergence of democratic South Africa, black leaders appealed to fellow blacks to forgive the whites for the atrocities they had committed while in power. They wanted to build up a new South Africa based on equality of all races.

(i) **Which type of tactics did the white recist government of South Africa used to continue their rule? What would have happened in South Africa if the black majority had decided to take revenge on the whites for all their oppression and exploitation? (2)**

(ii) **"The apartheid system was particularly bppressive for blacks." Justify by giving two reasons. (2)**

Section F (2 + 3 = 5)

37. **(a) On the map of the world, two countries are marked, these countries were Allied powers of the Second World War which were in Europe. Identify these countries. (2)**

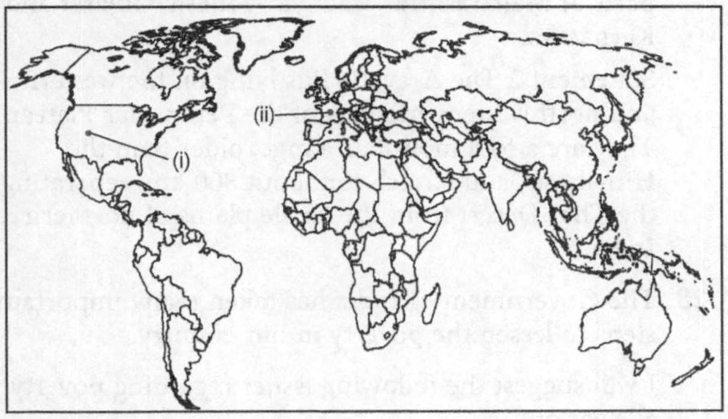

(b) Locate any three features with the help of the given information. (3)

(i) The capital of the state of Karnataka

(ii) Northern part of Western coastal plain

(iii) Neighbouring country of India

(iv) The Ghats on the South-Eastern part of India

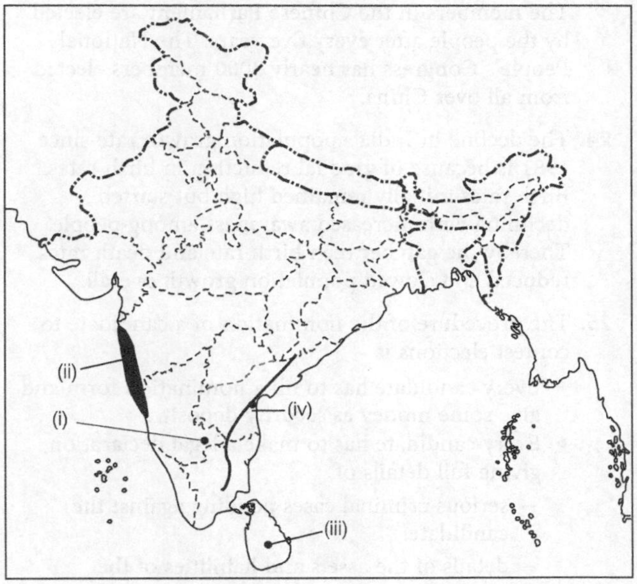

Answers

1. (a) Uttar Pradesh
2. (b) Clues I, II and III
3. (a)
4. (d) All of these
5. (d) Hilly, dissected and rocky nature of the terrain
6. (d) Both (a) and (b)
7. (a) Only I
8. (b) II, III and IV
9. (c) Dehradun
10. (d) All of the above
11. (b)
12. (c) Democratic government
13. (c) Elections are necessary and mandatory in all forms of government.
14. (d) Both statement I and statement II are correct
15. (d) All of the above
16. (d) Both statement I and statement II are correct
17. (b) IV, II, I, III
18. (c) development of human resources
19. (b) 1939
20. (c) 2011-12
21. Yes, Russia's industrialisation in the early 20th century increased the role of women in the urban workforce. By 1914 women comprised 31% of factory labour. Despite lower wages than men, their participation marked a significant shift in workforce dynamics, influencing social and economic roles in urban areas.
22. Lakshadweep islands differ from the Andaman and Nicobar islands in terms of geographical location and composition. The Lakshadweep islands are located in the Arabian sea. They are small coral islands covering 32 sq km with Kavaratti as their administrative capital. Whereas, the Andaman and Nicobar islands are larger and are scattered across the Bay of Bengal. They are known for their strategic importance and rich biodiversity.

23. Myanmar is not a true democratic country because it is ruled by military rulers. Democracy is a political structure in which people directly exercise power, or elect or members from among themselves to represent the people, such as a Parliament.

Or The name of the Chinese Parliament is National People's Congress ('Quanguo renmin Daibiao Dahui' in Chinese Mandarin language).

The members in the Chinese Parliament are elected by the people after every five years. The National People's Congress has nearly 3000 members elected from all over China.

24. The decline in India's population growth rate since 1981 is because of gradual reduction in birth rates. Birth rates initially remained high but started declining with increased awareness among people. Thereby the gap between birth rate and death rates reduced and slowed population growth overall.

25. The procedure of the nomination of a candidate to contest elections is

- Every candidate has to fill a nomination form and give some money as security deposit.
- Every candidate has to make a legal declaration, giving full details of
  - serious criminal cases pending against the candidate.
  - details of the assets and liabilities of the candidate and his or her family.
  - educational qualification of the candidate.

All this information has to be made public, which provides an opportunity to the voters to choose the desirable candidate.

Or All the political parties in our country have agreed to follow a set of norms and guidelines and these are known as model code of conduct. According to this, no party or candidate can

- use any place of worship for election propaganda.
- use government vehicles, aircrafts and officials for elections.
- lay foundation stones of any projects, take any big policy decisions or make any promises of providing public facilities after the date of elections are announced.

26. On 3rd March, 1933, the famous Enabling Act was passed in Germany.

This act established dictatorship of Hitler in Germany in the following ways

- This act gave Hitler all powers to sideline the Parliament and rule by decree.
- All political parties and trade unions, except the Nazi Party and its affiliates were banned in Germany.
- The new state machinery under Hitler established complete control over the economy, media, army and Judiciary of Germany.
- Special surveillance and security forces were created to control the society. These included the Gestapo (Secret State Police), the SS (The Protection Squads), Criminal Police and the Security Service (SD).

27. Both the statements are correct because- The Deccan Traps are a distinct feature of the Peninsular Plateau. They are an extensive volcanic region formed by lava flows millions of years ago. This volcanic activity resulted in the creation of fertile black soil regions in parts of Maharashtra, Madhya Pradesh, Gujarat and Karnataka.

Statement 2 The Aravali Hills lying on the western and northwestern margins of the Peninsular Plateau. They are a fold mountain range, older than the Himalayas, and stretch for about 800 km, separating the Thar Desert from the fertile plains of northern India.

28. The Government of India has taken many important steps to lessen the poverty in our country.

I will suggest the following issues regarding poverty alleviation

- **Stop Social Exclusion** Some communities are socially excluded so they do not reap the benefits of economic development. Certain groups like poor women, children and old people are deprived of basic needs and live in poverty. So, by stoping social exclusion will ensure decline in poverty level.
- **Generating Employment** By generating more employment opportunities in both rural and urban areas, the poverty level can decline.
- **Increase in Literacy Level** By raising the level of education in a country, more employment opportunities are generated. So, rise in literacy level raises the income which in turn reduces poverty.

29. Health is considered crucial because it directly impacts an individual's ability to realise their potential and contribute effectively to growth of organisations. Health is essential for individuals to achieve their potential and productivity.

For organisations, healthy workers are more efficient and contribute more effectively to overall growth.

Health supports well-being and is a priority in national policies aimed at improving healthcare accessibility and services.

30. When a person, skilled or non-skilled, willing to work as per the going wage, does not get work, the person is said to be unemployed. This situation is termed as unemployment.

Two types of unemployment found in rural areas are as follows

(i) **Disguised Unemployment** This prevails in agricultural sector in rural India, where all the members of the family are engaged on a plot of land belonging to them. Everybody seems to be working on that land, but production does not suffer if some of the family members are removed from work. The surplus persons are disguisedly unemployed.

(ii) **Seasonal Unemployment** It also prevails in agricultural sector in rural India. Labourers are busy during the period when sowing, harvesting, weeding and threshing is done. Other than this period, labourers hardly get any work as villages lack infrastructure, construction activities or other sources of employment.

Or The quality of population of a country depends upon some factors like, the literacy rate, health of a person indicated by life expectancy and skill formation acquired by the people. The quality of population ultimately decides the growth rate of the country.

Illiterate and unhealthy population becomes a liability for the economy. It can be justified in the following ways

- Illiterate and unhealthy people are not capable to use land and capital efficiently.
- Their employment potential is low compared to literate and healthy people and they earn much less than literate and helathy people.
- An unhealthy person has less productivity and has to spend more money on his medical care than a healthy person.

Thus, illiterate and unhealthy people are a liability for the economy by making the country poorer and retard the development of it.

31. Hitler's regime greatly influenced German youth through education organisation. He believed that a strong Nazi society could be established only by teaching children Nazi ideology.

To achieve this drastic changes were introduced in the schools which were as follows

- Jewish and politically unreliable teachers were dismissed.
- Jewish and non-Jewish children were segregated.
- Jews, the physically handicapped, Gypsies were regarded as 'undesirable children' and were thrown out of schools.
- Nazi ideology was promoted through rewritten textbooks.
- Racial science was introduced to justify Nazi ideas of race. Stereotypes about Jews were popularised even through maths classes where curricular were manipulated to include biased and distorted information reinforcing anti-semitic veiws.
- Children were taught to be loyal and submissive, hate Jews and worship Hitler. Hitler trained boys with aggressive values and hatred for perceived enemies.

The long-term implications of this systematic training was to ensure long-term submission to Nazi beliefs. It would encourage a population ready to support and enforce Hitler's totalitarian regime.

Or Nazi Germany rigidly enforced traditional gender roles among women. Girls were instructed to prioritise motherhood, racial purity and domestic duties. Women's fight for gender equality was regarded as detrimental. Women who experience racial discrimination and undesirable children had to face punishment, whereas those producing 'Aryan' offspring received rewards like medical benefits and discounts.

The consequences for those who deviated from these norms included public condemnation, severe punishments and loss of civic rights. Women maintaining ties with Jews or other targeted groups were publicly humiliated, sometimes jailed and separated from their families. This systematic enforcement aimed to mould women into instruments of Nazi ideology, strengthening societal control and racial purity through harsh measures and public shaming methods.

32. At the time of the French Revolution, women were part of the class of the unprivileged. To improve their condition, they started their own political clubs and newspapers. About sixty women's clubs were formed. The Society of Revolutionary and Republican Women was the most famous club.

Women demanded the same political rights as men. They were disappointed that the Constitution of 1791 reduced them to passive citizens. Thus, they demanded the right to vote, to be elected to the Assembly and to hold political office.

Only then, they felt, would their interests be represented in the new government.

The steps which were taken by the government of the time to improve their condition were as follows

- State schools were established for women.
- Schooling was made mandatory for all girls.
- They could not be forced to marry against their will.
- Marriage was made into a contract entered into freely and registered under Civil Law.
- Divorce was made legal and could be applied for both by women and men.
- Women were allowed to be trained for jobs and were allowed to run small businesses.

Or The following changes were seen in the regime of Robespierre's government

- Robespierre's government issued laws placing a maximum ceiling on wages and prices. Meat and bread were rationed.
- Peasants were forced to transport their grain to the cities and sell it at fixed prices by the government.
- The use of expensive white flour was forbidden and all citizens were forced to eat the equality bread, *i.e.* a loaf made of whole wheat.
- Instead of the traditional Monsieur (Sir) and Madame (Madam), all French men and women were called as Citoyen and Citoyenne (citizen).
- Churches were also shut down and their buildings were converted into barracks or offices.

33. The geological composition and features of the three main ranges of Himalayas are as follows

(i) **Great Himalayas** (Himadri) This range is the Northernmost range. Its core is composed of granite and its average peak height is 6,000 metres. Its folds are asymmetrical, forming glaciers and covered with perennial snow.

(ii) **Lesser Himalayas** (Himachal) It is located South of Himadri. It includes Pir Panjal, Dhaula Dhar and Mahabharat ranges, with altitudes of 3,700-4,500 metres. Famous valleys like Kashmir and Kangra are located in these ranges.

(iii) **Outermost range** (Shiwaliks) This range is 10-50 km wide and 900-1100 metres high. Shiwaliks are sediment deposits from the main ranges.These valleys are covered with thick gravel and alluvium. The longitudinal valley between lesser Himalaya and the Shiwaliks are known as Duns. Dehra Dun, Kotli Dun and Patli Dun are some of the well-known Duns.

Or The Himalayas are divided regionally from West to East by river valleys in the following ways

(i) **Punjab Himalaya** This section of himalayas lies between the Indus and Satluj river. They are also referred to as Kashmir and Himachal Himalaya regionally.

(ii) **Kumaon Himalayas** This part lies between the Satluj and Kali rivers.

(iii) **Nepal Himalayas** This part is demarcated by the Kali and Teesta rivers.

(iv) **Assam Himalayas** This section extends from the Teesta to the Dihang rivers.

(v) **Purvanchal Himalayas** These ranges are located to the East of the Brahmaputra river, where the Himalayas sharply bend Southward.

Major characteristics of Purvanchal hills include

- They are composed mostly of strong sandstones.
- They are covered with dense forests.
- They include the Patkai, Naga, Manipur, and Mizo hills, running in parallel ranges and valleys.

34. (i) Socialists were those people who were against private property and saw it as the root of all social ills of the time.

(ii) According to Karl Marx, the workers could free themselves from capitalist exploitation by constructing a radically socialist society where all property was socially controlled.

(iii) The features of socialists were

(a) Socialists were against the private property.

(b) Socialists regarded the private property as the root cause of all social evils.

35. (i) Punjab Himalayas lies between Indus and Satluj rivers.

(ii) The part of the Himalayas lying between Satluj and Kali rivers is known as Kumaon Himalayas and the part lying between Teesta and Dihang river is known as Assam Himalayas.

(iii) The Purvanchal mountain is the Eastern extension of the Himalayas lying in the Easternmost parts of India. These mountains are composed of sedimentary rock. They are covered with dense forests. The Purvanchal comprises the Naga Hills, Manipur Hills, Mizo Hills and Patkai Hills.

36. (i) The white racist government continued to rule by detaining, torturing and killing thousands of black and coloured people.

If the blacks had not forgiven the whites for all their oppression and exploitation and decided to take revenge upon them, there would have been bloodshed everywhere. It could have led to a division of the country and they would not be seen as a united and peaceful South Africa.

(ii) The apartheid system was particularly oppressive for blacks because of the following reasons

(a) They were forbidden from living in white areas. They could work in white areas only if they had a permit to do so.

(b) They could not even visit the Churches where the whites worshipped. Blacks could not form associations or protest against the terrible treatment.

37. (a)

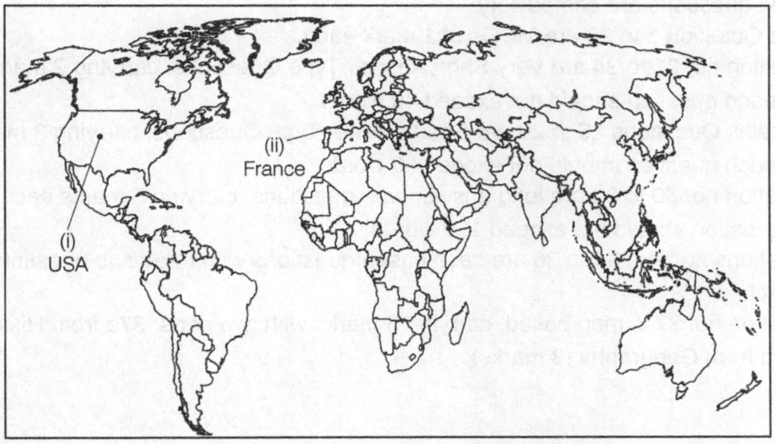

(b)

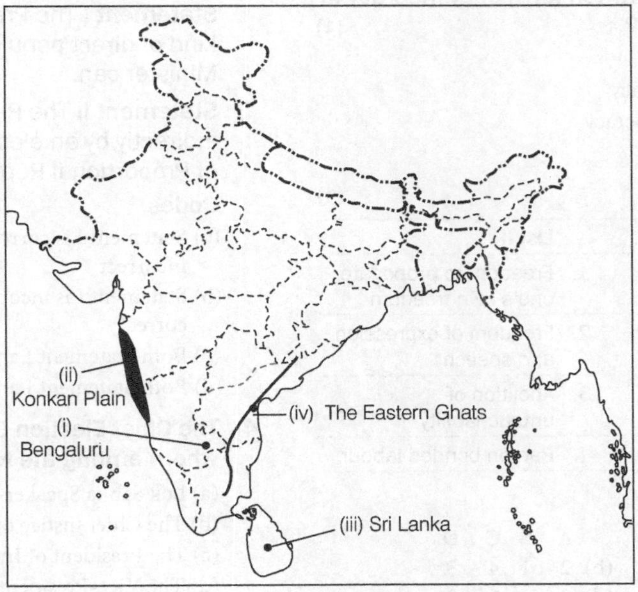

Sample Question Paper 2 (Solved)
Social Science

Time : 3 hrs	M.M. : 80

General Instructions

1 Question paper comprises Six Sections – A, B, C, D, E and F. There are 37 questions in the question paper. All questions are compulsory.
2 Section A – From Question 1 to 20 are MCQs of 1 mark each.
3 Section B – Question no. 21 to 24 are Very Short Answer Type Questions, carrying 2 marks each. Answer to each question should not exceed 40 words.
4 Section C – Contains Questions 25 to 29 are Short Answer Type Questions, carrying 3 marks each. Answer to each question should not exceed 60 words
5 Section D – Question no. 30 to 33 are long answer type questions, carrying 5 marks each. Answer to each question should not exceed 120 words.
6 Section E – Questions no from 34 to 36 are case based questions with three sub questions and are of 4 marks each.
7 Section F – Question no. 37 is map based, carrying 5 marks with two parts, 37a from History (2 marks) and 37b from Geography (3 marks).

Section A (1 × 20 = 20)

1. What is the most common form of democracy in contemporary times? (1)

(a) Direct democracy
(b) Participatry democracy
(c) Representative democracy
(d) Liberal democracy

2. Match the following. (1)

	List I		List II
A.	Right to Freedom	1.	Freedom to propogate one's own freedom
B.	Right to Freedom of Religion	2.	Freedom of expression and speech
C.	Right against Exploitation	3.	Abolition of untouchability
D.	Right to Equality	4.	Ban on bonded labour

Codes

	A	B	C	D		A	B	C	D
(a)	1	2	3	4	(b)	2	1	4	3
(c)	4	3	2	1	(d)	3	4	1	2

3. Consider the statements given below and choose the correct answer. (1)

Statement I The President can never claim the kind of direct popular mandate that the Prime Minister can.

Statement II The President of India is elected indirectly by an electoral college with the system of Proportional Representation.

Codes

(a) Statement I is correct and Statement II is incorrect
(b) Statement I is incorrect and Statement II is correct
(c) Both Statement I and Statement II are incorrect
(d) Both Statement I and Statement II are correct

4. The Chief Election Commissioner is appointed by whom among the following? (1)

(a) Lok Sabha Speaker
(b) The Chief Justice of India
(c) The President of India
(d) The Vice-President of India

5. Find the incorrect option from the following. (1)

(a) Dr. BR Ambedkar was the Chairman of Drafting Committee.
(b) Shyama Prasad Mukherjee was the founder President of the Bharatiya Jana Sangh.
(c) Mahatma Gandhi was a member of Constituent Assembly.
(d) HC Mookherjee was the Vice-Chairman of the Constituent Assembly.

6. Which age group is included in the work force population? (1)

(a) 21 to 50 years
(b) 16 to 60 years
(c) 14 to 50 years
(d) 15 to 59 years

7. Match the following. (1)

List I (States)	List II (Bordering country)
A. West Bengal	1. Myanmar
B. Manipur	2. Bangladesh
C. Gujarat	3. Pakistan
D. Uttarakhand	4. Nepal

Codes

	A	B	C	D		A	B	C	D
(a)	4	3	2	1	(b)	1	3	4	2
(c)	2	1	3	4	(d)	1	2	4	3

8. Sivaraman lives in a small village near Karur town in Tamil Nadu. Karur is famous for its handloom and powerloom fabrics. There are 100 families in the village. Sivaraman, an Aryunthathiyar (cobbler) by caste now works as an agricultural labourer for 160 per day. But that's only for five to six months in a year. At other times, he does odd jobs in the town. (1)

Why did Sivaraman need to do odd jobs in the town apart from agriculture?

(a) Agriculture only provides seasonal work
(b) Physical weakness
(c) Lack of skills to work in agriculture
(d) Aryunthathiyar caste is not allowed to work in agriculture for an entire year.

9. The Northernmost longitude of India is (1)

(a) 97°25'E (b) 8°4'E
(c) 82°32'N (d) 37°6'N

10. Interpret the table given below and choose the correct option for the following question. (1)

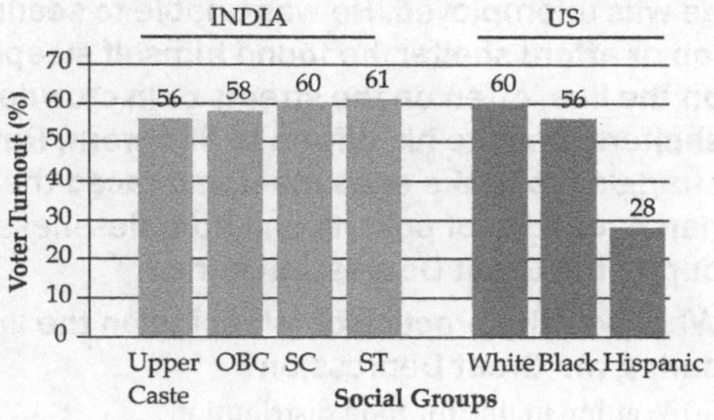

Why people from poor background vote in larger proportion in India?

(a) To demand better welfare policies.
(b) They have less access to educational resources.
(c) They are required by law to vote.
(d) They are more influenced by political advertisements.

11. Which of the following correctly defines deforestation? (1)

(a) The disappearance of forest
(b) Unplanned cutting of trees
(c) Cutting of trees for agriculture only
(d) None of the above

12. Arrange in sequence. (1)

I. Formation of Comintern
II. Formation of the Russian Social Democratic Workers Party
III. Beginning of Collectivisation

Codes

(a) II, I, III (b) III, II, I
(c) I, II, III (d) II, III, I

13. Consider the statements given below and choose the correct answer. (1)

Statement I The making of the Indian Constitution was a challenging process.

Statement II India emerged from colonial rule with a partition based on religious differences, leading to significant violence and uncertainty about the future.

Codes

(a) Statement I is correct and II is incorrect
(b) Statement I is incorrect and II is correct
(c) Both I and II are incorrect
(d) Both I and II are correct

14. Ravi, a labourer in the United States during the Great Depression, he faced some challenges as he was unemployed. He was unable to secure a job or afford shelter, he found himself sleeping on the line, often on the streets or in crowded shelters. Despite his efforts to find work, Ravi struggled to make ends meet and faced the harsh realities of poverty and homelessness during the Great Depression period. (1)

What was the practice of "sleeping on the line" during the Great Depression?

(a) Waiting in line for food distribution
(b) Sleeping in crowded shelters
(c) Paying for a place to sleep on the streets
(d) Standing in line for government assistance

15. This cartoon shows which of the following incident? (1)

(a) Jewish students are expelled from school.
(b) Jewish teacher and students are expelled from school.
(c) Racism is introduced in Nazi school.
(d) Jewish teacher and Jewish people are expelled from school under the jeers of German classmates.

16. Read the following data and select the appropriate option from the following. (1)

Trends in Literacy Rates in-Post Independent India

Year	Male	Female
Literacy Rate of 2018	73%	65%
Literacy Rate of 2017	78%	70%
Literacy Rate of 2011	72%	64%

Source : (Graph.2.1) Census of India, Office Register General, India 2021.

How much percentage of boys is not literate in 2018?

(a) 27% (b) 31%
(c) 17% (d) 37%

17. Find the incorrect option. (1)

(a) Poverty line is an imaginary line used by any country to determine its poverty.
(b) National Sample Survey Organisation was established in 1970.
(c) Poverty among social groups and economic categories varies widely in India.
(d) In 2011-12 estimates, all India HCR (Head Count Ratio) was 21.9%.

18. Sprinkling crops with insecticide is an activity of which sector? (1)

(a) Primary sector (b) Tertiary sector
(c) Secondary sector (d) Manufacturing sector

19. Read the given statements and select the correct option. (1)

I. Proportion of people below poverty line came down to about 22% in 2011-2012.
II. Proportion of people below poverty line is also same for all social groups and economic categories in India.
III. Scheduled caste or the scheduled tribe population highlights the seriousness of the problem.
IV. Karur city is famous for its handloom and powerloom fabrics.

Codes

(a) Only I (b) Both II and III
(c) I, III and IV (d) None of these

20. Foodgrains in buffer stock is procured by government through (1)

(a) Food Corporation of India
(b) State Government
(c) Ministry of Home Affairs
(d) None of the above

Section B (2 × 4 = 8)

21. How did the Jacobin club members distinguish themselves from the nobles in French society during the Revolution? **(2)**

Or What role did the Jacobins club play during the French Revolution, particularly in advocating for broader political rights?

22. Rahul, a resident of Varanasi, India, is deeply concerned about the pollution of the Ganges River, also known as the Ganga. Growing up, he witnessed the river's gradual degradation, affecting not only the environment but also the health and well-being of the communities relying on it for various purposes.

As Rahul, identify and analyse major sources of River Pollution? **(2)**

23. Elections are considered essential in a representative democracy. Justify the statement. **(2)**

24. Mr. Sharma notices irregularities in his local ration shop, including the sale of poor-quality grains and irregular opening hours. What problems arise from these malpractices in the Public Distribution System (PDS)? **(2)**

Section C **(3×5=15)**

25. Social exclusion contributes to the persistence of poverty. Justify the statement with valid points. **(3)**

Or What factors contribute to vulnerability to poverty?

26. Mention the constitutional provisions that make India a secular state. **(3)**

27. After reading a chapter about Nazism and Germany, Sumit wondered upon why the German Republic was not received well by its own people after the First World War. Identify the reasons for people's dissatisfaction with the new republic. **(3)**

28. Why is Indian Ocean named after our country? Give three reasons. **(3)**

29. What is a famine? How are people affected by a famine? **(3)**

Build your answer around these points
- Widespread deaths
- Shortage of food
- Increasing price of food

Section D **(5×4=20)**

30. In what ways, did the Nazi state seek to establish total control over its people? **(5)**

Or Describe the impact of Nazism on domestic and foreign policy of Germany.

31. Priya plans to visit Delhi in December. What seasonal weather will she experience during her trip? List the key characteristics of that season. **(5)**

Or

Priyansh plans to visit Delhi in June. What seasonal weather will he experience during his trip? List the key characteristics of that season.

32. Through the e-office implementation, FCI is making efforts towards a paperless office culture. These initiatives of integrated IT solutions serving as the core operational software for FCI, should provide a single source of information and streamline functions with a common digital backbone.

Source edited: The Hindu **(5)**

What are the major functions of the Food Corporation of India?

Or Explain the measures adopted by the Government of India to achieve self-sufficiency in foodgrains.

33. How has Indian Constitution embodied the basic values into its institutional arrangements? Discuss. **(5)**

Or "Indian Constitution is both rigid and flexible." Explain.

Section E **(4×3=12)**

34. Read the source given below and answer the questions that follow.

On 16th October, 1917, Lenin persuaded the Petrograd Soviet and the Bolshevik Party to agree to a socialist seizure of power. A Military Revolutionary Committee was appointed by the Soviet under Leon Trotsky to organise the seizure. The date of the event was kept a secret. The uprising began on 24th October. Sensing trouble, Prime Minister Kerenskii had left the city to summon troops.

At dawn, military men loyal to the government seized the buildings of two Bolshevik newspapers. Pro-government troops were sent to take over telephone and telegraph offices and protect the Winter Palace. In a swift response, the Military Revolutionary Committee ordered its supporters to seize government offices and arrest ministers. Late in the day, the ship *Aurora* shelled the Winter Palace. Other vessels sailed down the Neva and took over various military points. By nightfall, the city was under the committee's control and the ministers had surrendered.

At a meeting of the All Russian Congress of Soviets in Petrograd, the majority approved the Bolshevik action. Uprisings took place in other cities. There was heavy fighting especially in Moscow but by December, the Bolsheviks controlled the Moscow-Petrograd area.

(i) **The Military Revolutionary Committee was appointed by the Soviet. Suggest the reasons.** **(1)**

(ii) **Infer the importance of the control of the Military Revolutionary Committee over the Petrograd city.** **(2)**

(iii) **How did Lenin make the Petrograd Soviet and the Bolshevik Party to agree in October 1917?** **(1)**

35. Read the source given below and answer the questions that follow.

The Green Revolution in the late 1960s introduced the Indian farmer to cultivation of wheat and rice using High Yielding Varieties (HYVs) of seeds. Compared to the traditional seeds, the HYV seeds promised to produce much greater amounts of grain on a single plant. As a result, the same piece of land would now produce far larger quantities of foodgrains than was possible earlier. HYV seeds, however, needed plenty of water and also chemical fertilisers and pesticides to produce best results.

Higher yields were possible only from a combination of HYV seeds, irrigation, chemical fertilisers, pesticides, etc. Farmers of Punjab, Haryana and Western Uttar Pradesh were the first to try out the modern farming method in India. The farmers in these regions set up tubewells for irrigation and made use of HYV seeds, chemical fertilisers and pesticides in farming. Some of them bought farm machinery, like tractors and threshers, which made ploughing and harvesting faster. They were rewarded with high yields of wheat.

(i) **What method adopted by Indian farmers enabled them to grow more from same piece of land?** **(1)**

(ii) **Green Revolution is beneficial for the Indian farmers. Explain.** **(1)**

(iii) **Which modern implements and items were used by Indian farmers?** **(2)**

36. Read the source given below and answer the questions that follow.

A detailed account of the different physiographic units highlights the unique features of each region. It would, however, be clear that each region complements the other and makes the country richer in its natural resources. The mountains are the major sources of water and forest wealth. The Northern plains are the granaries of the country. They provide the base for early civilisations. The plateau is a storehouse of minerals, which has played a crucial role in the industrialisation of the country.

The coastal region and island groups provide sites for fishing and port activities. Thus, the diverse physical features of the land have immense future possibilities of development.

(i) **How are the coastal islands useful for India?** **(1)**

(ii) **In what way, the Himalayan mountains have become the major source of water?** **(1)**

(iii) **What role plains and plateau play in India's development?** **(2)**

Section F **(2 + 3 = 5)**

37. (a) **On the outline map of France, two features are marked. Identify them.** **(2)**

(i) A port city known for the slave trade.

(ii) The city which gave its name to the National Anthem of France.

(b) **On the outline map of India, locate and label any three of the following features.** **(3)**

(i) Standard Meridian of India

(ii) Capital of the state of Arunachal Pradesh

(iii) Mountain Peak-K2

(iv) The Satpura Range of mountains

Answers

1. (c) Representative democracy
2. (b)
3. (d) Boh Statement I and Statement II are correct
4. (c) The President of India
5. (c) Mahatma Gandhi was a member of Constituent Assembly.
6. (d) 15 to 59 years
7. (c)
8. (a) Agriculture only provides seasonal work
9. (d) 37°6′ N
10. (a) To demand better welfare policies.
11. (a) The disappearance of forest
12. (a) II, I, III
13. (d) Both I and II are correct
14. (c) Paying for a place to sleep on the streets
15. (d) Jewish teacher and Jewish people are expelled from school under the jeers of German classmates.
16. (a) 27%
17. (b) National Sample Survey Organisation was established in 1970.
18. (a) Primary sector
19. (c) I, III and IV
20. (a) Food Corporation of India
21. Jacobin club members distinguished themselves from the nobles by wearing long striped trousers. Nobles used to wear knee breeches. This was a way of demonstrating the end of the power held by the people who wore knee breeches. These Jacobins came to be known as the sans-culottes which means 'those without knee breeches'. Sansculottes men also wore the red cap that symbolised liberty.

Or The Jacobin club was a centre for discussing government policies and planning actions. They secured voting rights for all men over 21, regardless of their wealth. On 10th August, 1792, they attacked the Palace of Tuileries, held the king hostage, and later got the royal family imprisoned.

22. As Rahul, identified and analysed the major sources of pollution these are
    - A heavy load of untreated sewage and industrial effluents are emptied into the river.
    - The leakage of oil from ships.
    - Excessive use of pesticides and chemical fertilisers.
23. Elections are essential in a representative democracy because they allow people to choose their representatives, determine the government, and influence policy-making. They ensure accountability and the ability to change leaders based on public approval. Elections are crucial for upholding democratic principles.
24. These malpractices in the Public Distribution System cause unsold poor-quality grains to pile up with the FCI. These stocks often rot due to prolonged storage, further worsening food security issues.These actions undermine the effectiveness and reliability of the PDS.
25. Social exclusion intensifies poverty by systematically denying certain groups access to opportunities and resources available to more privileged segments of society. This exclusion prevents marginalised individuals from improving their economic and social status. Thus , the cycles of poverty and inequality continue to exist.

Or Vulnerability to poverty refers to the increased likelihood that certain communities or individuals will fall into or remain in poverty. These communities can be from marginalised groups or lacking adequate resources. This vulnerability arises from limited access to assets, education, healthcare and job opportunities. This makes them more prone to adverse events like natural disasters and economic downturns.

26. The constitutional provisions that make India secular are
    - The Constitution provides to all its citizens the freedom to profess, practice and propagate any religion of their choice.
    - There is no official religion for India.
    - There shall be no religious instruction in the government educational institutions. Every religious group or sect is free to manage its religious affairs.

27. The reasons for people's dissatisfaction with the new republic are as follows

- The peace treaty at Versailles with the Allies was a harsh and humiliating peace.
- Germany lost its overseas colonies, a tenth of its population, 13 per cent of its territories, 75 per cent of its iron and 26 per cent of its coal to France, Poland, Denmark and Lithuania.
- The War Guilt Clause held Germany responsible for the war and damages the Allied countries suffered. Germany was forced to pay compensation amounting to £6 billion.

28. Indian Ocean is named after India due to its important features which are –

- India has the longest coastline on the Indian Ocean.
- India has a central location between East and West Asia.
- India's Southernmost extension, the Deccan Peninsula, extends towards the Indian Ocean, which makes it significant to international trade done through the Indian Ocean.

29. A famine is characterised by widespread deaths due to starvation and epidemics caused by forced use of contaminated water or decaying food and loss of body resistance due to weakening from starvation.

This occurs due to a severe shortage of food resulting from crop failure or other calamity. This increases the price of food drastically, making it unaffordable for the weaker sections of the population.

30. The Nazi state sought to establish total control over its people in the following ways

- All political parties and trade unions were banned except the Nazi Party and its affiliates.
- The state established total control over the economy, media, army and Judiciary.
- Germany became almost a police state. Special surveillance, security forces, secret state police (Gestapo) were created to control the society.
- The Nazi rule glorified war and chose the path of war as a way out of the economic crisis. The Nazi rule targeted the Jews as the cause of all miseries and undertook Genocidal War against the Jews.
- Hitler introduced a massive programme of militarisation to enhance the military power of Germany and to restore its international honour and glory.

Or Nazism impacted domestic policies of Germany as follows

- Hitler indefinitely suspended civic rights like freedom of speech, press and assembly.
- He sidelined Parliament and ruled by decree.
- All political parties and trade unions were banned except for the Nazi Party and its affiliates.
- The state established complete control over the economy, media, army and judiciary.
- Special security forces like Gestapo were created to control the citizens.

Nazism had great impact on Germany's foreign policy. The changes due to this were

- Germany pulled out of the League of Nations in 1933.
- Germany reoccupied the Rhineland (1936) and integrated Austria and Germany (1938) under the slogan, One people, One empire and One leader.
- Hitler occupied the Sudetenland province of Czechoslovakia and later took over the entire country.

31. Priya will experience cold weather season during her trip to Delhi. The key characteristics of the cold weather season in Northern India are as follows

- **Temperature Range and Season Duration** Temperatures range lies between 10°C to 15°C in the Northern plains, with December and January being the coldest months. It lasts from mid-November to February.
- **Diurnal Temperature Variation** Days are moderately warm, but nights are cold.This often leads to frost formation in the early morning hours.
- **Weather Patterns and Winds** North-East trade winds dominate, resulting in dry weather over most of northern India. Tamil Nadu's coast may experience some rainfall during this period.
- **Impact of Cyclonic Disturbances** Cyclonic disturbances originating from the West and North-West bring winter rains to the plains and snowfall to the Himalayan slopes. These winter rains, locally known as 'mahawat', are crucial for the cultivation of 'rabi' crops.
- **Atmospheric Conditions** The Atmosphere is characterised by clear skies, low humidity levels, and variable winds, contributing to the distinct winter climate experienced in Northern India.

Or Priyansh will experience hot weather season during his trip. The key characteristics of the hot weather season (summer) in India are as follows

- **Gradual Temperature Increase** This season covers months from March to May and temperatures rise significantly across India. Temperature ranges from 38 degrees to 47 degrees in North India.
- **Formation of Low-Pressure Area** Rising temperatures in northern regions lead to falling air pressure. This creates a low-pressure area that extends from the Thar Desert to Eastern India.
- **Hot and Dry Winds ('Loo')** Strong, hot and dry winds known as 'loo' blow across North and North-Western India. It poses health risks due to their intensity and dryness.
- **Weather Phenomena** Dust storms and local thunderstorms with hail storms occur frequently during this season, offering temporary relief from the heat.
- **Pre-Monsoon Showers** They are referred to as 'mango showers' in Southern states, and occur occasionally. These showers help in the early ripening of mangoes and provide some relief from the heat.

32. The major functions of the Food Corporation of India are as follows

- Supporting and encouraging crop production by declaring MSP so that farmers can sell their crops to FCI.
- Distribution of foodgrains throughout the country through the Public Distribution System.
- Maintaining a satisfactory level of buffer stocks of foodgrains to ensure National Food Security.
- Intervention in the foodgrains market whenever required for regularising the prices.

FCI has played a significant role in India's success in providing food security by maintaining buffer stocks.

Or After independence, Indian policy makers adopted all measures to achieve self-sufficiency in foodgrains.

Following measures were adopted by Government of India to achieve self-sufficiency in foodgrains

- India adopted a new strategy in agriculture, which resulted in 'Green Revolution' especially in the production of wheat and rice.
- The government has made the provision of buffer stock meant to distribute foodgrains in the deficit areas and among the poorer strata of society at a price lower than the market price.
  This also helps to resolve the problem of shortage of food during adverse weather conditions or during the periods of calamity.
- The government has made provision of Public Distribution System (PDS). This is meant for distribution of foodgrains through government regulated shops among the poorer sections of the society.
- The government has also initiated several programmes like Poverty Alleviation Programmes (PAPs) and Food for Work Programme to ensure affordability of food by providing employment.

33. The Indian Constitution embodied the basic values into its institutional arrangements as

- Values that inspired and guided Indian freedom struggle and later developed by it formed the foundation of Indian democracy. These values were included in the Preamble to the Indian Constitution.
- The Indian Constitution begins with a short statement of its basic values. This is called the Preamble to the Constitution. Inspired by the American Constitution, Indian Constitution also begins with the Preamble.
- The Preamble guide all the articles of the Indian Constitution. It contains the philosophy on which the entire Constitution is dependent. The Preamble provides a standard to examine and evaluate any law and action of the government. It also determines whether it is good or bad.
- Indian Constitution embodies these values into institutional arrangement. But the laws of the Constitution are not static and unalterable. These can be changed with people's aspirations and changes in society.

Or Indian Constitution is both rigid and flexible, because the procedure of amendment is neither easy nor difficult. The Constitution has provided a federal structure for India. The jurisdictions of the centre and states have been defined and demarcated. Both the centre and the states have been authorised to exercise powers independently.

There are provisions which can change the federal structure into a unitary one. Amendments can be made only with the consent of both the centre and the states. A special majoriry of the Union Parliament, i.e. a majority of not less than two-third votes is required to amend the Constitution. Thus, Indian Constitution enjoys the advantages of a combination of flexibility and rigidity.

34. (i) The Military Revolutionary Committee was appointed by the Soviet under Leon Tratsky to organise the socialist seizure of power in Russia.

(ii) The importance of the control of the Military Revolution or Committee over the Petrograd city is explained in the following ways

- As the pro-government troops of Russia seized the building of two Bolshevik newspapers, the Military Revolutionary Committee ordered its supporters to seize government offices and arrest ministers.
- The Winter Palace was fired and various military points were took over. Ministers were surrendered. By night, the Petrograd city was under the committee's control.

(iii) Lenin feared that the provisional government would set-up a dictatorship in Russia. He wanted to arrange an uprising against the government. Thus he persuaded the Petrograd Soviet and the Bolshevik Party unitedly agree to a socialist seizure of power in Russia and both of them agreed to do that.

35. (i) The method of Green Revolution enabled the farmers to grow more from same piece of land.

(ii) The Green Revolution enabled the Indian farmers to cultivate wheat and rice using high yielding varieties of seeds, irrigation chemical fertilisers, insecticides and pesticides, etc. This increased their income from agriculture.

(iii) The modern implements used by the Indian farmers were tubewells, tractors, threshers and harvesters, which made ploughing and harvesting faster. The farmers also used fertilisers and pesticides to increase their farm yield.

36. (i) The coastal islands are useful for India as they provide sites for fishing and port activities.

(ii) In the following ways, the Himalayan mountains have become major source of water

- The mountains block the way of monsoon winds causing rains in the Northern part of India.
- Melting of snow in the mountains give rise to rivers which are sources of water.

(iii) Plains and plateaus play an important role in India's development in the following ways

- The Northern plains provide fertile land that is most suitable for agriculture.
- The Peninsular plateau provides minerals that are needed by the industries.

37. (a)

(b)

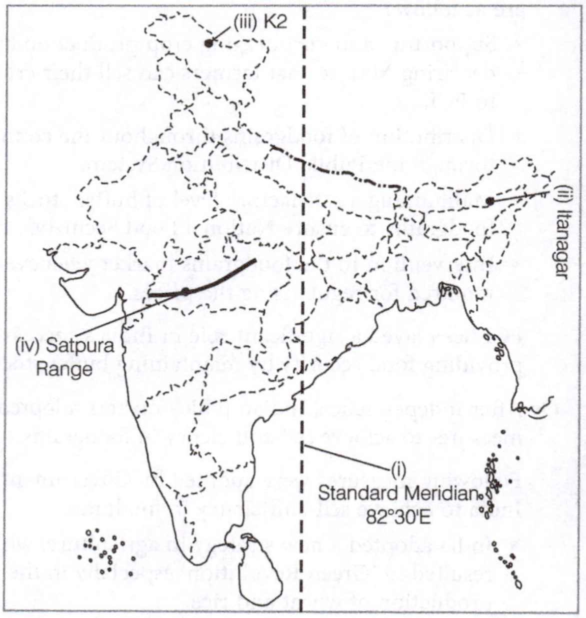

Sample Question Paper 3 (Unsolved)

Social Science

Time : 3 hrs M.M. : 80

General Instructions

1 Question paper comprises Six Sections – A, B, C, D, E and F. There are 37 questions in the question paper. All questions are compulsory.
2 Section A – From Question 1 to 20 are MCQs of 1 mark each.
3 Section B – Question no. 21 to 24 are Very Short Answer Type Questions, carrying 2 marks each. Answer to each question should not exceed 40 words.
4 Section C – Contains Questions 25 to 29 are Short Answer Type Questions, carrying 3 marks each. Answer to each question should not exceed 60 words
5 Section D – Question no. 30 to 33 are long answer type questions, carrying 5 marks each. Answer to each question should not exceed 120 words.
6 Section E – Questions no from 34 to 36 are case based questions with three sub questions and are of 4 marks each.
7 Section F – Question no. 37 is map based, carrying 5 marks with two parts, 37a from History (2 marks) and 37b from Geography (3 marks).

Section A (1 × 20 = 20)

1. Robert Mugabe was the President of (1)

(a) Ethiopia (b) Zimbabwe
(c) Algeria (d) Mozambique

2. When did French women march to Versailles and brought the king Louis XVI back with them to Paris? (1)

(a) 5th October, 1789 (b) 10th October, 1789
(c) 10th November, 1791 (d) 10th June, 1790

3. Find the incorrect option. (1)

(a) 'India Shining' by the Congress Party in the 1971 Lok Sabha elections.
(b) 'Land to the Tiller' by the Left Front in the 1977 West Bengal Assembly elections.
(c) 'Save Democracy' by the Janata Party in the 1977 Lok Sabha elections.
(d) 'Protect the Self-Respect of the Telugus' by the Telugu Desam Party in the 1983, Andhra Pradesh Assembly elections.

4. During the Industrial Revolution, various social and economic changes occurred. Which of the following accurately describes these changes? (1)

I. Factory owners were required to provide extensive social benefits to workers.

II. The rise of factories led to significant urbanisation and the growth of new cities.

III. Technological innovations led to improvements in agriculatural productivity.

IV. Working conditions in many factories were harsh, with long hours and low wages.

Codes

(a) Only I (b) Both II and III
(c) Both III and IV (d) Only IV

5. Consider the statements given below and choose the correct answer. (1)

Statement I Due to the apparent Southward movement of the Sun, the global heat belt shifts Northwards.

Statement II In March, the highest temperature is about 38° Celsius, recorded on the Deccan plateau.

Codes

(a) Statement I is correct and II is incorrect
(b) Statement I is incorrect and II is correct
(c) Both I and II are incorrect
(d) Both I and II are correct

6. Match the following. (1)

List I (Rivers)	List II (Originate From)
A. Narmada	1. Western Ghats
B. Tapi	2. Satpura range
C. Godavari	3. Amarkantak hills
D. Mahanadi	4. Highlands of Chhattisgarh

Codes

	A	B	C	D		A	B	C	D
(a)	1	2	3	4	(b)	4	3	2	1
(c)	2	1	3	4	(d)	3	2	1	4

7. What is the minimum buffer stock norm for the Food Corporation of India? (1)

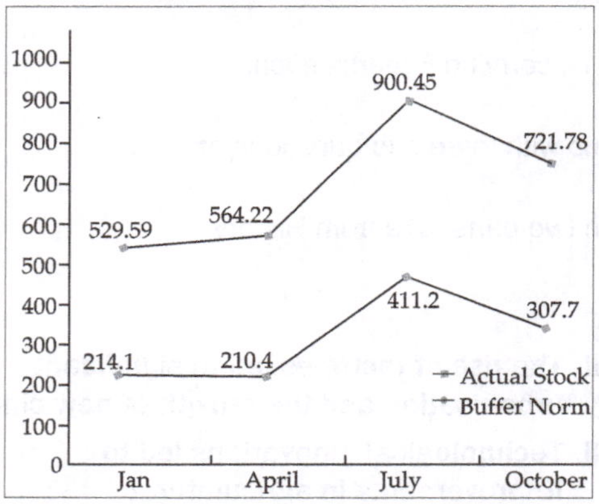

(a) 210.4 million (b) 214.1 million
(c) 307.7 million (d) 529.59 million

8. Arrange the following anti-poverty programmes in chronological order based on the year of their launch. (1)

I. Mahatma Gandhi National Rural Employment Guarantee Act (MGNREGA)
II. National Food for Work Programme (NFWP)
III. Prime Minister Rozgar Yozana (PMRY)
IV. Swarnajayanti Gram Swarozgar Yojana (SGSY)

Codes

(a) IV, III, I, II (b) II, IV, I, III
(c) II, I, III, IV (d) II, I, IV, III

9. Consider the statements given below and choose the correct option. (1)

Statement I 6000 Kalanga families were equally divided between the two kingdoms.

Statement II (R) The kalangas of Java were a community of skilled forest cutters and shifting cultivations.

Codes

(a) Statement I is correct and Statement II is incorrect
(b) Statement I is incorrect and Statement II is correct
(c) Both Statement I and Statement II are incorrect
(d) Both Statement I and Statement II are correct

10. Read the data and find out the increase noticed among the teacher in the year 2016-17. (1)

Year	No of Colleges	No of Universities	Students	Teacher
2015-16	41,435	753	284,84,741	14,38,000
2016-17	42,338	795	294,27,158	14,70,190
2017-18	41,012	851	366,42,378	12,84,957

***Source :** UGC Annual Report 2019-20 and selected Education Statistics, Ministry of HRD.*

(a) 5.7% (b) 12.28%
(c) 2.18% (d) 9.12%

11. What is the message given by the people in this image? (1)

(a) Equality of right to vote and equal value of each man's vote.
(b) Elections must offer a real choice between political parties.
(c) Political equality is a right of each individual.
(d) None of the above

12. Find the incorrect option regarding citizen's rights in Saudi Arabia. (1)

I. Citizens can form political parties or any political organisations.
II. There is no freedom of religion.
III. Women are subjected to many public restrictions.
IV. Every citizen is required to be a Muslim.

Codes

(a) Only I (b) Both I and III
(c) Both I and IV (d) II, III and IV

13. At the beginning of the twentieth century, the vast majority of Russia's people was (1)

(a) lawyers (b) agriculturists
(c) teachers (d) industrialists

14. Match the following. (1)

	List I (Seasons)		List II (Duration)
A.	Cold Weather Season	1.	Mid-November- February
B.	Hot Weather Season	2.	March-May
C.	Advancing Monsoon Season	3.	June-September
D.	Retreating/Post Monsoon Season	4.	October-November

Codes

	A	B	C	D		A	B	C	D
(a)	1	2	3	4	(b)	1	3	2	4
(c)	4	3	1	2	(d)	4	3	2	1

15. Consider the following statements about exhaustion of natural resources. (1)

I. Crude oil resources would last only 50 years more.

II. Oil extraction is undertaken by Middle East region at a very fast pace.

III. Non-conventional fuel sources should be encouraged that reduces use of crude oil.

Which of the above statements gives an idea of sustainable development?

(a) Only II (b) Only I
(c) Only I and II (d) Only III

16. What cause social exclusion in society? (1)

(a) Income (b) Education
(c) Family (d) Caste system

17. What does EVM stand for? (1)

(a) Electronic Vending Machine
(b) Electronic Voting Machine
(c) Electoral Voting Machine
(d) Electoral Volunteer Mechanism

18. Fixed capital of a dairy farmer is (1)

(a) buffaloes and cows (b) milk chilling machine
(c) tempo to transport milk (d) All of these

19. Dr. Priya Sharma, a wildlife biologist, is conducting research on the conservation of the one-horned rhinoceros found in .... and .... Her work aims to understand the challenges facing these majestic creatures and develop strategies for their protection. (1)

(a) Jharkhand and Odisha
(b) Chhattisgarh and Madhya Pradesh
(c) Assam and West Bengal
(d) Uttar Pradesh and Haryana

20. The Wular lake in Jammu and Kashmir is the result of which of the following activities? (1)

(a) Tectonic activity (b) Rainfall
(c) Human activity (d) None of these

Section B (2×4=8)

21. Nazis wanted only a society of pure and healthy Nordic German Aryans. They alone were considered as 'desirable', while other communities were classified as 'undesirable'.

(i) What was the Nazis' justification for persecuting these 'undesirable' communities?

(ii) How did the Nazis' racial policies impact the lives of those deemed 'inferior'? (2)

22. When was the Ganga Action Plan (GAP) launched? Why was the scope of the Ganga Action Plan expanded? (2)

23. The Pradhan Mantri Gramodaya Yojana (PMGY) aims to improve basic services in the villages. Justify the statement. (2)

Or When was the Swarnajayanti Gram Swarozgar Yojana (SGSY) launched? What was the aim of the scheme?

24. "Indian judiciary is considered one of the most powerful institutions in Indian democracy." Justify the statement. (2)

Section C (3×5=15)

25. How would you describe the topography of the Indian desert?

Build answer around these points

- Landscape
- Nature
- Streams (3)

26. What do you mean by direct democracy? Why it is not practiced in the present day world? (3)

or What is representative democracy? How is it significant in the contemporary world?

27. "Colonial rule and income inequalities are the causes of poverty." Comment. (3)

28. What is the Antyodaya Anna Yojana (AAY)? How did the scheme evolve over time to benefit eligible families?" **(3)**

29. Jews died many deaths even before they reached the gas chamber. Justify the statement with suitable reasons. **(3)**

Section D **(5×4=20)**

30. "Formation of Indian Constitution was no less struggle than that of Africa." Do you agree? Explain with five arguments. **(5)**

Or Why is the Preamble to the Constitution important?

31. What is the aim of production? Explain the four factors of production of goods and services. **(5)**

Or Sarah, a development consultant specialising in rural areas, has been tasked with analysing the critical role of transportation infrastructure in fostering rural development. With a passion for improving livelihoods in remote regions, Sarah studied intricate relationship between transport accessibility and rural prosperity.

How does improved transport connectivity contribute to economic growth in rural areas?

32. Analyse the key factors and events that led to the transformation of feudal France into a republic. **(5)**

Or Analyse the key factors and events that led to the transformation of the Republic of France into an empire under Napoleon.

33. Risha is planning to visit India in July . What type of weather can Risha expect to experience in India during July, and what are the characteristics of this season? **(5)**

Or Risha is planning to visit India in October. What type of weather can Risha expect to experience in India during October. What are the characteristics of this season?

Section E **(4×3=12)**

34. Read the source given below and answer the questions that follow.

The year 1904 was a particularly bad one for Russian workers. Prices of essential goods rose so quickly that real wages declined by 20 per cent. The membership of workers' associations rose dramatically. When four members of the Assembly of Russian Workers, which had been formed in 1904, were dismissed at the Putilov Iron Works, there was a call for industrial action. Over the next few days over 11,000 workers in St Petersburg went on strike demanding a reduction in the working day to eight hours, an increase in wages and improvement in working conditions.

When the procession of workers led by father Gapon reached the Winter Palace it was attacked by the police and the Cossacks. Over 100 workers were killed and about 300 wounded. The incident known as Bloody Sunday, started a series of events that became known as the 1905 Revolution. Strikes took place all over the country and universities closed down when student bodies staged walkouts, complaining about the lack of civil liberties. Lawyers, doctors, engineers and other middle-class workers established the Union of Unions and demanded a Constituent Assembly.

During the 1905 Revolution, the Tsar allowed the creation of an elected consultative Parliament or Duma. For a brief while during the revolution, there existed a large number of trade unions and factory committees made up of factory workers. After 1905, most committees and unions worked unofficially, since they were declared illegal. Severe restrictions were placed on political activity.

(i) Why the year 1904 was considered as particularly bad one for Russian workers? (1)

(ii) The procession of workers led by father Gapon attacked by the police and the Cossacks. Why? (1)

(iii) Why the Tsar allowed the creation of an elected consultative Parliament? (2)

35. Read the source given and answer the questions that follow.

A Constitution is not merely a statement of values and philosophy. As we noted above, a Constitution is mainly about embodying these values into institutional arrangements. Much of the document called Constitution of India is about these arrangements. It is a very long and detailed document. Therefore it needs to be amended quite regularly to keep it updated. Those who crafted the Indian Constitution felt that it has to be in accordance with people's aspirations and changes in society. They did not see it as a sacred, static and unalterable law. So, they made provisions to incorporate changes from time to time. These changes are called Constitutional Amendments.

The Constitution describes the institutional arrangements in a very legal language. If you read the Constitution for the first time, it can be quite difficult to understand. Yet the basic institutional design is not very difficult to understand. Like any Constitution, the Indian Constitution lays down a procedure for choosing persons to govern the country. It defines who will have how much power to take which decisions. And it puts limits to what the government can do by providing some rights to the citizen that cannot be violated.

(i) Why the Constitution is essential for a democratic country? (1)

(ii) Define constitutional amendments. (1)

(iii) Highlight the salient features of the Constitution of India. (2)

36. Read the source given below and answer the questions that follow.

The Northern plain is broadly divided into three sections. The Western part of the Northern plain is referred to as the Punjab plains. Formed by the Indus and its tributaries, the larger part of this plain lies in Pakistan. The Indus and its tributaries – the Jhelum, the Chenab, the Ravi, the Beas and the Satluj originate in the Himalaya. This section of the plain is dominated by the doabs.

The Ganga plain extends between Ghaggar and Teesta rivers. It is spread over the states of North India, Haryana, Delhi, Uttar Pradesh, Bihar, partly Jharkhand and West Bengal to its East, particularly in Assam lies the Brahmaputra plain. The Northern plains are generally described as flat land with no variations in its relief. It is not true. These vast plains also have diverse relief features. According to the variations in relief features, the Northern plains can be divided into four regions. The rivers, after descending from the mountains deposit pebbles in a narrow belt of about 8 to 16 km in width lying parallel to the slopes of the Shiwaliks. It is known as bhabar. All the streams disappear in this bhabar belt. South of this belt, the streams and rivers re-emerge and create a wet, swampy and marshy region known as Terai. This was a thickly forested region full of wildlife. The forests have been cleared to create agricultural land and to settle migrants from Pakistan after partition.

(i) Where does the Indus river originate? (1)

(ii) What do you mean by doab? (1)

(iii) Define 'Bhabhar'. (2)

Section F (2 + 3 = 5)

37. (a) Identify and label the markings on the map of france given below. (2)

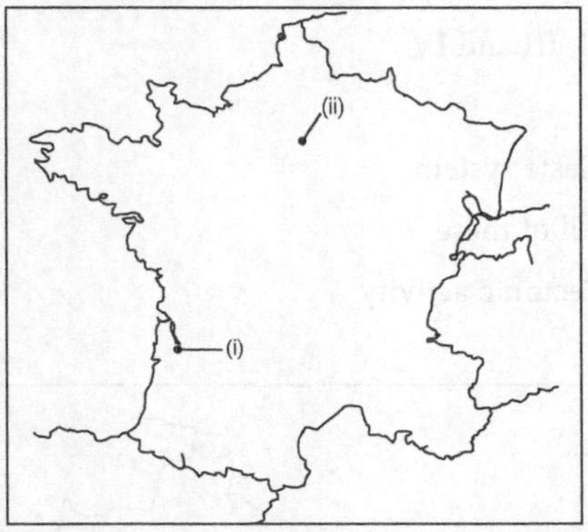

(b) On the given political outline map of India, locate and label any three of the following features marked and write their correct names. (3)

(i) A mountain range (ii) Plateau region

(iii) Coastal plain (iv) A mountain peak

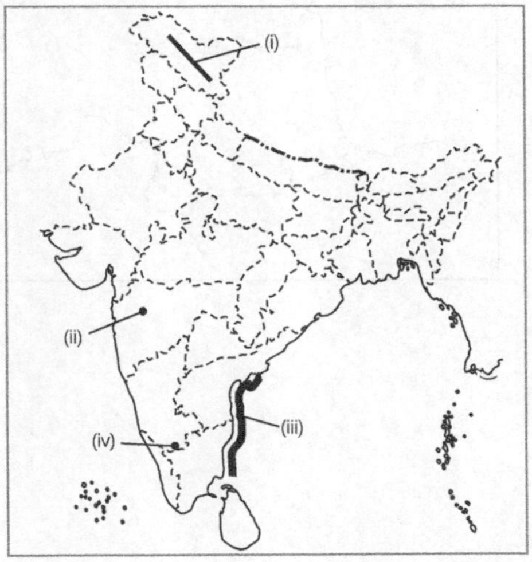

Answers

1. (b) Zimbabwe
2. (a) 5th October, 1789
3. (a) 'India Shining' by the Congress Party in the 1971 Lok Sabha elections.
4. (b) Both II and III
5. (b) Statement I is incorrect and II is correct
6. (d)
7. (a) 210.4 million
8. (a) IV, III, I, II
9. (b) Both A and R are true, but R is not the correct explanation of A
10. (c) 2.18%
11. (a) Equality of right to vote and equal value of each man's vote.
12. (d) II, III and IV
13. (b) agriculturists
14. (a)
15. (d) Only III
16. (d) Caste system
17. (b) Electronic Voting Machine
18. (d) All of these
19. (c) Assam and West Bengal
20. (a) Tectonic activity
37. (a)

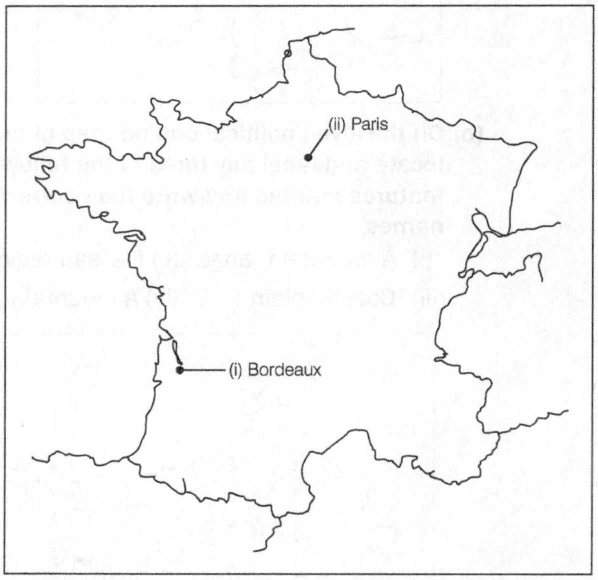

(b)

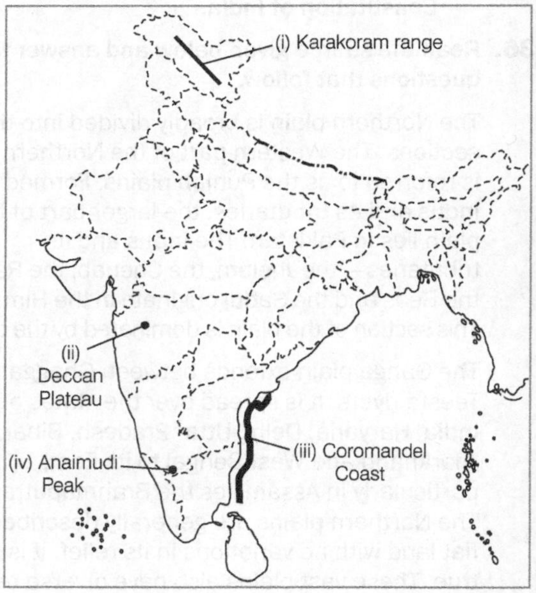

Sample Question Paper 4 (Unsolved)
Social Science

Time : 3 hrs	M.M. : 80

General Instructions

1 Question paper comprises Six Sections – A, B, C, D, E and F. There are 37 questions in the question paper. All questions are compulsory.
2 Section A – From Question 1 to 20 are MCQs of 1 mark each.
3 Section B – Question no. 21 to 24 are Very Short Answer Type Questions, carrying 2 marks each. Answer to each question should not exceed 40 words.
4 Section C – Contains Questions 25 to 29 are Short Answer Type Questions, carrying 3 marks each. Answer to each question should not exceed 60 words
5 Section D – Question no. 30 to 33 are long answer type questions, carrying 5 marks each. Answer to each question should not exceed 120 words.
6 Section E – Questions no from 34 to 36 are case based questions with three sub questions and are of 4 marks each.
7 Section F – Question no. 37 is map based, carrying 5 marks with two parts, 37a from History (2 marks) and 37b from Geography (3 marks).

Section A (1 × 20 = 20)

1. Rina Bhatt, the HR manager at a XYZ company, is facing staffing challenges due to a increase in demand for the company's products. The case revolves around Sarah's efforts to ensure compliance with staffing requirements while meeting the company's operational needs.

What legal considerations should Sarah Johnson keep in mind when hiring new employees to meet the increased demand? (1)

(a) Compliance with labour laws (b) Workplace diversity
(c) Employee satisfaction (d) Marketing strategies

2. Synagogue is the place of worship of (1)

(a) Christians (b) Buddhists (c) Jews (d) Parsis

3. Population as an asset for the economy rather than a liability. Population can be turned into a productive asset by (1)

I. Investment in healthcare and well-being
II. Education and skill development
III. Economic opportunities and entrepreneurship
IV. Social and political participation

Codes

(a) Only I (b) III and IV (c) I and II (d) All of these

4. Consider the following statements and choose the correct option. (1)

I. Hitler became Chancellor in 1930.
II. Hitler pulled out of the League of Nations in 1931.
III. Hitler was against the Versailles Treaty.

Codes

(a) Only I (b) Only II
(c) Both I and II (d) Only III

5. Based on the graph given below, which of the following statements best represents an observation about democratic participation in India? (1)

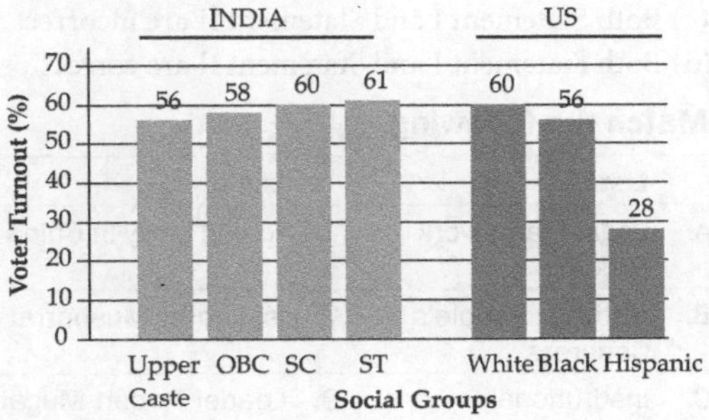

(a) The poor and underprivileged in India are less politically engaged than their counterparts in Western democracies.

(b) India's democracy shows signs of stronger grassroots participation compared to the United States, particularly among disadvantaged groups.
(c) Voter turnout in India is consistently lower across all social groups compared to the United States.
(d) The increase in election-related activities suggests a decline in the importance of voting among Indian citizens.

6. Which of the following is/are true meaning of the rule of law? (1)

(a) The government shall not deny to any person in India equality before the law.
(b) The laws apply in the same manner to all, regardless of a person's status.
(c) No person is above the law.
(d) All of the above

7. Arrange the following mountain ranges in the order of their location from West to East. (1)

I. Aravalli mountain range
II. Gir mountain range
III. Khasi Hills
IV. Patkai Bum mountain range

Codes

(a) IV, II, I, III (b) I, III, IV, II
(c) I, II, III, IV (d) II, I, III, IV

8. Consider the statements given below and choose the correct answer. (1)

Statement I The Election Commission (EC) has now begun to exercise all its powers and also expand them.

Statement II When on election duty, government officers work under the control of the EC and not the government.

Codes

(a) Statement I is correct and Statement II is incorrect
(b) Statement I is incorrect and Statement II is correct
(c) Both Statement I and Statement II are incorrect
(d) Both Statement I and Statement II are correct

9. Match the following. (1)

	List I		List II
A.	Legal Framework Order	1.	Ruling party in China
B.	National People's Congress	2.	Issued by Musharraf
C.	Institutional Revolutionary Party	3.	Leader Robert Mugabe
D.	ZANU-PF	4.	Formed in 1930 in Mexico

Codes

	A	B	C	D		A	B	C	D
(a)	2	1	4	3	(b)	1	2	3	4
(c)	4	1	2	3	(d)	3	4	1	2

10. Which one of the following is not a factor that makes an election democratic? (1)

(a) There should be something to choose from.
(b) Parties and candidates should be free to contest elections.
(c) The choice should not be offered at regular intervals.
(d) The candidate preferred by the people should get elected.

11. Identify the personality and name the famous programme introduced by him. (1)

(a) Joseph Stalin, Collectivisation Programme
(b) Vladimir Lenin, Commune (mir) Programme
(c) Karl Marx, Dictatorship of Proletariat
(d) Friedrich Engels, Communism

12. Many Gypsies and blacks living in Nazi Germany were considered as racial 'inferiors' who threatened the biological purity of the 'Superior Aryan' race. They were widely persecuted. What were the long-term effects of the persecution of 'undesirable' communities in Nazi Germany? (1)

(a) It led to the establishment of a homogeneous society
(b) It led to widespread global condemnation and the eventual downfall of Nazi Germany
(c) It led to an increase in the popularity of Nazi ideology
(d) It had no long-term effects

13. The book 'The Spirit of the Laws' was written by (1)

(a) John Locke (b) Rousseau
(c) Montesquieu (d) None of these

14. When did French woman march to Versailles and brought the King Louis XVI back with them to Paris? (1)

(a) 5th October, 1789 (b) 10th October, 1789
(c) 10th November, 1994 (d) 10th June, 1790

15. What is the effect of Green Revolution on soil? (1)

(a) It enhances soil fertility (b) It decreases soil fertility
(c) It decreases production (d) None of these

16. **Consider the statements given below and choose the correct answer.** **(1)**

Statement I Democracy improves the quality of decision-making by involving consultation and discussion.

Statement II Democratic governments are less accountable to the people. **(1)**

Codes

(a) Statement I is correct and II is incorrect
(b) Statement I is incorrect and II is correct
(c) Both I and II are incorrect
(d) Both I and II are correct

17. **'Tamil Nadu usually does not receive enough rain during monsoon, but this year, due to the formation of a weather system over South-West Bay of Bengal, Tamil Nadu has recorded a few good spells of rain.'** **(1)**

When does the Tamil Nadu coast receive a significant portion of its rainfall?

(a) June and July (b) August and September
(c) October and November (d) December and January

18. **Which Southernmost point of the Indian Union was sub-merged under the sea water in 2004 during the Tsunami?** **(1)**

(a) Kavaratti (b) Indira Point
(c) Port Blair (d) Kanyakumari

19. **Consider the following statements associated with poverty line and select the correct option.** **(1)**

(a) A common method used to measure poverty is based on the income or consumption levels
(b) Poverty line may not vary with time and place
(c) A person not having a car in India may be considered poor
(d) In 2011-12 the poverty line for a person was fixed at 916 per month for rural areas

20. **Read the data and select the appropriate option from the following some important features of PDS.** **(1)**

Name of Scheme	Year of Introduction	Coverage Target Group
Public Distribution System (PDS) was introduced	Upto 1992	Universal
Revamped Public Distribution System (RPDS) was introduced	1992	Backward Blocks
Targeted Public Distribution System was introduced	1997/2000	Poor and BPL APL

RPDS was introduced in how many blocks in India?

(a) 1,200 (b) 1,500 (c) 1,700 (d) 5,000

Section B **(2×4=8)**

21. Since poverty has many facts, social scientists look at it through a variety of indicators. Justify the statement. **(2)**

22. How does democracy offer a peaceful resolution to conflicts arising from social diversity? **(2)**

Or How does democracy improve the quality of decision-making?

23. The population, which accounts for world's 17.5 per cent population, comprises 623.7 million males and 586.5 million females, said a provisional 2011 Census report. China is the most populous nation accounting for .... **(2)**

Source (edited) : Economics Times

What significant demographic change is predicted for India in relation to China by 2045?

24. Ancient trade routes have influenced cultural exchange. Justify the statement. **(2)**

Section C **(3×5=15)**

25. How were the great plains of Northern India formed? **(3)**

Or Dr. Rajesh Gupta, a prominent environmental scientist, has initiated legal action against a commercial expedition company planning to conduct tourist activities in a fragile ecosystem within the Himalayan mountains.

What are the potential environmental impacts of tourists activities in fragile ecosystems of Himalayas?

26. The government under General Pervez Musharraf in Pakistan cannot be called a democracy. Why? **(3)**

27. Why do all the countries in the world not have the same poverty lines? State some suitable reasons. **(3)**

28. How did the representatives of the third estate respond when Louis XVI rejected their proposal for a new voting system in the Estates General in 1789? **(3)**

29. Why did the National Assembly in France declare war against Prussia and Austria in 1792, and what significance did the Marseillaise have during this period? **(3)**

Section D (5×4=20)

30. The 'Mid-Day Meal' scheme is one of the most successful schemes of the Indian Government. Explain by giving its purpose. **(5)**

Or What do you mean by NFWP? Explain its main features.

31. What landmark decisions were taken by the National Assembly led by the third estate on 4th August, 1789? **(5)**

Or Explain the causes for the empty treasury of France under Louis XVI.

32. India has a long coastline that is advantageous for the country. Explain. **(5)**

Or India has had strong geographical and historical links with its neighbours. Comment.

33. Rebecca Thompson, a small business owner, has filed a lawsuit against a multinational corporation for alleged patent infringement. The case has sparked debates regarding the extent of the Supreme Court's powers and its role in safeguarding intellectual property rights.

How does the Supreme Court's power of judicial review come into play in Rebecca Thompson's lawsuit against the multinational corporation? **(5)**

Or Why is there a need for political institutions? Explain.

Section E (4×3=12)

34. Read the source given below and answer the questions that follow.

The period from 1793 to 1794 is referred to as the Reign of Terror. Robespierre followed a policy of severe control and punishment. All those whom he saw as being 'enemies' of the republic-ex-nobles and clergy, members of other political parties, even members of his own party who did not agree with his methods-were arrested, imprisoned and then tried by a revolutionary tribunal. If the court found them 'guilty' they were guillioned. The guillotine is a device consisting of two poles and a blade with which a person is beheaded. It was named after Dr Guillotin who invented it.

Robespierre's government issued laws placing a maximum ceiling on wages and prices. Meat and bread were rationed. Peasants were forced to transport their grain to the cities and sell it at prices fixed by the government.

The use of more expensive white flour was forbidden; all citizens were required to eat the pain degalite (equality bread), a loaf made of whole wheat. Equality was also sought to be practiced through forms of speech and address. Instead of the traditional Monsieur (Sir) and Madame (Madam) all French men and women were hence forth Citoyen and Citoyenne (Citizen). Churches were shut down and their buildings converted into barracks or offices.

Robespierre pursued his policies so relentlessly that even his supporters began to demand moderation. Finally, he was convicted by a court in July 1794, arrested and on the next day sent to the guillotine.

(i) Enemies of the French Republic was tried by a revolutionary tribunal. Justify. (1)

(ii) Laws of Robespierre's government were very repressive. Explain it by giving an example. (1)

(iii) The ideas of equality was applied in French society. Justify the claim by giving an example. (2)

35. Read the source given below and answer the questions that follow.

While determining the poverty line in India, a minimum level of food requirement, clothing, footwear, fuel and light, educational and medical requirement, etc are determined for subsistence. These physical quantities are multiplied by their prices in rupees. The present formula for food requirement while estimating the poverty line is based on the desired calorie requirement.

Food items, such as cereals, pulses, vegetable, milk, oil, sugar, etc together provide these needed calories. The calorie needs vary depending on age, sex and the type of work that a person does. The accepted average calorie requirement in India is 2400 calories per person per day in rural areas and 2100 calories per person per day in urban areas.

Since people living in rural areas engage themselves in more physical work, calorie requirements in rural areas are considered to be higher than in urban areas. The poverty line is estimated periodically (normally every five years) by conducting sample surveys. These surveys are carried out by the National Sample Survey Organisation (NSSO).

(i) If a person wants to determine poverty line in India, then which factors should be used to determine for subsistence? (1)

(ii) How is the food requirement estimated in poverty line? (1)

(iii) Why is the calorie requirement of rural areas more than that in urban areas? (2)

36. Read the source and answer the questions that follows.

The Monsoon, unlike the trades, are not steady winds but are pulsating in nature, affected by different atmospheric conditions encountered by it, on its way over the warm tropical seas. The duration of the monsoon is between 100-120 days from early June to mid-September. Around the time of its arrival, the normal rainfall increases suddenly and continues constantly for several days. This is known as the 'burst' of the monsoon and can be distinguished from the pre-monsoon showers.

The monsoon arrives at the Southern tip of the Indian Peninsula generally by the first week of June. Subsequently, it proceeds into two–the Arabian Sea branch and the Bay of Bengal branch. The Arabian Sea branch reaches Mumbai about ten days later on approximately the 10th of June. This is a fairly rapid advance. The Bay of Bengal branch also advances rapidly and arrives in Assam in the first week of June. The lofty mountains causes the monsoon winds to deflect towards the West over the Ganga plains. By mid-June the Arabian Sea branch of the monsoon arrives over Saurashtra-Kuchchh and the central part of the country.

The Arabian Sea and the Bay of Bengal branches of the monsoon merge over the North-Western part of the Ganga plains.

Delhi generally receives the monsoon showers from the Bay of Bengal branch by the end of June (tentative date is 29th of June). By the first week of July, Western Uttar Pradesh, Punjab, Haryana and Eastern Rajasthan experience the monsoon. By mid-July, the monsoon reaches Himachal Pradesh and the rest of the country.

Withdrawal or the retreat of the monsoon is a more gradual process. The withdrawal of the monsoon begins in North-Western states of India by early September. By mid-October, it withdraws completely from the Northern half of the Peninsula. The withdrawal from the Southern half of the Peninsula is fairly rapid. By early December, the monsoon has withdrawn from the rest of the country.

The islands receive the very first monsoon showers, progressively from South to North, from the last week of April to the first week of May. The withdrawal. takes place progressively from North to South from the first week of December to the first week of January. By this time the rest of the country is already under the influence of the winter monsoon.

(i) Why is monsoon considered pulsating in nature? (1)

(ii) Evaluate the characteristics of the two branches of the South-West monsoon. (1)

(iii) Why is withdrawal of monsoon is considered a more gradual process in the Indian sub-continent? (2)

Section F (2+3=5)

37. (a) On the map of the world, two countries are marked which were under German expansion (Nazi power). Identify them. (2)

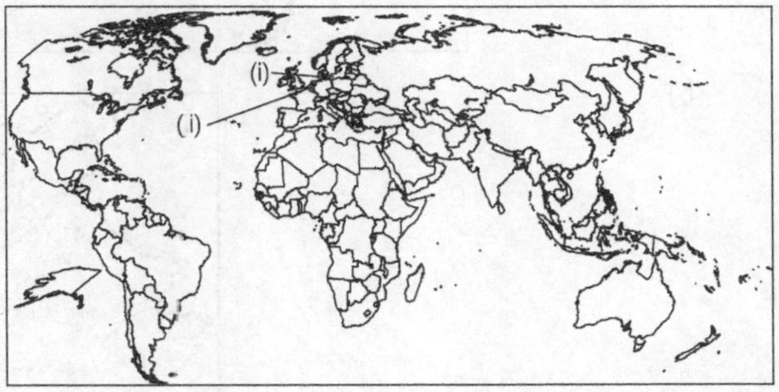

(b) Locate and label any three of the following features on the map of India. (3)

(i) The capital of Uttar Pradesh
(ii) Kanchenjunga
(iii) Konkan coast
(iv) Chota Nagpur Plateau

Answers

1. (a) Compliance with labour laws
2. (c) Jews
3. (d) All of these
4. (b) Only II
5. (b) India's democracy shows signs of stronger grassroots participation compared to the United States, particularly among disadvantaged groups. coast.
6. (d) All of the above
7. (b) It led to widespread global condemnation and the eventual downfall of Nazi Germany IV
8. (b) Statement I is incorrect and Statement II is correct
9. (a)
10. (c) The choice should not be offered at regular intervals.
11. (a) Joseph Stalin, Collectivisation Programme
12. (b) It led to widespread global condemnation and the eventual downfall of Nazi Germany
13. (c) Montesquieu
14. (a) 5th October, 1789
15. (b) It decreases soil fertility
16. (a) Statement I is correct and II is incorrect.
17. (c) October and November
18. (b) Indira Point
19. (a) A common method used to measure poverty is based on the income or consumption levels
20. (c) 1,700
37. (a)

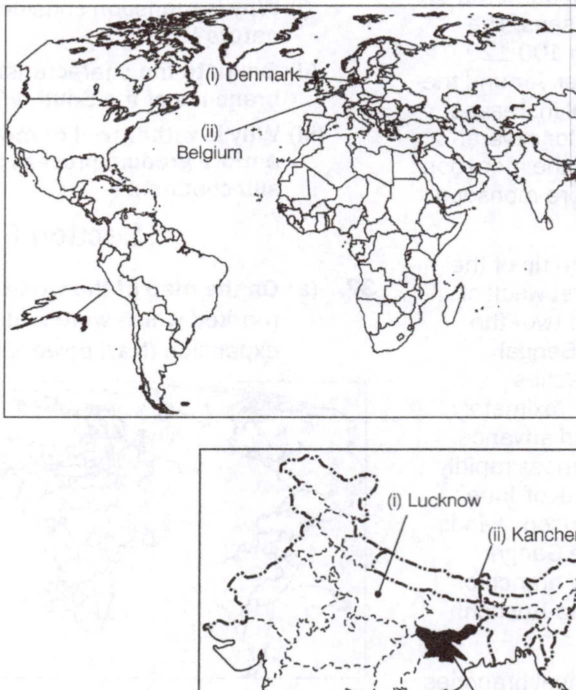

(b)

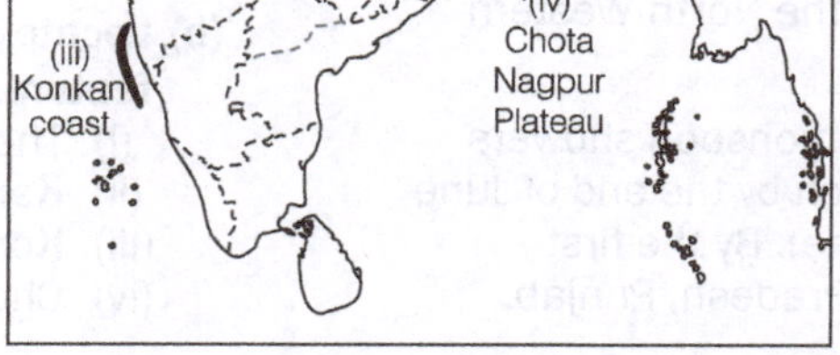

Sample Question Paper 5 (Unsolved)

Social Science

Time : 3 hrs	M.M. : 80

General Instructions

1 Question paper comprises Six Sections – A, B, C, D, E and F. There are 37 questions in the question paper. All questions are compulsory.

2 Section A – From Question 1 to 20 are MCQs of 1 mark each.

3 Section B – Question no. 21 to 24 are Very Short Answer Type Questions, carrying 2 marks each. Answer to each question should not exceed 40 words.

4 Section C – Contains Questions 25 to 29 are Short Answer Type Questions, carrying 3 marks each. Answer to each question should not exceed 60 words

5 Section D – Question no. 30 to 33 are long answer type questions, carrying 5 marks each. Answer to each question should not exceed 120 words.

6 Section E – Questions no from 34 to 36 are case based questions with three sub questions and are of 4 marks each.

7 Section F – Question no. 37 is map based, carrying 5 marks with two parts, 37a from History (2 marks) and 37b from Geography (3 marks).

Section A (1×20=20)

1. The Western part of the Northern Plain is referred to as the Punjab Plains. Formed by the Indus and its tributaries, the larger part of this plain lies in Pakistan. The Indus and its tributaries - the Jhelum, the Chenab, the Ravi, the Beas and the Satluj originate in the Himalaya. This section of the plain is dominated by the doabs. (1)

The Northern plain is broadly divided into how many parts?

(a) 3 (b) 2

(c) 5 (d) None of these

2. Which of the following Union Territories has the largest number of Lok Sabha seats? (1)

(a) Puducherry

(b) Delhi

(c) Lakshadweep

(d) Chandigarh

3. Which of the following is correctly arranged in terms of their population density (highest density to lowest density)? (1)

(a) Assam, Kerala, Arunachal Pradesh

(b) Kerala, Assam, Arunachal Pradesh

(c) Assam, Arunachal Pradesh, Kerala

(d) Kerala, Arunachal Pradesh, Assam

4. Raj is planning a trip and wants to experience a place with minimal temperature fluctuations between day and night. Which of the following destinations should he choose? (1)

(a) Jaisalmer, Rajasthan (in the Thar Desert)

(b) Kerala

(c) Mount Abu, Rajasthan

(d) Ladakh, Jammu and Kashmir

5. Consider the statement given below and choose the correct answer. (1)

Statement I Poor people suffer from chronic hunger because of their very low income and in turn inability to buy food even for survival.

Statement II Seasonal hunger is related to cycles of food growing and harvesting.

Options

(a) Statement I is correct and II is incorrect.

(b) Statement I is incorrect and II is correct.

(c) Both I and II are incorrect.

(d) Both I and II are correct

6. Match the following. (1)

	List I		List II
A.	Maasailand was cut in to half	1.	1919
B.	Tanganyika came under British control	2.	1964
C.	Formation of Tanzania	3.	1885

Codes

	A	B	C		A	B	C
(a)	1	2	3	(b)	3	2	1
(c)	3	1	2	(d)	2	1	3

7. Arrange the following events in the correct chronological order due to which General Musharraf established his rule in Pakistan. (1)

I. Musharraf issued a 'Legal Framework Order' by which the President can dismiss the national or provincial assemblies.

II. Musharraf overthrew a democratically elected government by a military coup and declared himself Chief Executive of the country.

III. Elections were held to the national and provincial assemblies.

IV. Musharraf changed his designation to President.

Codes

(a) IV, III, I, II (b) II, IV, III, I
(c) II, I, III, IV (d) II, IV, I, III

8. Which of the following is not true regarding China's election? (1)

(a) Elections are regularly held after every five years.
(b) Before contesting elections, a candidate needs the approval of the Chinese Communist Party.
(c) The government is always formed by the Communist Party.
(d) Every party has fare chance to come into power.

9. Consider the statements given below and choose the correct option.

Statement I Poverty line is an imaginary line used by any country to determine its poverty. **(1)**

Statement II It varies time to time, place to place and country to country.

Codes

(a) Statement I is correct and Statement II is incorrect
(b) Statement I is incorrect and Statement II is correct
(c) Both Statement I and Statement II are incorrect
(d) Both Statement I and Statement II are correct

10. Consider the following statements about Deccan Plateau and choose the correct option. (1)

I. Deccan Plateau has a triangular landmass.

II. Deccan Plateau lies South of the Narmada river.

III. Satpura range lies North of the Deccan Plateau.

Codes

(a) Only I (b) Only II
(c) I and II (d) All of these

11. Match the following. (1)

List I	List II
A. Punjab Himalayas	1. Teesta-Dihang rivers
B. Nepal Himalayas	2. Satluj-Kali rivers
C. Assam Himalayas	3. Kali-Teesta rivers
D. Kumaon Himalayas	4. Indus-Satluj rivers

Codes

	A	B	C	D		A	B	C	D
(a)	4	1	3	2	(b)	4	3	2	1
(c)	4	3	1	2	(d)	3	4	2	1

12. Find the incorrect option. (1)

(a) In 1920, Hitler joins the German Worker's Party.
(b) In 1922, Nazi Youth League was founded.
(c) In 1933, the Enabling Act was passed.
(d) In 1911, Germany attacks USSR.

13. See the picture and choose the title that closely relates to the given picture. (1)

(a) In sufficiency in food grains
(b) Fair Price Shops
(c) Massive starvation and food insecurity
(d) Types of hunger

14. When was slavery finally abolished in the French colonies? (1)

(a) 1845 (b) 1845 (c) 1848 (d) 1850

15. When was grazing tax introduced in India? (1)

(a) In the mid-19th century
(b) In the 18th century
(c) In the 19th century
(d) None of the above

16. When did Napoleon Bonaparte crown himself as Emperor of France? (1)

(a) 1798 (b) 1800
(c) 1804 (d) 1802

17. Which of the following is agriculturally is the most productive part of India? (1)

(a) Northern Plains
(b) Indian Desest
(c) Coastal plains
(d) Peninsular Plateau

18. Who gave a historical speech 'Tryst with Destiny' on 15th August, 1947? (1)

(a) Mahatma Gandhi
(b) Jawaharlal Nehru
(c) Shyama Prasad Mukherjee
(d) Dr BR Ambedkar

19. Which of the following statements is best supported by the data in the graph? (1)

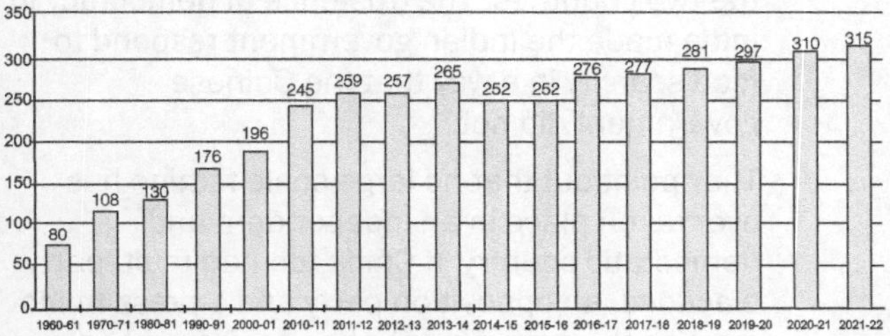

(a) India's foodgrain production has shown consistent year-on-year growth from 1960 to 2010.
(b) The Green Revolution had its most significant impact on foodgrain production in the 1970s.
(c) Foodgrain production in India is more than tripled between 1960-61 and 2010-11.
(d) The rate of increase in foodgrain production was highest in the 2000s decade.

20. Read the following data and select the appropriate option from the following. (1)

Estimates of Poverty in India		
Year	Poverty Ratio (%)	
	Rural	Urban
Poverty Ratio in 1993-94	50	32
Poverty Ratio in 2004-05	42	26
Poverty Ratio in 2009-10	34	21

Source : 2018 Government of India Central Statistics Affair.

During which year, the poverty ratio is minimum?

(a) 1993-94 (b) 2004-05
(c) 2009-10 (d) None of these

Section B (2×4=8)

21. Describe the Hitler's foreign policy before the Second World War? **(2)**

Or What does the term 'Genocidal War' refer to?

22. India shares its land boundaries with Pakistan and Afghanistan in the northwest, China (Tibet), Nepal and Bhutan in the north and Myanmar and Bangladesh in the east. Our southern neighbours across the sea consist of the two island countries........ **(2)**

(i) Which island countries are our southern neighbours?

(ii) Describe India's physical position in relation to its neighbouring countries on a map of Asia?

23. 'India celebrated its 75th Republic Day on 26th January, 2024.'
Why is January 26 celebrated as Republic Day in India? **(2)**

24. "Recently , the government has announced an increase in agricultural subsidies to support farmers". What is a subsidy and how does it benefit consumers and producers?" **(2)**

Section C (3 × 5 = 15)

25. On polling day, Ravi asked his friends Arun to come along for casting their votes together. When Arun denied doing so, Ravi told him that he should vote as voting is his right. Identify the reasons why are rights essential in a democracy. **(3)**

26. Saurabh, a recent college graduate, has been struggling to find employment in his field despite his qualifications. The case delves into the challenges of unemployment, job search strategies, and the impact of economic factors on individual careers. **(3)**
Describe how does unemployment have a negative effect on the economic development of a country.

Or Enumerate three features of the National Health Policy, 2002.

27. The North-West India receives rainfall during winters. Why? State any three reasons. **(3)**

28. How did the representatives of the third estate respond when Louis XVI rejected their proposal for a new voting system in the Estates General in 1789? **(3)**

29. In the wake of the high incidence of poverty levels, as reported by the NSSO in the mid-1970s, three important food intervention programmes were introduced.

Name these programmes and what impact they had on food security and poverty alleviation? **(3)**

Section D **(5×4=20)**

30. Name the two coastal strips that flank the Peninsular plateau. Distinguish the two by giving five characteristics of each. **(5)**

Or Read the information about New Print Technology and answer the question that follows.

The Himalayas, geologically young and structurally fold mountains stretch over the northern borders of India. These mountain ranges run in a west-east direction from the Indus to the Brahmaputra. The Himalayas represent the loftiest and one of the most rugged mountain barriers of the world.

How do regional names contribute to a better understanding of the diverse sections of the Himalayan mountain range? Discuss their significance in geographical and cultural contexts?

31. "Hunger is an important aspect indicating food insecurity." Justify the statement with suitable arguments. **(5)**

Or Give detailed insight into the rationing system of India.

32. "Elections in democracy are all about political competition." Is this competition always good? Analyse the statement. **(5)**

Or "The rulers of non-democratic countries also need to hold elections." Explain.

33. "Jacobins emerged as a radical force in French politics during the Revolution." Examine the statement. **(5)**

Or "Robespierre's Reign of Terror significantly altered French society and governance." Examine the statement.

Section E **(4×3=12)**

34. Read the source given below and answer the questions that follow.

China's famine of 1958-1961 was the worst recorded famine in world history. Nearly three crore people died in this famine. During those day, India's economic condition was not much better than China. Yet India did not have a famine of the kind China had. Economists think that this was a result of different government policies in the two countries. The existence of democracy in India made the Indian government respond to food scarcity in a way that the Chinese government did not.

They point out that no large-scale famine has ever taken place in an independent and democratic country. If China too had multi-party elections, an opposition party and a press full to criticise the government, then so many people may not have died in the famine.

This example brings out one of the reasons why democracy is considered the best form of government. Democracy is better than any other form of government in responding to the needs of the people. A non-democratic government may and can respond to the people's needs, but it all depends on the wishes of the people who rule.

(i) **Policies adopted by a democratic government can change the condition of people in the country. Comment.** **(1)**

(ii) **Explain with example, that democratic government is more responsive.** **(1)**

(iii) **What did the economists think on comparing the situation of India and China?** **(2)**

35. Read the source given below and answer the questions that follow.

On 16th October, 1917, Lenin persuaded the Petrograd Soviet and the Bolshevik Party to agree to a socialist seizure of power. A Military Revolutionary Committee was appointed by the Soviet under Leon Trotsky to organise the seizure. The date of the event was kept a secret. The uprising began on 24th October. Sensing trouble, Prime Minister Kerenskii had left the city to summon troops.

At dawn, military men loyal to the government seized the buildings of two Bolshevik newspapers. Pro-government troops were sent to take over telephone and telegraph offices and protect the Winter Palace. In a swift response, the Military Revolutionary Committee ordered its supporters to seize government offices and arrest ministers. Late in the day, the ship *Aurora* shelled the Winter Palace. Other vessels sailed down the Neva and took over various military points. By nightfall, the city was under the committee's control and the ministers had surrendered.

At a meeting of the All Russian Congress of Soviets in Petrograd, the majority approved the Bolshevik action. Uprisings took place in other cities. There was heavy fighting especially in Moscow but by December, the Bolsheviks controlled the Moscow-Petrograd area.

(i) The Military Revolutionary Committee was appointed by the Soviet. Suggest the reasons. (1)

(ii) Infer the importance of the control of the Military Revolutionary Committee over the Petrograd city. (1)

(iii) How did Lenin make the Petrograd Soviet and the Bolshevik Party to agree in October 1917? (2)

36. Read the source given below and answer the questions that follow.

The Brahmaputra rises in Tibet East of Mansarowar lake very close to the sources of the Indus and the Satluj. It is slightly longer than the Indus, and most of its course lies outside India. It flows Eastwards parallel to the Himalayas. On reaching the Namcha Barwa (7757 m), it takes a 'U' turn and enters India in Arunachal Pradesh through a gorge. Here, it is called the Dihang and it is joined by the Dibang, the Lohit, and many other tributaries to form the Brahmaputra in Assam.

In Tibet, the river carries a smaller volume of water and less silt as it is a cold and a dry area. In India, it passes through a region of high rainfall. Here, the river carries a large volume of water and considerable amount of silt.

The Brahmaputra has a braided channel in its entire length in Assam and forms many riverine islands. Every year during the rainy season, the river overflows its banks, causing widespread devastation due to floods in Assam and Bangladesh. Unlike other North Indian rivers, the Brahmaputra is marked by huge deposits of silt on its bed causing the riverbed to rise. The river also shifts its channel frequently.

(i) How does the Brahmaputra river enter India? (1)

(ii) Which situations make the Brahmaputra to carry smaller volume of water in Tibet and more water in India? (1)

(iii) Evaluate the important features of the Brahmaputra river. (2)

Section F (2+3=5)

37. (a) On the given map of the world, two features are marked. These are the countries that were Allied powers in the First World War. Identify these countries. (2)

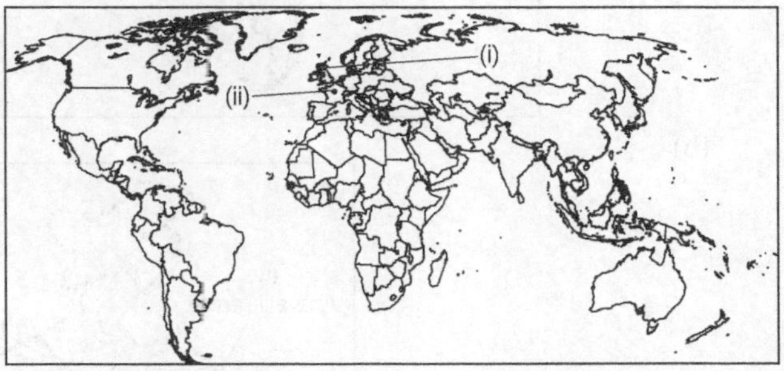

(b) Locate Label any three features of the following on the map of India. (3)

(i) The capital of Rajasthan

(ii) The capital of Maharashtra

(iii) Coastal Plains in Kerala

(iv) Aravalli range

Answers

1. (a) 3
2. (b) Delhi
3. (b) Kerala, Assam, Arunachal Pradesh
4. (b) Kerala
5. (d) Both I and II are correct
6. (c)
7. (d) II, IV, I, III
8. (d) Every party has fare chance to come into power.
9. (d) Statement I is incorrect and Statement II is correct
10. (c) I and II
11. (a)
12. (a) In 1920, Hitler joins the German Worker's Party.
13. (c) Massive starvation and food insecurity
14. (c) 1848
15. (a) In the mid-19th century
16. (c) 1804
17. (a) Northern Plains
18. (b) Jawaharlal Nehru
19. (c) Foodgrain production in India is more than tripled between 1960-61 and 2010-11.
20. (a) 1993-94
37. (a)

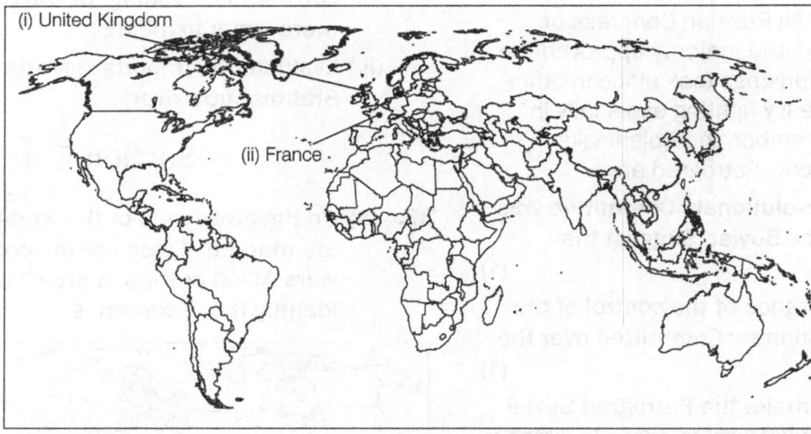

(b)

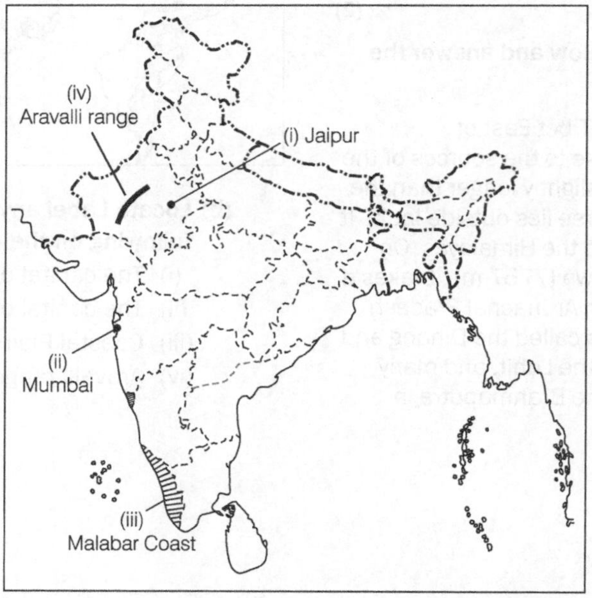